The Best of
NEVADA

A witty, definitive and remarkably useful guide to Las Vegas, Reno-Tahoe and beyond

By Don W. Martin and Betty Woo Martin

Pine Cone Press • Columbia, California

OTHER BOOKS BY DON & BETTY MARTIN

THE BEST OF THE GOLD COUNTRY • Pine Cone Press (First printing, 1987; second printing, 1990; revised 1992)
THE BEST OF THE WINE COUNTRY • Pine Cone Press (1991)
INSIDE SAN FRANCISCO • Pine Cone Press (1991)
COMING TO ARIZONA • Pine Cone Press (1991)
THE BEST OF ARIZONA • Pine Cone Press (1990)
THE BEST OF SAN FRANCISCO • Chronicle Books (1986; revised 1990)
SAN FRANCISCO'S ULTIMATE DINING GUIDE • Pine Cone Press (1988)

Copyright © 1992 by Don W. Martin and Betty Woo Martin
All rights reserved. No written material, maps or illustrations from this book may be reproduced in any form, other than brief passages in book reviews, without written permission from the authors. Printed in the United States of America.

Library of Congress Cataloging-in-Publication Data
Martin, Don and Betty—
The Best of Nevada
Includes index.
1. Nevada—description and travel
2. Nevada—history
3. Gambling—history and techniques
ISBN 0-942053-13-3
Library of Congress card catalog number 91-67256

Cartography • **Dianne Shannon,** Columbine Type and Design, Sonora, Calif.

THE COVER • *Nevada rings in the New Year in typically flamboyant fashion, with a fireworks display over downtown Las Vegas.*
— Photo courtesy Las Vegas News Bureau

CONTENTS

1. NEVADA: GETTING TO KNOW YOU
The way it was — 11
The way it is — 20
Getting there — 22
Getting married — 23
Getting ?? — 24
Beating the heat — 26
Just the facts — 29

2. BEATING THE ODDS
The nervous art of gambling — 31
Money management — 33
Shifting the odds — 34
Blackjack — 46
Craps — 46
Baccarat — 50
Roulette — 54
Slot machines, video poker, video blackjack & keno — 58
Books on gambling — 64

3. LAS VEGAS: DYNAMIC, SEXY LADY OF THE DESERT
The way it was — 65
The way it is — 73
Getting there & around — 73
Getting hitched — 77
Where to shop — 78
Affordable Las Vegas — 79
Las Vegas ABCs — 82
Touring Las Vegas — 85
The casinos — 90
The big shows — 122
Other attractions — 128
Activities — 136
The ten best restaurants — 140
Where else to dine — 143
The ten best buffets — 148
Where to sleep — 150
Local favorites — 155
Where to camp — 158

4. LAS VEGAS NEIGHBORS: FIRE, ICE AND WATER
Valley of Fire-Lake Mead-Hoover Dam loop — 159
Lake Mead & Hoover Dam — 162
South to Laughlin — 167
Red Rock-Pahrump-Mount Charleston loop — 174
A run for the borders: Stateline, Jean & Mesquite — 180

5. THE WESTERN EDGE: BOOMTOWNS, BOMBS & BASQUES
Las Vegas to Beatty — 183
Goldfield — 189
Tonopah — 190
Hawthorne & Walker Lake — 194
Yearington to Gardnerville — 196
Historic Genoa — 202

6. SILVER CITIES: CARSON & VIRGINIA
The way they were — 205
Carson: the way it was — 206
The way it is — 208
Carson City attractions — 209
The casinos & dining — 212
Where to sleep — 215
Where to camp — 216
North & east of Carson — 216
Virginia City — 219
The way it was — 221
The way it is — 222
Attractions & tours — 226
Interesting saloons — 229
Where to dine & sleep — 230

7. RENO: STILL THE BIGGEST LITTLE CITY

The way it was — 233
The way it is — 237
Getting there & around — 238
Getting hitched — 239
Where to shop — 239
Affordable Reno — 239
Reno's ABCs — 240
Touring Reno — 241
The casinos — 243
Other attractions — 251
Where to dine — 259
Where to sleep — 262
Where to camp — 264
Neighboring Sparks — 265

8. LAKE TAHOE: PINE TREE PLAYGROUND

The way it was — 267
The way it is — 269
Getting there — 270
The north shore, Incline — 271
Unspoiled east shore — 276
South shore, Stateline — 277
Taking a ride on the
   California side — 284

9. THE I-80 CORRIDOR: COWBOYS AND PAIUTES

The way it was — 285
Northeast to Pyramid Lake — 287
Lovelock — 291
Winnemucca — 295
Elko — 302
Jackpot & Wendover — 308

10. THE U.S. 50 CORRIDOR: HIGH LONESOME

The way it was — 315
Fallon — 318
Austin — 323
Eureka — 326
Ely — 329
Great Basin Nat'l Park — 335
Pioche, Cathedral
   Gorge & Caliente — 338

11. GLOSSARY

Nevada gaming dictionary — 345
Other useful books — 348

MAPS

Nevada — 10
Nevada counties — 30
Las Vegas Strip — 86
Downtown Las Vegas — 89
Tonopah — 191
Carson City — 204
Virginia City — 225
Reno — 232
Lake Tahoe — 275
Winnemucca — 297
Elko — 304
Ely — 335

INTRODUCTION

"Nevada."

Say the word and two quick images come to mind: glittering casinos and vast deserts as bare and beige as a showgirl's tanned bottom.

Other guidebook authors protest that Nevada is much more. It is, they insist, an appealing place peppered with alpine lakes, pine-thatched hills and lofty peaks painted with a perpetual patina of snow.

Well, of course it is. You will learn in Chapter 1 that Nevada is home to nearly 200 mountain ranges and one of America's largest lakes, that it is ribboned with rippling rivers, that it has lofty peaks reaching to Calvary, that its dry deserts are absolutely soaked with Western history.

These, however, are not the primary reasons Nevada has become the nation's third most popular tourist destination. The mountains are higher in California and wider in Colorado, the snow is drier in Utah, the rivers are more ripply in Oregon, and Arizona practically *invented* Western history.

People go to Nevada to raise legal hell. From the casinos of Las Vegas and Reno to the hot tubs of Tahoe to the government-regulated cathouses of Elko and Ely, they go to *party*.

In **The Best of Nevada** we focus on the best places to do so. We cover the action in Las Vegas, Reno-Sparks and Lake Tahoe. We take you by the hand and lead you through the gaudiest of the casinos, permitting you to dawdle at a blackjack table and shake hands with a one-armed bandit. We encourage you to linger in a lounge show and enjoy the glitziest skin revues this side of Paris. In consultation with experts, we teach you how to gamble, all the while warning you that you'll probably lose. We tell you where to get a great steak at a bargain price, and where to get into trouble, if you're so inclined.

Certainly, we have not neglected the other side of the Nevada coin. Although we spent considerable time exploring Las Vegas from our havens at the Mirage and Excalibur, although we wandered at length the streets of Reno and prowled the pines of Tahoe, we also covered the rest of the state. We trekked over the vast Great Basin Desert, explored mining camps too stubborn to die, hiked the heights of one of America's newest national parks and followed the Pony Express across the loneliest road in America.

Nevada is a great state to explore by car, since the highways are generally in excellent shape and rarely crowded. Two of them, Interstate 80 and U.S. 50, are rich in history, following the routes of pioneer trails. You'll learn about them in chapters 9 and 10. Throughout the state, Nevada does a fine job of marking and interpreting its historic spots. Look for "Point of Historical Interest" signs as you travel. These Nevada-shaped signs offer considerably more detail than most states' historic plaques.

One of Nevada's great lures is that it is a true two-season vacation state. In summer, revelers, families and rugged outdoor types are drawn to the Reno-Tahoe area. In winter, Las Vegas is the playground of the rich, the famous and folks just like us. And of course, Tahoe shelters some of America's great ski resorts.

We've done it all, examined it all and explored it all. We've sorted through the wonders of this amazing state, and saved **The Best of Nevada** just for you.

THE WAY THINGS WORK

Dining

Our intent here is to provide a selective dining sampler, not a complete list. You will note that many of our recommendations are in casinos, since many of these gaming resorts have taken the trouble to install rather good restaurants. Actually, *most* of Nevada's dining parlors are in casinos. We used several methods to select cafe candidates for inclusion: Inquiry among locals, suggestions from friends and our own experiences. Our choices are based more on overviews of food, service and decor, not on the proper doneness of a specific pork chop.

One has to be careful about recommending restaurants. Obviously, people's tastes differ, and it's difficult to judge a cafe by a single meal. Your well-done fish is someone else's artgum eraser. The chef might have a bad night, or a waitress might be recovering from one. Thus, your dining experience may be quite different from ours. We graded the restaurants with one to four little grins, for food quality, service and ambiance.

☺ **Adequate**—A clean cafe with basic but edible grub.

☺☺ **Good**—A well-run establishment that offers good food good service.

☺☺☺ **Very good**—Substantially above average; excellent fare, served with a smile in a fine dining atmosphere.

☺☺☺☺ **Excellent**—We've found heaven, and it has a good wine list!

Price ranges are based on the tab for an average dinner, including soup or salad (but not wine or dessert). Obviously, places serving only breakfast and/or lunch are priced accordingly.

$—Average dinner for one is $9 or less
$$—$10 to $14
$$$—$15 to $24
$$$$—$25 to $34

Ø—**Non-Smoking section** available in dining room. Double symbol means entire dining room is smoke-free.

Many casinos, seeking to lure patrons, offer great food bargains, particularly all-you-can-eat buffets. You'll find an abundance of these in the popular gaming centers of Las Vegas, Laughlin, Reno and Lake Tahoe.

Casinos

We also apply "grin ratings" to casinos, based on their visitor appeal. They're explained in greater detail when we begin our casino listings in Chapter 3 on page 91.

Lodging

We list most of the major casino hotels for those of you who want to be close to the action. We also recommend budget places for those seeking to save funds for Nevada's version of the good things in life—gaming, girlie shows and Wayne Newton. In choosing lodgings, we often rely on the judgment of the Nevada division of the California State Automobile Association (AAA) because we respect its high standards. We also include some budget places that may fall short of Triple A ideals but still offer a clean room for a fair price. Of course we can't anticipate changes in management or the maid's day off, but hopefully your surprises will be good ones.

⌂ **Adequate**—Clean and basic; don't expect anything fancy.
⌂⌂ **Good**—A well-run place with comfortable beds and most essentials.
⌂⌂⌂ **Very good**—Substantially above average, often with facilities such as a pool and spa.
⌂⌂⌂⌂ **Excellent**—An exceptional lodging with beautifully-appointed rooms, often with a restaurant and extensive amenities.
Ø—**Non-Smoking rooms** available. Double symbol means the entire facility is smoke-free (common with bed & breakfast inns). Most bed & breakfast inns do not allow pets. Inquire when you make reservations so your poor pooch doesn't have to spend the night sulking in the back seat of your car.

Price ranges are listed for rooms during the most popular visitor months, which is winter in Las Vegas and summer in the Reno-Tahoe area. Of course, many places reduce their rates during slower periods. Bed & breakfast inns, for instance, often have lower weekday rates. Conversely, some hike their prices for holiday peaks or local celebrations. Price codes below indicate the cost of a standard room for two during high season. All prices were furnished to us by the establishments, so you'll know who to scold if they're way off base.

$—a double for under $25
$$—$25 to $49
$$$—$50 to $74
$$$$—$75 and beyond

It's always wise to make advance reservations, particularly during weekends and local celebrations (listed at the end of each community write-up). If you don't like the place and you're staying more than a day, you can always shop around after the first night and—hopefully—change lodgings.

MISCELLANY

TIMES AND PRICES • Don't rely too much on times listed in this book because many places seem to change their hours more often than a dead-beat changes his address. Prices change, too, inevitably upward, so use those shown only as guidelines. Also, restaurants seem to suffer a rather high attrition rate, so don't be crushed if one that we recommended has become a laundromat by the time you get there.

CAMPING • Nevada offers a good assortment of campsites, from commercial RV parks in most towns and cities to U.S. Forest Service campgrounds. Further, many casinos offer RV parks or free RV parking, but don't plan on pitching your pup tent on these patches of asphalt.

ATTRACTIONS • We list the best attractions, those you should include on your must-see list if your visit is limited, followed by "the rest" if you have more time to prowl.

NUGGETS • These are lesser known, often overlooked attractions, shops, historical monuments, wide places in the road and other things that we felt had special appeal.

Incidentally, we've cleverly edged this introductory section in a **black border** so you can thumb quickly back to it.

A FEW WORDS OF THANKS

In a sense, guidebooks are written by committee. We only provide the research, the adjectives and the editing, while hundreds of other sources furnish the facts and background information.

We'd like to thank the **Nevada Commission on Tourism** and the dozens of **chamber of commerce** folks who gave us useful material (sometimes without their knowledge, since we often travel as accidental tourists). Among other helpful souls were staff members of the **Nevada Division of State Parks** and Nevada offices of the **National Park Service, U.S. Forest Service** and **Bureau of Land Management.**

We'd particularly like to thank **Don Payne, John Reible** and **Stephen Allen** of the Las Vegas News Bureau, **Tracey A. Turner** and **Carol Infranca** of the Reno-Sparks Convention & Visitors Authority, and librarian **Lee Mortensen, Nita Phillips** and other helpful members of the Nevada Historical Society in Reno.

CLOSING INTRODUCTORY THOUGHTS

Nobody's perfect, but we try. This book contains thousands of facts and a few are probably wrong. If you catch an error, let us know. Also, drop us a note if you discover that a museum has become an auto repair shop or the other way around; or if a restaurant, motel, casino or attraction has opened or closed.

All who provide useful information will earn a free copy of the revised edition of *The Best of Nevada* or one of our other publications. (See listing in the back of this book.)

Address your comments to:
Pine Cone Press
P.O. Box 1494 (11362 Yankee Hill Rd.)
Columbia, CA 95310

A BIT ABOUT THE AUTHORS

This is the eighth guidebook by the husband and wife team of Don and Betty Martin. Don, who provides most of the adjectives, has been a journalist since age 17. He was a Marine correspondent in the Orient, then he worked for several West Coast newspapers and he served as associate editor of the travel magazine of the California State Automobile Association. He now devotes his time to writing, photography, travel and—for some curious reason—collecting squirrel and chipmunk artifacts.

Betty, who does much of the research, photography and editing, offers the curious credentials of a doctorate in pharmacy and a California real estate broker's license. She also is a free-lance travel writer and photographer who has sold material to assorted newspapers and magazines.

A third and most essential member of the family is *Ickybod*, a green 1979 Volkswagen camper, the Martins' home on the road. Without *Ick*, they might have been tempted to solicit free lodging and meals, and this guidebook wouldn't be quite so honest.

TRAVEL TIPS

Whether you travel by car, RV or commercial transit, these tips will help make any trip anywhere more enjoyable and economical.

Reservations • Whenever possible, made advance room reservations. Otherwise, you'll pay the "rack rate," the highest rate that a hotel or motel charges. Also, with a reservation, you won't be shut out if there's a convention or major local celebration.

Car rentals • The same is true of car rentals; you'll often get a better rate by reserving your wheels ahead. **Important note:** Car rental firms may try to sell you "insurance" (actually collision damage waver) to cover your rental car. However, you may already have this protection through your own auto insurance company. Check before you go and take your insurance policy as proof of coverage.

Trip insurance • If you're flying, trip insurance may be a good investment, covering lost luggage, accidents and missed flights (essential if you have a no-refund super saver). Most travel agencies can arrange this coverage.

Medical needs • Always take spare prescription glasses and contacts. Take prescriptions for your lenses and for any drugs you may be taking. Don't forget sun protection if you're going from a cold to a hot climate, such as wide-brimmed hat and sunblock. Otherwise, your pale winter skin will sizzle in a hurry.

Cameras and film • If you haven't used your camera recently, test it by shooting a roll of film before you go. Test and replace weak camera and flash batteries. Protect your camera and film from extreme heat; don't leave them shut up in a car on a hot day. If you're flying, hand-carry your camera and film through the security check.

Final checklist

There's more to trip departure than putting out the cat. Check off these essentials before you go:

___ Stop newspaper and other deliveries; put a hold on your mail.
___ Lock off or unplug your automatic garage door lifter.
___ Arrange for indoor plant watering, landscaping and pet care.
___ Make sure your phone answering machine is turned on; most of these devices allow you to pick up messages remotely.
___ Don't invite burglars by telling the world via answering machine or voice mail that you're gone. Put several lights on timers and make sure newspapers and mail don't accumulate outside.
___ If you're going on a long trip, arrange for future mortgage and other bill payments to avoid late charges.
___ Take any food from the refrigerator that may spoil and turn the temperature down to save energy.
___ Double-check the clothes you've packed (extra shoes, matching belts); make sure your shaving and cosmetic kits are complete.
___ Take more than one type of credit card, so you won't be caught short if one is lost or stolen.
___ Get travelers checks and/or take your bank card.
___ Have your car serviced, including a check of all belts, tires and fluid levels. For long desert stretches, take extra water and oil.
___ Turn out the lights, turn off the heat and put out the cat.

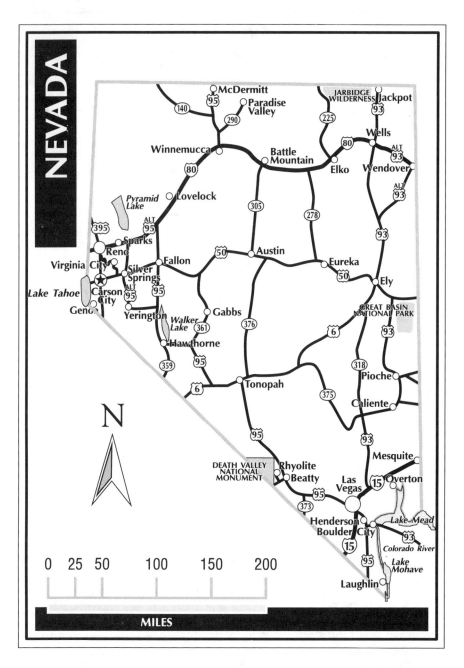

Dorothy: "Toto, I don't think we're in Kansas anymore."
Toto: "Sweetheart, I don't think we're even on the same planet..."

Chapter One
NEVADA
Getting to know you

Let's say you've been captured by aliens, blindfolded and spirited away from Topeka or Tulsa or possibly even Temecula. You're beamed up into a darkened room; the blindfold is removed but the drapes are drawn.

"Get some sleep," the chief alien warns. "You'll need it."

A rustle of Gore-Tex and they're gone, right through the door without opening it.

Sleep? Who can sleep?

You flick a switch and light bathes a nicely appointed room done in warm tropical colors. Hmmm; neat prison!

A throaty rumble draws you to the window. You throw back the drapes and your eyes widen in amazement. Below you, a volcano is spewing fire and steam! All around it, the night sky is glittering with a dazzling rainbow of color. Psychedelic towers pierce the darkness, blinking and winking enticingly. Your Seiko says it's past midnight, yet the street below is busy with traffic. A tall sign stands in the foreground. "The Mirage," it reads.

"You can say that again!" you mumble under your breath.

Intrigued, you cross the room and try the door. It's unlocked. You inhale deeply, step into the hallway and flatten yourself against the wall. No guards! Only a guy carrying a dinner tray set with fancy silver service. He nods, smiles and continues walking.

You step into an elevator; it's crowded with revelers.

"Going down?"

A young woman giggles and offers you her champagne glass. You take a tentative sip and your head begins to clear. The elevator doors open and you're catapulted with the others into a huge room decorated with palm trees and glittering lights. It's filled with milling people and strange looking machines with glowing, blinking disks and panels.

You wander about, staring in fascination, no longer wanting to flee. Your path takes through an indoor rain forest, past a huge aquarium and a white tiger lair. You pause before one of those whirring, blinking machines. Instinctively, you grope into your pocket, find a coin and insert it in a slot. The apparatus flickers and purrs contentedly, then it expels five similar coins.

12—CHAPTER ONE

A pretty girl, wearing an abbreviated floral costume and carrying a drink tray, pauses beside you and flashes her Colgate ivories.
"Cocktail?"
"What?"
"Would you care for a cocktail, sir? Compliments of the Mirage."
Welcome to Nevada.

As you wander about the busy, pulsing Mirage casino in Las Vegas, you may find it difficult to believe that you're in one of the least populated states in America. Nevada has a mere nine human critters per square mile, the third lowest rate in the country.

That's one of its great attractions. Nowhere else in America, perhaps in the world, can you find such a range of vacation extremes. Las Vegas offers the greatest concentration of posh resort hotels on the globe. Yet within minutes, you can be in a pristine desert. Up north, Reno and Tahoe offer similar extremes, from fancy casinos to an alpine wilderness.

Because legalized gambling underwrites many of the expenses in these fancy casinos, Nevada offers the best tourist bargains in America. It has been said, with authority, that Las Vegas and Reno are the least expensive cities for visitors in the developed world. Where else can you get breakfast for $1.49, all-you-can-eat buffets for $2.49 and nice hotel rooms for the price of a motel?

A latter day discovery

Despite its fame, Nevada was one of the last areas in America to be explored. As a matter of fact, 49ers rushing to the newly discovered California gold fields regarded Nevada as a large pain in the donkey—an inhospitable barrier of icy mountains and hot, yucky deserts.

For a couple of decades, Nevada was merely something to get *across*, not something to develop. The Pony Express, transcontinental telegraph and railroad were difficult ventures because they had to cross Nevada to reach the "real" promised land, California.

This might have given the first Nevadans something of a complex. If so, their spirits are having the last laugh, and their descendants are laughing en route to the bank. The 1990 U.S. census revealed that, percentage-wise, Nevada was the fastest growing state during the previous decade. The state has led the nation in new job growth for the past four years. Both *Money Magazine* and the National League of Cities rank Nevada as one of the country's best tax havens.

Much of this prosperity is focused around Las Vegas, which gains about 5,000 new residents a month. It was rated the nation's top economic growth area by *Inc., Magazine,* and by Alphametrics Corporation, a Pennsylvania-based economic research group.

Although many businesses are moving to the state, tourism is the primary fuel that fires the Nevada machine. More than 25 million people a year are drawn here, 22 million to Las Vegas alone. Tourism and related services employ nearly three out of four Nevadans.

What transformed Nevada from the overlooked to the sought-after? Luck and tough-minded individualism. People who are rugged enough to settle one of America's last frontiers are *survivors*.

The luck came with the massive Comstock Lode silver strike in 1859. It yielded so much wealth that the "civilized" part of the country took quick notice, particularly since the nation was headed into a civil war that needed financing. Nevada was rushed to statehood in 1864. By contrast, southern cousin Arizona, more explored and settled, had to wait until 1912.

The "Nevada individualism" developed through the boom and bust years that followed. When the Comstock and other strikes went sour late in the century, Nevadans kept looking and digging. They found more silver and gold in Tonopah and Goldfield, and copper way out east in Ely. Then, when everything went bust in 1929, they encouraged tourism by legalizing gambling, liberalizing marriage and divorce laws and condoning prostitution. In later years, red light districts were formally sanctioned in many Nevada counties and they're frisky to this day. Residents even coddled the Mafia a few decades ago to encourage the development of its gaming industry.

Damned the moralistic torpedoes and full speed ahead. Nevada is a survivor!

That's an interesting attitude for a state whose first town was established by Mormons. Those good Christians would be, and probably are, appalled to learn that gambling is Nevada's primary tourist draw and that it has the highest per capita booze consumption of any state in the Union.

Nevada is known as the Silver State or the Sagebrush State. But get real, folks. It's actually the Party State.

THE WAY IT WAS • In the beginning, there was darkness and light and rainfall and great seas and maybe even Mormons. Nevada and most of neighboring Utah lay under water 500 million years ago, the eastern reaches of a paleo-Pacific. Through the eons, the earth's fragile crust shifted and drifted like a brittle ocean, uplifting Nevada to drain off the seawater, then letting it settle to create valleys and basins. Magma spewed through the cracked surface to form volcanoes, or cooled in the depths to become granite, rich in crystallized minerals.

About 175 million years ago, ancestors of the Sierra Nevada were formed when the Pacific Plate jammed under the Continental Plate, tilting it on edge and shattering it into high peaks and narrow valleys. In the mega-centuries that followed, the peaks were worn down by erosion, only to be raised again by another tectonic twitch. East of the mountains, a great landlocked depression was formed, riddled with north-south mountain ranges like the casings of giant moles.

The plates ground together again 18 million years ago, creating a bulge in the basin. Then they began pulling apart, threatening to flood Nevada and turn California into an island. (Some residents of America's most populous state think that wouldn't be a bad idea. Nevada would quickly build a bridge, of course, because most of its visitors come from the Golden State.)

Then, ten million years ago, the plates began reversing direction, giving the Sierra Nevada its present-day tilt. This created a fractured fault zone which to this day generates earthquakes and anxiety in both states. After the final uplift, much of the state fell under the Sierra Nevada rainshadow and a primeval version of the Great Basin Desert was born.

However, cooling effects of the Pleistocene ice ages two million years ago brought lush grasslands, huge lakes and great forests of conifers, ferns and mosses. Sabre-toothed cats, camels, musk ox, woolly mammoths and mastodons wandered about. A gigantic lake, called Lahontan by geologists, covered much of western Nevada about 50,000 years ago. It then gradually shriveled, leaving Pyramid, Walker and Winnemucca lakes as its residue.

None of the ice ages actually reached Nevada, but their presence to the north altered the state's climate. Glaciers formed in many interior mountain ranges, carving bowl-shaped valleys that survive today. The Ruby Mountains (Chapter 9) and Great Basin National Park (Chapter 10) offer fine examples of glacier-sculpted valleys. The last ice age retreated about 15,000 years ago, leaving Nevada in its present-day shape.

The lay of the land

The Great Basin occupies nearly 80 percent of Nevada's land surface. It's one of north America's largest topographic features, covering more than ten percent of the lower 48 states. About 500 miles wide and 750 miles long, it bulges into northeastern Oregon, sweeps east to Salt Lake City and south to a point just above Las Vegas. There, the land tilts down into the Mojave Desert, whose arid expanses cover much of southern California and parts of western Arizona.

Hardly a basin, Nevada's central mass is corrugated with mountains, cut by valleys and ribboned by rivers. It might better be described as a rugged plateau that droops at the edges, like a badly-done pumpkin pie. Its center averages more than 2,000 feet higher than the outer fringes. Like real basins, it *is* completely landlocked. No moisture falling here ever reaches the sea. Rivers flow into lakes or simply evaporate into alkaline sand, creating acrid bowls such as the Carson and Humboldt sinks. This was the feature that inspired explorer John C. Frèmont to christen it the Great Basin in 1844.

Of Nevada's rivers, the Truckee is best known, originating in the Sierra Nevada's Lake Tahoe and flowing northeast into Pyramid Lake. Originally called the Salmon Trout by Frèmont, it was later named either for the chief of the northern Paiutes or for an emigrant train's Indian guide (depending on your historian). The name means "all right" or "very well", which certainly was appropriate for California-bound pioneers through this area. The Truckee provided water and streamside grazing for their stock after a withering desert crossing, and it was a major pathway into the Sierra Nevada.

The Walker and Carson rivers also begin in the Sierra; one forming Walker Lake, the other dying in Carson Sink. The only rivers entirely within Nevada are the Humboldt and its main tributary, the Reese. The Humboldt is born in the northeastern corner, near the Great Basin's outer rim, and it flows into Humboldt Sink. The Reese flows northward out of the Toiyabe Range south of Austin and joins the Humboldt near Battle Mountain.

With its lowlands nearly a mile high, the basin is cold country in winter. Temperatures often plummet well below zero. Many of its mountain ridges top 10,000 feet and snowcaps are common from spring through fall. Mount Wheeler in Great Basin National Park wears one the year around.

In contrast to the Great Basin Desert, the Mojave drops below 1,000 feet in areas, making Nevada's southern tip the hottest part of the state. It also houses 85 percent of the state's residents, clustered in and about Las Vegas.

Two other enclaves complete Nevada's geophysical features. The far northeastern edge tilts into the southern Idaho's Columbia Plateau. Its Owyhee River drains into the Snake River and ultimately into the Pacific. And of course, the great wall of the Sierra Nevada forms much of Nevada's southwestern horizon.

Surveyors gave California the high ground when they drew an angular line from Lake Tahoe to the Colorado River to set the two states' borders. Virtually all of the Sierra's ramparts are in California. However, Nevada's slice of Tahoe provides its third most popular tourist destination after Las Vegas and Reno. The foothill slopes of Toiyabe National Forest below Lake Tahoe offer an important alpine playground as well.

The coming of man

As elsewhere in America, Nevada's first residents came not in search of silver, loose dice or looser women. Wandering across from the Asian land bridge, probably lost but not really caring, the Native Americans worked gradually southward.

The earliest evidence of human habitation has been traced to 11,000 B.C., suggesting that these hunter-gatherers had been pushed southward by the last ice age. They likely fished along the shores of Lake Lahontan and hefted their crude spears at caribou, mastodons and woolly mammoths. Only a few projectile points and bones of their quarry have been found.

The first group identified by archaeologists were the Lovelock People, named for a cave near that town. It yielded several human remains and an exciting collection of tools, shell work, fish hooks and weapons points, plus baskets and even duck decoys made from tules. The Lovelocks probably worked the neighborhood about 4,000 years ago and may be the ancestors of the present-day Paiutes, Nevada's largest Native American group.

Paiutes co-mingled peacefully, for the most part, with Washoe and Shoshone tribes, ranging over most of northern and central Nevada. All were basically hunter-gatherers and no evidence of a major settlement has been found.

Meanwhile, predecessors of Arizona's Anasazi roamed Nevada's southern tip, around present-day Las Vegas. They evolved into an agricultural society, creating shelters of rock and adobe. The Anasazi developed one of pre-Columbian America's most advanced cultures, fertilizing their crops, using irrigation, enjoying a balanced protein diet of corn, beans and squash and creating large communities of several hundred residents.

Mysteriously, they disappeared around 1100 A.D., only four centuries before the Spanish began kicking up a fuss among the Mayans of Mexico. Drought, disease and internal strife may have led to their demise. Some archaeologists suggest that Arizona's present-day Hopi Indians may be their descendants. Arizona claims most of the significant Anasazi pueblo sites, particularly around the Grand Canyon-Flagstaff area. However, some ruins have been found near Overton, northeast of Las Vegas. Relics from the site are on display in the town's Lost City Museum.

The Spanish, having done in the Mayans and Toltecs, began migrating northward to pester North America's natives. That 30-year-old troublemaker, Francisco Vasquez de Coronado, came looking for legendary golden cities in 1540. He passed through present-day Arizona and got as far north as Kansas before returning home empty-handed; he bypassed Nevada.

The first outside visitor probably was Padre Francisco Garcès, who nipped the southern tip of the state headed for California in 1775. Spanish missions had been established there by this time, and he was looking for a better route to the coast. The Spanish never attempted a settlement in Nevada, although it was arbitrarily was included in Spain's claim to all of the Southwest.

When Mexico won independence in the 1820s, it assumed Spain's claim to Nevada and the rest of the American Southwest. This area remained Mexican territory until it was ceded to the United States in the 1848 Treaty of Guadalupe Hidalgo. The treaty was basically an internationally-sanctioned land grab after the U.S. won the Mexican War. Nevada was lumped in "Washoe Country," vaguely a part of the California territory. Then it was included with Utah Territory, created in 1850. Nevada finally gained its own territorial status in 1861.

The Intruders

After Garcès, Nevada suffered no more trespass until 1826, when fur trapper Jedediah Strong Smith passed through, following a route similar to the padre's. He continued on to California to spend the winter, a practice that many still follow. Trapper Peter Skene Ogden came the next year, entering from the north, and did a bit more exploring. Old Jed returned from his California vacation in 1827, making a thirsty, near-fatal crossing through the middle of the state. This experience began building Nevada's reputation as more of a barrier than a destination.

Ogden was the first to work Nevada from north to south, following the grain of the mountains in 1829. Legendary scout Kit Carson was blazing an east-west route to California about this time, following Garcès' sandal tracks. Joseph Walker did a bit of fur trapping along the Humboldt and his namesake Walker River in 1833. Like Jedediah, he wintered in California.

The first recorded wagon train crossing was made by the Bidwell-Bartleson party in 1841, roughly following a course that would become the Emigrant or California Trail. Bidwell descendants are still active in communities north of Sacramento. A few more trains straggled across, attracting little attention until the tragedy of the Donner Party. Heading for California in 1846, the group was delayed in its Nevada desert crossing, then it became trapped on the wrong side of the Sierra Nevada by an early snowstorm.

"The starving emigrants ate everything available," wrote Robert Glass Cleland in *Wilderness to Empire* (© 1944), *"Boiled strips of ox hide, tiny field mice, the barks and twigs of trees, and finally even the flesh of their dead companions."*

Only 45 of the 79 pioneers lived through the terrible winter. Although this is more of a California story, it has a Nevada irony. If the emigrants had retreated to the grassy lowlands (across the present-day Nevada border), all likely would have survived.

Legendary explorer, map-maker and pathfinder Lieutenant John C. Frèmont left his mark on Nevada in the decade of the 1840s. He was sent by the U.S. Army to map the vast, unexplored West, since more and more Americans were being drawn here. With Kit Carson as his guide, he arrived in 1843, gave the Great Basin and Pyramid Lake their names and mapped substantial chunks of the state. He spent most of the rest of his days in California, exploring, mapping, politicking and promoting.

Note that all these people are passing *through* Nevada. That seemed to be the state's fate in those days. Wander through, maybe trap a few muskrats, shoot a pronghorn for supper, stagger across a hot and rock-bound desert, struggle up and over the Sierra Nevada, then head for the beach.

The California Gold Rush intensified this rite of passage, and tens of thousands crossed the state between 1848 and 1860. The Pony Express and telegraph eased the passage of communication, then the transcontinental railroad finally made the trip easier for people. It also encouraged a few folks to linger and explore Nevada bit. With so much gold on the other side of the mountains, it seemed logical that something of value should be on *this* side.

Actually, it was men of the Bible looking for land who established Nevada's first community. Mormon pioneers, pursuing their own version of manifest destiny, spread westward from Salt Lake City to expand the boundaries of Brigham Young's Deseret. The first settlement was an emigrant trading post called Mormon Station, established in 1850 and later named Genoa.

Salt Lake's territorial government seemed too removed to provide protection for these westward settlers, so they petitioned to set up their own administration. The Mormon-controlled Utah legislature offered a compromise in 1855 by creating Carson County, covering most of present-day Nevada, and turning its rule over to local church officials. However, the federal government served notice that expansion of the Mormon empire, a clear violation of the separation of church and state, would not be tolerated. In 1857, a sulking Young began calling many of his flock home, virtually abandoning early settlements such as Mormon Station and Las Vegas.

Meanwhile, prospectors were poking about in earnest, resulting in the world's largest silver strike in 1859. Finally, Nevada became the place to *be*. The Comstock Lode spawned one of the biggest, wildest and rowdiest mining towns ever to hit the wild West—Virginia City. Still rowdy, a little bit wild but not very wicked, it is today a major tourist destination.

Silver brought the expected hordes and whores, and clashes between miners and the remaining Mormons were inevitable—and ironic. The Mormons couldn't abide the miners' womanizing and drinking, while the miners felt the Mormon practice of polygamy was an absolute abomination.

The glitter of Virginia City silver caught the eye of Washington officials, who needed allies and funds to fight the Civil War. They sawed Utah in half in 1861 (further blunting Brigham's power) and created the Nevada Territory. Three years later, it became America's 36th state, with Carson City as its capital.

The beginning of Reno

While all this was happening in and about Carson City, the new transcontinental railroad opened more of Nevada to settlement. A toll station on the Truckee River was picked as a distribution center for the new railroad. Named for Civil War hero Jesse L. Reno, it would be the largest city in the new state for many years. With rail transportation now available, huge free-range ranches spread through the valleys of the Great Basin. Basque shepherds came to spread their flocks, and to clash with the cowmen in plots right out of an old Roy Rogers Western. Prospectors, encouraged by the Comstock strike, ranged throughout the state, finding more strikes, creating more communities.

As Mormons continued withdrawing from local governments, their seats were filled with *nouveau riche* miners, cattlemen and businessmen, who dominated state politics well into this century. And that, bygawd, meant Republican! To a considerable degree, it still does.

The rich mineral deposits began playing out in the 1880s and Nevada went into a 20-year tailspin. Things picked up in 1900 with a major silver

— photo courtesy **Nevada Historical Society**

Could this be Glitter City? Kuhn's Store became a temporary bank as preparations were made for the 1905 lot sale that gave Las Vegas its start.

strike at Tonopah Spring, midway between Reno and Las Vegas. A gold find just to the south at Goldfield soon followed, and monster copper deposits in Ruth near Ely brought more people.

It was time to party again! Nevada nearly doubled its population in the first ten years of the new century.

Although agriculture played third fiddle to mining and ranching, it has some historic roots in Nevada. By a political non-coincidence, America's first Federal Bureau of Reclamation project dampened the desert around Fallon in 1903. Nevada rancher-Congressman Francis Griffin Newlands spent years campaigning for a program to irrigate the growing, thirsty West. His efforts resulted in passage of the Federal Reclamation Act and creation of the U.S. Reclamation Service in 1902. A year later, the Newlands Project was initiated, diverting water from the Truckee to the Carson River to irrigate the dry Carson Sink Valley.

The modern era

As Nevada galloped into the 21st century, it was still a place to *cross*, since California was galloping even faster. However, it now benefited from the West Coast's transportation needs. More railroads were laid, north to south and east to west. The Union Pacific, following the old Mormon Trail, reached from Los Angeles to Salt Lake City, cutting through southern Nevada. In 1905, a division point was established near a former ranch settlement. Its name translates from the Spanish as "The Meadows." We've come to know it better as Las Vegas.

A rail line was sent northward from here to serve the mines of Goldfield, Tonopah and Rhyolite, and Las Vegas began to take shape as a shipping center. It wasn't much of a shape—a collection of tents and whipsaw board shacks built on lots that had been sold off by the railroad. For decades, it was a scruffy little desert crossroad, a poor cousin to bustling Reno, Carson City and Virginia City.

Cross-country highways became vogue as motorcars proliferated early in this century. After ten years of pushing dirt around, a road from Los Angeles through Las Vegas to Salt Lake was completed in 1924. Lonely towns along the two old pioneer routes, the Emigrant Trail across northern Nevada and the Overland Route through the middle, campaigned for a transcontinetnal highway. Both groups got their wish. In 1927, the Victory Highway (U.S. 40 and now I-80) and the Lincoln Highway (U.S. 50) were completed. Reno celebrated the event by erecting an arch over Virginia Street that later carried its famous "Biggest Little City in the World" slogan.

Two years later, on Wednesday, October 28, 1929, Nevada and the rest of the Nation awoke with a hangover.

Although Nevada's economy was chugging right along during the first third of this century, this was still one of the least developed states in the Union. Thus, the Wall Street crash hit here particularly hard. The mine-oriented economy went down with the stock market and nearly every bank in the state shut its doors. Asset-poor Nevada had little to fall back on. The small farming oasis around Fallon put food on local tables, but provided little for export. A drought in the early 1930s decimated the Great Basin cattle herds. And the state had virtually no manufacturing industry.

Legalizing sin

Ever the maverick, Nevada sought bold and offbeat solutions to its economic crisis. While the rest of the country had been shocked by the sins of the Roaring Twenties, then sobered by the Depression, Nevadans decided to keep the party rolling.

In 1931, Humboldt County Assemblyman Phil Tobin, a 29-year-old Winnemucca cowboy, introduced a bill to legalize gambling. Assembly Bill 98 was signed into law by Governor Fred Balzar on March 19. It sanctioned every form of gaming except lotteries which, ironically, are now legal in many other states. Gaming provided a further lure for celebreties, who came to the Party State for quickie divorces, often followed by quickie marriages to their traveling companions. Word began spreading through the gossip columns, and often on the front page, that Nevada was the place to have a good time.

Initially, gambling casinos were rather dingy little places—little more than scruffy card rooms. Picture a scene from an old black and white Western and you get the idea. Then a front-page article in a 1941 edition of *Variety* heralded a change: "WHITEMAN GOES TO STIX."

Commercial Hotel owner Newton Crumley, Jr., decided to change the casino image by brightening up his place, serving food and hiring big-name entertainers from Hollywood. Bandleader Paul Whiteman, Ted Lewis and his Rhythm Rhapsody Revue, Sophie Tucker and Lawrence Welk appeared on Crumley's stage. The Commercial Hotel, incidentally, wasn't in Reno or Las Vegas, but way out in the stix in Elko.

Of course the idea soon caught on in the two larger cities, setting the trend for the headliners and glittering, glamorous revues that make Nevada the Party State.

During the early Thirties, while Reno began to glitter as the Biggest Little City in the World, Las Vegas remained a scruffy railroad crossing. Then the stock market crash handed southern Nevada a giant recovery project: Hoover Dam. It was already on the drawing boards when the market collapsed, and the resulting Depression provided a steady stream of men willing to work in the hot desert sun for 50 cents an hour. To discourage malingering, the government created a company town—Boulder City—and prohibited gambling and whoring. However, Las Vegas was a short drive away. By the time the dam was completed in 1935, a good many of the 5,000 men who built it had left a goodly chunk from their pay envelopes in the town's brothels and casinos. Incidentally, Boulder City is still the only town in Nevada where gambling is prohibited.

The dam offered another advantage: plenty of hydroelectric power to light those gaudy marquees that would come in the decades ahead. World War II brought the military to Nevada, looking for wide open spaces to train for desert warfare and test weapons of death. Many of the troops remained or returned after the war, contributing to the state's growing numbers.

The two big bosses

Two country boys, Winnemucca's Phil Tobin and Elko's Newton Crumbly, Jr., got Nevada's gambling game started. Reno's Raymond and Harold Smith kept it rolling. They built an attractive main street casino and promoted Nevada gambling by scattering "Harold's Club or Bust" signs from coast to coast.

However, it was two outsiders who made Nevada style gambling internationally famous. Through their influence, Las Vegas would become the biggest city in Nevada and the largest city in America founded within this century. One, a notorious mobster, built the first of the glamorous hotels along the Strip, which has become the world's largest entertainment center. The other, a notorious recluse and eccentric, brought corporate respectability. The only thing the two and Las Vegas had in common was their year of birth—1905.

Bugsy Siegel of the movie of the same name arrived in 1946 to construct the Fabulous Flamingo, a gaudy gaming resort that would attract the stars of Hollywood and the hoods of Chicago and New York. It promoted that enticingly sinister George Raft-style glamour that focused the eyes of the world on Las Vegas.

Two decades later, billionaire Howard Hughes—who had completed his transition from movie maker, playboy and aviation pioneer to eccentric germaphoebic recluse—arrived in town in a curtained ambulance. Seeking total privacy, he leased the high-roller floors of the Desert Inn, where he surrounded himself with a retinue of stone-faced Mormon guards.

In 1967, when Desert Inn officials asked him to move, he became indignant and bought the place. That opened the financial floodgates and he didn't stop buying until he owned a six-pack of Las Vegas Strip hotels. All at once, owning a Nevada casino was not only legitimate, it was downright respectable. Corporations moved in. Hilton, MGM and—good grief—even Holiday Inn, began appearing on those gaudy marques.

And that's the way it started.

THE WAY IT IS • "Recession? What recession?"

That was the response from our longtime friend Don Payne, boss of the Las Vegas News Bureau, when we asked how tourism was faring. Seemingly recession-proof, scandal-proof and probably bullet- proof, Nevada tourism is booming like a latter day Comstock silver strike. The economic slump of the early 1990s slowed the state's growth only slightly. Nearly 25 million visitors left behind a $5 billion profit for the gaming industry in 1990.

Apparently, many of these visitors decided to stay, perhaps to keep an eye on their money. During the decade of the Eighties, Nevada led the nation in growth, increasing nearly 40 percent from about 850,000 to 1.2 million. Most of this occurred in Clark (Las Vegas) and Washoe (Reno) counties, where eight of ten Nevadans live. This migratory flood is evident in the fact that three out of four Nevada residents were born somewhere else. That's the highest rate in the nation.

Considering that the state has a population density of only nine people per square mile, imagine how thinly settled the rest of the state is! In fact, more than 85 percent of its land area—nearly 60 million acres—is public land, held by federal and state governments. That's second only to Alaska's ratio, just slightly higher. You'll discover this wonderful remoteness in chapters five, nine and ten as we explore a Nevada beyond the glitter.

Nevada is expected to gain another 200,000 citizens by the end of the century. It may rival Oregon as the West's fourth most populous state, after California, Washington and Arizona.

Not all of this growth has been spurred by tourism. A 1980s resurgence in mining activities has reawakened many of the interior towns. Old company housing has been dusted off among the tailing pits of Ruth. The almost-ghost towns of Eureka and Austin are hosting prospectors of a different stripe. They're college grads, armed with portable chemical labs and lap-top computers. With major improvements in recovery and smelting technology, old tailings are being sifted for new wealth.

The new golden state

For the first time in their closely-linked mining histories, Nevada has passed California as America's largest gold producer. In fact, the Silver State now produces more than half of the country's gold, about six million troy ounces per year. That's twice as much as California yielded in 1850, the peak year of its gold rush. Copper, silver, diatomaceous earth, brucite, magnesite, barium and many other metals are being pulled scientifically from Nevada's earth. Several open pit gold mines have been started and some of the old copper pits are being reactivated.

Long the maverick, willing to bend society's rules to survive, Nevada today finds itself more in stride with the rest of the nation. With its new successes, it shares the rest of the nation's headaches: traffic congestion, shortages and environmental concerns. Reno and Carson City are spreading toward one another across Truckee Meadows and the Washoe Valley. Las Vegas has plenty of room to grow, but not enough water for future residents.

Agreeable Nevada allowed itself to become an atomic test site after World War II. Now, tests have been driven underground and health-conscious environmentalists would like to drive them out. Lawsuits were filed in past years over possible radioactive contamination. Conservationists lock ecological horns with the mining and cattle industries, which no longer have free reign over the Nevada landscape.

Some folks are even voting Democrat these days!

Nevada's high-flying lifestyle takes its toll on residents, and their marriages. Some find it difficult to cope with the pressure of an ongoing party. Nevada suffers the distinction of America's highest divorce, suicide and incarceration rate. On the other hand, hundreds of thousands live quiet, productive lives in quiet homes in Reno and Las Vegas suburbs.

Nevada's history and sociology have closely paralleled that of neighbor California. Both came to statehood because of mining discoveries, both were

North-South pawns during the Civil War, and mining revenues from both helped the Union win that conflict. Similarities remain to this day. Both states are major vacation destinations and both have a penchant for catching glamour headlines. Between the two, they capture more tourists than any other area of the country.

There are some fears that California may put a damper on Nevada's party by legalizing gambling. In fact, Assemblyman Tom Bane of Van Nuys introduced a bill in 1992 to create a "gambling zone" along a ten-mile strip of the Nevada-California border.

"Californians are driving over the border and losing their money," said a Banes aide. "Why not stop them a little bit before they get there?"

The bill didn't fly and it will be many years—if ever—before California legalizes unlimited gaming, since it would require a constitutional amendment. But with Nevada's neighbor suffering chronic budget deficits, it's a nagging temptation that probably won't go away.

In the meantime, the party's still in Nevada, so let's go find it!

Getting there

As the California-bound emigrants discovered, Nevada is hard *not* to miss. And with all its attributes, who would want to?

BY CAR • Two major freeways serve Nevada's pair of metropolitan centers. I-80 passes through Reno-Sparks on its long journey from San Francisco to the east coast and I-15 takes carloads of southern Californians to Las Vegas. North-south U.S. 95 ties the two together. U.S. 395, angling northward from California, links the capital at Carson City to Reno.

Many of these highways were built over pioneer trails, and Nevada's Commission on Tourism has given them pet names and prepared special milepost brochures. We've patterned our interior explorations along some of these routes. Tourist officials call I-80 the Wagon Master Trail and I-15 is the Los Angeles Highway, of course. U.S. 95 is the Silver Trail; U.S. 93, running north from Las Vegas to Wells, is the Caravan Trail. Route 50 through the middle of Nevada is the Loneliest Road, a title earned from a 1986 Life Magazine article. I-80 and 15 are the state's only freeways, except for short links around Reno, Las Vegas, Lake Tahoe and Carson City.

BY AIR • Las Vegas and Reno are served by many major national and international airlines. McCarran International in Las Vegas hosts more than 35 scheduled or chartered carriers, handling 30 million passengers a year. Call (702) 798-5410 for flight information. Reno-Cannon International is served by a dozen carriers. Call (702) 328-6400.

BY TRAIN • Amtrak's *Desert Wind* serves Las Vegas from Los Angeles, headed for Salt Lake City and beyond. The cross-country *California Zephyr* serves Reno and towns along Interstate 80 from San Francisco-Oakland. Call (800) USA-RAIL.

BY BUS • Greyhound pauses in most major communities, but few of Nevada's smaller towns enjoy bus service. Call (702) 322-4511 in Reno and (702) 382-2640 in Las Vegas.

BY EL CHEAPO BUS TOUR • Some large Las Vegas, Reno and Lake Tahoe casinos sponsor super-cheap bus tours from southern and northern California. They underwrite most of the cost of the bus ticket and then give you cash or casino chips, plus discount books, making the trip practically free. Some are overnighters with cheap hotel rates; others are one-day

— photo courtesy Las Vegas News Bureau

If you can't come to the wedding, the wedding will come to you in marriage-easy Nevada. This "marriage a la cart" is in Las Vegas.

round-trippers that give you several hours to gamble. Most travel agents have details on these trips.

Getting married

With liberalized divorce laws in many states, Nevada is no longer a mecca for dissenting couples. However, it's still fashionable to get hitched there. Las Vegas is the marriage mecca of the state; more than 70,000 couple a year tie the knot in Glitter City. Nevada weddings can be wonderfully romantic in one of Las Vegas or Reno's grand churches, or wonderfully tacky in one of the neon-piped "marriage mills."

Nevada has no waiting period and requires no blood test. All that is needed is a driver's license for identification and $35 for a marriage license (available at court houses throughout the state) and a willing couple. Those 16 and 17 need a notarized affidavit of parental consent. For a quickie wedding, a justice of the peace or marriage commissioner (or deputy) will do the deed at the courthouse for a $25 to $30 fee. Or, check out one of the state's hundreds of marriage mills. You'll find them in the Yellow Pages, under "Wedding Chapels" (right after "Weather Stripping"). The Reno-Carson City Nevada Bell directory has eight pages of chapels; the Las Vegas phone book has a dozen.

Several large casino hotels have their own chapels. The Excalibur in Las Vegas, for instance, offers a Medieval English themed wedding. You can get married aboard the Tahoe Queen and Lake Mead Ferry Service or at Ponderosa Ranch tourist park at Lake Tahoe. Scenic Weddings of Las Vegas will marry you anywhere you want, on or off the ground.

One call does it all for many of the chapels. They'll arrange music, still and video photography, limo service, a reception, proper witnesses, tuxedo rental, gifts, flowers and accessories, even a ring selection. Many chapels never close. If you're really in a hurry, Little White Chapel in Las Vegas features the "original drive up wedding window."

Ministers make the rounds from chapel to chapel on a tight schedule, tying the knot, shaking hands, kissing brides, signing documents, accepting fees and moving on. Some ministers will come to you. Weddings among the slots are not uncommon. About 500 people in Nevada are licensed to perform marriages. For years, anyone with a "congregation" of five or more could be licensed, giving rise to a legion of "Marryin' Sams." Laws were tightened a few years ago, saying that marriages must be "incidental" to a pastor's other duties. Still, Sams and Mrs. Sams perform about 56,000 marital mergers a year in Las Vegas alone.

Cost? You can get married on the cheap for about $65 ($35 license fee plus $25 or $30 for the ceremony) if you go to a deputy justice of the peace. At a commercial wedding chapel, figure on a minimum of $100, including $35 for the license, $40 to $60 for the chapel and maybe $25 to $40 for the padre's pocket. The basic fee buys you about half an hour of chapel time. Of course, once you start the add-ons, the cost goes into the hundreds or even thousands. Most chapels take credit cards, although the minister's fee should be paid in cash.

Compared with a big ceremony at home, a Nevada wedding is a bargain. Further, you won't have to feed all those relatives and listen to Aunt Ethel's gossip at the reception. Besides, haven't you *always* wanted to get married under a waterfall? Las Vegas Wedding Gardens has one.

All types of marriages are available: Protestant, Catholic, Jewish, heathen, generic. Bi-lingual, multi-lingual, write your own script or just stand numbly and nod your head. Nevada's most popular wedding days? Valentine's Day (ah, romance), followed by New Year's Eve (ah, tax break).

Getting—??

Nevada is one of the few places in the Western Hemisphere with areas that legally sanction the world's oldest profession. Naturally, it arouses curiosity (and perhaps other things) among visitors.

The most famous of Nevada's bawdy houses is Joe Conforte's Mustang Ranch, in Story County, ten miles east of Reno. In 1971, after years of legal battling, this Sicilian-born entrepreneur of intimacy from Oakland, California, convinced local officials to formally legalize prostitution.

However, the trade itself goes back to the state's earliest days. The first whorehouses likely were in Virginia City. At the peak of Comstock silver output in the 1860s, as many as 300 "fallen angels" were putting out as well. Naturally, they followed the flow of gold and silver and cattle to Reno, Winnemucca, Elko, Ely, Tonopah, Goldfield, Austin and Eureka.

Some of the places were grimy little cribs, but others were classy places. Whores had a special place in the hearts of those randy miners, and not just for the obvious reasons.

"The miners—hands calloused, boots worn, having smelled only sagebrush and sweat—why, the poor bastards knew that the one place they could get a welcome, a smile, a bed with springs, clean sheets, the smell of perfume, was the crib," wrote 1920s Governor James Scrugham.

However, if the cat houses were havens for miners, they could be hell for the girls.

"All night, men have pawed and used her and not one has given a damn about her feelings," writes George Williams III, in *Rosa May: The Search for a Mining Camp Legend* (©) 1980). "She may start to drink hard, snuff cocaine or take laudanum (an opium derivate), to ease the pain of her loneliness."

Suicide rates were high among prostitutes and many died of disease contracted from their customers. Others' health deteriorated from poor diet, abuse or chronic depression. In those days before planned parenthood, hookers used concoctions such as bichloride of mercury, potassium permagnate, lysol and mercuric cyanide to prevent infection and pregnancy.

During this century, most of the rest of the West outlawed prostitution. Neighboring California never formally legalized the trade, although some of its gold rush towns condoned it until the 1950s. Meanwhile, Nevada just kept going along its randy way.

Interestingly, the U.S. military was the first agency to bring real pressure on this Nevada-style contact sport. Bases that opened here during World War II initially were a boon to the ladies of the night. Frisky troops on liberty hurried to the cribs along the banks of the Truckee River in Reno and the notorious Block Sixteen of Las Vegas.

However, increases in social diseases and complaints from wives about wayward husbands brought action from base commanders. They had no authority over local communities, but they could—and did—put them off limits to their troops. The locals cooperated by closing down their decades-old houses of the night. To this day, Nevada's four most populous counties—Washoe, Douglas, Carson and Clark—containing Reno, Lake Tahoe, Carson City and Las Vegas, are the only ones that specifically outlaw prostitution.

Many of the smaller counties, more liberal and probably needing the business, continue to let the ladies operate. However, legal whoring is hardly rampant (if that's the proper word) in the state. As of this writing, only 36 cathouses were county licensed. An assortment of local ordinances outlaw pimping, set up zones, and limit sign sizes and advertising. When a regulation in Beatty required that cribs had to be at least 300 yards from a school or church, the locals complied by moving the school.

Legalizing lust

Today, Storey and Lyon counties have formal pro-prostitution laws. Many of the other "cow counties" continue to operate under their old codes which imply: "We aren't saying you should be doing this, but since you are, you must follow certain standards."

Red light districts are strictly zoned and cat houses usually gather in small clusters not far from downtown areas. On the surface, most appear to be rather modest little bars. Which is what they are, with bedrooms attached. If you're curious, you could stop in for a drink, although you may be distracted by a scantily-clad, alarmingly friendly "hostess."

In Reno, Carson City, Las Vegas and Tahoe, you'll probably get a blank stare from a cab driver, desk clerk or elevator operator if you ask where the frisky action is. Or they may suggest that you check the Yellow Pages under "Escort Services" or "Massage." If the ad says the place is "county licensed," it's across the line, where anything goes. Otherwise, all you may get is an escort, or maybe even a massage.

In Las Vegas, most of the adult action can be found under "Entertainers." The phone book contains 40 pages of ads offering adult dancers, hostesses, strippers, convention escorts, dream girls, calendar girls, centerfold kittens and—oh yes—breathless males. More explicit ads fill the pages of free adult pleasure tabloids in news racks throughout the city. Their primary gigs are personalized strip tease, dirty dancing or just getting naked in the privacy of your hotel room, which is not illegal. Options include nude aerobics, bondage, whips and chains, and oil wrestling (oil included).

Are these ladies prostitutes? Knowledgeable sources in Glitter City say many of them will perform extracurricular activities for an additional fee. They're busted occasionally by vice cops posing as horny conventioneers, but their business continues to thrive. And yes, many take credit cards.

The frisky districts aren't hard to find in Nevada's "legal counties." They're pinpointed in *Best Cat Houses in Nevada* by J.R. Schwartz, © 1991, available at many Nevada bookstores. Or check under "Brothels" in the phone book covering Elko, Humboldt, Lander & Pershing counties. At least, you won't get an accidental massage.

Beating the heat

The idea, folks, is to visit northern Nevada in the summer and southern Nevada in the winter. However, you may be tempted by some great room rates and special packages during Las Vegas' slower summer season. Why not? Everything but your luck is protected by air conditioning.

Also, Nevada's desert interior deserves exploring, which will take you into some remote and warm areas. Therefore, some comments about heat, desert driving and desert survival are in order.

Sizzling summers don't seem to bother the state's residents since the majority of them live in the Las Vegas area. With air conditioning and a little common sense, they do just fine.

Heat is not a problem if you keep a cool head. For one thing, desert heat is dry. Humidity, not heat alone, causes the greatest discomfort. It inhibits perspiration, which is the body's natural air conditioner. For instance, at zero humidity, 115 degrees has a "discomfort rating" of only 103. (Only?) It's like a wind-chill factor in reverse. However, if the mercury hits 115 and the humidity is 40 percent, the discomfort factor spirals to 151, which would make survival impossible. Fortunately, that combination never occurs in the Nevada desert.

Follow these steps to keep your cool when the weather's not:

✹ Don't be a mad dog or an Englishman. Plan your outdoor activities in the early morning and evening. Save the noonday sun for the casinos and swimming pool.

✹ Avoid dehydration by drinking plenty of water. And we mean *plenty*. A gallon a day will keep heatstroke away.

✹ If you're out in the heat, avoid sweet drinks or alcohol, which speed up dehydration. Besides, you chubby little rascal, the average soft drink contains *twelve teaspoons* of sugar. The best thing to drink is plain old water. Some of those athletic drinks are useful, since they replace minerals and electrolytes.

✹ Don't take a lot of salt, despite what they told you in boot camp. Salt causes your body to retain water, and you *want* to perspire. That's what keeps you cool. It's important to keep plenty of fluid circulating through your system.

* Don't exert yourself on a hot day. Your body will lose more fluid than you can replace.

* Wear light-colored, reflective clothing, preferably cotton or linen. Avoid nylon and polyester, since these fabrics don't "breathe" and this traps body heat against your skin.

* If you must work or play outdoors in the heat, dip your shirt or blouse in water frequently. The garment's evaporation, along with that from your body, will help keep you cool.

Shielding the sun

Southwestern states such as Nevada and Arizona suffer high skin cancer rates. Because of their southern latitude and clear air, more of the sun's damaging ultraviolet rays reach the earth. Skin cancer can develop late in life, years after you've stopped getting your annual tan. One form, melanoma, can be deadly. Even if you don't get skin cancer, which is nearly 100 percent preventable, excess sun exposure will lead to premature wrinkling.

Some drugs increase your skin's sensitivity to the sun, so check with your pharmacist. Among the suspect items are hormone-based drugs including birth control pills, some tranquilizers, diuretics, sulfa drugs and antibiotics such as Vibramycin and Tetracycline. Even some artificial sweeteners and perfumes are suspect.

Take these precautions to keep your hide from being fried:

* Use sunscreen with a high SPF (sun protection factor). Anything above 15 is a virtual sunblock. Even if you're working on a tan, use sunblock on sensitive areas, such as your lips, nose and—yes—the tops of your ears. Also, if you have a bald pate, remember to protect that, preferably by wearing a hat instead of a sun visor.

* Bear in mind that suntan lotion tends to rinse off in water, so re-lather yourself after you've taken a dip.

* If you spend a lot of time outdoors, some specialists recommend getting a careful, light tan. Moderately tanned skin will resist sunburn, up to a point. You can still get singed from prolonged exposure, however. Get your tan *very slowly*. After all, you're on vacation, so what's the rush? Limit your initial exposure to a few minutes a day. Do your tanning in the morning or late afternoon.

* Always wear a broad-brimmed hat or visor outdoors. It'll protect your eyes from sun glare and shield your face from sunburn. The *vaqueros* knew what they were doing when they created the sombrero.

I prefer to keep moving as I work on my tan—walking, swimming, bike-riding and such. If you baste yourself in the sun, you may doze off and get too much exposure. Besides, it's boring.

Incidentally, clouds don't block all of the sun's ultraviolet rays. Also, reflections from sand, pool decks or water can intensify burning. Wet T-shirts may look rather fetching on the right bodies, but they offer almost no sun protection.

If you *do* get burned, ease the pain with a long dip in the pool or a lingering, cool shower, then use one of those over-the- counter anesthetic sprays. (However, repeated use of anesthetics can create allergic reactions in some people.) Antihistamine will relieve the itch. That's right; the same stuff that you take for the sniffles. Also, keep your skin out of the sun until it's fully healed. Catch a lounge show, order a tall gin cooler and try to forget the itchy burn.

Surviving the desert

Nevada's interior occupies thousands of square miles of open spaces. These can be intimidating places if you're stranded. If you're tempted, as we often are, to explore this remote and beautiful world, save the urge for fall, winter or spring. Southern and interior Nevada summers are for poolside lounging, not desert prowling. When you venture into the wilds, let someone know where you're going, and when you intend to return.

Keep these pointers in mind if you wander off well-traveled asphalt:

* First, foremost and always, take plenty of *water*. Water to drink, to soak your clothes, to top off a leaky radiator. It's cheap, it's easily portable and it can save your life.

* Give your vehicle a physical before going into the boonies, to ensure that it'll get you back.

* Take extra engine oil, coolant and an emergency radiator sealant. Include spare parts such as fan belts, a water pump, radiator hoses and tools to install these things. Toss an extra spare tire into the trunk, along with a tire pump, patching and sealant, and that universal item of survival gear—duct tape.

* Take food with you—stuff that won't spoil. If your vehicle breaks down, you may be out there for a while. Also pack matches, a small shovel, aluminum foil (for signaling), a can opener, a powerful flashlight and a space blanket so you can snooze in the shade of your car.

* A CB radio or cellular phone can be a life-saver. Remember that channel 9 is the emergency CB band, monitored by rescue agencies.

* ***Never*** drive off-road, particularly in an on-road vehicle. Loose, sandy desert soil can trap your car in an instant, even if the ground looks solid. We don't leave established roadways as a matter of principle, because tires are hell on the fragile desert environment. And no, we don't approve of "off-road" areas.

* Even if you keep to the roads, you might get stuck in a sand-blown area or a soft shoulder. Carry a tow chain and tire supports for soft sand, like strips of carpeting. An inexpensive device called a "come-along," sort of a hand-winch, can get you out of a hole, if you can find something for an anchor.

* If you do become stranded in the desert, stay in the shade of your car—*not* in the vehicle itself. Otherwise, you'll get a painful lesson about the greenhouse effect. Don't try to walk out of the desert, particularly during the heat of the day. Besides, a vehicle is easier to spot than a lonely hiker. Use a mirror or aluminum foil as a signal device, and build a signal fire. A spare tire will burn, and a douse of oil will make the fire nice and smoky. Start your blaze in a cleared area away from your vehicle. You don't want to launch a wildfire that might compound your predicament.

* If you're on a road and you know that you can reach civilization on foot, do your walking at night. Take all the water you can carry.

Incidentally, heat isn't your only problem in the desert. Flash floods can roar down dry washes and across roadway dips, particularly during the late spring and summer. If you're driving or hiking in the desert and a sudden rainstorm hits, keep to the high ground until it passes.

Avoiding "heat sickness"

Heat exhaustion and its lethal cousin heatstroke are real dangers on hot summer days. Both are brought on by a combination of dehydration and sun. And these aren't just risks of the remote desert. Heat sickness can strike on a hot day in downtown Las Vegas.

Signs of heat exhaustion are weariness, muscle cramps and clammy skin. The pulse may slow and you may become unusually irritable. If left untreated, heat exhaustion can lead to deadly heatstroke. The skin becomes dry and hot, the pulse may quicken and you'll experience nausea and possibly a headache. Convulsions, unconsciousness, even death can follow.

At the first sign of heat sickness, get out of the sun and into the shade. Stay quiet and drink water—plenty of water. If you're near a pool, faucet or stream, douse your face and body with water, and soak your clothes. You *must* lower your body temperature quickly!

JUST THE FACTS

Size • 109,590 square miles; seventh largest state. Measures 320 miles wide by about 483 miles long.

Population • About 1.2 million (1990 census); largest city is Las Vegas with about 750,000 residents.

Population density • About nine people per square mile; ranks 49th among the states, after Alaska.

Elevations • Highest point, Boundary Peak in the Sierra Nevada southeast of Carson City—13,143 feet. Lowest point, Colorado River at the Nevada-California-Arizona border—470 feet.

Admitted to the Union • October 31, 1864, as the 36th state.

Time zone • Pacific, except in a few small enclaves along the Idaho border that run on Mountain time.

Taxes • Seven percent sales tax levied on most purchases, except grocery items. (No, gambling revenue doesn't pay all the state's bills.)

Telephone area code • (702) for the entire state. (So why do we keep repeating the area code? To label it as a phone number, and to separate local numbers from toll-free ones.)

Official things • **State motto**—"All for our country"; **state song**—Home Means Nevada (which we've never heard; has anyone?); **state colors**—blue (for the wide open skies) and silver (for the mineral); **state bird**—mountain bluebird; **state animal**—desert bighorn; **state reptile**—desert tortoise; **state flower**—sagebrush; **state tree**—bristlecone pine (also the single leaf pinyon); **state gems**—turquoise and black fire opal; **state mineral**—silver; **state rock**—sandstone; **official fish**—Lahontan cutthroat; **official fossil**—ichthyosaur.

State nicknames • Silver State and Sagebrush State.

Motorists' laws • Safety belts must be worn (enforcement is secondary, which means you must first be stopped for another violation). Children under four or weighing less than 40 pounds must be secured by a child restraint. Speed limit is 55 mph; 65 where posted on rural freeways.

Indian reservations • They're considered sovereign territories, with their own laws, which generally agree with those of the rest of the state. They pay federal taxes on sales items, but not local taxes. Some reservations earn funds by operating smoke shops, selling tax-free cigarettes, along with

30 — CHAPTER ONE

arts and crafts items and sometimes fireworks. State hunting and fishing licenses aren't needed on reservations, but most require local permits, so make sure you inquire.

TO LEARN MORE

Dial (800) NEVADA-8 (638-2328). Also check these sources:

Nevada Commission on Tourism, Capitol Complex, Carson City, NV 89710; phone number above.

Las Vegas Convention & Visitors Authority, 3150 Paradise Rd., Las Vegas, NV 89109; (702) 733-2323.

Reno-Sparks Convention & Visitors Authority, 4590 S. Virginia St., Reno, NV 89502; (800) FOR-RENO outside Nevada or (702) 827-RENO.

Lake Tahoe Visitors Authority, P.O. Box 16299, South Lake Tahoe, CA 95706; (800) AT-TAHOE outside Nevada or (916) 544-5050.

Outdoor pursuits

Nevada Division of State Parks, Capitol Complex, Carson City, NV 89710; (702) 687-4387.

Great Basin National Park, Baker, NV 89311; (702) 234-7331.

Lake Mead National Recreation Area, 601 Nevada Hwy., Boulder City, NV 89005; (702) 293-8907.

Red Rock Canyon National Conservation Area, P.O. Box 26569, Las Vegas, NV 89126; (702) 863-1921.

Bureau of Land Management, P.O. Box 1200, Reno, NV 89520; (702) 785-6402; and Box 26569, Las Vegas, NV 89126; (702) 647-5000.

Nevada Department of Wildlife, 1100 Valley Rd. (P.O. Box 10678), Reno, NV 89520-0022; (702) 688-1500.

Pyramid Lake Fishing, c/o Pyramid Lake Fisheries, Star Route, Sutcliffe, NV 89510; (702) 673-6335.

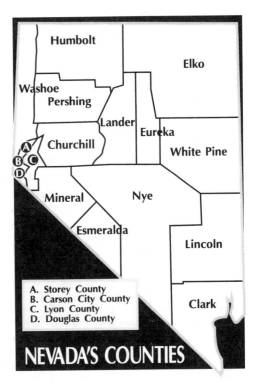

A. Storey County
B. Carson City County
C. Lyon County
D. Douglas County

NEVADA'S COUNTIES

"Of all the seductive vices extant, I regard that of gambling as the worst. It captivates and ensnares the young, blunts all moral sensibilities, and ends in utter ruin." — **Nevada territorial governor James Nye, 1861**

Chapter Two
BEATING THE ODDS
The nervous art of gambling

We begin this chapter with two thoughts:

1. By playing the right game right, you often can win money in Nevada's gaming parlors.

2. The vast majority of people who gamble lose. If this weren't so, Nevada gaming revenues in 1991 would not have topped four *billion* dollars.

It is gambling—more specifically, it is *losing*—that supports the lavish casinos of Las Vegas, Reno and Lake Tahoe. It is losing that underwrites the elaborate girlie revues and the multi-million dollar paychecks of big room entertainers. Losing subsidizes the hotel rooms and meals that make Nevada the least expensive tourist destination in the developed world.

Three out of four Nevada jobs are tied to tourism which, in turn, is tied mostly to gambling. And gambling would not be profitable without that simple three-word phrase that says it all: ***the house advantage.*** Some call it the house edge.

Simply put, the house advantage means that in the long run, the house will win. It will win because a percentage of coins fed into slot and video poker machines drop into a galvanized bucket hidden in the base, never to be paid out. It will win because in blackjack, despite near-even odds, the dealer takes the last hit, giving him or her the edge in most cases. It will win because wheels of fortune, keno and bingo games are heavily weighted in the house's favor. Even in roulette, where an odd/even bet should be 50-50, the house has an advantage because of the "zero- double zero."

Of course, the longer you stay at the machines or tables, the better the house's odds (unless you're on a rare hot streak). To keep you at your station, most casinos have created a pleasure vacuum. You're surrounded by glitter and pretty drink girls and jingling jackpot bells and the sound of money. There are no clocks, and most casinos have no windows to the outside world. Your every need is met: food, drinks, entertainment, clean restrooms. You need never go outside; just stay there and try to win!

Have you ever kept track of how much money you lose to your slot machine or at a table while waiting for that leggy girl to return with your "free" drink? Also, you may be interested to know that in some casinos, a dealer

— photo courtesy Las Vegas News Bureau

Many casinos offer free gambling lessons to familiarize novices with their games. The standing gentleman here is probably offering unwanted advise.

may quietly summon a drink girl for you, whether you request her or not, when you have a streak going. The philosophy is basic: keep the players happy and perhaps a little foggy and above all, *keep them!*

There's an old saying in Nevada (adjusted for inflation): "The foolish gambler comes to town in a $25,000 automobile, then leaves in one worth $100,000—a Greyhound bus."

So what accounts for the great popularity of Nevada's casinos? Why do so many people travel so far just to lose money? Simply put, the casinos play on human nature. To paraphrase a cliché, "to gamble is human." We gamble every day of our lives—with the stock market, with a business investment, with traffic, with our sanity in marriage. So what's so radical about investing a few dollars in the machines or tables in Nevada?

Further, there's something maddeningly tempting about trying to turn money into more money. Back home, we labor for an hour to make a few dollars, after laboring for years to achieve the education and skills needed to perform our jobs. If we build a business, it requires a big investment in time and money. Thus the idea of putting a dollar on a table or into a machine and having it come back multiplied; the idea of getting something for nothing—*that's* a seductive temptation!

It's likely that gambling has been tempting mankind since the beginning. Anthropologists will lay you odds that some primitive implements found in prehistoric digs were gaming devices. Crude dice have been discovered in Stone Age cultures of African bushmen, Australian aboriginals and American Indians. Egyptian records show that dice were rolled in 3000 B.C. and Chinese gambling has been traced to 2300 B.C. There is historical evidence that an ancient form of keno helped finance construction of the Great Wall. Ancient Hebrews drew lots to determine God's will, which got Jonah thrown into the briny. With God as the pit boss, Moses used a lottery to divide up the nations of Israel. Roman soldiers gambled over Christ's robe.

Chinese, avid gamblers to this day, are credited with the creation of playing cards, along with paper money, around 1000 A.D. Early explorers brought examples back to Europe, from which evolved the tarot cards, used both for fortune telling and gambling. The four suits are probably of Chinese origin, while face card royalty started in Europe.

Should you wonder, the jack, queen and king wear costumes of the 1400s, and for very good reason. In 1486, King Henry VII decreed that his wife, Elizabeth of York, was to be the playing card queen. According to the Guinness Book of Records, her's is the world's most published portrait, being printed about 500 million times a year!

Christopher Columbus' crew played cards to kill time and supposedly made a crude deck in the New World from the leaves of the copas tree. John Montague, the fourth Earl of Sandwich, invented fast food in 1762 when he became so engrossed with gambling that he had his servant bring him meat and cheese between chunks of bread.

Gambling came to America early, lurking in the holds of the colonists' ships. Not quite pure Puritans saw no harm in card games and an occasional throw of the dice, while the Southern gentry preferred the more fast-paced horse racing and cock fighting. Lotteries helped finance the Revolutionary War. Way out west, Spanish *Californios* placed bets on gruesome bill and bear fights. The great California Gold Rush drew people from all over the world and they brought their games of chance. The Chinese introduced keno and *pai gow*. Mississippi riverboat gamblers migrated across the Sierra Nevada to set up gambling halls in San Francisco. Tinhorn gamblers and faro tables became the stereotype of Western movies.

When silver was discovered in the Comstock, gamblers quickly followed the prospectors, dreamers, whores and the rest of the mining crowd back to the eastern side of the Sierra. Gambling—and cheating—became so rampant that Nevada territorial Governor James Nye led the fight to have it outlawed in 1861. However, the law was largely ignored in the booming Comstock lode and it was repealed in 1869. Outlawed again in 1910, gambling remained in the back rooms until that fateful day in 1931 when Governor Fred Balzar signed Assembly Bill 98.

Money management

Today, sociologists estimate that nearly 50 percent of all adult Americans gamble. With the rising popularity of state-run lotteries, those numbers probably are even higher.

Most of us get a kick out of making an affordable bet—putting up five cents or five dollars or fifty dollars, with the hope of seeing it increase. If we win, we've made money. If we lose, we've enjoyed the thrill of trying to win. It's that simple. Note that we used the term "affordable bet." Gambling should be treated like any other form of recreation. You should invest only what you can afford.

When you plan a vacation or weekend getaway, you budget a certain sum for lodging, food and entertainment. You wouldn't order a $30 lobster and champagne dinner when you've only allowed $15 per meal. You certainly won't check into the Ritz when the budget cries out for Motel 6. By the same token, when planning a trip to Nevada, decide how much you can afford to *lose*. Set aside that amount and don't go beyond it. Make that an absolute rule!

One "method" used by gamblers to try and break a losing streak is to start doubling their bets. The theory is that the next win will cover the previous loss. However, most gambling experts agree that this can add up to quick disaster. Although the laws of probability say that, with 50-50 odds, you'll win half the time, wins and losses come in streaks. They almost never alternate. Try flipping a coin 20 times and you'll invariably see a streak pattern—three tails, two heads, two tails, four heads, one tail, and so on.

Thus, if you lose a $10 bet at blackjack, then double it and lose again, you're out $30. Try it a third time and you're down by $70. A four-time loser is suddenly short $150! Even if you finally win, you've only broken even. And if you start winning and keep doubling to try and build up your stake, every loss takes you back to zero.

On the other hand, if you start winning, don't get greedy. Some gamblers set a strict limit on how much of their winnings they'll "re-invest," perhaps 25 or 50 percent. Then if the cards or dice go sour, they quit while their original investment and a certain percent of their winnings are still intact.

The key to money management is simple: quit when you get too far behind and even when you get too far ahead. Don't become one of those Damon Runyon characters, grubbing around for a five-spot so he can place just one more bet on a sure thing.

We all know that the only sure things in life are death and taxes. And incidentally, in a typically brazen act of unfairness, the Internal Revenue Service will tax you on your winnings (casinos report big winners), but won't allow you to deduct gambling losses.

SHIFTING THE ODDS

With all these warnings, why on earth do we call this chapter "Beating the odds?" Because if you play your cards right (forgive the cliché), you can greatly reduce the house advantage and, in one game at least, shift the odds in your favor.

We are not expert gamblers. However, in the months spent researching this book, we consulted every available source on gambling and winning. We've read the now-legendary *Beat the Dealer* by Dr. Edward O. Thorp, and many other gambling books. We've digested all the "friendly gaming advice" offered by the individual casinos and we've attended casino-sponsored gambling classes. Several years ago, Betty sampled life on the other side of the table by taking blackjack dealing lessons in Reno.

From all of this has emerged some mathematical realities. Gambling is basically a venture into the laws of probability. We can't promise that you'll win, but we can tell you which games offer the best and the worst odds; which are good bets and which are sucker bets.

The best bets

Blackjack is the one game in which you can shift the odds in your favor if you—literally—play your cards right. Also, it's the easiest of the table games to learn, and the most popular.

Craps is a simple game with complicated betting procedures. However, if you bet "pass or don't pass," combined with a free odds bet (to be explained below), the house advantage is less than one percent.

Baccarat is a glamorous game particularly attractive to high rollers. Although the rules are complicated, betting is simple. You either bet with the bank or the player, and the average house advantage is between one and two percent.

The sucker bets

Roulette is a simple game of betting on numbers, either individually or in combinations. However, it takes a good lucky streak to overcome the 5.26 percent house edge. It's more popular in Europe than here, although virtually all Nevada casinos of any size have the wheel.

Alas, **slot machines** and my favorite **video poker** fall into the sucker category. Unlike table games, slot odds can be rigged by the house and there is no guarantee of payback. Overall, the one-armed bandits keep 16 to 20 percent of what they're fed. However, some $1 carousel slots promise a 97 to 98 percent payout. Video poker and **video blackjack** offer some player control, since you can decide how many cards to draw (poker) and whether to take a hit (blackjack).

The colorful **Big Six** or wheel of fortune is one of gambling's biggest sucker bets, making a fortune only for the casino. Depending on where you place your bets, the house edge ranges from 11 to 24 percent.

Champion of the sucker bets is **keno**, offering lousy odds. The house edge ranges from 20 to more than 40 percent. The more "spots" you pick, the worse your odds.

Bingo odds can be somewhat better than keno, since someone wins the pot at the end of each round. Odds vary, depending on the number of cards that have been issued.

Other games people play

In addition to the games above, many medium to large casinos have a **poker room,** carrying on a tradition that has been stylized by nearly every Western movie ever filmed. The method of play has changed little, except that sore losers rarely kick over the table and cheaters don't get shot by irate cowhands.

The house basically conducts the game and collects a five percent commission (vigorish) from each winning hand. Players compete among themselves, just as they did in the old John Wayne movies. **Seven card stud** is the most popular game, in which each player is dealt seven cards and plays his best five. In a variation called **Texas hold 'em**, five cards are placed face up in the middle of the table. Then each player is dealt two face down, which he uses in concert with those in the pen to build a winner. A third version is **pai gow,** in which a player receives seven cards, which he plays as two separate hands—a two-card and a five-card.

Since poker is not played against the house and is really a game for experts if serious money is involved, we don't cover it here. **Five card draw**, played in some casino poker parlors, also is the basis for **video poker,** which we cover below.

Sports and race books are popular in Nevada casinos. They provide opportunity for betting on virtually every professional and amateur game in the country and every horse race on the globe, and even on special events such as elections.

The biggest day for Nevada sports books? Superbowl Sunday. Each year, about $50 million is bet on the game. The largest wager on record was a cool $1 million, bet on the San Francisco 49ers over the Cincinnati Bengals in 1989. Surprisingly, the bold gambler was not an Arabian oil sheik or an

36—CHAPTER TWO

Asian millionaire; it was a casino owner, Bob Stupak of Vegas World. As any sports fan knows, the 49ers and Stupak won. Incidentally, much of the Superbowl betting action isn't based on the outcome of the game. Sports books will accept wagers on which team will score first, how it will score, who will be ahead at halftime and so on.

There are two bets you can't place in a Nevada sports book. Bets aren't accepted on sporting events within the state or on the Presidential election.

Satellites beam the action to a dozen or so TV monitors and odds are written on tote boards. Some of the larger sports/racing lounges look like a cross between a TV production studio and the New York Stock Exchange. I've counted as many as *fifty* built-in TV monitors in some lounges. Even if you aren't betting, they're great places to sit and watch a game or horse race. Most have bars and snack bars nearby, creating the ideal sports bar environment.

Tradition says that the handicappers at the Stardust in Las Vegas set the basic odds, which are picked up throughout the state. The biggest sports and racing lounges are in the Las Vegas Hilton, Caesars, the Mirage and, of course, the Stardust.

Those are the games people play. Now, the specifics of how to win, or at least how to avoids losing so much.

BLACKJACK

In 1962, UCLA professor Edward Thorp, a non-gambler, became curious about blackjack and decided to put it to the computer. After running through tens of thousands of electronic hands, he discovered that, based on the value of cards already played out of a deck, the odds in a blackjack game could be shifted in favor of the player. Simply put, if a deck is rich in high-value cards, the dealer is more likely to "bust." At that stage of the game, one has a slightly better chance of winning than losing.

Thorp wrote all this down in his book, *Beat the Dealer*. From the moment it hit the streets, card-counting became all the rage. Thorp fans won so consistently that casinos began taking countermeasures. Known "card counters" were banned from playing, and dealers used multiple decks to make card counting more difficult. Some changed rules on splitting and doubling down to increase the house advantage, or simply shuffled the deck more frequently.

Card counters then came up with measures to counter the countermeasures. Instead of keeping tabs on the specific number of ten-spots, they followed the general flow of cards or assigning point values to make it easier to keep track when multiple decks were used.

Although the card-counting fad has diminished, many of the faithful are still out there (and still being banned from casinos). Thorp and his followers insist that their system works. Then why aren't all the casinos in Nevada and Atlantic City bankrupt? Because even for the card counter, the odds change only slightly in their favor, and winning is a time-consuming job. Further, there are still thousands of players content to just let the cards fall where they may. In fact, many casinos have gone back to single-deck games. However, they may shuffle more frequently, which breaks the rhythm the card counter is following.

Before getting into playing techniques, we'll discuss the basic rules of blackjack, which are pretty simple. Incidentally, if you're a novice, avoid

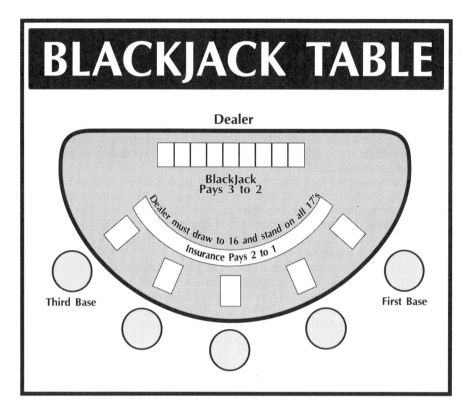

"first base" (the first seat to the dealer's left), because you'll have to play first. If you're anything like me, math doesn't come easily, particularly when you're a bit nervous. However, sitting at the opposite end (third base) can make quick enemies of the other players, since you may take a stupid hit that otherwise would have gone to the dealer. (Gamblers are *very* superstitious.) It's best to sit somewhere in the middle.

Here's how the game works: The dealer perches behind a table, facing one to seven players on the outer rim. (To keep things simple, we'll identify the dealer as "she," since many of them are women and we don't want to be accused of chauvinism.) Players place their bets, then she starts on her left and deals one card to each player and one to herself, all face down. Then she deals a second card face down to the players and one to herself, face up.

In some casinos, both dealer cards are face up. On the surface, this seems to be a tremendous advantage to the player. However, the casino usually has other rules to offset this advantage, such as paying only one-to-one on blackjacks, or counting a tie as a loss for the player. If you encounter a "double exposure" table, always ask for the fine print.

The object of the game is to get as close to 21 as possible without "busting," or going over. Each card has a value based on its number. Face cards count ten and aces can be counted as either one or eleven. A hand containing an ace is called a "soft" hand because it's flexible. One with no aces or one in which the ace is counted as one point is a "hard" hand.

An ace and ten-card dealt in the initial round is a "natural" or a blackjack, since it amounts to 21. A player getting this combo is an immediate winner and is awarded $3 for each $2 that is bet. Otherwise, bets are paid on a one-to-one basis. When the dealer also has a natural, the hand is a "push" and neither wins.

If the dealer gets an ace or ten, she checks her hole card to see if she has a blackjack, in which case everybody immediately loses—except the lucky guy who also was dealt a natural. When her upcard is an ace, before looking at her hole card, she'll ask if anyone wants "insurance." This is a side-bet in which the players can wager that the dealer has a blackjack. Players can post up to half of their original bet and they're paid two-to-one if the dealer indeed has a natural. This allows them to break even.

If she does have a blackjack, the winning insurance bets are paid and the round ends, since a dealer blackjack stops the play. She collects all losing bets from the players' hands, lets the "pushes" stand (players' blackjacks, if any), and starts dealing another round. If she doesn't have a blackjack, insurance bettors lose this side-bet and the hand continues. (We'll talk more about the wisdom insuring or not insuring later.)

After the initial two cards are dealt, each player has the option of "standing," playing the cards he's received, or taking a "hit" to try and get closer to 21. This, of course, is where all the strategy is involved. A player can call for as many hits, one at a time, as he wishes. This is done by a simple gesture such as brushing his cards on the table or tapping them. If he goes bust, he is expected to immediately turn over his cards and surrender his bet. When all players have taken or rejected a hit, the dealer turns over her hole card and completes her hand. If she busts, everybody wins except players who busted earlier. If she has 21 or less, you must beat her score to win.

Once all of this is determined, the dealer pays out her losses, takes in her winnings and starts dealing the next hand.

At the onset, the house has three basic advantages:
1. You must beat the dealer; a tie is a push and your bet rides into the next hand.
2. The dealer is the last to take a hit, so she can collect from players who have already busted, even if she busts herself.
3. Many inexperienced players, and people like myself who can't add up to ten without shedding socks, will increase the house edge by making stupid plays.

The player has two advantages:
1. Dealers must follow specific rules. Generally, they must hit 16 or below and stand on 17 or above. Thus, they can't employ any sort of strategy; their dealing is virtually automatic.
2. Players see at least one of the dealer's cards before deciding on their own strategy.

Incidentally, although both of your cards are face down, this offers no disadvantage to the dealer. The pre-set rule dictates whether or not she takes a hit, so she could care less.

There are three variations on blackjack betting:
Doubling down—After seeing your first two cards, you can double your original bet. You must do this before requesting additional cards. In most casinos, you can then draw only one more card. To double down, you simply announce your intention, turn over your cards and double your bet, or simply turn them over and nod; the dealer will get the message.

Splitting pairs—Any matching pair (two threes, two fours, etc.) can be split, allowing you to play two separate hands. If you get a third identical card (three fours, for instance), you can split again in most casinos, and wind up playing three hands. For splitting purposes, ten-value cards are regarded as pairs; thus, you can split a ten and king. However, this is really dumb, since you already have a 20.

To split, turn over both cards and separate them. You must then make a bet on the new hand equal to your original wager. The dealer treats the hands independently, hitting on each as many times as you request. The exception is when you split aces, which can be hit only once each. Also, if you split aces and are dealt a ten, it's not considered a blackjack. It pays only one-to-one, not three-to-two.

Surrendering—If you feel you've been dealt a lousy hand, you can "surrender" and forfeit half your bet. You must do this before calling for additional cards. Not all casinos permit surrendering.

Rule variations

In addition to the standard rules of play, there are variations that change from area to area, and even from casino to casino. Thus, a rather simple game can become pretty complicated.

The Nevada Gaming Commission doesn't set standards for the games people play; that's left to individual casinos. By tradition, rules in northern and southern Nevada tend to differ. Serious gamblers say the Las Vegas Strip casinos offer the state's most liberal blackjack rules. These are the major variations:

Dealer hitting—On the Strip, a dealer must stand on both hard and soft 17s (an advantage to the player), while in most downtown Las Vegas casinos and in northern Nevada, dealers hit soft 17s (an advantage to the house).

Doubling down—A player may double down on any of the first two cards he's dealt on the Strip and in downtown Las Vegas. In northern Nevada, doubling is permitted only on tens and 11s, which favors the casino. However, these rules can vary from casino to casino, even in the same area. For instance, not all places permit surrendering and some don't allow insurance bets.

If you're going to play serious blackjack, seek out places with the most liberal rules. Houses with rules favoring the players generally post them rather prominently, both outside and inside the place. And by all means, if you're card counting, seek out a place that uses single decks.

Incidentally, *never* become hostile at a dealer because you're losing. Keep in mind that she's not making you lose; she's merely laying out the cards. The way they're played, cleverly or stupidly, is your doing.

MAKING THE ODDS WORK FOR YOU

We'll begin with basic strategy, which any good player employs whether they count cards or not. Actually, there are parallel strategies in blackjack: avoiding busting and hoping the dealer busts. Remember, students, the dealer has only two options—to hit 16 and stand on 17. You, on the other hand, have all sorts of alternatives.

If you're lucky, the dealer will slap you with a pair of tens or at least something in the high teens. These hands don't require much strategy. You pat your cards, smile smugly and challenge her to beat you, or go bust trying. However, most of the time, you'll be dealt something less. With any

40—CHAPTER TWO

hand totaling 12 to 16, the odds are *not* favorable. But you have to play it, or exercise the surrender option.

To help guide you through these troublesome moments, we offer a "hit-or-stand" chart. Compiled from an assortment of gamblers' books and diagrams, it's based on your hard total and the dealer's upcard. Remember that a hard total is one without an ace, or one in which the ace is counted as one point. (Example: If you're dealt an ace-three, your total can be either four or 14. However, if you draw a third card and it's a nine, you must count the ace as one for a total of 13, since counting it as 11 would break you.)

Before going to the chart, if your total is four through 11, ALWAYS take a hit, since you can't bust. Once you reach 17 or more, STOP! Don't take another hit, no matter what the dealer shows, because the odds are that you'll go over.

Otherwise, follow the guidelines outlined below. The left hand column represents your *total* card count, whether you've achieved it with your first two cards or with subsequent hits.

Hitting for percentages
(H=hit, S=stand, O=optional)

Hard total	Dealer shows	Hit or stand
12	2 or 3	H
12	4 thru 6	S
12	7 thru ace (including 10)	H
13	2 thru 6	S
13	7 thru ace	H
14	2 thru 6	S
14	7 thru ace	H
15	2 thru 6	S
15	7 thru ace	H
16	2 thru 6	S
16	7 thru ace	O
17 and above	Anything	S!

As the chart indicates, you should sit on a 12 when the dealer is showing four through six. At first, this may seem illogical. After all, you're still nine points from 21. Of the 52 cards in a deck, 36 have a value of nine or less (counting the flexible ace). So the odds are nearly two to one that you won't bust, right? Wrong!

Let's look at the odds like a cold, calculating computer. Other than the dual-value ace, half the cards in a deck are valued at eight or more (eight through king). So it's likely that the dealer has eight or more in the hole. (Betty's late uncle, an excellent blackjack player, always worked on the premise that the dealer had ten in hiding.) With a four, five or six showing, the dealer's total is probably somewhere in the early to mid teens. If it's 16 or under, she *must* take a hit. Since half the cards in the deck are valued at eight, nine or ten, the odds are pretty good that she'll bust. So you should ride it out and not take a hit. *Did you follow that?*

Note that the chart seems more concerned with the dealer's hand than with yours. No matter what your hard total (other than the option we put on 16), it alternates between hit and stand. You stand if the dealer has two through six showing, hoping that she'll bust because she has to hit 16. Conversely, you take a hit when she shows seven through ace, since she likely has 17 or better and will stand. Your only salvation is to try and beat her.

The strategy above is intended to help you struggle through those miserable 12-16 hands. At best, you'll win half of them by following the charts, and better hands will follow. If you keep getting bad hands, quit before you get in too deep, pocket what's left of your chips and go play video poker.

Doubling down

As you recall from the paragraph above, you double down by turning both cards over, doubling your bet and taking a single hit. The odds dictate that you should double down only when you have a hard total of nine, ten or 11. Also, this decision should be dictated by the dealer's upcard. Here are the guidelines:

Double a nine only if the dealer has a two through six showing. Double a ten only if she has a two through nine showing. Always double an eleven, no matter what the dealer shows.

Basically, you double down when the odds suggest that the dealer may bust, and/or when you feel the deck is still rich in tens. Never double down when the hit (which you must take) will break you. If you're card-counting, you can be more liberal in doubling down (see below).

Soft hits

That flexible little ace offers some options, giving you a soft total that can stay soft or become hard. Yes, lady, we're still talking about blackjack here.

As we said above, your total becomes firm when you must value the ace as one point to keep from busting. The advantage of the soft ace is that it gives you a shot at escaping those miserable 12 to 16 hands. For instance, ace-four counts as either five or 15. You don't want that disgusting 15, so you have the option of improving it.

Generally, you should hit any soft total of less than 17 (an ace plus a two through six). Even if you're hit by a ten, it will merely put you back where you started. If you draw a small card, it can improve your hand. For example: ace and six equals seven or 17. If you take a hit and get an ace through four, *voila!* You've got a very desirable hand, from 18 to 21. With anything above 17, the odds of getting a sufficiently small card diminish.

If you're dealt an ace plus seven, stand pat if the dealer shows two through eight. Take a hit if her upcard is a nine or ten, because she'll be hard to beat anyhow. *Always* stand on ace plus eight or nine, no matter what the dealer shows, because you've got a nice, soft 19 or 20. (Beginners sometimes tote up ace-eight or ace-nine as a nine or ten and take a hit, which could put them in the mid-teens and cripple a good winning hand.)

Soft hands also offer opportunities for doubling down. Remember, always stand on ace plus eight or nine. Otherwise, follow these strategies, say those in the know (and their computers):

When to go double

D=double down; H=hit without doubling; S=stand

Dealer's upcard:	2	3	4	5	6	7	8	9	10	Ace
Your soft hand: A+2, 3, 4 or 5	H	H	D	D	D	H	H	H	H	H
A+6	H	D	D	D	D	S	H	H	H	H
A+7	S	D	D	D	D	S	S	H	H	S

Splitting pairs

Remember students, splitting consists of turning one hand into two when you have two of a kind. You turn the cards face up, side by side, and match your original bet on the second hand. The dealer plays the hands one at a time, making hits as you request.

You can take as many hits as you want, with one exception: If you split aces, you're permitted only one hit on each card. And if you draw a ten-card, it's not a blackjack, but merely a hand amounting to 21. If you're dealt additional matched cards (a third four, for instance, after you've split fours), most casinos will allow you to split again, for a total of three hands. Also, some casinos allow you to double down on a split hand. You're matching your original bet with each split, so use caution here. You've got a lot to lose if the cards don't cooperate.

Once you've started your split hands, play them based on the strategy outlined in the first chart above. But when to split? Most gamblers agree on these rules of the road:

Always split **aces** because they can count as 11 and the odds of getting a high-value card are very good. Also split **eights** because those miserable things add up to 16, the worst hard hand in the game; *anything* is an improvement.

Never split **tens** because you're breaking up a good 20-point hand. By the same token, don't split **fives** because you're likely to draw to the low or mid-teens. If you keep the fives as a ten, there's a good chance that you'll draw a high-value card.

Here are the basics:

To split or not to split
H=hit; SP=split; S=stand; D=double down

Dealer's upcard:	2	3	4	5	6	7	8	9	10	Ace
Your pair: 2's & 3's	H	SP	SP	SP	SP	SP	H	H	H	H
4's	H	H	H	H	H	H	H	H	H	H
5's	D	D	D	D	D	D	D	D	H	H
6's	SP	SP	SP	SP	SP	H	H	H	H	H
7's	SP	SP	SP	SP	SP	SP	H	H	H	H
8's	SP	SP	SP	SP	SP	SP	SP	SP	SP	SP
9's	SP	SP	SP	SP	SP	S	S	SP	S	S
10's	S	S	S	S	S	S	S	S	S	S
aces	SP	SP	SP	SP	SP	SP	SP	SP	SP	SP

Would you buy insurance from this person?

Our last sermon, before we get into card-counting, concerns the logic of buying insurance. As you recall, if the dealer's upcard is an ace, she gives you a chance to cover your fanny by offering an insurance bet. You can bet up to half the amount of your original wager. If she has a blackjack, you win. Further, the insurance bet pays double, covering your initial bet, which you're destined to lose to her natural. The whole thing's a wash. Seems like a painless way to get out of a bad situation.

But is it? Some blackjack disciples think not. They apply logic, somewhat convoluted, in this manner:

You aren't really hedging your own bet. You are in fact making a second bet. The odds dictate that a dealer with an ace showing doesn't have a blackjack, because fewer than one-third of the cards in a deck have a value of ten. You're bucking odds of two to one, students.

Thus, you'll probably lose your insurance bet. And because the dealer has an ace showing, she's in a good position to beat your regular hand as well, so you lose *twice* in one round. Ouch!

Even if you have a matching blackjack, the insurance bet isn't a good deal. On the surface, it appears that you're protecting your blackjack from a push by betting that the dealer has one, too. In fact, you're likely to give away your blackjack bonus.

Let's suppose your original wager was $10. You put up another $5 on the insurance bet, so you're at risk $15. If you both have blackjacks, you collect $10 on the insurance bet and your original wager is a push, so you've made $10 on the hand. But remember, the odds are two-to-one that she doesn't have a blackjack. And since you *do* have one, you would have won $15 for your $10 bet because of the three-for-two payoff policy.

Since the odds are two-to-one that your blackjack will win, why give away $5 by betting against yourself?

Still with us? We told you the logic was convoluted.

COUNTING THOSE CARDS

We saved card-counting until last because it's really very simple, despite all the mystique surrounding it. We'll begin by pointing out that card counting does not require total recall, or anything approaching it. What you're really doing is tracking the "rhythm" of the cards. Remember our comments about the laws of probability? Although a flipped coin has a 50-50 chance of showing heads or tails, it tends to run in streaks. The same is true in cards. And that's what you'll be counting—the streaks.

Each deck has 16 cards with a value of ten, plus 32 with fixed lesser values and four aces that count 1 or 11. Thus, about a third of the cards have a ten-value. During the course of each hand, you'll see every card played, since the players and the dealer turns over their cards when they bust or at the end of the round.

In a normal deal, you should see half as many ten-cards as lower value cards. But the laws of probability say deals are rarely normal. They'll probably vary between flows of low-value cards and flows of high-value cards. When a lot of low cards appear in a hand, the odds say that a batch of ten-cards will arrive in the next round.

In card counting, you don't have to sit there mumbling under your breath: "There's a ten, a king, a jack, and gee whiz another ten..." Use a simple formula by checking the cards on the table to determine if a third of them are face cards. Even simpler: On average, each player uses three cards in a round, so each player should have played at least one face card. If they haven't, the next hand should be rich in tens. If lots of tens appear in the current round, expect some little stuff the next time out.

Although this method is most effective in single-deck blackjack, it also can be applied to multiple decks because you're counting the *flow* of the cards. Even if a six-deck wad is being dealt from a shoe, not uncommon these days, those probability patterns will still emerge.

When is a deck considered rich or poor? When the two-to-one ratio is off by three or more cards in a given round. If several hands go by and the lopsided trend continues, expect all heck to break loose at any minute. If the ratio is off by only one card, most experts play it as a neutral deck.

Another counting method is to assign plus or minus values to cards. It works this way: Whenever you see a ten card, give it a minus-one. Give every three through six a plus-one. Ignore the rest of the cards for counting purposes. This system works because a deck has the same number of three-to-six cards as tens. And it's the smallest cards that really favor the dealer.

At the end of each hand, the plus-or-minus tells you which cards were played more frequently—tens or little guys. If you come up minus three, a lot of tens were played so expect small stuff in the next deal. A plus factor tells you that few face cards fell. It's time to cross your fingers and increase your next bet.

Wait until the hands are played out before making your count. You can take a quick tally as the dealer flips over the players' cards. Of course, if a player goes bust, you need to check his card values before the dealer scoops them away.

Counting aces can shift the odds your way as well, since an ace-rich deck offers a better likelihood of blackjacks. And of course, soft hands offer more flexibility. This process is even simpler than counting ten-cards. No matter how many decks are being played, ever 13th card should be an ace. If a couple of hands go by an no aces appear, expect a batch to show up shortly.

When the deck becomes rich in both tens and aces, that's when the blackjacks *really* begin to fall, so increase your bets. The dealer will get some, too. But she has to pay off three-to-two if you get a natural.

Making things work

So how do you put this information to use? By knowing what's coming, you can alter the size of your bets. Further, after the cards have been dealt, a plenitude or scarcity of tens can determine whether to double down, split or buy insurance. If you've just finished a high-value round, make a minimal bet on the next hand. A possible rash of little cards may favor the dealer while giving you a lousy 15. Conversely, if you've just tiptoed through a batch of twos and threes, fatten your bet on your next hand.

In single-deck blackjack, the smaller the deck shrinks before it is re-shuffled, the more effective card-counting becomes. If only a few cards remain and you know several tens are still out, that may be the time to double down on a seven and three, even if the dealer has a nine or ten showing.

We've said that a deck rich in ten-value cards favors the player, and one with a lot of low value cards favors the dealer. But why? Aren't both drawing the same cards?

Certainly, but remember that the dealer must hit 16 and stand on 17. With a deck rich in high-value cards, she's more likely to bust, and with a lot of little cards in the deck, she's more likely to stay under 21.

On the other hand, you don't have to stand or hit on a set amount. You can do anything you want, short of kicking over your chair and going into hysterics if you're dealt a 15. Here are examples of player advantage:

With many ten-cards due in the next deal, you're more likely to hit a blackjack. Further, if both you and the dealer are dealt 12 to 16-point hands, you can stand pat, while she must take a hit. With a lot of ten-cards out, she's more likely to bust.

Also, if the dealer shows a seven through ten and you've got a bad hand, you can surrender, knowing that you may draw a ten and bust. You've saved half your bet. Another example: If the dealer shows a four, five or six and you have a hard total of eight, consider doubling down. If you draw a ten, you're in the high teens. The dealer, having to hit 16 or less, may draw a ten and bust. Further, if the deck is rich in tens and the dealer shows an ace, this is a good time to buy insurance.

When the deck shifts to your favor, don't jump all over the charts with your bets. You'll tip your hand as a card-counter and be asked to absent yourself from the premises. Remember, the dealer may be watching the card flow, too. If you suddenly jump from a $5 to a $50 bet, you've likely blown your cover. Sometimes, the pit boss won't be so inhospitable as to ask you to leave. He'll simply instruct the dealer to shuffle after every hand or so, effectively destroying your count.

Unless you're ready to take your last shot and run with it, don't hike your bets by more than double; triple at the most. If you keep winning, you might be able to double your bets without tipping your hand. The dealer may just think you're reckless and greedy.

Finally, bear in mind that card counting shifts the odds only slightly in your favor, so you'll need patience. Don't expect to make a quick killing. If that were possible, all those experts would be out playing cards instead of writing books. So would we!

Where to sit

Seasoned card-counters like to sit at third base, since they'll play last. Also, that's a good place for viewing the other cards, since you only have to look in one direction. As players take hits and/or bust and their cards are turned up, you can check the flow of the deal. This helps you decide whether to split, double down or punt. If you see four ten-spots fall in front of you, don't expect to get one.

Conversely, suspicious dealers *expect* card counters to be perched on their right, and they may watch you more closely. So if you aren't going to be subtle about it, sit in the middle and put your peripheral vision to work.

Incidentally, even if you don't count cards, so-called good and bad streaks often can be attributed to the typically irregular flow of a deal. You may join a game when the deck is ten-rich and wow! You keep hitting those double tens and winning. Or you may go into a skid because somehow the dealer keeps drawing a three, four or five to her "lousy" 14, 15 or 16.

To review, students, you can utilize your card-counting knowledge in two ways:

First, by following the basic rules we outlined in the beginning of this section, you should have a one percent edge over the house. By increasing your bets when the deck becomes favorable, you can use that edge to magnify your winnings. Conversely, when the deck is unfavorable, you can reduce your bets and protect your pot.

Second, you can alter your playing strategy regarding splitting, doubling and insurance bets, based on your knowledge of what's coming. Dozens of variations on this can be applied, according on the strength or weakness of the deck. Dozens of books have been written to describe them. If you want to get serious about this business, we suggest that you buy one, since they offer much more detail that we have given here. Several are listed at the end of this chapter.

Whether you take our second-hand advice or read the books by the experts, the key is *memory*. Memorize the charts, the odds and the variations.

46—CHAPTER TWO

Play hundreds of hands at home, with your mate, your buddy or your computer as the dealer. Watch how the cards fall, watch the patterns, the ebb and flow of big cards and little cards. Keep tally of your hits and misses, your busts and wins. You'll see that odds which seem illogical are borne out by the laws of probability.

Practice card-counting, hour after hour, hand after hand. To be effective in the busy, rushed environment of a casino, counting must be second nature. Keeping track of tens must become as automatic as scratching an itch.

Then, take thee to a casino, head for a table, smile confidently at the dealer, surrender some of your hard-earned cash and say: "Chips, please."

She'll tell you then what we tell you now: "Good luck."

After all, it's only money.

Blackjack proprieties

- Always keep your cards on the table, in full view of the dealer.
- Once you've placed your chips in the betting box, keep your mitts away from them. You might be accused of altering your bet after play has begun.
- To request a hit, scrape the cards toward you, or nod and tap them with your forefinger.
- To stand pat, slide your cards under the chips in your betting box or simply use a gentle "stand off" gesture with your hands.
- To double down, turn your cards over and place the new bet beside the chips in your betting box.
- To split a pair, turn both cards over and make sure they're separated, to avoid confusion with doubling down. Place the new bet on one of the split cards.
- To make an insurance bet, place your chips (up to half of your original bet) in the marked area.
- Turn your cards over immediately upon receiving a blackjack, or when you bust. Otherwise, let the dealer turn your cards over at the end of play, and remove them. If you've won, she'll add a stack equal to your chips and push them toward you.
- It's considered proper form to tip the dealer, either by offering a chip or two at the end of a hand, or by making a side-bet for her. This won't alter the course of play, and don't expect her to slip you an ace off the bottom of the deck. However, it creates a pleasant rapport. She'll likely be more patient if you're a slow learner, and perhaps even point out a stupid move you've made. Further, if the cards seem to be falling your way, she may be less inclined to shuffle the deck and break up the pattern.

CRAPS

The liveliest and noisiest of gambling games, craps is life in the fast lane. It's definitely *not* a game for the timid or the bewildered novice. Unlike sedate, quiet blackjack and baccarat, craps is a vocal, high-spirited enthusiastic party. Players scream for their numbers to come up, the stickman calls out the numbers and taunts people to make their bets. It's easy to find a craps table in a casino. Just follow your ears.

This game is a high rollers' delight. Bets can be made on every throw of the dice, so money changes hands very quickly. Fortunes can be won or lost in a blink with those lightning-fast rolls. Played conservatively (which seems like a contradiction after the above description), the game offers the second best odds in Nevada, after blackjack.

By conservative, we mean you should bet on "pass" or "don't pass." You're betting that the shooter (the one throwing the dice) will or won't make his point. House advantage for either is very low—1.41 percent for pass (the shooter wins his point) and 1.40 percent for don't pass (the shooter loses his point). Also, you can match or double your pass-don't pass bet with a "free odds" bet, in which the house has no edge at all.

Confused? So were we. Let's see how things work.

Unlike blackjack, craps is a standing game, and often a standing-room-only game at a hot table. It's also the only game in which players execute the action, by throwing those little ivory cubes. However, until you learn the game thoroughly, we recommend that you focus on making bets and leave the shooting to others.

Once a player receives the dice, he keeps rolling until he "craps out" out and fails to make his point. They are next passed to the player on the left. That individual can decline the invitation and pass them on. You can play craps all day and all night and never touch the dice.

The premise is simple. A player throws the dice down the high-rimmed table, hard enough so that they bounce off the opposite wall before coming to rest. That first roll is called "coming out." If he rolls a seven or 11, he wins whatever bet he's placed on the pass line. If he rolls a two, three or 12, he craps out and loses. If he rolls any other number, that becomes his "point." He keeps rolling until either that point comes up (he wins), or the seven comes up (he loses).

The rest of the action consists of betting, either with the shooter (pass) or with the house (don't pass), or on individual rolls of the dice. Many of the quick fortunes in craps are made by people "riding a winner," betting on a shooter with a hot hand.

Since dice have one through six spots, seven is the number most commonly hit, with six possible combinations. Next best are six and eight (five ways to hit), five and nine (four ways), four and ten (three ways), three and 11 (two ways) and two and 12 (one way). If you bet on specific numbers, casinos create their advantage by offering odds that are slightly worse than the possibility of that number being rolled.

The best bets

Pass or don't pass—You're betting either that the shooter will or won't make his point. The bet must be made before his first roll. House advantage is 1.414 percent for pass and 1.402 percent for don't pass.

Come or don't come—Similar to pass or don't pass, except that you make this bet *after* the shooter has come out and established his point. Again, you bet either for or against the shooter. House advantage is the same as for pass and don't pass.

Free odds bet—This bet can only be placed as a backup to a pass or come bet. It backs up a pass/don't pass bet if it's placed before the shooter comes out, or a come/don't come bet after the shooter establishes his point. It's called "free odds" because the house grants the bettor the exact odds involved in the shooter making his point. For instance, if a shooter's point is a ten, the odds of him making it before rolling a seven are two to one, and that's what the free odds bet pays. Thus, a free odds bet combined with a pass/come bet offers the lowest house advantage of all, less than a percent. You can bet either for or against the shooter.

In some casinos, the free odds bet is limited to an amount equal to the original bet, and is called "single odds." Others permit doubling the amount originally wagered, hence a "double odds" bet. The house edge (in concert with the pass/come bet) is .08 percent for single odds and .06 for double odds.

Borderline bets

Place bets—Made after the initial roll, it's similar to the come bet, except that you pick any number four through ten (except a seven). You bet that the shooter will roll it before hitting his point or a seven. The house payoff is slightly worse than the actual odds of that number being hit, so the advantage ranges between about 1.52 and 6.6 percent, depending on the number you select. Place bets can be made and called off at any time between rolls.

Buy bets—You pay five percent commission (vigorish) to get true odds on any number you bet. It's only a good bet on numbers four and ten, which *still* only trims the house edge to 4.76 percent.

The field—You bet that one of the numbers in the "field" on the table—2, 3, 4, 9, 10, 11 or 12—will come up on the next roll. It's a borderline bet because the numbers most often hit—five, six, seven and eight—are excluded. The two and 12 pay double. House edge is 5.5 percent. In some casinos, the two and 12 pay triple, lowering the edge to 2.7 percent.

Sucker bets

Big Six and Eight—You bet that the six or eight will be rolled before a seven. Since a winning bet is paid in even money, the odds are lousy; house edge is nearly ten percent.

Hard ways—These pay high odds, as much as nine to one, but they come up infrequently, giving the house an 11 percent advantage. You select the four, six, eight or ten and bet that it will come up as a double before it is "thrown easy," or before a seven is thrown. Example: If you pick a six and the shooter rolls three and three, it's a double and you win. If he throws a two and four or five and one (or a seven), you lose. Dumb bet.

Any craps—It's a single roll bet; you get seven to one odds that the shooter will roll a two, three or 12. House advantage is 11.11 percent.

Seven—It's another one-roll bet. Despite the seven's flexibility, it comes up only once in every five rolls, yet the house pays only four to one, giving itself a 16.6 percent advantage. *Very* dumb bet.

Eleven—Like the seven above, it's a one roller. It pays 14 to one; real odds are 17 to one. Again, the house helps itself to a 16.6 percent edge.

Horn bet—It's a multiple bet. The player wagers an equal amount on each of four numbers, betting that the two, three, 11 or 12 will come up in the next roll. Again, the house takes a 16.6 percent bite. Do not pass go; do not collect $200; go directly to jail for making another stupid bet.

Craps proprieties

• Keep your hands away from the table surface while the shooter is shooting, and be careful not to spill anything there. That will earn a piercing glare from the boxman. Nothing should disturb with the erratic journey of the thrown dice.

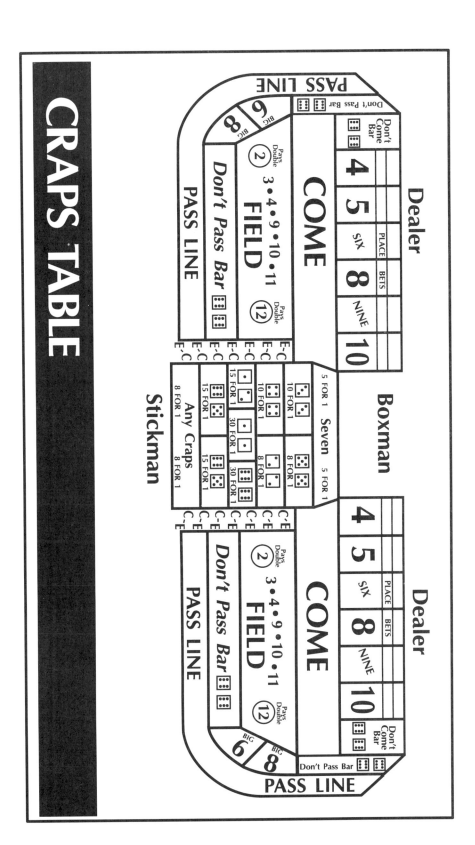

- Never hand chips directly to the dealer; place them on the table within his reach.
- Make your own line and come bets, putting your chips down in the right area. You can add additional bets to the come box between rolls. To make place bets and most other wagers, put your chips near a dealer and tell him where you want them to go.
- If you win, the dealer will place your winning chips in front of you; he *won't* hand them to you. Pick them up quickly, lest they accidentally take a ride on the next toss of the dice.
- If you roll the dice, give them some elbow grease; make sure they hit the opposite end and bounce back with authority. Otherwise, the boxman will frown and regard you as a wimp.
- Tip the dealers, particularly when they've been helpful and patient with you.
- Join the chorus and make all the noise you want. Unlike other games, craps requires little concentration.

BACCARAT

Like bridge, baccarat strikes us as one of those card games that started out with a simple concept, then was made unnecessarily complicated.

It is a quiet, elegant and rather boring game preferred by Europeans and by Asian high rollers who in recent years have made their presence known in Nevada casinos. Because it attracts big-money players, it has been surrounded with glamour and elegance. Baccarat tables are often shielded from the rest of the casino, in posh little rooms. (However, insiders inelegantly call it the baccarat pit.) The dealers wear tuxes instead of casino uniforms. And it's definitely a high stakes games, often with a $20 minimum bet, up to a maximum $2,000 and beyond.

Unlike blackjack or craps, baccarat allows very little player input. Players take turns dealing, but that is mere ritual. Indeed, there is nothing a player can do to change the course of the game. The cards literally fall where they may.

The game originated in Italy and is very popular in European casinos. It came to Las Vegas in the 1960s in a version called *chemin de fer*. This is identical to baccarat except that players take turns holding the bank, and play against the other participants. That's akin to passing the deal around in blackjack. *Chemin de fer* is no longer played in Nevada; only baccarat, in which the casino is always the banker.

The word baccarat is based on the French pronunciation of the Italian *baccara,* meaning zero. And this is one of the game's curious complications. All tens and face cards have a value of nothing. So why aren't they merely removed from the deck? Who knows.

The game progresses thusly:

One tuxedoed dealer runs the game, passing the shoe from player to player. He receives cards dealt by a player and places them in their proper position. Two other dealers take in and pay off bets.

Players take turns dealing from the hefty eight-deck shoe, although one can elect to pass it on. While dealing, a player must bet on the bank. Also, he continues dealing as long as the bank continues to win. When the bank loses, the shoe is passed counterclockwise.

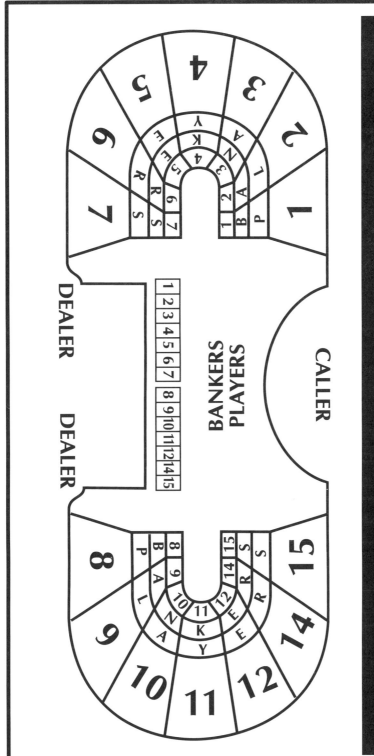

52—CHAPTER TWO

Cards are placed in one of two areas, "bankers" or "players." The object of the game is for the dealt cards to add up to nine, or as close to it as possible. Any hand totaling eight or nine is a natural and an automatic winner. If the count is ten or more, only the last digit is counted for the score. In other words, a six and four equals zero, a six and five are one, a face card and seven are seven, and so on.

A draw might go this way: Player draws two and three for a five; bank hand draws seven and jack for a seven. Player draws a four and *voila,* you have nine and a winner. As we mentioned above, if the count goes over ten, only the last digit counts. Thus, if player had a score of five and drew a nine, the total of fourteen would roll back to four to create a losing hand. Thus, the fall of the cards can become rather intriguing. It's sort of like busting in reverse.

Complex rules, printed and available to the players, determine when to draw and not to draw, and when the dealing's done. Participants bet on whether the banker or the player wins each hand. Because of some vague complexity in the rules, the banker has a slight edge so a five percent commission (vigorish) is collected on any banker bets.

With all this, the house edge is a minuscule 1.37 percent on player bets and 1.17 percent on bank wagers. Essentially, a baccarat participant is betting on streaks, gambling on whether bank or player wins.

That's about the extent of the strategy in this game. From our standpoint, it seems to be about as scientific as betting on coin flips, since the house edge is practically even. If you feel the bank's on a roll, you might adjust your bets upward and go with the flow. If bank and player alternate winning, you might bet minimally until you see a streak developing. Many systems have been devised for betting baccarat. However, since there is no set pattern to the laws of probability, most are probably based on a combination of superstition and luck.

Despite the low house odds, baccarat must be making money for the casinos, since their venues are the most elegant in the place. Some casinos offer mini-baccarat, an informal version of the game with a single dealer operating at a blackjack style table. Players sit facing the dealer and place bets on player or bank; they do not handle the cards. Mini-baccarat tables generally are located in the main casino.

Baccarat proprieties

- When you arrive at the table, select a seat, wait for the current hand to finish, then request chips from a dealer.
- Sit quietly and try to look dignified.
- If you're holding the shoe, don't peek at the cards as you deal them.
- If you win a bank bet, don't pay your five percent vigorish. A dealer keeps track of your fees and collects after the shoe has been emptied and cards are being re-shuffled.
- Since baccarat is such a slow-paced and genteel game, it's considered proper to request food, as well as drinks. Don't neglect to tip for this service.
- As in other table games, it's apropos to tip a dealer. Do it discreetly here. Don't flip a chip through the air and say: "Here, catch!"
- Look properly solemn and courtly, even if you win a huge bet and feel like yelling. (Perhaps you could excuse yourself, run over to the nearest craps table and let out a war whoop.)

Lifestyles of the rich and risky:
A DAY IN THE LIFE OF A HIGH ROLLER

Your accommodations are, in a word, stunning. You may choose between spacious, tropically elegant lanais or palatial European villas. All are complete apartments with kitchens, sensually done bedrooms with separate men's and women's bathrooms, impeccably furnished dining and sitting rooms, and private patios with swimming pool and spa. Maid and butler service are included, of course.

These are the "preferred guest" suites at the Mirage, the most opulent casino hotel in Las Vegas. The European villas, built at a cost of $3 million each and occupying 5,000 square feet, are particularly striking. They are visions from the Palace of Versailles. In my quarter of a century as a travel writer, I have never seen such lavish elegance.

Yet, even if you are a multi-millionaire, you cannot rent one of these palatial suites. A head of state, eminent industrialist or world-famous entertainer might be permitted to do so, with the permission of the chairman of the board. However, if you are an established high roller, they're free. The entire glorious package is yours—the apartment, the 24-hour maid service, plus all meals, liquor, shows, perhaps even shopping in the casino arcade.

"I assume that includes a limo from the airport," I quipped to Mirage public relations vice president Alan Feldman.

He grinned. "A limo? We'll send our jet for you."

"How far? All the way to Tokyo, maybe?"

"If necessary," he said. "Of course, many of our preferred guests have their own personal jets."

I mentioned Tokyo because most of today's top gamblers are Asians—from Japan, Hong Kong, Taiwan and Singapore. A few American and Latin players also qualify for this highest echelon of the gaming elite. Arabian oil sheiks? They don't gamble that much. (It is the Asians who prefer the Mirage's European suites. Grass cloth and hand-carved mahogany are no novelty around the Pacific Rim.)

High rollers, in casino parlance, are people who love to gamble and will risk substantial sums at the tables. Alan identifies these "preferred customers" as players whose bets range from $25 and beyond. Of course, only those in the highest strata are invited to the Mirage lanais or villas.

"These are people who, over a weekend, will commit a million dollars to gambling," he said. "We don't care if they win or lose; only that they spend a reasonable amount of time at the tables."

"What's the game of choice for high rollers?"

"Baccarat," Alan said. "We've seen players bet $200,000 on a hand, which would amount to a $14 million an hour rate. We also have blackjack players who'll bet $50,000."

Most large casinos, including the Mirage, offer perks to lesser players as well. Gratuities range from free shows and meals to room discounts or free rooms. Some casino hotels arrange junkets, bringing in plane loads of high stakes gamblers for a few days of action. However, only a few of the major hotels have suites reserved exclusively for high rollers, and none are as lavish as those at the Mirage.

For convenience, casinos allow high rollers to establish lines of credit. Once it has been set, a gambler simply steps up to a table, signals a pit

54 — CHAPTER TWO

boss and signs a marker for a few hundred or a few thousand dollars in chips.

"All right, Alan, I'm ready for the good life," I said hungrily. "How do I become one of your 'preferred customers,' as you call them."

"Simple. You can open a credit line at the casino cashier, which is even easier than opening a department store account. You also can bring cash or transfer funds to be placed on deposit. Finally, you could just sit at a table and ask to be rated. The pit boss takes down your name and follows your play. The average amount of your bets and your length of play is evaluated and we come up with an equation. Over a period of time, this establishes a rating."

After some quick calculations, I determined that, based on my typical commitment to gambling, my rating might qualify for a free hamburger at a casino snack bar.

ROULETTE

Favored in Europe but only moderately popular here, roulette is another quiet, dignified game. As with baccarat, the player has absolutely no input and can take no action to alter the course of play. The game has been around for centuries in Europe and, since it was popular in England, it soon found its way to the Colonies.

Although roulette is portrayed as a glamorous game in films, with perhaps a stunning redhead leaning over the shoulder of her current jet-set prince, nibbling his left earlobe and urging him on, it's really just a numbers game. It's about as scientific as blindfolding yourself and throwing a dart at a bingo card. Entire books have been written about roulette "systems," which mystifies us, because players are simply playing tag with the laws of probability. The game works thusly:

A handsome wooden wheel is marked with 36 numbered black or red slots, randomly placed around its perimeter, plus zero and double zero slots. It is these zeros that give the house its edge, for it pays off 35 to one, while the layout has 38 numbers. That makes the house advantage 5.26 percent. European wheels have only a single zero, so the house edge drops to 2.7.

The *croupier* spins the wheel and sends a little white ball in the opposite direction. Centrifugal force holds it in a groove on the wheel's outer edge. The *croupier* will announce: "Place your bets, gentlemen" as the little ball zings along. As it loses momentum and starts dropping toward the inner wheel, he will advise: "No more bets, please" or "All bets down." Bets placed after that moment will not be accepted.

The ball tumbles down into the dished wheel and settles into one of the slots. The *croupier* calls out the winning digit and places a marker on that number on the layout.

Players can bet on either odd or even numbers or black or red and win even money. Remember, the odds aren't even because a zero or double zero is a loser. Other combinations include the first, second or third dozen numbers, or the first, second or third column on the betting layout.

One can bet on two numbers by placing a chip on the border between them, or on four by placing it on the four corner intersection. Other combinations can be bet as well; the *croupier* will explain. These bets have higher

ROULETTE TABLE

			0	00	
11 to 18	1st 12		1	2	3
			4	5	6
EVEN			7	8	9
			10	11	12
◇	2nd 12		13	14	15
			16	17	18
◆			19	20	21
			22	23	24
ODD	3rd 12		25	26	27
			28	29	30
19 to 36			31	32	33
			34	35	36
			2-1	2-1	2-1

payoffs than odd-even or black-red, but of course the odds of hitting specific numbers are much greater. In the long run, those wicked little zeros, which are automatic losers (unless you bet on them), still give the house the edge.

Some casinos use the European *en prison* rule, meaning that even money bets aren't collected when the zeros come up. They're "imprisoned" and carried over to the next spin. Or the house may take only half of these bets. This, obviously, improves the odds for the player.

Participants purchase special colored chips, which usually have a set value of 25 to 50 cents. Colors are assigned because a good scattering of chips generally winds up on the playing surface. Generally, players place their own bets. And with all those numbers floating around, it's difficult to determine whose chips are whose.

Although chips have a low value, that doesn't represent the minimum bet, which is posted at the table and can run from $1 upwards. However, you can spread a bet. For instance, you can put four 25-cent chips on four different numbers or combinations to meet a one-dollar betting minimum. Of you want higher values, the *croupier* will designate it by marking a sample of your color chip and placing it on the edge of the wheel. Further, players can use other casino chips to bet larger amounts.

If you insist on playing this leisurely, dignified game, you're better off catching a plane to England or the Continent, where the single zero and *en prison* rule prevail. The game is even more ritualistic there, running at a slower pace, perhaps 30 to 40 spins per hour, compared with 60 to 90 in Nevada.

Busy European tables may have both a *tourneur* who will set the wheel and ball in motion and a *croupier* who settles bets. The *croupier* uses a stylish little wooden rake to haul in losers' chips. Hence, the expression, "raking in the chips."

Roulette proprieties

• Get chips only at the table you're playing, and cash them in there.

• You will place most of your own bets, except on areas out of your reach. The *croupier* will place winning chips beside your bet and nudge them in your direction; you then pick them up.

• Do not try to place a bet once the ball starts descending. Obviously, you're expected to keep your hands away from the betting area at this point. Late bet changes are *verboten*.

• There's no "system paranoia" at a roulette table, so the *croupier* won't mind if you make a list of previously hit numbers.

• Tipping is appreciated after a big win, or when you cash in your chips and depart.

SLOT MACHINES

It's interesting that the Nevada Gaming Commission has all sorts of regulations governing the conduct of casinos and their owners, but none concerning the house advantage. Odds in most table games are governed by mathematics, habit, custom and convention. They're fairly standard from casino to casino.

However, houses set their own odds on slot machines, and they are not required to post them. No wonder that these devices have earned the nickname one-armed bandits!

Casinos love these little rascals, since they require no attendant and are great money-makers. In a good year, an average nickel machine will generate $2,500 or more in profit. Some smaller casinos operate only slot machines, perhaps along with keno, another form of legal banditry. They do quite well, thank you.

On average, slot machines pay out 84 percent. The other 16 percent drops into a container in the bottom, never to be seen again. Sometimes, you'll hear that metallic clunk, particularly early in the morning, after the buckets have just been emptied and the coins are hitting the bottom.

Despite their reputation for banditry, slot machines are the world's most popular gambling device. Some large Las Vegas casinos have literally thousands of them. On a busy weekend, when the blue rinse insurance widows hit town, you'll be hard-pressed to find a single free handle to pull.

When picking your particular bandit, you might want to follow these tips to increase your odds of winning.

- Go to a casino that concentrates on slots and not table games. It wants to attract customers and generally does so with generous payouts. When those jackpot bells keep ringing, the word gets around. Downtown Reno and Las Vegas have the highest concentration of slot-focused casinos
- When you've selected a machine, read the graphics describing the various payouts. Do you want infrequent, big jackpots or do you prefer a lot of little payouts to nurse your nickels along? Machines of the same design and denomination have different yields. Some, for instance, may be jackpot only machines, while others have the full range of cherries, plums, oranges and other fruits.
- The most liberal slots are the dollar carousels, which often advertise a 97 percent payout or even higher. Carousels are oval islands of inter-linked slots with an operator on a raised platform within the oval. It is the attendant's function to make change, pay off large jackpots and urge you to keep pulling. Some slot islands have shiny new cars parked above them, yours to drive home if you hit the right combination.
- Avoid "convenience" slots near exits, restaurant and show lines or other heavy traffic areas. They're designed to catch your loose change and usually aren't very generous.
- By the same token, *never* play slots in supermarkets, drugstores, convenience marts, airport terminals and other non-casino businesses. Again, these are pocket-robbers and rarely offer good odds.
- On machines that increase their payout with multiple coins, always give them the maximum "feed," since these offer special bonuses. Thus, if your budget is a quarter per feed, play a nickel machine and give it five at a time. Graphics on the device will outline the increased payouts.
- Don't get drawn into high-pressure places where hawkers try to drag you off the streets with "free" bonus books, unless that place has a solid reputation for liberal slots. You're interested in payoffs, not free key chains and free pulls on gimmick machines.
- If you hit a jackpot, *stay with your machine* until an attendant comes over, since it may not be set to pay out the full amount. One will arrive shortly, because bells and gongs have heralded the blessed event. Do not—repeat—do not feed it again until your win has been verified.
- This is a judgment call, but if a machine fails to yield after ten pulls, I move to the next one. Conversely, if a machine keeps paying, even in pid-

dling amounts, I stay with it. The law of averages say it eventually should yield its jackpot.

We won't pretend that there's a science to winning at slots. There is not, despite several books that claim otherwise. The best odds are offered by the dollar carousels, but bear in mind that these critters are hungry, taking one-dollar tokes per pull. If a machine gets cold, you can lose money quicker than at a frenzied craps table.

Also, with a 97 percent payback, the critter keeps $3 for every hundred you feed it. Then it keeps $3 of your remaining $97 and so on. Thus, this cruel mathematical law dictates that, without a little bit of luck, the machine eventually will eat it all.

If you like long odds without much risk, try one of the "progressive" slots. These carousels, with names like "Megabucks," are linked statewide by telephone lines and can pay more than a million dollars at a single jerk. A reader board ticks off the jackpot, and it can be exciting and tempting to watch it build. However, only one nickel is added to the jackpot for every dollar played, so you *know* who's making most of the money. Also, conventional payouts on these machines are traditionally poor.

The basic slot machine has three reels with 20 symbols, offering a possibility of 8,000 combinations. Thus, if there is only one jackpot bar per reel, the odds of hitting it are 8,000 to one. If it's a four-reeler, it shoots up to 160,000 to one.

However, most machines aren't *that* tightfisted. They offer an assortment of bars—single, double and triple, with payoffs at various levels. The super jackpot is generally a special bar, perhaps with a seven or the casino's logo overprinted. The current trend is toward jackpot only machines, offering a variety of different payoffs.

Many modern slots allow you to play on "credit," meaning it keeps a record of the coins you've won instead of issuing them. To play, you merely push a button to draw down from your winnings. At any time, you can hit another button (usually marked "collect") to receive your winnings in cash. Being a paranoid gambler, I never let credit accumulate within the machine. What happens in case of a power failure? However, if you have faith in the power company, the credit machines allow you to rest your feeding fingers and your weary right arm.

The vast majority of slots take nickels, quarters or dollar tokens. Ten-cent machines are rare, for reasons that are obscure to us. Naturally, in this age of electronics, slot machines have become more sophisticated. Some display video images instead of reels. Others are activated by pushing a button instead of pulling that familiar handle. (Somehow, the term "one-button bandit" doesn't sound quite right.) A few of the new machines even play you a song as they yield their treasure.

VIDEO POKER & VIDEO BLACKJACK

Introduced a few years ago, video poker is quickly becoming one of the more popular games in Nevada. We may soon see the day when these machines outnumber the slots. Incidentally, the first reeled gaming devices, developed toward the end of the last century, were poker machines.

The reasons for the popularity of video poker machines is obvious. Like slots, they're easy to use and they appeal to cautious low-rollers, since they take nickels and quarters. (The Gold Spike in downtown Las Vegas even has

HIGH TIMES FOR LOW ROLLERS

You don't need to have a lot of juice or be a big-time gambler to earn special privileges in Nevada's gaming parlors. Many casinos, particularly in Las Vegas and Reno, offer slot clubs that provide bonuses to regular players. Also, some hotels offer junkets to low rollers who will commit a set amount of time and money to gambling.

Slot club members are issued plastic cards, which they insert into electronic readers attached to designated slot machines. The card records the amount of coins played, which earns bonus points for the player. Depending on the club, points can be redeemed for cash, merchandise, airfare to the resort, free meals and shows, and either comp lodging or room upgrades. Some clubs pay back a percentage of the money wagered, or pay bonuses on jackpots. Slot club members may be invited to special parties or promotions. They can become eligible for drawings for sports cars and other major goodies.

Obviously, clubs are intended to keep slot players at their posts for extended periods. For instance, one club promises $10 cash back for spending two hours pulling the handle of a dollar machine. That's a lot of dollars to feed but of course, a good share of that loot is coming back in payoffs. In most clubs, bonus points are based on the amount you feed, whether you're winning regularly or not. Generally, quarter and dollar machines are set up for club members.

The Tropicana's club rewards both slot and table players. When members register with a pit boss, points are accumulated based on the time played and wagers made. Some clubs are geared to brief visitors who don't have a lot of time to play the machines. For instance, the Sahara issues Comp Cards which are stamped each time players exchange folding money for coins or chips. These stamps add up to free meals and bonuses.

Joining a slot club is simple. Just walk up to the cashier's cage and you'll be directed to the club booth. If you're checking into a hotel with a slot club, you'll likely get a brochure with your room key.

Among Las Vegas casinos with clubs are the Lady Luck and Four Queens downtown; the Tropicana, Stardust, Riviera, Hilton, Sands, Sahara and Westward Ho on the Strip. The Pioneer Hotel and Harrah's Del Rio in Laughlin have clubs. Among Reno's casinos with programs are Bally's, Harrah's, Fitzgerald's, the Flamingo Hilton and the Riverboat Casino.

Low roller junkets go a step further than slot clubs, providing free airfare, room, meals and cocktails. An example is the Riviera's "Gambler's Spree," which offers vacation packages to players who will gamble eight hours during a two-night, three-day. The longer they gamble, the more the freebies.

To learn about these mini-junkets check with a travel agent, or simply dial a few hotel 800 numbers and see what they offer.

60—CHAPTER TWO

penny video poker, along with penny slots.) Unlike slots, they allow player input, so you can control your fate to a degree.

With no handle to pull, video games lend themselves to a horizontal format, so many are built into casino bar tops. Table tops in keno and sports book lounges may have video screens as well, allowing you to spend your money twice as fast.

Both video poker and blackjack are electronic versions of the table games. Since we've already dealt in detail with blackjack, we've focus here on video poker. Besides, you can't count cards on a video screen; the rascal shuffles after every deal.

Video poker

Unlike slot reels, video poker combinations can't be altered. The machine contains a 52-card electronic deck which is shuffled after each hand. Your odds, then, are based on the generosity of the payout for the various winning hands. They vary from 87 percent and up.

This essentially is five-card draw poker, which you may have played for match sticks as a kid. In case you haven't, we'll review the steps briefly. You're dealt five cards, then you can discard those you don't want and replace them with new ones. The idea is to get a winning combination. They're posted, in order of significance, on the machine.

To play video poker, you feed the machine one or more coins; some take up to ten. The payout generally builds in precise proportion to the number of coins fed. However, they pay large bonuses for royal flushes if you feed them the maximum. As in slots, I like to use a five-coin machine and coin it to the max.

Once you've fed the machine, push the "draw/deal" button and a video image of five cards will appear. On machines that accept a maximum of five coins, the deal is automatic after a full feed. Beneath each card is a "hold" button. Push it for the cards you want to save. The word "held" will appear above or below that card. Then push "draw/deal" again and new cards will replace your discards.

If you push a hold button, then change your mind, push it again and it'll clear. Also, when you're dealt a crappy hand and want all new cards, just push the draw/deal button again.

Important note: If you get a full-hand winner on the first deal, such as a flush, straight or full house, *make sure* you push the hold button for each card! If you just hit draw/deal (which I accidentally did once), you'll get a new hand and erase your winner.

Since video poker is rather new, most machines allow you to play on credit, electronically accumulating your winnings. Some have a button allowing you to bet five credit coins with a single push.

If you've played draw poker at a table, bear in mind that there are variations in video poker. Among pairs, only jacks or better are winners (sometimes tens or better), and they merely return the amount of your bet. Also, you're playing against the machine, not against other players. Thus, the numerical value of a pair isn't important. (In regular poker, the highest pair wins the hand, so you would go for aces instead of jacks, for instance. In video poker, it makes no difference.)

Some machines have jokers, or deuces wild which gives you, in effect, four jokers. Individual payoffs are much lower and you have to get at least three of a kind to win anything. For instance, on a straight machine, four of a kind may pay 125 coins after a five-coin feed, while on a deuces wild machine, that combination may pay only 25. However, those four wild cards make the machine pretty loose and—depending on the amount of the payoffs—these can be the most generous of the video poker games.

Before beginning play, read the payoff chart, since pots vary from casino to casino. This basic strategy should give you the best chance of winning; it's similar to that used in regular draw poker:

- If you draw a low pair, discard the other three cards in hopes of getting three of a kind. The exception: if you have four of the same suit, keep them and try to draw a flush. Do the same if you have four "legs" of a straight flush.
- If you get a junk hand with a face card or ace, keep that and discard the rest, with the hopes of drawing jacks or better. If you get both a face card and an ace, keep either one but not both. The more cards you draw, the better the odds of getting a pair. However, if you draw the jack, queen and king, keep all three with the hopes of getting jacks-or-better, a straight, three of a kind or two pair.
- If you draw a junk hand with no possibilities, discard the whole thing and take five new cards. (Hit deal/draw without pushing a hold button.) The exception: if you have three cards toward a straight flush, keep them.
- Always draw to an outside straight or straight flush, but *never* to an inside straight. However, you should draw to an inside straight flush and particularly a royal flush, because of the potential high payoff. (An outside straight is one you can complete on either end, such as an eight-nine-ten-jack. A seven or queen will complete it. An inside straight would be an eight-nine-jack-queen; only a ten will complete it, so the odds are twice as great.)
- Keep jacks or better and discard the other three cards, since it will return your bet and you might draw three of a kind or two pair. The exception: dump a pair to draw to an outside straight flush because of the high payoff.
- Always draw to a three-card or four-card four-card straight flush, and particularly a royal flush. Although the odds of hitting a royal are 30,000 to one, the payoff is a whopper. Using the same logic, draw to a three-card royal if you don't have a winning combination in your hand.
- If you're dealt a straight or flush containing four cards toward a royal flush, what the hell, I'd go for it! (Example: ten-spade, jack-spade, queen-spade, king-spade, ace-heart.)

We prefer video poker over slots because it permits player input. Also, it's a comfortable game. Many are table-top style, with armchairs instead of stools. In our experience, video poker seems to have a bit better odds than slots (other than the dollar carousels, which have better odds but are more expensive.) Invariably, we get more mileage out of a roll of coins with a video poker game than with a one-armed bandit. This is not a scientific or computer-generated study. It's merely a personal observation.

Video blackjack

This game machine isn't very popular because it gives the house a big advantage. It shuffles after every hand, making card counting virtually impossible. The rules are pretty much the same. A push is a tie and you get

62—CHAPTER TWO

your money back, or you can let it ride as the next bet. Some, but not all, offer the options of surrender, splitting, doubling down and insurance.

If you're tempted by video blackjack, follow the same rules we outlined for the table game. We've never had much luck with these machines and regard them as nasty little quarter-eaters. Since they're uncommon in most casinos, we suspect that others haven't won much from them, either. One reason for their lack of popularity is that, unlike other gaming machines, they don't offer big payoffs. You can't hit a jackpot or deal yourself an electronic royal flush.

Slot machine & video poker proprieties

- Remember, if you hit a jackpot or poker hand larger than what the machine pays out, *don't touch that dial!* All the commotion will soon bring an attendant. Further, don't leave your machine until the attendant asks you to "play it off." If you go wandering off, trying to find someone, some nerd may come by and feed your machine, erasing your evidence.

- An attendant will never take your word if you say a machine malfunctioned and didn't pay the proper amount. Don't even try to argue. In fact, every machine has a sign that states, in effect: "malfunctions void pay-outs."

- If you need coins, push the change button on the machine. Someone one will arrive shortly.

- Just because it's a silly superstition, I never leave a "smile" on a machine. Always play off a winning combination.

- Make sure a machine is free before playing it. Someone may be working several in a row (although this is frowned upon when casinos are crowded). Multi-users become irrational when you coin one of their machines and hit something.

- Expect to be offered a free drink if you stay at one machine for any length of time. It's proper to tip when the libation arrives. It's not customary to tip a change person.

- Don't sit at a machine unless you intend to play it. If you're leg-weary, seek out a seat in a keno lounge or sports book; folks are less fussy there.

KENO

We'll devote little space to keno because it's strictly a sucker game. We'll ignore bingo all together, since every Protestant child and Catholic adult knows how to play it. Keno originated in China centuries ago, and was brought to California during the 1849 gold rush. It is thus one of the West's oldest gambling games.

The premise is simple. You pick up a blank keno ticket which contains 80 numbers and mark from one to 15 of them with a crayon provided by the casino. You mark the amount you want to bet in the square provided, usually in the upper right hand corner. Bets generally range from 70 cents upward, although some places offer keno tickets as low as a dime. On the right edge of the ticket, jot down the number of "spots" you've selected.

Take the completed ticket to the keno lounge, or hand it to a runner, along with your bet. These fast-moving folks, invariably women, cover the coffee shops, bars, gaming tables and slot machine areas, so you can play keno and do something else simultaneously. A keno writer makes a duplicate of your ticket and gives that to you. Note that he or she has stamped the date, ticket number and number of the game played on both copies. This is to prevent forgeries.

Remember, students, only the original, held at the keno lounge, is used to determine the winner. Equally important, if you have a winning ticket, ***it must be cashed in before the next game starts***, or your win will be forfeited. March right up to the keno lounge and cash that puppy in.

Note the game number on your duplicate. It should match the one on the electronic keno boards, which are placed throughout the casino. That is the game currently in progress. If the runner is late, or if you're late getting your ticket to a runner, it may be held over for the next game, so make sure the numbers match.

The 80 keno numbers are marked on ping pong balls held captive in a "blower" or air machine. When the game starts, the machine is turned on and the balls come alive. They bounce around in their little wire prison like excited molecules, eventually to be blown one at a time into a capture chute. The first 20 numbers are collected by a keno operator, announced and flashed on the reader boards. They also are punched out of a master keno card, to be used to verify winners.

The amount you win is based on three things: the number of spots you picked, the number you "caught" and the sum you bet. It should be apparent that the odds are poor, since 20 numbers are drawn from a possible 80, giving you only a 25 percent chance of hitting a given number. If you mark one spot on a 70-cent game and catch it, the payoff is $2.10. For even odds, it would be $2.80. The odds of catching several marks become astronomical. The more numbers you mark, the worse the odds of winning.

Various combinations and groups of numbers can be marked as well. You've got your split ticket, your king ticket, your combination ticket, your way ticket and your special ticket. Brochures list the bewildering variety of betting combinations. They're tucked into racks along with blank keno forms, scattered through the casino. They don't mention the terrible odds.

Why is the game so popular? Because the payouts can be astronomical, too. Where else can you invest 70 cents and win $25,000? Also, it's an easy game to play, a leisurely way to kill time and hope for a killing. As we pointed out, runners will happily bring the game to you, wherever you are.

You might make a fortune even before the ice in your drink melts.

Keno proprieties

- It's good form to tip a keno runner, particularly if she runs a winning ticket for you.
- If you sit in the keno lounge, free drinks may be offered and again, tipping is proper.
- As you're following the game, do not scribble all over your duplicate ticket. It should match the original being held at the keno lounge. If you want to record the drawn numbers, tick them off on another keno blank.
- To replay the same numbers, you can turn in your dupe, which becomes the original for the upcoming game.
- If you've got a winner, get your buns to the keno lounge as quickly as possible. It's not the casino's rule that voids a winning ticket after the start of the next game. It's federal law, intended to prevent forgeries.
- If you come up a big winner, Big Brother will know, because you'll be asked to complete a form and reveal your social security number.

TO LEARN MORE

This chapter should prove useful to the novice gambler. However, it only scratches the surface of the vast complexities of this business. And despite the provocative titles of some of our source books (and the title of this chapter), following these steps will by no means guarantee you a winner.

At worst, however, they will cut your losses and extend your fun. And if trying to win isn't fun, then maybe you're not cut out for this sort of thing.

Many casino hotels offer free lessons, teaching you the rules and procedures of various games. Among them are the **Hilton, Imperial Palace, Fitzgerald's, Sahara, Holiday Casino** and **Barbary Coast** in Las Vegas, in Reno at **Bally's, Fitzgerald's, Circus Circus, Flamingo Hilton** and the **Peppermill** and at south shore Lake Tahoe's **Harvey's Resort.** Further, you can learn simply by watching TV in your hotel room, since some casino hotels offer gambling lessons via closed circuit.

If you want to learn more about the individual games, you'll find a host of gambling books and even videos in various Nevada outlets. They'll assail you with theories, plots, charts, graphs and complex numerical sequences that would give a mathematical genius Excedrin Headache #13.

Two good sources in Las Vegas are **Gamblers General Store,** 800 S. Main Street, (800) 322-CHIP or (702) 382-9903; and **Gamblers Book Club,** 630 S. Eleventh, just off Charleston, (702) 382-7555. In Reno, try the **Gambler's Bookstore** at 195 Virginia St., (800) 323-2295 or (702) 786-6209; it also publishes a mail order catalog.

If you want to follow this business month to month, you might consider subscribing to **Win,** a magazine published by Gambling Times, Inc., 16760 Stagg St., Van Nuys, CA 91406; (818) 781-9355. The firm also offers an impressive assortment of books on gambling; write or call for a list.

Some books you might try:

Beat the Dealer by Dr. Edward O. Thorp, © 1962, 1966; Vintage Books. This is the one that started the card-counting rage; it's been updated, with some tear-out quick reference charts.

The Gambler's Playbook by Avery Cardoza, © 1991; Cardoza Publishing. A slim book with not much depth, it's handy mostly as a quick reference guide to games and their terminology.

Win at the Casino by Dennis R. Harrison, © 1982; Fell Publishers. Written with wit and humor, it explains card-counting in detail and discusses the odds of other gambling games.

The Winner's Guide to Casino Gambling by Edwin Silberstang, © 1980; New American Library. This presents a good overall picture of the games people play and the odds of winning.

A closing thought: Don't go to Nevada expecting to win. Go expecting to have fun and *hoping* to win. Above all, *never* commit more than you can afford to lose. Grantland Rice once wrote:

"When the One Great Scorer comes to mark against your name,
He writes—not that you won or lost—but how you played the Game."

However, he probably never got tapped out at a craps table a thousand miles from home.

(For a complete glossary of gambling terms, see Chapter 11.)

> *"No attempt has been made to introduce pseudo-romantic architectural themes, or to give it artificial glamour and gaiety. Las Vegas is itself—natural and therefore very appealing..."*
>
> — From *Nevada, a Guide to the Silver State*, 1940

Chapter Three
LAS VEGAS
The dynamic, sexy lady of the desert

If Nevada is the party state, then Las Vegas is Party Central.

It is the world's largest gambling and entertainment center—a city where adults can legally fulfill their fancies. It encourages them to loosen their hair and let it fly in the desert wind. It allows them to drop a dollar into a slot and pray for a million more, or throw a pair of dice with legal abandon. It permits them to watch lovely naked bodies onstage, and to order a double martini at four a.m.

It even provides places to park the kids while they're chasing these adult fancies. With new theme parks and even theme casino hotels, the town is becoming an enticement for youngsters, as well as those who conceived them.

Las Vegas is the only city in the modern world devoted primarily to revelry. Never mind that it also has ordinary industries, auto parts shops, paint stores, convenience marts, churches and even museums, like other American cities. Never mind that many of its 805,000 residents live in ordinary bungalows with maybe a tricycle tipped over in the front driveway. These are byproducts of its primary function—to give the world a place to party. And the world answers the city's siren call, at the rate of more than 22 million people a year.

In Las Vegas, the party comes in many sizes and enticing shapes. On any given weekend, visitors can see spectaculars such as Siegfried and Roy's multi-million-dollar magic at the Mirage, the Riviera's technically intriguing "Splash," the long running topless "Les Folies Bergere" at the Tropicana or an Arthurian jousting tournament at the Excalibur. They might catch Sinatra, Cher, Cosby, Minnelli, Goulet, Humperdinck, Iglesias, Rogers (Kenny, not Roy) or the perennial Wayne Newton.

There are confirmed Elvis sightings every night at the Imperial Palace's "Legends in Concert." Reagan, Bush and other public figures have been heard from as well, emerging from Rich Little's larynx at the Sahara.

THINGS TO KNOW BEFORE YOU GO

BEST TIME TO GO • The best weather and highest hotel prices are in the spring and fall; Christmas/New Year is the single busiest period of the year. You'll get great bargains in early December and January/February. Summer is hot but everything's air conditioned, and you can get some good room deals. Although Las Vegas is balmy in winter, it gets nippy at night because of its relatively high altitude— 2,174 feet.

WHAT TO SEE • Downtown Casino Center at night and the Vegas Vic "howdy" sign; the Strip at night from the Mormon Temple on Bonanza Street; the Mirage Volcano erupting (dusk to 1 a.m.); the Auto Collection at the Imperial Palace; Liberace Museum; Siegfried and Roy show at the Mirage; King Arthur's Tournament at Excalibur; million dollar currency exhibits at Binion's Horseshoe and Vegas World; world's largest gold nugget display at the Golden Nugget.

WHAT CASINOS TO SEE • The Mirage, with its dolphin and tiger habitat, indoor rain forest and giant fish tank; Caesars Palace for its Roman statuary and general grandeur; Circus Circus, with its big top look, circus acts and carnival midway; Excalibur for its great size, medieval castle motif and midway; Tropicana for its lush Polynesian look; Las Vegas Hilton for its monumental chandeliers and overall elegance; the Golden Nugget for its brass, marble and gold opulence; the Barbary Coast, with leaded glass and Victorian glitz.

WHAT TO DO • Learn to gamble at one of the many casinos' free gaming lessons; get wet and cool at Wet 'N Wild water park; play a round of mini-golf at Scandia Family Fun Center; tour the Ethel M Chocolate Factory; bowl at the 106-lane Showboat Bowling Alley; catch a scenic flight over the Grand Canyon; turn the kids loose at the Lied Children's Museum; shop 'til you drop at Fashion Show Mall; pig out at a buffet; greet the sunrise in Glitter Gulch.

Useful contacts

Las Vegas Convention and Visitors Authority, 3150 Paradise Rd., Las Vegas, NV 89109; (702) 892-0711.

Las Vegas Chamber of Commerce, 711 Desert Inn Rd., Las Vegas, NV 89109; (702) 735-1616 or (702) 457-4664.

Las Vegas radio stations

KENO-AM, 1460—pop music of 50s to 70s
KFM-AM, 1410—country & Western
KNUU-AM, 970—news and talk
KORK-AM, 920—60s-80s top 40
KVEG-AM, 840—news and sports
KEYV-FM, 93.1—new age, jazz
KFM-FM, 102—country & Western

KILA-FM, 90.5—Christian radio
KJUL-FM, 104.5—40s-60s hits
KOMP-FM, 92.3—rock
KNPR-FM, 89.5—National Public Radio
KRLV-FM, 106.5— nostalgic soft hits
KRRI-FM, 105.5—oldies, rock
KVNR-FM, 95.5—country & Western

This around the clock party shows little sign of waning. Even the recent recession caused only a blip on the Las Vegas revelry meter. Bold entrepreneurs, gambling that more people will be drawn by the biggest, the classiest and the brassiest, keep building larger and more opulent casino resorts.

Nine of the world's ten largest hotels line the Las Vegas Strip (New construction will give the city the top ten largest hotels by 1993.) Steve Wynn opened the posh, 3,049 room Mirage in 1989, with its own white tiger habitat, rain forest and erupting volcano. The $630 million price tag exceeded the cost of all the other Strip hotels *combined*, plus Hoover Dam. Less than a year later, the 4,032-room Excalibur—the world's biggest resort hotel—opened its doors, with special lures for kids as well as adults.

In 1990, with the arrival of the Excalibur and major expansions of other hotels, room capacity increased by 10,000 to a total of more than 76,000. In fact, during a two-year period, 1988 to 1990, the room count jumped by 13,000. This gives Las Vegas more rooms than any other city of its size in the world. And when a major convention hits, all of them may be full. In fact, the occupancy rate averages over 90 percent.

And there's more to come, insist these entrepreneurial optimists. A massive pyramid-shaped hotel is planned next door to the Excalibur. America's tallest tower may jut skyward near Vegas World at the upper end of the famous Las Vegas Strip. A family-oriented Treasure Island resort will open next door to the Mirage in 1994, and a $1 billion, 5,000-room MGM Grand Hotel and Hollywood theme park is in the works, to be the grand daddy of them all.

Gaming revenues exceeded $3.87 billion in 1990, an all-time record; 20,297,382 people came to Las Vegas to play that year. Many come to stay as well, at the rate of a thousand a week. Greater Las Vegas (Clark County) is the fastest growing major metropolitan center in the United States, shooting from about 100,000 in 1960 to more than 805,000 in 1992. It has been America's fastest growing large city in this century. Of course, this is no great trick, since it only came into existence in this century.

How did all this happen? How did a patch of sun-fried sand far from civilization become the entertainment center of the world? In fact, how did it become anything?

THE WAY IT WAS • It took a series of coincidences, unrelated events, non-events and dumb luck to create America's largest new city. During these formative years, this shallow Mojave Desert valley hosted an eclectic collection of sinners, winners and losers: frontier scouts, miners and Mormons who tried and failed, railroaders, gangsters and one reclusive billionaire.

For tens of thousands of years, a small spring seeped from a desert basin, creating a pleasantly green oasis. It trickled wearily for about ten miles and disappeared into the hot sand, apparently ignored by generations of desert wanderers. Even the well-traveled Anasazi, who built sturdy pueblos in northern Arizona and southern Nevada ten thousand years ago, never developed this tempting spot. Later hunter-gatherer tribes of Paiutes pitched their mobile settlements in this Mojave Desert valley and utilized the spring.

When the Spanish established missions in Arizona and California in the 17th and 18th centuries, they forged a trail between them that passed through present-day Yuma, Arizona. In 1829, seven years after Mexico gained independence from Spain, trader Antonio Armijo led a 60-man party farther north, seeking a more direct route to missions in the Los Angeles basin. The group made camp in south central Nevada on Christmas Day, and scout Rafael Rivera was dispatched in search of water.

Young Rivera wandered southwesterly for two weeks until, a hundred miles from camp, he sighted a desert miracle—a hundred-acre grassland fed by an artesian well. *Vegas*, Spanish for meadow, soon became a vital link on the Old Spanish Trail. Eventually, it was marked on maps as Las Vegas, "The Meadows." The well itself became known as Big Springs, later Las Vegas Springs.

In the spring of 1844, celebrated explorer-topographer John C. Frèmont became the first American to visit Big Springs. Then in 1855, Mormon missionary William Bringhurst was sent by Brigham Young to "teach the Indians hygiene and religion" and to plant crops. What Young really wanted was a way station midway between Salt Lake City and Los Angeles. By this time, the region was in American hands, initially as part of the New Mexico Territory, and then the Arizona Territory. The basin was known by the curious Yankee redundancy of Las Vegas Valley. (The Meadow Valley?)

An early beginning for gambling

The Mormons built a 150-foot square adobe fort along the creek, two miles east of the spring. They planted crops, built stock corrals and discussed salvation and tithing with the local Paiutes. The Indians resisted conversion; they preferred spending idle hours playing a primitive gambling game with sticks and bone fragments—true precursors of today's Las Vegans. Meanwhile, the Mormon's crops withered in the hot summer sun, a lead mining venture in nearby Mount Potosi failed and the mission was abandoned in 1857. A piece of the adobe fort survives, now an historic site just off North Las Vegas Boulevard and Washington Avenue.

Enter Octavius Decatur Gass, who was to become the valley's first citizen of substance. A prospector who'd found a bit of gold along the Colorado River, he arrived in 1865 and built Las Vegas Rancho on the site of the old fort. He planted alfalfa and food crops and served briefly as head of the Arizona territorial senate. However, he lost his seat in 1867 when boundaries were redrawn and the valley became part of the new state of Nevada.

Octavius was a generous, hospitable individual and his home became an important way station for travelers along the Old Spanish Trail. Perhaps he was too generous. In 1879, he had to borrow $5,000 from Archibald Stewart, a Scotsman who'd made his money as a freighter in the California gold fields. Gass couldn't cover his debt, and certainly not the Scotsman's 30 percent interest rate. He lost the ranch in 1881; Archie and his wife Helen became the new masters of the Meadows manor.

Then in 1884, in a scene that might have been scripted for a low budget Western movie, Archie confronted a cowboy from a neighboring ranch, accusing him of making a play for Helen. The Scotsman obviously was better at business than gunslinging; the cowboy shot him out of the saddle.

Widowed Helen, mother of Archie's four children and carrying his fifth, carried on. She ran the ranch, established a campground and dining hall for travelers and functioned as the *grande dame* of Las Vegas which, in 1900, boasted a population of 30. She scrimped and saved to buy more land, hoping that a railroad eventually would reach this desert outpost.

This wasn't mere speculation. For years, construction of a line between Los Angeles and Salt Lake City had been underway, in fits and starts. With water from the artesian well and timber in the adjacent mountains, Las Vegas Springs was a logical stop. Mrs. Stewart's patience was rewarded in 1904. Montana copper king, Senator William Clark, took control of the San Pedro, Los Angeles and Salt Lake Road and set about to complete the 35-year-old project.

The coming of the rails

Clark paid Helen $55,000 for her water rights and most of her ranch land. He designated the site as Railroad Watering Stop Number 25. Construction on this final segment was completed in January of 1905 and a golden spike was driven at Jean, near the California border.

The railroad formed the Las Vegas Land and Water Company to conduct an auction of town site lots on May 15. Las Vegas was born. Taking advantage of discounted rail fares, 3,000 hopefuls flocked here to buy a piece of a brand new town. The sale of 700 lots, conducted over two days, brought in $265,000, proving that Mr. Clark was a much better real estate speculator than Mrs. Stewart. However, the first lady of Las Vegas remained a social and cultural leader in the emerging community until her death in 1926.

The land company promised a right and proper town, with streets and curbs and water systems; with banks, churches and churches and stores. To keep sin in its place, the sale of liquor would be limited to Block 16, an area bounded by First, Second, Ogden and Stewart. This was to become the town's den of depravity, particularly after "the niftiest house of joy on the Pacific Coast" was opened on the second floor of the Arizona Club in 1912.

Like the railroad that created it, the new community suffered through fits and starts. Its population surged and fell like a stock market graph on a nervous Tuesday. Even in the best of those early times, it was still miles from nowhere. It was just a hot and dusty town in a hot and dusty desert, hardly the sort of place that would attract jet-setters. A spur line Clark had built to Tonopah was shut in 1917 after that area's mines played out. He sold his interest in the Los Angeles-Salt Lake line to Union Pacific in 1921. The firm closed a large local repair facility, putting hundreds out of work.

Las Vegas went into what appeared to be a terminal skid. Even if it survived, it seemed destined to be nothing more than a grubby railroad crossing. However, like the heroine in a paperback novel, the dusty lady of the desert kept finding rescuers.

Build it, dam it

For decades, man had been trying to tame the mighty Colorado River, which went on periodic rampages and flooded farm settlements around Yuma. Two narrow gorges, Black Canyon and Boulder Canyon, offered ideal dam sites and both were within miles of Las Vegas. A federal program to construct a dam was approved in 1928.

When the Stock Market took a dive in 1929, it should have taken Las Vegas down for the count. Instead, the Depression provided a steady flow of unemployed men, willing to work in the hot sun for fifty cents an hour to build the world's highest dam. Work started in 1931, the same year that Governor Fred Balzar signed the law legalizing gambling. By this time, Block 16 had become a ghetto of sin, legal and otherwise. The conservative Feds wanted their workers clear of such diversions, so they built the company town of Boulder City to house the dam builders. To this day, it's the only city in Nevada where gambling is illegal.

— photo courtesy **Nevada Historical Society**

"If you haven't seen the Fabulous Flamingo, you haven't seen Las Vegas," reads the message on this postcard from Bugsy Siegel's "carpet joint."

Of course, Las Vegas was a mere 26 miles away, a short drive for a construction worker with a paycheck and a powerful desert thirst. Block 16 thrived as never before. The town's population jumped to 7,500 during the peak of dam construction as satellite services grew to support the flood of nearby workers. However, Hoover Dam's major contribution to Las Vegas was more lasting. It offered a next-door source of water and power, and a popular recreation facility on Lake Mead.

The city suffered the expected slump at the completion of the dam, then it settled down, to patiently waited out the Depression. To quote from a graphic in the UNLV natural history museum: "Las Vegas was a sleepy, dusty railroad town from 1905 to 1940. Legal gambling did little to change its appearance."

A few casinos were focused around the old railroad station on Fremont Street, but these little sawdust joins were hardly tourist lures.

In 1941, Southern Californian Thomas Hull established El Rancho Vegas Hotel, way out on the Los Angeles Highway (Route 91), where land was cheap. It was little more than an auto court and casino with a Western motif, yet it incorporated the essential elements of a gambling resort: casino, restaurant, a gift shop, showroom and swimming pool. Texas movie theater magnate R.E. Griffith followed in 1942 with the Last Frontier Hotel, a larger and much more elaborate gaming parlor. These were the early stirrings of the Las Vegas Strip, although their success was only moderate because of wartime rationing. In 1944, Griffith booked Sophie Tucker, the area's first big-name entertainer, to lure more gamblers.

Many of the early Las Vegas casino owners were southern Californians and historians say Pair-O-Dice owner Guy McAfee first called this area "The Strip." The former Los Angeles policeman supposedly named it after the Sunset Strip.

The Strip offered several advantages over downtown. It was—and still is—out of the city limits, where building codes were more lenient and taxes were lower. Land was cheaper, providing ample space for attractive landscaping and parking. Finally, this was the first area encountered by Californians who were—and still are—the town's greatest source of visitors.

While Las Vegas gradually gained momentum, rival Reno thrived. Harold Smith had scattered "Harold's Club or Bust" signs across the country. William Harrah brought class and dignity to casinos with his stylish downtown club. Celebrities came to Reno for quickie marriages and divorces. The town laid cocky claim to "The Biggest Little City in the World" and Renoites looked down their collective noses at their ugly stepsister.

The dusty lady of the desert, now jealous, needed another rescuer.

World War II helped, bringing the U.S. Army Air Corps and its million-acre aerial gunnery range, and Basic Magnesium, a major military contractor. The town's population, having reached 8,500 by 1940, exploded to 35,000 by war's end.

The military put pressure on the sin centers of Block 16, and Clark County outlawed prostitution to avoid having the entire town put off limits. The downtown gaming center grew much more quickly than the Strip during this period, since servicemen and train passengers could more easily reach the action here. By war's end, Fremont Street had earned its Glitter Gulch nickname.

Don't call him Bugsy

The Strip got its rescuer in 1946, but he didn't ride in on a white charger. In fact, he didn't ride in at all. Benjamin Siegel, born in the same year as Las Vegas, had been hanging around town since the early 1940s. (He despised the name Bugsy. "My friends call me Ben," he once growled to a reporter who had mentioned the hated nickname.)

He grew up as a street punk on the wrong side of Brooklyn and soon teamed up with boyhood buddy Meyer Lansky, along with Frank Costello and Charles "Lucky" Luciano. This unholy quartet became the underlords of New York and Chicago, eventually joining forces with two dozen others to form a coast-to-coast organized crime ring. The group was simply known as the Combination. They also operated legitimate businesses, providing new profits and safe havens for their illegal gains.

Lansky posted Siegel to Los Angeles in 1938 to consolidate mob activities and "discourage" competition. Tall, handsome and persuasive, he fell in easily with the Hollywood crowd, hanging out with George Raft, Cary Grant and Barbara Hutton, and seducing wide-eyed starlets. Here, he met Virginia Hill, made her mistress of the mob and moved her into a Beverly Hills mansion. As America entered World War II, Ben started another war, shifting to Las Vegas to muscle in on its profitable race book action.

This town was no Beverly Hills—but the potential! Many of the mob's felonious activities—gambling, bookmaking, sports betting—were legal here. Siegel's arrival in Las Vegas began a mob infiltration that continued until the Kefauver Commission investigations of the 1950s.

Siegel bought into several downtown casinos and began raising funds to build his Fabulous Flamingo. It was named for the hot pink birds that had brought him luck at Florida's Hialeah Racetrack. Flashy Ben wanted none of the Western décor that dominated the town's other casinos. The Flamingo would be a "carpet joint," a classy place for classy gamblers, with a flashy California-Miami look.

The sticky-fingered mobster began skimming construction funds and the initial $1 million price tag skyrocketed to $6 million. Hampered by cost overruns, postwar material shortages and Ben's skimming, the project fell behind schedule. A nervous Siegel kept putting the touch on Combination members for more money. The disgruntled gang bosses, led by Lucky Luciano, met in Havana and voted to ice Siegel unless his Fabulous Flamingo was a fabulous success. The place had great potential; it would set the pace for the glorious and glitzy Las Vegas Strip hotels to follow, with their shimmering neon, stylish casinos and landscaped pool decks.

A confident Siegel told the local press: "Las Vegas will be proud of the Flamingo. It will become one of the world's greatest playgrounds."

Pressured by his bosses, Siegel opened his playground before it was finished, on a wet and rainy December 26, 1946. Even with stars like Jimmy Durante, Rose Marie and Xavier Cugat, the carpet joint drew poorly. It lost so heavily in those first few days that Ben shut it down to complete construction. Reopened in March, it soon began showing a profit. However, Benjamin Siegel's lot had been cast. On a warm June evening, as he relaxed with a copy of the *Los Angeles Times* in his girlfriend's Beverly Hills mansion, someone emptied a .30 caliber Army carbine through a trellised window. He took four slugs, two in the chest and two in the head. It was the gang's first, but certainly not the last, execution of one of its leaders.

Las Vegas gangland infiltration continued. Tennessee Senator Estes Kefauver brought his Committee to Investigate Organized Crime to town in 1951. The probe generated some curious results. It spurred other communities to clean out their illegal gambling nests, sending a flood of illegal casino owners, dealers and other gambling pros in a lemming like march to Nevada. At the same time, it prompted Nevada state officials to take command of the games, which had been under control of counties.

All of this bad press may have hurt Las Vegas' pride, but not its growth. With the Fabulous Flamingo setting the pace, lavish casinos began springing up along Las Vegas Boulevard, like cactus flowers after an April rain. The city's population bounced from 45,000 to 65,000 between 1955 and 1960.

Finally, Las Vegas fulfilled its promise as the ultimate party town. A dozen new casino resorts went up between 1950 and 1958. Topless came to town, in the shapely form of Paris girlie shows. Hookers, illegal but tolerated, roamed the sidewalks of the Strip and Fremont Street, along with 11 million annual visitors. Sinatra, Davis, Bishop and others of the Rat Pack performed by night and hung out in the casinos by day.

Out across the desert, in bizarre cadence to this merry madness, atomic bombs were being exploded at the Nevada Test Site. Las Vegans, jarred by these contaminated temblors, weren't speaking figuratively when they asked which way the wind was blowing.

Enter Howard

By the time reclusive billionaire Howard Hughes arrived in 1966, many of the mobsters had been filtered out of the gambling scene. Or at least, they were going straight and causing no trouble, under the wary eye of the Nevada Gaming Control Board. Many of those who weren't screened out were bought out by Hughes, to usher in the era that rules today: Corporate Las Vegas.

Arriving late at night in a curtained ambulance, Hughes took over the high roller suites on the ninth floor of the Desert Inn. His Mormon *samurai* even kept hotel employees at bay, along with an inquiring press and the rest of the world. Hughes managed to keep so thoroughly under raps that no known photo of The Man in Las Vegas exists.

After several months, Desert Inn boss Moe Dalitz advised Hughes' retinue that he needed his high roller suites for *real* high rollers. (Neither Hughes nor his Mormon entourage gambled.) The guest who overstayed his welcome solved the problem simply; he bought out the aging casino boss for $13.2 million.

Over the next three years, Hughes' Summa Corporation bought the Frontier, Castaways, Sands, Silver Slipper, Landmark and great chunks of land along Las Vegas Boulevard and elsewhere. Hughes spent $300 million and he intended to spend more, on a supersonic jet airport and on a space age city called Husite, to occupy one of his 27,000-acre chunks of nearby desert.

Loving this new corporate image, city officials chased the hookers off the streets and began promoting Las Vegas as an all-family destination.

In the end, Hughes built nothing for the town except new respectability. He left in 1970 the way he came, on a stretcher, under veil of night, exactly four years to the day after he'd arrived. He died on April 5, 1976, a secretive, paranoid hypochondriac—the distorted darling of the Safeway tabloids.

THE WAY IT IS • If we were visiting Las Vegas for the first time, we would arrive at night. By plane, we'd see a great shimmer of diamonds scattered across a black basin, a night sky turned upside down. By car we would see, after endless miles of shadowy desert monotony, awesome towers of neon rising above the glimmering wake of Las Vegas Boulevard.

We would cruise in slow motion along Las Vegas Boulevard, then adjourn downtown and walk Fremont Street, beneath the brilliant canopy of Glitter Gulch (more formally known as Casino Center). Next, we'd head east out Bonanza Street, more than six miles to the Las Vegas Mormon Temple, glowing boldly from the flanks of Sunrise Mountain. We'd walk the landscaped grounds of this impressive $18 million structure, staring upward at its six lighted spires. We'd gaze back down the valley at the incredible carpet of city lights below, like a million fireflies crawling over black velvet.

This is Las Vegas personified: a high rollers' town where even the churches are showy and imposing. Surprisingly, this supposedly wicked city has one of the highest church-to-population ratios in the country. Does this reflect a need for frequent confession? Or does it suggest a peaceful coexistence among the good, the bad and the beautiful?

GETTING THERE

A six or seven-hour drive on Interstate 15 will fetch you to Las Vegas from most points in southern California. The highway continues on to Salt Lake City. U.S. 95 links Las Vegas with Reno to the north and Phoenix to the south. Party Central is about 600 miles from San Francisco, 325 from San Diego, less than 300 from Phoenix, 425 from Salt Lake and 442 miles south of little sister Reno.

Seventeen scheduled and about 20 charter airlines serve the attractive **McCarran International Airport**, alongside the Strip about five miles south of downtown. Scheduled service includes most of the majors and large regional carriers—**American,** (800) 433-7300; **America West,** (800) 247-5692; **Continental,** (800) 525-0280; **Delta,** (800) 221-1212; **Hawaiian Air,** (800) 277-7110; **Midway Air,** (800) 621-5700; **Southwest,**

(800) 531-5601; **TWA,** (800) 438-2929; **United,** (800) 631-1500 and **USAir,** (800) 428-4322.

We'd recommend booking your flight through a travel agent, who will know of the best package deals available. (See **Getting Situated**, below.)

Recently remodeled, the airport is an attraction itself, a pleasing study in palm landscaping, sculptures and leading-edge design. A $7.50 ticket surcharge helps pay for all of this. Of course, slots beckon as soon as you deplane, but do not expect generous payouts; save the urge for the casinos. Although Las Vegas ranks somewhere in the 70s in American city size, McCarran is the 20th busiest airport in the nation.

Since the airport is right on the Strip, not far from downtown, taxis and limo services are cheap. Gray Line airport shuttle is $3 to most Strip hotels and $4.50 downtown (384-1234). Bell Trans limo is more plush and has similar fares (385-LIMO); it offers service to most hotels every 30 minutes. Cab rides range from $6 to the nearest Strip hotel to about $12 downtown.

Amtrak and **Greyhound** both serve the city. The Amtrak depot (386-6896 or 800-USA-RAIL) is in Jackie Gaughan's Plaza downtown, on the site of the old Union Pacific station. Greyhound (382-2640) is next door, at Main and Fremont streets. Amtrak's *Desert Wind* stops here once a day, following the route carved by Senator Clark's railway between Los Angeles and Salt Lake City. Incidentally, Las Vegas boasts the only railway station in the world located within a gaming parlor.

It's the climate

Although Las Vegas is a desert resort and the climate's wonderful in spring and fall, it can get nippy during the winter. Bear in mind that it's high desert country at 2,174 feet. If you want a December-January tan, try your luck in Laughlin on the Colorado River at 540 feet (next chapter).

January is the coldest and wettest month in Las Vegas, but that's not very wet. Annual rainfall is 4.19 inches, which can come as a December soaker or summer shower. It never (well, almost never) snows and temperature drops below freezing only about 33 nights a year.

Figure on about 320 days of sunshine a year, one of the highest rates in the nation. Yes it gets hot in summer but not scalding. The all-time high was 117, recorded way back in 1942. (Phoenix routinely gets into the 120s.) Average summer high is usually in the 90s, and it's a dry heat.

GETTING SITUATED

If you're on a budget, some books recommend jumping into your car, driving to Las Vegas and checking around for a cheap room. *Nyet!* Unless you're wearing a backpack and seeking a youth hostel, ignore that advice.

Las Vegas is the one city in the world where hotel rooms are competitive with mom and pop motels. Never, repeat *never* approach the city without making prior arrangement. To go without reservations is to pay "rack rate" (walk-in rate), the highest that hotels charge. Further, the city has few slow seasons since conventions can hit at any time of the year, so you may find rooms hard to get.

Many hotels offer inexpensive packages, sometimes in conjunction with airlines, so book through a travel agent, who can tell you who has best deals. Even if you're driving, check with your travel agent about special room packages. During our many visits to compile this work, we regularly found hotel rates right on Las Vegas Boulevard from $20 to $35.

There are other reasons for choosing hotels over motels in Las Vegas. You're in the middle of the action, surrounded by restaurants and cheap buffets, and many have special attractions for the kiddies. Further, all casino hotels offer free parking, either valet or do-it-yourself.

The toughest times to find rooms are the two weeks of Christmas Vacation and Easter week. Most of spring and fall are tight as well. Midsummers are better, but with the increase of family-oriented lures, summer rates aren't the bargains they used to be. The slowest periods? The first half of December and early January, from the day after New Year's up to but definitely *not* including Superbowl weekend. That's the hottest betting weekend of the year. Things go slow through February and start picking up in March.

Getting camped

Even the RV crowd can enjoy casino hotel convenience. You'll find RV parks at **Circus Circus** and **Hacienda** on the Strip, **California Hotel** downtown and **Sam's Town** out on the Boulder Highway toward Hoover Dam. **Excalibur** and **Stardust** hotel folks don't object if campers use outer parking lots, as long as they're self-contained. But please don't try to pitch a tent at any of these places. The stakes raise havoc with the asphalt.

Several other RV parks are on the edge of town. Check under **Where to camp**, much farther along in this comprehensive chapter. Incidentally, RV parks fill up very fast in spring and fall, particularly those at the casinos.

GETTING AROUND

We've already established that casinos are focused in two areas, on the Strip and downtown along Fremont Street. A few others sit near I-15 off ramps, west of the Strip.

Despite some twists and turns, the city streets are easy to negotiate. As the map shows, I-15 roughly parallels Las Vegas Boulevard for all of its length.

To migrate downtown from the Strip, simply head north on the boulevard to the point where it intersects with Main Street. You can fork left onto Main and follow it a couple of miles to Fremont (in front of Jackie Gaughan's Plaza), or stay on the boulevard, and turn left onto Fremont, which carries you right down Glitter Gulch. The Main Street route is probably slightly faster.

For those in a marriage mood, many of the city's wedding chapels are along Las Vegas Boulevard, between its intersection with Main and Fremont streets. Several smaller motels and cabarets are clustered here as well. The stretch of Main between the boulevard and Fremont looks like that of any ordinary commercial suburb, with a slightly scruffy mix of carpet stores, radiator shops and the like.

Downtown is obviously an area in transition. New or expanding casinos and modern office buildings are gradually displacing the few remaining dog-eared pawn shops, discount stores and cheap souvenir shops.

If you need the familiar comforts of suburban shopping centers with their supermarkets and super drug stores, head east on any of the major east-west streets—Charleston Boulevard, Sahara Avenue, Desert Inn Road, Flamingo Road and Tropicana Avenue. Much of the city's new growth is in that direction.

Growth means traffic jams, so it's best to stay off Las Vegas Boulevard and its major cross streets during the evening rush hour. The commute rush

76 — CHAPTER THREE

isn't nearly as bad in the morning. Weekend Strip traffic is particularly thick and Friday nights are essentially awful. If you have to get back to the Strip from downtown during the early evening or if you have a plane to catch, try jumping on the freeway and getting off at the exit nearest your destination. Or consult a map and use Paradise Road to the east of Las Vegas Boulevard or Industrial Road to the west.

Another tip: Whenever you've scheduled a show or some such thing on the Strip, allow yourself extra time, even if it isn't a weekend evening. Although all the casino hotels offer free parking, it's often a long hike from your car to the casino. Then you must shoulder through the merry crowd to reach the showroom. We came close to missing a couple of openings by being tardy. Of course, using valet parking will hurry things along. (Since our 1979 camper *Ickybod* has a few idiosyncrasies, we're reluctant to do so.)

Things aren't quite as hectic downtown since it's more compact and the larger hotels have parking structures. But these can fill up on weekends.

A very pedestrian thought

Downtown is park-and-walk country; all the casinos are easily reached on foot. Also, if you're a serious walker, you'll enjoy hiking the busy sidewalks of Las Vegas Boulevard, taking in the sights and basking in the gaudy glimmer of the lights.

The **Four Corners** area (Las Vegas Boulevard's junction with Dunes and Flamingo roads) is a great walking neighborhood. Some of the biggest and most lavish casinos are clustered here—**Caesars Palace, the Mirage, Bally's** and the **Flamingo Hilton**. From Four Corners, it's an easy hike to the **Imperial Palace Auto Collection** and to the shops of **Fashion Show Mall**.

A note of caution, however. We suspect that most Las Vegas cab drivers were expelled from New York for being too crazy. (When they watch old World War II movies, they probably root for the *Kamikaze*.) They have little regard for crosswalks and absolutely none for jaywalkers. They apparently think the "Strip" means a drag strip.

Transit, public and otherwise

Las Vegas Transit System operates out of an attractive new hub at Stewart Avenue and Casino Center Boulevard, within a block of Glitter Gulch. From here, buses fan out in all directions, with regular service along Las Vegas Boulevard. With their frequent stops, they tend to be rather slow, however. Fare is $1.10 and you'll need exact change, so withhold some silver from the slots. Or you can buy a ten-ride commuter card from the driver for $7.30. The **Strip Shuttle** runs from the downtown hub along Las Vegas Boulevard every 15 minutes from 6 a.m. to 12:45 a.m., then every half hour from 2:45 a.m. to 6 a.m. Call 384-3540 for transit information.

The privately operated **Las Vegas Strip Trolley** (382-1404) runs from the Las Vegas Hilton down Las Vegas Boulevard to the Hacienda, dropping you at the doorstep of 25 major hotels. Fare is an even dollar and the rigs run on the half hour from 9:30 a.m. to 2 a.m. Look for old fashioned trolleys, like San Francisco cable cars with tires.

Taxis and limos

Have you ever noticed that cabs always disappear when it rains? Do they melt? Fortunately, showers are rare in Las Vegas. Here, cabs disappear on

Friday and Saturday nights. They're readily available most other times and fares are $1.70 at flag fall and $1.20 for additional miles.

Don't try to flag a cab along Las Vegas Boulevard. You'll find plenty of them clustered at any of the hotels, sometimes even on Friday and Saturday evenings. The main cab companies are **Whittlesea** (384-6111), **Yellow/Checker** (873-2227) and **Desert Cab** (736-1702). Eight different firms offer limo service, the fancy way to go in this flashy town. The three majors are **Presidential Limo** (731-5577), **Bell Trans** (385-LIMO) and **Lucky Seven** (739-6177). For the ultimate ride, call 735-5211 for **Villa Roma's** 32-foot double stretch Lincoln, with a plush red velvet interior, rumble seat and hot tub. Hourly limo rates are from $22, all the way to $120 for the super stretch.

Rental cars

If you arrive by plane, train or bus, we'd recommend renting a car because of the plenitude of free parking in Las Vegas. Further, you may want to explore the surrounding area (see Chapter 4). Again, plan ahead. Nearly every rental car in town can vanish during a big convention weekend. Even during quieter times, you may have to take a more expensive model because all of the little guys have been checked out by the time you arrive. Also, most agencies offer better rates for those who reserve in advance.

Several locals claim lower rates than the majors, which may or may not be the case, depending on the kind of package deal you swing through your travel agent. Among the larger independents are **Fairway**, (800) 634-3476; **Rebel Rent-A-Car**, (800) 372-1981; **U.S./RentRite**, (800) 777-9377; **Showcase Rents**, (702) 387-6717; **Brooks Rent A Car**, (800) 634-6721; **Abbey Rent-A-Car**, (800) 736-4988, **Valley Car Rental**, (800) 221-4447 and good old **Rent-A-Wreck**, (702) 736-0040.

Bear in mind that some independents may not offer cars or service as reliable as the established agencies, or they may have mileage charges that will add up to higher rates. Also, most have no airport offices, although they may offer airport pickup and delivery.

GETTING HITCHED

We discussed the simplicity of Nevada marriage laws in Chapter 1. All that is required is a driver's license or other identification if you're 18 or older. There's no waiting period or blood test requirement. A notarized parental consent is needed if you're between 16 and 17.

About 75,000 marriages are performed each year in Las Vegas; 56,000 by "Marryin' Sams" that work the dozens of marriage mill chapels, and the rest by state marriage commissioners. You'll be in good company if you come here for a quickie nuptial fix. Among those who have tied a hasty Las Vegas knot are Bruce Willis, Bette Midler, Joan Collins and Lisa Bonet.

The **Clark County Marriage License Bureau** is at 200 S. Third Street downtown; phone 455-3156 during working hours or 455-4415 after 5 p.m. Office hours are 8 a.m. to midnight Monday through Thursday, then continuously from 8 a.m. Friday to midnight Sunday. License fee is $35, and you can then stroll a block to the **Commissioner of Civil Marriages** at 309 S. Third. There, a deputy justice of the peace will perform the deed for a $25 to $30 fee. The office is open the same hours as the license bureau. For something a bit more frilly, adjourn to any of the dozens of **commercial wedding chapels** in town; the phone book lists 12 pages of them.

WHERE TO SHOP

Las Vegas may not rival San Francisco as a shoppers' mecca. However, it offers several fine havens for credit card abuse, including the three largest covered malls in Nevada.

The most attractive is the stylish **Fashion Show Mall** at South Las Vegas Boulevard and Spring Mountain Road, next to the Mirage. In a hurry to spend? It offers valet parking, in addition to ample self-parking off Spring Mountain Road. Store hours are Monday-Wednesday 10 to 6, Thursday-Friday 10 to 9, Saturday 10 to 6 and Sunday noon to 5; phone (702) 369-8382. Major tenants are Bullocks, Neiman Marcus, Saks Fifth Avenue, the May Company and Dillards. Another 140 shops, boutiques and restaurants are tucked into this air- conditioned shelter, including high fashion shops like Lillie Rubin, Victoria's Secret, Chez Magnifique, La Perfumerie and Christian Bernard. Waldenbooks, the only bookstore on the Strip, is tucked among the boutiques.

Maryland Parkway, a mile east and parallel to Las Vegas Boulevard, is one of the town's main shopping streets. This palm-graced boulevard is lined with proper boutiques, clothing stores, ordinary stores and fast food places. Its cornerstone is **Boulevard Mall** at Maryland Parkway and Desert Inn Road. Size- wise, it's right up there with Fashion Show Mall, offering 144 stores. Shops here are more family oriented and the mall is popular with locals. Anchor stores are Sears, Penney's and The Broadway. Store hours are weekdays 10 to 9, Saturday 10 to 6 and Sunday 11 to 5; phone (702) 735-8268. It offers both valet and self parking.

The city's third covered biggie is **The Meadows** on Meadows Lane between Decatur and Valley View west of town. To reach it, take the Valley View exit from Freeway 95, go south to Meadows Lane and continue west. It's anchored by Sears, Penney's, The Broadway and Dillards. A hundred smaller shops and more than 20 restaurants cluster about fountains and patios. Like Boulevard Mall, it draws more locals than tourists, although it's a good place for visitors to seek out specialty shops. Hours are weekdays 10 to 9, Saturday 10 to 6 and Sunday noon to 5; phone (702) 878-4849.

Many casino hotels offer stylish shopping malls, in addition to the usual news stand-souvenir shops. **Caesars Palace** and **Bally's** have the largest collection of shops and boutiques. Caesars opened its new Forum Shops in mid-1992 with 70 boutiques and restaurants, and Bally's has a 40-shop arcade. Others with a goodly selection are the **Imperial Palace, Stardust, Mirage, Flamingo Hilton, Desert Inn, Las Vegas Hilton, Riviera** and the **Excalibur.**

If you're into **antiques**, you'll find several yesterday shops on East Charleston between Maryland Parkway and the Boulder Highway.

Souvenirs: shopping yourself silly

If you think San Francisco's Fisherman's Wharf is awash with tacky souvenir stores, wait until you shop the streets of Las Vegas. Entire shopping centers are devoted to these supermarkets of schlock.

Consider the **Bonanza** at Las Vegas Boulevard and Sahara Avenue (385-7359), which claims to be the world's largest souvenir store. Not a single store, it's a collection of several shops, most of them inter-linked. Each is stuffed with great ranks of curios, ranging from genuinely curious to tasteless. It also offers convenience foods and liquor, although prices are rather high. (See **Liquor** below.)

International Boutique at 2303 S. Las Vegas Boulevard (731-4716) is another sizable souvenir complex. Others are scattered up and down Las Vegas Boulevard, tucked between flashy casino hotels like gaudy little bits of cheap costumed jewelry. Downtown offers another large collection of trinket parlors. You'll find one of the larger souvenir assortments in good old **F.W. Woolworth** at Fremont Street and Las Vegas Boulevard.

The most popular tourist items appear to be 99 cent sunglasses, Elvis Presley clocks, things velveteen and "I lost my ass in Las Vegas" T-shirts. Topless cigarette lighters, dice toothpick holders, dice clocks, Chicken Ranch whorehouse T-shirts and calendars, inflatable Wayne Newton dolls and roulette ash trays are quite vogue as well. It's interesting to note that many of the large "gift shops" have armed guards.

Who'd want to steal this junk?

Gambling shops

Where but in Las Vegas would you find stores devoted exclusively to the nervous art of gambling?

The largest is the **Gamblers General Store** at 800 S. Main Street, phone (800) 322-CHIP or (702) 382-9903. It's open daily from 9 to 5. You'll see it on your left as you follow Main from the Strip to the downtown casino center. Want a handful of used casino dice, a crap stick, complete *pai gow* set, roulette wheel or book on gambling? It's all here, plus a selection of used slot machines, priced from $1,000 up.

Gamblers Book Club, at 630 South Eleventh, is open daily from 9 to 5, phone 382-7555. It's just off Charleston Boulevard, opposite Ed and Ralph's Market. This dusty little place is stuffed to the rafters with new and used books on gambling, plus local guidebooks and a good selection of gambling videos. Interested in learning about the city's sinful side? You'll find a good selection of Las Vegas exposès and books on the mob, written by Mario Puzo and the like.

Other book stores

Yes, people take time to read in Las Vegas, although apparently not very often. **Waldenbooks** in Fashion Show Mall is the only bookstore on the Strip, and we found none downtown except those devoted to gaming. For other book sources, you'll have to adjourn to suburbia. **Waldenbooks** has outlets at The Meadows, at 3783 S. Maryland Parkway (in front of Mervyn's and just south of Boulevard Mall) and at Decatur and Sahara west of Las Vegas Boulevard. Rival **B. Dalton** has branches at The Meadows and Boulevard Mall. An excellent source of Nevada lore is the **Barnes and Noble** book shop in the Moyer Student Union on the **UNLV** campus.

AFFORDABLE LAS VEGAS

Unless you've thumbed recklessly through this book and skipped directly to this spot, you already know that Las Vegas offers great visitor bargains. And you know why: Casino operators will bait you with free drinks, cheap meals and cheap lodging to get you inside. They hope to offset their impulsive generosity with that golden phrase, **the house edge.**

The next several paragraphs comprise a where-to and how-to guide. In general, downtown casino hotels are less expensive than those on the Strip.

However, this is a town about which you can never make assumptions. Many major hotels offer remarkable bargains during the slow season.

If you plan to visit Las Vegas more than once a decade, you may want to subscribe to Anthony Curtis' **Las Vegas Advisor.** It's a monthly newsletter focusing on the town's best bargains, from cheap rooms to free meals to rental car deals. You can subscribe or order the most recent issue for $3 by contacting: Las Vegas Advisor, P.O. Box 28041, Las Vegas, NV 89126; phone 871-4363. Visa and MasterCard phone orders are accepted for $10 or more. (This isn't a commercial endorsement; we've never met Mr. Curtis. We do know that he takes no ads and accepts no comps.)

When to come

The best bargain season is the first two weeks of December, following the National Finals Rodeo. As my friend Don Payne of the Las Vegas News Bureau says: "The hotels practically give rooms away then." By contrast, the absolute *busiest* season is the Christmas-New Year holiday.

Early January through February also are good bargain-seeking periods, although the huge Consumer Electronics convention in mid-January convention tightens things a bit. The next slowest period is mid-summer, but that advantage is fading as more visitors defy the heat and rely on air conditioning. And of course, that's when you can bring the kiddies.

Preparing for your visit

Before heading out, check with a travel agent, who should know which hotels are offering the best slow-season deals. During a recent winter period, rooms at the Excalibur and Aladdin dropped to $20 for a double. The Stardust offered $22 rooms, *including* free tickets to "Enter the Night," one of the better shows in town. These are just random examples; check with your travel agent for others. To get great rates such as these, you have to book in advance. Many packages are tied to discount airfares, offering a double saving. Further, many of them include discounts or freebies for shows, meals and drinks.

Year around, the least expensive rooms are at the **Excalibur, Circus Circus** and **Imperial Palace,** plus many of the older downtown hotels. One of the best buys, if you don't mind driving to the far end of Las Vegas Boulevard, is the new **Vacation Village,** offering attractive rooms all year for as little as $20 Sunday through Thursday. The **Boardwalk** has an all-year Sunday-Thursday rack rate of $32 to $34. Downtown, the **Gold Spike** offers doubles and kings for $20, including breakfast; extra bodies are just $3. When you arrive, you can play penny slots and video poker. (Not all of these room deals are booked through travel agencies; see phone numbers under **Where to sleep** later in this chapter.)

Couponamania

And then there are the coupons. Bushels of them, acres of them, *tons* of them. The coupon is the greatest single weapon used by casinos to lure warm bodies. You can get coupons anywhere, everywhere—with a gasoline fill-up en route, as you check into your hotel, at official and unofficial visitors bureaus, from the sweaty palms of street hawkers downtown, from brochure racks.

Some offer a free slice of nothing, like a gratis pull on a slot machine that pays off in more coupons, or a free keno game with ridiculous odds. But much of the stuff is real: free food, free drinks, free mini-rolls of nickels, show discounts. Incidentally, coupons are valid for adults only. These people want you to play the machines and sit the tables, and you must be 21 to do that.

The freebies begin at the border. The **Welcome Center** three miles inland from California on I-15 will hand you a pound or so of coupons with no strings attached. So-called visitors bureaus up and down the Strip pass out the freebies as well. However, they may try to sell you a tour or charge a commission for hotel or show reservations.

We stopped at one of these "bureaus," said no thanks to the sales pitch, and received—wrapped in a handy map of Las Vegas—coupons good for the following:

- Free hip pack from Circus Circus • Free popcorn and souvenir from Silver City • Free beer, popcorn, souvenir and gaming guide from Slots A Fun • Free souvenir and deck of playing cards from the Excalibur • Free shows or meals for one hour of slot play at the Riviera • Free drinks at O'Sheas Casino • Free drinks and nickels from the Flamingo Hilton • Free gift (unidentified, $7 value) from the Sands • Free mini-hamburger from the Boardwalk • Free hat and mug from Fitzgerald's • Two-for-one meal at Jason's Bar and Grill • Free meal, shrimp cocktail, popcorn, drink and split of champagne from Anthony's.

In addition, we received coupons good for bonus books from the various sponsoring casinos that contained still more freebies and discounts.

Bargains with no coupons attached

Las Vegas is Bargain City even without coupons. During the course of our research for this book, we jotted down the following goodies, and this is only a partial list. (Obviously, many may no longer be in effect, and some have hour limitations.)

On the Strip (or nearby)

Barbary Coast—A $1.95 breakfast and 75 cent drinks.
Bourbon Street Casino—A 99 cent breakfast served all day.
Dunes—Pizza and beer for $1; free apple cider.
Boardwalk—Probably the cheapest place on Las Vegas Boulevard, with mini "Castle burgers" at three for a dollar, spaghetti for $1.59 and breakfast for $1.29.
El Rancho—Breakfast special for $1.79.
Hacienda—Breakfast 99 cents to $1.99; all you can drink wine with $6.95 dinner buffet.
O'Sheas Casino—Fifty cent beer.
Palace Station—Margaritas for 99 cents, $1 shrimp cocktail, $1.50 chili dog.
Sahara Hotel—Seventy-five cent hot dogs with all the trimmings.
Silver City—A $1.99 buffet from 11:30 p.m. to 11 a.m.; one of the cheapest in town. Also, a 99 cent shrimp cocktail and 75 cent drinks. Further, it's the town's only smoke-free casino.
Slots A Fun—Free popcorn and sandwich wedges; 99 cent shrimp cocktails and hot dogs, and 75 cent imported beer.
Vacation Village—One of the Strip's better bargain places, with ten cent draft beer from midnight to 7 p.m., $2 steak and eggs from midnight to 6 a.m., $9.99 buffet dinner with a show.

Westward Ho—Scrambled eggs, biscuits and gravy for 49 cents and a hot dog and beer for 99 cents.

Downtown

Binion's Horseshoe—A $2 New York steak with salad and baked potato from 10 p.m. to 4:45 a.m.

Fitzgerald's—A $1.50 chili dog, with Tabasco sauce on the side (nice addition).

Golden Gate Casino—A 99 cent shrimp cocktail; claims to have sold 25 million of them; $1.95 meatball sandwich.

Golden Nugget Casino—A $1.99 New York steak dinner 11 p.m. to 5 a.m.

Gold Spike Casino—Low rollers' paradise with penny slots and video poker, five cent bingo and keno, 50 cent bar drinks.

Main Street Station—Draft beer for 75 cents.

Jackie Gaughan's Plaza—Bar drinks for 75 cents, breakfasts for 49 and 99 cents.

THE LAS VEGAS ABCs
All numbers (702) unless otherwise indicated

Adult entertainment—News racks all over town offer guides to adult lures, complete with provocative photos. These tend to get scattered about, making this one of the few cities in the world with R-rated litter. "Entertainers" who'll come to your hotel room for adult encounters are listed in the Yellow Pages under that heading—40 pages of them. (See **Getting—??** in Chapter 1.) The town has its share of topless bars, listed under Cocktail Lounges. Several small motels, particularly along Las Vegas Boulevard downtown, offer adult movies as part of their in-room services.

Auto clubs—American Automobile Association members are served by the Nevada Division of the California State Automobile Association. District office is at 3312 W. Charleston Blvd.; 870-9171. Office hours are 8:30 to 5 weekdays. For emergency road service call locally 878-1822 or out of town, (800) 336-HELP. The National Automobile Club is at 2306 Crestline Loop, North Las Vegas; 649-5030.

Babysitting—Among sitters that provide service in your hotel room or in their facilities are Las Vegas Babysitting Agency, 457-3777; Reliable Babysitting, 451-7507; Sandy's Sitters Service, 731-2086; Vegas Valley Babysitting, 871-5161 and Nanny's & Granny's, 368-7741. Others are listed under "Baby sitters" in the Yellow Pages. Many hotels can arrange sitters for tykes and virtually every major casino has a video arcade. Those with extensive facilities for children are Circus Circus and Excalibur.

Bicycling—The flat residential streets of Las Vegas and roads in the suburbs make nice bike routes. Don't try cycling on Las Vegas Boulevard or its busy cross streets; they have no bike lanes. For conducted bicycle tours and bike rentals, contact CitySpokes at 596-2489.

Big rooms—These are the major show lounges, often seating a thousand or more and featuring either top-name entertainers (headliners) or big, splashy revues. In the past, one had to grease the palm of the maitre d' to get a good seat, but many of the big rooms are now going to ticketed assigned seating.

Bus service—See **Transit**, below.

Cash machines—Virtually every casino has credit card cash advance machines and autotellers that will respond to your bank card. The autotellers are a much better deal, operated by local banks and charging only a dollar per transaction. Credit card machines charge as much as 10 percent of the amount advanced. For a better cash advance deal, take your MasterCard or VISA to any issuing bank during regular hours.

Checks and credit—Most casinos will cash out of state checks if you apply at the cashier's cage and give them 24 hours to verify your account. If you're in the high roller category, you also may be able to establish credit, then you merely sign an IOU for chips. (See **A day in the life of a high roller** in Chapter 2.)

Currency exchanges—Three firms offer foreign currency exchange: American Foreign Exchange in the Las Vegas Hilton on Las Vegas Boulevard (731-4155), Foreign Money Exchange at 3025 S. Las Vegas Boulevard (791-3301) and Nevada Coin Mart just off Las Vegas Boulevard at 750 E. Sahara Avenue (369-0500). Most hotel cashiers will exchange foreign currency, but the rates generally aren't very favorable.

Dental services—Misery with a molar? Call the Clark County Dental Society at 435-7767 for a dentist referral.

Desert driving—You have to go through at least 150 miles of it to reach Las Vegas. Most modern cars whisk along with no problems, but if yours tends to overheat, accomplish that stretch in the early morning or evening. Also, take a five-gallon can of water along. Before hitting that last, long stretch to Las Vegas, swing into a service station to top off your tank and check your water, oil and belts. You'll be driving as much as 70 miles between services in some areas. (Also see **Surviving the desert** in Chapter 1.)

Gambling lessons—Many casinos offer them, including the Imperial Palace, Caesars Palace, Circus Circus, Fitzgerald's, the Sahara, Stardust, Harrah's Las Vegas, Hilton and Barbary Coast. They range from blackjack, craps and baccarat study sessions to tips on handicapping the ponies. Check the individual casinos for schedules. Also, some hotels offer gaming instructions in the room via their TV systems.

Hotel reservations—Las Vegas has no official reservation service; your best bet is to book through a travel agent. The Yellow Pages lists several commercial booking outfits: Las Vegas Hotel Reservation Center, (702) 736-1666; Las Vegas Reservation Bureau, (800) 826-3010; Las Vegas Reservation Systems, (800) 233-5594; and Las Vegas Room Reservations, (702) 732-3455. Most charge a fee for their services.

Liquor—Booze used to be a bargain in Nevada until California removed its price controls and became competitive. That shut down a lot of big Nevada discount liquor stores. Booze is still cheap here, compared with most other states' prices. If you want a room bottle, avoid stores on the Strip or downtown, however. Best prices, often by many dollars, are in ordinary suburban supermarkets. For a wide selection of wine at good prices, check out Lee's Discount Liquor at 3480 E. Flamingo Road. Drive four miles east on Flamingo, cross Pecos and you'll see a red and white building on the left; do a U-turn and come back to it.

Medical services—Clark County uses the 911 number for medical and other emergencies. Major hospitals with 24-hour emergency rooms are University Medical Center, 1800 W. Charleston at Shadow Lane (383-2000) and

84 — CHAPTER THREE

Humana Hospital Sunrise, 3186 Maryland Parkway near Desert Inn Road (731-8080). For non-emergencies, call the Clark County Medical Society at 739-9989 for a physician referral.

Neighborhood casinos—Do locals gamble? Many do not, while others do so only occasionally. You'll most likely find them at neighborhood casinos where, it is said, slot odds are better. They range from plain to fancy, and they're appealing havens for low rollers. Ask casino people where they gamble and you'll probably get some pretty good recommendations.

Newspapers—The *Las Vegas Review-Journal* is the morning sheet and the *Las Vegas Sun* is the afternoon paper. The two combine for a ten-pound Sunday edition. The R-J's Friday issue offers a good rundown on what's happening in town.

Pets—Few casino hotels allow them; some smaller motels do. Animal Inn offers boarding service; call 736-0036.

Photography—Photos inside casinos used to be strictly forbidden, but that's no longer the case. Although most still follow the old rule (which is a custom, not a law), other places permit you to unholster your Instamatic. The **Excalibur** and **Tropicana** are a couple. For others, simply ask in the casino.

Police services—Dial 911 in an emergency. Otherwise, Las Vegas Police Department number is 795-3111; Nevada Highway Patrol is 486-4100.

Poison emergency—Humana Hospital Sunrise has a poison information center at 732-4989.

Road conditions—Call 486-3116.

Show reservations—These can be made through individual hotels, or use one of these agencies (which may charge a fee): Club Guides, 384-6400; J&K Show Tickets, 796-2326; or Ticketmaster with two numbers—893-3033 for show information and 474-4000 to charge by phone. Popular shows book up early, so make your arrangements as soon as you hit town.

Time—Casinos never have clocks, figuring you're having too much fun to care what time it is. Ask an employee or dial a three-digit number: 118. You probably know that Nevada runs on Pacific Time.

Tipping—Many of the big rooms have gone to pre-assigned seating, eliminating the need to tip the maitre 'd for a select table. For those still using the old fashioned system, a $10 to $20 tip is suitable and $40 will get you into the bald headed row. Elsewhere, tipping follows standard practice—15 percent for most services rendered, a dollar or two for valet parking and 20 percent for limo drivers. As mentioned in Chapter 2, it's proper to tip dealers, drink girls and casino runners.

Visitor information—The Las Vegas Chamber of Commerce operates an information center at 2301 E. Sahara Avenue, open weekdays 8 to 5; 457-4664. Commercial visitor centers are listed in the Yellow Pages under Tourist Information. Free weekly guides provide comprehensive intelligence on what's happening where, listing "big room" shows, lounge shows, kids' attractions, buffets, brunches and restaurants. You'll also find advertisers' coupons good for discounts on tours, meals, lodging and such. These guides available at hotel desks and in news racks throughout Las Vegas. Among the many are *What's On, Tourguide Magazine of Las Vegas* and *Las Vegas Today*. What's On is the thickest, a 100-pager listing everything from bingo games to cultural events; it even provides a weekly TV guide.

Weather—Call 736-6404 or 734-2010.

ON TOUR: STRIP ATTRACTIONS

We'll lay you odds that you'll arrive in Las Vegas via the Strip. If you're driving from the east, south or north, we lose the bet, because I-15 and U.S. 95 intersect in the heart of downtown. Also, the Amtrak and Greyhound stations are there. However, most motorists approach from California and folks who fly wind up at McCarran International, on the southern end of Strip.

Let's say you're steering your Belchfire V-6 eastward on I-15. For endless miles, the only distractions from the seemingly endless Mojave Desert have been billboards touting the favors of Las Vegas. As you approach the Nevada border, huge electronic billboards invite you to **Whiskey Pete's** and **Primadonna** casinos, linked by a linked by a Disney-style monorail.

Press on, since Las Vegas is 42 miles away and we deal with these border places late in the next chapter. Three miles inland is a rest stop and **Welcome Center** run by the Las Vegas Convention and Visitors Authority, where you can pick up your first few pounds of free coupons and literature. It's open daily from 8 to 5; until 4 in winter. You next pass the non-town of Jean and two more large casinos, **Gold Strike,** and the impressive riverboat-shaped **Nevada Landing.** Then it's back to monotonous desert.

Just beyond the turnoff to **Henderson** (State Highway 146), you see the promise of Vegas—the towers of Las Vegas Boulevard. Take the first freeway exit (South Las Vegas Boulevard) and your adventure has begun. You first encounter **Vacation Village,** a new casino hotel way down on the tail end of the boulevard. At this end of the Strip, you can imagine what it was like before Bugsy came, for it is little more than wind-ruffled sand and an occasional building.

Hughes Executive Air Terminal is on your right, with the runways of **McCarran International Airport** behind it. (To reach McCarran's passenger terminal, you must continue on to Tropicana Avenue and turn left.) Short of Tropicana, you see the recently remodeled Spanish-style **Hacienda,** which was the southernmost of the Strip hotels until Vacation Village opened. Next come the **Excalibur** with its imposing Arthurian towers and **Tropicana** with a lush Polynesian setting; both are worthy of exploration.

If you've flown in and picked up a rental car, you can join our tour at this spot. Before you leave the attractive, modernistic air terminal, note the giant teapot and cup sculptures in the departure area. (Suggesting that Las Vegas is a mad tea party?)

From this point, you can take a side trip about two miles east on Tropicana to the **University of Nevada at Las Vegas,** with its impressive **Thomas & Mack Center,** home of the Runnin' Rebels basketball team. Nearby is the university's excellent **Marjorie Barrick Museum of Natural History.** Continuing out Tropicana, you'll find the **Liberace Museum,** in a Spanish style shopping center on your right.

Back on Las Vegas Boulevard, note the "Free aspirin and tender sympathy" sign at a Union 76 service station on your left, a couple of blocks beyond the Excalibur. It has been featured in newspapers and magazines since the 1950s.

Next, also on the left, is a pleasantly scruffy little casino called the **Boardwalk.** Beyond is **Aladdin Casino Hotel** on the right and the **Dunes** on the left. You're approaching the **Four Corners** area, with a gag-

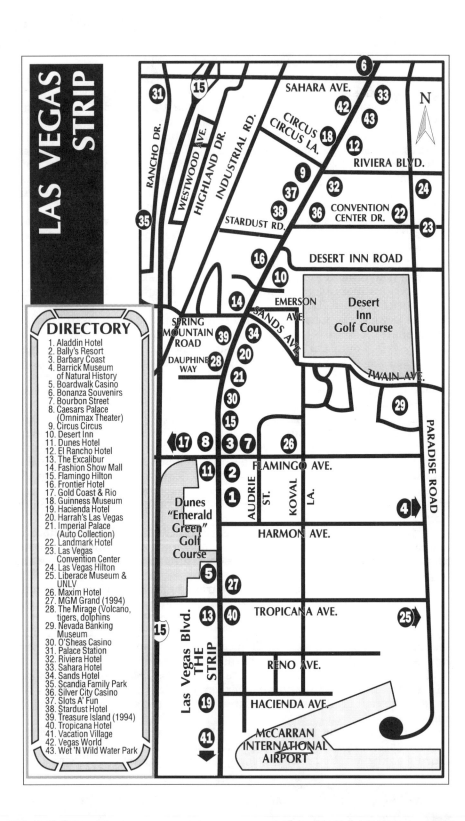

gle of major casino hotels, where Dunes road from the west and Flamingo Road from the east bump into Las Vegas Boulevard. Opposite the Dunes, set back a bit on Flamingo Road, is the large and quite opulent **Bally's,** the former MGM Grand.

Flamingo Road is something of a mini-Strip, with the cheerfully marqueed **Barbary Coast, Bourbon Street Casino** and **Maxim Hotel** lined up, across from Bally's. The imposing brown granite highrise you see to the northeast is the new **First Interstate Tower,** the only tower on the Strip not devoted to gaming and hotel rooms. The **Nevada Banking Museum** is on the ground floor. To reach it, continue on Flamingo to Paradise and turn left, then go left again onto Corporate Drive and curl around to the right until you wind up in the parking lot.

Back on Las Vegas Boulevard, the legendary **Flamingo Hilton** is next door to the Barbary Coast. It has been redone many times since Ben's day, although the original four-story **Fabulous Flamingo** still survives within the complex.

Beyond the Flamingo are **O'Sheas Casino,** the **Imperial Palace,** with its excellent **Auto Collection,** and **Harrah's Las Vegas,** one of the more attractive mid-sized casinos on the Strip with its sparkling showboat motif. The long-established **Sands,** now remodeled and expanded, is just beyond.

Two of Nevada's most luxurious casino resorts are across the boulevard, occupying the entire one-mile stretch between Dunes Road and Spring Mountain Road. Resplendent in marble and splashing fountains is the Romanesque **Caesars Palace,** and next door is the imposing **Mirage.** The **Fashion Show Mall** is next, on the boulevard at Spring Mountain Road. Las Vegas performers have left hand prints and signatures in cement in the **Stars on the Strip** at the Las Vegas Boulevard entrance.

Beyond the mall, still on your left, is the Spanish-style **Frontier,** recently remodeled and expanded. Originally the Last Frontier, it was the second casino on Las Vegas Boulevard. The quietly elegant **Desert Inn,** former lair of Howard Hughes, is across the boulevard. Just up from the inn at 302 E. Desert Inn Road is the **Guardian Angel Cathedral.** Here, gamblers drop chips in the collection box and confess their sins, and probably leave a tip for Lady Luck. The **Stardust** is back across Las Vegas Boulevard to the north. Next door is the only **McDonald's** in the country with a gaudy neon sign, plus a large kids play complex.

Inland from the Stardust, up Convention Center Drive, you'll see the huge **Las Vegas Convention Center** and the curious **Landmark Hotel**, resembling a flying saucer that crash-landed on a silo. A landmark is all it is these days; the place is closed. Tucked in behind the convention center is the plush, green **Las Vegas Country Club.**

Circus Circus, next door to the Stardust, draws families by the legions with its free circus acts and midway games. The small **Slots A Fun** is adjacent. Across the boulevard is the Western motif **Silver City,** the world's only smoke-free casino. Next door is the **Riviera** and the **Candlelight Wedding Chapel,** probably one of the busiest in town, is just beyond. Then comes **El Rancho,** with its pioneer town façade. To the east on Riviera Boulevard is the large, stylish **Las Vegas Hilton.**

Back on the main drag, the Strip begins to merge into Las Vegas proper. **Guinness World of Records Museum** is on the left side of the boulevard, behind an Arby's and opposite El Rancho. **Wet 'N Wild** water park is on the right, and the long-standing **Sahara Hotel and Casino** stands just beyond.

The **Bonanza** souvenir complex is across the Strip at the corner of Sahara Avenue. A bit farther along, still on the left, is the celestial-surrealistic **Vegas World** casino. Take a peek at its **million dollar jackpot** exhibit. The casino is at the junction of Las Vegas Boulevard and Main Street.

ON TOUR: DOWNTOWN ATTRACTIONS

Our momentum has carried us toward central Las Vegas, so you can keep on touring, or follow our advice above and save it for after sunset. You can tell day from night here quite easily, because it's much brighter after dark.

To reach downtown from the strip, we recommend the Main Street approach. Watch for the **Gamblers General Store** on the left at 800 South Main. Continuing on, you'll soon see the cornerstone of Glitter Gulch, **Jackie Gaughan's Plaza,** (formerly the Union Plaza) standing at the head of Fremont Street. This is an historic spot, where agents of Senator Clark's railroad stood to auction off the first Las Vegas lots on May 15, 1905.

Find a place to park, because everything of interest here is within walking distance. Many of the larger casinos have free parking structures and the Plaza has a large lot with validated parking. Also, street parking costs a mere quarter an hour, although you'll have to remember to return and feed the meter until 6 p.m. Downtown action is essentially contained within an eight-block square, cradled by Main Street, Stewart Avenue, Fourth Street and Carson Street.

The cadence is different here than on the Strip. Downtown has more of a carnival atmosphere, where Sassy Sally's and Coin Castle street hawkers try to lure you into their casinos with coupon books and free pulls on Big Bertha machines. Downtown is a low rollers' haven, with low table stakes and lots of nickel slots and video poker. Many casinos here feature slot and video machines only and it is said (but never proven, as far as we know) that downtown machines are more generous. Certainly, many of the hotels are less expensive. The **Gold Spike** at Fourth and Ogden for instance, offers $20 rooms, and it features penny slot and video machines.

However, some of the casinos are quite stylish, equal to the Strip's gaming parlors. The Golden Nugget, Jackie Gaughan's Plaza and Fitzgerald's come to mind.

Starting at the Plaza, let's take a hike down Fremont Street. The **Golden Gate,** home of the "famous" 99 cent shrimp cocktail, and the small **Coin Castle** are on the right. Across the street is the friendly **Las Vegas Club** with a **Sports Hall of Fame.** At the end of the block, the **Pioneer** occupies the corner of Fremont and First Street. And here stands the legendary **Vegas Vic,** the tall neon cowboy who says: "Howdy, welcome to downtown Las Vegas." A newer neon girl friend, **Vegas Vickie,** is across the street, above a topless nightclub called **Glitter Gulch.**

Staying on the Pioneer side of the street, we next encounter the **Golden Nugget.** It's easily the most attractive downtown casino, with its glossy and handsome New Orleans décor. Check out the **world's largest nugget** display here, between the hotel lobby and main casino. **Binion's Horseshoe,** another large complex, is across Fremont from the Nugget. Check out its

DOWNTOWN LAS VEGAS

DIRECTORY

1. To Gambler's General Store
2. Union Plaza
3. Golden Gate & Pioneer (Vegas Vic)
4. Las Vegas Club
5. Golden Nugget
6. Binion's Horseshoe
7. Four Queens (Ripley's Believe It or Not)
8. Fremont Casino
9. Fitgerald's
10. El Cortez Hotel
11. Gold Spike
12. Lady Luck
13. Block 16 (Former red light district)
14. California Casino
15. Main Street Station
16. Transit Center & Post Office
17. County Courthouse
18. City Hall
19. Lied Children's Museum (City Library)
20. Las Vegas Natural History Museum
21. Old Mormon Fort
22. Cashman Field
23. To Mormon Temple & Sunrise Mountain
24. To Sam's Town & Boulder Highway

million dollar currency display. The next cross street is Casino Center Boulevard, with the **Four Queens** on one corner and the **Fremont** on the other. The Queens houses **Ripley's Believe it or Not Museum.** Beyond the Queens, the towering **Fitzgerald** is the tallest building in Nevada, with 33 stories stacked 400 feet into the sky.

A few blocks down Fremont, you'll encounter the venerable **El Cortez** casino and hotel, just beyond North Las Vegas Boulevard. It's downtown's oldest survivor, dating from 1941. If you walk north on Las Vegas Boulevard and double back along Ogden Avenue, you'll encounter several small to medium-size casinos. None offer noteworthy visitor attractions. They are for the most part focused on slots, if that's your game. **Lady Luck** (bright, busy and cheerful) and **California Casino** (with a California-Hawaiian look) are the larger places along this stretch. Your hike back will take you to **Main Street Station,** an attractive Victorian style place on Main Street.

En route, walk a squared circle around Ogden, First, Stewart and Casino Center Boulevard (formerly Second Street) and try to imagine it as the infamous **Block 16,** a ramshackle ghetto of saloons and brothels. You'll really have to stretch your imagination, for the entire block now contains parking facilities. The **Downtown Transportation Center** is in this area, at Stewart Avenue and Casino Center Boulevard. Also note the bronze statue of the late gaming pioneer **Benny Binion** on horseback, at the corner of Ogden and Casino Center.

ATTRACTIONS ELSEWHERE

Other off-the-Strip Las Vegas lures are rather scattered so we won't try to stitch them together as a driving tour. They're listed below under **Attractions** (best and otherwise). However, since you're in the neighborhood, fire up your Belchfire V-6 and motor north on Las Vegas Boulevard.

Note the modern new half-circle **Las Vegas City Hall** at 400 W. Stewart Avenue on your left. Pass under the U.S. 95 freeway and you'll be in the vicinity of several attractions. The new **City Library** and **Lied Children's Museum** are on your left in **Whipple Cultural Arts Center.** A short distance beyond, on the right, is the **Las Vegas Natural History Museum.**

Now, turn right onto Washington Avenue, then right again into **Cashman Center**. Drive through the parking lot opposite the center's entrance, heading back toward Las Vegas Boulevard. Pass through a gate in a cyclone fence, bump up a short dirt road and you're sitting where it all began, at the **Old Mormon Fort.** The fort is just behind the natural history museum, but you have to take this round-about route to reach it.

Having done all this, follow North Las Vegas Boulevard back downtown, turn left onto East Bonanza Road and drive about 6.5 miles to the **Las Vegas Mormon Temple.** We raved about this locale and this view a few pages back. It's a great place to witness Las Vegas at sundown, sunup or after dark.

THE STRIP CASINOS

Well, of course Las Vegas has some fine museums, a couple of wanna-be-museums, nice parks and the other things that draw tourists. However, casino resorts are the main attractions in this one-of-a-kind city. We'll use a rating system to separate the exceptional from the merely fascinating. We aren't judging them by their greatness as gaming parlors or hotel rooms (viewed separately under **Where to sleep**.) Our ratings are based on the bounty of their facilities and their overall appeal to visitors.

☺☺☺☺—Simply awesome; a required stop.

☺☺☺—A major casino resort with all the goodies.

☺☺—Quite interesting, perhaps with some special appeal.

☺—An okay place to visit with a roll of nickels, but I wouldn't want to live there.

K—of special appeal to kids.

Ø — Casinos with non-smoking gaming areas.

Most of the city's restaurants are in casino hotels, and we list them within each write-up. Price ranges are for dinner with soup or salad, not including drinks or dessert. Dining salons located outside casinos are covered farther down in this chapter, under **Where else to dine.**

The larger resorts offer considerable dining variety, from the ubiquitous "gourmet room" (which it may or may not be) to 24-hour coffee shops and pig-out buffets. Many gourmet rooms require jackets and perhaps ties for gentlemen; check when you make reservations. Incidentally, Clark County law requires all restaurants to offer no smoking areas.

Aladdin Hotel & Casino • ☺☺☺ Ø

3667 S. Las Vegas Blvd. (below Flamingo Road, opposite the Dunes), (800) 634-3424 or (702) 736-0111. The first foreign-owned casino hotel in town, the Aladdin carries its Arabian nights theme from the rooftop magic lamp to the bare-midriff casino change girls right out of *I Dream of Jeanie*. Korean-born Ginji Yasuda of Japan bailed the Aladdin out of bankruptcy for $51.5 million in 1987. He installed his family into the penthouse and pumped several million more into a complete renovation. It is thus one of the more showy of the Strip casino resorts.

The hotel was opened in 1966 by Milton Prell, a former partner in the Sahara who decided he wanted his own Mideastern desert-theme resort. He was a longtime friend of Elvis Presley and hosted his marriage to Priscilla in his private suite in 1967. Prell sold out after suffering a stroke, the hotel began to skid and was shut down by the Nevada State Gaming Commission for alleged underworld links in 1979. Perennial Las Vegan Wayne Newton and a financial partnership ran it for a while, but it never thrived until Yasuda's checkbook entered the picture.

The casino: The large gaming facility has an appealing Casbah look with those fetching change girls, Islamic arches and lots of beaded chandeliers. All the basic gaming devices are available ($2 table minimums), including a new poker room and high stakes sports and race book. Non-smokers tables are available. Of course, there are enough slots to keep Lawrence of Arabia's Arabians occupied.

Entertainment: The 7,000-seat Aladdin Theater is the biggest showroom in town, booking headliners ranging from Rudy Nureyev to Tina Turner. The 700-seat Baghdad Room featured the "Alakazam" magic show at this writing, and the comfortable Sinbad Lounge offers combos, singers and such until the wee hours. Other regulars are a "Sex over Forty" adult comedy in the afternoon and "Comedy Underground" in the evening.

Dining: The Aladdin offers three rather stylish dining salons. **Wellington's** is English in motif and American in menu, with assorted steak and barbecue selections; dinner entrées $12 to $25; nightly 5 to 11. **Fisherman's Port** is one of the town's better seafood restaurants; the look is New

England nautical, although the menu tilts toward Cajun; figure on $14 and up; Friday-Tuesday 5 to 11. **The Florentine** is a classy Italian dining salon with lots of crystal and frosted glass; dinners are $11.50 to $22; Thursday-Sunday 6 to 11. **The Oasis** is the Aladdin's 24-hour coffee shop and the **International Buffet** offers a good selection of Oriental dishes in addition to the usual salads and heat lamp meats.

Rooms: Doubles $45 to $95.

Bally's Las Vegas • ☺☺☺☺

3645 S. Las Vegas Blvd. (at Flamingo Road); (800) 634-3434 or (702) 739-4111. This gleaming monster with nearly 3,000 rooms, a casino the size of a football field and mega-tons of marble and crystal, began life on a grand scale as the MGM Grand. With mega- millionaire Kirk Kerkorian at the helm, Metro-Goldwyn-Mayer spent $120 million into the project. When it opened in late 1973, it was the world's biggest resort hotel.

Better than any MGM film, it was a smash hit from the beginning, earning $22 million in profits during its first full year. Then on November 21, 1980, a fire swept through its main hotel wing, trapping hundreds in their room; 84 people died. After rebuilding, MGM sold the hotel for more than $500 million (with 20 percent earmarked to settle fire lawsuits) to Bally Manufacturing Corporation, the world's leading maker of slot machines and lottery products.

Set back from Las Vegas Boulevard, it covers more than 42 acres, with a large "Swimpark," tennis courts, a 40-store shopping arcade, two main showrooms, six restaurants, health spas and other amenities. Nearly 4,000 employees run this city-sized resort. You will note as you explore the imposing complex that many of the movie themes survive from the MGM days.

Casino: Marble columns and striking two-ton chandeliers embellish Bally's 56,200-square-foot casino. All of the games are here, from baccarat to *pai gow* to 1,400 slot and video poker and blackjack machines, plus a large race and sports book. Should you need to learn, craps, baccarat, blackjack and roulette lessons are conducted frequently. This is a medium to high roller establishment, with $3 minimums and 25 cent and up slot and video machines.

Entertainment: Another Bally superlative: it's the only Nevada casino with two "big rooms." The 1,100-seat Ziegfeld Theatre is home to Donn Arden's *Jubilee!* with 100 singers and dancers. The Celebrity Room hosts assorted headliners and the nearby Celebrity Lounge offers live entertainment from early afternoon to around 4 a.m. *Catch a Rising Star* is a comedy club, downstairs among the boutiques of the large shopping arcade.

Dining: With half a dozen restaurants, Bally claims to serve 18,000 meals a day. **Cafè Gigi** is very French in appearance and menu; expect to part with $25 to $40 per entrèe; Wednesday-Sunday 6 to 11. A Venetian setting enhances **Caruso's,** where Italian specialties are $12 to $26; Friday-Tuesday 6 to 11. **Barrymores'** is an essentially American steaks, chops and seafood place with a clubby New York look; $18 to the forties; dinner nightly 6 to 11. A new entry is **Grapes,** a California-theme wine and seafood bar featuring Wolfgang Puck's "gourmet California pizza." The **Coffee Shop** is called just that, open for 24 hours, and the buffet goes by the name of **Big Kitchen.**

Rooms: Doubles $84 to $175.

Barbary Coast • ☺☺☺

3595 S. Las Vegas Blvd. (Flamingo Road); (800) 634-6755 or (702) 737-7111. Almost in the shadow of Bally's but certainly not dimmed by it, the Barbary Coast is one of the little jewels of the Strip. This vision in 19th century San Francisco opulence was opened in early 1979 by Michael Gaughan, whose father Jackie owns three downtown casinos. Its canopy of lights is one of the more brilliant marquees on Las Vegas Boulevard and the interior is a pleasing study in stained glass and crystal chandeliers. The 30-foot-long "Garden of Earthly Delights" glass mural on the west wall of the casino, depicting a Victorian fantasy, is the largest of its type in the world.

Casino: It's quite complete for a small casino, offering craps, roulette, keno, *pai gow* poker, baccarat and a race and sports book. Although this place appeals to low rollers, with low table stakes and nickel slots, the look is definitely upscale. Globe chandeliers, plush red velvet and that famous stained glass accent the Gay Nineties interior.

Entertainment: In the interest of space, the casino's sports and race book does double duty as a show lounge at night. The Irish Show Band is one of the regulars here.

Dining: A Big Mac, followed by strawberries Romanoff? A **McDonald's** occupies one corner of the Barbary Coast, and **Michael's,** one of the town's more stylish restaurant, sits in another. The menu is upscale American-continental; dinners $25 to $95; 6 to 11 nightly. The 24-hour **Victorian Room** fills the niche between these two restaurant extremes, featuring American and Chinese fare.

Rooms: Doubles $50 to $75.

Boardwalk Hotel & Casino • ☺☺

3750 S. Las Vegas Blvd. (near Harmon Avenue, between the Excalibur and Dunes); (800) 635-4581 or (702) 735-1167. What's a scruffy little place like this doing with a double grin rating? We like it because it's one of the cheapest places on Las Vegas Boulevard, offering inexpensive rooms and foods and lots of low-roller slots and tables.

Dining: Typical of the 24-hour coffee shop's food prices are $1.95 for spaghetti and $3.59 for a catfish or prime rib dinner. Our favorites are Castleburgers at three for a dollar. If you've never waded east of the Mississippi, you probably don't know that Castleburgers are mini hamburger and onion patties on buns about the size of dinner rolls. They're great quickie snacks, which you can embellish with catsup, onions and relish at a condiment table. **Rooms:** Doubles are $32 to $70.

Bourbon Street Casino • ☺

120 E. Flamingo Rd. (just east of Las Vegas Boulevard); (702) 737-7200. There's little of visitor interest here, although it's a good hangout for low rollers, with $1 and $2 tables, lots of nickel slots, ten cent keno and cheap food. A 99-cent breakfast is served all day and the dinner buffet is $4.99. Bourbon Street offers a sparkling old New Orleans façade, although it's a bit smoky and dingy inside.

Caesars Palace • ☺☺☺☺

3570 S. Las Vegas Blvd. (at Dunes Road); (800) 634-6001 or (702) 731-7110. Caesars Palace successfully marries grace with glitter, opulence with flamboyance. It's an odd mix of Roman statuary, spewing fountains, a Brahman shrine, a space age theater and people movers that all seem to work in some sort of understated garish harmony. This is the domain of the high rollers, the hangout of stars and wanna-be stars, the lair of Mohammed Ali in his prime. It was opened (without the apostrophe) by motel baron Jay Sarno (with alleged help from the Teamsters pension fund) in 1966. The Lum Corporation, restaurant chain owners, bought it in 1969 and has greatly expanded the original 680-room resort.

Devote a goodly slice of time to this place. Start out front, noting the absence of a gaudy marquee and the presence of a 20-foot marble statue of Caesar. The grand entry is graced by 50-foot cypress trees and gushing fountains that spill over the formal drive on blustery days. (One writer called it Nevada's most elegant Italian car wash.) The works of Michelangelo and sundry other marble chippers are replicated throughout the expansive interior. Arcaded people movers move people from the sidewalk to the grand domed entryway (and away from the next-door Mirage; they only travel in one direction).

Select the central moving sidewalk through the domed Caesars World. It carries you past several Romanesque scenes done in holography and laser sound (note that Cleopatra looks suspiciously like Liz Taylor). Inside the roomy and lavish casino, scrutinize the marble statuary (including the figure of boxing legend Joe Lewis with accompanying fight films), Cleopatra's Barge show lounge surrounded by a moat, and the huge sports and race book. Stroll the marbled hallway of the Forum Shops, the new 70-store shopping and dining complex opened in mid-1992. Caesars also has tennis courts, a large "Garden of the Gods" swimming complex, an Omnimax movie theater, a health club and even a jogging trail at the rear.

Casino: Make that plural. Gaming parlors are spread throughout the sprawling interior and they are intended for serious gamblers. It's the only casino in town with $10,000 denomination baccarat chips, plus those $100 and $500 slot machines. Surprisingly, you'll find a few nickel slots in these handsomely coiffed oval gaming areas, plus great Roman ranks of the quarter and dollar variety. If you're willing to risk $3 per pull to chase near impossible odds, you might become an instant millionaire at the "Million Dollar Baby" slots.

Entertainment: The Sports Pavilion hosts world champion boxing matches and other major athletic events. Top stars, from Cher to Sinatra, appear in Circus Maximus and Cleopatra's Barge features live music for dancing. The ultra wide-screen **Omnimax Theater** occupies a circular platform high above one of the gaming areas (see **Attractions** below).

Dining: Three of Caesars' restaurants are worth bending your budget, just to experience the setting. A lighted pool, fluted columns and red leather booths set off the sumptuous **Bacchanal**, where "wine goddesses" pour your wine from shoulder-high chalices. Seven-course *prix fixe* dinners are around $65. Art treasures enhance the circular, garden-like **Palace Court**; American-continental entrées are $25 to $45. The **Empress Court** is upscale Chinese, done up in Asian art treasures; entrées start at $15, and *prix fixe* from $40 to $50. All three restaurants require reservations, with set seatings.

The rest: **Primavera** offers a view of the Garden of the Gods swimming pool; upscale Italian cuisine $12; daily 9 a.m. to 11 p.m. For gimmick, knife-wielding Benihana-style teriyaki steak, try the **Ah' So Steak House;** 6 to

11 nightly. **Spanish Steps** serves just what the name implies (although the Spanish steps are in Rome); $16 to $45; nightly 5:30 to 10:30. Other places in which to masticate are **Cafè Roma** coffee shop, **La Piazza Food Court** with assorted foreign dishes, **Palatium** buffet and **Post Time Deli** near the large race and sports book. Sunday brunch is served in **Circus Maximus** from 9:30 to 2.

Rooms: Doubles $95 to $145.

Circus Circus Hotel • ☺☺☺ K ∅

2880 S. Las Vegas Blvd. (upper Strip, opposite the Riviera); (800) 634-3450 or (702) 734-0410. From the sublime of Caesars, we go to—well—the circus. The giant pink clown out front is your first clue that this place is family-oriented. The free monorail ride, the circus acts above the casino and the circular carnival midway confirm it. Not surprisingly, it's a low rollers' haven. (Who can afford to feed kids and face a $5 table minimum at the same time?) Rooms start as little as $19, the place has one of the cheapest buffets in town and the casino is awash with nickel machines.

Interestingly, both Caesars and Circus Circus are the creations of Jay Sarno. However, it was the second owner, Arizona furniture tycoon William Bennett, who turned it into the big top success that it is today. Sarno opened in 1968 without a hotel, and he even charged admission for gamblers and their kids to see the elephant, along with the trapeze acts and clowns. In 1974, Bennett took his idea and ran with it, expanding into highrise hotel towers, an RV park, a monorail and the world's biggest buffet.

High stakes tables? High roller suites? Sorry sir, you've got the wrong circus tent.

With nearly 100 percent occupancy and happy parents feeding great shiny buckets oceans of nickels into 3,000 slot machines, Circus Circus is one of the greatest money shows in Nevada. The company built a second Circus Circus in Reno, two more casinos in Laughlin, and the Excalibur, the world's biggest resort hotel, just down Las Vegas Boulevard.

Casino: Originally, it was open to the big top, directly beneath the high wire acts. However, that made the handle-pullers nervous, so a ceiling was added, partially shielding the second floor midway and performance arena. The casino below offers all the typical action, with ranks of slots, the standard table games, a large keno parlor and a poker parlor. Even down here, life's a circus. A cocktail lounge and a slot machine section are mounted on revolving carousels. You might want to avoid them if you've just pigged out at the buffet. The west casino has non-smoking areas.

Entertainment: Are you kidding? Aerialists, jugglers, acrobats, magicians, clowns and swallowers of assorted swords perform on or high above the raised circus arena. It's rimmed by a cheerfully raucous carnival midway of coin-pitches, ring tosses, balloon bustings, hoop throws, ball throws and sundry other games of chance. Cabaret shows and headliners? Sorry, you're still in the wrong tent.

Dining: Who need gourmet when you can attract 12,000 buffet diners a day? (However, management insists that its giant food line loses money.) In addition to the **Circus Circus Buffet,** the place offers two more conventional restaurants. The **Skyrise Dining Room** issues inexpensive steak and potato fare nightly 5 to 11 and the **Steak House** offers more steak and potatoes, 5 to midnight. It's a bit more posh with an open hearth, brass and leather trim. Prices start around $7 at the Skyrise and $12 at the Steak

House. Other dining areas are predictably kid-oriented: **Circus Pizzeria**, **Snack Train** fast food service and the **Pink Pony** 24-hour restaurant.

Rooms: One to four people, $19 to $44.

The Desert Inn • ☺☺☺

3145 S. Las Vegas Blvd. (Desert Inn Road, opposite the Frontier); (800) 634-6906 or (702) 733-4444. One of the oldest hotels on the Strip has become one of the most opulent. It's a picture of Southwestern elegance, sheathed in bronzed glass bay windows and beige stone. The "DI" offers few attractions for the casual visitor. However, you might enjoy stepping inside to enjoy its atmosphere of understated elegance, which is more typical stately Palm Springs than flashy Las Vegas.

In fact, it was named for a Palm Springs luxury resort when it was opened by Walter Clark in 1950. Actually, Clark was only the front man for the hotel and a minority owner. Cleveland gang figure Morris Dalitz held the juice and ruled for decades as one of the big men on the Strip. The Inn caught a lot of ink when Howard Hughes moved upstairs in 1966 and captured more when Howard bought out Dalitz to begin his own Las Vegas empire. Kirk Kerkorian picked it up from Hughes' Summa Corporation in 1988 and completed a multi-million dollar refurbishment that has made it the most elegant mid-sized property on the Strip.

A golf course open to guests (and others with advance appointment), 200 acres of garden-like grounds, a swimming pool and several spas, one of the town's best health clubs and a large shopping arcade complete this picture of affluence.

Casino: No one-dollar blackjack tables here. The rather small and roomy casino is high roller country, elegantly coiffed in understated Southwestern garb, with striking circular chandeliers. Table stakes start at $3 and most are higher. Surprisingly, you can ferret out a few nickel video poker machines while taking in the look of this posh habitat. Note the special area with $5, $25 and $10 slots, with a nicely attired attendant standing by to provide the proper tokens.

Entertainment: The Desert Inn recently dropped its "Showstopper" revue in favor of top headliners such as Sinatra and Cher. The Winners Choice casino lounge offers live entertainment into the early hours.

Dining: The restaurants are upscale with prices to match. **La Vie en Rose,** with hand-painted murals and a rose garden theme, offers continental fare for $25 to $50; four seatings, at 6, 6:30, 9 and 9:30. **Portofino** is styled in burgundy and baroque, with northern Italian fare $14 to $30; Tuesday-Saturday 6 to 11. Tropical fish aquariums greet diners at **HoWan,** serving Asian dishes $11 to $40; Wednesday-Sunday 6 to 11. **La Promenade** is 24-hour coffee shop, properly upscale with velvet booths and golden umbrellas **Champions' Deli,** out by the tennis courts and golf course in the country club, serves breakfast, lunch and drinks.

Rooms: Doubles $75 to $175.

Dunes Hotel & Country Club • ☺☺☺

3650 S. Las Vegas Blvd. (Dunes Road, adjacent to Caesar's Palace); (800) 634-6971 or (702) 737-4110. The Dunes is another longtime gambling den with a golf course and extensive grounds. However, it does not enjoy such a checkered past. Not quite. Opened in 1955 by New England financiers with no casino experience, it promptly went broke, then was reopened by Major

Riddle, a gent with Teamster pension fund ties. Riddle introduced topless to the Strip and the Dunes was an immediate hit.

Several owners put it through an economic roller coaster ride, climaxed by a 1985 bankruptcy. It was purchased three years later by Masao Nangaku, a Japanese investor with lots of yen to spend. The Tokyoesque influence is evident in the clamshell motif Dome of the Sea restaurant and the smoked glass Oasis casino with its hot pink neon and gold lamè palms. It's a pretty place, but without the elegance or the high roller atmosphere of the Desert Inn.

Casino: Lots of nickel and quarter video poker machines, slots and dollar blackjack draw folks into the attractive Arabian nights theme gaming parlor. One area, much flashier than anything in Arabia, is called Xanadu, a glittering study in gaudy neon. The casino offers all the usual table games and a sports book.

Entertainment: The Persian Room, the Dunes' big showplace, was dark at this writing but it may be featuring either headliners or a major revue by the time you arrive.

Dining: The **Dome of the Sea** provides a very aquatic dining experience, with swimming fishies projected onto the walls. Prices swim from $13 to $36; hours are 6 to 11 daily. The ubiquitous 24-hour coffee shop is the **Savoy,** specializing in American and Chinese fare. The long popular Sultan's Table gourmet room is gone, replaced by the **Sultan's Buffet.**

Rooms: Doubles $39 to $109.

El Rancho Hotel & Casino • ☺☺

2755 S. Las Vegas Blvd. (just south of Wet 'N Wild water park); (800) 634-3410 or (702) 796-2222. A handsomely contrived Old Mexico façade sets El Rancho apart from the *neon moderne* gambling castles along Las Vegas Boulevard. Western and Spanish dècor blend nicely in the main casino.

If one is tempted to assume that this gaming parlor is a descendant of El Rancho Vegas, one would be wrong. It *does* have a long history, dating back to 1948 as the fourth hotel on the Strip. However, it was opened as the Thunderbird and later had its license jerked by the Nevada gaming commission for gangland ties. After passing through several owners, it is now the property of Ed Torres, local hotel operator, who renamed it in honor of El Rancho Vegas. The original sat across Las Vegas Boulevard until it burned in 1960 and was never rebuilt.

Casino: The attractive casino, with Spanish tile false roofs and other old Mexico touches, offers lots of low-roller slots, $2 minimum blackjack and roulette buy-in for $10. A large bingo parlor flanks one side of the casino and a 52-lane bowling alley is at the other.

Entertainment: El Rancho has a "big room" but it was inactive when we visited. In fact, the whole place seemed rather quiet, which is a pity since it's attractive in its rustic South of the Border way. The casino lounge offers live entertainment most evenings.

Dining: The 24-hour **Alamo Coffee Shop,** with a sort of Mexican/American Naugahyde look, offers a rural American menu of southern fried chicken, barbecued ribs and the like; $4 to $6, with a $1.79 breakfast special. Snack bars offer Mexican and American snacks and pizza and the buffet is appropriately called the **Chuckwagon.**

Rooms: Doubles $35 to $70.

— **Betty Woo Martin**

Arthurian towers mark the imposing entrance to the Excalibur, the world's largest resort hotel with 4,032 rooms.

Excalibur • ☺☺☺☺ K

3850 S. Las Vegas Blvd. (Tropicana Avenue); (800) 937-7777 or (702) 597-7777. We'll start with a single superlative. This $290 million medieval family fun castle is the world's largest resort hotel, with 4,032 rooms. Ready for more? How about 100,000 square feet of gaming space, 2,630 slot and video machines, seven restaurants and 7,000 parking spaces, all spread over 117 acres. It was opened in June, 1990, by Circus Circus Enterprises.

Excalibur is *circus extremus* in the King Arthur manner, with a dinner jousting tournament, turreted castle façade complete with a moat, cobblestone foyer, a casino trimmed in neon knights, and simulated stone walls decorated with shields, suits of armor and knightly weapons. Costumed performers may appear at any moment about the Medieval Village shopping complex. In planning Excalibur, designers checked out 20 real English castles to get the right look.

Did we say this place was family-oriented? Kids and parents can root for the white knight and hiss the black one at King Arthur's Pageant. One can engage in assorted ring tosses and coin pitches at Fantasy Faire or invest quarters in the Wizard's Video Arcade. The Magic Motion Machine effectively simulates the Colossus roller coaster at California's Magic Mountain.

Casino: Set on the ground floor between the mezzanine Medieval Village and the basement Fantasy Faire, the casino is one of the biggest in town, with lots of nickel and quarter action and low stakes tables. All the games are here, including a race and sports book. A 200-foot registration desk occupies a nearby landing, so you can check in, send the kids off to Fantasy Faire and hit the tables.

Entertainment: King Arthur's Tournament, a family dinner show presented twice nightly, is a state-of-the-art jousting match, with costumed knights doing battle to the beat of lasers and Merlin-inspired illusions. Diners eat with their hands and scream enthusiastically for the good guys. However, one is not encouraged to throw bones at the Black Knight. Lipizzaner stallion shows also are presented in the arena. After the kiddies are tucked in, adults can catch live entertainers at the Minstrel's Lounge in the casino.

Dining: Trimmed in rich woods, stone and floral carpeting, **Camelot** is Excalibur's upscale dining salon; entrèes from $11 to 20; Sunday-Thursday 5 to 11 and Friday-Saturday 5 to midnight. Other restaurants with assorted themes are the 24-hour **Sherwood Forest** cafe with an essentially American menu; **Sir Galahad**, an olde English style place featuring prime rib, Yorkshire pudding, trifle *et al*; **Oktoberfest** with German fare and a live "oompah" band; **Lance-A-Lotta Pasta**, obviously an Italian place and **Robin Hood's** Snack Bar. The **Roundtable Buffet**, rivals the one at Circus Circus in size and food variety, with four serving lines and seating for 1,400.

Rooms: Doubles $29 to $69.

Flamingo Hilton • ☺☺☺

3555 S. Las Vegas Blvd. (near Flamingo Road); (800) 732-2111 or (702) 733-3111. Ben Siegel wouldn't recognize his "real class joint" today, with its monumental neon blossoms, highrise towers with bronzed windows and a casino large enough to swallow the original Fabulous Flamingo. Built "out in the middle of nowhere" miles from downtown Las Vegas, the first pink lady had a mere 105 rooms, compared with today's 3,530. It was a grand showplace for its day, however—$6 million worth of luxurious sparkle. Siegel outfitted every employee in tuxedos, even the janitor. Restaurant guests dined with sterling silver.

After Siegel was iced by the mob, his Fabulous Flamingo became a quick success. His boss Meyer Lansky took charge, operating behind the scenes through an assortment of fronts and managers. Thomas Hull, who started the Strip with El Rancho Vegas, held title briefly. Then Kirk Kerkorian picked it up in 1967 and sold to the Hilton Corporation three years later.

The first hotel chain to own a Nevada casino, Hilton dropped the name "Fabulous" even while making it so. Sinking mega-millions into expansion, the corporation created the second biggest hotel in the world, after Excalibur. A 1990 tower brought the room count to 3,530.

Several original structures survive, across from the main swimming pool in the shadow of the towers. Siegel's old room, now the called the Bugsy Suite, is the fourth-floor penthouse of the Oregon building. If you're curious to see it (from the outside only, of course), cross the pool deck behind the main casino, step into the Oregon building and take the elevator to the fourth floor. The doors will open onto a small ante room outside the locked door of the suite, room 44000 (which you can rent). The building itself is worth a look, with a huge chandelier practically filling a second-floor rotunda. If you want more of the flavor of Siegel's day, you can adjourn to the Beef Barron restaurant and order Bugsy's Speakeasy Special, consisting of rib, beef or chicken with veggies, salad and wine or beer for $14.95.

Beyond the Bugsy suite, the resort offers all the Vegan amenities, including an indoor-outdoor pool, formal gardens, health club and tennis courts.

Casino: The bright game room is a huge layout, with half a dozen roulette wheels, and several craps tables and several dozen blackjack venues. A lot of high stakes tables draw serious gamblers, although there are some $3 games and lots of slots for mere mortals. Follow the neon rainbows—Hilton's trademark—to the Pot of Gold Machines, which have made instant millionaires out of a lucky few.

Entertainment: "City Lights" in the Flamingo's big room is one of the few dinner shows left in town. It's a nostalgic American musicale, Las Vegas style, with topless showgirls, big production numbers and a magician or two. The Hilton Lounge offers a mix of singers and combos playing dance music from mid-evening until 4 a.m.

Dining: Despite its aura of affluence, the Flamingo focuses more on affordable food. **Beef Barron** is a Hilton chain regular, with an Old West look and American fare; $8 to $40; 5 to 11:30 nightly. **Alta Villa** is Italian country style, with $8 to $20 entrèes; 5 to 11:30. **Peking Market** ($8 to $30; 5 to 11:30) is obviously Chinese, with a pleasing open market dècor and the adjoining **Spirits of Dr. Wu** serves potent tropical potions. Sushi's the thing at **Sushi Bar Hamada, Lindy's** is a New York style deli and the **Flamingo Room** offers a large American-continental menu. The **Crown Room Buffet** is just what it says, and **Food Fantasy** is a cafeteria style international food court.

Rooms: Doubles $59 to $119.

Frontier Hotel & Gambling Hall • ☺☺

3120 S. Las Vegas Blvd. (Stardust Road opposite the Desert Inn); (800) 634-6966 or (702) 734-0110. The Frontier's 200-foot sign is nearly as large as the hotel, which has a "mere" 986 rooms. Many are in a horseshoe shaped structure, appropriate to the casino's Western dècor. It encloses an attractive garden with a swimming pool, patios and fountains.

The Frontier is a descendant of the oldest surviving hotel on Las Vegas Boulevard. It traces its lineage to the Last Frontier, opened by Texas movie theater mogul R.E. Griffith in 1942. (Nothing remains of the first Strip hotel, the 1941 El Rancho Vegas.)

It was rebuilt and re-christened the New Frontier in 1956 and totally redone again in 1967 to become just plain Frontier. During this period, it switched from hokey cowboy to space age Italian marble, then back to its present Western look. Howard Hughes was one of several owners who steered its irregular course through the decades; he bought the third metamorphism immediately after its emergence. Margaret Elardi purchased the hotel it in 1988, closed the big show room where Wayne Newton and Siegfried and Roy once romped, and returned the focus to down-home Old West.

Casino: An abundance of nickel slots, $1 table minimums and inexpensive food appeal to the Chevrolet set in the large, comfortable casino. It has a poker parlor, appropriate to its Western heritage, and beginning poker lessons are conducted Monday through Saturday.

Dining: Folks eat cheap where Wayne Newton once sang. Part of the Elardi down-scaling was the conversion of the showroom into a buffet. On the other end of the scale is **Justin's,** a fancy Victorian gourmet room with crystal chandeliers and plushy booths; continental fare is $18 to $50; hours 6 to 11:30 nightly. In the middle is **Margarita's,** one of the town's more appealing Mexican restaurants, with a pleasing Southwest dècor and "live" tortilla oven, just off the casino.

Rooms: Doubles $35 to $125.

Hacienda Hotel • ☺☺☺

3950 S. Las Vegas Blvd. (just below Excalibur); (800) 634- 6713 or (702) 739-8911. While it's no major visitor attraction, the medium-sized Hacienda has some exceptionally pretty touches, such as hand-painted Spanish floral designs on its walls and arches. The old Spanish look is carried throughout, with colonnaded walkways and heavy beam ceilings. A splashing waterfall at the entrance greets casino guests. Other facilities include a swimming pool and six tennis courts.

California motel owners Warren and Judy Bayley opened the Hacienda in 1956 and set the friendly, low-key atmosphere that remains today. Since it was way out in the boondocks (the last casino on Las Vegas Boulevard at the time), they used their own fleet of planes to bring in folks for inexpensive "Hacienda Holidays." After their passing, it went through a series of owners, finally winding up in the hands of Paul Lowden, a musician-entrepreneur and the landlord of the Sahara Hotel. He's been expanding and sprucing up the place.

The hotel's large **Camperland,** one of several casino-operated RV parks in town, has its own country store, swimming pool and kiddie playground.

Casino: It's a friendly place with special appeal to low rollers such as ourselves, with low stakes tables and lots of nickel slots and video poker machines. The Spanish floral touches add a cheerful ambiance to the gaming parlor, and periodic free champagne parties cheer things even further.

Entertainment: Hacienda's mid-sized Fiesta Theatre featured magician Lance Burton's "Magical Journey" show at this writing.

Dining: Black leather booths and brick walls offer a cozy Latin setting for the **Charcoal Room,** featuring steaks and American dishes; $20 to $35; 6 to 10:30 nightly. The **Cactus Room** is the 24-hour eatery and **El Grande Buffet** offers something grand for friends of the grape, all-you-can-drink wine with dinner.

Rooms: Doubles $41 to $81.

Harrah's Las Vegas • ☺☺☺ Ø

3475 S. Las Vegas Blvd. (opposite the Mirage); (800) 634-6765 or (702) 369-5000. Harrah's, formerly the Holiday, wins our neon piping award as the most delightfully gaudy structure on the Strip. It's fashioned in the shape of a riverboat, complete with red and black smokestacks, tied up to a convincing looking riverfront dock. The hotel portion, hidden in Harrah's shining shadow is the world's largest Holiday Inn, with a 1,721 room count.

The place caters to families, with a complete separation of the paddle wheeler casino and the highrise hotel. You can't hear the jingle of slot machines from the lobby. The complex includes a shopping arcade, swimming pool, health spa and kids' video arcade.

Casino: It's one of the more cheerful on the Strip, carrying the riverboat theme indoors with flocked wallpaper, white enamel carved woods and beaded chandeliers. River gambler attire adorns dealers, who are said to be among the more friendly and helpful in town. This is a comfortable, low-key place for beginners, with plenty of nickel slots, low stakes tables, a race and sports book, poker room and bingo parlor. It has smoke free gaming tables.

Dining: Joe's Bayou offers deep South ambiance and Cajun cookin'; $10 to $15; daily 5:30 to 11. **Claudine's** is more intimate, candle lit and with an American steak and seafood menu; $15 to $25; Thursday-Monday 5:30 to 10:30. The **Veranda Cafe** functions as the requisite coffee shop and **All That Jazz** serves $7 to $11 Cajun fare for breakfast, lunch and dinner. Folks line up to stuff themselves at the **Galley Buffet,** which has an all-day, all-night breakfast for $2.99.

Rooms: Doubles $59 to $115.

Imperial Palace • ☺☺☺ K

3535 S. Las Vegas Blvd. (between Sands Avenue and Flamingo Road, opposite Caesar's Palace); (800) 634-6441 or (702) 731-3311. While not lavish, the Palace is one of the Strip's more appealing resorts, with its interesting East-West look, curled up eves to ward off Chinese demons and sexy *cheongsam*-clad cocktail waitresses to lure them back. It earns its "K" because of the outstanding **Auto Collection** and a rather good second-floor hamburger joint. If you're a serious car nut, the auto exhibit is worth a special trip to Las Vegas. Wait until you see the Duesenberg collection!

The Palace began life modestly as the Flamingo Capri, then became "Imperial" in 1979. Tucked between Harrah's and the Flamingo Hilton, it has expanded considerably in recent years, nearly overflowing its five-acre site.

Casino: It's fun to look for the Oriental doo-dads here—snarling dragons, quasi-temple shapes, beaded curtains, even pagoda-roofed slot machines. It's an Asian potpourri with a Teahouse Coffee Shop, the Sakè Bar, the Ginza Bar, the Mai Tai Lounge and Geisha Bar. If you're superstitious and Asian, you'll like all the red for good luck. The casino has lots of low stakes tables and a fair amount of nickel machines. A high-tech race and sports book with a TV monitor at each seat was added recently. It also has a **School of Gaming** open to the public on the fourth floor. The race and sports book probably holds the record for the number of video screens; there's one at every seat!

Entertainment: The "Legends in Concert" features convincing lookalike sound-alikes of Elvis, Marilyn, Elton, et al. The many cocktail lounges focus more on drinking than entertainment.

Dining: You'd expect to find a good Chinese restaurant here and you'd be right; **Ming Terrace** serves Cantonese and Mandarin fare; $7.75 to $14, daily from 5 p.m. It's on the fifth floor Dining Plaza, along with other appropriately named places: the **Embers** steak and lobster house, $11 to $30, Wednesday-Sunday 5 to 11; the **Rib House,** specializing in barbecue, $10 to $17, Thursday-Monday 5 to 11; and the **Seahouse,** whose fare is obvious, $12 to $28, Friday-Tuesday 5 to 11. **Burger Palace** on the second floor serves quite good hamburgers and extremely good fries. The 24-hour joint is called the **Teahouse,** naturally, and the **Imperial Buffet** is just that.

Rooms: Doubles $20 to $125.

Las Vegas Hilton • ☺☺☺☺

3000 Paradise Rd. (east of Las Vegas Boulevard, next to Las Vegas Convention Center; (800) 732-7117 or (702) 732-5111. Like Caesars, the Hilton is an intriguing blend of posh and flash. Monumental beaded chandeliers, Greco-Roman friezes and neon Hilton rainbows send a mixed decorator's message across the huge casino. The Hilton demands exploration, from its double-lobby hotel with elegant European furnishings to its rooftop recreation area with a pool, six tennis courts and an 18-hole putting green.

The world's largest sports book, 14 different dining areas, a 220,000 square foot convention complex, a health club and a huge show lounge complete the heady Hilton picture.

This immense property began life in 1969 as the International, created by super entrepreneur Kirk Kerkorian. The Hilton chain purchased it in two stages, in 1970 and 1971. It's interesting to note that Hilton officials never built a casino from scratch. However, by the time they'd finished buying and expanding the Flamingo and International, the firm owned the world's two largest resort hotels—for the moment, at least.

Casino: This is high roller country, with most table stakes beginning at $5. Thousands of slots and videos, generally from 25 cents up, attract handle-pullers. Even if you're a modest gambler, the casino is worth a stroll. Admire the huge chandeliers over the gaming tables and the bronzed statue of Man of War, greeting visitors to the Super Book.

Entertainment: The biggest of the big names have appeared in the big room of the Hilton (and the International that preceded it): Elvis Presley, Bill Cosby, Crystal Gale, Gloria Estefan, Eddie Murphy and Engelbert Humperdinck. It's Wayne Newton's perennial hangout for 12 weeks of the year. The Casino lounge offers live music, including some minor luminaries such as the Checkmates.

Dining: We haven't the room to list all 13 eating venues. **Le Montrachet** is the upscale place, with entrées starting around $35 and *prix fixe* dinners $50 and beyond. The **Hilton Steak House** and **Barronshire Room** focus on steaks and American Southwest fare; their prices are $18 to $35. **Andiamo** is an upscale northern Italian restaurant with an open kitchen; dinners are $15 to $30. Oriental gardens complement the **Garden of the Dragon** Chinese restaurant and **Benihana Village** features knife-flashing table side prep and cooking, plus an animated bird show. **Socorro Springs Cafe** is the ubiquitous 24-hour coffee shop and **Paco's,** a recent edition, serves assorted Mexican fare. The **Buffet of the Champions** is self-explanatory.

Rooms: Doubles $80 to $175.

Maxim Casino ● ☺☺

160 E. Flamingo Rd. (just east of Las Vegas Boulevard); (800) 634-6987 or (702) 731-4300. This medium-sized casino features a sleek, modernistic façade and cheery contemporary interior. Offering all the resort essentials—a highrise hotel, swimming pool, showroom and shops, it arrived on the scene in 1977.

Casino: Locals say this is one of the more friendly places on the Strip, with generous slots. Players who hang in there will be tabbed by casino employees for free meals and shows, in addition to the usual complimentary drinks. Table minimums are $2, and the place has a large, comfortable keno lounge. **Entertainment:** At this writing, Maxim's lounge featured nightly comedy shows at 7 and 9 p.m.

Dining: Maxim's gourmet room is **Da Vinci,** an attractively modern place with mirrored walls and velour booths, continental fare, focusing on a finish of flaming desserts; $14 to $30; nightly 6 to 11 nightly. The **Tree House** fills the 24-hour coffee shop role. With smoked mirror glass, lots of hanging greenery and butcher block tables, it's a cut above the ordinary.

The Mirage ● ☺☺☺☺ K

3400 S. Las Vegas Blvd. (adjacent to Caesars Palace); (800) 627-6667 or (702) 791-7111. It begins with a throaty growl; jungle critters chatter nervously. Then a sidewalk-shaking rumble; fire, steam and water squirt skyward; "lava" cascades over the side (via gas jets) and spills hissing into the lagoon.

Mirage indeed.

— photo courtesy Las Vegas News Bureau

Crowds gather to watch periodic eruptions of the volcano outside the Mirage, one of the strip's most elaborate resorts.

Las Vegas Boulevard is lined with casinos that have blossomed into resorts. The Mirage is a world class resort that just happens to have a gaming license. With its performing volcano, white tiger lair, dolphin habitat and indoor rain forest, it rivals anything we've seen in Hawaii, the Caribbean or Mexico. It's amazing what you can do with a little imagination and $630 million.

Steve Wynn of the downtown Golden Nugget spent more than all of the other Strip casinos *combined* to create this impressive destination resort. Nervous bean counters told him it was impossible; the place would have to generate a million dollars a day just to break even and meet its debt service. Since its opening in 1989, it has done more than a $1.75 mil per diem.

The Mirage catches them all: the high rollers tucked into multi- million dollar suites that you can't even rent, hoards of tourists who stare in awe at the volcano and lagoon and are thus drawn inside, mom and pop and the kiddies who love to ogle the white tigers and dolphins.

The façade has not a shred of neon. With a traffic-stopping volcano, who needs colored piping? Incidentally, it performs every 15 minutes from dusk until 1 a.m.

Mirage creator Wynn is *the* bright young success story of Las Vegas. The son of a Maryland bingo parlor operator, he came to town in 1967 and began speculating in real estate. He acquired controlling interest in the Golden Nugget in 1973, at the tender age of 31, then launched a total refurbishment to create the largest, most opulent property along Glitter Gulch. Later, he built and then sold the Golden Nugget in Atlantic City, then purchased Del Webb's Nevada Club in fast-growing Laughlin and converted it into yet another Golden Nugget.

The Mirage, of course, is his most ambitious project. By most measures, it's the town's most expansive resort, on a 100-acre site with a half-mile front, 7,300 employees and glossy Y-shaped 30-story hotel towers. Beyond the resort's palm-lined causeway, past the white tiger habitat, visitors will find a 20,000-gallon aquarium as a backdrop to the registration desk, palms real and simulated beneath a 90-foot glass atrium, scores of shops, half a dozen restaurants and a landscaped multi-pool swimming grotto.

Oh, yes. There's a casino in there someplace.

Casino: The gaming center isn't hard to find, since it's rather large and bright, with a Polynesian theme. Suspended roofs break it up into a series of smaller areas, with the usual slots, video machines and tables. Both high and low rollers will find action here, with nickel slots and affordable table stakes. If you're *really* serious about gambling, can spend as much as $500 a pull on special token slot machines or request an elegant private room where the smallest denomination chip is $1,000. Baccarat is the highest of the high stakes game here.

Entertainment: Siegfried and Roy present the town's most spectacular show, a multi-million dollar mix of animals and illusions, performed in a specially designed theater. When they take an occasional one-week break, big-name entertainers fill the big room void. Various singers and combos function in the Lagoon Saloon, from noon until well past midnight. The dolphin habitat is open from 11 to 7 on weekdays and 9 to 7 weekends for a $3 admission fee. It's not a show, but discussions and demonstrations of dolphin behavior. The facility has both above and underwater viewing areas.

Dining: The Mirage's tropical theme carries into most of its cafes. **Kokomo's** is a restaurant under glass adjacent to the rain forest, featuring steaks and seafood with Polynesian accents; dinners $9 to $16; daily 11:15 to 2:30 and 5:30 to 11. **Moongate** (5:30 to 10:30 nightly) and **Mikado** (5:30 to 11:30 Tuesday-Saturday) are fancifully done Chinese and Japanese restaurants; prices are $15 to $30. **Caribe Cafe** is the 24-hour place and the Mirage buffet is set in a Caribbean village. The **California Pizza Kitchen** serves "gourmet" pizza from a wood fired oven. North of the tropics appetites can head for **Ristorante Riva,** primarily northern Italian and **The Bistro,** frankly French; prices are $11 to $30.

Rooms: Doubles $79 to $225.

O'Sheas Casino • ☺

3555 S. Las Vegas Blvd. (just north of the Flamingo Hilton); (702) 733-3111. This is essentially an extension of the Flamingo, with an Irish accent. Hilton officials built this mid-sized casino in 1989 to catch their overflow. The décor is strictly from Erin, working on the premise that anyone who ventures in here will enjoy the luck o' the Irish.

More than 600 slot and video poker machines, a couple dozen gaming tables and a keno parlor occupy this 30,000 square foot facility. The **Shamrock Cafe** serves essential American fare at reasonable prices 24 hours a day. The place also houses the **Donnybrook Buffet,** and a snack bar is nearby. **O'Sheas Pub** provides live music and a dance floor.

Riviera Hotel • ☺☺☺

2901 S. Las Vegas Blvd. (Riviera Boulevard, opposite Circus Circus); (800) 634-6753 or (702) 794-9451. Just when you thought we were running short of superlatives, the alphabet brings us to the Riviera, which has—are you ready?—the world's largest casino. Completed in March, 1990, it covers 125,000 square feet, bigger than a football field with the sidelines and end zones thrown in.

Like an adult Topsy, the Riviera just keeps on growing, with a collection of add-on towers that give it the look of a Las Vegas Leggo set. It began life in 1955 as the tallest highrise on the Strip, jutting skyward for a dizzying nine stories. Financed by Miami hoteliers, the hotel had a Mediterranean flair and catered to high rollers. The new owners didn't have flair for Vegas action, however. They rented Liberace's famous smile for an astounding $50,000 a week, hoping to pack the house. Even with the flamboyant showman in the big room, the place went broke.

An assortment of shady characters moved in to run things, including Gus Greenbaum, late of the Fabulous Flamingo. Like the other early hotels, it eventually went legit, reining for decades as one of the Strip's class acts. Present owner Meshulam Riklis, operator of a major travel company, decided to appeal to a broader economic spectrum.

Casino: It is indeed huge, spreading in several directions, with coffered, lighted ceilings, brass columns and pink neon. Naturally, all the games are here in all the denominations, plus a race and sports book. And should feel the need, there's a wedding chapel off to one side.

Entertainment: The "Splash" revue is one of the town's better shows, a technically intriguing extravaganza both above and under water. The Riviera also has three other shows in smaller venues: "An Evening at La Cage," featuring female impersonators; "Crazy Girls—Fantasie de Paris," a rather erotic musical; and "An Evening at the Improv," an adult comedy club. Also, live entertainment is presented until 3 a.m. at LeBistro Lounge.

Dining: Ristorante Italiano is the Riviera's posh eatery, with a handsome Venetian look; $8 to $28; nightly 6 to 11. Handsome **Kristopher's** offers a pool-side view and demonstration kitchen, with prix fixe American dinners for $19.95; 5:30 to 11 nightly. The 24-hour place, **Kady's Brasserie,** is a deli style pool-side cafe. **Rik' Shaw** (5:30 to 11:30) features inexpensive Oriental fare and the **Mardi Gras Food Court** offers assorted fast foods, including that Burger King and other major franchises. The **Riviera Buffet** serves breakfast, lunch, dinner and a show special.

Rooms: Doubles $59 to $95.

Sahara Hotel & Casino • ☺☺☺

2535 S. Las Vegas Blvd. (Sahara Avenue, at the top of the Strip); (800) 634-6666 or (702) 737-2111. This is one of the few places in town where you can learn what time it is, not inside but outside. A time and temperature sign atop the 24th story has long been a familiar Strip landmark.

One of the most stable of the Las Vegas resorts, the Sahara was opened in 1952 by Los Angeles jewelry baron Milton Prell. It enjoyed its brief moment in the sun as the biggest, most elaborate, etc., of the new Strip joints. Del Webb's company did the construction, and he gained controlling interest in 1961, then sold out to Las Vegas musician-entrepreneur Paul Lowden in 1982. It is thus one of the few early hotels never tainted by gangland ownership. Through the tumultuous decades, it simply sits there, making money, digesting it and expanding.

The ten-building complex includes a pair of pools, a major showroom, convention center and the usual shops and boutiques. Neither drab nor ostentatious, it's a bright and cheerful place that's full most of the time. Not ostentatious? Well, it *does* have the world's tallest free-standing sign, spelling out its name in a 222-foot stack of letters.

Casino: High ceilings, good lighting, pink neon and light paint merge to provide an open, almost breezy feeling. Slots and tables accommodate rollers both high and low and a large race and sports book attracts the handicappers. In the midst of all this glitter, there's an earthy touch—a vendor issuing hot dogs for 75 cents, with all the trimmings.

Entertainment: Headliners appear in the Congo Theatre; mimic Rich Little had an indefinite engagement the last time we checked. "Island Magic" is a Polynesian revue served with dinner at 5 and 7 p.m. Friday-Wednesday for $14.95. The Casbar Lounge offers a mix of vocalists and combos, including an occasional vintage group such as the Four Freshmen.

Dining: Shades of tropical old L.A. **Don the Beachcomber** out-does the original with elaborate Polynesian décor and lots of rum drinks sprouting little paper umbrellas South seas, steak and seafood menu, $12 to $26; Tuesday-Saturday 5 to 11. On the upscale side is the **House of Lords**, terribly British and one of the town's better-regarded restaurants with continental entrées $15 to $35; nightly 6 to 11. The **Caravan Room** is the around-the-clock coffee shop and the **Turf Club Deli** offers walk-up food. If you're looking for the all-you-can-eat line, it's called the **Garden Buffet**.

Rooms: Doubles $55 to $100.

Sands Hotel Casino • ☺☺☺ ∅

3355 S. Las Vegas Blvd. (Sands Avenue, opposite the Mirage); (800) 446-4678 or (702) 733-5000. It's *deja vu* all over again if you saw that great film *Ocean's Eleven,* about an attempt to knock over a Las Vegas casino. The Sands is one of the grand old Strip hotels, dating back to 1952. The greats of show biz played the legendary Copa Room. Frank Sinatra and Dean Martin briefly owned a piece of the hotel and it was a popular hangout for their Rat Pack buddies—Peter Lawford, Joey Bishop and Sammy Davis Jr. (If you missed *Ocean's Eleven,* the Rat Pack was the cast.)

A confusing assortment of people was involved in the Sands' creation, some probably gang-related, some not. As the darling of the Rat Pack and visa versa, it was *the* hangout of the Fifties. Howard Hughes' Summa Corporation purchased the hotel in 1967, and the familiar conical tower was completed, topped by a giant "S" that serves as a handy Strip beacon. In 1988, Summa sold out to Kerkorian, who turned right around and dealt it off to the Interface Group, a large trade show conglomerate. Naturally, the group immediately announced major expansion plans.

The indoor Sands is a cheerful space, all a-glimmer with neon piping and mirror tiled ceilings. Much of the 1950s elegance survives in the extensive swimming pool gardens. They're rimmed by low-rise garden rooms and shadowed by a single circular hotel tower, one of the city's most enduring landmarks. Facilities include shuffleboard, night-lighted tennis, a nine-hole putting green and serious mens' and womens' fitness clubs.

Casino: Bright and high tech, the casino has a large sports and race book, the usual ranks of slots and just about every table game played in town. In a clever decorator touch, various denominations of slot and video poker machine areas are marked by pink, green, yellow, blue and red neon piping. Table stakes start at $2 and the casino offers areas for non-puffers. Blackjack games are "double exposure," meaning that both dealer's cards are dealt face up.

Entertainment: The famous Copa Room recently switched from big-name bookings to a lady magician, "Melinda and her Follies Revue." The musical, "Viva Las Vegas," plays there in the afternoon. The Winners Circle cabaret features a wide range of lounge acts, ranging from the comedy improvisational Committee to combos and vocal groups.

Dining: An authentic award winner (Travel-Holiday Magazine), the **Regency Room** serves French-continental fare in a properly clubby setting. It would not be difficult to picture Sinatra and Lawford perched at a favored table; the restaurant, in fact, dates back to the Rat Pack era. It's not as pricey as it looks, with complete dinners for $18 to $27; nightly 6 to 11 nightly. The **House of Szechwan** issues predictably spicy Chinese fare, starting at $12; nightly 6 to 10 nightly. **Ristorante Regency** issues Italian luncheons; $9 to $12; Monday-Friday 11:30 a.m. to 2:30 p.m. The **Garden Terrace** is the all-night place.

Rooms: Doubles $69 to $79.

Silver City ☺☺ ØØ

3001 S. Las Vegas Blvd. (opposite the Stardust); (702) 732-4152. They've finally done it; a smoke-free casino! Silver City is a likable and funky mid-sized club that asks you to please leave your butts outside. Further, it's a laid-back low rollers' delight with nickel slots and video poker, $1 single deck blackjack and cheap food. Instead of a blue haze in the rafters, you see mannequins of miners practicing their craft. Clever! Further, it's the only casino we've ever seen with a bike rack out back.

Dining: Silver City offers one of the Strip's cheapest buffets, featuring Mexican and American food, priced at $1.99 from 11:30 p.m. to 11 a.m. and $2.99 from 11:30 a.m. to 11 p.m. Also, you can get a shrimp cocktail or hot dog for 99 cents, and a sauerkraut or chili dog for $1.30.

Slots A Fun ● ☺

2880 S. Las Vegas Blvd. (beside Circus Circus); (702) 734-0410. This place catches the adult overflow from Circus Circus, and it's owned by the same outfit. If you've seen one too many aerial acts or heard one too many childish shrieks of delight, it's a handy retreat. You can find plenty of low roller action—nickel slots and video poker, $1 blackjack and rare ten cent slot machines with the old fashioned bells, plums and oranges on the reels. The food is cheap here, starting at zero: free popcorn and little sandwich wedges. If you insist on paying, you can get 99 cent hot dogs and cocktails and 75 cent imported beer.

Stardust Hotel ● ☺☺☺

3000 S. Las Vegas Blvd. (Stardust Road); (800) 634-6757 or (702) 732-6111. My earliest recollection of Las Vegas is of the dazzling horizontal marquee of at Stardust, largest in the world. It's been replaced by a more modern neon facade to match the new tower, still one of the brighter spots on the Strip. I also recall being astonished to learn that the hotel was the largest in the world, with *1,400 rooms!*

I didn't know at the time that this magical place (at least to a kid from Idaho) was among the most scandal-ridden of all the early Las Vegas carpet joints. Tony Cornero, who ran gambling ships off the California coast, floated a stock scheme to finance its construction in 1955. Unlike Siegel, he didn't survive to see the opening. But he wasn't rubbed out; he died from a heart attack with a pair of dice in his hands at a Desert Inn craps table.

Back room maneuvering, financing problems and gangland involvement became so entangled that the place didn't open its doors for three years. And that required a massive bail-out by Max Factor's brother John, who may have been fronting for yet another batch of racketeers. Howard Hughes put chips on the table in 1968, but the Justice Department killed the sale, ruling that Howard was on the verge of creating a monopoly. The place finally went legit after decades of gangland involvement. It was purchased in 1985 by the highly respected Boyd Group, owner of several other Nevada casino properties.

Instead of starting small and expanding, the Stardust started big and stayed that way for decades. It opened in 1958 with 1,032 rooms, then more were added to round off the number at 1,400, and it remained that way for years. The current owners recently completed a new tower to round it off again at 2,500 rooms. With a dramatic "slash" color scheme, the tower is one of the most attractive buildings on the Strip.

The Stardust has all the trimmings of a first rate casino-resort: handsomely gaudy casino, a major revue, a six-pack of restaurants, two Olympian pools and an athletic club.

Casino: It's among the most attractive in town, with mauve, pink and amber neon, mirrored columns and black matte ceilings sparkling with starpoints. Minimums and maximums accommodate the full range of gamblers. The large sports and race book, looking like Mission Control, is the most influential in the state. Here, "the line is made" (odds and point spreads are set) for all the others to follow. A sports handicappers' library is next door, with printouts of the latest stats on the games and the nags. Handicapping classes are conducted Tuesday at 3 and Thursday at 10; free table gaming lessons also are offered.

Entertainment: When the Stardust opened in 1958, Donn Arden opened a lot of eyes with one of the town's earliest topless revues, "Lido de Paris." The show broke every longevity record in town, finally replaced in 1990 by "Enter the Night," even more sensuous and certainly more high tech. Sandy Hackett's Comedy Club offers stand-up mirth nightly (he's the son of comic Buddy Hackett) and the Starlite Lounge features the usual assortment of combos and singers from late afternoon until about 3 a.m.

Dining: Restaurants are quite affordable here. **William B's,** a steak house with a stylish turn-of-the-century motif, offers entrées from $14 to $25; daily 5 to 11. Folks go to **Tres Lobos** for things Mexican; done in an attractive Spanish courtyard motif; $6 to $16; Sunday-Thursday 5 to 11 and Friday-Saturday 5 to midnight. The franchised **Tony Roma's** is (according to the sign) the place for ribs. **Ralph's Diner** is right out of Stardust's earliest years, with a Fifties style soda fountain, and **Toucan Harry's** is a 24-hour coffee shop with an Oriental slant. The **Warehouse Buffet** caters to storage-shed sized appetites. The **Shortstop Snack Bar**, near the big sports and race book, is just what the name implies.

Rooms: Doubles $40 to $200.

Tropicana Hotel & Casino ● ☺☺☺☺ K

3801 S. Las Vegas Blvd. (Tropicana Avenue, opposite the Excalibur); (800) 634-4000 or (702) 739-2222. They call it the "Island of Las Vegas" and it's one of the town's most appealing resorts. The old "Trop" has a lush new look, with thick south seas vegetation, lagoons, pools and contentedly chattering tropical birds. A $70 million conversion from European art *nouveau* to the south seas look was completed in 1986. With a tennis club, dinner show, multiple restaurants, health club, shopping arcade and 1,908 rooms, the Trop qualifies as one of the town's few true destination resorts.

Focal point is a landscaped five-acre water park with three pools (including one indoors for chilly weather), several waterfalls, three spas, flamingos, swans, penguins and a water slide. It also has a swim-up bar, in typical Hawaiian fashion, plus something not permitted in the Islands—the world's only swim-up blackjack game.

The gangland era of the 1950s gave birth to the original Tropicana. It blossomed in 1957 under the hand of a Frank Costello underling, "Dandy" Phil Kastel. Far from town but conveniently near the airport, the $15 million jewel earned the title of "Tiffany of the Strip" for its pseudo-Miami opulence. After a typical gangland roller coaster ride, it wound up in the hands of the conservative Ramada Corporation in 1979. The firm created the European look, then reversed itself and spent a mega-bundle to take it back to—and beyond—its original tropical glory.

Some of the stained glass of the "European era" remains, including a dazzling leaded glass canopy over the casino. All this glitz works well with the lush tropic vegetation, creating a sort of "Tiffany goes to Hawaii" look.

Casino: Even if you've never gambled and don't intend to start now, walk beneath the casino's great glass roof. If you haven't sworn off wagering, you'll find a complete array of tables with stakes at $3 and beyond, plus lots of slots and video poker from a nickel and beyond. Incidentally, the Trop has one of the most elegant baccarat rooms on the Strip. If you need gaming instruction, blackjack, craps, roulette and baccarat lessons are conducted daily.

Entertainment: Think of it as *Les Folies sans Brassiere*. With the closing of the Lido show at the Stardust, "Les Folies Bergere" at the Tiffany Theatre is the town's oldest revue. It's also one of three remaining dinner shows on the Strip. You'll find other entertainers (more fully garbed) at pool side and in the garden-like Atrium Lounge. Another entertainment feature is "The Comedy Stop," a stand-up laugh show.

Dining: The Trop offers the predictable array of restaurants, beginning with the upscale **Rhapsody** with continental fare ranging from $13 to $30; Friday-Monday 6 to 11. On Sunday, the place becomes a Sunday brunch venue. **El Gaucho** offers Argentine dècor and American steaks, plus ribs and seafood, in the $15 to $30 range; daily 6 p.m. to 11 p.m. Less formal dining choices include the 24-hour **Java Coffee Shop,** the **Tropics** with Polynesian fare and a view of the island water park, **Di Martino's** for things pasta, the Benihana-style **Mizuno's** with table-side chopping and cooking, and the **Island Buffet** for all-you-can-eat.

Rooms: Doubles $65 to $95.

Vacation Village • ☺☺

6711 S. Las Vegas Blvd. (far end of Las Vegas Boulevard, near I-15 exit 34); (800) 658-5000 or (702) 897-1700. The Vacation Village opening in 1990 extended the Strip's casino resorts all the way to the end, or to the beginning, depending on your geographic point of view. There's still a lot of empty space between the village and the next two majors, the Tropicana and Excalibur.

Since Vacation Village offers some of the best prices on the Strip, budget-conscious visitors shouldn't mind the couple of extra miles. For thirsty folks, it's really worth the effort, since the place offers ten cent beer on tap. The village is quite attractive for a budget layout; it's simple, yet modern with a pleasing Southwestern look. Facilities include two swimming pools and a spa, four restaurants and three lounges.

Casino: A Mayan-style vaulted ceiling rises from the open, airy gaming facility, which offers an abundance of low stakes tables and nickel slots and video poker machines.

Dining and entertainment: "Comics on Vacation" is one of the town's better showroom deals. The show and a buffet are only $9.99. Another food bargain is a $2 steak and eggs breakfast between midnight and 6 a.m. The 24-hour **Anasazi Dining Room** with a Southwest look features assorted American entrées and some of the town's better Mexican fare; prices are very modest, starting at $4.75 for complete meals. The **Pasta Village** features all you can eat pasta, pizza and salad; $3.99 for lunch and $4.99 for dinner.

Rooms: Doubles $20 to $45.

Vegas World Hotel & Casino • ☺☺

2000 S. Las Vegas Blvd. (upper end, at Main Street junction); (800) 634-6277 or (702) 382-2000. By alphabetic coincidence, Vacation Village and Vegas world are the Strip's bookends, the first or last casinos you encounter. Vegas World, opened by high stakes gambler Bob Stupak in 1979, is considerably more showy. (What's a high stakes gambler? This is the guy who bet a cool million on Joe Montana's arm in the Superbowl.)

Stupak's casino is, well, curious. It appears that he started out to build a planetarium and changed his mind. Satellites, asteroids, planets and an occasional astronaut float about a domed starry ceiling. You almost expect Darth Vader to be dealing blackjack in this place, or at least Mr. Spock. The space age look carries outdoors to the starkly modern Cape Kennedy facade. Stupak still wants to reach for the stars. A sign announces that he'll soon build America's tallest free-standing tower.

Casino: This high-stakes gambler apparently believes in giving his customers the edge. Both dealer cards are face up in blackjack and craps is a "no bust" game, meaning the shooter can't lose on his come out throw. Tables have low minimums and the slots are reportedly very loose. Stupak offers other lures as well: a **$1 million currency exhibit** and the opportunity to win it on special slot machines. (It hasn't happened.) Vegas World also features the world's largest (here we go *again*) wheel of fortune, measuring 25 feet in diameter. Stupak scatters a lot of coupon books around town to get people inside and keep them there.

Entertainment: The Galaxy Showroom has two different shows nightly. "Memories of Elvis" begins at 6, followed by "The Legendary Allen Rossi" at 9. Vegas World Lounge features assorted musicians and vocalists between 5 p.m. and 4 a.m.

Dining: The intimate **Kelly and Cohen's Gourmet** is the gourmet restaurant. Its stylish Victorian décor offers curious contrast to the extraterrestrial look of the rest of the place; dinners are $12 to $30; nightly 5 to 11. **Daisy's Cafe** is the ubiquitous 24-hour coffee shop and the all-you-can eat place naturally is called the **Moon Rock Buffet**, serving from 5 p.m. to 10 p.m. only.

Rooms: Doubles start at $35.

THE DOWNTOWN CASINOS

Downtown is the lair of old time Las Vegas gamblers, since this is where gaming began. As we mentioned earlier, the Glitter Gulch casinos are generally more informal and less elaborate than their newer neighbors on the Strip. They're also smaller and more compact in these limited confines. An exception is the posh and ornate Golden Nugget.

Table stakes are lower, food bargains abound and lodging is rather inexpensive in Glitter Gulch. However, with the likes of the Golden Nugget and the Plaza, it would be unfair to stereotype the area as a blue collar hangout.

Binion's Horseshoe Hotel & Casino • ☺☺

128 E. Fremont St. (at Casino Center Boulevard); (800) 622-6468 or (702) 382-1600. Benny Binion was a high-stakes Texas gambler and rum-runner who arrived decades ago to become one of the legendary characters of Las Vegas. Although he was nailed with a tax evasion rap in the 1950s, he was generally regarded as one of the gentlemen of Nevada gaming, untainted by the Chicago and New York underworld. He built the Horseshoe into one of downtown's most successful operations, then he bought out the next-door Mint in 1988 to create one of the area's largest casinos.

Benny passed to that great casino in the sky in 1989 at the age of 85. He's enshrined in bronze, on horseback, opposite the parking structure in the family's growing downtown empire.

Casino: This may be the most serious gambling establishment in town, with great ranks of slots, no-limit tables and no fancy lounge shows. Benny didn't even like the term "gaming," insisting that his was a *gambling* establishment. "Calling it gaming is like calling a whorehouse a brothel," he once said. Not surprisingly, Benny's gambling hall hosts the World Series of Poker each April. Incidentally, low rollers needn't be intimidated by the high stakes here. The Horseshoe offers plenty of nickel machines and dollar minimum tables. If you want to feel rich, you can have your picture taken standing before a **million dollar cash exhibit**. Casino personnel shoot the pic, and it's free.

The Western style look of the original Horseshoe and the more contemporary décor of the Mint form an interesting contrast. It's easy to see where Binion kicked out a wall to merge the two facilities.

Dining: The Horseshoe's highrise hotel houses the **Skye Room** restaurant, offering a basic American menu and one of the best views in town; dinners $12 to $25. The downstairs **Steak House** issues similar fare at similar prices. Both are open from 5 to 11 nightly. Inexpensive pasta is dished up at **Spaghetti Red's,** while tacos and the like emerge from the **Mexican Bar;** dinners are $5 to $14. Binion's also offers the usual all-night coffee shop and a buffet.

Rooms: Doubles $25 to $55.

California Hotel & Casino • ☺☺

12 Ogden Ave. (at First Street); (800) 634-6255 or (702) 385-1222. The names say old California—San Francisco Pub, Market Street Cafe and Redwood Bar and Grill. However, the look is strictly Hawaiian. California Casino's harmless identity crisis has come about because this is a favorite hangout for gamblers from the Aloha State.

Sam Boyd, one of the town's highly respected gaming citizens, opened the place in 1975. Sam settled in Las Vegas in 1940, after several years as a carnival worker and bingo club operator in California and Hawaii. He ran bingo parlors downtown, operated a roulette concession at the Eldorado, became a Sahara and Mint executive, then he built the Union Plaza in 1971. His Boyd Group of selected friends and family members is one of Nevada's most successful locally-based gaming corporations. It owns the Fremont, Stardust and Sam's Town.

Casino: About a thousand slots and video poker machines, ranging from a nickel to $5, occupy the good-sized casino floor. They're joined by a couple dozen blackjack tables, craps, roulette, mini- baccarat, keno and a sports book. Dark woods, coffered ceilings, brick walls and palm trees carry out the California-goes-to-the- Islands theme.

Entertainment: Singers, combos and pianists provide live music at the Redwood Bar and Grill from 6 p.m. to midnight.

Dining: The **Redwood Bar and Grill** is the requisite gourmet room, serving upscale American fare from 5:30 to midnight; $11 to $27. **Pasta Pirate,** with a California Cannery Row décor, offers seafood and pasta from 5:30 to 11:30 and **Market Street Cafe** fulfills the 24-hour coffee shop role, with American and Oriental food.

Rooms: Doubles $40 to $50.

El Cortez Hotel • ☺

600 Fremont Street (at Sixth); (800) 634-6703 or (702) 385-5200. Older but well maintained and with recently refurbished rooms, the venerable Cortez is one of the better "buys" downtown. Don't expect anything of tourist interest here, but do expect rather liberal slots, cheap food and lodging and friendly folks. The Cortez dates back to 1941 and briefly was part of Ben Siegel's fragile empire. It looks a bit lonely, sitting out there by itself, several blocks from the multi-colored glare of Fremont Street. One gets the impression that it's quietly basking in former glory days.

Casino: Coffered ceilings speak of more elegant moments, when Siegel and his crowd followed the action here. Today's action consists of $1 and $2 tables and nickel through quarter slots and videos, plus keno, of course. Relatively unchanged, the casino is a genuine Las Vegas old-timer, occupying the same space for more than half a century.

Dining: Locals get in line with tourists and tour groups to take advantage of the cheap prices at **Roberta's Café.** Dinner is served nightly from 4 to 11; $10 for hefty steaks, up to $13 for other entrèes. The **Emerald Room** is the never-close coffee shop.

Rooms: Doubles $23 to $40.

Fitzgerald's Casino Hotel • ☺☺

301 E. Fremont St. (at Third); (800) 274-5825 or (702) 382-6111. The luck of the Irish is rampant here, in theme if not in fact. Shamrocks and leprechauns abound, particularly in the Lucky Forest. Blarney's Castle dollar carousel claims a 97 percent payback, but it doesn't say which machines offer this largess.

Fitzgerald's hotel structure joins the Las Vegas list of superlatives as the tallest (34 stories, 400 feet) building in Nevada. It began life as the Sundance Hotel, built by Moe Dalitz in 1980. The Reno-base Fitzgerald group purchased the property in 1987 and promptly stuffed it with good luck charms. In the "Lucky Forest," one can hope for the best by tossing a coin in

114 — CHAPTER THREE

a wishing well, paying homage to a horseshoe and rubbing a genie's lamp or a Buddha's lucky tummy.

Casino: This good-sized facility offers the predictable range of games of chance, plus—appropriate to its theme—an Irish Sweepstakes racing game. Among its slot machines are some rare ten-centers, complete with oldstyle fruit salad on the reels.

Entertainment: The lounge offers music alive from 6 to midnight weekdays and noon to midnight weekends.

Dining: Leprechauns give way to cowboy regalia in **Cassidy's Steak House,** with a mix of American and Mexican food. Dinners are $10 to $24; daily 8 a.m. to 11 p.m. **Chicago Joe's** is lace-curtain Italian with the usual pastas; 11:30 a.m. to 11 p.m. **Molly's** is vaguely Irish in décor, serving a dual function as the 24-hour coffee shop and eat-until-you-drop buffet.

Rooms: Doubles $30 to $125.

Four Queens Hotel & Casino • ☺☺

202 E. Fremont St. (at the corner of Third Street); (800) 634-6045 or (702) 385-4011. This block-long casino below a hotel tower contributes substantially to the glitter of Glitter Gulch. Its canopy-style New Orleans façade is one of the more brilliant along Fremont Street. The Queens casino opened in 1965; a 720-room highrise hotel was added later. It's home to a couple of curiosities that make it worthy of a visit—the **Ripley's Believe it or Not Museum** and the world's largest slot machine.

Casino: This is one of the more luminous gaming parlors in town, with white paneled ceilings, globe chandeliers, mirrored columns and—get this—pink felt on the gaming tables. The look is Mardi Gras, with the usual array of slots, videos and table action. The late Robert A. Ripley certainly would have written up the Queens Machine, the world's largest gaming device. Measuring nearly 10 by 19 feet, this monster can accommodate six players at one time. An attendant pulls the handle after this big Bertha is fed a fistful of dollars.

Entertainment: The French Quarter Lounge is one of the town's hottest jazz spots. The hotel also features other combos and singing groups, including occasional oldies such as the Platters, from mid-afternoon until the early hours.

Dining: American fare occupies the menu at **Hugo's Cellar,** whose gimmick is a table side salad bar; dinner prices are $20 to $37; nightly 6 to 10. **Magnolia's Veranda** is one of downtown's more attractive coffee shops, with a Southern garden look and a view of the casino. Elaborate calorie-laden treats are served at the oldstyle **Ice Cream Shoppe.**

Rooms: Doubles $47 to $57.

Fremont Hotel & Casino • ☺

301 E. Fremont St. (between Third and Casino Center); (800) 634-6182 or (702) 385-3232. The Fremont opened in 1956 as downtown's first highrise. However, little remains of the original look, thanks to a $15 million face lift after the Boyd Group purchased it in 1985. During the casino's early years, a couple of brothers named Newton performed in the now-defunct Carnival Lounge. One of them—Wayne—is still around town, on the verge of becoming an institution.

Casino: This long, narrow and busy gaming establishment is a-brim with slots, tables and other devices, with table minimums starting at $2. A sign promises loose and liberal slots. The Western-style casino is a bright, almost gaudy place, splashed with red neon trim. Incidentally, it also offers downtown's only bingo parlor.

Entertainment: Roxie's Bar is alive with live entertainment from noon until around 4 a.m.

Dining: The 24-hour **Overland Stage Café** a good selection of American fare and some Chinese dishes; prices run from $5 to $12/ **Tony Roma's** serves ribs and such nightly from 5 and the **Paradise Buffet** is the all-you-can-stuff-into-your-face place.

Rooms: Doubles $36 to $50.

Gold Spike Hotel & Casino • ☺

400 E. Ogden Ave. (at Fourth Street); (800) 634-6703 or (702) 384-8444. This is the darling of the budget set, a slightly scruffy and exceedingly friendly little casino that offers the cheapest ride in town.

Casino: Slot machines and video poker begin at one entire penny, all tables have a dollar minimum and you can play keno for 40 cents or roulette and electronic keno for a dime. Although it's difficult to make much at a penny machine, some of the longshot payoffs actually amount to thousands of dollars. Any royal flush in video poker earns you a free meal at the coffee shop, in addition to a generous payoff.

Dining: Prices at the small coffee shop follow the low-roller trend. For instance, a hot roast beef or ham dinner sets you back $3.

Rooms: Doubles $20; perhaps the best room buy in town.

Golden Nugget Hotel & Casino • ☺☺☺☺

129 E. Fremont St. (at Casino Center Boulevard); (800) 634-3454 or (702) 385-7111. Nothing on the Strip matches the studied elegance of the Nugget. Cloaked in white Grecian marble with white and gold-leaf canopies, it is a vision in French New Orleans chic. The carriage style entrance off Casino Center Boulevard would do justice to a grand hotel in Europe. The interior is richly done in polished marble, beveled mirrors and Tiffany style glass, with brass-on-white accents. Gold-leaf elevator walls and gold plated pay phones add wonderfully ostentatious touches.

Occupying two city blocks and surrounded by potted palms, the Nugget is an island of elegance amidst the bright lights and honking traffic of downtown. A major show room, pool, spa, sauna and complete health club are among its amenities. Check out the **world's largest nugget display**, midway between the casino and the hotel lobby. Revolving on a Plexiglas turntable is the "Hand of Faith," a 875 troy ounce nugget found near Wedderburn, Australia, in 1980. Several other nuggets are included in the exhibit.

All of this is the work of Steve Wynn, who obtained controlling interest in the property in 1973. Founded in 1946 by Los Angeles gambler Guy McAfee, the Nugget initially sported a gaudy Barbary Coast cum Wild West look. It boasted the largest neon sign in Glitter Gulch, which was a postcard fixture for decades. Today, like Wynn's Mirage, the Nugget façade has not a shred of neon.

Casino: The Nugget features more than 30,000 square feet of gaming space, all done up in white, brass and beveled glass. Despite its opulence, it's affordable. Nickel slots and videos abound, table stakes start at a dollar and blackjack is dealt from single decks.

Entertainment: The Golden Nugget Cabaret, one of two downtown showrooms, features headliners such as Mel Tillis and Don Rickles.

Dining: Restaurants carry out the Nugget's upscale image. **Elaine's** is French in décor and menu and **Stefano's** is northern Italian, with a pleasing garden setting. Prices at the three are $15 to $35; all serve dinner only. **Carson Street Café** is the 24-hour place and the **Buffet,** not surprisingly, is served in a stylish setting, with chandeliers, booths and greenery.

Rooms: Doubles $50 to $110.

Lady Luck Casino Hotel • ☺☺ ∅

206 N. Third St. (at Ogden Avenue; (800) 523-9582 or (702) 477-3000.
Although the Lady Luck offers little for the casual tourist, it provides plenty for the casual gambler. With its thick coupon book and gratis goodies, it has one of the most liberal freebie policies in town. The Lady started as a small "grind joint" in the 1960s and has ballooned into the third largest downtown facility, with a large casino and a 796-room hotel.

Casino: With windows on the street, rare for a casino, the place is particularly bright and open. It's cheerfully decorated with neon piping, beaded lights and mirrored ceilings. Table stakes start at $1 and nickel slots and video poker games are plentiful. You can even gamble (for nothing) with your parking validation ticket; every 200th one earns $25. To load up on various freebies, show out-of-state identification at the welcome center. The casino has non-smoking areas, and it features free gaming lessons.

Dining: The **Burgundy Room** is a virtual mini-art gallery with a 1930s look and originals by Dali, Poucette and Le Verrier. The menu is American-continental; $11 to $20; nightly except Wednesday, 5 to 11. The **Emperor's Room,** decorated with replicas of the Xian terra cotta warriors, serves Szechwan and Cantonese fare; $6.50 to $15; from 5 to 11 nightly except Tuesday. **Brasserie** is the 24-hour place and the **Lady Luck Prime Rib Room** serves prime rib with an all-you-can-eat salad bar in the evening, plus buffets at breakfast and lunch.

Rooms: Doubles $39 to $75.

Las Vegas Club Hotel & Casino • ☺☺

18 E. Fremont St. (at Main Street); (800) 634-6532 or (702) 385-1664.
Two things distinguish the Club: the Sports Hall of Fame and the most liberal blackjack rules in Nevada. This is one of the oldest gaming parlors in the state, opened shortly after gambling was legalized in 1931. Present owner Mel Exder has modernized and expanded it, creating a rather attractive little downtown casino with a stack of affordable hotel rooms.

Casino: We won't repeat the liberalized blackjack rules here, which make sense only to serious players. They're emblazoned on a big sign hanging right above the tables, so you'll get the message quickly. Lots of splitting and doubling down and that sort of thing. The small casino is pleasing to the eye, with chandeliers, mirrored walls and a high lavender ceiling. Within are the usual ration of slot and videos from a nickel up, tables from $2 up, a sports book, keno and other games of choice and chance.

The **Sports Hall of Fame** occupies a hallway between the casino and restaurant. You'll find dozens of photos of your sports heroes, Maury Wills' gilded baseball shoes, trophies and assorted autographed baseballs and footballs. It reportedly has the largest collection of baseball memorabilia outside of Cooperstown.

Dining: The **Great Moments Room** is done up in "country English" with a continental menu and dinner fare from $13 to $20; nightly from 5:30. The 24-hour **Dugout** carries on the Sports Hall of Fame look and the menu carries American, Hawaiian, Chinese and Mexican specialties.
Rooms: Doubles $40 to $50.

Main Street Station • ☺☺
300 N. Main St. (Ogden Avenue); (702) 387-1896. This stylish old New Orleans style casino may or may not be functioning as you read this. Local word was that the Station was having a financial struggle. 'Tis a pity if it has closed, since its elaborate décor is certainly worth your perusal. It's all dressed up in leaded glass, simulated Tiffany lamps, carved and polished woods, pressed tin ceilings and wrought iron.

Casino: Several authentic artifacts decorate the medium-sized casino and its pub, including bronze and crystal chandeliers from the San Francisco Opera House, bronze doors from the Kuwait Royal Bank of London and a carved oak fireplace from Scotland's Preswick Castle. A brochure available at the hotel registration door will guide you to these items. The usual gaming tables (some under leaded glass canopies) and machines are there to challenge your gaming skills, including a new game imported from Australia called "two up."

Entertainment: Rosie O'Grady's Good Time Emporium features Dixieland/can-can/red hot mamma shows nightly at 7, 9 and 11. Even if there's no show, stop in for a 75-cent beer and admire the artifacts and Gay Nineties look of this large pub with its surrounding gallery seats.

Dining: White-painted iron arches hold up the ceiling of **Apple Annie's**, a large, open restaurant serving basic American fare around the clock and the **Cascade Parlor Car** serves American and Italian fare ($8 to $15) for lunch and dinner. **Lilie Marlene's** is done in a railcar and early aviation theme with American-continental fare, specializing in prime rib; $10 to $20; Wednesday-Sunday 5 p.m. to 11 p.m. Prix fixe dinners are served for $28 in the **Louisa Alcott Dining Car.** Try the **Morning Glory** deli for *beignets* (traditional New Orleans square powdered doughnuts), pastrami sandwiches and other light fare; 11:30 a.m. to 10 a.m.
Rooms: Doubles $30 to $50.

Pioneer Club • ☺
25 E. Fremont St. (First Street); (702) 386-5000. We have only one reason for listing this small place. The club boasts the town's most enduring image: Vegas Vic. This 60-foot neon cowboy is often featured in movies, videos and assorted promos, welcoming people to Las Vegas with his recorded baritone. (Actually, he says "Howdy, welcome to *downtown* Las Vegas," exhibiting obvious provincialism.)

Vic has been around since 1951 and the club itself goes back even farther, to the late 1930s. Today, the Pioneer is an ordinary Western-style casino catering to low rollers, with red coffered ceilings, lots of glitter-lights and a **Carl's Jr.**, hamburger joint.

Don't forget to say "Howdy" to Vic on your way in.

Jackie Gaughan's Plaza • ☺☺☺
One Main St. (at Fremont); (800) 634-6821 in California, (800) 634-6575 elsewhere, or (702) 386-2110 locally. Talk about location! Historically and visually, the Plaza occupies the best spot downtown. It was here that

agents of Senator William Clark stood on May 15, 1905, to auction off the first lots. This was the site of the historic Union Pacific railroad station. Today, the Plaza is the glistening capstone of Glitter Gulch—the beginning or the end of Fremont Street, depending on your vantage point.

Amenities here are comparable to those of a Strip casino resort: health club, shopping arcade, 650-seat showroom, swimming pool and a sports deck with a jogging track and lighted tennis courts. It stretches for nearly three blocks along the face of Main Street. Occupying land leased from Union Pacific, it's the world's only casino with a railroad station (Amtrak); Greyhound is nearby.

Sam Boyd spent a hefty $20 million to build the Union Plaza in 1971; it was downtown's largest until Wynn completed his Golden Nugget expansion. Enlarged to its present 1,037 rooms in 1983, the facility is now owned by Jackie Gaughan's Plaza Corporation.

Casino: The brilliant casino entrance lights up the sky at the end of Fremont, drawing folks into a roomy, high-ceiling interior. All the games and machines are here, in all the price ranges, plus a 300-seat sports and race book. Even on busy days, when the tour buses and conventions hit town, the casino has a spacious feel, with wide aisles and enough machines and tables to go around.

Entertainment: The showroom featured "Boy-lesque," a female impersonator revue, at this writing. The show had been moved uptown from the Strip. The Omaha Lounge offers live music from 11 a.m. until 4 a.m.

Dining: Plan a sunset dinner at the **Center Stage** beneath the hotel's glass dome and ask for a front row seat; the Fremont Street view is impressive. The food isn't bad, either: American-continental fare ranging from $15 to $35; daily 5 to midnight. Other culinary venues include **Kung Fu Plaza,** with Chinese-Thai fare, served from 11 a.m. to 11 p.m. with prices ranging from $5 to $25, and the **Plaza Diner,** offering inexpensive American fare and a cheap around-the-clock breakfast.

THE OUTLYING CASINOS

Las Vegas gaming action reaches well beyond the Strip and Glitter Gulch. Several casinos, large and small, are scattered about the neighborhoods or poised near freeway off ramps. Many are folksy little places appealing to locals, who like to avoid the tourist crowds. Others are major operations, competing for the attention of visitors and residents alike.

The outlying casinos generally offer rather good room and restaurant prices and generous odds, since they must work to lure visitors away from the established areas.

Arizona Charlie's Hotel & Casino • ☺

740 S. Decatur Blvd. (near west Charleston); (800) 342-2695 or (702) 258-5200. This small, ordinary-looking Western-style casino offers lots of nickel slots, low table stakes and, typical for a neighborhood casino, a bowling alley. Opened in 1988, it features a view window into the counting room. You can press your nose to the glass and say goodbye to your quarters as they're being rolled and wrapped.

Dining and entertainment: Inexpensive American fare is dished up at **Mae's Diamond J** 24-hour coffee shop; meals $4.55 to $11, and you can get a filling breakfast for a mere 49 cents. The **Wild West Buffet** serves all-you-can eat breakfast, lunch and dinner. Live entertainers hold forth nightly at the **Palace Grand Lounge;** the spicy Naughty Ladies Revue was the feature when we visited.

Rooms: Doubles $25 to $35.

Gold Coast Hotel & Casino • ☺☺

4000 W. Flamingo Rd. (about half a mile west across I-15); (800) 331-5334 or (702) 367-7111. One of several casinos reached by I-15 freeway off ramps, the colonial Spanish style Gold Coast was opened in 1986 by the Gaughan family. Although it enjoys a rather good tourist draw, it's also popular with locals, who claim that it has very generous slots.

Facilities include a large free-form pool with a tropical bar, a 72-lane bowling alley, video arcade and twin-screen movie theater.

Casino: The place has a pleasing Spanish look with stucco and pink tile. Massive brass chandeliers dangle from a vaulted roof over the gaming tables; the look is bright and open. Table minimums are low, nickel slots and videos are numerous and the place features a large bingo parlor. It also has one of the town's larger race and sports books; we counted 49 flush-mounted video screens, giving the place a Mission Control look.

Entertainment: Two attractive lounges, simply named East and West, offer assorted live entertainments, ranging from Dixieland to pop vocal groups. Music happens from 11 a.m. to 4 a.m. The town's largest dance hall features Western, rock & roll and big band music.

Dining: Gold Coast's Spanish look carries into the **Cortez Room** restaurant, although the menu is more American than Latino. A basket of warm sourdough bread precedes generous and inexpensive entrées; dinners $6 to $16; open daily for breakfast, lunch and dinner. The **Mediterranean Room** features seafood and Italian fare from $4 up; nightly 5 to 11; and the **Monterey Room** is the 24-hour venue, serving American and Chinese fare; an all-you-can-stuff **buffet** is presented daily.

Rooms: Doubles $35 to $50.

Palace Station Hotel-Casino • ☺☺☺

2411 W. Sahara Ave. (just west of I-15 Sahara interchange); (800) 634-3101 or (702) 367-2411. Locals flock to this attractive railroad-themed place. In fact, if you're to believe readers' polls conducted by the *Las Vegas Review-Journal,* it's the hottest spot in town. It offers much for the visitor as well—an interesting railroad motif with a depot-styled hotel lobby, rail car restaurants and train snouts poking from the façade. Two swimming pools, spas and a shopping area complete the amenities.

The operation began as a small casino and bingo parlor in 1975, opened by local-boy-makes-good Frank Fertitta, Jr. He started as a Stardust dealer in 1960 and worked his way right up to chairman of the board of the Palace Station's family-held corporation.

Casino: The huge casino offers 2,100 slots and videos, all the table games (with modest minimums), a poker room, sports and race book and the town's most popular bingo parlor, with 600 seats. To keep the folks coming, a free $25,000 bingo session is held once a week.

Entertainment: The Loading Dock Lounge features live music nightly from 8 p.m. to 4 a.m. Piano tinklings and occasional performers are part of the scene in the Palace Saloon, from 7 p.m. until 1 a.m.

Dining: Five restaurants, low priced and frequent favorites in those reader polls, offer assorted fare. **Fishermans Broiler** peddles freshly flown-in seafood; $8.75 into the mid-teens; daily 11 a.m. to 11 p.m. **Pasta Palace** features the ambiance and fare of northern Italy; from $6.95; nightly 5 to 11. Mexican grub emerges from **Guadalajara Bar & Grille,** with dinners starting at $7; nightly 5 to 11. **Iron Horse Cafe** is the we-never-close place, serving American and Chinese food, and **The Feast** is the all-you-can-eat place.

Rooms: Doubles $35 to $65.

Rio Casino & Suite Hotel • ☺☺☺ Ø

3700 W. Flamingo Rd. (at Valley View Boulevard, opposite the Gold Coast); (800) 888-1808 or (702) 252-7777. This is one of the most striking casino hotels in Las Vegas. Find a moment to drive west on Flamingo Road to check out this striking gaming venue. It has a dazzling look of *Brazil moderne*, accented by a curving red and blue glass sweep to its hotel tower and a rainbow casino entrance flanked by mirror glass walls. One of the newest kids on the block and the town's most attractive off-Strip resort, it was completed in early 1990.

Casino: "Jackpot Jungle" is trimmed in palm trees, plastic parrots and pastel tropical colors. The place is alive with upbeat South American sounds and the drink girls in their scanty flowered wraps look straight off the beach at Ipanema. Juan Peron would have loved it here. Of interest to fresh air fans: it has non-smoking gaming areas.

Entertainment: "Tropical Heat," one of the town's most sensuous topless revues, warms things in the main showroom, while live performers make music in the Ipanema Bar from 1 p.m. until 2 a.m. The Game Hut video arcade provides a stash for the kiddies.

Dining: The 24-hour pool side **Beach Cafe** offers American and Polynesian-Chinese fare from $3 to $9 and the all-you-can eat buffet is the **Carnival,** served in an appropriately decorated venue. **Antonio's** is an upscale Italian place with entrèes ranging from $11.50 to $19; nightly 5 to 11. The bright yet clubby looking **All American Bar and Grill,** with sports memorabilia and built in TV screens, serves American fare from $8 to $14.

Rooms: Doubles $81 to $99.

Sam's Town Hotel & Gambling Hall • ☺☺☺ Ø

5111 Boulder Highway (five miles east; at Flamingo Road); (800) 634-6371 or (702) 456-7777. This place covers several acres alongside the Boulder Highway. Its Western façade is so long and extensive that you might take it for a movie set. Out here in the low rent district, the prices are cheap, the look is cowboy, the folks are friendly and Sam's is thriving. Started in 1978 by the Boyd Group, the place has been on a non-stop expansion kick for more than a decade.

Current facilities include 198 hotel rooms, five restaurants, three floors of gambling, a Western dance hall, swimming pool, two RV parks and a 56-lane bowling alley. The Western Emporium provides 2,500 square feet of old West style shopping, from cowboy hats and Southwestern pottery to tourist curios. It's worth the short drive (follow Fremont Street, which becomes Boulder Highway or take Flamingo Road from Las Vegas Boulevard) just to see this place. Also, locals say the machines are pretty loose.

Casino: This is a *gambling hall*, partner, not a fancy-pants casino. The 58,000 feet of gaming space accommodates more than 2,000 slots and videos; three dozen blackjack, four crap, three roulette and four pai gow poker tables; a 590-seat bingo parlor with a non-smoking section, plus a poker room and race and sports book.

Entertainment: Live country music rattles the rafters of the Western Dance Hall Monday through Saturday from 9 p.m. until 3 a.m. Free dance lessons are conducted from 7:30 to 9 to help improve your cowboy two-step. The place becomes a disco on Sundays.

Dining: Diamond Lil's has a Western-Victorian look and an American menu; $10 to $35; nightly 5:30 to 10 (until 11 Friday and Saturday). **Willie and Jose's Mexican Cantina** needs no further introduction; $5 to $10; nightly 4 to 10 (until 11 Friday and Saturday). **Mary's Diner** exudes nostalgic Americana, with 1950s blue plate specials, and **Smokey Joe's Market and Cafe** has American entrées and an all-you-can-eat salad bar. Both are open 24 hours. **Calamity Jane's Ice Cream House** also is a Coca-Cola museum.

Rooms: Doubles $40 to $45.

Santa Fe Hotel & Casino • ☺☺☺

4949 N. Rancho Dr. (at Highway 95 north); (800) 872-6823 or (702) 658-4900. If ya gotta have a gimmick, how about two, or maybe three? The Santa Fe is a strikingly handsome new casino with at least three distinctive features: a skating rink, a bowling alley and a very contemporary Southwest look. Opened in February, 1991, it sits at the convergence of Highway 95 and Rancho Drive—easy to find and probably worth the short drive north of town.

Casino: Santa Fe's sleek Southwestern look carries throughout the large casino, with requisite turquoise and salmon colors and clean geometric designs. It offers the usual assortment of machines, gaming tables, a sports book, bingo room and poker room.

Entertainment: The Ice Lounge, just off the skating rink, features live entertainment, frequently country and Western. It may one of the few places on earth where you can listen to good down-home music and watch skaters at the same time.

Dining: Opening on the casino, **Pablo's Cafe** has the predictable Southwestern trim with Spanish tile accents. Its busy menu jumps from basic American to Cajun, Southwestern, Mexican and Italian—everything from baby back ribs to shrimp Creole. It never closes and dinner prices are $5 to $10.

Rooms: Doubles $35 to $45.

Showboat Hotel, Casino & Bowling Center • ☺☺

2800 E. Fremont St. (at Charleston, about two miles east of downtown); (800) 826-2800 or (702) 385-9123. Far from the madding crowd, this New Orleans style facility is rather a sleeper. With pleasing pastel colors and an ornate curved, coffered ceiling, it is one of the town's more attractive medium sized casinos. Yet most tourist miss this place, which appeals mostly to locals, bingo players and bowlers. In fact, it hosts one of the country's oldest major bowling tournaments, covered by network TV each year.

The "boat" was launched in 1954 and recently was expanded and remodeled to offer 500 hotel rooms, a video arcade, huge bingo parlor and spruced up bowling alley with 106 lanes.

Dining: Di Napoli, Wednesday-Monday 5:30 to 11, is an exceptionally pretty place, done in ornate Venetian floral pastels, serving northern Italian fare from $10 to $18. The **Plantation** has a luscious Southern belle look and Deep South fare; $7 to $14; Thursday-Sunday from 5:30 to 11. American and Chinese entrèes are served at the 24-hour **Coffee Shop.** The **Captain's Buffet** features cholesterol-free desserts as well as the usual wide assortment of edibles, served in a New Orleans French market.

Rooms: Doubles $36 to $45; they dip to $20 in the off-season.

THE BIG SHOWS

If Las Vegas has a signature, it's the big revues, with leggy showgirls wearing elaborate head dresses, feathers on their fannies and little else. These spectaculars, which in fact are known the world over as "Las Vegas-style revues," generally follow a fixed format. Expect to see big, splashy production numbers with draped and semi-draped singers and dancers, a magician, a brace of acrobats or jugglers and perhaps an animal act. Most magicians will have a shapely female assistant whose primary function seems to be the removal of excess doves, produced from hankies, balloons and the ear canals of audience volunteers.

The revues are increasingly more high tech these days, and lasers are *de rigueur* for the nineties. Some shows are built around magicians or animal acts, such as "Siegfried and Roy" at the Mirage.

Many of the big rooms book big name entertainers instead of these long-running reviews. Since stars demand salaries in the tens of thousands a week, these headliner shows often are as expensive to stage as the revues, reflected in ticket prices as high as $75. Don't expect to see an hour and a half of your favorite star during a 90-minute show. Lesser luminaries often start the action. In fact, several acts may precede the star attraction. Some of these "starters" have gone on to their own fame. Several years ago, while waiting for Glen Campbell to step onstage, we enjoyed several songs by a barefoot newcomer from Nova Scotia named Ann Murray.

If you haven't been in town for a few years, you'll note some changes in the big rooms. First, dinner shows are now a rarity, replaced by two-drink cocktail service. This is no great loss, since many of these repasts consisted of overdone fish and veggies that died on the way in from the steam table.

The only dinner shows remaining at this writing were "City Lights" at the Flamingo Hilton, "Les Folies Bergere" at the Tropicana and "King Arthur's Tournament" at the Excalibur. Of these, the Excalibur offers the best fare—an eat-with-your-hands rock cornish game hen and baked potato.

Ticketed seating

Another significant change: Most big rooms have gone to a ticket policy with pre-assigned seating. In the past, you made reservations, got into a long line at show time and slipped the maitre d' $5 to $20 to get a decent table. This is still done in some places, but most issue a theater-style ticket. (Insiders say the annual take of many a Las Vegas maitre d' has slipped from more than $125,000 to $25,000.)

The best way to get a good seat for a ticketed show is to make reservations as early as possible. Generally, tickets don't go on sale until the day of the show, so check the box office hours and get there early. Up front booths are the best, since most seats are at long tables perpendicular to the stage, requiring everyone to swivel sideways when the show starts. Booths often are reserved for comps or larger groups, however.

— photo courtesy **Riviera Hotel**

Las Vegas showgirls are legendary for their pulchritude. This crew exhibits a lot of skin in "Crazy Girls—Fantasie de Paris" at the Riviera.

If you're doing quite a bit of gambling and you've established a rating at a particular casino, ask the pit boss for a comp (a freebie) or at least for preferred seating. Often, nearly half the seats in a particular show may be comped to high rollers, assorted dignitaries, convention organizers, occupants of fancy suites and even an occasional travel writer. If you're holding a comp, go straight to the VIP side, bypassing all those plebeians who are in a waiting line extending across the casino.

The big shows aren't the bargains they were a few years ago. Expect to pay more than $50 for a top headliner. Siegfried and Roy's animal/magical show, easily the most spectacular revue in the state, commands $72.85. However, some of the smaller shows are still quite affordable, costing less than $15, including a pair of drinks. Vacation Village offers a show and dinner buffet for under $10 and Rio's sizzling "Tropical Heat" adult revue is just $17.15 with a buffet or $12.95 without. Also, look for package deals (see **Couponamania** above) that include show discounts.

Incidentally, you can reserve most of the ticketed shows through local agencies such as TicketMaster, 474-4000.

And now, the good news for non-smokers: Most of the big rooms are now smoke-free. Curiously, leggy cigarette girls still make the rounds, selling cigars, cigarettes and possibly even Tiparillos, along with snacks and souvenirs.

Most ticket prices include two drinks, which will be delivered shortly after you're seated. Since you'll nurse them through 90 minutes of entertainment, you might want to order something straight up, like a good sippin' brandy or wine. Cocktails will get watery and warm. You can order additional drinks, but the management discourages too much waiter/waitress movement once the show is underway. If you're at a ticketed show, you'll be presented a check for additional drinks either just before the show begins or immediately at its conclusion. Virtually all big rooms accept credit cards, so just slap the plastic on the tray, and figure on a 15 percent tip. (If you're comped, you'll be given a voucher to sign; base your tip on the value of the show tickets.)

We saw every major show in town just before this book went to press. After long nights of double drinks, double-takes during magic acts and double-breasted showgirls, we present our favorites.

The best Las Vegas shows

The best overall show: SIEGFRIED AND ROY • *Mirage Showroom; Thursday-Tuesday at 7:30 and 11 with ticketed seating; $72.85 including two drinks; kids six and older admitted; no smoking;* **792-7777.** It's a stunning show in a stunning setting, worth the high price. A free-form stage juts into the audience, surrounding pods of patrons, drawing them into the action. Siegfried and Roy have been performing their combined animal-illusion act for more than a quarter of a century, making elephants vanish, sawing assorted beautiful women in half and nuzzling beautiful white tigers (who share Siegfried and Roy's mansion in the suburbs). The show is leading-edge high tech, spiced with a bit of Wagner opera. Our heroes do battle with a giant metallic dragon right out of *Star Wars*, and they dance, prance, vanish and unvanish in a netherworld of lasers, smoke, fire and probably even brimstone. This is an noisy, upbeat show with lots of exaggerated animal growls, Wagnerian wailing and a wall-shaking sound track.

The best family show: KING ARTHUR'S TOURNAMENT • *Excalibur; nightly shows at 6 and 8:30 with ticketed seating; $24.95 including dinner; suitable for kids; a no-smoking theater;* **597-7600.** You'll have fun with the family here, eating game hens with sticky fingers, rooting for your assigned hero (based on your seating) and hissing the black knight, who looks suspiciously like Darth Vader. The show opens with a procession of nubile maidens looking like the playing card characters from *Alice in Wonderland*. It quickly shifts to a laser-enhanced jousting tournament as Sir Lancelot does battle against challengers for the magical sword Excalibur. The lances are balsa and nobody gets hurt, although the swords are real, requiring a fancy bit of choreography for the combatants. You'll see some good examples of horsemanship and a bit of magic as ringmaster Merlin struts about, setting off puffs of smoke and lasers. The show ends with acrobatics and an impressive trick riding demonstration.

The best high tech revue: DONN ARDEN'S JUBILEE • *Bally's Zeigfeld Theatre; nightly except Wednesday at 7:30 and 11 with maitre d' seating; $30 including two drinks; adults only (18 and over); no smoking;* **739-4567.** The sinking of the Titanic and Sampson's long-haired temple destruction produce great high tech effects in this Donn Arden spectacular. He's been producing shows here since 1952 and Jubilee has been running for more than a decade. Between his choreographed disasters, showgirls under 40-pound head dresses put their best fronts forward, magicians produce an alarming number of doves and acrobats and jugglers twist and juggle. It's the biggest show in town, with a cast of 100. Many are semi-clad in lavish costumes done by Cher's favorite dress designer, Bob Mackie.

The best low tech revue: CITY LITES • *Flamingo Hilton Showroom; nightly except Sunday; dinner show at 7:45 for $27.50 and cocktail show at 11 for $19.95; parental guidance suggested because of topless dancers; no smoking;* **733-3333.** Typical of the oldstyle Las Vegas Revues but with a modern theme, "City Lights" features a good mix of nubile show girls, flashy costumes, plumed bonnets, magicians and acrobats. The dance numbers are focused around Broadway show tunes, highlighted by a Radio City Music Hall style chorus line; great stuff for the nostalgia buff. "Lites" also features the town's only topless ice skaters, making us wonder if the updraft makes things a bit nippy. A particularly intriguing segment of the show employs the Garza Brothers, bodies bronzed and thoroughly entangled, moving in slow motion under special lights to create statues come to life.

The most energized dance revue: SPLASH • *The Riviera's Versailles Theatre; nightly at 8 p.m. for $27.50 and 11 p.m. for $24.50; $3 surcharge on Saturdays and holidays; includes two drinks. Maitre 'd seating. Kids OK for early show; late show is topless. No smoking;* **794-9301.** Although this is billed as an aquatic show, it features some of the most highly-charged dance numbers in town. An MTV-style rap dance with an inner city theme is particularly impressive. The aquatic sequences are noteworthy as well, with dancing waters, dancing mermaids and an occasional dancing clam. You'll see lots of supple bodies, particularly in the 65,000-gallon onstage aquarium. It's not exactly "The Little Mermaid," but the ladies are sufficiently covered during the early show to earn the show a PG rating. Some shed their tops (or jiggle out of them) for the late show. "Splash" is the most contemporary show on the Strip, with lots of upbeat Top Forty music. Not surprisingly, producer Jeff Kutash is a choreographer by trade.

The most sensuous show: ENTER THE NIGHT • *The Stardust Theatre; nightly at 7 and 11 with ticketed seating; $33.25 including two drinks; adults only (21 and over); no smoking;* **732-6111.** The original stars of this show, longtime Las Vegas regulars Bobby Berosini and his orangutans, quit (or were discharged) in early 1992. We can understand why. Watching a bunch of ugly little apes flipping off their trainer wasn't very entertaining. What remains—highly-charged laser dance numbers, slinky topless costuming, a sensual male aerial artist and a brilliant ice skating sequence—are a collective knockout. The skaters and a black female lead singer carry the show, with a lot of boost from a pair of singing/dancing brothers. One of these acts may have star billing by the time you read this, or producers may bring in someone else to anchor this very sensual and fast-paced revue. The show's focus, as suggested by the title, is adult frolic after dusk.

The best nostalgic Las Vegas revue: LES FOLIES BERGERE • *Tropicana's Tiffany Theatre; nightly except Thursday, dinner show at 8 for $26.95 and cocktail show at 11 for $18.95; maitre d' seating; parental guidance suggested because of topless dancers; no smoking;* **739-2411.** Need a trip down a Las Vegas memory lane? It's all here: the $50 bill to the maitre d' to get into the bald-headed row, the beautiful showgirls, the French style dance numbers, the magician with his doves, the quickie breast of chicken dinner. (There's also a cocktail show.) It opens with a classic French can-can and evolves nicely into an American nostalgic musical review. Some of the most beautiful and bountiful women in town prance about in great and sensual dignity. With the recent closing of the Lido at the Stardust, *Les Folies Sans Brassiere* is the senior show on the Strip, dating back to 1959. That was long before most of today's titillating showgirls were a twinkle in *anyone's* eye.

The best Elvis sighting: LEGENDS IN CONCERT • *The Imperial Palace Theatre; nightly except Sunday with maitre d' seating; 7:30 and 10:30; $17.95 including cocktails; suitable for kids; no smoking;* **794-3261**. Out in the foyer, a John Wayne clone drawls with some ladies from Iowa, waiting for the show to start. Inside, the curtain goes up and there's Bobby Darrin's twin in a shiny suit, singing "Mack, the Knife." He's followed by a balding Elton John; then Marilyn Monroe in hot pink, who slinks into the audience to squirm into a gentleman's lap. Next comes a writhing and undulating Tom Jones and a vibrant Blues Brothers act with a very believable John Belushi. They're followed by a sparkly-shirted Neal Diamond. The show ends with a replicated Elvis, rivulets of sweat and all, singing a medley of his hits. The performers are remarkably convincing in look and gesture and they don't lip-sync; they do their own singing. This is one of the best shows for the price in town.

When you've got to do it all
AROUND THE CLOCK IN GLITTER CITY:

You have to catch that damned plane first thing tomorrow. You're going home, back to that lousy job, back to back taxes, back to the wife that snores and the dog that sheds. (Or is it the other way around?) But there's still so much to do, so much to see, so little time! That crummy convention took kept you too busy. Twenty-four hours left; you want to do it all!

9 a.m.—You stuff yourself at the Excalibur breakfast buffet. Apple pancakes, waffles, bacon, sausage, ham, fruit, rolls, bagels, more rolls; it's essential to carbo-load.

9:45 a.m.—Waddling downstairs, you settle into the Magic Motion Machine for a simulated roller coaster ride to settle your stomach.

10 a.m.—You check out the glitter at the Liberace Museum, wondering how you'd look in a gold lamè jacket, sequined boxer shorts and ostrich plume cape.

11 a.m.—At Caesar's Palace Omnimax Theater, you watch volcanoes belch liquid stone on an ultra-wide screen; it does nothing to calm your tummy.

Noon—You hike to the Circus Circus and watch several big top acts. Aerialists swing above a sea of slot machines, ignored by the players below. You invest two dollars on a coin toss game, win a medium-sized panda and—on an impulse—hand it to a passing child.

1 p.m.—You simmer with harmless envy, admiring the $50 million Duesenberg exhibit at the Imperial Palace Auto Collection. But you're not rich. You're an ordinary guy with an ordinary job, a wife and a dog that sheds. The spicy bloody Mary at the auto collection bar finally calms your stomach.

2:30 p.m.—Your cultural side demands equal time and you drive downtown to the Nevada State Museum. You want to learn more about this intriguing place where the sun shines in January.

4:30 p.m.—Poking about the downtown casino center, you pause at the Union Plaza. After failing to win the $402,639.95 progressive jackpot at the video poker carousel, you retire to the lounge. You order a 75 cent drink and listen to the music and voice of Dusty Barron. He plays one of those electronic guitars that sounds like everything but a guitar.

6 p.m.—Your stomach has finally dispatched that last sweet roll, so you gulp down a 99 cent shrimp cocktail at the Golden Gate Casino, chased by a $1.50 chili dog at Fitzgerald's. Who has time for formal food? The plane leaves tomorrow. The plane, boss, the plane!

7 p.m.—Your cabbie, apparently bent on suicide, lurches crazily through Saturday night traffic. He delivers you barely in time for the Siegfried and Roy show at the Mirage. Maybe it was the shrimp cocktail and chili dog, but you'd swear you saw an entire elephant disappear. You order another tequila and orange, but that damned pachyderm never comes back.

10 p.m.—You step into the cool January night and witness another spectacle—the hissing and spewing eruption of the Mirage volcano. Then you sprint across the street to the Sands to catch Rich Little. He starts to do an impression of Willie Nelson, but he accidentally slips into a post-Watergate Richard Nixon.

12:30 a.m.—Another kamikaze cab delivers you to the Aladdin for the Comedy Underground show. You're early so you grab a butter pecan ice cream cone and slice of pepperoni pizza at the "I Scream for Pizza" parlor. Your stomach wants to go home but you're just getting started. The comic tells a gag about a guy in a sawmill who lost all of his fingers; he was unable to have them re-attached because he couldn't pick them up. That's sick, so why are you laughing?

2 a.m.—You settle in at the Sinbad Lounge in the Aladdin and listen to the music of the Irish Show Band. It occurs to you that bars are closing in the rest of the world, but Las Vegas seems to be catching its second wind. So are you.

3 a.m.—Yet another cab delivers you to the Tropicana at the lower end of the Strip, where a sax and keyboard duo plays fine swinging years dance music. You sit there under a simulated palm tree, wishing you'd brought your wife.

3:30 a.m.—The little combo calls it a night, so you spirit yourself back upstream to the Flamingo Hilton. There, you catch the last show of a black singing group called the Four Winds.

4:30 a.m.—Feeling wonderfully nocturnal, you return downtown and drift from casino to casino. Images of Frank Sinatra singing *My Time of Day* flicker through your mind. Fremont Street is bathed in glitter brighter than the sun, which sleeps somewhere beyond Sunrise Mountain. You like the gentle laughter of the pre-dawn few in the casinos; replacing the raucous noise of earlier crowds. You can hear the brittle rattle of the dice, the click of a roulette wheel. Sinatra was right; it's a nice time of day.

6 a.m.—Suddenly famished, you walk to the Fremont Casino cafe and order steak, two eggs, hash browns and toast. Awaiting its arrival, you mark a $7 keno ticket, with the promise of winning $100,000. The promise is not kept, but the breakfast isn't bad for $2.89.

7 a.m.—You step outside and pay your respects to the rising sun,

128 — CHAPTER THREE

which—inadequate to the task—fails to outshine Fremont Street.

7:10 a.m.—Comfortably fed, you settle into a seat before a video poker terminal at the Golden Gate, whose machines have been kind to you in the past. This machine is not unkind today, providing more than an hour's amusement before capturing your final nickel.

8:35 a.m.—Your cabbie weaves recklessly through the morning rush hour, aware that you have a plane to catch. You doze in the back seat with visions of $402,639.95 jackpots, Duesenbergs, gold lamè jackets, hissing volcanoes and butter pecan ice cream dancing in your head.

9 a.m.—The cab lurches to a stop in front of the Excalibur, jerking you back to reality. You smile and tip the driver generously. You're remarkably alert, pleased that you have seen the elephant.

Even if the damned thing disappeared on you.

Author's note: This 24-hour marathon was performed during an early January weekend, proving that even in the off-season, Las Vegas is a city that never sleeps.

We caution you not to try this at home.

THE BEST ATTRACTIONS

Certainly Las Vegas offers tourist attractions other than casinos (including some within the gaming parlors). We present here a list of the best in alphabetical order, followed by the rest. Our third list, called "Nuggets," features lesser known, often overlooked attractions or perhaps curiosities may not even make the list in ordinary guidebooks.

Of course, prices are subject to change and hours often flex with the seasons. That's why we list phone numbers right up front.

Clark County Heritage Museum ● *1830 S. Boulder Hwy. (just north of the highway's merger with U.S. 93/95 expressway), Henderson; (702) 455-7955. Daily 9 to 4:30; adults $1, kids and seniors 50 cents.* This is one of Nevada's finer historic museums, well worth the short drive out Boulder Drive to neighboring Henderson. Or, take the expressway and double back a mile or so on Boulder Highway. Plan several hours to explore this 25-acre indoor-outdoor museum, and save a few moments to poke about the gift and book shop. If you have time to visit only one museum in southern Nevada, this is it. Nowhere else can you learn more about this fascinating corner of the Party State.

A handsome *adobe moderne* houses fine, professionally-done exhibits relating to Southern Nevada's yesterdays. Check out the Pleistocene diorama with it camels and ground sloths, the Anasazi artifacts and Paiute camp complete with sound effects. Move right along to displays on the Mormon settlement, mines and mining camps, the wheelhouse of a Colorado River boat and—of course—gambling exhibits. This is a hands-on place where kids can grind meal with a *metate* and legally feed a slot machine (since it yields no prizes; the pennies go to the museum). Spin the wheel of fortune and try your luck at chuck-a-luck.

Outside, you can stroll through fully furnished period homes, like the 1912 Beckley house; a 1905 miner's home from Goldfield and one of the company houses from Boulder City, equipped with original 1930s appliances. (Remember when, Dearie?) All are originals, moved to this site. Step into the 1931 Boulder City railroad depot (which used to house the main museum), a Paiute brush shelter and an 1890 print shop, and walk the dusty streets of a ghost town.

Guinness World of Records Museum • *2780 S. Las Vegas Blvd. (opposite El Rancho, behind Arby's); 792-3766. Daily 9 a.m. to 10 p.m. Adults $4.95; seniors, military and students $3.95, kids (under 12) $2.95; MC/VISA, DISC.* You'll meet Robert Wadlow, the world's tallest man at eight feet, 11.1 inches (in life-sized plastic and on video) and other record-setters at this place. This kind of museum could be tacky and boring, but this one isn't. With lots of videos, models of the biggest this and smallest that and fun statistics, it's surprisingly entertaining. Watching videos of world domino toppling competitions will consume several intriguing minutes, and sports films will use up several more. Exhibits concerning all-time popular movies, songs and TV shows will fortify you with a treasure chest of trivia. You'll come away with wonderful bits of useless information, like the fact that Oreos are the world's top-selling cookies (100 billion since their introduction in 1912). Life Savers top the candy list, with 33,431,236,300 rolls sold between 1913 and 1987. If they were stacked on end, their little holes would form a tunnel to the moon and back three times.

Fancy that.

Imperial Palace Auto Collection • *Fifth floor of the Imperial Palace parking garage at 3535 S. Las Vegas Blvd.; 731-3311. Daily 9:30 to 11:30. Adults $6.95, seniors and kids (4-12) $3.* Auto nuts may never want to leave this place. Voted one of the ten best auto exhibits in the world, the Imperial Palace collection covers a broad spectrum, from horseless carriages to a rare Tucker to cars of the rich and famous. Antique freaks will love the 1910 Thomas Flyer and nostalgia nuts will ogle the 1954 baby blue Chevy Bel Aire convertible. More than 200 vehicles are on display, part of a collection of 700 that is rotated periodically. Among personality cars are the 1937 Cord in which Tom Mix met his doom in 1940, limos that toted Presidents Eisenhower and Kennedy, Hitler's 1939 armored Mercedes parade car, Juan Peron's and Emperor Hirohito's Packards, and Jack Benny's legendary Maxwell. One room is stuffed with $50 million worth of Duesenbergs. A bar at one end peddles great sinus- clearing bloody marys and other libations.

Las Vegas Mormon Temple • *827 Temple View Drive (end of Bonanza, east of downtown); 452-5011. Grounds open Tuesday through Friday 5:30 a.m. to 10 p.m. and Saturday 5:30 a.m. to 3:30 p.m.; closed from 3:30 Saturday through Monday.* Only the faithful may enter this baronial temple. However, visitors can stroll the beautifully landscaped grounds and enjoy an awesome view of Las Vegas, fanning out from the base of Sunrise Mountain. Completed in 1989 at a cost of $18 million (including land), this is one of the most imposing church structures in America. Six fluted spires thrust skyward from the granite edifice, presumably toward heaven. One is topped by a ten-foot Fiberglas and gold plated Angel Moroni. Visit this place at night when the temple is bathed in white light and the city sparkles below like a Technicolor universe.

Liberace Museum • *1775 E. Tropicana Ave. (in a small shopping center at Spencer Avenue, about three miles from Las Vegas Boulevard); 798-5595. Monday-Saturday 10 to 5, Sunday 1 to 5. Adults $6.50, seniors $4.50, students $3.50, kids (6-12) $2.* Think of this place as a monument to garish extravagance. Because Walter Valentino Liberace was such a flamboyant character given to outlandish dress, and because he became so ridiculously rich, this is one of the most interesting one-man museums in the country. Plan a couple of hours to check out "Mr. Showmanship's" pearl-encrusted, rhinestone-shrouded, crystal-covered fantasy land. Stare with proper curiosity at his jeweled patriotic hotpants, capes of white fox and mink, rhinestone Baldwin piano and million dollar mirror-tiled Rolls Royce. In a sense, Liberace's ludicrous taste was an extension of the flamboyant town that nurtured him. Although he lived in Palm Springs, he performed here for decades, starting at the age of 23. Despite his extravagance (and obvious insensitivity to furry animals), he was a gentle and generous soul and he remains so, even in death. Proceeds from the museum go to the Liberace Foundation for Creative and Performing Arts.

Lied Children's Museum • *833 N. Las Vegas Blvd. (in the new library complex on the left, just under the freeway); 382-5437. Tuesday-Saturday 10 to 5 (until 7 Wednesday), noon to 5 Sunday, closed Monday. Adults $4; students, military and seniors $2.50, (kids 4-11) $1.50.* Turn the kids loose in this large new facility (pronounced *Leed*) and you may lose them for the day—which is probably not a bad idea. Scores of interactive exhibits will teach your little rat pack about the nature of things. More than 100 kinetic, computer-driven, video and other devices cover everything from athletic prowess to space science to career selection. Kids can inflate a hot air balloon, blow bubbles with dry ice and engage in assorted other educational kinetics. The museum even teaches them how to open a savings account and write checks. This could come in handy if your luck turns bad at the tables.

Marjorie Barrick Museum of Natural History • *On the UNLV clampus at 4505 S. Maryland Parkway (follow Harmon Avenue east into the campus); 739-3381. Weekdays 9 to 5 and Saturday 10 to 5; free.* Behind that stuffy title lurks one of the more interesting museums in town. Exhibits cover such a broad range that one is tempted to put a comma between "natural" and "history." Among its displays are live desert critters in glass cages, an excellent exhibit on the early days of Las Vegas and the creation of the Strip, graphics concerning our threatened planet, changing art and photo exhibits, Indian basketry and projectile points, dance masks of Mexico, Navajo rugs, stuffed birds and animals of Nevada and—for reasons that escape us—a stuffed polar bear. It may occur to you as you stroll about this bio-diverse collection that the exhibit hall seems rather cavernous. For good reason: this was home court for the Runnin' Rebels basketball team before they moved to the new Thomas & Mack Center.

A small exhibit concerning the gambling history of Las Vegas is housed in the James Dickinson Library, a short walk from the natural history museum. See **Nuggets** below for specifics.

Mirage Dolphin Habitat • *At the Mirage, 3400 S. Las Vegas Blvd. (Spring Mountain Road); 791-7111. Weekdays 11 to 7, weekends and holidays 9 to 7. Adults and kids $3, under three free.* When Steve Wynn built his Mirage, he spent more on this dolphin environment ($14 million) than earlier entrepreneurs spent on entire resorts. The 1.5 million gallon complex is a dolphin study center, not a Sea World-type show. Handlers discuss these sleek sea creatures and demonstrate their remarkable intelligence, then they escort visitors into an underwater viewing chamber. Other Mirage exhibits worthy of visitor attention are the white tiger habitat near the main entrance, the "rain forest" beneath a 90-foot glass atrium, a 20,000 gallon coral reef aquarium that forms a backdrop to the hotel registration desk and, of course, the volcano and waterfall lagoon out front.

Nevada Banking Museum • *In the First Interstate Tower, 3800 Howard Hughes Parkway (off Paradise Road between Sands Avenue and Flamingo Road); 385-8011. Monday-Thursday 10 to 4 and Friday 10 to 5:30; free.* Located in the banking lobby on the ground floor, this is one of the finest mini-museums in the state. Carefully done exhibits trace the history of banking and thus the economic growth of Nevada. Items include early drafts of the silver-seekers, old currency and coins, gambling tokens, gold scales, crude adding machines and a wonderfully archaic and complicated 1911 loan processing calculator.

Nevada State Museum and Historical Society • *700 Twin Lakes Drive in Lorenzi Park (Take Bonanza Road west from downtown, across bottom of Lorenzi Park, right onto Twin Lakes then right to museum parking lot); 486-5205. Daily 8:30 to 4:30; adults $2, under 18 free.* This nicely done museum traces the evolution of southern Nevada from pre-history through the present, with a good mix of artifacts, graphics and historic photos. Of particular interest is an extensive exhibit on Nevada gambling, with old gaming machines and photos. Other displays cover the building of Hoover Dam and those troubling days of atomic testing. A film clip shows Ronald Reagan in *Rear Gunner,* a hokey World War II film shot partly on location here in 1942. In the Hall of Biological Science, you learn more than you ever wanted to know about desert denizens, from barrel cactus to bighorn sheep.

Omnimax Theater at Caesars Palace • *3570 S. Las Vegas Blvd. (at Dunes road); 731-7901. Daily; shows hourly from 2 to 10 p.m. Adults $4.50; Caesar hotel guests, seniors, kids (4-18) and military $3.* Omnimax is one of those monster movies that projects a 70mm image onto a curved screen. Viewers recline in tilt-back chairs like astronauts about to blast off. At this writing, the show was *Ring of Fire,* with predictably graphic photos of volcanic and earthquake activity around the Pacific Rim. It's particularly timely, covering the big blast at Mount St. Helens and the Loma Prieta earthquake that rattled the San Francisco Bay Area in 1989. Among the show's highlights are spectacular scenes of Hawaii's Kilauea lava flows.

Ripley's Believe It or Not! • *In the Four Queens Hotel, 202 E. Fremont St. (at Third Street); 385-4011. Sunday-Thursday 9 a.m. to midnight, Friday-Saturday 9 a.m. to 1 a.m. Adults $4.95, seniors and military $3.95, kids (6-12) $2.50.* Robert A. Ripley roamed the earth for three decades, looking for the strange, the bizarre, the grotesque and other synonyms. His heirs opened this and other museums to display his collection of oddities or facsimiles thereof. Here, you'll meet some of the same folks that amazed you at Guinness museum—the world's tallest, fattest, oldest, etc. We preferred the Guinness place because its many videos made it more animated. The collection here is rather static and some of it is post-Ripley, such as a 14,000-jelly bean mosaic of a roulette table and a 77,069 match stick space shuttle. You'll find Ripley classics as well: the requisite shrunken head, a two-headed calf and lots of his old *Believe It or Not!* cartoon panels. You'll certainly be pleased to learn that a guy from Germany consumed 25 pounds of cheese and three pounds of hay within two hours. A yucky chamber of horrors section depicts a man who survived a cranial crowbar impalement and it regales visitors with jolly facts about mass murderers.

Plan your visit between meals.

THE REST

Bethany's Celebrity Doll Museum • *1775 E. Tropicana Ave. (adjacent to Liberace Museum); 798-3036. Daily 9 to 5; free.* This small museum and gift shop specializes in dress-up dolls of movie idols such as John Wayne, Shirley Temple, Mae West and Elvis, of course. One of the features of this modest little place is a *Gone With the Wind* doll collection.

Broad Street Memorabilia Collection • *4501 Paradise Rd. (across Harmon Avenue from Hard Rock Cafe, in the St. Tropez Center); 733-7601. Monday-Saturday 11 to 6; free.* This is a collector shop focused on rock and roll nostalgia, with a large selection of items from the 1960s to the present. The stuff ranges from Beatles memorabilia to Michael Jackson posters.

Historic Las Vegas self-guiding tour • *Preservation Association of Clark County, 385-0115.* A small, nicely-written brochure/map available from the visitors bureau and various museums will guide you past 24 historical sites. Most are old buildings that have somehow survived the town's tumultuous growth. If you can't find a brochure, call the preservation association.

Las Vegas Museum of Art • *3333 Washington Ave. (in Lorenzi Park); 647-4300. Tuesday-Saturday 10 to 3 and Sunday noon to 5. Free; donations accepted.* This isn't the Louvre, but it's a noble attempt by Las Vegans to give their town a cultural face. It offers a modest collection of Western art and rotating exhibits that feature many for-sale items. If you're a semi-serious art patron, plan a visit each time you come to town, since exhibits change frequently.

Las Vegas Natural History Museum • *900 N. Las Vegas Blvd. (at Washington); 384-3466. Daily 9 to 4; adults $5, seniors and military $4, kids (4-12) $2.50.* Recently moved to bigger quarters in the old Elks Club building, this museum—like nature itself—is still evolving. When we visited, it consisted primarily of a large stuffed critter collection and major changing exhibits that focus on the natural world around us. Recent examples are dinosaurs and sharks. Kids will like the hands-on room where they can fondle things from nature and dig in a sandbox to pretend they're unearthing fossils.

Old Mormon Fort • *North Las Vegas Boulevard at Washington Avenue (behind the Natural History Museum; enter from Cashman Field Parking Lot B); 386-6510. Memorial Day through Labor Day: Saturday and Monday 8 to 2 and Sunday noon to 3; the rest of the year: Saturday and Monday 10 to 2 and Sunday 1 to 4. Adults $1, kids 50 cents.* This small adobe is more interesting for what it represents than for what it is. You'll see a modest museum with a few dusty furnishings, graphics and artifacts concerning the town's earliest days. What you'll learn is more important—that this is the oldest structure in Las Vegas, the sole remnant of the Mormon mission established in 1855. It's a miracle that it survived, having gone through a number of uses and abuses. It served as a ranch outbuilding, store, barracks, storage shed, and a Hoover Dam testing lab. The Elks Club bought the property in 1955 and demolished everything except this small remnant. After passing through the hands of several do-gooder organizations, it became state property in 1989. Nevada has plans, but no funds, for its restoration.

Scandia Family Fun Center • *2900 Sirius Ave. (off west side I-15 frontage road, between Spring Mountain and Sahara); 364-0070. Monday-Thursday 10 a.m. to 11 p.m. and Friday-Saturday 10 a.m. to 1 a.m. Free admission;*

THIS IS KID STUFF!

Although Las Vegas may be an adult playground, many facilities are geared for children. Since state law prohibits anyone under 21 from loitering in casinos, many resorts are targeting the family trade by providing video parlors and other youth-oriented diversions away from the gaming areas.

Of course, the town also has a good selection of parks, museums and such. Many of the attractions covered in this chapter are suitable for kids. We'll group them in this handy box for quick reference.

The best budget family resorts are **Circus Circus**, with its ongoing circus acts and large carnival midway; and **Excalibur,** with midway games and rides, an all-family jousting tournament and large video parlor. On the upscale side, the **Mirage** will appeal to kids with its white tiger and dolphin habitat and growling volcano. As for feeding the tribe, buffets at **Circus Circus, Excalibur, Gold Strike Inn, Lady Luck** and **Silver City** are among the least expensive. The **Aladdin** and **Hilton** buffets offer special children's rates.

Casino resorts with large video and game rooms include **Bally's, Caesars Palace** and the **Riviera.** The large swimming complex at the **Tropicana** has youth appeal as well. Shows that are suitable for kids are **King Arthur's Tournament** at the Excalibur, **Siegfried and Roy** at the Mirage, **Splash** at the Riviera and **Legends in Concert** at the Imperial Palace.

Under our **Attractions** listings, you'll find these lures most appealing to the younger set: **Guinness World of Records Museum** at 2780 Las Vegas Boulevard, **Imperial Palace Auto Collection** for those old enough to appreciate fine automobiles, the glitter of the **Liberace Museum** east on Tropicana Avenue, **dolphin and white tiger habitats** at the Mirage, **Omnimax Theater** at Caesar's Palace, **Ripley's Believe It or Not!** at the Four Queens, the **Las Vegas Natural History Museum** children's discovery room, and the little critter zoo at **Southern Nevada Zoological Park.**

Lied Children's Museum in the new library complex at 833 N. Las Vegas Boulevard, is engineered precisely for curious children. **Wet N' Wild** water park adjacent to the Sahara Hotel and **Scandia Family Fun Center** on the west I-15 frontage road between Spring Mountain and Sahara also are directed to the younger set. **Kidd Marshmallow Factory Tour** will appeal to anyone who has ever made "s'mores" over a campfire. **Bonnie Springs Ranch and Old Nevada,** 18 miles west out Charleston Boulevard, has a petting zoo and other children's lures. We give it more detail in the next chapter.

If you need a **Babysitter,** these firms provide service either in your hotel room or at their facilities: Las Vegas Babysitting Agency, 457-3777; Reliable Babysitting, 451-7507; Sandy's Sitters Service, 731-2086; Vegas Valley Babysitting, 871-5161 and Nanny's & Granny's, 368-7741. Others are listed under "Baby sitters" in the Yellow Pages. Many hotels can arrange sitters.

fee for games. This is a good place to park the kids while you play adult games, or you can join them in a round of miniature golf. Facilities at this good-sized complex include two mini-golf courses, mini-Indy racers, bumper boats, baseball batting cages, a snack bar and dozens of video games.

Southern Nevada Zoological Park ● *1775 N. Rancho Dr. (at Melody Lane, two miles west of downtown); 648-5955. Daily 9 to 5; adults $5, kids under 17 and seniors $3.* Nevada's only zoo is a rather scruffy little place. Its animals dwell in oldstyle cages that would bring a frown to the face of a modern zoo keeper. One gets the impression that the folks here try hard, but there just isn't much money. One also gets the impression that the animals might prefer to be somewhere else, particularly on hot summer days. The collection consists of about 150 critters spread over a shabby three acres. You'll see a Bengal tiger, a cougar (hungrily eying a grivet monkey in the next case), a brace of wallabies and a goodly collection of tropical birds. Volunteer chickens, peacocks, pigeons and other feathered friends probably outnumber those in cages, so be careful where you step.

Wet 'N Wild Water Park ● *2601 S. Las Vegas Blvd. (adjacent to Sahara Hotel); 737-3819. Open May through October, 10 to 8 daily. Adults $14.95, kids (3-12) $11.95. MC/VISA, AMEX.* This is a great place to soak your head and the rest of your body on a hot desert day. Corkscrew water slides, water roller coasters and twisting flumes will keep you happily wet. Or you can just loaf beside a lagoon and pretend you're at the beach. Raft and tube rentals are available, along with lockers and a snack-souvenir shop.

NUGGETS

We've already covered many of these special interest items in our casino explorations. We've group them here in case you missed any.

Brahman shrine ● *Outside Caesars Palace, 3570 S. Las Vegas Blvd. (at Dunes Road).* This four-ton, four-faced, eight-armed shrine is behind the statue of Caesar, near the domed Caesars World central entrance to the casino. It was donated by a Thai millionaire in 1984 to promote good luck, presumably for himself as well as other hotel guests. Passersby often pause and pay homage to the bronze, gold-plated shrine and many leave offerings. When we last checked, the offering dish contained three bags of airline peanuts and a packet of Grandma's oatmeal applesauce cookies.

Coca-Cola Museum ● *Sam's Town Hotel and Gambling Hall, 5111 Boulder Highway (five miles east; at Flamingo Road). In Calamity Jane's Ice Cream House; free.* Coke memorabilia fans will want to visit the casino's ice cream parlor, where dozens of artifacts, logo items and posters of the venerable beverage are on display. They go all the way back to the turn of the century, when the original Coca-Cola contained the narcotic coca (thus the name) and was touted as the "ideal brain tonic."

Gallery of History ● *In the Fashion Show Mall (main floor, walk to the right from the Strip entrance), South Las Vegas Boulevard and Spring Mountain Road; 731-2300. Weekdays 10 to 9, Saturday 10 to 6 and Sunday noon to 5.* Even if you can't afford the $175,000 document signed by President Lincoln just before his assassination, you'll enjoy browsing through this unusual store. It offers dozens of framed document and other bits of memorabilia for sale, including items such as John Wilkes Boothe's signature for $15,500, an autographed photo of the cast of television's *Honeymooners* for $1,799 and a baseball signed by Babe Ruth for $15,000.

Hard Rock Cafe • *Paradise Road and Harmon Avenue. Weekdays 11:30 a.m. to 1 a.m., weekends 11 to 1.* Most cafes Hard Rock were installed into existing buildings. This one was built from the ground up, with a dramatic barrel-arched ceiling and a free-standing 40-foot guitar as a marquee. Check out the virtual museum of rock and roll memorabilia inside as you sip a beer or pick at your baby back ribs. Guitars, gold records, concert posters and rock stars' clothing adorn the walls, and a gold flake 1960 Cadillac convertible is parked atop the sunken bar.

Million dollar currency exhibits • *Vegas World at the head of the Strip (2000 S. Las Vegas Boulevard at Main Street) and at Binion's Horseshoe downtown (128 E. Fremont at Casino Center).* At **Vegas World**, several slots promise a million dollar payoff and the money's right there for the taking. However, at this writing, no one had scored the mil since the exhibit was installed in 1984. At **Binion's Horseshoe,** you can at least take home a vision of the million. Casino personnel will photograph you standing before this Plexiglas-framed collection of $10,000 bills and give you the picture free. It's in the rear right corner of the casino.

Casino history exhibit • *James Dickinson Library, UNLV campus (off Harmon Avenue); 739-3252. Monday-Thursday 8 to 8, Friday 8 to 5, Sunday 1 to 5; free.* A display case in the special collections department of the UNLV library contains graphics and artifacts concerning the gaming history of Las Vegas, with stuff from El Rancho Vegas and other early casinos. A nearby wall is lined with posters from films made in or about Las Vegas. If you're a real nut on the history of gambling or the history of Las Vegas, the special collections department can bury you in facts and trivia, with books, Las Vegas movie manuscripts and videotapes, old casino brochures, mobster biographies and whatever. The department also contains the Gaming Research Center, the world's most extensive gambling study facility.

To reach the library, walk through the cactus garden of the Barrick Museum of Natural History (see **Attractions** above), swing to the right around two *avant garde* buildings (one very round, the other very red and rectangular), enter the rectangular one—the library—and take the elevator to the fourth floor.

Neon junkyard • *Young Electric Sign Company, 5119 Cameron St. (go west on Tropicana for 1.7 miles beyond the freeway, then left on Cameron for a few blocks); 876-8080.* Think of this as a "junky jewel" instead of a nugget. Over the years, YESCO has produced most of the town's gaudy and gargantuan neon creations, and Reno's latest "Biggest Little City in the World" arch. The factory is on the right side of Cameron Street, and a large lot just beyond serves as a junkyard of its yesterday signs. They don't do tours but you can peek through the fence at a scatter of old Colonel Saunders chicken buckets, marquees from early-day casinos and motels and other businesses.

Sports Hall of Fame • *Las Vegas Club, 18 E. Fremont St. (at Main Street); 385-1664. Open 24 hours; free.* The world's only collection of World Series bats (1946 until 1958) highlights this gathering of sports memorabilia, covering a wall between the restaurant and gaming area of the casino. Autographed photos, baseballs and footballs, assorted trophies and Maury Wills' bronzed base stealing shoes are among the dozens of items on display.

Vegas Vic neon sign • *On the Pioneer Club at 25 E. Fremont Street downtown (at First Street).* You've got to stop and say howdy to the most famous neon sign in Nevada. He'll say howdy right back when he's turned on (which isn't always). Sixty-foot "Vegas Vic" was installed here by YESCO in 1951 and he's been featured in countless films and promotions. He has said "Howdy, welcome to downtown Las Vegas" several million times.

FOOD FACTORY TOURS

These two outings deserve a special listing because we can't figure out where else to put them. They're both southeast of town so plan a joint visit.

Ethel M Chocolate Factory tour • *Two Cactus Garden Dr. (off Sunset Way); 458-8864. Self-guiding tours daily from 8:30 to 7; free.* To get there, drive to the bottom of Las Vegas Boulevard, turn east at the last traffic light (below the airport, near a Texaco station) and follow Sunset Road for just under six miles. Where it makes a 90-degree right turn, continue straight ahead onto Sunset Way and take the second left onto Cactus Garden Drive.

How do they get the filling inside the chocolates? You'll discover the secret during this picture-window tour of one of the world's leading chocolate firms. The "M" is for Mars (the name of the founder) as in Mars Bars, M&Ms, Three Muscateers and Milky Way. The factory is located here because good old liberal Nevada is one of the few places where liquor-filled chocolates can be produced and sold. You'll get a free sample of these tasty little "adult truffles" after the tour. You can buy more, along with assorted souvenirs, in a gift shop. Best time to see chocolates in production is on weekday mornings. An attractive cactus garden out front invites strolling and exploring; you can buy your very own prickly plant at the cactus shop. Although Sunset Road/Sunset Way lead right to Ethel M from lower Las Vegas Boulevard, there are more direct routes from downtown. Call from wherever you are and the nice folks will give you specific directions.

Kidd Marshmallow Factory tour • *8203 Gibson Road in Henderson; 564-5400. Self-guiding tours weekdays 9 to 4:30 and weekends 9:30 to 4:30.* To get here from Ethel's, backtrack to the Sunset Way/Sunset Road intersection, turn left and continue southeast out Sunset Road for 2.3 miles to U.S. 95 freeway. Head south just over two miles until the freeway ends and turn right onto Lake Mead Drive. Follow it less than a mile, go right onto Gibson Road, then left onto American Pacific Drive and follow it into an industrial park. The Kidd place is in a copper brown building, one of only three structures in the park. It's adjacent to a Cami'z sportswear factory outlet, so follow the Cami'z signs. Call before you go, since production occasionally shuts down during slow periods—although the factory remains open to visitors.

Marshmallows may seem rather one-dimensional, but this tour was more interesting than we'd expected. Through picture windows, you see candied gelatin extruded through a machine like long white worms. They're dusted with cornstarch, chopped into little white nuggets and packaged. You'll get a mini-packet at the end of the tour, and you can buy more at a gift shop, along with souvenirs. A wall display records a rather disastrous day in the life of Kidd marshmallows. In 1988, an adjacent rocket fuel plant exploded, knocking the Kidd place flat. It was back in operation a year later.

ACTIVITIES

You mean besides gambling, seeing naked women onstage, pigging out at buffets and partying at 4 a.m.? Here's a sampler of what *else* you can do in Las Vegas. Most of these outings can be booked a day or two before. Many casino resorts have tour desks, usually in their hotel lobbies.

— photo courtesy **Las Vegas News Bureau**

Flights over Hoover Dam and the Grand Canyon are popular pastimes for southern Nevada visitors.

SIGHTSEEING FLIGHTS • With the Grand Canyon only 150 miles by air, overflights are among the most popular tours operating out of Las Vegas. Local carriers also have "flightseeing" trips to other areas. (Also look under **Tours** below.) When you book a flight, ask what type of aircraft is being used. The "high wing" type offers the best viewing; choppers are good, too. Also, if you're on a budget, ask about standby flights, often offered at substantial discounts.

Adventure Airlines (736-7511) has Grand Canyon air-ground flights to the Hualapai Indian Reservation, with barbecues on the rim.

Air America Tours (736-6260) offers all-window seat flights over Grand Canyon, Hoover Dam and Lake Mead.

Canyon Flyers (293-3446) has Grand Canyon flights operating out of Boulder City Airport, with free Las Vegas pickup.

Helicop-Tours (736-0606) has chopper flights over the canyon, including landings within the canyon.

Price-Les Travel offers flights over Grand Canyon, Hoover Dam and air-ground tours to Death Valley and Valley of Fire State Park.

Scenic Airlines (597-2295) is one of the oldest and largest of the Grand Canyon flightseeing firms, dating back 25 years. It offers overflights and air-ground combinations. All craft have high wings and large windows for good viewing.

Silver Air (891-0346) offers turbine helicopter flights over the Grand Canyon and day and night flights above the Strip.

TOURS • Several companies offer guided tours in, about and beyond the city. Some examples:

Boat Tours of Las Vegas (565-7333) has sightseeing, lunch, dinner and sunset paddle wheeler cruises on Lake Mead.

Desert Action, Inc. (796-9355) has four-wheel drive tours of the desert; the firm also rents FWD's and sends you on your way.

Grand Canyon Specialists (383-4010) offers ground and air Grand Canyon tours and Hoover Dam tours.

Gray Line (384-1234) is one of the area's largest operators, offering city tours, trips to Hoover Dam with Lake Mead cruises, Laughlin, Old Nevada, Red Rock Canyon and Valley of Fire, plus Grand Canyon flights and treks to nearby national parks.

Guaranteed Tours (739-9585) has air and ground Grand Canyon tours including one with an Indian-hosted luncheon, Lake Mead cruises, a desert tour and trips to Calico Ghost Town, Death Valley and Zion National Park.

Interstate Tours (293-2268) specializes in motor coach, helicopter and aircraft tours to the Hualapai Indian Reservation and the Grand Canyon.

Key Tours (362-9355) has trips to Laughlin, daytime and sunset cruises on Lake Mead and Hoover Dam visits.

Lake Mead Cruises (293-6180) features sightseeing and dinner voyages across the lake in a Mississippi-style paddle wheeler.

Las Vegas Flyers (736-4554) offers ground and air tours to the Grand Canyon, Valley of Fire, Death Valley, Bryce and Zion canyons, plus Lake Mead cruises and Las Vegas overflights.

Silver Line Tours (877-8966) has trips to the Grand Canyon South Rim, Zion National Park, Death Valley and Calico Ghost Town.

GOLF • Several of the area's golf courses are private, or are limited to hotel guests only. These are open to the public:

Angel Park Golf Club, 100 Rampart Blvd., Las Vegas; 254-4653. Two courses; green fees $60 with cart.

Black Mountain Golf and Country Club, 501 Country Club Dr., Henderson; 565-7933. Fees $18, cart $10.

Craig Ranch Golf Course, 628 W. Craig Rd., North Las Vegas; 642-9700. Fee $11, cart $5.

Desert Rose Golf Course, 5843 Club House Dr., Las Vegas; 431-4653. Fee $21.50, cart $7.50.

Dunes Country Club, 3650 S. Las Vegas Blvd., Las Vegas; 737-4749. Fee $60 including cart.

Las Vegas Golf Club, 4349 Vegas Dr., Las Vegas; 646-3003. Fee $11.50, cart $15.25.

Las Vegas Indian Wells Country Club, One Country Club Dr., Henderson; 451-2106. Fee $50 including cart.

Legacy Golf Club, 130 Par Excellence Dr., Henderson; 897-2187. Fees $55 including cart.

Los Prados Country Club, 5150 Los Prados Circle, Las Vegas; 645-5696. Fee $17, cart $9.

North Las Vegas Golf Course, 324 E. Brooks, North Las Vegas; 649-7171. Fee $3 for a par three course, no carts.

Painted Desert Golf Course, 5555 Painted Mirage Way, Las Vegas; 645-2568. Fee $55 including cart.

Sahara Country Club, 1911 E. Desert Inn Rd., Las Vegas; 796-0013. Fee $60 including cart.

Sun City Summerlin Golf Club, 9201-B Del Webb Blvd., Las Vegas; 363-4373. Fee $60 including cart.

TENNIS • Most hotel courts are for guests only, or they have guest privileges extended to other hotels. These courts are open to the public. Guests have priority at hotel courts so call well in advance for a spot.

Aladdin Hotel, 3667 S. Las Vegas Blvd., 736-0111; open from sunrise to 10 p.m.

Caesars Palace, 3570 S. Las Vegas Blvd., 731-7110; open from dawn to dusk.

Center Court Racquet Club, 3890 Swenson St., 735-8153; indoor and outdoor lighted courts, open from 7 a.m. to 10 p.m. weekdays and until 6 weekends.

Desert Inn, 3145 S. Las Vegas Blvd.; 733-4444, courts available from 8 a.m. to 8:30 p.m.

Las Vegas Racquet Club, 3333 W. Raven Ave., 361-2202; six lighted courts, 10 a.m. to 10 p.m.

Sands, 3355 S. Las Vegas Blvd., 733-5000; courts are open from 9 a.m. to 10 p.m.

Sports Club Las Vegas, 3025 Industrial Rd. (behind the Stardust, near the freeway), 733-8999; open 24 hours; facilities for tennis, racquetball and squash.

Jackie Gaughan's Plaza, One Main St., 386-2110; 9 a.m. to 6 p.m.

University of Nevada at Las Vegas, Tropicana and Harmon, 739-3150. Courts open to the public at various hours; students and faculty have priority.

CASINO BOWLING • Las Vegas is one of the few places on earth that mixes bowling and gambling. These casinos offer bowling alleys: **Showboat Hotel,** 2800 E. Fremont St. (385-9153); **Arizona Charlie's,** 740 S. Decatur Blvd. (258-5200); **Gold Coast,** 4000 W. Flamingo Rd. (367-7111); **Santa Fe,** 4949 N. Rancho Dr. (658-4900) and **Sam's Town,** 5111 Boulder Highway (456-7777). The Showboat is the largest with 106 lanes; it's the site of a major national bowling tournament.

Horseback riding is available at Bonnie Springs Ranch, 18 miles west of town (follow West Charleston Boulevard); 875-4191.

ANNUAL EVENTS

New Year's Eve Celebration downtown with a major fireworks show behind Jackie Gaughan's Plaza (which generated this book's cover); call 382-6397.

LPGA Invitational Golf Tournament in March; 382-6616.

Clark County Fair in April at Logandale, 60 miles north; 477-0123.

World Series of Poker in the Spring at Horseshoe Casino; 366-7397.

PGA Senior Classic Golf Tournament in May at the Desert Inn; 382-6616.

Helldorado Days and Rodeo in June, the city's major Western-style celebration with parades, contests and old West dress-ups, at Thomas and Mack Center; 870-1221.

Las Vegas Invitational Golf Tournament in October; 382-6616.

U.S. and World Invitational Triathlon in mid-October; 731-2115.

National Finals Rodeo in early December, plus other Western festivities, at the Thomas and Mack Center; 731-2115.

THE CITY'S TEN BEST RESTAURANTS
By Stephen Allen

Las Vegas has come a long way from the day when dining out meant hitting the ubiquitous "Chuckwagon." In addition to its dozens of buffets (see box below), the city offers some of the best—if unsung—restaurants in the country. It had more than 850 dining parlors at last count. With so many choices, how can a visitor find the best places to eat?

Obviously, by consulting a local dining expert. We asked restaurant writer Stephen Allen to pick his ten favorite places. He begins with the best of the bunch, the Palace Court, and follows with the next nine in alphabetical order.

Stephen is certainly qualified to discuss Las Vegas dining. He has penned scores of newspaper and magazine articles on the subject, and he has authored restaurant sections for Fodor and Birnbaum travel guides. In addition to his freelance writing, he serves as media director for the Las Vegas News Bureau.

1. PALACE COURT • *Caesars Palace, 3570 S. Las Vegas Blvd.; (702) 731-7547. Classical French; dinner $30 to $35; full bar service. Dinner only, 6 to 11 nightly. Reservations essential; jacket and tie required. Major credit cards.* Caesars Palace has been the Las Vegas standard bearer for excellence for a long time; the hotel recently celebrated its 25th anniversary. Thus, it's no surprise that the Palace Court is regarded as the city's top restaurant. The quality of the food and attentive service never vary in this award-winning establishment.

This circular restaurant under a stained glass dome is a peaceful retreat on the second floor of Caesars, far removed from the casino. Overlooking a swimming pool, it's a virtual garden of trees, bushes and flowers—real, of course. The atmosphere is one of *haute cuisine* in a private French courtyard, with fine crystal and china. The fare is classical French, although it's a bit on the lighter side, without heavy sauces.

Among its specialties are *Navarin de Coquille St. Jacques* (bay scallops baked in white wine), *Gratin of Crayfish St. Charles* (crayfish tails baked in vermouth and cognac), *Hommard Vivant Selon Desir* (live Maine lobster, steamed or baked), whole quail baked in crockery and the ever popular veal Oscar. The Court has an extensive wine list and a *sommelier* to assist with your selection. (In old Las Vegas, they wouldn't have known the meaning of the word.)

No matter what you order, leave room for one of the desserts; they're simply the best in the city. When they roll that cart to your table, you won't be able to resist.

2. ANDRE'S • *401 S. Sixth St.; (702) 385-5016. Classical French; dinners $30 to $40; full bar service. Lunch weekdays, dinner nightly 5 to 11. Reservations essential; jacket and tie required. Major credit cards.* This restaurant, tucked into a home on a downtown side street, is the loving creation of Andre Rochat. Styled like an elegant French country house, it's more popular with well-heeled locals than tourists—a haven to many of the city's movers and shakers.

Some of the specialties are *chateaubriand* for two, stuffed pork tenderloin and rack of baby lamb. Andre also has one of the best wine cellars in the city.

3. BATTISTA'S HOLE IN THE WALL • *4041 Audrie St. (opposite Bally's Casino); (702) 732-1424. Northern Italian; dinners $15 to $25; full bar service. Daily 5 to 10 p.m. Reservations suggested; major credit cards.* Once upon a time, there was an Italian opera singer from Bergamo named Battista Locatelli. He came to America, worked as a truck driver, soon grew weary of that, moved to Las Vegas and took over operation of a tiny 14-seat cafe. Then who should move across the street but the 2,000-room MGM Grand Hotel (now Bally's). *Mama mia,* what a break!

Battista now takes in about $4.5 million a year. It's a friendly and sparkling clean restaurant, and the northern Italian food is one of the city's best bargains, since it includes all the Italian wine you can drink. (Go easy, now!)

Perhaps it's the proximity to Bally's, but through the years the place has become popular with show people. Pictures of Battista with the visiting stars cover the walls. Some of his specialties are *cioppino*, veal *piccante* and chicken *cacciatore.* While the restaurant is open only for dinner, Battista operates the best pizza parlor in town during the day—Pizza-Rio, right next door.

4. CHIN'S • *In Fashion Show Mall (3200 S. Las Vegas Blvd.); (702) 733-8899. Gourmet Chinese; dinners $20 to $30; full bar service. Daily 11 a.m. to 10:30 p.m. Reservations suggested; MC/VISA, AMEX.* This handsome, plant-filled atrium restaurant is in a rather odd location—in a shopping mall. However, it was a hit with both locals and visitors the day it opened. Owner Tola Chin's classic Chinese menu and attention to detail are the keys to its success.

Don't expect to find chow mein and chop suey here. This is a stylish restaurant with creative dishes typical of more elegant Hong Kong dining salons. Some of the specialties are Chin's beef, lemon chicken and strawberry shrimp. You'll find many dessert choices; our favorite is the tasty and unusual "crispy pudding." Try Chin's *dim sum* for lunch. Translated as "little hearts," *dim sum* consists of a variety of intriguing foods served in small, tasty morsels. Fortunately, the price for the lunch is a dim sum as well!

5. MANFREDI'S LIMELIGHT • *2340 E. Tropicana Ave. (at Eastern, in the Renaissance Center); (702) 739-1410. Northern Italian/Continental; dinners $10 to $20; full bar service. Daily 4:30 to 11. Reservations suggested; major credit cards.* This is a little family-owned cafe with a terrific reputation among locals. The Manfredis are highly-regarded members of the community; their affection for their work shows in the quality of food and service in this cozy and comfortable place.

Others obviously share the town's enthusiasm. A special dining issue of *Bon Appetit* listed Manfredi's as one of the best Italian restaurants in the West. Some of the specials are veal *provimi*, *calimari* with garlic and herbs and *agnolotti*. All the pasta and sauces are homemade.

6. PAMPLEMOUSSE • *401 E. Sahara Ave.; (702) 733-2066. Classical French; dinners $25 to $35; full bar service. Dinner only, nightly from 6 to 10. Reservations essential; jacket and tie required. Major credit cards.* This cozy restaurant with the strange name is quite simply the most intimate and romantic place in Las Vegas. More than anything else, it will remind you of a little French cottage.

Pamplemousse is owned—and carefully tended—by Georges LaForge, who worked as a *maitre d'* in several of the city's better hotels. It was named as a tribute to his close friend, the late singer Bobby Darin, who said "pamplemousse" was the most beautiful word in the French language. (It means grapefruit, about the only thing the restaurant doesn't serve.)

Taking a page from California *chic,* this place has no menu. The waiter recites the dishes and how they're prepared; he also takes your order by memory. The specialty here is roast duckling with green peppercorns and armagnac; you shouldn't miss it. If you aren't a duck fan, try the salmon with orange and curry, or the veal *sauce Moutarde.*

A fine French restaurant should send you into the night feeling that all is right with you and the world. Pamplemousse can do just that.

7. RALPH'S DINER ● *Stardust Hotel (3000 S. Las Vegas Blvd.); (702) 732-6111. American Fifties fare; meals $5 to $10; no bar but drink service is available. Daily 7 a.m. to 10 p.m. No reservations; major credit cards.* You probably never expected to find something like this in a casino, but we love the place! Hey, could da Fonz and Opie be wrong? They'd feel right at home in this recreation of a Fifties diner, complete with 'burgers and fries in plastic baskets, "choklit" malts, meat loaf and fried chicken.

Two specials are catfish with hushpuppies, and mini-burger "Sliders." Occasionally, the wisecracking waitresses will stop and do the Watusi to the Fifties style jukebox.

While we're on the subject of good food, the Stardust also is home to the best ribs in Las Vegas, at Tony Roma's. Although it's a chain, the ribs are excellent, and corporate headquarters calls it the best Tony Roma's in the world. We don't know how the execs arrived at that conclusion, but we'll take their word for it.

8. RICARDO'S ● *2380 E. Tropicana Ave. (Renaissance Center); (702) 798-4515. Mexican; dinners $10 to $15; full bar service. Daily 11 a.m. to 11 p.m. (to midnight Friday and Saturday). Reservations suggested; major credit cards.* The Las Vegas *Review Journal* conducts an annual readers poll to determine the city's best restaurants, casinos, attractions and such. Ricardo's is always the winner in the Mexican restaurant category.

The reasons are obvious: a large menu, reasonable prices with well-prepared traditional Mexican food and terrific drinks, served by a friendly staff. Everything on the menu is good, and we especially like *burrito Colorado, sizzling fajita* chicken and the *chimichangas.* For dessert, try the deep fried ice cream.

If someone in your party is having a birthday, the strolling mariachis will gather around to sing *Esta son las manitas.*

9. SAVOIA ● *4305 Paradise Rd. (near St. Tropez Hotel); (702) 731-5446. Continental; dinners $20 to $30; full bar service. Daily 11 to 11. Reservations suggested; major credit cards.* This large, bright and attractive place also is owned by Georges LaForge of Pamplemousse, which probably explains why it's so good. You'll receive the same care and attention to detail, although this place is more informal and a bit less expensive.

Some of the specials are *Savoia* teaser appetizers (oysters, clams and mussels sautéed in garlic sauce), vegetable lasagna, broiled Norwegian salmon and hobo steak (baked in a salt crust then sliced and served with Dijon mustard sauce, cognac and fresh herbs). Live jazz is featured on Thursday, Friday and Saturday nights.

10. THE TILLERMAN • *2245 E. Flamingo Ave.; (702) 731-4036. Seafood; dinners $20 to $30; full bar service. Daily 5 to 11 p.m. No reservations; major credit cards.* Who would believe that a desert city has a really good seafood restaurant? You've found it at the Tillerman. Although it doesn't take reservations, the place is large so the wait is usually short. And the lounge is cozy and comfortable, serving good, generous drinks.

This is a high-ceiling, plant-bedecked place with youthful, friendly and efficient waiters and waitresses. They're trained to take your order without writing it down, which we always find impressive but scary. The Tillerman is a bit off the beaten track, a few miles from the Strip, but it's worth the trip if you're a seafood fan. Although the menu is extensive, ask about the specials, which are flown in daily. Two of our favorites are yellowfin tuna and broiled salmon.

WHERE ELSE TO DINE

Las Vegas may be the cheapest place to eat in the developed world. Where else can you pig out at a buffet for less than $3, get a shrimp cocktail for 99 cents and popcorn for nothing? Of course, you'll find plenty of regular restaurants as well. In fact, the town abounds with them.

Following our friend Stephen Allen's favorites, we offer additional selections. Since we've already covered casino dining, these are restaurants outside the gaming areas. Incidentally, Clark County law requires that all restaurants provide non-smoking sections, so we dispense with our symbol, except to indicate dining rooms that are completely smoke-free (ØØ).

American

Alias Smith & Jones • ☺☺ $$

541 E. Twain Ave. (in Twain Plaza between Paradise and Swenson); 732-7401. Basic American; dinners $10 to $15; full bar service. Daily 11 a.m. to 6 a.m., plus 11 to 2 Sunday brunch. Reservations accepted; MC/VISA, AMEX, DISC. Popular all-night place named for a long-gone TV show, with a homey cedar panel-hanging plant-crackling fireplace look. It's eclectic menu features remarkably good hamburgers and chicken wings and a choice of two dozen omelettes, plus typical American steaks, chops and seafood.

Celebrity Deli • ☺☺ $$

4055 Maryland Parkway (near Flamingo Road); 733-7827. New York style deli; dinners $10 to $14; wine and beer. Daily 9 a.m. to 9 p.m. Reservations accepted; MC/VISA, AMEX. Typical kosher deli offering pastrami, corned beef, lox and bagels, potato *knish* and other classics. Try one of the multi-decker sandwiches, followed by New York style cheesecake.

Coachman's Inn • ☺☺ $$

3240 S. Eastern Ave. (a mile southeast of the Strip); 731-4202. American with some Italian; dinners $10.50 to $26; full bar service. Open 24 hours. Reservations essential for dinner; major credit cards. Longtime local favorite, noted for its prime rib. Also features assorted steaks, plus seafood and several Italian entrées. Cozy mountain hideaway setting with fireplace and warm wood décor.

Dickinson's Wharf • ☺☺ $$$

953 E. Sahara Ave. (near Commercial Center Drive, just off Las Vegas Boulevard); 732-3594. Seafood and steaks; dinners $15 to $29; full bar service. Nightly 5 to midnight. Reservations accepted; major credit cards. Family-run seafood restaurant with a nautical look and a New England accent to the menu. Entrées include whole Maine lobster, crab Newburg, orange roughy and seafood combination dinners. Also steaks and Italian fare.

Elephant Bar & Restaurant • ☺☺ $$

2797 S. Maryland Parkway (between Sahara and Desert Inn roads, near Hilton Hotel); 737-1586. American-Polynesian; dinners $9 to $14; full bar service. Sunday-Thursday 11:30 to 10, Friday-Saturday 11:30 to 11. Reservations accepted; major credit cards. Pleasing South Seas look, complete with a waterfall and cheerful patio for warm-weather dining. Menu is mixed American with tropical accents; try the featured macadamia mahi mahi.

Famous Pacific Fish Company • ☺☺☺ $$

3925 Paradise Rd. (two blocks north of Flamingo Road); 796-9676. Seafood; dinners $10 to $20; full bar service. Monday- Thursday 11 to 10, Friday-Saturday 11 to 11, Sunday 4 to 10. Reservations accepted; major credit cards. Inviting "open beam *nouveau*" look, bright and open. Extensive seafood menu ranges from blackened Cajun things to broiled fish filets to shrimp stir fry. Fresh fish is flown in daily.

The Flame • ☺☺☺☺ $$$

One E. Desert Inn Rd. (at Las Vegas Boulevard, opposite the Stardust); 735-4431. Steak house; dinners $15 to $45; full bar service. Open 24 hours. Reservations accepted; major credit cards. One of the town's legendary restaurants, popular with locals, show people and tourists for more than 30 years. Clubby leather interior with open charcoal broiler and framed photos of celebs and sports heroes. Varied steak menu, plus seafood and inexpensive brunch and lunch specials such as breakfast steak and potatoes and French dip sandwiches. It's easy to find this place; just watch for the flickering neon flame.)

The Golden Steer • ☺☺ $$$

308 W. Sahara Ave. (just west of the Strip); 384-4470. American-Italian; dinners $20 to $25; full bar service. Nightly 5 to midnight. Reservations accepted, essential on weekends; major credit cards. Large, rambling steak house with a Western-Victorian look is a local institution, meaning that it's been around for more than 30 years. With 24- hour notice, you'll be served pheasant, chukkars or guinea hen. Quail is on the regular menu, along with assorted steaks, prime rib and several typical Italian entrées.

The Green Shack • ☺☺ $$

2504 E. Fremont St. (east of downtown); 383-0007. Basic American; dinners $8 to $14; full bar service. Nightly except Monday, from 5. Reservations accepted; MC/VISA. It claims to be the "oldest and best kept secret in Las Vegas" but it's hardly a secret. Folks have been coming here since 1930, when it served Hoover Dam construction crews. The town's oldest restaurant has a basic American roadhouse look with a menu to match: southern fried chicken (reputedly the best in town), chicken gizzards, batter fried shrimp and top sirloin. Hefty dinners are served with biscuits and honey.

Jerome's • ☺☺☺ $$$
4503 Paradise Rd. (at Harmon Avenue); 876-1963. American- continental; dinners $14 to $25; full bar service. Nightly 6 to 11. Reservations accepted; major credit cards. Expatriate San Franciscans such as ourselves love this place, featuring great chunks of sourdough bread and Italian-style seafood such as cioppino and scampi. Other menu specials are blackened swordfish, grilled shrimp with garlic and chicken piccata. The place has expansive feel, with white nappery and mahogany chairs.

Keifer's • ☺☺☺ $$$
105 E. Harmon Ave. (in the Carriage House just off Las Vegas Boulevard), 739-8000. California nouveau; dinners $12.50 to $20; full bar service. Nightly 5 to midnight, also open for breakfast. Reservations accepted; major credit cards. Large, modern and stylish restaurant offering an awesome ninth floor view of the Strip; the look is sort of "Polynesian modern." Creative California/American regional menu has continental accents. Specialties include French onion soup in a hollowed sourdough bowl, blackened catfish, halibut with avocado and shrimp, and chicken cordon bleau.

Port Tack • ☺☺☺ $$$
3190 W. Sahara Ave. (Valley View Boulevard); 873-3345. American with seafood tilt; dinners $15 to $18; full bar service. Daily 11 a.m. to 6 a.m. Reservations for five or more only; major credit cards. The place reminds us of a San Francisco-style seafood house with lots of brick and wood, a salad bar, and an oyster bar with a large saltwater aquarium. Fish is flown in from San Diego; shellfish from the east coast. Also steak, ribs, chicken and pasta.

Asian, East Indian

A Touch of Ginger • ☺ $
4001 S. Maryland Parkway (near Flamingo Road); 796-1779. Vietnamese; dinners $3.50 to $9; wine and beer. Daily 11 to 10. No reservations; MC/VISA, AMEX. Small family style place featuring spicy southeast Asian fare. Vietnamese food is influenced by French wine sauces, Indian curries and Chinese ginger, plus Vietnam's lemon grass and peanut sauce. Try spicy seafood dishes, pork and shrimp crepes and *satay* (skewered meats and veggies with peanut sauce).

Beijing Restaurant • ☺☺☺ $$
3900 Paradise Rd. (across from First Interstate Tower); 737-9618. Chinese; dinners $7.50 to $27; full bar service. Monday- Saturday 11:30 to 11, Sunday 5 to 11. Reservations accepted; major credit cards. Handsomely decorated place with museum- quality furnishings and artworks. It's worth a visit just to admire the jade, cloisonne, carved ivory and embroidered silk. Large menu features classic Peking duck, shark's fin soup, black pepper steak, pine nut shrimp and crab leg in black bean sauce, plus an extensive selection of vegetarian dishes.

China Doll • ☺☺ $$
2534 E. Desert Inn Rd. (near Eastern Avenue); 369-9511. Chinese; dinners $7 to $14; full bar service. Weekdays 11:30 to 10, weekends 3 to 10. Reservations accepted; MC/VISA. Simple, appealing little family restaurant offering a

mix of mild Cantonese and spicy Szechwan/Hong Kong dishes. Specialties include orange flavored chicken, spicy *sha-cha* beef and black pepper steak *kew*. Very modest prices; four-item combo dinners are under $10.

Shalimar Restaurant • ☺☺ $$$
3900 Paradise Rd.; 796-0302; also at 2605 Decatur Blvd.; 252-8320. Indian; dinners $12 to $18; full bar service. Lunch Monday- Friday 11:30 to 2, dinner nightly 5:30 to 10:30. Reservations accepted; major credit cards. Tandoori style cooking served amidst attractive East Indian décor, to the tune of a *sitar*. A tandoor is a clay oven from which emerges spicy fat-free lamb, chicken and shrimp dishes. They're served with hot, puffy bread cooked on the side of the oven. Menu also features 20 vegetarian dishes.

French & continental

Alpine Village Inn • ☺☺☺ $$
3003 Paradise Rd. (opposite Las Vegas Hilton); 734-6888. German-Swiss-American; dinners $9.50 to $18; full bar service. Nightly 5 to midnight. Reservations accepted; major credit cards. A local favorite since 1950, it's about as Alpine as you'll find in the desert. It has a Swiss chalet look inside and out and a snowy mountain-cable car scene in the dining room. Expect someone in *liederhosen* at any moment. Menu is mostly German-Swiss, with a few American steaks. Try the *bauernplatte* (farmer's plate) with various sausages, smoked pork chops, roasted chicken and breaded cubed beef.

The Bootlegger Restaurant • ☺☺☺☺ $$$ ØØ
5025 S. Eastern Ave. (near Tropicana); 736-4939. Continental-Italian; dinners $10 to $19; full bar service. Tuesday-Sunday 11:30 to 10:30, closed Monday. Reservations accepted; major credit cards. Long-established restaurant with "Mamma" Maria Perry in the kitchen, creating her own sauces and healthy low-cal pastas. She recently earned the "Nevada Restaurateur of the Year" title. Assorted seafood, veal, beef and chicken entrées served in a romantic setting with brick walls, cozy booths and crackling fire. Extensive wine list; smoke-free dining room.

Phillip's Supperhouse • ☺☺☺ $$$ ØØ
4545 W. Sahara Ave. (2.5 miles west of Las Vegas Boulevard); 873-5222. Continental and seafood; dinners $15 to $36; full bar service. Nightly 5 to 11. Reservations accepted; major credit cards. Handsome Victorian-New England décor with warm woods, print wallpaper and intimate alcove seating. It's divided into several dining areas; some are smoke-free. Busy menu offers several Italian dinners, plus fresh seafood, lamb chops, steaks and prime rib.

2nd Story • ☺☺☺ $$$
4485 S. Jones Blvd. (between Tropicana and Flamingo); 368-2257. French-continental; dinners $12.50 to $25; full bar service. Nightly 6 to 10:30. Reservations accepted; major credit cards. Intimate dining salon with a dramatic picture window view of the Strip; great spot for a sunset dinner. Also features an enclosed patio with retractable roof. Menu focus is French, plus rack of lamb, fresh seafood and a fine whisky-marinaded filet mignon.

Swiss Cafe • ☺☺ $$$
1431 E. Charleston Blvd. (15th Street); 382-6444. Continental; dinners $14 to $19; wine and beer. Lunch Monday-Friday 11:30 to 2, dinner Tuesday-Saturday 6 to 9:15. Reservations accepted; MC/VISA. Cozy chef-owned cafe

featuring a continental mix, ranging from veal Zurich and chicken curry Bombay to Jäger schnitzel and Dijon sea scallops. A well-chosen wine list features a variety of wines by the glass.

Tony's Greco-Roman Restaurant • ☺☺ $$$

220 W. Sahara Ave. (just west of Las Vegas Boulevard); 384-5171. Greek and Italian; dinners $8 to $19; wine and beer. Daily 11 a.m. to 10 p.m. Major credit cards. More Greek than Roman, this little cottage restaurant features specialties such as *souvlaki* (marinated lamb or beef), *riganato* (chicken oregano) and *dolmathes* (stuffed grape leaves). Don't miss the *baklava* for dessert. From the Italian side emerges *marinaras, parmigianas* and *picatas*.

Waldemar's Restaurant • ☺☺ $$$

2202 W. Charleston Blvd. (in Galleria Center at Rancho); 386-1995. Central European; dinners $7 to $19; wine and beer. Weekdays 9 to 4, Monday-Saturday 5 to 11. Reservations accepted; MC/VISA, AMEX. Nicely rustic old European look with brick arches, long dining tables and soft background music. Mostly Swiss-German menu, with *schnitzel* and German potato salad, veal *cordon bleau*. and *rouladen*.

Italian

Carluccio's Tivoli Gardens • ☺☺☺ $$

1775 E. Tropicana Ave. (at Spencer, behind Liberace Museum, 2.5 miles off Las Vegas Boulevard); 795-3236. Northern Italian; dinners $10 to $12; full bar service. Tuesday-Sunday 4:30 to 10, closed Monday. Reservations accepted; MC/VISA, AMEX. Once the site of Liberace's restaurant, it still retains some of Mr. Showmanship's flashy flamboyance, particularly in the cocktail lounge with a glittering grand piano. Specials include veal Florentine, seafood *Diablo* and crab-stuffed shrimp. It's also noted for desserts.

Cipriani • ☺☺☺ $$$

2790 E. Flamingo Rd. (near Eastern Avenue); 369-6711. Dinners $18 to $25; full bar service. Lunch weekdays 11:30 to 2, dinner Monday-Saturday 6 to 10:30. Reservations essential for dinner, not needed for lunch; major credit cards. One of the town's classiest Italian restaurants, with an open kitchen, stylish furnishings, chandeliers and hanging plants. Full range of Italian fare, from *osso buco* to fresh pastas; also *prix fixe* dinners.

Fortunato's • ☺☺ $$

3430 E. Tropicana Ave. (at Pecos Avenue); 458-3333. Dinners $6 to $13; full bar service. Monday-Friday 11 to 10, Saturday 4 to 10, closed Sunday. Reservations accepted; major credit cards. Pleasant little family-run cafe with husband Steve Whisler in the Kitchen and wife Nancy up front. Typical Italian veal, chicken, seafood and pastas, plus a variety of soups and desserts.

Pasta Shop Ristorante • ☺☺ $$

2495 E. Tropicana Ave., (near Eastern Avenue); 451-1893. Dinners $9.50 to $18; wine and beer. Monday-Saturday 5 to 9:30, closed Sunday. Reservations accepted; MC/VISA. Cozy, intimate cafe that makes its own pasta; very popular with locals. The small menu offers typical Italian entrées, ranging from seafood to chicken *Davida*; however, go primarily for the pasta.

Romeo's • ☺☺☺ $$ ØØ

2800 W. Sahara Ave. (west of I-15 in The Plazas); 873-5400. Northern Italian; dinners $12.50 to $18.50; full bar service. Lunch 11:30 to 2:30, din-

ner 5:30 to 10:30. Reservations accepted; major credit cards. Very stylish place with fountain entryway, spacious dining room with high ceiling; patio for warm-weather dining. Menu specials include *osso buco,* veal with raspberry champagne sauce, Dover sole and fresh pastas. Smoke-free dining.

Mexican and assorted Latino
El Sombrero Cafe • ☺ $
807 S. Main St. (downtown between Charleston and Fremont); 382-9234. Mexican; dinners $6 to $7.50; wine and beer. Daily 11 to 10. Reservations not needed; MC/VISA, AMEX. Good basic smashed beans and rice place; the oldest Mexican restaurant in Las Vegas. Remarkably large and inexpensive dinners, including specials such as *carne asada* and *camarones* (shrimp with tomatoes). The look is *cantina tourista,* complete with sombreros of course.

Macayo Vegas Restaurant • ☺☺ $$ ØØ
1741 E. Charleston Blvd. (between Maryland Parkway and Eastern Avenue); 382-5605. Mexican-American; dinners $5 to $12; full bar service. Daily 11 a.m. to midnight. Reservations accepted; major credit cards. One of four lively, decorative restaurants belonging to a locally-owned chain. Some American dishes, plus the usual generous-sized Mexican fare; the pork, chicken and beef fajitas are specialties. Two dining areas; one is smoke-free.

Yolie's Brazilian Steakhouse • ☺☺☺ $$$
3900 Paradise Road (Citibank Park, upper level); 794-0700. Brazilian churrascaria; dinners $13 to $21; full bar service. Lunch weekdays 11:30 to 3, dinner nightly 5:30 to 11. Reservations accepted; major credit cards. It's interesting for the ritual as well as the food. If you order the $20.95 *prix fixe* Brazilian dinner, waiters pass by your table, slicing chunks of chicken, beef, sausages and lamb from sword skewers; the meal also includes black bean soup, salad and assorted side dishes. One also can order from the menu.

The joy of pigging out:
THE TEN BEST CASINO BUFFETS
By Stephen Allen

They used to call them "chuckwagons." Nearly every Las Vegas casino had one, offering all-you-can-eat beans, bread, salad and slabs of meat. Today, they're elaborate buffets, featuring dozens of items at incredible bargains. You couldn't eat at home for these prices! How can the casino hotels make any money on the buffets, you may ask? They can't, but it sure keeps you close to the casino, which is the whole idea.

The idea started in the early 1940s with the town's first resort style casino, El Rancho Vegas. Owner Beldon Katelmen, seeking to keep his customers in the casino after the cocktail show, came up the Midnight Chuck Wagon Buffet—"All you can eat for a dollar." The idea quickly spread to other casinos, and the "chuck wagon" soon became a universal ritual throughout the state. The buffets are a bit more than a dollar now, but they're still great food bargains.

As a result, Las Vegas and other Nevada cities may be the only places in the civilized world where you can enjoy an all-you-can eat buffet for less than the price of a Big Mac, fries and shake.

LAS VEGAS — 149

In addition to buffets, you'll want to check out the many hotel Sunday brunches, which also are great bargains. Most include all the champagne you can drink. For a listing of all the buffets, with times and prices, pick up a copy of the free tourist publication, **What's On**. It's available at news racks, information desks and hotel lobbies, or call 385-5080. At last count, the magazine had tallied 36 buffets and 24 brunches. *Bon appetit!*

We list our top selection first, with the next nine in alphabetical order.

1. BALLY'S STERLING BRUNCH • *Sunday 9 a.m. to 2:30 p.m.; $22.95. On the Strip at 3645 Las Vegas Blvd. (at Flamingo Road); 739-4111.* This is the most expensive brunch in the city, and it's worth it! The food is not just abundant; it's the quality and variety that will amaze you, topped off by those fabulous Bally's desserts. They don't stint on the champagne here, so you might want to make this the highlight of your day. The Sterling Brunch has been rated the best buffet/brunch in Las Vegas by a number of food critics, and we agree.

2. Bally's Big Kitchen Buffet • *Brunch 7:30 to 2:30 for $5.95; dinner 4:30 to 10 for $10.95.* Bally's has done it again with their regular daily buffet, featuring good quality food at reasonable prices. This buffet is unique: You go right into the Big Kitchen to load up. Nothing could be fresher than going to the source. The brunch features all-you-can-eat shrimp. Chinese selections highlight the dinner, since Bally's Chinese restaurant once was located here.

3. Caesars Palace Champagne Brunch • *Sunday 8:30 a.m. to 2:30 p.m.; adults $13.50, children $10.50. On the Strip at 3570 Las Vegas Blvd. (at Dunes Road); 731-7110.* In keeping with the Caesars tradition of abundance, the champagne flows like water. The ample buffet features an array of egg dishes, along with waffles, cold salads and desserts.

4. Circus Circus Buffet • *Breakfast 6 to 11:30 for $2.29; lunch noon to 4 for $2.99; dinner 4:30 to 11 for $3.99. On the Strip at 2880 Las Vegas Blvd. (opposite the Sahara); 734-0410.* This is the world's largest buffet, serving as many as 10,000 people a day. In fact, the buffet feeds more people a year than the entire population of Ireland! Several serving lines are available, so the wait isn't long. A sister to this buffet is at the other Circus Circus Enterprises property, **Excalibur,** the world's largest hotel.

5. Flamingo Hilton Crown Room Buffet • *Breakfast 7 to 11:30 for $3.95; dinner 4:30 to 9:30 for $5.95. On the Strip at 3555 Las Vegas Blvd. (near Flamingo Road); 733-3111.* This buffet offers a distinctive twist: Every month, a different international specialty is featured, such as Italian, German, Mexican and such. Another nice point: you can dine indoors or out, in the "Little Vienna" area overlooking the pool. (Why Little Vienna? The hotel president is Austrian.)

6. Fremont Seafood Fantasy • *Fridays only, 4 to 11 p.m. for $10.95. Downtown at 200 E. Fremont St. (Third Street); 385-3232.* One of the town's newest buffets, the Seafood Fantasy was an instant hit with locals as well as visitors. It seems that everyone who lives in the desert *loves* seafood. Lobster, crab, shrimp, clams, oysters, smoked salmon, catfish and calamari—it's all here, plus some delicious homemade soups.

7. Golden Nugget buffet • *Breakfast 7 to 10:30 for $4.75; lunch 10:30 to 3 for $7.50; dinner 4 to 10 for $9.95; Sunday 8 a.m. to 10 p.m. for $9.95.*

Downtown at 199 E. Fremont St. (at Casino Center Boulevard); 385-7111. Las Vegas citizens have voted this the best buffet in town for several consecutive years, in a poll conducted by the *Review Journal*. A sister to this feast is served at the other property owned by Steve Wynn, the **Mirage**.

8. Las Vegas Hilton Buffet of Champions • *Breakfast 7 to 9:30 for $6.25, lunch 11 to 2:30 for $7.25; dinner 5 to 10 for $8.99; children half price. Just off the Strip at 3000 Paradise Rd. (adjacent to the convention center); 732-5111.* Located near the race and sports book, the buffet has a sports decor and offers a wide selection of carved, broiled or grilled entrées, three salad bars and a big display of desserts, including ice cream.

9. Showboat Seafood Spectacular • *Wednesday and Friday 4:30 to 10 p.m. for $7.45. East of downtown at 2800 Fremont St. (near Charleston Boulevard); 385-9123.* This is the oldest of the Las Vegas seafood buffets, and many local fans say it's still the best. Tons of shrimp, crab, clams and oysters are offered in a new and attractive setting.

10. Tropicana Island Buffet • *Breakfast 7 to 11 for $3.95; lunch 11 to 2:30 for $3.95; "Caribbean Nights" dinner Friday and Saturday only, 4 to 10 for $7.95. On the Strip at 3801 Las Vegas Blvd. (at Tropicana Avenue); 739-2222.* This Polynesian style buffet is somewhere between a luau and a smorgasbörd. Among its delights are hand-carved roast beef, fresh fish, fried chicken, salad bars and of course, sinful desserts.

WHERE TO SLEEP

The price ranges listed below are intended only as rough guidelines, generally indicating low to high season. Casino room rates often go lower during special off-seaon promotions, often with dinner and/or show packages. Many hotels follow a "whatever the traffic will bear" policy. They change rates so often—with the season, with the holidays and perhaps even with the mood of the manager—that they don't print rate cards. Further, it's pretty much a given that you'll pay one rate for Sunday through Thursday and another for Friday and Saturday. Many have a third rate—higher, obviously—for peak holiday periods.

This list covers lodgings within and outside of casino resorts. For details on the casinos, review the listings above. Price ranges are for a double, midweek to weekend, during the normal tourist season; they often go substantially lower. The Ø symbol indicates the place has non-smoking rooms. The bold-faced **K** indicates properties with special attractions for **k**ids.

Most hotels and motels without gaming parlors offer discount coupon books to various casinos.

Rooms from $70 and up

Bally's Las Vegas • △△△△
P.O. Box 19030 (3595 S. Las Vegas Boulevard at Flamingo Road), Las Vegas, NV 89109; (800) 634-3434 or (702) 739-4111. Doubles $84 to $175, suites $175 to $1,250. Major credit cards. One of the more luxurious of the large Strip resorts, with 2,832 attractively furnished rooms, done in mirrored ceilings and bright colors. Large 42-acre complex with 40-store shopping arcade, health clubs, two main showrooms, six restaurants, large swim complex and tennis courts.

Caesars Palace • ⌂⌂⌂
3570 S. Las Vegas Blvd. (at Dunes Road), Las Vegas, NV 89109; (800) 634-6001 or (702) 731-7110. Doubles $95 to $145, suites $150 and beyond. Major credit cards. Another of the more luxurious Las Vegas Boulevard resorts. Most of the 1,524 rooms are very elegant with mirrored walls, platform beds and vivid colors. Remember that scene from *The Rain Man*, when Dustin Hoffman and Tom Cruise were given a two-story Caesar suite with an elevated spa? It can be yours for $750 a night—or nothing if you're a *very* high roller. Extensive casino complex includes marble statuary, Omnimax theater, tennis courts, health club and some of the town's most luxuriant restaurants.

Desert Inn Hotel & Casino • ⌂⌂⌂
3145 S. Las Vegas Blvd. (at Desert Inn Road), Las Vegas, NV 89109; (800) 634-6906 or (702) 733-4444. Doubles $75 to $175, suites up to $1,500. Major credit cards. With 821 units, it's the most stylish of the smaller Strip resorts. Elegantly furnished rooms and suites with all the amenities. Howard Hughes' penthouse is available for around $300. Complex includes the usual casino, multiple restaurants and live entertainment, plus a golf course, jogging track, tennis courts and health club.

Las Vegas Hilton • ⌂⌂⌂ Ø K
P.O. Box 91347 (3000 Paradise Road, just off Las Vegas Boulevard), Las Vegas, NV 89193-3147; (800) 732-7117 or (702) 732-5111. Doubles and singles $80 to $175, suites $290 to $710. Major credit cards. One of the world's largest resorts, with 3,174 rooms, ranging from rather stylish to completely elegant. Full amenities, including pool, spa, tennis courts, putting green, large shopping arcade, 13 restaurants, headliner room and world's largest race and sports book.

The Mirage • ⌂⌂⌂ Ø K
P.O. Box 7777 (3400 S. Las Vegas Boulevard at Spring Mountain Road), Las Vegas, NV 89177-0777; (800) 627-6667 or (702) 791-7111. Doubles $79 to $225, suites $365 and up. Major credit cards. Step up to the desk even if you aren't checking in; you'll want to see the 20,000-gallon saltwater aquarium behind it. The Mirage is most elaborate resort complex in Nevada, with 3,044 nicely furnished rooms and suites. Large casino complex, several restaurants, indoor "rain forest," white tiger and dolphin habitats, major showroom, swimming pool complex and other amenities. Room décor continues the Polynesian theme with muted splashes of tropical color

Rio Suite Hotel • ⌂⌂
3700 W. Flamingo Rd. (opposite the Gold Coast), Las Vegas, NV 89103; (800) 888-1808 or (702) 252-7777. Doubles $81 to $99. Major credit cards. All units are mini-suites in this attractive new tropical Brazilian style highrise. The 430 two-room units have refrigerators, safes, free coffee and remote controlled TV. The Amazon-Ipanema theme carries through the room décor, casino, restaurants and showroom.

Sands Hotel • ⌂⌂ Ø
3355 S. Las Vegas Blvd. (Sands Avenue, opposite the Mirage), Las Vegas, NV 89109; (800) 446-4678 or (702) 733-5000. Doubles $69 to $79, suites $135 to $327. Major credit cards. One of the longtime Strip resorts, with 716 attractive rooms surrounding appealing landscaped grounds. Several garden

152 — CHAPTER THREE

rooms available. Amenities include a major showroom, health club, putting green, shuffleboard and tennis courts. As we type this, the hotel is about to expand from 755 to more than 2,000 rooms with the opening of a new tower.

Rooms from $50 to $69

Aladdin Hotel & Casino • ⌒⌒ ∅
3667 S. Las Vegas Blvd. (near Flamingo Road), Las Vegas, NV 89109; (800) 634-3424 or (702) 736-0111. Doubles $45 to $95, suites $250 to $350, penthouse $2,500. Major credit cards. A 1,100-room resort with stylishly new or refurbished rooms and suites; most are rather luxurious. The Aladdin is one of the more glimmery of the Strip casino resorts with a headliner room and assorted amenities.

Barbary Coast Hotel & Casino • ⌒⌒
3595 S. Las Vegas Blvd. (at Flamingo Road), Las Vegas, NV 89132; (800) 634-6755 or (702) 737-7111. Doubles and singles $50 to $75. Major credit cards. A 200-unit casino hotel with attractively furnished rooms; TV movies. Bright New Orleans style casino complex with entertainment, dining, race and sports book. Rooms follow the casino's 19th century theme with canopied four-posters, white lace and patterned wallpaper.

Dunes Hotel & Country Club • ⌒⌒ ∅
P.O. Box 93298 (3650 S. Las Vegas Boulevard at Flamingo Road), Las Vegas, NV 89119; (800) 243-8637 or (702) 737-4110. Doubles and singles $49 to $109, suites to $1,800. Major credit cards. Full-service casino resort with 1,100 large, color coordinated, nicely appointed rooms and suites. Complete resort amenities including a large gaming area, golf course, entertainment and several restaurants.

Flamingo Hilton • ⌒⌒
3555 S. Las Vegas Blvd. (Flamingo Road), Las Vegas, NV 89109; (800) 732-2111 or (702) 733-3111. Doubles $59 to $119, suites from $240 to $480; Bugsy Siegel's suite is $400. Major credit cards. Among the largest of Nevada's plush casino resorts with 3,555 rooms and suites; largest hotel in the Hilton chain. Most rooms are new or redecorated, with all the amenities. Resort features a large landscaped pool area, major showroom, several restaurants, tennis courts, health club and other amenities.

Golden Nugget Hotel & Casino • ⌒⌒⌒
P.O. Box 2016 (downtown at Fremont Street and Casino Center Boulevard), Las Vegas, NV 89125; (800) 634-3454 or (702) 385-7111. Doubles $58 to $110, suites $130 to $800. Major credit cards. Roomy, sumptuous units in downtown's largest and finest resort complex. Victorian style with four-poster beds and print wallpaper. Extensive resort facilities with a swimming pool, showroom, handsomely bright casino, spa and sauna and several restaurants.

Harrah's Las Vegas • ⌒⌒ ∅
3475 S. Las Vegas Blvd. (opposite the Mirage), Las Vegas, NV 89109; (800) 634-6765 or (702) 369-5000. Doubles $59 to $115. Major credit cards. Comfortable pastel rooms, with a showboat style casino up front. The 1,725-unit hotel is popular with families since the hotel is well-separated from the gaming area. Large video arcade, pool, spa and shops.

LAS VEGAS — 153

Riviera Hotel & Casino • ⌂⌂⌂
2901 S. Las Vegas Blvd. (Riviera Boulevard, opposite Circus Circus), Las Vegas, NV 89109; (800) 634-6753 or (702) 794-9451. Doubles $59 to $95, suites $125 to $310. Major credit cards. One of the Strip's senior resorts, featuring the world's largest casino, plus multiple restaurants and a major show lounge. When we last checked, the constantly-expanding Riviera had 2,200 rooms and counting. With all the expansion, it offers a wide mix of accommodations with various decorator looks.

Sahara Hotel & Casino • ⌂⌂⌂
2535 S. Las Vegas Blvd. (at Sahara Avenue), Las Vegas, NV 89119; (800) 634-6666 or (702) 737-2111. Doubles $55 to $100, suites $200 and up. Major credit cards. Another of the longtime Strip resorts, offering a good selection of new and older refurbished rooms; most are quite posh for the price. Other amenities include a landscaped pool area, major showroom, large casino and half a dozen restaurants. With its attractive lower-end prices, the hotel is booked every weekend of the year.

Stardust Resort & Casino • ⌂⌂⌂ Ø
3000 S. Las Vegas Blvd. (at Convention Center Drive), Las Vegas, NV 89109; (800) 634-6757 or (702) 732-6111. Doubles $40 to $200, suites $150 to $350; some older motel units in $30s off-season. Major credit cards. Extensive full-service complex with 2,500 nicely furnished rooms. Large showroom, comedy club, free gaming lessons, shopping arcade and all the other resort amenities.

Tropicana Hotel & Casino • ⌂⌂⌂⌂ K
P.O. Box 97777 (3801 S. Las Vegas Blvd. at Tropicana Avenue), Las Vegas, NV 89193; (800) 634-4000 or (702) 739-2222. Doubles $65 to $95, suites $260 to $525. Major credit cards. Pleasing tropical look accents the 1,908 rooms in this lush "Island of Las Vegas" resort. Amenities include a large swimming complex, major showroom, several restaurants and an impressive leaded glass ceiling in the main casino.

Rooms from $25 to $49

Arizona Charlie's Hotel & Casino • ⌂⌂ Ø
740 S. Decatur Blvd. (at West Charleston), Las Vegas, NV 89107; (800) 342-2695 or (702) 258-5111. Doubles and singles $25 to $35. Major credit cards. Small hotel with 100 rooms and pool; TV, some with refrigerators. Adjacent casino with restaurants, bowling alley, bingo and nightly live entertainment.

Binion's Horseshoe Hotel & Casino • ⌂⌂
128 E. Fremont St. (at Casino Center Boulevard), Las Vegas, NV 89101; (800) 622-6468 or (702) 382-1600. Doubles $25 to $55. Major credit cards. Rooms aren't fancy, but neither are the prices. A 380-unit hotel with a block-long casino in the heart of downtown. Room count was boosted to 380 with the acquisition of the 26-story Mint highrise. Rooftop pool on one of the towers.

Boardwalk Hotel-Casino • ⌂⌂ Ø
3750 S. Las Vegas Blvd. (near Harmon Avenue), Las Vegas, NV 89109; (800) 635-4581 or (702) 735-1167. Doubles $32 to $70, weekly rates available. Major credit cards. Simple but clean and comfortable rooms in this

201-unit hotel; one of the better buys on the Strip. Two pools and a coin laundry. Adjacent casino features some excellent food bargains.

California Hotel & Casino • ⌂⌂
P.O. Box 630 (12 Ogden Avenue at First Street), Las Vegas, NV 89125-0630; (800) 634-6255 or (702) 385-1222. Doubles and singles $40 to $50. Major credit cards. A 650-unit downtown casino hotel with pool and spas. The hotel is popular with Hawaiians and pastel floral patterns in the large rooms help make them feel at home. Adjacent casino with restaurants, entertainment, video game room, Hawaiian specialty shop; downtown RV park (see below).

Capri Motel • ⌂
3245 E. Fremont St. (east of downtown), Las Vegas, NV 89104; (702) 457-1429. Doubles $30 to $35, singles $20 to $25, kitchenettes $120 to $140 a week, suites $65. MC/VISA, AMEX, DISC. A 19-unit motel with TV, room phones and a pool.

Center Strip Inn • ⌂ ∅
3688 S. Las Vegas Blvd. (at Flamingo Road), Las Vegas, NV 89109; (800) 777-7737 or (702) 739-6066. Doubles $35 to $70, singles $25 to $70, suites $70 to $100. Major credit cards. A 92-unit motel with TV movies, VCRs, small refrigerators and continental breakfast.

Circus Circus Hotel • ⌂⌂ ∅
P.O. Box 14967 (2880 S. Las Vegas Boulevard, near Sahara Avenue); Las Vegas, NV 89109; (800) 634-3450 or (702) 734-0410. One to four people $30 to $44, sometimes as low as $19 during slow periods, the cheapest casino hotel rooms in town; some more expensive suites. Major credit cards. Simply furnished, inexpensive rooms draw families to this bright and cheery "big top" casino. Even with 2,800 rooms, they fill up fast during high season. Ongoing circus acts, carnival midway and full casino and dining facilities.

Crest Budget Inn • ⌂ ∅
207 N. Sixth St. (at Ogden Avenue), Las Vegas, NV 89101; (800) 777-1817 or (702) 382-5642. Doubles $32 to $45, singles $27 to $30, kitchenettes $135 to $155 a week. Major credit cards. A 155-unit motel with TV movies, VCRs, continental breakfast and refrigerators.

El Cortez Hotel • ⌂
600 Fremont St. (at Sixth Street), Las Vegas, NV 89101; (800) 634-6703 or (702) 385-5200. Doubles $23 to $40, extra person in room $3. Major credit cards. Older 308-unit hotel with small but neat and clean rooms; among the better buys downtown. Recently refurbished, it boasts one of the oldest original casinos in Las Vegas.

El Rancho Hotel & Casino • ⌂⌂
2755 S. Las Vegas Blvd. (just south of Wet 'N Wild water park); Las Vegas, NV 89109; (800) 634-3410 or (702) 796-2222. Doubles and singles $35 weekdays, $45 weekends and up to $70 for peak holidays. Major credit cards. A Mexican-Western style casino hotel with 1,000 rooms. Not fancy but fair-sized and comfortably furnished.

Excalibur Hotel & Casino • ⌂⌂ ∅ K
P.O. Box 96778 (3850 S. Las Vegas Blvd. at Tropicana Avenue), Las Vegas, NV 89193; (800) 937-7777 or (702) 597-7700. Doubles $29 to $69, suites

SO, WHERE TO THE LOCALS GO?

There is a theory, sometimes valid, that the best way to find the top attractions in a city is to ask someone who lives there.

The *Las Vegas Review-Journal* conducts a readers' poll each year to determine the best that the city has to offer. The paper admits that the results may be skewed, since some casino hotels encourage their employees to stuff the ballot box. Even without the stuffing, we wonder about the selections, since readers pick places like Wendy's for the best hamburger and 7-Eleven for the best coffee. (No gourmet burger joints in Las Vegas?)

However, for what it's worth, here some results from the most recent poll (1992). We're listing only items of likely interest to visitors.

Restaurants

Italian—The Olive Garden, 1545 E. Flamingo Road, 735-0082; and 1361 S. Decatur Blvd., 258-3453.
Asian—Chins, 3200 S. Las Vegas Blvd. (Fashion Mall), 733-8899.
Mexican—Ricardo's, 2380 E. Tropicana Ave., 798-4515.
Breakfast—Omelet House, 4850 W. Flamingo Rd., 251-3171.
Casino buffet—Golden Nugget, 199 E. Fremont St., 385-7111.
Seafood—Red Lobster, 2325 E. Flamingo Rd., 731-0119; and 200 S. Decatur Blvd., 877-0212.
Steak house—Circus Circus, 2880 S. Las Vegas Blvd., 734-0410.

Entertainment and recreation

Family attraction—Wet 'n Wild, 2600 Las Vegas Blvd., 737-3819.
Free entertainment—Circus Circus circus acts, 734-0410.
Best place to go on a budget—Red Rock Canyon.
Best place to dance—Shark Club, 75 E. Harmon Ave., 795-7525.
Singles bar—T.G.I. Friday's, 1800 E. Flamingo Rd., 732-9905.
Sports bar—Sneakers, 2250 E. Tropicana Ave., 798-0272.
Quiet Bar—Peppermill Inn, 2895 S. Las Vegas Blvd., 735-4177.
Museum—Lied Discovery Children's Museum, 833 N. Las Vegas Blvd., 382-KIDS.
City view—Sunset Mountain, at the end of Bonanza Street.
Weekend getaway/picnic area—Mount Charleston.

Casino hotels

Production show—"Splash" at the Riviera, 2901 S. Las Vegas Blvd., 794-9301.
Sports book—Las Vegas Hilton, 3000 Paradise Rd.
Comedy club—Catch a Rising Star at Bally's, 3645 S. Las Vegas Blvd., 739-4111.
Slot machines, keno lounge and video poker—Palace Station Hotel and Casino, 2411 W. Sahara Ave.
Poker room and blackjack tables—Binion's Horseshoe, 128 Fremont St.
Slot club—Gold Coast Casino, 4000 W. Flamingo Rd., 367-7111.
Neon display—Rio Casino Hotel, 3700 W. Flamingo Rd.
Architecture/Visitor photo opportunity—The Mirage, 3400 S. Las Vegas Blvd.

156 — CHAPTER THREE

$100 and up. Major credit cards. The world's largest resort hotel with 4,032 units. Simply furnished, inexpensive rooms are popular with families; more elaborate suites available. Family resort with a medieval castle theme; carnival midway, large casino, several restaurants, jousting tournament.

Fitzgerald's Casino Hotel • ⌒⌒
301 E. Fremont St. (at Third Street), Las Vegas, NV 89101; (800) 274-5825 or (702) 382-6111. Doubles $30 to $125. Major credit cards. Tall 650-unit hotel tower in the heart of downtown casino row. Neat "motel-modern" rooms; some have whirlpools for $10 extra. Irish-theme casino beneath.

Four Queens Hotel Casino • ⌒⌒ ø
202 E. Fremont St. (at Third), Las Vegas, NV 89101; (800) 634-6045 or (702) 385-4011. Doubles and singles $47 to $57. Major credit cards. A 170-unit downtown hotel. Rooms have modern décor or New Orleans look; TV movies, radios; refrigerators on request. Full casino facilities downstairs.

Fremont Hotel & Casino • ⌒
301 E. Fremont St. (at Third Street), Las Vegas, NV 89101; (800) 634-6182 or (702) 385-3232. Doubles $36 to $50. Major credit cards. Older 450-unit casino hotel with neat and prim rooms, recently refurbished. Not fancy, but good buys in the heart of Glitter Gulch.

Frontier Hotel & Gambling Hall • ⌒⌒
3120 S. Las Vegas Blvd. (Stardust Road opposite the Desert Inn), Las Vegas NV 89109; (800) 634-6966 or (702) 734-0110. Doubles $35 to $125, suites $210 to $300. Rooms have an earthy Southwestern look and reasonable prices; some rather fancy pool-side suites. Full casino and restaurant facilities adjacent.

Gold Coast Hotel & Casino • ⌒⌒⌒ ø ø
P.O. Box 80750 (4000 W. Flamingo Road, half mile west of I-15), Las Vegas, NV 89180; (800) 331-5334 or (702) 367-7111. Doubles $35 to $50, suites $100 to $400. Major credit cards. Appealing and inexpensive Spanish style rooms in attractive new 750-unit casino hotel just west of Las Vegas Boulevard. Large casino, movie theater, bowling alley and entertainment.

Hacienda Hotel • ⌒⌒
3950 S. Las Vegas Blvd. (south of Excalibur), Las Vegas, NV 89109; (800) 634-6713 or (702) 739-8911. Doubles $41 to $81, suites $135 to $375. Major credit cards. An 814-room resort offering several simply-furnished, comfortable and inexpensive units, along with fancier suites. Attractive resort with Spanish look to the rooms and casino; RV park adjacent.

Imperial Palace • ⌒⌒⌒ K
3535 S. Las Vegas Blvd. (near Flamingo Road), Las Vegas, NV 89109; (800) 634-6441 or (702) 731-3311. Doubles $25 to $125, suites $50 to $275. Major credit cards. Large 2,700-room casino resort. Simply furnished, attractive rooms with Oriental décor, plus some fancier suites with sunken Japanese "Luv Tubs." Asian theme casino with showroom, several restaurants and cocktail lounge; Imperial Palace Auto Collection in parking garage.

Palace Station Hotel Casino • ⌒⌒⌒ ø
P.O. Box 26448 (2411 W. Sahara Avenue at I-15 exit), Las Vegas, NV 89126-0448; (800) 678-2846 or (702) 367-2411. Doubles $35 to $65, suites $85 to $105. Major credit cards. New full-service casino resort with 1,041 at-

tractively furnished rooms. Restaurants, two swimming pools and spas, kids' arcade, other amenities.

Lady Luck Casino Hotel • ⌒⌒ ∅
P.O. Box 1060 (206 N. Third Street at Ogden Avenue), Las Vegas, NV 89125; (800) 523-9582 or (702) 477-3000. Doubles $39 to $75, suites $75 to $500. Major credit cards. A 792-room downtown casino hotel; TV movies, radios, refrigerators. Full casino facilities adjacent.

Las Vegas Club Hotel & Casino • ⌒⌒
P.O. Box 1719 (18 E. Fremont Street at Main), Las Vegas, NV 89125; (800) 634-6532 or (702) 385-1664. Doubles and singles $40 to $50, suites from $125. Major credit cards. Newly refurbished rooms with Southwestern décor; TV, radios and room safes. Casino, restaurants and entertainment.

Sam's Town Hotel & Gambling Hall • ⌒⌒ ∅
5111 Boulder Highway (east of downtown at Nellis Boulevard), Las Vegas, NV 89122; (800) 634-6371 or (702) 456-7777. Doubles and singles $40 to $45, suites $91 to $100. Major credit cards. A 197-room Western-style resort hotel with nicely furnished rooms, casino, bowling center, kids' playroom, the Western Emporium shopping complex, pool and other amenities.

Santa Fe Hotel & Casino • ⌒⌒ ∅
4949 N. Rancho Dr. (at Highway 95 north), Las Vegas, NV 89130; (800) 872-6823 or (702) 658-4900. Doubles and singles $35 to $45. Major credit cards. Attractive new 200-room casino hotel with a sleek Southwestern look. complex includes a skating rink, bowling center and large casino.

Showboat Hotel, Casino & Bowling Center • ⌒⌒ ∅
2800 Fremont St. (at Charleston), Las Vegas, NV 89104; (800) 826-2800 or (702) 385-9123. Doubles $36 to $45, as low as $20 in the off-season; suites $110 to $165. Major credit cards. A 500-unit hotel with neat, simply furnished rooms. Pool, casino, bowling center, kids' arcade, restaurants.

Jackie Gaughan's Plaza • ⌒⌒⌒
P.O. Box 760 (One Main Street at Fremont), Las Vegas, NV 89101; (800) 634-6821 or (702) 386-2110. Doubles $30 to $60. Major credit cards. Attractive, well-furnished and quite inexpensive rooms in one of downtown's top casinos. Facilities include pool, jogging track, tennis courts and showroom.

Vegas World Hotel-Casino • ⌒⌒
2000 S. Las Vegas Blvd. (at Main Street), Las Vegas, NV 89104; (800) 634-6277 or (702) 382-2000. Doubles and singles from $35, suites from $65. Major credit cards. A 1,313 unit hotel with full casino facilities, plus restaurants, kids' arcade and swimming pool. Simply attired, well-equipped room.

Villa Roma • ⌒⌒ ∅
220 Convention Center Dr. (just off Las Vegas Boulevard, near the Hilton), Las Vegas, NV 891009; (800) 634-6535 or (702) 735-4151. Doubles and singles $25 to $75. Major credit cards. A 100-unit motel on the Strip, with TV, in-room refrigerators and coffee makers. Pool, wedding chapel

Rooms under $25

Downtowner Motel • △ ∅
129 N. Eighth St. (at Ogden Avenue), Las Vegas, NV 89101; (800) 777-2566 or (702) 384-1441. Doubles $20 to $42, singles $20 to $30, kitchenettes

$135 to $155 a week. Major credit cards. A 200-unit motel with TV movies, VCRs, room refrigerators, continental breakfast and pool.

Gold Spike Hotel Casino • △
400 E. Ogden Ave. (at Fourth Street), Las Vegas, NV 89101; (800) 634-6703 or (702) 384-8444. Doubles $20, mini-suites $30; rates include breakfast. MC/VISA. Among the best room buys in town; small, neat and clean units with TV and phones. Low roller casino with penny slots and such.

Vacation Village • △△
6711 S. Las Vegas Blvd. (far southern end of Las Vegas Boulevard), Las Vegas, NV 89193; (800) 658-5000 or (702) 897-1700. Doubles $20 to $45. Major credit cards. Basic but neat and attractive rooms in a new 315-unit complex; one of the better bargains on the Strip. Southwest style casino adjacent with a couple of restaurants and a show lounge.

WHERE TO CAMP

Las Vegas RV parks, particularly those at the casinos, fill up quickly during peak fall and spring periods, particularly on weekends. Get there early in the day or make advance reservations.

California Casino RV Park • P.O. Box 630 (12 Ogden Avenue at First Street), Las Vegas, NV 89125-0630; (800) 634-6255 or (702) 385-1222. RVs only, full hookups $12. Reservations accepted; major credit cards. Showers, phones, laundry, recreation room, rec facilities, dog run and dump station. Adjacent to California Casino downtown, two blocks off Casino Center.

Circusland RV Park • At Circus Circus Casino, 500 Circus Circus Drive (just off Las Vegas Boulevard), Las Vegas, NV 89109; (800) 634-3450 or (702) 794-3757. RVs only, full hookups $10. Reservations advised well in advance; major credit cards. Showers, pay phones, laundry, provisions, Propane, dump station, swimming pool, sauna and spa. Monorail to main casino complex. Free RV parking is permitted nearby when RV park is full (which it almost always is); this does not include access to the pool, spa, laundry and shower facilities.

Hacienda Camperland • 3950 S. Las Vegas Blvd. (at Tropicana Avenue), Las Vegas, NV 89119; (702) 793-8214. RVs only, full hookups, $9.68 June through September and $14.95 the rest of the year. Reservations accepted in summer only; major credit cards. Showers, some picnic tables and barbecues, pay phones, laundry, Propane delivery, dump station, swimming pool and spa, tennis, horseshoes, volleyball, playground. Casino adjacent.

Las Vegas KOA • 4315 Boulder Hwy. (Desert Inn Road), Las Vegas, NV 89121; (702) 451-5527. RV and tent sites; full hookups $21.95 water and electric $19.95, tent sites $17.95. Reservations accepted; MC/VISA. Showers, picnic tables, pool, spa, pay phones, Propane, convenience store with slots, rec room with video games and pool table, kids' playground; free shuttle to the Strip.

Sam's Town RV Park • 5111 Boulder Hwy. (at Nellis Boulevard east of downtown), Las Vegas, NV 89122-6089; (800) 634-6371 or (702) 454-8055. RVs only, full hookups, $7.50 June through September, $10 the rest of the year. Reservations accepted; major credit cards. Two separate parks with showers, phones, laundry, recreation rooms, horseshoes, swimming pools and spas and pet runs. Casino adjacent.

> *"Only two commodities have allowed the vast populating of the arid Southwest—water and hydroelectric power."*
>
> — Dexter K. Oliver, *Desert Lifestyle Magazine*

Chapter Four
LAS VEGAS NEIGHBORS
Exploring lands of fire, ice and water

We're going to assume that you're comfortably entrenched into affordable lodging in Las Vegas and will use that as your base for further exploration. We have thus fashioned this chapter into a series of day trips from Glitter City.

These treks will carry you through a land of surprising variety, from the russet ramparts of the Valley of Fire to the snowy reaches of Mount Charleston and the booming "desert Riviera" of Laughlin. You'll explore the shoreline of Lake Mead and the towering mass of Hoover Dam, so essential to the survival of Las Vegas. Had men not battled to tame the Colorado River and fought for their share of its water and electricity, there would be no Glitter City.

Incidentally, Nevada's southwestern tip is a great place to explore in winter, since you can skid down the slopes of Lee Canyon Ski Area and skitter across the surface of Lake Mead on the same day.

VALLEY OF FIRE-LAKE MEAD LOOP

This 150-mile round trip takes you northeast along Interstate 15, then south to the Lost City Museum at Overton, to Valley of Fire State Park, then through Lake Mead National Recreation Area to Hoover Dam and Boulder City. You can make it a two-day outing by continuing 80 miles south to Laughlin.

Interstate 15 provides a quick vehicular shot through the bland creosote bush desert northeast of Las Vegas. At the **Moapa River Indian Reservation**, you might pause at a smoke shop to load up on fireworks and other essentials. Continue on to **Glendale,** then turn south on State Highway 169 toward **Logandale** and **Overton.** This green farming valley along the Muddy River, a refreshing break from the beige desert, was settled more than a century ago by Mormons.

Earlier Americans realized the valley's agricultural potential as well. The Anasazi farmed along the Virgin and Muddy rivers ten centuries before,

THINGS TO KNOW BEFORE YOU GO

BEST TIME TO GO • As in Las Vegas itself, these neighbors attract most of their visitors from fall through spring. Climate varies considerably, of course, from the snowy heights of Mount Charleston to the sizzling depths of Laughlin. Because it's 1,500 feet lower than Las Vegas, Laughlin is consistently warmer, with very balmy mid-winter temperatures.

WHAT TO SEE • Overton's Lost City Museum, Henderson's Clark County Heritage Museum, the sculpted wonderlands of Valley of Fire State Park and Red Rock Canyon, plus Red Rock's Spring Mountain Ranch State Park, Lake Mead National Recreation Area's Alan Bible Visitor Center and Hoover Dam, of course, and perhaps Davis Dam.

WHAT CASINOS TO SEE • In Laughlin, the Riverside, Colorado Belle, Golden Nugget, Ramada Express, Flamingo Hilton, Gold River and Harrah's Del Rio; plus the Nevada Landing at Jean and Peppermill Resort in Mesquite.

WHAT TO DO • Skid the slopes of Lee Canyon Ski Area and perhaps take a winter sleigh ride at Mount Charleston Village; have a sunset dinner at the Mount Charleston Hotel; hike to the White Domes area at Valley of Fire and crawl among the rocks of the Calico Hills of Red Rock Canyon; sip wine at the Pahrump Valley Winery; cruise Lake Mead on the Desert Princess and rent a speedboat, fishing boat or house boat at any of several Lake Mead National Recreation area marinas; take the Hoover Dam tour.

Useful contacts

Boulder City Chamber of Commerce, 1497 Nevada Hwy., Boulder City, NV 89005; (702) 293-2034.

Lake Mead National Recreation Area, 601 Nevada Highway, Boulder City, NV 89005-2426; (702) 293-8907.

Laughlin Visitors Bureau, P.O. Box 29849, Laughlin, NV 89029; (702) 298-3321.

Mesquite City Hall, P.O. Box 69, Mesquite, NV 89024; 346-5295

Las Vegas Ranger District, Toiyabe National Forest, 550 E. Charleston Blvd., Las Vegas, NV 89104; (702) 388-6255; for the Mount Charleston area.

Red Rock Canyon National Conservation Area, Bureau of Land Management, P.O. Box 26569, Las Vegas, NV 89126; (702) 647-5000

Valley of Fire State Park, P.O. Box 515, Overton, NV 89040; (702) 397-2088.

Area radio stations

You can pick up the Las Vegas stations, of course; see previous chapter. Also, these come through in various neighborhoods:

KREC-FM, 98.1, Brian Head, Utah (areas east of Las Vegas)—top 40

KWEST-FM, 97.7, Laughlin-Bullhead City—60s through 90s pop hits

KRRI-FM, 105.5, Boulder City—vintage rock and pops

building a 30-mile-long string of pueblos, romantically and erroneously labeled the Lost City. They are indeed lost now, melted back into the soil from which they were formed; some are drowned under Lake Mead. However, excavations have yielded a trove of Anasazi and later Paiute relics, now on display at one of Southern Nevada's finer museums. You'll find it on a rise to your right, a mile south of Overton; watch for the rather small sign.

Lost City Museum • *P.O. Box 807, Overton. NV 89040; (702) 397-2193. Daily 8:30 to 4:30; $1 for anyone over 18. Native American crafts and gift shop.* Built as a Civilian Conservation Corps project during the Depression, the adobe museum with its log and brush ceiling bears a fair resemblance to the "lost" pueblos that it commemorates. The interior contains excellent displays concerning the agriculture, weapons, social lives, arts and crafts of the Anasazi and later groups. Particularly interesting are exhibits concerning the excavations, accomplished mostly by the "CCC boys" who worked for a dollar a day, plus meals and tent shelter. Minerals, fossils and petroglyphs complete this extensive collection. Outside, one can climb a notched log ladder into a pit house and poke into a above-ground adobe. These are reconstructions, since only foundations of the original villages were found.

Travelers had known of the ruins for more than a century; Jedediah Smith came across them in the 1820s. Serious excavations began in the 1920s, and were accelerated with the realization that Lake Mead would forever bury some of the relics. To spur interest in the project and draw visitors to the museum, state tourist officials came up with the "Lost City" tag.

South of the museum, Highway 160 enters the upper reaches of **Lake Mead National Recreation Are**a. However, before becoming too engrossed with this water-and-desert playland, follow signs west to one of our favorite Nevada haunts:

Valley of Fire State Park • *P.O. Box 515, Overton, NV 89040; (702) 397-2088. Visitor center open daily 8:30 to 4:30. Scheduled ranger programs. Campground beautifully situated among red rock formations; with flush potties at section "A" and pit toilets in unit "B"; both have water, tables and barbecues. No hookups; $4.* Although we've described this outing as a one-day loop tour, you might be tempted to spend most of that day marveling at the incredible red rock shapes of the Valley of Fire. In fact, we spent two full days here, returned for part of a third and left reluctantly, still wanting to explore more. Whatever your schedule, be here during early or late light when shadows accent the myriad shapes. New drama comes after sunset, as the russet formations emit an eerie alpenglow.

Approaching the park from the west, you'll first encounter an interpretive shelter and **Elephant Rock,** a much-photographed formation that's everybody's favorite stone pachyderm. In the shelter, you'll learn that the valley was created not by fire, but by deposits of iron-laced sandstone 150 million years ago. Contoured by winds and later smothered by ocean deposits of limestone, the land has been warped and eroded into a wonderland of shapes and colors. Predominately red, the terrain also reveals marbled streaks of limestone beige, sexy magentas from manganese deposits, along with yellows and greens from assorted other minerals.

From the main drive you can explore some **stone cabins** built by those CCC boys during the park's early days, the **Seven Sisters monoliths**, several **petrified logs**, the **stone "Beehives"** and **Atlatl Rock**, rich with pre-Columbian petroglyphs. At the visitor center, tucked into the base of a

— Betty Woo Martin

Petrified pachyderm towers over the author at Valley of Fire State Park.

fiery weather-sculpted escarpment, pick up a brochure listing the park's features and hiking trails, then drive out to Rainbow Vista. En route, a short walk takes you through a narrow, convoluted canyon to **Mouse's Tank**, a natural water hole where a drop-out Indian once sought sanctuary.

At **Rainbow Vista**, follow a 1.5 mile trail along the edge of Fire Canyon to **Silica Dome**. A seven-mile round trip hike delivers you to our favorite part of the park, the remote **White Domes** area, rich in multi-colored formations. Both trails are former roads, starting at the edge of the Rainbow Vista parking area. For Silica Dome, stay on the main road/trail; for White Domes, take a left branch after a few hundred feet.

From the White Domes Trail, hike up some of the fantastically eroded dry washes. (Off-trail hiking is permitted in this park.) Get down on your knees to study subtle marbling of cross-bedded deposits left by ancient sandstorms, now cast in soft stone. Note the subtle burgundies, pinks, magentas and rosès, swirled together in a petrified confection.

Once you've explored the park, retrace your route out the eastern entrance. It's time to patronize a lake and a dam that have changed the face of the West more than any other object created by man.

Lake Mead and Hoover Dam

The story of the West is the story of water. Range wars were fought over water rights. Rich placer mines lay idle for lack of water to separate gold from gravel. Farms shriveled and died during drought years or when cities stole their upstream water.

"Whiskey is for drinking; water is for fighting," Mark Twain once observed.

Nowhere is the role of water more evident than in this arid corner where Nevada, California and Arizona converge. Here, the mighty Colorado

River, now backed up by Lake Mead, forms a squiggly state border. Walk a hundred feet from the shoreline, and you're in a thirsty desert. Annual rainfall, as little as three inches, supports creosote bush and a few critters with the good sense to keep out of the noonday sun, and not much else.

Rio Colorado once ran untamed through this desert, drying to a trickle in late summer, then flooding downstream farmlands during spring runoff. Now, it has been harnessed by nearly a dozen dams along its extended reach from Colorado's rocky mountain high to the Gulf of California.

The grandest of these is Hoover Dam, built during the Depression as one of the largest public works projects in history. The completion of the 762-foot concrete dam in the narrow, steep-walled Black Canyon marked the end of the free-flowing Colorado and the beginning of major development along its shorelines. And certainly, it pulled neighboring Las Vegas from its dusty doldrums, first providing construction jobs, and then water and power for future growth.

More than 5,000 men, working in shifts around the clock, finished the massive structure two years ahead of schedule. When it was completed in 1935, it was the world's highest dam, holding back the world's largest manmade reservoir. It has been declared one of America's seven civil engineering marvels. It was alternately called Boulder Dam and Hoover Dam until Congress made the Hoover name official in 1947.

Lake Mead National Recreation Area

As you depart Nevada's first state park, you soon enter America's first federal recreation area, established in 1935 as Boulder Dam Recreation Area. Now Lake Mead NRA, it's the third largest unit of the National Park System outside Alaska, with more than 1.3 million acres. It's also the fourth most-visited, drawing nine million souls a year.

Although Lake Mead National Recreation Area is named for one of the world's largest artificial lakes, 87 percent of its surface is land area, taking in great slices of Nevada and Arizona desert. However, with balmy spring and fall climate and temperatures routinely topping 100 in summer, most folks head for the wet. Both the Nevada and Arizona shorelines are lined with marinas. Similar facilities touch the shorelines of **Lake Mohave** to the south, also part of Lake Mead NRA. Fishing is excellent on the two reservoirs, according to people who do that sort of thing. Fisherpersons often catch their limits of striped and largemouth bass and rainbow trout.

Heading south from Valley of Fire, you'll note that Lake Mead's **Northshore Scenic Drive** doesn't skim the edge of the reservoir. It remains some distance inland to avoid desert washes that cut the irregular shoreline. Short drives will take you to the assorted marinas. Most offer boat launching and rentals, serious bait shops, camping, picnic areas, swimming and sundry other services. Here's a review of marinas and other lures, in order of appearance along Northshore Drive:

Overton Beach ● *Picnic area, marina, store, RV Park with full hookups, $15 per night; (702) 394-4040.* Overton also offers free primitive camping on a scraped-away chunk of desert, down near the water.

Echo Bay ● *Oleander-shaded campsites for $6, with water, tables and barbecue grills; no hookups; also full service RV park for $17.* This large marina complex also has a motel and restaurant (listed below), convenience store, speed boat and houseboat rentals.

Callville Bay • *Camping for $6, with water, tables and barbecue grills; no hookups.* Other facilities include a marina and launch ramp, houseboat, speed boat and fishing boat rentals, a convenience mart, snack shop and attractive cocktail lounge with a deck overlooking the lake. The former Mormon settlement of Callville lies under the lake, just offshore.

Las Vegas Wash • *A $6 campground with the usual facilities, no hookups; plus a marina and picnic area.*

Lake Mead Fish Hatchery • *Daily 8 to 4; free.* The hatchery is worth a brief browse if you to like to view zillions of fingerlings in concrete rearing troughs. Graphics in the visitor center discuss the art of fish farming.

Lake Mead Resort and Marina • *Floating dock complex, with boat and water ski equipment rentals, snack shop, convenience store and Tail O' the Whale restaurant (listed below), plus onshore motel; (702) 293-3484.* **Desert Princess** *cruises; $12 for adults, $5 for kids. Also breakfast, dinner and dance cruises, from $16.50 to $32; (702) 293-6180.* The Desert Princess is a handsome quasi-paddlewheeler offering hour and a half voyages to the face of the dam and back. The flatwater excursion is about as stimulating as a trip on a moving sidewalk. However, the narration is interesting and so are the views. The paddlewheeler chugs past the Precambrian schist of narrow Black Canyon and pauses before the face of the dam, providing a fishes eye glimpse of this great concrete wall and its giant Art Deco intake towers.

Boulder Beach • *Campsites at Hemenway Harbor for $6; picnic tables, barbecues, water and flush potties, with no hookups. A trailer village offers full hookups for $17, with showers and such.* Other facilities include a swimming area, picnic tables, marina and boat launch.

Alan Bible Visitor Center • *At the corner of North Lakeshore Drive and U.S. 93; daily 8:30 to 5.* This is an excellent interpretive center, with films on Lake Mead and Hoover Dam construction, wildlife exhibits, gift shop and bookstore and a botanical garden out front. A fifty-cent *Lake Mead Auto Tourguide* booklet, available here, details driving trips on the Nevada and Arizona sides of Lake Mead and Lake Mohave. Lake Mead NRA brochures list the area's nine marinas—six on Mead and three on Mohave. For a complete list of marinas and their facilities, contact: Lake Mead National Recreation Area, 601 Nevada Highway, Boulder City, NV 89005-2426; (702) 293-8907.

Hoover Dam • *Phone (702) 293-8367. Guided tours $1 for adults; kids under 15 free. Daily 8 a.m. to 6:45 p.m. Memorial Weekend through Labor Day; 9 a.m. to 4:15 the rest of the year; closed Christmas Day. Small visitor center on the Nevada side open 8 a.m. to 7:30 p.m. Memorial Weekend through Labor Day; 8:30 to 5 the rest of the year. (All times are Pacific.)*

The dam is three miles down Highway 93 from the Alan Bible Visitor Center. Rough hewn hills cradle Black Canyon, providing a dramatic setting for this great spade-shaped wedge of concrete. The highway twists through craggy peaks into narrow canyon, then crosses the dam into Arizona. If you park and look dizzily down the curving sweep of concrete, you'll sense the immensity of this project.

Expect traffic jams during the early 1990s, since construction is under way to improve parking and to build a new visitor center. Completion, depending on the whims of federal funding, is anticipated at mid-decade. During busy periods (any weekend and most summer days), you'll have to park some distance away and catch shuttles to the dam. Most of the parking is on the Arizona side (including RV parking). Also, you'll likely have to wait for an available tour. To avoid the rush, get there early.

You'll be assaulted by friendly tour-guide superlatives as you're taken through this engineering marvel. The dam is 660 feet thick at the base, tapering to 45 feet at the top and it contains 4.4 million cubic yards of concrete. Behind it, Lake Mead can hold ten trillion gallons of water, enough to cover Pennsylvania a foot deep. (Ever wonder who figures out these things?) The lake reaches 110 miles north and east toward the Grand Canyon and has a surface area twice the size of Rhode Island.

"At peak capacity, 118,000 six-packs per second go through penstocks that feed 17 generators," our guide burbled happily.

She said the dam was built beyond specifications, designed to last 2,000 years. She didn't add that Lake Mead likely would be silted up by then, and Hoover Dam would be holding back nothing but a giant alluvial fan.

The dam is a handsome structure, finished with striking Art Deco trim. Copper doors, ornate grill work, fluted intake columns in the forebay and sleek winged statues seem designed for a world's fair instead of a flood control project. Further, it was built with tourism in mind. Visitors are taken deep into the concrete wedge on oversized elevators and escorted through the dam's innards along terrazzo-tiled hallways. From balconies, they stare down into the giant generator rooms, where millions of kilowatts are sent humming throughout the Southwest.

If the tour works up an appetite, visit the "Snacketeria" built over the dam's forebay, offering hot dogs, hamburgers and similar fare. There's a gift shop adjacent. For $3.95, you can take home a souvenir coffee mug that tells all your friends (unfortunately): "I ate a dam dog at the Hoover Dam Snacketeria."

Boulder City

Population: 2,500 **Elevation: 1,232**

One of America's first planned communities, Boulder City sits on a knoll seven miles from the dam. It's a pretty little place, fronted by a park that adds a rich splash of green to this tawny desert.

Like the dam, this company town was built with esthetics in mind. The old arcaded business district along Arizona Street is a well- preserved Art Deco Main Street USA. Downtown's centerpiece is the gleaming white Dutch colonial Boulder Dam Hotel, with a handsome turn of the century lobby. Old Boulder City has earned a spot on the National Register of Historic Places. Its newer suburbs are more modern, typical of any middle class community.

Boulder City is, as we mentioned earlier, the only community in Nevada that prohibits gambling. However, a gaming parlor between the dam and the town fills that need:

Gold Strike Inn, Hotel & Casino • ☺☺

Highway 93, Boulder City, NV 89005; (800) 245-6380 or (702) 293-5000. The casino has a bright, cheerful Western look with a frontier town façade, brass chandeliers and red flocked wallpaper. All the table games are here: one craps, one roulette and several blackjacks. You'll find a good selection of nickel slots and video poker machines, plus some rare ten-cent slots. A fine display of old gaming machines and ornate cash registers occupies one wall. See below for dining and lodging specifics.

ATTRACTIONS

Boulder City/Hoover Dam Museum • *444 Hotel Plaza (P.O. Box 516), Boulder City, NV 89005-0516; (702) 294-1988. Daily 9 to 5; admission $1 for adults; 50 cents for seniors and children under 12.* This small museum in the Boulder City historic district exhibits photos, documents and artifacts concerning Hoover Dam's construction. A gift shop sells souvenirs, and a film relates the story of the dam project. Nearby, along Arizona Street and Hotel Plaza, you can stroll beneath the sidewalk overhangs of the Art Deco shops and stores of old Boulder City.

Boulder Dam Hotel • *1305 Arizona St., Boulder City, NV 89005; (702) 293-1808.* Restored to its 1930s Art Deco look, this fine old hotel is worth a peek even if you don't need a room. Step into the fashionable lobby with its oak paneling, period furnishings and brick fireplace. Have a drink beneath the heavy wood beams of the Spillway Lounge, decorated with pictures of the dam and early Boulder City.

WHERE TO DINE
Boulder City and Lake Mead

Carlos Mexican Dining • ☺☺ $$
1300 Arizona St. (Hotel Plaza), Boulder City; (702) 295-5828. Mexican; dinners $8 to $15; full bar service. Tuesday-Sunday 4 to 10 p.m. MC/VISA. Attractive little Mexican cafe with bentwood chairs, white nappery and silk flowers on the tables. Typical smashed beans and rice, plus steak, *fajitas* and crab tostadas.

Echo Bay Restaurant • ☺☺ $$
Echo Bay Resort, Lake Mead; (702) 394-4000. American; dinners $9 to $15; full bar service. Monday-Thursday 7 a.m. to 8:30 p.m., weekends and holidays 7 to 9:30. MC/VISA. Nautical-looking place with a seafood menu and enough lanyards, halyards and other rigging to launch a four-master.

Gold Strike Steakhouse • ☺☺ $$
At Gold Strike Inn Casino, Highway 93, Boulder City; (702) 293-5000. American-continental; dinners $8 to $15; full bar service. Major credit cards. Elegant, clubby restaurant with high backed chairs and dark woods. Lunch and dinner buffets $4.23.

Tail O' the Whale • ☺☺ $$
At Lake Mead Marina, Lake Mead; (702) 293-2074. American; dinners $9 to $15; full bar service. Sunday-Thursday 7 a.m. to 9 p.m., Friday-Saturday 7 to 10. MC/VISA. Mostly seafood, with specials such as sautéed skillet shrimp and brochette of shrimp in tomatoes and peppers. Typical nautical decor.

WHERE TO SLEEP

Boulder Dam Hotel • ⌂⌂ $$
1305 Arizona St., Boulder City, NV 89005; (702) 293-1808. Doubles $30 to $50. Major credit cards. Many guest rooms have been redone with period decor such as wrought iron beds, lace curtains and print wall coverings. Facilities include restaurant, cocktail lounge, pool and spa.

Echo Bay Resort • ⌂⌂⌂ $$$
On Lake Mead, c/o Overton, NV 89040; (800) 752-9669 or (702) 394-4000. Doubles $69 to $89. Major credit cards. Attractive large rooms with TV,

phones, many with lake view. Laundry, restaurant and marina facilities adjacent.

Gold Strike Inn • ⌒⌒ $$
Highway 93, Boulder City, NV 89005; (800) 245-6380 or (702) 293-5000. Singles and doubles $31 to $57. Major credit cards. Part of the Gold Strike Casino; rooms have TV, phones and oversized beds.

Lake Mead Resort • ⌒⌒ $$$
322 Lakeshore Rd., Boulder City, NV 89005-1204; (800) 752- 9669 or (702) 293-2704. Doubles $50 to $65. Major credit cards. Simple but comfortable rooms with phones, TV; many with lake views. Restaurant and marina facilities adjacent; Desert Princess cruises (see above).

BACK TO LAS VEGAS VIA HENDERSON

To complete your loop, continue west on Highway 93 and then northwest on U.S. 93/95 to **Henderson,** a pleasantly nondescript Las Vegas suburb. You'll pass **Railroad Pass Hotel Casino** just short of the town; it's worth a browse if you have some loose change. Just beyond Railroad Pass, you have a choice of two routes—Boulder Highway, which delivers you into the heart of downtown Las Vegas (after an eternity of stoplights) or the U.S. 93/95 expressway, which gets the job done quickly.

Boulder Highway will take you past **Clark County Heritage Museum,** which you must see if you haven't already. (Details under **The best attractions** in the previous chapter.) You'll also pass several suburban casinos, topless bars, "fantasy" video shops and "official" Las Vegas visitor centers.

Several more casinos are gathered around downtown Henderson, where low-rolling locals cash their Friday paychecks, put aside the rent (hopefully) and try their luck. Among the more attractive places here is the El Dorado Casino at 140 Water Street. It offers 25-cent keno, ten-cent roulette, 94-cent hot dogs, 99-cent breakfasts and other food bargains. It's also the only place in southern Nevada where I won substantially at video poker, which can be attributed either to dumb luck or generous payouts. To find the downtown gaming parlors, turn west off Boulder Highway onto Lake Mead Drive, then south onto Water Street after a couple of blocks.

SOUTH TO LAUGHLIN

Before returning to Glitter City, you may choose to continue south on Highway 95 to Laughlin, that new riverside community that's growing like a well-watered weed.

The route south is quick, straight and uneventful, through the dreary creosote bush desert of a bowl-shaped valley. You'll pass through **Searchlight,** which offers a bit of history and little else. Gold was discovered there at the end of the last century and mining continued until wartime demands shut it down in the 1940s. Today, it is little more than a slight widening of the road, with a few weathered buildings housing a general store and a small saloon-casinos. If you like remote marinas, you can follow a paved road 14 miles east of here to **Cottonwood Cove** on the Lake Mohave shore of Lake Mead National Recreation Area. It offers camping ($6), a trailer park, marina, restaurant, mini-mart, picnic area, swimming beach, laundry and boat rentals.

Ten miles south of Searchlight is **Cal-Nev-Ari,** a planned hamlet started along an abandoned airstrip in 1965. Despite its namesake homage to the three states that converge nearby, it hasn't grown much. Another ten miles takes you to State Highway 163, and a 20-mile drive over the Eldorado Mountains to Don Laughlin's curious dream town.

Laughlin

Population: 3,000 **Elevation: 540 feet**

What started as a bankrupt bait shop in a nameless riverside hamlet may soon become the second largest gambling center in Nevada. That's right, students. Laughlin is expected to pass Reno in both visitor traffic and gaming revenue within the next few years. It's already in third place, ahead of Lake Tahoe, drawing two million visitors a year.

Why is this town in the hot, dusty southern tip of Nevada growing so quickly? What's attracting Nevada's biggest casino operators to spend millions on glitzy new gaming parlors and high-rise hotels, way out in the middle of noplace?

The river itself provides one of the answers. Rio Colorado, its flow slowed here by downriver Parker Dam, adds an appealing dimension to this booming desert community. A river walk links many of the gaming resorts, and shuttle boats scurry about, stopping at various casinos and bringing visitors from large parking lots on the Arizona side. We aren't suggesting that the river is beautiful. The banks are barren and Arizona's Bullhead City across the way is rather unsightly. But it *is* cool and inviting, offering an abundance of water sports. Many hotels rent water play equipment.

Price and location add to the Laughlin success picture. Hotel rooms and food are much cheaper here than in Las Vegas, and the town is ideally situated to draw both Arizona and California visitors. In fact, 70 percent of Laughlin's tourists come from those two states, and 80 percent of them treat it as a destination resort. Since Laughlin is less than 25 years old, most of the casinos are modern and spacious, unlike the stuffy gaming parlors of yore. Many have picture windows on the river.

Laughlin is a particular favorite of senior citizens, since neighboring Bullhead City is one of Arizona's largest winter snowbird roosts. And these are folks with time on their hands and discretionary income in their pockets. Many spend the warm winter in their motorhomes, filling dozens of RV parks along Bullhead's shoreline. Laughlin is a virtual RV city from fall through spring and the casinos appear to be hosting geriatric conventions.

Although the town has only one "formal" RV park, most larger casinos invite RVers to park free, providing night lighting, refuse barrels and other conveniences. In fact, this section of our book was researched with our VW camper *Ickybod* resting in the Gold River RV lot, his blunt nose nearly hanging over the Colorado River. Where else can you get free camping with a river view?

Most towns are named for some long-expired pioneer, but the founder of Laughlin is alive and well and laughing all the way to the bank. Michigan-born Don Laughlin came to Las Vegas in 1954, tended bar, dealt cards, saved his money and bought a small gaming parlor. In 1966, at age 33, he sold the club and, with an unlimited gaming license in his pocket, he began casting about for a place to increase his fortunes.

He was drawn to a small beach called Sandy Point, across the Colorado River from Bullhead. There was no town here; only a bankrupt bait shop and a scruffy motel. He put $35,000 down on the complex (including six acres of river front), moved his family into some of the motel rooms and began building a small casino hotel called the Riverside. It drew little attention at first, but a few folks liked the Riverside's riverside location. They began coming over from Bullhead City and other nearby points in California and Arizona. Within a few years, Laughlin was booming as if someone had discovered gold in the river's sands. Indeed, Mr. Laughlin had!

The young entrepreneur practically built Laughlin's infrastructure, spending $1 million on street improvements and $3 million on a bridge to Bullhead City, plus $6 million to expand Bullhead's airport, thus encouraging feeder lines to establish scheduled air service.

Eight casinos now line a two-mile stretch along the river bank, ranging from the small Pioneer Gambling Hall to the smart new Harrah's Del Rio, easily one of the most attractive gaming resorts in the state. A ninth casino, Ramada Express, is parked across Casino Drive, the main street.

Where's the *real* Laughlin?

Your first question upon arrival may be: "Where's the rest of the town?" Other than casinos, Laughlin has virtually no business district, although a few facilities are emerging inland. Bullhead City, an unplanned scatter as ugly as its name, provides most of the bedrooms and supermarket services for Laughlin's 10,000 (and growing) employees. Bullhead is experiencing its own boom, now topping 35,000 population.

The best way to commute among the casinos is to catch the 50-cent **casino bus** operated by Laughlin Transit. Free shuttle boats that churn across the river to large Bullhead City parking lots also cruise between casinos; ask individual operators where they go. Catch one of the shuttles after dark and watch the casino lights cast rippling reflections across the water. That's as close to pretty as Laughlin ever gets. From midstream, the riverboat-shaped Colorado Belle Casino almost looks believable.

You can pick up Laughlin literature and discount goodies at the **Laughlin Visitors Bureau,** across the street from the Riverside Casino. It's operated jointly by the Las Vegas Convention and Visitors Authority and the Laughlin Chamber of Commerce. Helpful ladies will try to find hotel space for you. It's a good idea to make advance reservations, however. Except in mid-summer, hotel occupancy rates hit 98 percent! Even in summer when it sizzles, occupancy remains rather high.

Laughlin's casinos offer no Las Vegas style revues, although some headliners—mostly country stars—perform here. Lounges offer the usual assortment of musicians and singers, and Sandy Hackett (comedian Buddy's kid) has opened a comedy club at the Gold River. Touring Laughlin's casinos is simple, since they're neatly aligned along the river. We offer a preview, starting from the first—and certainly the most historic.

Don Laughlin's Riverside Hotel & Casino • ☺☺☺

P.O. Box 500, Laughlin, NV 89029; (800) 227-3849 or (702) 298-2535. This is the casino that hatched the town—at least, a smaller and earlier version of it. Not surprisingly, the town board meets in an upstairs room here. The casino's Gay Nineties look is bright and cheery, with coffered ceiling, globe chandeliers and mirror tiles. The large complex has three movie theaters, two swimming pools, a Western dance hall (where you can learn the cowboy two-step), and a 600-unit RV park (listed below).

Check the display of antique gaming devices in the main casino. And if you want to relieve houses guests of their loose change, you can buy antique or relatively new slots at a shop here, from $1,700 and up.

Entertainment: Country stars such as Charley Pride, Waylon Jennings and Mel Tillis perform in the Celebrity Theatre, the only major showroom in Laughlin. Things get lively after hours in the Losers' Lounge.

Dining: The stylish, clubby **Gourmet Room** features American and continental fare from $16 to $25, serving Sunday-Thursday 5 to 10 and Friday-Saturday 5 to 11. An all-you-can-eat salad bar is a **Prime Rib Room** feature, where dinners are $7 to $20. The **buffet** offers river views.

Lodgings: The 660 rooms offer a pleasing Southwest look with warm fall colors; doubles are $34 to $42 Sunday-Thursday and $53-$62 Friday-Saturday; lower in summer. No-smoking rooms available.

Flamingo Hilton • ☺☺☺

1900 S. Casino Dr. (P.O. Box 30630), Laughlin, NV 89029; (800) 292-3711 or (702) 298-5111. The requisite flamingo pink even carries to the tinted windows in this large, sleek Florida-modern high rise. The casino decor is clean, bright and spacious with high, pink coffered ceilings, beaded lighting and picture windows on the river. Resort facilities include a swimming pool, spa, tennis courts, gift shops, large video arcade and summer "Funland Carnival."

Entertainment: Club Flamingo features celebrity clones in the "American Superstars" show, brightened with special multi-media effects.

Dining: The Hilton **Beef Barron** is replicated here, with a rustic log look and antler chandeliers; the menu is mostly beef and barbecue; prices are $10 to $14; daily 4 to 9 p.m. The 24-hour **Lindy's** is a pleasing rendition of a New York/Miami deli with black and white tile on the floor and corned beef and pastrami on the menu. The **Flagship Buffet** has river view seating.

Lodging: Attractive rooms, many with river views, are $18 to $35 Sunday-Thursday and $45 to $75 Friday-Saturday. Non-smoking units available.

Edgewater Hotel & Casino ☺☺

2020 S. Casino Dr. (P.O. Box 30707), Laughlin, NV 89028; (800) 67-RIVER or (702) 298-2453. The lofty Edgewater Hotel has a sleek Southwestern look, although the large casino is rather plain. It's a Circus Circus enterprise, with little of the glimmer and trappings of its downriver cousin, Colorado Belle. Facilities include a swimming pool, spa and water sports.

Dining: The **Hickory Pit** offers American barbecue, veal and seafood from $12 to $18; open 4 to midnight. The 24-hour **Garden Room** has good dining deals, such as orange roughy dinner for $4.25 and all you can eat hot wings for $3.95. There's also a breakfast-lunch-dinner **Buffet**.

Lodging: The Edgewater is one of Laughlin's larger properties, with 1,450 rooms tucked into its tower. Simple, nicely appointed units with a Southwestern look go for $22 to $27 Sunday-Thursday and $44 to $49 Friday-Saturday. No-smoking units are available.

Ramada Express Hotel-Casino • ☺☺☺

2121 S. Casino Dr. (P.O. Box 658), Laughlin, NV 89028; (800) 2-RAMADA or (702) 298-4200. The only casino on the west side of the street, Ramada

Express is a pleasing study in "early American railroad." The exterior has the green and cream façade of an oversized stationhouse and the interior is a-brim with railroading memorabilia, tulip chandeliers with brass trim and wafting ceiling fans. The registration desk suggests an oldstyle ticket counter and the casino is fashioned into a high-ceiling waiting room, with appropriate railroading signs. Employees complete this turn-of-the-century vision, wearing striped shirts with gartered sleeves and long dresses.

Entertainment: An oldstyle saloon features periodic live entertainment. For outdoor amusement, you can catch a free train ride around the parking lot; it's also useful as a shuttle for arriving patrons.

Dining: The **Steakhouse** reflects the early railroading theme with burgundy walls and brass accents, suggesting a fancy salon car; prices are $13 to $22 for mesquite broiled steaks, freshwater trout and other American fare; daily 5 to 10 (until 11 weekends). The **Dining Car** is the requisite 24-hour coffee shop with essential American grub from $5.25 to $12. You can get a bit rounder at the **Roundhouse Buffet.**

Lodging: Much roomier than Pullman berths, the fashionable units are done in warm greens and dark woods, with prices from $29 to $34 weekdays and $49 to $59 weekends. Smoke-free rooms are available.

Colorado Belle • ☺☺☺

2100 Casino Dr. (P.O. Box 2304), Laughlin, NV 89028; (800) 458-9500 or (702) 298-4000. A bright and cheery paddlewheeler run aground, the Belle also is a Circus Circus operation. More cheerful than the next-door Edgewater, it carries a pleasing riverboating theme from bow to strobe-lighted paddlewheel. Inside, red flocked wallpaper, sweeping grand staircases and beaded staircases transport gamblers downriver to New Orleans. Facilities include two swimming pools and spas in enclosed courtyards and water sports.

Entertainment Brassy-voiced can-can girls show a lot of leg, bloomer, garter and gusto at a thrice-a-day Bourbon Street Review on a stage open to the casino. This place *jumps!*

Dining: The Belle offers some of the best and most varied dining buys on the river. The **Orleans Room** is the gourmet place, with Southern fare such as seafood Creole and blackened red snapper, plus continental dishes; $14 to $20. The **Mississippi Lounge** features seafood and **Mark Twain** peddles barbecued chicken and ribs; price range at both is $5 to $7. You can get $6.95 prime rib and lobster tail and other entrées for $5 to $10 at the 24-hour **Paddlewheel.** It gets even cheaper at the **Captain's Food Fare,** with meals from $1.99 to $4.99.

Lodging: Doubles are $22 to $32 weekdays and $49 to $59 weekends. The 1,288 rooms have that old-timey nautical look, many with balconies.

Pioneer Hotel & Gambling Hall • ☺

P.O. Box 29664, Laughlin, NV 89028; (800) 634-3469 or (702) 298-2442. Looking rather out of place among the gleaming new Laughlin fun parlors, the Pioneer is a modest little joint. With its woodsy Western look, it must have floated downriver from downtown Las Vegas. A covered wagon on the front lawn completes the down-home look, and the interior is busy, crowded and smoky. Outdoor facilities include a pool and tennis courts. A reincarnation of the Pioneer's original Vegas Vic stands out front. However, he doesn't wave and say: "Howdy, welcome to downtown Laughlin."

Dining: Granny's is the most attractive entity in the smoky, rather drab casino, with a pleasing Victorian-American look. Granny must be a helluva shot, because pheasant, buffalo steak, venison and elk are featured on the menu. Prices are $12 to $22; hours are 5:30 to 9:30. Lunch **buffet** is $3.75, dinner buffet and Sunday brunch go for $4.45.

Lodgings: Vaguely Western in look and quite comfortable, the 415 low-rise, fair-sized rooms go for $28 to $35 weekdays and $39 to $45 weekends. Riverfront rooms range from $55 for doubles to $75 for mini suites. All prices are for one to four people.

Golden Nugget-Laughlin • ☺☺

2300 S. Casino Dr., Laughlin, NV 89028; (702) 298-7111. We'll have to wait and see what Steve Wynn of Mirage fame has in store for the Golden Nugget. A major renovation project may be finished by the time this chapter inspires you to travel to Laughlin.

Wynn purchased Del Webb's Nevada Club recently and quickly built a multi-level garage to shelter patrons' cars from the summer sun. He's begun remodeling the casino and plans are laid for an elaborate $200 million highrise hotel. When we visited, we were greeted at the casino entrance by a Wynn trademark—a smaller version of his Mirage rain forest. The theme will expand as renovation and new construction continue.

Dining: The tropical transition continues in the 24-hour **River Cafe,** offering inexpensive American fare from $6 to $10, such as veal Acapulco, Southern fried chicken and liver and onions. There's also a **buffet.**

Gold River Gambling Hall & Resort • ☺☺☺

2700 S. Casino Dr. (P.O. Box 77700), Laughlin, NY 89029-7770; (800) 835-7904 or (702) 298-2242. Like the Golden Nugget, the Gold River is a casino in transition. Built by the Boyd Group as Sam's Town Gold River, it now has new owners who are busy with refurbishment and remodeling. It was at this writing an imposing 21-story tower with "mine shaft modern" decor in and out. Some of the webbed steelwork and work shed façade may have been removed by the time you arrive.

The casino is (or was) very spacious, with industrial strength beam ceilings, from which dangle (dangled) neon names of famous Nevada mines and mining companies. The new brochure suggests that it will have a "Gold Rush era Victorian theme." Whatever the look, the resort offers an abundance of slots, some with river views, swimming pool and spa. Sandy Hackett's Comedy club features stand-up comics and Roxy's Saloon offers live entertainment and music for dancing.

Dining: An interesting stone and log cabin motif embodies **Sutter's Lodge** serving American and continental fare; $13 to $19. **Smokey Joe's** is the 24-hour coffee shop and the **Opera House** buffet features $3 breakfast, $4 lunch and $6 dinner.

Lodging: Roomy rooms with Southwestern touches are $22 to $27 weekdays and $35 to $40 weekends. Non-smoking rooms are available.

Harrah's Del Rio • ☺☺☺☺ ∅

2900 S. Casino Dr. (P.O. Box 33000), Laughlin, NV 89028; (800) 447-8700 or (702) 298-4600. Set in its own little cove apart from the other casinos, elegant Spanish-style Harrah's is the classiest place in town. High beamed ceilings, tile floors, gleaming white walls and strolling mariachis create a convincing south-of-the-border ambiance. It even has a Spanish courtyard and tolling mission bell. Colors, of course, are predominately salmon and turquoise. The spacious gaming venue is divided into twin riverview casinos; one is smoke-free.

It's also the only resort with a real beach on the river (as opposed to concrete beach walks). A pool and patio are adjacent. On a slope above, the RV Plaza Convenience Center offers fuel, a mini-mart, free RV parking and even a free shuttle down to the riverside casino. With all these appointments, Harrah's can properly call itself Laughlin's only true destination resort.

Dining: The cozy, river-view **William Fisk's Steakhouse,** open at 5 p.m., offers assorted seafoods, chops, venison and quail, from $15 to $20. **Cafe Colorado** features American dishes and lots of sandwiches; $8 to $14; open 24 hours. Of course there's a Latino place—**El Hacienda,** with stuff such as stuffed *sopatilla* and lobster enchiladas; $7 to $19; nightly 5 to 10. **Del Rio** is the buffet, serving breakfast, lunch and dinner.

Lodging: Harrah's 957 rooms offer warm Latin colors and all the usual resort amenities at bargain prices: $29 to $55 weekdays and $49 to $70 weekends and holidays. Suites and patio rooms range from $75 to $90. Smoke-free units are available.

WHERE TO CAMP

Riverside Resort RV Park • P.O. Box 500, Laughlin, NV 89029; (800) 227-3849 or (702) 298-2535, ext. 645. Full hookups, $14. Reservations accepted with three weeks' advance notice; major credit cards. Across the street from and operated by Laughlin's Riverside Resort. Laundry, showers, dump station, access to resort's swimming pools and other amenities.

Sportsman Park • Just below Davis Dam, north of Laughlin. No hookups, $6. Flush potties but no showers; river access. Run by Clark County Department of Parks and Recreation.

Free RV parking • Limited facilities at Harrah's Del Rio, Gold River, Flamingo Hilton and Ramada Express.

ATTRACTIONS & ACTIVITIES

Antique slot machine exhibit • *Inside Laughlin's Riverside Casino; free.* Devices include a rare 1892 carousel floor machine and some of the quasi-legal slots that were popular after gaming machines were outlawed. They include as a 1922 Mills slot machine that issued mints and a 1931 Jennings that dispensed golf balls.

Davis Dam • *Just north of Laughlin; for information, write: Superintendent, Davis Dam, Bullhead City, AZ 86430. Free self-guiding tours daily, 7:30 a.m. to 3:30 p.m. (Arizona time)* Sixty-five miles downstream from Hoover Dam, Davis forms craggy, steep-walled Lake Mohave, the lower pond of Lake Mead National Recreation Area. It provides flood control and sends hydroelectric power into the Southwest. Tours take you into the concrete and earthfill structure, where you can look down the line of huge humming turbines. Stepping onto the dam's lower deck, you can watch the water boiling up from their penstocks. From here, it flows briefly downstream past Laughlin's casino row before bumping into another reservoir formed by its near twin, Parker Dam.

River cruises • **Blue River Safaris,** *P.O. Box 507 (in Laughlin's Riverside Hotel & Casino), Laughlin, NV 89029; (800) 345-8990 or (702) 298-0910.* Hour and a half narrated motor launch cruise up to Davis Dam, then downriver past the casinos. **Laughlin River Tours, Inc.** *P.O. Box 29279*

174 — CHAPTER FOUR

(at the Edgewater Casino), Laughlin, NV 89029; (800) 228-9825 out of state only, or (702) 298-1047 and 298-2453, ext. 3877. The Little Belle *150-passenger sidewheeler offers cruises along the riverfront to Davis Dam.*

Free river cruises • They're offered by most major hotels between Laughlin and Bullhead City and among the casinos; some operate 24 hours.

RED ROCK-PAHRUMP-MT. CHARLESTON LOOP

Looking for a little variety? This 200-mile round trip takes you through wondrous geological shapes, to a pretend wild west town and Nevada's only winery, past a few cat houses, then from cactus to pines and back to cactus.

The loop trip circles the Spring Mountains, a dramatic alpine island rising 35 miles northwest of Las Vegas. We suggest an early start to catch first light at Red Rock Canyon, and perhaps a late finish, with dinner in either of two sky view restaurants in the ramparts of Mount Charleston. Also, plan the trip over a weekend, Friday through Monday, so you can tour the Spring Mountain ranch house in Red Rock Canyon.

To begin, head west out Charleston Avenue (State Highway 159), passing the Southwest-style suburbs of expanding Las Vegas. After about ten miles, you'll see the folded, russet ramparts of our first attraction.

Red Rock Canyon National Conservation Area • *c/o Bureau of Land Management, P.O. Box 26569, Las Vegas, NV 89126; (702) 647-5000. Visitor center open daily 9 to 4; free. Conducted hikes and nature programs. Loop drive open 8 a.m. to 6 p.m. Free primitive camping along Oak Creek Road..*

More of an eroded cliff face than a canyon, Red Rock is a 13-mile fault extending along the base of the Spring Mountains. A BLM brochure describes it best: "At Red Rock Canyon, the gray carbonate rocks of an ancient ocean have been thrust over tan and red sandstone in one of the most dramatic and easily identified thrust faults to be found."

Around 65 million years ago, the Keystone Fault was jammed upward; it then weathered through the centuries, creating an incredibly convoluted face. Narrow canyons invite hikers to explore nature's sculptures. Most are reached from a 13-mile **scenic drive** starting at the **visitor's center**, which you see on your right, shortly after entering the preserve. Bunkered into a desert slope, the sandstone-colored center offers fine exhibits on flora and fauna and the geological and human history of the canyon.

Your first stop on the scenic drive is most dramatic: a tumbled collection of red, gray and beige rocks appropriately called the **Calico Hills.** The red slash of Calico's upper strata is a vivid landmark, visible for miles. Short trails take you down into this twisted, swirling strata, which suggests a stone marble cake or perhaps a storm-tossed petrified ocean.

Continuing around the drive, you can pause for hikes into **Lost Creek, Icebox** and **Pine Creek canyons**. Each takes you into sculpted desert washes of the Keystone Fault. The circular drive returns you to the main highway about two miles south of the visitor's center. Before continuing on south, backtrack briefly to **Red Rock Overlook,** where graphics describe the forces that created the natural wonder before you.

Following Highway 160 south along the face of the fault, you'll encounter two significant attractions tucked into this rough-hewn escarpment.

Spring Mountain Ranch State Park • *P.O. Box 124, Blue Diamond, NV 89004; (702) 875-4141. Grounds open daily 8 a.m. to 5 p.m.; ranch house* open Friday-Monday 10 to 4, closed Tuesday-Thursday; $3 entry fee. Picnic area, self-guiding tours of house and grounds.

The presence (or non-presence) of Howard Hughes adds a special mystique to this attractive ranch oasis, which sits at the base of Spring Mountain's craggy face. Views from the ranch house and grounds are awesome. The ranger on duty admitted spending a good share of his time staring out the windows. Visitors can stroll through furnished rooms, admire a free form swimming pool, loaf under the sheltering shade of poplars, olives, sycamores and cottonwood, or take a picnic down by the parking lot.

Spring Mountain Ranch dates from 1876 when one James B. Wilson homesteaded the land. Initially a working ranch, it later became a hideaway for people of means. Chester Louck, the Lum of Lum and Abner, owned it from 1948 to 1955 and built the present cut sandstone and redwood ranch house. German actress Vera Krup lived here from 1955 until her death in 1967. The next owner was billionaire Howard Hughes, then living in a Desert Inn high roller suite. There is no record that he ever set foot on his ranch, although it was used as a Summa Corporation hideaway by Robert Mayhew and other execs. It was sold to the state of Nevada in 1972.

Old Nevada and Bonnie Springs • *Old Nevada, NV 89004; (702) 875-4191. Old Nevada western town open daily from 9:30; adults $5.50, kids 3 to 11 and seniors $4.50. Stagecoach rides $5 for adults and $3 for kids. Petting zoo free. Bonnie Springs Motel rooms $55 to $75 for doubles, $85 to $95 for kitchenettes and up to $125 for suites (rates include Old Nevada admission). Breakfast rides for motel guests $15. Bonnie Springs Restaurant serves Western style fare; dinners $11 to $16; full bar service. Daily 8 a.m. to 10 p.m. MC/VISA, AMEX.*

Bonnie Springs is a good example of what happens to an historic ranch without preservation-minded owners or state park protection. Like Spring Mountain Ranch, it occupies a dramatic setting at the base of red rock ramparts. It traces its origins to 1843, when it served as a way station on the Old Spanish Trail. It is today a large, busy and rather scruffy tourist complex with features good and bad. The restaurant is pleasingly rustic, filled with Western doodads. Its adjacent bar is festooned with neckties surrendered by dudes foolish enough to arrive in city duds. Rooms at the adjacent motel are clean and neat, with nice Western touches.

On the down side, the petting zoo is ratty and one feels quick sympathy for its inmates. Next-door Old Nevada is a wanna-be frontier town built for tourists. It offers the requisite shoot-outs and false-front stores selling worry stones, plastic cactus, cowboy hats and other pointless curios. Although it's supposed to be rustic, it could use a tad of paint here and a fresh nail there. The Opera House invites patrons to watch "mellerdramas" while seated on folding gym chairs and the styrofoam silver mine needs work. However, the wax museum offers a nice quick study of Nevada history. You can get hamburgers, snacks and real sarsaparilla at the **Miner's Restaurant**.

At least, the place presents a positive attitude. As folks approach the ticket booth, they're greeted by exuberant young men in cowboy clothes, who may announce: "Welcome folks! You're just in time to see a real live hangin'! At least, it starts out that way."

From Old Nevada, your route takes you south past **Blue Diamond,** a company town for the James Hardie Gypsum Mine. At State Highway 160, swing right and begin a quick climb up to **Mountain Springs Summit,** past the scalloped cliff faces of **Potosi Mountain.** This is the area where—if you'll recall our Las Vegas history—members of the early Mormon settlement tried unsuccessfully to get the lead out of a mine.

Pahrump

Population: 12,000   **Elevation: 2,695 feet**

From the pass, you descend quickly into the **Pahrump Valley.** The curious name comes from the Paiutes, who occupied an oasis here; it means "plenty of water" or "water on a flat rock." You shortly enter the scrawny suburbs of Pahrump, an unplanned scatter of a community strewn across the high desert. Once an alfalfa and cotton growing area, this valley now sprouts double-wides, prefabs and a few real houses.

Two miles short of the small business district, on an upslope to the right, you'll encounter Nevada's vinicultural pride and joy:

Pahrump Valley Winery ● *Highway 160 at Homestead Road, Pahrump; (702) 727-6900. Free tours and tasting daily 10 to 4:30. Gift shop, wine sales and Tastings restaurant (see below); MC/VISA.* Opened in mid-1990, Nevada's first and only winery is housed in a striking mission-style structure, gleaming white with a blue tile roof. The winery is strictly state of the art, a study in stainless steel and polyurethane. The building interior is state of the decorator's art, with brass sconces and artworks on crisp, white walls.

Everything is classy about this place except the wine, which is produced mostly from an ordinary hybrid white grape called Symphony. It's a well-made wine—crisp, clean and quite drinkable, but don't expect the taste of an awesome Chardonnay or provocative Chenin Blanc. Ten acres of Symphony vines are being nurtured on the rocky desert slopes, although the wine we sipped was produced from juice trucked in from California.

Continuing on into Pahrump, you can gamble away a some time in the **Saddle West Casino-Hotel** downtown. It's rather new, with a Western motif, offering the usual array of games, with plenty of nickel machines and low table minimums. Antique slot machines, weapons and arrowheads are displayed in the casino's **Old West Showroom.**

Across the street is **Blackjack Fireworks,,** one of Nevada's few fireworks stores not on an Indian reservation. This place is so loaded with explosives that you feel nervous just walking in with a book of matches in your pocket. Bins are filled with strings of ladyfingers, nasty-looking cherry bombs and other holiday weapons we haven't seen since we were kids.

WHERE TO DINE AND SLEEP

Tastings Restaurant ● ☺☺☺ ∅∅

At Pahrump Valley Winery; (702) 727-6900. American-continental; dinner $10 to $20; wine and beer. Daily noon to 2 and 5 to 9, (until 8 on Sunday). Reservations accepted; MC/VISA. Stylish dining room done in white, beige and brass, with mirrored walls and arched windows; warm-weather patio. Busy menu ranges from filet and scampi to duck l'orange, almond chicken and assorted pastas.

Days Inn ● ⌂⌂ ∅

P.O. Box 38 (Highway 160 at Loop Road); (800) 325-2525 or (702) 727-5100. Doubles $29 to $40. Major credit cards. New 45-unit motel with TV, room phones; some spa tubs and efficiency units; pool.

Saddle West Hotel-Casino ⌒⌒
P.O. Box 234, Pahrump, NV 89041; (800) 522-5953 or (702) 727-5953. Doubles $19 to $29, suites $49 to $89. Major credit cards. Good-sized rooms in a new complex that includes a casino, showroom with live entertainment, kids' video arcade, pool and spa. **Silver Spur Restaurant** serves American fare 24 hours; dinners $5 to $9, plus specials for as little as $2. The outdoor **Redwood Patio** serves Western style barbecue.

WHERE TO CAMP

Pahrump Station RV Park • *P.O. Box 38 (Highway 160 and Loop Road), Pahrump, NV 89041; (702) 727-5100. RVs only; $12 for full hookups. Reservations accepted; MC/VISA.* Adjacent to Days Inn; showers, cable TV, pull-throughs, laundry, pool.

Saddle West Hotel-Casino • *P.O. Box 234, Pahrump, NV 89041; (702) 727-5953. Free RV parking, no tents or hookups.* Facilities in adjacent casino.

Although most of the Pahrump Valley is in Clark County, the western edge and the town of Pahrump are in Nye County, where prostitution is legal. Since bustling Las Vegas is a short drive away, the valley has developed a dual personality. It shelters one of the state's larger concentrations of brothels and one of its fastest-growing retirement communities. **Venus Massage and Bath** cat house is just north of town, opposite the Pahrump Valley Winery on Homestead Road. If you follow Homestead west, you'll encounter the legendary **Chicken Ranch,** which inspired the *Best Little Whorehouse in Texas* movie and Jeannie Kasindorf's book, *Nye County Brothel Wars.*

As you continue this loop trip north on Highway 160, you'll pass into the Amargosa Valley and see more evidence of Nye County's naughtiness. Signs invite motorists to the remote hamlet of **Crystal**, whose population is devoted primarily to copulation. Its **Cherry Patch Ranch** is popular with Las Vegas high rollers. You'll likely see a limo rolling along the one-mile road to this lonely sanctuary of sex, which consists of a few bungalows and doublewides. Signs point down a short lane to **Mable's Whorehouse,** although the place appeared to be closed when we passed through. Crystal also has an airstrip, handy for those seeking a jetset application of the term "quickie."

"Cherry Patch House of Prostitution" a large sign reads simply. The Patch is open 24 hours and credit cards are accepted. Next-door Madame Butterfly's Bath and Massage Salon needs no further introduction. If you're more curious than frisky, you can stop for a friendly drink at the nicely appointed Cherry Patch cocktail lounge. You also can pull a few slot machine handles (probably safer and less expensive than having yours pulled).

Mount Charleston

Five miles from the Crystal turnoff, you hit U.S. Highway 95. Turn south to begin the final leg of your loop around the Spring Mountains. After 40 miles of boring greasewood desert, turn right onto State Highway 156 to begin a rapid transition from spines to pines. Incidentally, there is no gasoline on the mountain, so you might want to tank up in Pahrump.

Toiyabe National Forest's Spring Mountains playground offers welcome and sometimes snowy relief from the desert lowlands. Its centerpiece is Mount Charleston, Nevada's third highest peak, at 11,918 feet. Folks flock to this area the year around, to hit Lee Canyon's slopes in winter and to camp,

— **Betty Woo Martin**

Mount Charleston's forests offer quick refuge from the summer desert heat.

picnic and play among the pines in summer. Don't expect solitude at this altitude; more than a million people are drawn here each year.

The arrow-straight climb up Highway 156 offers an intriguing botanical transition. You leave the yucca and creosote bush desert floor, climb through stands of hairy-armed Joshua trees, segue into a pinon-juniper woodland and complete the transition into ponderosa pines. In less than an hour, you pass through four life zones. After the snow melts, a fifth can be reached on foot, if you have the gear, patience and inclination to hike nine miles to Charleston's crest. Unless you're in excellent shape, it should be taken in two days.

Most visitors are content to admire these craggy heights from the lowlands, pitching tents and parking RVs at assorted campgrounds, hiking less demanding trails and enjoying the alpine comforts of area resorts.

Highway 156 passes Charleston's craggy crest and ends at a parking lot in **Lee Canyon.** In summer, you can hike to a small grove of **bristlecone pines,** or trek five miles to a larger bristlecone stand high in Charleston's flanks. In winter, you can strap on the sticks and schuss the slopes of **Lee Canyon Ski Area.** This small complex offers three lifts; a ski shop, rentals and lessons and a coffee shop and cocktail lounge with an appealing view of the slope. Skiers can choose from a dozen runs, ranging from beginner to advanced. (Details below.)

From Lee Canyon, backtrack briefly and take the crossover road (route 158) to Highway 157. You'll enjoy some awesome desert floor views from here, particularly if you pause to take the short **Desert View Senses Trail.** Near the juncture with Highway 157, note the striking **Mount Charleston Hotel,** a monumental chalet perched on a mountain shelf.

Above the hotel, route 157 takes you past the pine-shaded summer homes of **Mount Charleston Village** in Kyle Canyon. The road terminates at **Mount Charleston Restaurant,** a Swiss chalet-style lodge (see below). From a nearby picnic area, a pair of two-mile round-trip trails lead to **Cathedral Rock** and **Echo Cliff.** Another trail at the end of a gravel road in upper Kyle Canyon takes you two miles to **Mary Jane Falls.** These trails are moderately steep; the views are worth the exertion.

From here, a quick downhill run on Highway 157 returns you to U.S. 95, which gets you back to Las Vegas within 20 minutes. If you've followed our suggestion to have dinner at the Mount Charleston Hotel or Mount Charleston Restaurant, you'll witness a dazzling display of night lights as you approach Glitter City.

WHERE TO DINE AND SLEEP

Mount Charleston Hotel • ⌂⌂⌂ $$$

Mount Charleston Village, NV 89124; (702) 872-5500. Doubles $49 to $69, suites to $150. Major credit cards. This handsome, monumental log structure is akin to some of the grand national park chalets. It's a tempting retreat, either overnight or for dinner in the octagonal dining room with its lofty pitched ceiling. Views from the Cliffhanger cocktail lounge and from the picture-window restaurant are properly stirring. Hotel facilities include a spa, sauna and small gaming area with a few slot machines. The **Canyon Dining Room** serves American-continental fare from 8 a.m to 10 p.m.; dinners $12 to $20; full bar service. Reservations accepted.

Mount Charleston Restaurant & Lounge • ☺☺ $$$

Mount Charleston Village, NV 89124; (800) 955-1314 or (702) 386-6899. American-continental; dinners $16 to $26; full bar service. Daily 8 a.m. to 9 p.m.; bar open 24 hours. Reservations accepted; MC/VISA. This rustic mountain hideaway has been drawing Las Vegans for a quarter of a century. Try the roast breast of wild duck, sautéed buffalo medallions, the "Wild Mountain Platter" of rabbit, quail, venison and pheasant, or more domesticated dishes. Or sit and sip an Irish coffee at the circular fireplace, and perhaps listen to the brassy melodies of a Swiss band.

MOUNTAIN ACTIVITIES

Camping, hiking, picnicking and the like • *Contact the Las Vegas Ranger District, Toiyabe National Forest, 550 E. Charleston Blvd., Las Vegas, NV 89104; (702) 388-6255; office open weekdays 8:30 to 5. Trail guides, maps and general information available.* Mount Charleston campsites are at **Kyle Canyon, Fletcher View** and **Hilltop**, $7 per night, pit potties with no hookups, seven-day limit. Generally closed by snow in winter. You'll also find several picnic areas and hiking trails on the mountain, described above.

Horseback riding and sleigh rides • *Mount Charleston Riding Stables, Highway 157 (in Kyle Canyon, near Mount Charleston Restaurant), Mount Charleston, NV 89124; (702) 872-7009. Open daily all year; major credit cards.* Horseback rides starting at $18 per hour, plus Fletcher Canyon wilderness ride for $38 (three hours), hay wagon rides and winter sleigh rides.

Skiing • *Lee Canyon Ski Area, State Highway 156, Mount Charleston, Las Vegas, NV 89124; (702) 646-0008; ski school 872-5462; snow and road conditions 593-9500. Open daily from Thanksgiving to Easter, with snow machines to ensure good skiing. Lifts operate 9:30 to 4. All-day tickets $23 for adults and $15 for kids and seniors; half-day $18 and night skiing $20.* If you've flown into Las Vegas, you can catch a bus to the slopes by calling

646-0008. The ski facility also operates **Ski Lee Rentals** at 2395 N. Rancho Road in Las Vegas, offering rental equipment, lift tickets and whatever else you might need for this desert-to-ski experience.

Winter visitors will find snow play areas just below the ski area, suitable for tubing, sledding and cross-country skiing.

MAKING A RUN FOR THE BORDERS

In recent years, large casino-hotels have bloomed like neon flowers on Nevada's highway frontiers. Most of these places appear to be thriving, suggesting that Nevada-bound travelers can't wait to get inland to find some action. Busy Interstate 15 nurtures two such complexes, on either side of Las Vegas at the California and Arizona borders. Because land is cheap out here, food and rooms at these places are very inexpensive. We're listing them here because we don't know where else to put them.

Stateline and Jean

Population: thousands of slot machines   Elevation: 2,200 feet

Sixty percent of southern Nevada's visitors are from southern California. If you're part of this majority and you're driving, you'll encounter your first Las Vegas neighbors at Stateline (a non-place) and Jean (barely a place).

Stateline is merely a geographic expression, describing the point at which I-15 pierces the skin of Nevada. Here, investors have built two large casinos smack on the border, **Whiskey Pete's** and **Primadonna**. That's all there is to Stateline, folks: two casinos and a freeway interchange. They're linked by a free monorail—supposedly the only one in America crossing an interstate freeway.

Whiskey Pete's Casino Hotel ● ☺☺

P.O. Box 93718, Stateline, NV 93718; (800) 367-PETE or (702) 382-4388. Major credit cards. This place seems to have an identity problem, with a medieval castle façade, and an old West theme inside. Visitors are greeted at the door by the bullet-riddled "Bonnie and Clyde car." Outlaws Bonnie Parker and Clyde Barrow were slain in this 1934 Ford V-8 during a Louisiana shoot-out with the law. Beyond, you'll find a Western-style casino with the usual machines and table games, featuring plenty of low-roller action.

Dining: The low-roller theme carries into the 24-hour coffee shop, where you can get a $3.25 prime rib dinner and other fare from $4 to $10. **Ernesto's Cantina** serves basic smashed beans and rice dishes at similar prices. There's also a **buffet** for breakfast, lunch and dinner.

Lodging: Room rates are a bargain as well: singles and doubles for $16 Sunday-Thursday and $29 Friday-Saturday. Suites go up to $150. Guest facilities include two swimming pools and a spa.

Camping: Pete's offers free RV and truck parking, with no hookups.

Primadonna Resort & Casino ● ☺☺

Mailing address: P.O. Box 95997, Las Vegas, NV 89193-5997; (800) 367-7383 or (702) 382-1212. Major credit cards. Primadonna has a bright New England carnival theme, with a Ferris wheel out front. If you have kids in tow, you may prefer it to Pete's, since it also has a large video arcade, an indoor merry-go-round and a circus-theme restaurant. While your rug-rats ride the plastic carousel horses, you can find a good selection of gaming devices in the main casino.

Dining: The 24-hour **Animal Crackers** restaurant serves basic American fare at very basic prices: as little as $1.95 for a huge platter of fried chicken and biscuits. (Mine had run out of steam on the steam table, but I *like* chewy chicken.) Other meals range up to $10. The **Skydiver**, with an oldstyle aviation theme, peddles pasta, barbecue and steak dinners for $5 to $10; it opens nightly at 5.

Lodging: Primadonna's rooms are $18 Sunday-Thursday and $31 Friday-Saturday; a pool and spa are in a landscaped area behind the hotel.

A dozen miles inland, after passing the Las Vegas Convention & Visitors Authority's **Nevada Welcome Center** (open daily 8 to 5), you'll encounter the tiny hamlet of **Jean**. Again, you're greeted by a pair of casinos, **Nevada Landing** and **Gold Strike**, shimmering like neon mirages in the greasewood desert.

Nevada Landing Hotel & Casino • ☺☺☺

P.O. Box 19278, Jean, NV 89019; (800) 628-6682 or (702) 387- 5000. Major credit cards. This paddlewheel steamer ran aground a long way from water, bringing the dock with it. The brightest thing between Baker and Las Vegas, Nevada Landing has a neon- draped steamship and highrise pier facade. The interior is stylish as casinos go, with large beaded chandeliers, plush red wallpaper and knurled ceiling beams.

Dining: A pleasing oldstyle riverboat cafe, simply called **The Restaurant,** serves assorted American fare from $4.50 to $9; open nightly 4 to 9. The **Chinese Restaurant** is open Friday-Tuesday 5 to 11; dinners are $6 to $12. Or you can hit the 24-hour **coffee shop** or the **buffet** line.

Lodging: Attractive and rather spacious rooms are $16 Sunday- Thursday and $29 Friday-Saturday; there's a pool out back.

Gold Strike Hotel & Gambling Hall • ☺☺

P.O. Box 278, Jean, NV 89109; (800) 634-1359 or (702) 477- 5000. Major credit cards. Gold Strike's bright and busy façade suggests a cross between a Western movie set and Tune Town. The interior look is Gay Nineties, with rusty reds and dark woods. In addition to the usual gaming assortment, the place features live entertainment and a kids' arcade.

Dining: The **Dante** restaurant is one of the more attractive in this borderland limbo, with a clubby look of burgundy and dark woods. The menu is American-continental; $8 to $19. A **buffet** and **Burger King** complete the dining selection.

Lodging: Rooms with a "modern Gay Nineties" look go for $16 weekdays and $29 weekends, with suites from $19 to $45. There is, of course, a pool and spa.

Mesquite

Population: 2,000   **Elevation: 1,597 feet**

Sitting on Interstate 15's Nevada-Arizona border eighty miles east of Las Vegas, Mesquite is another popular casino crossing, luring visitors from both Arizona and nearby Utah. Unlike Stateline/Jean, it's a town of some substance, dating from 1880 as a Mormon farming and ranching center. It has experienced explosive gains of late, doubling its size to become Nevada's statistical growth champion between 1980 and 1990.

The rural enclave sits near the banks of the Virgin River in a rural valley, backdropped by the 8,000-foot **Virgin Mountains.** A few buttes and other eroded shapes mark this area as a gateway to the nearby Arizona-Utah canyon lands. Take time to pause at the town's one cultural lure:

Desert Valley Museum • *31 W. Mesquite Blvd. (346-5705); open Monday through Saturday from 9 to 4. Free; donations appreciated.* The museum shelters the usual collection of old photos, elderly slot machines, farm machinery and—good grief—an antique birthing table. The building is a museum piece as well, constructed in 1941 as a library and later used as a hospital.

An alarming chunk of downtown Mesquite is occupied by the extensive **Peppermill Casino** complex, about a mile from the border. The town's only other gaming parlor of note is the new **Virgin River Casino,** just inside the state line. A **Nevada Welcome Center,** operated jointly by the Las Vegas and Visitors Authority and the Nevada Commission on Tourism, is across the freeway from the Virgin River place. When we visited, a third casino was under construction, next door to the welcome center.

Peppermill Resort • ☺☺☺

Mesquite Boulevard (P.O. Box 360), Mesquite, NV 89024; (800) 621-0187 or (702) 346-5232. Major credit cards. Rivaling many of the larger casino resorts in Las Vegas, the attractive Peppermill complex includes a large gaming area, tennis courts, golf course, putting green, six swimming pools, spas, a mini-mart and shopping arcade, kids video parlor, miniature golf, three restaurants, a 728-room hotel and nearby riding facilities at Arvada Ranch.

Dining: The **Steakhouse** serves American-continental fare Sunday-Thursday 5 to 10 and Friday-Saturday 5 to 11; dinners $12 to $20. **Peggy Sue's Diner** is right out of the Fifties, complete with the snout of a 1956 Chevy; it serves Reuben and Denver sandwiches and other edible nostalgia; Sunday-Thursday 7 a.m. to 9 p.m., Friday- Saturday 7 to 10; meals $3 to $9. The 24-hour **coffee shop**, with a giant Noma Bubblelight decor, offers a mix of American and Italian fare from $5 to $12.

Lodging: Attractive, good-sized rooms are $36 to $48, with mini- suites from $64 to $72.

Camping: Next-door **Western Village RV Park,** owned by the Peppermill, has full hookups for $12, with barbecues and picnic tables. Free RV parking with no hookups is available across the street.

Virgin River Hotel-Casino • ☺☺

Interstate 15 exit 122 (P.O. Box 1620), Mesquite, NV 89024; (800) 346-5232 or (702) 346-7777. Major credit cards. Attractive with a vague sort of Grecian-modern look, the mid-sized Virgin offers the usual assortment of games of chance. We liked the coffered reflective ceilings and mirrored walls that accent the bright, cheery gaming area. An attractive pool complex is tucked between the hotel section and a backdrop of russet brown hills.

Dining: The 24-hour restaurant features oldstyle American fare such as grilled liver and onions and chicken fried steak; dinners from $5.50 to $11.50, plus the usual loss leader specials.

Lodging: Simple, nicely furnished rooms are $20 Sunday-Thursday, jumping to $45 Friday-Saturday.

"I recall an early morning in 1957, seated with my family around the breakfast table. Suddenly, an atomic blast lit up the sky. My mother stopped stirring the Wheatena, peeled back the curtain...and peered out. Dad arose and padded to the back door. 'A-bomb,' he grunted and went back to blotting the bacon.— A Hometown Grows Up, Nevada Magazine, 1987

Chapter Five
THE WESTERN EDGE
Boomtowns, Bombs & Basques

Nevada state tourism prompters like to call U.S. Highway 95 running between Las Vegas and Reno the Silver Trail. Indeed, many of the desert-scorched hills along this lonely route were—and most likely still are—laced with silver.

Tonopah, one of the few towns of substance on this road, was known as "Queen of the Silver Camps" during its glory days. These mean, rocky hills yielded gold as well. Goldfield, now little more than a weary relic, was Nevada's largest gold mining center and the biggest city in the state around the turn of the century, claiming more than 20,000 citizens.

Although it travels between Nevada's two largest cities, the Silver Trail isn't a heavily used route. Perhaps folks in Las Vegas and Reno don't have that much to say to one another. Most traffic still runs the width of the state, not the length, as it has since California gold drew the first substantial human herds across its deserts.

Significantly, there is no north-south pioneer trail, except in the fertile minds of tourist promoters. Railroads provided the first mass transit. The Virginia & Truckee line reached south to Hawthorne in 1890 and Senator William Clark stretched his Las Vegas & Tonopah route northward in 1906 to haul wealth from the mines of Rhyolite, Goldfield and Tonopah. Highway 95, fused together from game trails, Indian paths and rail-side wagon trails, came later.

The highway doesn't quite link Las Vegas and Reno. It passes several miles to the east of the Biggest Little City, only to disappear under the four-lane asphalt of Interstate 80. It crawls free again in Winnemucca and wanders through the remote southeastern tip of Oregon and on into Idaho, seeking sanctuary in Canada. In our upstate Nevada trip, we'll peel off just above Walker Lake and head west toward Carson City, which we're saving for the next chapter.

THINGS TO KNOW BEFORE YOU GO

BEST TIME TO GO • The southern portion of the "Silver Trail" is hotter than the hinges of Hades in summer; it becomes more temperate as you approach Minden/Gardnerville/Genoa. The northern area is suitable for all-year visits, although Genoa's state historic park and court house museum are closed in winter.

WHAT TO SEE • The rustic ruins of Rhyolite, Tonopah's excellent Central Nevada Museum, Yerington's extensive Lyon County Museum, the Genoa Courthouse Museum and Mormon Station State Historic Park in Genoa.

WHAT CASINOS TO SEE • The lake-view casino at Topaz Lodge, Gardnerville's Sharkey's Casino with its clutter of Western and boxing memorabilia and Minden's Danish/Western themed Carson Valley Inn.

WHAT TO DO • Drive from Beatty/Rhyolite on over to Death Valley National Monument (although you're in the wrong guidebook); hike the heights of Mount Oddie in Tonopah; bend an elbow in the historic Santa Fe Saloon in Goldfield and the Genoa Bar and Saloon in Genoa; stuff yourself with a Basque supper at the Overland Hotel in Gardnerville; explore the high Sierra above Carson Valley.

Useful contacts

Beatty Chamber of Commerce, P.O. Box 956, Beatty, NV 89003; (702) 553-2225.

Carson Valley Chamber of Commerce, 1524 Highway 395 North, Suite #1, Gardnerville, CA 89401; (702) 782-8144.

Death Valley Chamber of Commerce, No. 2 Post Office Row, Tecopa, CA 92389; (619) 852-4524.

Goldfield Chamber of Commerce, P.O. Box 225, Goldfield, NV 89013; (702) 485-9957.

Mineral County Chamber of Commerce, P.O. Box 1277, Hawthorne, NV 89415; (702) 945-5896.

Tonopah Chamber of Commerce, P.O. Box 869, Tonopah, NV 89049; (702) 482-3859.

Area radio stations

KGBM-FM, 99.3, Minden-Gardnerville—top 40 of yesterday and today

KPAH-FM, 95.9, Tonopah—light rock

KTPH-FM, 92.7, Tonopah—National Public Radio

KVLV-FM, 99.3, Fallon—top 40, country music and news

KVLV-AM, 980, Fallon—country and Western

There is good reason to drive north on Highway 95. After you've spent days visiting the crowded Las Vegas Strip and its popular neighbors, the Silver Trail's remoteness may be incentive enough. Further, you'll discover an interesting assortment of old mining towns, a shimmering desert lake, some great Basque restaurants and Nevada's first settlement. Don't expect a lot of beauty as you make a northward transition from the low Mojave Desert to the higher Great Basin. Do expect a certain amount of ugly. You'll see some of Nevada's scruffiest towns and most ravaged landscape, where hungry men tore at the earth to extract its riches, then left it like a cast-off lover.

LAS VEGAS TO BEATTY AND RHYOLITE

If you took our Red Rock-Pahrump-Mount Charleston Loop in the previous chapter, you ran the first leg of this route in reverse. You'll recall that there isn't much to see as Highway 95 knifes northwestward through a creosote bush desert.

The inviting alpine island of **Mount Charleston** rises to the left, but your companion ahead and to the right is the most remote terrain in all of Nevada. It's remote for a reason. Beyond the locked gates of **Mercury**, which you'll see on your right, stretches the forbidding wastes of the **Nevada Test Site.** Here, death angel mushrooms grew from the desert floor as atomic scientists perfected America's ultimate killing machines. Aboveground testing continued on this 1,350-square mile site from 1951 until 1962, when an international nuclear test ban treaty drove the explosions underground. The blasts routinely rocked the casinos of Las Vegas and send radioactive clouds wafting over Utah.

As we drove past, we were morbidly curious about the look of the test site, where mock cities and armaments had been constructed for destruction. Considering the likelihood of long-term contamination, it could prove to be a fatal attraction. It is of course off limits.

Conventional weapons scatter jackrabbits and other luckless residents across the landscape of the **Nellis Air Force Range,** just beyond the Nevada Test Site. A tiny tip of California's **Death Valley National Monument** nudges into Nevada to the west of here. **Amargosa Valley,** your first shred of civilization since leaving Las Vegas, promotes itself as one of the monument's gateways, at the juncture of State Highway 373. Not a town, it's merely a mini-mart, Cowboy Joe's Restaurant and Bar and an Indian trading post.

Thirty miles beyond, you'll encounter Beatty, the first of several drab little towns along the Silver Trail.

Beatty

Population: 3,500 **Elevation: 3,300 feet**

A collection of small casinos, service stations and RV parks, Beatty sits at the junction of U.S. 95 and State Route 374. It's obviously a former mining center, surrounded by rough-hewn peaks with their tell-tale tailing dumps. However, little remains of its better days; the look is dreary-modern.

It is useful today as a short term and long term winter Snowbird roost and a gateway to Death Valley and the nearby ghost town of Rhyolite. It may assume a more significant and macabre role in the future, as gateway to the Department of Energy's long-term nuclear waste dump, on nearby Yucca Mountain ridge.

Montillus Beatty and his Paiute bride settled at a spring along the seasonal Amargosa River at the turn of the century. They built up a small ranch that became an important provisioning center after the nearby Bullfrog/Rhyolite gold discovery in 1904. Senator Clark hurried his tracks northward and Beatty became a major supply center, with three railroads fanning out to area mines. Although Rhyolite's boom went bust by 1910, Beatty survived as a railroad watering stop and later as a highway fueling stop and Death Valley gateway.

For a place with limited visitor appeal, Beatty has a surprising number of visitor centers. Three of them are lined up near the town's main intersection, just west of Highway 95 on State Route 374.

At the Department of Energy's **Yucca Mountain Information Office,** (weekdays 10 to 3, weekends noon to 5) you'll be inundated by leaflets, brochures and videos describing the wonders of atomic power. Tours of the proposed site are conducted periodically, by reservation. For information, contact: Yucca Mountain Information Office, P.O. Box 69, Beatty, NV 89003; (702) 794-7434. "I'm smart about nuclear energy," it says on ballpoint pens, passed out by the dozens at the center, along with reams of paper. One could gather enough free material here to write a doctoral thesis on nuclear waste disposal—albeit a very biased one. Considering the generosity of the handouts in this public relations overkill, it's easy to see why site selection alone is costing us taxpayers more than a billion dollars. Wait'll they start digging.

The material assures us that the proposed storage site, about 30 miles east of Beatty, would provide safe haven for 70,000 metric tons of radioactive nuclear power plant garbage for 10,000 years. It would be stored in canisters in tunnels 1,000 feet below the surface. What the leaflets don't stress is that thousands of trucks must pass through Nevada with the lethal stuff on board, that DOE can't guarantee that the canisters won't leak, and that the nuclear waste will still be hot and deadly after the 10,000 years have elapsed.

The free pens don't work worth a damn. I hope the engineering is better at the dump site.

Much less alarming is the **Beatty Visitor Information Center,** (daily 10 to 5). Despite its name, it's more of an interpretive center for Death Valley National Monument, run by the Death Valley Natural History Association. You'll find displays and photo exhibits on the valley and other subjects, plus a goodly supply of books, brochures, videos and topo maps either for free or for sale. Next in line is the **Beatty Chamber of Commerce Visitor Center,** open weekdays 9 to 5. It offers brochures on the area which, again, seem preoccupied with Death Valley.

WHERE TO GAMBLE, DINE & SLEEP

Most of the restaurants and lodgings in Beatty are in the three casinos, so we'll lump them together for convenience.

Burro Inn ● ☺☺

Highway 95 (south end of town; P.O. Box 7), Beatty, NV 89003; (800) 843-2078 or (702) 553-2445. MC/VISA. This is the only casino of the three with personality. It's done up in old Western style, with artifacts, period photos and tulip chandeliers. Two blackjack tables and a few ranks of slots and video poker machines complete the gaming selection. A cute oldstyle restaurant offers modest prices: $4.50 to $14; basic American menu; open 24 hours. **Lodging:** Basic, clean rooms with wood panel wall insets to add a rustic touch; singles $32, doubles $34.50 to $40.

Exchange Club of Beatty • ☺
Downtown at Highway 95/372 junction, P.O. Box 97, Beatty, NV 89003; (702) 553-2368 for casino and restaurant, (702) 553-2333 for motel. MC/VISA. One of the town's few historic structures, this venerable saloon has been around since 1906. However, it has been extensively remodeled and it's almost too sleek and cheerful for an historic structure. One might say that it has been modernized to death. Gaming devices consist of two blackjack and one poker table, plus slots. The **restaurant** offers an interesting mixed menu with stuff like honey-dipped fried chicken, beef and cabbage pocket pita, liver and onions; $5 to $11. Beige Naugahyde coffee shop look; open 24 hours; non-smoking tables. **Lodging:** Simple, very clean rooms with TV, phones and refrigerators; doubles and singles $35 to $38.

Stagecoach Hotel and Casino • ☺☺
Highway 95, north end (P.O. Box 836), Beatty, NV 89003; (702) 553-2419. MC/VISA. The largest of the three, this new casino has an old Western town façade, although the inside is rather spartan, with low ceilings and mirrored walls. It offers blackjack, roulette and dice tables, plus slots, a small gift shop and ice cream parlor. The **restaurant** has an American menu with the usual pork chop, spaghetti, meatball and steak fare, $7 to $14, plus a $4.95 breakfast buffet. Attractively austere with Naugahyde and brick; open 24 hours. **Lodging:** Singles $30, doubles $35 to $40.

WHERE TO CAMP

Burro Inn RV Park • *Highway 95 (south end of town; P.O. Box 7), Beatty, NV 89003; (800) 843- 2078 or (702) 553-2445.* RV sites with full hookups, $10. Showers, flush potties; casino and restaurant adjacent.

Rio Rancho RV Park • *North end (P.O. Box 905), Beatty, NV 89003; (800) 448-4423 and (702) 553-2238.* Hookups $14, tent sites $12.95. Showers, cable TV, laundromat, Propane and supplies, rec room, horseshoes, barbecues and picnic tables.

Rhyolite

A seven-mile trip southwest on State Highway 374 will carry you past LAC Corporation's new $100 million **open pit gold mine**, where science is extracting the gold that Rhyolite prospectors missed. The graveled tailing dumps are so massive that they're forming their own new mountain. A right turn will deliver you to Rhyolite, where hopeful men grubbed for that same gold 90 years earlier.

The town was built to last; unfortunately, the gold didn't. Rhyolite today is a sad old relic of brick and stone shells and a few shacks losing their battle with gravity. Even latter-day attempts at tourism seem to be failing. When we visited, the **Original Rhyolite Ghost Museum** was closed and the **Red Barn Museum of Artifacts** down the road was shuttered as well. The grounds of the Ghost Museum were adorned with a car-part sculpture called "Desert Flower" and a Last Supper scene of ghostly shrouded plaster of Paris figures. We didn't find much Rhyolite history here, but it's worth a stop—open or not.

This Spanish colonial railroad station is one of the few structures still intact in the former mining boomtown of Rhyolite
— Don W. Martin

A group called Friends of Rhyolite (P.O. Box 85, Amargosa Valley, NV 89020; 533-2424) is working to resurrect the town. Unfortunately, there isn't much left to salvage. Only two structures of substance survive. The green mission revival **Rhyolite Depot** is privately owned and is thus receiving some care. When we lasted visited, it was being used as a set for a film called *Painted Desert*; watch for it at your local cinema. The other surviving relic is the **Bottle House,** with walls constructe entirely of whiskey bottles, which must have required a powerful amount of drinking. It's badly vandalized and is fenced off to prevent further destruction.

Photographers and others with poetic eyes will find Rhyolite to be an intriguing, almost haunting place—a lonely scatter of shattered walls and sagging roofs, set against a mean, rocky desert slope. It wasn't always thus.

"What a procession!" the *Rhyolite Herald* recalled. *"Men on foot, burros, mule teams, freights, light rigs, saddle outfits, automobiles, houses on wheels—all coming down the line from Tonopah and Goldfield, raising a string of dust a hundred miles long!"*

Two prospectors, Frank "Shorty" Harris and Ernest L. Cross, found gold-speckled green rocks here in August of 1904. They hurried to "Old Man" Beatty's ranch to announce their find. Soon, scores of men were camped at Beatty's place, then came the long procession later described by the *Herald*. Goldfield and Tonopah to the north were practically emptied out in the rush to the Bullfrog and Rhyolite gold fields. By March of 1905, five new tent cities had sprung up: Bullfrog, Amargosa, Bonanza, Rhyolite and Gold Center.

Rhyolite became the center of activity; substantial stone and brick buildings rose from the rocky desert dirt. The town soon had an opera house, several banks and even its own stock exchange. Three railroads served the fancy new Spanish-style depot. Surely the boom would last for decades!

It lasted only six years. By 1910, the mines had fizzled out and only $2 million had been pulled from the earth. That much had been spent in the building of the hasty communities. One by one, the towns withered and died. The *Herald* summed it up poetically: *"Verily, the Bullfrog Croaketh."*

RHYOLITE TO TONOPAH

The mountainous desert terrain goes flat as you continue north, completing the transition from the Mojave to the Great Basin. **Scotty's Junction** at State Highway 267, yet another gateway to Death Valley, offers basic provisions and—of course—Death Valley information. Sixteen miles beyond, at the juncture of State Route 266, is **Cottontail Ranch,** sitting as bold as brass, right on the main highway. At night, its shining red light is visible for 50 miles. *"A lighthouse in a sea of sand,"* exudes *Best Cat Houses in Nevada* author J.R. Schwartz, who gets carried away with his descriptions.

Leaving behind carnal thoughts of credit card love, you leave the desert flat and climb to **Goldfield Summit.** Just beyond is a town that, like Rhyolite, enjoyed precious few years in the golden limelight. Unlike Rhyolite, it's still hanging on—if only just barely.

Goldfield

Population: 400 **Elevation: 5,690 feet**

Sitting on a low mountain shelf, Goldfield looks more like a survivor of the *Blitzkrieg* than a former gold rush town. The hills are pocked with tailing dumps and coyote holes; several brick and stone structures stand abandoned and neglected.

Only one building of substance is occupied: the fortress-like **Esmeralda County Courthouse,** built in 1907. With its 400 folks, Goldfield is one of the smallest county seats in America. That's appropriate since Esmeralda, with a mere 1,300 citizens, is among the nation's least populated counties. This indicates a long downhill skid, since Goldfield once was Nevada's largest city, with a population topping 20,000. If you're in town during court house business hours (weekdays 9 to 5), step inside to see its carved wainscoted hallways and genuine Tiffany lamps.

Other buildings of note, shuttered and fenced, are the imposing three-story brick 1908 **Goldfield Hotel,** the brick and cut stone **high school** and the 1906 **Southern Nevada Consolidated Telephone Company** building; it managed to keep on functioning until 1963. Various investors have tried to refurbish and resurrect the hotel, so it just might be in business when you pass through.

Betwixt and between these structures are assorted shacks, modest bungalows, mobile homes and hundreds of empty lots where the town once thrived. Stop by **Gloryhole Antiques** for an animated conversation with proprietress Virginia Ridgway, who can tell you where to prowl and what to see in the old town and its surrounding desert. To call it an antique shop is a simplification; Virginia runs an antique-jewelry-gift-curio store-bookstore-information center.

Another worthy stop is the 1905 **Santa Fe Saloon,** four blocks east of the highway on Fifth Avenue. It's a weather-battered wooden false front drinking establishment, held up mostly by habit and determination. The wonderfully shabby interior offers a dusty scatter of antiques, a mirrored back bar and elbow-worn "plank" and contemporary accouterments like hundreds of truckers' hats hanging from the rafters. A few cribs survive out back, reminders of the days when the Santa Fe was one of the town's more lively bawdy houses.

A brief drive out Columbia Street will deliver you to a mining moonscape, a ruined region of tailing dumps, molehills and coyote holes. The earth's exposed innards run the full spectrum of a perverted rainbow: curdled pea soup green, emergency room red, terminal gray and yucky yellow. More than any other town in Nevada, Goldfield reflects the mining cycle of boom, bust and abandonment. Here, the earth was ravaged, ripped inside out by greedy men, then left to die in the desert sun.

THE WAY IT WAS ● Columbia Mountain was a peaceful if barren place when Messrs. Billy Marsh and Harry Stimler arrived in 1904 on a buckboard pulled by a horse and a mule. The pair had been grubstaked by Jim Butler, who'd turned neighboring Tonopah into a silver boom town two years earlier. They found some surface gold that assayed at only $12 per ton, but it held promise of richer treasures beneath.

The usual rush followed and within two years, Goldfield was a substantial town of stone and brick. In 1907, the county seat was assigned here, taken from the protesting citizens of Hawthorne. Corporations were formed to finance the extensive underground mining operation, which led to the inevitable problems: "high-grading" by miners smuggling nuggets from the mines, and a violent clash between union miners and mine owners. The U.S. Army was sent to bring order and the corporations eventually broke the back of the unions. Soon, the town's back was broken as well. The gold began to run out in 1919; a fire in 1923 ruined what was left of the economy.

Where to eat and sleep

Mozart Club ● ☺☺ $
Highway 95 (north end); (702) 485-3219. American; dinners $4 to $8; full bar service. Tuesday-Sunday 10 a.m. to 8 p.m. No credit cards. Prim little white tablecloth place with an oldstyle Western bar. Menu features liver and onions with bacon (very tasty), chicken fried steak, catfish and other down home cookin'.

Sundog Bed & Breakfast ● △△ $$
P.O. Box 486, (211 Sundog St.) Goldfield, NV 89103; (702) 485-3438. Doubles $30 to $50, singles $30 to $35. Private and share baths; continental or full breakfast. No credit cards. A 1906 gold rush era home furnished with American and European antiques. Comfortable library with extensive music collection.

Tonopah

Population: 4,017   **Elevation: 6,050 feet**

If Goldfield is withering, its sister community 25 miles to the north is thriving.

Tonopah is the Humphrey Bogart of Nevada's mining camps. It's so hound dog homely that it's almost handsome. The town is stuffed into and scattered about the clefts of rough-hewn Mizpah Hill and Mount Oddie. It's an incongruous blend of modern bungalows, apartment houses, thriving businesses, shanties, double-wides, rusting mining machinery and tailing dumps. The business district is scattered carelessly along Highway 95, in a

TONOPAH

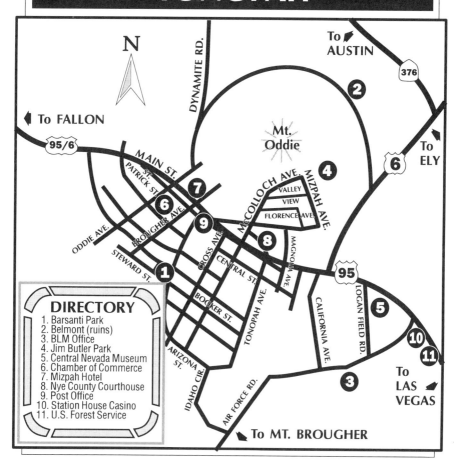

DIRECTORY
1. Barsanti Park
2. Belmont (ruins)
3. BLM Office
4. Jim Butler Park
5. Central Nevada Museum
6. Chamber of Commerce
7. Mizpah Hotel
8. Nye County Courthouse
9. Post Office
10. Station House Casino
11. U.S. Forest Service

mix of old brick and modern buildings. The town exhibits no more sense of order than the mines which gave it birth.

THE WAY IT WAS • We've heard this story before, about other mining towns, and it's probably a campfire fib. But it's too cute not to repeat.

It seems that in 1900 a rancher and part-time prospector named Jim Butler was working south from Belmont, looking for paydirt. Nevada's economy was in the doldrums, for there hadn't been a significant strike in decades. Butler took shelter under a ledge from a windstorm and—here's where the campfire talk starts. His mule wandered off, so he fetched a rock to give it a lesson in obedience and—that's right—the rock was laced with silver.

However it happened, Butler filed several claims and returned to his ranch to get his hay baled. He came back the following year, tailed by other hungry miners, and Tonopah's boom began. Butler and a friend named Tasker Oddie staked dozens of claims, most of which were leased out to other miners. An eastern firm bought out the pair for several hundred thousand dollars and formed the Tonopah Mining Company, with Oddie as manager. He later would become Nevada's U.S. senator. Butler bought a ranch in nearby Inyo, California, and lived the good life until his passing in 1922.

192 — CHAPTER FIVE

THE WAY IT IS • Although the predictable slump hit Tonopah in the 1930s and mining ceased completely during World War II, the town has survived rather well. An Army air base was built nearby and Tonopah became an important junction, with Highway 6 feeding in from eastern Nevada and continuing into California.

Mining is again live and well and the town calls itself "Miningtown USA." Assorted corporations are working molybdenum, copper, gold and silver deposits in the surrounding hills. The nearby Tonopah Test Range, where the Stealth bomber and a renegade Soviet MIG were test flown, provides government jobs. Also, Tonopah is the seat of expansive Nye County, the second largest in America, covering 18,064 square miles. A glance at a map will confirm that the town is a little bureaucratic tail wagging a huge geographical dog. It sits barely on the western edge of the county that stretches from southern to central Nevada.

Begin your Tonopah exploration by stopping at the **Chamber of Commerce** (Monday-Friday 9 to 5), offering an extensive collection of brochures about Nevada and a couple of states beyond. It's on Brougher Avenue, two blocks southwest of the highway; turn at the **Mizpah Hotel**. A leftover piece of brick refinement built in 1907, the Mizpah is certainly worth a browse, with its restored turn-of-the-century interior.

You'll also want to visit the **Central Nevada Museum,** reached by turning south off the highway on to Logan Field Road. For a view of Tonopah from on high, continue past the museum to Air Force Road and follow its twisting course to the ramparts of **Mount Brougher.** The pavement ends quickly and the road is rough, so take your time and enjoy the rocky desert mountain scenery.

To see the opposite heights, return to the highway and go north up McCulloch Avenue (near a Texaco station). Pause for a look at the silver missile-domed **Nye County Courthouse,** then continue upward and turn right onto Mizpah Circle, which delivers you to **Butler Park.** Beside the park, a left onto Occidental takes you to the base of **Mount Oddie,** up near the town water tanks. You can hike Oddie's barren face for an impressive view of the scattered community, its tailing dumps, headframes and surrounding hills.

There's not a serious forest in sight, although the **Tonopah Ranger Station** of Toiyabe National Forest sits on the south end of town; open weekdays 8:30 to 5. You can pick up a map for $2 and other stuff on the **Toiyabe, Toquima** and **Monitor mountain ranges** of the national forest, which lie to the north. State Highway 376 leaves U.S. 6 just east of Tonopah, taking you through the **Smoky Valley** between the Toiyabe and Toquima ranges. The highway delivers you to the mining town of Austin, which we visit in Chapter 10. The route is pretty and remote, and you'll encounter (or pass near) pioneer towns of **Manhattan, Round Mountain** and **Carver** along the way.

THE ATTRACTION

Central Nevada Museum • *Logan Field Road (P.O. Box 326); (702) 482-9676. October through April noon to 5 Tuesday-Saturday; May through September 11 to 5 daily. Free; donations appreciated.* Housed in a metal-sided building, this is one of Nevada's better community museums. Thematic exhibits cover the town's mining history, railroads, fraternal orders

— Betty Woo Martin

Mine headframes and tailing dumps are part of the landscaping in the rough-hewn old town of Tonopah.

and unions, business community, sociology and wildlife. Displays are clean and uncluttered, exhibiting items such as old slot machines, assayers' tools and chemicals, decorative checks from early banks and a copper still used by Tonopah bootleggers. A special section features the town's "fancy women".

THE CASINOS

Mizpah Hotel • ☺☺
100 Main St. (P.O. Box 952), Tonopah, NV 89409; (702) 482-3261. MC/VISA. A small Western-style gaming parlor occupies the ground floor of this handsome five-story yellow brick and cut stone structure. Casino features include a long bar with big-screen TV, a few gaming tables and the usual slots and video poker machines. Jack Dempsey once worked as a bouncer here; you'll find a small photo exhibit concerning the great fighter at the entrance to the **Jack Dempsey Room** restaurant downstairs. This elegant little Victorian dining room features American and Italian fare; nightly 5 to 10; $10 to $14. **Lodging:** Simple, neat rooms are $27 to $33.

Station House Casino • ☺☺☺
1100 Main St. (P.O. Box 1351), Tonopah, NV 89409; (702) 482-9777. This extensive complex harbors many of Tonopah's shopping facilities as well as its largest casino. The look is early Western railroad, with a pleasing interior of barnwood, leaded glass and glitter lights. Blackjack, craps and lots of slots comprise the gaming action, and there's a video parlor for the kiddies. A small **museum** features an exhibit of ancient slot machines and a few other frontier artifacts. A shopping arcade is adjacent, and the town's only supermarket is just beyond that.

Dining: Dinners at the early American style **Mary's Kitchen** are $7 to $11; open 24 hours. **Lodging:** Rooms with Western decor are $32 to $42.

WHERE ELSE TO DINE

El Marqès Restaurant • ☺☺ $
North Main St.; (702) 482-9947. Mexican with some Italian; dinners $5 to $9; full bar service. Daily 11 a.m. to 9 p.m.; MC/VISA, AMEX. Cute little place

with brick arched windows and cozy tables with votive candles. The inexpensive menu features chili Colorado, beef steak *en Pampas, carne asada* and Italian items such as breaded steak *a la Milan*.

Rex Chinese Cafe • ☺ $
Main Street (opposite the Mizpah); (702) 482-5377. Chinese; dinners $5 to $10; full bar service. Monday-Saturday 11 to 9; closed Sunday. Basic family-style Chinese place, serving mostly mild-flavored Cantonese dishes at very modest prices. Rex Club cocktail lounge adjacent.

WHERE ELSE TO SLEEP

Jim Butler Motel • ⌂ ∅
P.O. Box 1352 (100 S. Main at Brougher), Tonopah, NV 89409; (800) 635-9455 or (702) 482-3577. Doubles $32 to $34, singles $26 to $28. Nicely maintained 25-room motel with TV movies and room phones. Non-smoking rooms available.

Silver Queen Motel • ⌂ $$ ∅
255 Main St. (P.O. Box 311), Tonopah, NV 89049; (702) 482-6291. Doubles $34 to $46, singles $30 to $34, kitchenettes and suites $10 extra. Major credit cards. An 85-unit motel with TV movies, room phones and swimming pool. Antique shop on premises. **Terry's Restaurant** serves American fare, specializing in barbecued ribs and chicken; open 7 a.m. to 9 p.m.; dinners $6 to $10.69; full bar service.

WHERE TO CAMP

Lambertucci-Roma RV Park • *Highway 95 north; (702) 482-3356. RV spaces; no hookups $5, water and electric $8.* Scruffy but neat little park with tree-shaded pull-throughs; basic but clean restrooms and showers; gasoline.

Station House RV Park • *Highway 95 South (at Station House Casino); (702) 482-9777. Full hookups $12; MC/VISA.* Showers, laundry, phones, rec room, adult lounge; shopping, dining and casino facilities adjacent.

TONOPAH TO YERINGTON

This section of Highway 95 doesn't exactly brim with visitor interest. However, you'll encounter a museum or two and a major desert lake recreation area en route. And you will begin to see, on your left, the steep eastern ramparts of that magnificent mountain range, the Sierra Nevada (Snowy Peaks, if you're speaking Spanish).

Several highways branch into the Sierra at points along the route. Although it's difficult to define on the skyline, you'll be passing near **Boundary Peak,** the highest point in Nevada at 13,140 feet. It's on the horizon as you motor westward from Tonopah to the non-town of **Coaldale.** At this point, U.S. 6 splits off for a climb through Montgomery Pass into California. Highway 95, now graced with a Sierran view to the west, continues through the wide spot of **Mina** to the ugliest town in Nevada.

Hawthorne

Population: 3,700 **Elevation: 4,375 feet**

Poor old Hawthorne! Not only is it hound dog homely, it suffers the privilege of being hemmed in by explosives, courtesy of the **U.S. Army Ammunition Plant.** Bunkers, pillboxes, cones, overgrown mounds, humps and assorted other root cellars of death encircle the town. The place look like it was landscaped by giant gophers, with the aid of cement contractors.

The main army ammo depot sits at the town's south end, along with the **Naval Undersea Warfare Engineering Station.** Which is strange, since there's no sea to be under. North Hawthorne is anchored by the military complex of **Babbitt,** with more ammo bunkers, rows of Butler buildings where they assemble the stuff (no smoking, please) and more rows of austere barracks—some in use, some boarded up.

Hawthorne dates from 1881 when it was chosen as a railroad freight stop to serve nearby mines, although nothing of yesterday remains. It gained enough importance to become the Esmeralda County seat in 1883, lost it to Goldfield, then got it back when Mineral County was created in 1911.

The town today is a dreary collection of low-rise business buildings with 1950s brick fake fronts and little flat top houses squatting on treeless and cheerless lots. The commercial district sits askew of the highway, requiring a right and then a left turn for passage. A single casino, **El Capitan,** is a basic, smoky place downtown, with a few blackjack tables, one craps table and assorted machines. A coffee shop, open 24 hours, serves essential American fare for $6.50 to $11.50 and it takes MC/VISA. The casino is generally crowded with ordnance personnel, since there's little else to do here.

But wait! There's a museum, and it's somewhat interesting.

Mineral County Museum • *Tenth and D streets (north end, just left of the Highway 95 curve); (702) 945-3185. Open weekdays, 11 to 5 in summer and noon to 4 in winter. Free; donations appreciated.* You get the feeling that you're walking the aisles of a supermarket as you study the assorted exhibits in this place. Maybe that's because this plain cinderblock building once housed a Big T. Exhibits are unprofessional but interesting and varied. The list includes mounted butterflies, old family photos, typewriters, Hawthorne's original fire truck, a mimeograph machine (remember when, Dearie?) and a pair of brass knuckles on loan from the Mineral County sheriff's office. (They'll want them back?)

Walker Lake

Immediately north of Hawthorne, you'll discover that there's something blue in this lonely desert besides the sky. Walker Lake will be your roadside companion for the next 30 miles. Depending on your state of mental poetry, it is either a great, shimmering mirage-come-true in a thirsty desert, or a dull flat body of water with a drab, treeless shoreline.

The lake is part of the fabric of the Nevada saga, both current and prehistoric. It's one of the remnants of ancient Lake Lahontan, which once covered much of western and central Nevada. Early explorers Peter Skene Ogden and Jedediah Smith noted the lake's presence during their 1820s wanderings. Joseph Walker encountered it in 1833, desperately needing a drink after being lost for days in the desert. A decade later, he led Captain John Frèmont's surveying party through here. The great Western topographer named the lake and its river to the north in honor of the frontier scout.

The federal government granted the lake and 300,000 acres to the Paiutes in 1874, then naturally took a good chunk of it away as mines were discovered in the area. The Walker River Paiutes still own the upper third of the lake and reservation lands to the north. Most of the southern two-thirds are held by the Bureau of Land Management and the state of Nevada.

You'll find a mini-mart, lakeside motel and RV park at the hamlet of **Walker Lake,** near the south end. **Walker Lake State Recreation Area** offers facilities at **Sportsman's Beach** (sheltered picnic areas, campsites with pit potties, no hookups; fishing access) and at **Tamarack Point** (picnic sites and a launch ramp). An historic marker at the entrance to Sportsman's Beach discusses the lake's past. Anglers catch hefty Lahontan trout in this pond, courtesy of a Nevada Department of Wildlife fish hatchery.

The Paiute community of **Schurz,** just beyond the lake's north end, offers a mini-mart and fuel. Here, you'll fork west onto U.S. 95 alternate, headed into Mason Valley and the pleasantly ordinary hamlet of Yerington, the seat of Lyon County. You shed the desert and enter a farming valley, thanks to the miracle of Walker River irrigation.

Yerington

Population: 2,021 **Elevation: 4,380 feet**

Approaching from the south, swing left onto Yerington's Main Street, leaving 95-A. The drive down Main will set you to mind of a quiet little Midwestern brick front farming town, complete with a farm equipment store, Sprouse Reitz and Rexall Drug.

You'll shortly see the town's two gaming parlors, **Dini's Lucky Club Casino** and **Casino West.** Dini's is Western-style, with high ceilings and turn-of-the-century artifacts, including a collection of old clocks near the restaurant entrance. Casino West is an attractive carpet joint done in maple, with mirrored columns; sort of Middle America Modern. Both have the usual machines, gaming tables and restaurants. They don't do the 24- hour thing, although they do serve from around dawn until 10 p.m., offering inexpensive casino-subsidized fare.

The **Lyon County Courthouse** at Main and Grove streets downtown is a picturesque study in American Federalist Greek architecture, with its pediment and fluted columns. Farther along, just beyond Surprise Street, you'll see the **Lyon County Museum** on your right and **Lyon County Information Center** on your left. At the information center (weekdays 9 to 5), you can pick up brochures and a newsprint Mason Valley guide with maps directing you past some of the town's old buildings.

Lyon County Museum • *215 S. Main St.; (702) 463-2150. Saturday 10 to 4 and Sunday 1 to 4. Free; donations appreciated.* Housed in former church, this good-sized repository contains an extensive collection of Mason Valley's yesterdays, from mining and farming exhibits to a country kitchen. Among its curios are an old pump organ, Paiute folk crafts and a leather-covered money box that just may have belonged to George Washington.

Yerington began life as a cattle and farming settlement in 1869, and it had a great name—Pizen Switch. This was inspired by one of the settlement's first businesses, a saloon called the Switch because it was made of willows and tules. Legend says that when the barkeep's whisky barrel ran low, he'd top it off with whatever was handy—straight alcohol, assorted liniments, maybe a dash of turpentine. *"Let's go over to the Switch fer a cup o' pizen,"* the local boys would say.

Seeking more dignity, folks later called the place Greenfield, then in 1880, it was named in honor of H.M. Yerington, general manager of the Virginia & Truckee Railroad. Citizens hoped to flatter him into routing his Carson & Colorado spur line through their town. He wasn't moved by the gesture; the railroad skipped the Mason Valley and went through Hawthorne. However, the name stuck.

Yerington's fortunes weren't always tied to railroading and ranching. Until recently, it was a major copper producing center. The Anaconda Copper Company discovered ore in a nearby hill in the 1950s and chewed a hole into it for 20 years before moving on. To visit the company town of **Weed Heights** and a gaping open pit, drive north from town on 95-A for a couple of miles. Turn left at a small green sign, just beyond a Propane tank farm. Drive about a mile up the hill, swerving left to bypass a company guard station, and you'll wind up at the base of the housing area. Turn left at a stop sign, go a few hundred feet past a rank of mailboxes, then go left again at a giant ore truck tire embedded in concrete. You'll shortly find the overlook to the great hole in the ground. The terraced pit is almost attractive, with a lake of blue-green rainwater forming in its basin.

Although the weeds definitely are taking over some of the drab little flat top company houses, the community was named for Clyde Weed, an Anaconda vice president. Some of the pre-fab structures are occupied, giving Weed Heights the look of a semi-abandoned military housing project.

YERINGTON TO GENOA

From Yerington, you leave Highway 95-A and head southwest through alternating swatches of farmland, cattle graze and desert, on a collision course with the great wall of the Sierra Nevada. A two- mile run through steep-walled **Wilson Canyon,** cut by the Walker River, offers dramatic respite from the level Mason Valley.

You enter the **Smith Valley,** passing through pioneer hamlets of **Smith** and **Wellington** and come to a stop at U.S. 395. Swing briefly south and you'll hit **Topaz Lake**, just short of the California border. You can almost reach out and touch the Sierra Nevada here, and a short drive south would deliver you quickly to piney ramparts. The lake, however, is rimmed by brushy desert—a Walker Lake in miniature.

Topaz Lodge Casino (266-3338) offers Highway 395 travelers a first or last chance to gamble. It's an appealing little place with a knotty pine/Western interior and a picture window onto the lake. It offers a few blackjack tables and slots, including some hard-to-find dime machines. Other facilities include a 24-hour coffee shop, service station, lodge rooms (doubles $39 to $45) a mini-mart and RV park with lake-view sites (showers, cable TV; $7 with hookups, $4 without).

Topaz Lake Recreation Area, operated by Douglas County, offers camping, picnicking, boating and fishing. The lake is noted for its hefty cutthroat trout. For fishing and hunting guide service, get in touch with the **Topaz Sportsman's Club,** 3851 State Highway 208, Wellington, NV 89444; (702) 266-3512.

Minden-Gardnerville

Population: 5,400   **Elevation: 4,720 feet**

Since this is a Nevada guidebook, we stop short of the California line and head north on U.S. 395 into the **Carson Valley** and the heart of one of Nevada's Basque regions. Save room for dinner.

198 — CHAPTER FIVE

THE WAY THEY WERE • Nothing separates Minden and Gardnerville except their names. Their geographic and historic ties go back to Carson Valley's earliest days. John Gardner homesteaded a chunk of land along the Walker River in 1861. In 1879, one Lawrence Gilman left the troubled Mormon settlement of Genoa (which we'll visit shortly), bought a few acres from Gardner and opened a hotel.

The hotel became a settlement, which became Gardnerville. Danish, Bavarian and then Basque ranchers and shepherds were drawn to the area, and the valley soon became an important agricultural center. In 1905, another Mormon Station refugee, rancher H.F. Dangberg, donated right-of-way land for a spur of the Virginia & Truckee Railroad to haul the area's produce and livestock to market. The town that grew up around the railroad station was named Minden to honor Dangberg's hometown in Prussia.

Some say the twin towns never joined because of bad blood between the Gardners and Dangbergs. For whatever reason, they grew up side by each. Minden got the seat of Douglas County in 1916, snatching it from fading Genoa. However, Gardnerville is now thrice its size. The surrounding valley is still agricultural, and its population remains about one-fifth Basque, including the family of former senator and governor Paul Laxalt.

THE WAY THEY ARE • Originally a couple of miles apart, the two communities are now fused. In fact, they're spreading in several directions. They've become popular with retirees and with commuters from the capital of Carson City, just 12 miles north. Folks have discovered that this cool, high valley with its dramatic Sierra Nevada backdrop is rather a nice place to live. A short drive south on State Highway 88 takes one past the historic Pony Express station of **Woodfords** to the cute California mountain hamlet of **Markleeville.** The wild beauty of the high Sierra is within easy reach at **Ebbetts Pass** and **Carson Pass.** A brief drive west carries the traveler up **Kingsbury Grade** to the mountain playground of **Lake Tahoe.**

Before you're lured to the mountains, take time to explore these twin cities. While they're not tourist meccas, they offer a certain amount of rural charm. Approaching from the south, slow down to admire Gardnerville's handsome brick business district, sitting right on Highway 395. You'll see hints of cross-timbered architecture left over from the town's Danish-Bavarian past. Stop for brochures at the **Carson Valley Chamber of Commerce** at 1524 Highway 395 North, between Gardnerville and Minden (at Centertowne Street; weekdays 10 to 4).

As you blend from Gardnerville into Minden, fork left onto **Esmeralda Avenue** to view its sturdy business district—a mirror of the 1930s Midwest. You'll note a piece of automotive history on your right, in the "vee" between Esmeralda and Highway 395. **C.O.D. Garage,** named for founder Clarence O. Dangberg, is the oldest continually operating auto dealership in Nevada and one of the oldest in America. It dates from 1910 when Clarence, son of H.F. Dangberg, opened a Model-T showroom; he later switched to Buicks. Check out the oldstyle Union 76, Buick and American Automobile Association (AAA) signs. A few blocks beyond is **Minden Park,** donated to the town by Dangberg Senior. It's surrounded by fine old 1920s and 1930s style Carpenter Gothic homes. The austere Depression Federalist **Douglas County Courthouse** is just beyond at Eighth and Esmeralda. Note the ornate white British-style **Coventry Episcopal Church** nearby.

THE CASINOS

Carson Valley Inn • ☺☺☺
1627 Highway 395, Minden; (702) 782-9711. Dominating a good share of downtown Minden, this extensive facility is one of Nevada's more attractive "rural casinos." The exterior is brick and wood Danish-Bavarian, appropriate to Minden's heritage. The large gaming area has a stylish turn of the century look with warm woods, hurricane lamps and mirrored columns. Facilities include a sunken bar with a huge projection TV, assorted slots, blackjack, roulette and craps, plus a kids' video parlor and supervised play center. The lounge offers live entertainment and music for dancing nightly. The restaurant, motel and RV park are listed below.

Sharkey's • ☺☺
Highway 395, downtown Gardnerville; (702) 782-3133. Casino or museum? Take your pick. This scatter of a place, spread through three storefronts, is the closest thing to an archive that you'll find in a Nevada gaming parlor. Just off the gaming room, a couple dozen handsome saddles, some silver mounted, occupy a "Tribute to the American cowboy" exhibit, along with Will Rogers' lariat and other regalia. Step into the video room and you'll be surrounded by boxing memorabilia, from Jack Sharkey mementos (the casino's namesake) to *Rocky* movie posters. The rest of the place is filled with sailing ship models, old photos, a cigar band collection and other relics. Owner Milos Begovich even found room for lots of slots, a few blackjack and two poker tables. His 24-hour coffee shop and **Rib Room** serve affordable fare from bargain breakfasts to prime rib.

WHERE TO DINE

Fiona's steak & Seafood Lounge • ☺☺☺ $$
Highway 395 (adjacent to Carson Valley Inn), Minden; (702) 782-4347. American-continental; dinners $10 to $16; full bar service. Lunch Tuesday-Friday 11:30 to 2, dinner Tuesday-Sunday 5:30 to 9, Sunday brunch 9 to 2, closed Monday. Reservations accepted; MC/VISA, AMEX. Very stylish place with tropical atrium entry, bentwood chairs, drop lamps and booths—some under greenhouse windows. Menu ranges from lamb chops and baby back ribs to shrimp *primavera* and chicken *cordon bleau*.

J.T. Bar and Basque Restaurant • ☺ $
Main and Eddie Streets, Gardnerville; (702) 782-2074. Basque-American; dinners $8 to $14; full bar service. Daily 11:30 a.m. to 9 p.m. No credit cards. Curious combination of Basque restaurant and barbershop, a bit on the scruffy side. All-you-can-eat Basque menu, plus a some American dishes. Bar up front with a few slots, beneath a ceiling decorated with dollar bills.

Katie's Restaurant • ☺☺ $
In Carson Valley Inn, 1627 Highway 395, Minden; (702) 782-9711. American; dinners $5 to $10; full bar service. Open 24 hours; MC/VISA, AMEX. Pleasing casino cafe with leatherette booths, warm woods and hurricane lamps. Basic American fare, plus a $6.95 all-you-can-eat barbecued beef rib dinner nightly from 4 to 10.

Overland Hotel Basque Restaurant • ☺☺ $$
691 S. Main St., Gardnerville; (702) 782-2138. Basque-American; meals $8 to $16, Basque dinner $14; full bar service. Open Tuesday-Sunday, lunch

12 to 2, dinner 4:45 to 9:30. MC/VISA. Clean and trim dining room with high pressed tin ceilings in an historic Basque boarding house. All-you-can eat Basque dinners include a split of wine (see below) and choice of entrées. Family-style or individual tables; American menu for lunch.

BASQUE DINING: A CAPACITY FOR RAPACITY

You pick a spot at a long, family-style table set with simple china, flatware, soup bowls and what appear to be over-sized shot glasses. Half a dozen people have arrived at the same time and will dine concurrently with you. You look about for a menu but there is none.

Thunk! A cauldron of soup the size of a small washtub hits the table. One of the strangers, a friendly lady from Reno, takes your bowl and returns it filled and steaming.

Whap! Napkin-wrapped baskets of French bread land at each end of the table. Diners tear off pieces like hungry, polite collies and pass the basket down. Thonk, thonk, thonk! Loosely corked bottles of chilled red wine land at three appointed places. With comforting clinks of glass-on-glass, strangers fill one another's tumblers. The wine is dangerously close to sweetness, yet curiously tasty and refreshing.

The waitress, dark haired and smiling, has taken position at one end of the table. "Your entrée choices tonight are lamb chops, lamb steak, fried chicken, shrimp or steak. There's garlic in the shrimp, but we can hold it back. The side dish is brisket of lamb."

You order the chicken, others make their choices and she disappears. Soup is slurped, bread is torn and munched, wine is sipped and conversation moves easily among the strangers.

A procession of food

Thunk! A salad bowl the size of a wine vat lands at one end of the table. It's laced with slices of cold hardboiled egg, with a light oil and vinegar dressing. Thwack! A cauldron heaped with steaming brisket of lamb is deposited at the other end. Both are passed quickly, meeting midway at your station. The salad is garden crisp and the lamb perfectly overdone, falling off the bone, delicately flavored and smothered in mushroom buttons and mild red chilies.

Thwap, whap, thump, plunk! The entrées arrive on large platters. The table and diners groan under the weight of the culinary blitz. Your chicken is southern style and tasty; the fries are hot, salty and crisp, among the best you've ever had.

Driven by the good aromas and flavors, you push ahead mindlessly, unable to stop eating, even as your stomach begins to push you back from the table. Somehow, you find room for a scoop of butter pecan ice cream. Grunting contentedly, you sip hot tea and make idle conversation with new friends. The waitress, noting your pleasant discomfort, suggests a picon punch, a curious concoction of amer picon and grenadine.

This scene occurs every night at the Overland Hotel in Gardnerville and elsewhere in the state. Basque dining has been a Nevada tradition ever since the first Pyrenees shepherds migrated to the state in the 1860s. The Basques, whose roots disappear into antiquity, were drawn to Nevada's gold and silver strikes from their native highlands in France and Spain. Later, they resumed their traditional roles as shepherds, drawn by the great high desert grasslands of Nevada.

Their cuisine can be distinctive, since it's lamb-oriented, with spicy Spanish and saucy French influences. However, Basque dinners relate more to a style of serving than to specific foods. American French fries, New York steak, prawns and ice cream are common. Traditionally, Basque dinners are *prix fixe*, served family style and feature four or five meat choices, soup, salad, dessert and coffee or tea, plus one or more side dishes. If you prefer not to rub elbows with strangers, many cafes (including the Overland) offer individual tables as well as banquet-style seating. However, we feel that the camaraderie, flowing conversation and wine, are part of the Basque dining experience.

Some Basque restaurants are more than a century old, survivors of boarding houses and hotels where many bachelors congregated after leaving the mines and sheep pastures. They're still called hotels, although some no longer rent rooms.

A Basque meal should be a part of the Nevada experience. Best places to find the traditional old boarding house restaurants are in Gardnerville, Reno, Carson City, Winnemucca and Elko.

WHERE TO SLEEP

Carson Valley Inn • ⌂⌂⌂

1627 Highway 395 (P.O. Box 2560), Minden, NV 89423; (800) 321-9711 outside Nevada or (702) 782-9711. Doubles and singles $49 to $79, spa suites $99 to $149. Major credit cards. Large rooms with print wallpaper, flowered matching drapes and spreads; TV, room phones; glass-enclosed spa; full casino and dining facilities adjacent.

The Nenzel Mansion Bed & Breakfast • ⌂⌂⌂ ØØ

U.S. 395 and Eddy Street (P.O. Box 2498; a block south of Sharkey's), Minden, NV 89427; (702) 782-7644. Doubles $75 to $85, singles $70 to $80. Four rooms, two with private and two with shared baths; full breakfast. Imposing three-story 1910 mansion with widow's walk, owned by an early Minden banker. Guests' rooms done in a mix of early American and modern furnishings. Sitting room with marble fireplace; old fashioned sitting porches.

Westerner Motel • ⌂⌂ $$

1353 Highway 395 South, Gardnerville, NV 89410; (702) 782-3602. Doubles $32 to $43, singles $30 to $35. Major credit cards. Small, nicely maintained 25-unit motel with TV, room phones; swimming pool.

WHERE TO CAMP

Carson Valley Inn RV Park • *1627 Highway 395 (P.O. Box 2560), Minden, NV 89423; (800) 321-9711 outside Nevada or (702) 782-9711. RVS only, full hookups $14. Reservations accepted; Major credit cards.* Adjacent to Carson Valley Inn casino (see listing above), with laundry, showers and dump station.

GENOA

Population: 150 **Elevation: 4,789 feet**

If you drive four miles north on U.S. 395 from Minden, you'll soon see a sign directing you west, to the place where Nevada began.

THE WAY IT WAS • In 1851, a band of 18 Mormon merchants opened a trading post here to sell supplies and fresh teams to the California-bound masses crowding the Carson branch of the Emigrant Trail. They certainly chose an appealing spot.

"It stands upon a little slope at the very base of the mountains, which rise abruptly from the valley to a great elevation. It commands a view of almost the entire valley and the prospect is really beautiful. The serpentine course of the Carson River can be traced by the willows that border either bank." Thus wrote James Hutchings in 1859.

The trading post, initially called Mormon Station, was so successful that Brigham Young dispatched a colonizing group of 100 families to homestead the valley in 1855. They were led by Judge Orson Hyde, who saw visions of Italy in the imposing hills and re-named the settlement Genoa. Subsequent generations have warped the pronunciation to "ge-NO-uh". If you say it with the accent on the first syllable, locals will assume you're from California.

When Genoa was colonized, the area was part of the great Utah Territory, dominated by Young's clan. As more non-Mormons settled here, demanding non-sectarian government, Brig saw that he was losing his grip on his far-flung empire, which he called *Deseret*. He began calling the faithful home to Salt Lake, virtually emptying many of the Mormon settlements.

Genoa residents received their notice in 1857, forcing many to sell their land quickly and cheaply to the intruding gentiles. Some of the new owners didn't bother to pay at all, inspiring Judge Hyde to write a rather salty collection letter:

"You shall be visited of the Lord of Hosts with thunder and with earthquakes and with floods, with pestilence and with famine until your names are not known among men. You have rejected the authority of God, trampled upon his laws and given yourselves up to serve the god of this world; to rioting and debauchery, drunkenness and corruption. You can pay and find mercy, or despise the demand (for payment) and perish!"

The check's in the mail, sir.

Nevada's oldest settlement became one of its first casualties. It lost population to better-located communities in the Carson Valley, and the main emigrant trail shifted northward to Donner Pass. It enjoyed brief respite as a Pony Express station in 1860- 61. A fire devoured most of the town in 1910 and it lost its county seat six years later to Minden. Genoa may have become a non-town, surviving only as a bucolic bit of countryside with memories. However, the state of Nevada stepped in to construct a replica of the original trading fort shortly after World War II.

THE WAY IT IS • Genoa today has much of the bucolic look that moved James Hutchings to poetic prose more than a century and a half ago. However, it's beginning to lose its pastoral charm. Growing Carson City, just 12 miles north, is spreading to its edges. You'll note several modern new homes cropping up among Genoa's black locusts and amur maples.

Plan an hour or few to prowl about and poke into its court house museum and reconstructed fort. Other lures include several Victorians—mostly restored, an antique shop or two, the attractive **Pink House Restaurant**, the great old **Genoa Country Store** and snack shop dating from 1879, the 1862 **Masonic Hall** and the **Genoa Bar,** reaching back to 1863.

THE ATTRACTIONS

Mormon Station State Historic Park • *Main Street; (702) 782-2590. Open May 1 to October 15, daily 9 to 5; donations accepted.* This vertical-pole stockade is a reasonably authentic replica of the original. Exhibits in the log trading post museum tell the story of the fort, the Mormons and the California-bound pioneers who paused here. There isn't much to see in the stockade. ; you'll have to use your imagination to picture ox and mule-drawn wagons at rest; bustling and nervous immigrants gathering provisions, strength and courage for that last terrifying pull over Carson Pass.

Genoa Courthouse Museum • *Fifth and Main streets, opposite the fort; (702) 782-4325. Open May 15 to mid-October, daily 10 to 4:30. Free; donations appreciated.* This red brick, balconied structure houses an interesting assortment of collections gathered by the Carson Valley Historical Society. In addition to the usual pioneer lore, you'll find such curiosities as Henry Millam's collection of 200 years of American hats, a stuffed tiger, Washoe Indian baskets, an old school room and jail cell. One exhibit concerns George Ferris of Carson City, who invented the Ferris wheel, first exhibited at Chicago's Columbia Exposition in 1893. The upstairs courtroom has been restored and staffed with mannequins. A **Pony Express marker** out front of the museum declares that those "swift phantoms of the desert" hurried through here with the mail during 1860 and 1861.

Genoa Bar and Saloon • *Main Street, near the fort; (702) 782-3870.* This weathered, brick- front place bills itself as Nevada's oldest thirst parlor. It looks believable, with a long weathered plank and backbar, high ceilings, oiled wooden floors and two dogs snoring beside a sheet metal stove. Old photos, prints and a moth-chewed deer head decorate the walls; a small gift and antique shop occupies one side. The saloon was built in 1863 by Al Livingston and called Livingston's Exchange. The pub has a more contemporary claim to fame, as well. It was featured in a 1989 Coors beer commercial because an advertising exec decided that it "had a personality all its own."

WHERE TO SLEEP

The Genoa House Inn • △△△ $$$$ ØØ

180 Nixon St. (P.O. Box 141), Genoa, NV 89411; (702) 782-7075. Doubles $85 to $120, singles $75 to $110. Two rooms with private bath; full breakfast. yellow and white-trimmed 1872 Victorian, carefully restored and furnished with American and European antiques; built in 1872 by the valley's first newspaper publisher and listed on the National Register of Historic Places.

Wild Rose Inn • △△△ $$$$ ØØ

Main Street (P.O. Box 256), Genoa, NV 89411; (702) 782-5697. Doubles $85 to $105, singles $75 to $95. Four rooms with private baths; full buffet breakfast. Queen Anne Victorian handsomely restored and furnished with "country Victorian" antiques. The hillside setting offers views of the valley and mountains.

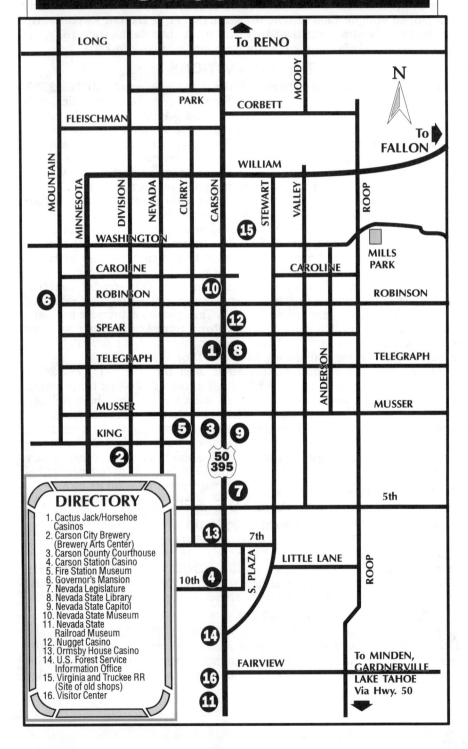

"Six months after my entry into journalism, the grand flush times of Silverland began. Joy sat on every countenance, and there was a glad, almost fierce intensity in every eye... Money was as plenty as dust; every individual considered himself wealthy, and a melancholy countenance was nowhere to be seen."
— Mark Twain, describing Virginia City in *Roughing It*

Chapter Six
THE SILVER CITIES
Carson and Virginia

Never mind the fact that emigrants struggled across the state's vast reaches, that young Pony Express riders galloped over the land like the winds of fury, and that Mormon pioneers established the first outposts. Nevada was not born of these people. The emigrants and pony lads were just passing through and many of the Mormons went back to Salt Lake City.

Nevada was born of silver miners and silver barons. It was the creation of men who dug the blue mud in Virginia City's Comstock Lode, and men who assayed and minted it in Carson City.

The two "silver cities" comprise a nice package for the Nevada traveler. About 12 miles apart, they're linked geographically and historically and both offer many visitor attractions. They're linked journalistically as well, by one of history's grand American writers. Twenty-six-year-old Sam Clemens stepped off a dusty stagecoach in Carson City on August 14, 1861. He was in the company of his older brother Orion, who had been appointed secretary to the new Nevada Territory. After 14 fruitless months as a prospector, Sam accepted a job as a reporter for Virginia City's *Territorial Enterprise*. He covered, among other things, the nearby Nevada legislature, where his brother obviously provided useful contacts.

Although Clemens spent a fair amount of time in Carson City, he is more closely associated with Virginia City, where he worked and where he adopted his famous pen name. Any fifth grader can tell you that "mark twain" is a riverman's cry that he has measured two fathoms, safe water for a paddlewheeler.

Today, the two communities are rather curious cousins, with little in common physically or socially. Carson City is at once prim and affable, looking more like a prosperous old Midwestern farm town than a frontier survivor. Virginia City is garish and tacky, an unabashed parody of its earlier days as a booming silver camp.

If you want to experience sociological time warp, stroll along one of Carson City's old residential streets, past elm-shaded Victorians. Then drive a dozen miles and clump down a Virginia City boardwalk, licking a "Cowboy Cone" and shouldering through legions of videocamera-clutchers.

Carson City

Population: 40,400 **Elevation: 4,660 feet**

Although it's Nevada's third largest community, right up there with Las Vegas and Reno, Carson City is fueled not by tourism and gaming, but by bureaucracy. Most of the games played here are political, as a growing Nevada shapes its future.

Certainly, tourists are drawn to this dignified brick-front community, and certainly there are a few casinos along Carson Street. The visitors are lured by the marble halls of the old capitol, the fine state museum and the equally fine railroad museum. They're drawn by history, not by craps table hysterics. In a sense, it has always been thus.

THE WAY IT WAS • Carson City never was a very exciting or excitable place. No boom followed by bust, no randy miners whooping it up in rows of cathouses. The town began life deliberately and carefully, as the visionary effort of one Abraham Z. Curry.

A New York businessman, Curry felt there was more money to be made in mining the miners and other settlers than in the mines themselves. Arriving in 1858, he set about to buy land and lay out a town. Prices were too high around already-established Mormon Station, so he and three partners bought a ranch that covered most of the Eagle Valley, just to the north. It had served since 1851 as Eagle Station Trading Post on the southern branch of the Emigrant Trail.

Curry beefed up the trading post operation and hired a surveyor to lay out a town. Ever the optimist, he instructed the surveyor to set aside ten acres for the future state capitol.

Capitol? Nevada wasn't even a territory, and it apparently had no prospects of becoming one in the near future. In fact, Brigham Young had recalled most of the Mormon settlers back to Salt Lake City and the area was in a bit of a slump. However, up in the rocky slopes of nearby Sun Mountain, gold-seekers were about to shape Carson City's fate. They kept encountering a sticky blue-black mud that clogged their sluices and fouled their mining operations. In 1859, a sample was carried across the mountains to Nevada City, California, where an assayer determined it to be a blend of silver sulfide and gold.

In the rush to the nearby gold *and* silver fields, Abe Curry's carefully laid out town became a major provisioning center. The new community, which Curry named for frontier scout Kit Carson, took the county seat away from Genoa in 1851. That same year, Washington officials sliced Brigham Young's Deseret in half to create Nevada Territory. Curry assured Carson City's selection as territorial capital by donating his Warm Springs Hotel, built over a mineral spring, as a legislative building. (What bureaucrat could resist an office with a natural hot tub next door?)

Pressing on with entrepreneurial fervor, Curry built a second hotel, established a brick yard and sandstone quarry and opened a toll road to the base of Sun Mountain. He later sold officials his other hotel to serve as both a courthouse and legislature. Warm Springs became the state's first prison, with Curry as warden. In 1869, construction started on a permanent state capitol—on that plot of land set aside years earlier by "Uncle Abe." When the Virginia & Truckee Railroad was built from Carson to the Comstock mines, Abe's quarry provided sandstone for the rail shops here. He also convinced federal officials to construct a mint in Carson City to handle the incoming flood of silver. Guess who served as its first superintendent?

Ambitious, successful, generous, quick to make a buck and share it, Abe Curry should have become the most powerful man in Nevada. However, he was struck down by a stroke in 1873 at the age of 58.

THINGS TO KNOW BEFORE YOU GO

BEST TIME TO GO • Carson City is an all-season place with mild climate; museums and other tourist lures are open year around. However, several attractions in Virginia City are closed from the end of October until early May. At 6,220 feet, it can get nippy in winter.

WHAT TO SEE • In Carson City, the State Capitol, Nevada State Railroad Museum and Nevada State Museum in the Old Carson Mint, the raw gold display in the Carson Nugget and the campus of the Stewart Indian School. Also travel to Fort Churchill State Park to the east and Bowers Mansion to the north. In Virginia City, check out The Castle, Fourth Ward School, Nevada Gambling Museum, The Way It Was Museum and St. Mary's Church.

WHAT CASINOS TO SEE • The Ormsby House and Carson Station in Carson City. In Virginia City, visit out the Bucket of Blood, Delta, Old Washoe House and Silver Queen saloons.

WHAT TO DO • Follow the historic homes tour with a brochure from the Carson City Convention & Visitors Bureau, and soak your buns at Carson Hot Springs. In Virginia City, take the trolley tour, Ponderosa Saloon mine tour and Virginia & Truckee steam train ride, then hike up the flanks of Mount Davidson.

Useful contacts

Carson City Convention & Visitors Bureau, 1900 S. Carson St., Carson City, NV 89701; (800) NEVADA-1 or (702) 687-7410.

Virginia City Chamber of Commerce, P.O. Box 464, Virginia City, NV 89440; (702) 847-0311.

Toiyabe National Forest, Carson Ranger District, 1536 S. Carson St., Carson City, NV 89701; (702) 882-2766; for information on the Sierra Nevada east of the city.

Area radio stations

Most Reno radio stations come in loud and clear in this area; see list in the next chapter. Also, you can tune in these locals:

KGBM-FM, 99.3, Minden/Gardnerville—classic hits
KNIS-FM, 91.3, Carson City—Christian radio
KODS-FM, 104, Carson City/Reno—oldies
KOZZ-FM, 105, Sutro—top forty
KONE-AM, 1450, Sutro—top forty
KTPL-AM, 1300, Carson City—popular music and news

Carson City never suffered the fate of boom-and-bust mining towns, since it was fortified with bureaucratic payrolls, and it also remained an important provisioning center. Of course, it shrank substantially when the Virginia City mines played out late in the last century, and it continued dwindling during the Depression. From a Comstock peak of 8,000, it shriveled to 2,000 in the 1930s. As late as 1950 it could boast (or complain) of being America's smallest capital city, with fewer than 5,000 citizens.

THE WAY IT IS ● Carson City today is a charming demographic curiosity. The heart of town, with its brick-front stores and gracious neighborhood Victorians, is little changed from yesterday. In fact, it still *looks* like a town of less than 5,000. However, the suburbs have grown considerably in recent years. The 1990 census revealed that Carson's population had galloped past 40,000. You'd think someone had found another silver strike in the hills!

With this sudden growth surge, it has passed the baton of America's smallest capital to Montpelier, Vermont. Size-wise, Carson is technically one of America's larger "cities," since it has combined old Ormsby County and Carson City into a single entity. Its boundaries stretch nearly 30 miles east to west and 12 miles north to south. Driving around the countryside, you'll see "rural Carson City" signs, marking the boundaries of the city-county.

Downtown Carson City remains relatively intact, except for the loss of a few old buildings to casino parking lots. Most of the growth is occurring to the north and south, and a disorderly procession of Walmarts and K-Marts have risen to greet mushrooming subdivisions. Driving along busy Carson Street—Highway 395—one gets the impression that all of the north Carson people shop in south Carson and visa versa. Despite thick cross-town traffic, it's easy to get around in this little city. Uncle Abe's grid is simple to navigate and there's ample parking on side streets and in casino lots.

If you've been following this book as we've written it, you'll approach from the south on U.S. 395. A few miles below town, it widens into four lanes to accommodate the city's fast-growing suburbs.

Quickie Carson tour

You can see most of what Carson City has to offer by following Highway 395 through downtown, and sprouting off at the proper intersections.

Just north of the U.S. 395-50 junction, watch for Snyder Avenue on your right and a sign indicating **Stewart Indian School** and museum. This interesting century-old fieldstone complex is about a mile east of the highway. Returning to 395 and continuing north, you'll see the large train sheds of the **Nevada State Railroad Museum** on your left.

Carson City Convention and Visitors Bureau's **Information Center** is just north of the museum; the same entry road serves both. It's open weekdays 8 to 5 throughout the year, plus weekends from 10 to 3, May to December. Just north on the highway is the **U.S. Forest Service** information office (Toiyabe National Forest), also on your left.

You're now entering old Carson City; many of its attractions and all of its casinos stand alongside Carson Street. Starting on the left, you see **Carson Station Casino** at Tenth Street, then the **Ormsby House casino** three blocks beyond at Seventh. The new **Nevada legislative buildings** and old **State Capitol** appear on your right and the Grecian-style **Carson County Courthouse** is on the left, at the corner of Musser Street.

Turn left onto Musser and you'll hit the Carson City Fire Department with its **Fire Station Museum** on the second floor. Continue on Musser to Division Street, go left a block and you'll see the old yellow brick **Carson City Brewery,** with two art galleries attached.

Return to Carson Street on Musser and continue north. You're now flanked by the city's three other casinos, **Cactus Jack** and the **Horseshoe** on your left and the **Nugget** just beyond on your right. Opposite the horseshoe is the attractive red brick Gothic **Nevada State Library**. The sturdy sandstone **Carson Mint** housing the **Nevada State Museum** is up a block from the Nugget, on the left.

Turn left onto Robinson Street (beside the mint) and follow it several blocks to Mountain Street. Before you is the quasi-plantation style **Governor's Mansion,** with its Grecian columns and circular drive. Go right onto Mountain, then right again onto Washington (after two blocks) and follow it across Carson to Stewart Street. On your left is the site of the **Virginia & Truckee Railroad shops**, built of solid sandstone by Carson City's solid citizen Abe Curry.

If you feel the urge to soak in a hot spring and see the site of Abe Currey's **Warm Springs Hotel**, return to Carson Street and continue north. Drive off our locator map and watch for Hot Springs Road, which forks to the right near a Safeway. Follow it eastward for about a mile and you'll see **Carson Hot Springs** on your left.

THE BEST ATTRACTIONS

Nevada State Capitol • *Carson and Musser streets; (702) 687-5000; open 9 to 5.* This is a state capitol in the grand manner, constructed of Abe Curry's cut sandstone, with bold Grecian columns and a lofty dome—once copper, now Fiberglass. The statehouse sits in its own personal park shaded by sugar maples and fir trees. Completed in 1870 and beautifully restored in 1977, it's both a working capitol and a museum. Offices of the governor, lieutenant governor and secretary of state are still within, all dressed up in 19th century furnishings. Walk the capitol's marbled halls and admire its carved wooden bannisters, deeply paneled wainscoting, rows of governors' portraits and decorative frieze representing the state's minerals and other resources.

The old senate chamber is now an excellent museum focusing on Nevada's history and the capitol's construction. You'll see the 36-star flag that flapped when Nevada became a state, the wine glasses used by Curry and Governor James Nye to toast statehood and significant other relics. There's a detailed mock-up of the office of Emmett Boyle, son of a prominent Comstock family and the first native Nevadan to become governor (1915-1922).

Nevada State Museum (Carson Mint) • *600 N. Carson St. (at Robinson Street); (702) 687-4810. Daily 8:30 to 4:30. Adults $1.50; kids under 18 free.* This is, in a sense, a double museum. The original cut sandstone building houses an outstanding numismatic exhibit. Displays focus on the days when Carson City minted coin of the realm. You'll see old coin presses, a complete set of scarce Carson City Morgan dollars and other coins bearing the rare "CC" mint mark. During its operation, from 1870 to 1893, it cranked out $49,274,434.30 in coins, most made from Comstock silver.

An attached building, added in later years, houses a fine museum of Nevada's natural and social history. You'll meet some of the state's earliest residents, such as an *ichthyosaur* skeleton and a *mammoth imperator*. A fine six-minute film in the Hall of Regional Geology describes the workings of plate tectonics. Bringing things up to date, the museum displays artifacts of Native Americans, early settlers and mining barons. In a special "Feminine Frontier" exhibit, you'll learn about Nevada's famous ladies, including one Katherine Patricia Ryan, born at a mining camp near Ely in 1912. She's better known today as Pat Nixon, wife of America's only unseated President.

Nevada State Railroad Museum • *2180 S. Carson St. (opposite Silver City Mall); (702) 687-6953. Wednesday-Sunday 8:30 to 4:30. Adults $1; kids under 18 free. Train rides around the grounds weekends from late May through Labor Day, plus a "Santa Train" in December.* Two beautifully restored choo-choos are centerpieces of this fine museum, which is built around rolling stock of the Virginia & Truckee Railroad. Admire the impeccable, brass-accented 1870 "Inyo" and the big, black and bold Number 25, a 150,000-pounder built in 1905. Both have restored rolling stock attached. The Inyo worked until 1925, then became a film star. For those of us who can remember, Gregory Peck wrecked her in *Duel in the Sun*. Exhibits also include meticulously crafted miniatures of the V&T's engines and lots of historic railroading photos. Several other engines and cars are housed in nearby sheds, which are open to visitors during warm weather. A gift shop bursting with railroad memories occupies a corner of the main museum.

The Virginia & Truckee was built in 21 zig-zagging miles up to Virginia City by Chinese laborers. It became the richest short line in America, hauling the wealth of the Comstock mines to riverside smelters. The railroad eventually branched over to Reno, down to Hawthorne and up to Lake Tahoe; it shut down in 1950.

Stewart Indian Museum • *5366 Snyder Ave. (a mile east of U.S. 395, south of town); (702) 882-1808. Daily 9 to 4. Free; donations appreciated.* The extensive grounds of the Stewart Indian School are perhaps more interesting than the museum itself. Several ruggedly handsome cut stone buildings stand about a park-like setting, shaded by ancient trees. Nevada Senator William Stewart, troubled by the West's cruel treatment of Native Americans, convinced Congress to fund the facility, which opened in 1890. The extensive complex served as an Indian boarding school until 1980, when it was closed by the Bureau of Indian Affairs "with no explanation," according to graphics in the museum. More than 3,000 Indian children received liberal arts, vocational and agricultural educations here.

The museum, unprofessional but lovingly done by the Stewart Indian community, occupies the old superintendent's house. Exhibits range from Indian crafts and sepia photos of the first graduating class to contemporary school band uniforms and cheerleaders' megaphones. A fine little gift shop sells Indian jewelry, weavings and other crafts.

THE REST

Carson City Brewery • *449 W. King St. (at Division Street). Brewery Arts Center open Monday-Friday 9 to 5, (702) 883-1976; Nevada Artists' Association Gallery open Monday- Saturday 10 to 4, (702) 882-6411. Both free.* The Carson Brewing Company turned out suds in this yellow brick building for thirsty Nevadans from 1864 until 1948, with a brief intermission for Prohibition. "Tahoe Beer, as famous as the lake," was quaffed from Reno to Ely to Pioche. Sadly, the old structure is now boarded up, although two art gal-

— Betty Woo Martin

The city's namesake, Kit Carson, bows to a visitor (lower left corner) on the grounds of the Carson City capitol.

leries occupy an attached building. Step inside to check out the works of local artists and admire a few relics from the brewery, on display in the Nevada Artists' Association Gallery. A drive is underway to refurbish the brewery.

Carson Hot Springs • *1500 Hot Springs Rd.; (702) 882-9863. Daily 7 a.m. to 11 p.m.; mineral pool use $8, seniors 55 and over and kids 12 and under, $6; other fees for private hot tubs and massages.* Not a shred of Abe Curry's Warm Springs Hotel survives, so you'll soak up more mineral water than history at this place. It's a plain but pleasant old facility, with a walled-in outdoor pool, sunning benches and hot tubs. The waters are a relaxing 100 degrees with none of the sulfuric rotten egg smell of some mineral springs. A motel, restaurant and RV park are part of the complex.

Fire Department Museum • *111 N. Curry St. (at Musser); (702) 887-2210. Free; open daily 1 to 4 or whenever one of the firemen happens to be in an adjacent office.* Warren Engine Company Number One began fighting Carson City's fires in 1863, and it's descendants have been doing it ever since. Relics of the old company, including its first motorized fire truck, are on display on the fire department's second floor. The 1913 Seagrave was, in fact, the first fire truck in the entire state. Other exhibits include hand-

212 — CHAPTER SIX

drawn hose carts, old photos, helmets and Currier and Ives prints of fire laddies in action. The original cut stone fire station is still intact, located across the street and housing professional offices.

Historic homes tour • *"Carson City Historic Tour" guide maps available at the visitor's center.* This newsprint style map will steer you past some of the most exquisite Victorians structures in Western America. Most are on the west side of Carson Street, running north from Second up to Washington streets.

NUGGETS

Governor's Mansion • *Mountain and Robinson streets.* You'll enjoy a glimpse of this handsome, dazzling white Classic Revival building, with its Ionic columns, second-story porch and curved, landscaped drive. The structure was built in 1908 and restored in 1968. Public areas of the mansion are sometimes open for tours.

Jack's Bar • *Fifth and Carson streets (just north of the Ormsby House).* Rare iron columns front this old-fashioned bar. An interesting clutter of collector whisky bottles occupy the backbar inside, along with a fetching gallery of nude paintings. It's one of Carson City's few surviving oldstyle bars.

Nevada State Library Building • *Northeast corner of Carson and Telegraph streets.* "French Gothic" might properly describe this ornate, steep-roofed, bell-towered brick building. Built in 1889, it houses the state's archives and a fine collection of books on Nevada.

Nugget display • *At the Nugget Casino, 507 N. Carson St.; (702) 882-1626. Open 24 hours.* Step inside the Nugget's Carson and Robinson Street entrance and you'll see fine examples of gold in curious shapes and styles formed by Mother Nature. The collection includes leaf gold, ribbon gold, gold-embedded quartz and unusual crystallized gold.

THE CASINOS

Cactus Jack's Senator Club • ☺

420 N. Carson St.; (702) 882-8770. The Senator Club is a basic sawdust joint the with the usual slots, a smoky poker room and three blackjack tables. Its 24-hour **Corner Cafe** is a simple coffee shop; dinners $4 to $8.

Carson Nugget • ☺☺

507 N. Carson St.; (702) 882-1626. Old but well maintained and only slightly smoky, the Nugget offers the usual tables games, lots of slots and videos, plus a bingo parlor, souvenir shop and a kids playroom. The look is 1960s modern, with recessed cone lamps and low ceilings. Stop by to admire the fine exhibit of unusual gold formations (see "Nuggets" above). A casino lounge features live entertainment and the City Center Motel nearby (listed below) provides lodging. The **Steak House** is an appealing brick and dark wood place with items ranging from tournados of beef to stuffed chicken breast. It's open Sunday-Thursday 5 to 9 and Friday-Saturday 5 to 10; dinners $10 to $15, plus early bird specials. The **Oyster Bar** is a small nautical style seafood place with ocean fare from $5 to $9. There's also a 24-hour **coffee shop** and a lunch and dinner **buffet**.

Carson Station • ☺☺

900 S. Carson St.; (702) 883-0900. The newest place in town, the Station is a medium-sized gaming parlor with slots and videos, of course, plus a sports book and the essential gaming tables—one dice, one roulette and several blackjack. A country band twangs from a lounge open to the casino. The **Restaurant** is rather attractive, with seating under greenhouse glass. It's open Sunday-Thursday 6 a.m. to 11 p.m. and Friday-Saturday 6 to 1 a.m. The menu is basic American, with dinners ranging from $6 to $10. Rooms are available at Carson Station's Best Western hotel (listed below).

Horseshoe Club • ☺
402 N. Carson St.; (702) 883-2211 Occupying the same block as Cactus Jack's and similar in size, temperament and smokiness, the Horseshoe is primarily a low rollers' slot and video poker place. The **Snack Bar,** open from 9 a.m. to 10 p.m., offers some of the town's best food prices, such as an 89-cent pancake, bacon and egg breakfast. Light entrées range from $3 to $6.

Ormsby House • ☺☺☺
600 S. Carson St.; (702) 882-1890. One of Nevada's most historic hostelries, the frontier-elegant Ormsby dates to 1859, when it was opened by Major William Ormsby (later killed in a Paiute skirmish at Pyramid Lake). The place survived into the 20s, closed, then reopened as a casino when gambling was legalized in 1931. The Paul Laxalt family has owned it for decades, expanding it and creating its present Victorian look.

The Ormsby has the proper look of a 19th century grand hotel, with cut stone walls, a columned portico out front and a grand, sweeping stairway, chandeliers and red flocked wallpaper inside. Gamblers will find slots and videos a-plenty in the roomy casino, plus the usual table games. Live music, often country 'n' Western, emanates from the Mark Twain Bar. A hotel tower (listed below) offers plenty of pillows. The **Supper Club** has a nice Victorian look and an Italian-American menu with savories such as bacon-wrapped prawns and blackened prime rib, $6 to $15, open from 5 p.m. A **buffet** is open for lunch and dinner and of course the place has the ubiquitous 24-hour **coffee shop.**

WHERE ELSE TO DINE

Adele's Restaurant & Lounge • ☺☺☺ $$$ Ø
1112 N. Carson St.; (702) 882-3353. American-continental, dinners $18 to $30; full bar service. Monday-Saturday 11 to 4:30 and 5 to 10, closed Sunday. Reservations accepted; MC/VISA, AMEX. Carson's most elegant restaurant, housed in Victorian splendor in a former supreme court justice's home. It features oak trim, leaded glass windows, crystal beaded lamps and other finery, with an appealing red and white color scheme. The menu ranges from good American steak and European classics to an outstanding and expensive *chateaubriand*. This is where the boys from the legislature (just across the street) convene their power lunches.

Bodine's Restaurant & Saloon • ☺☺ $$ Ø
5650 S. Carson St. (south of town at U.S. 395/50 junction); (702) 885-0303. American; dinners $10 to $20; full bar service. Lunch 11:30 to 3:30, dinner 5 to 10 (to 9 in the off-season). Reservations accepted; MC/VISA. Country style place with back patio featuring a waterfall and tableside pond. Essential steak and seafood menu focusing on things barbecued.

El Charro Avitia • ☺☺ $ Ø
4389 S. Carson St. (a mile and a half south, just beyond Walmart, off Clearview Drive); (702) 883-6261. Mexican; dinners $6 to $11; full bar service. Lunch Monday-Friday 11 to 5, dinner nightly from 5, various closing

hours. MC/VISA. Locally popular place serving excellent Mexican fare; well worth the drive south from town. Entrèes include specialties such as *torta* (sirloin with peppers), *chimichangas* and taco *nacionales* with chicken, almonds and cream cheese. The dining room is warm, cute and cozy, done in brick and dark woods.

Grandma Hattie's ● ☺ $ ∅

2811 S. Carson St. (south edge of town); (702) 882-4900. American; dinners $5 to $10; wine and beer. Daily 5 a.m. to 9 p.m. Reservations accepted; no credit cards. Simple, friendly family-style restaurant serving basic American chicken, steaks and chops. Generous portions of home-style cooking at reasonable prices; a local favorite.

Hawaiian Cactus Club ● ☺☺ $$

At Carson Hot Springs, 1500 Hot Springs Rd.; (702) 882-8963. American-Polynesian; dinners $8 to $14; full bar service. Tuesday-Thursday 10 a.m. to 11 p.m., Friday 11 to midnight, Saturday noon to midnight, Sunday 5 to 12. MC/VISA, AMEX. As the name implies, the look and the menu are a blend of Western America and Polynesia. The place was being remodeled when we visited, so you should be greeted by new palm trees, cactus and menu.

Heidi's Dutch Mill ● ☺☺ $ ∅

1020 N. Carson St.; (702) 882-0486. American; meals $4 to $7. Breakfast and lunch only, served from 6 a.m. to 2 p.m.; wine and beer MC/VISA. Pretty little Dutch style place, with wainscoting, print wallpaper, floral trim and high backed booths. It's the best breakfast cafe in town. Try the Belgian waffles, strawberry crepes or do-it-yourself omelettes.

Marrone's ● ☺☺ $$ ∅∅

2729 Carson St.; (702) 883-7044. Italian; dinners $4.75 to $14; full bar service. Lunch weekdays 11 to 2, dinner Monday-Saturday 5:30 to 9, closed Sunday. Reservations accepted; MC/VISA, AMEX. Cozy family-style place with a menu of select Italian dishes such as veals *parmigiana* and *Marsala*, chicken *Marrone* (marinated in beer, garlic and parsley) and various pasta dishes. Smoke-free dining room.

Miramar House ● ☺ $ ∅

202 Fairview (at Carson Street); (702) 882-0262. Chinese-Thai; dinners $5 to $13; full bar service. Monday-Thursday 11 to 9, Friday 11 to 10, Saturday noon to 10, closed Sunday. Major credit cards. Small place with a big menu; extensive selection of Chinese and Thai dishes, plus a few American items. Chinese combo dinners from $7.95 to $8.95 a person are a good buy, or try Thai specials such as beef, chicken or pork in curry with coconut milk and green chili.

New Pine Cone Restaurant ● ☺ $

3449 S. Carson St.; (702) 882-4110. Chinese; dinners $5.50 to $7.74; wine and beer. Daily 11:30 to 9. No credit cards. Simple family-style Chinese restaurant with an extensive Mandarin and Cantonese menu. Mix and match your dishes, or order individual dinners for as little as $5.55 for five items.

Scotty's Family Restaurant ● ☺ $ ∅

1480 N. Carson St.; (702) 882-2982. American; dinners $6 to $8.50; wine and beer. Daily 6 a.m. to 8 p.m. No credit cards. Basic family-style Naugahyde cafe serving ample portions at reasonable prices. Stuff the kids with spaghetti, chicken strips or hamburger steak for $2.95 while you dine on "Papa John Parmesan" (chicken fried steak) for $6.95 or grilled beef liver for $6.25.

Silvana's Italian Cuisine • ☺☺ $$$ ∅
1301 N. Carson St. (at Corbett); (702) 883-5100. Italian-American; dinners $13 to $20; full bar service. Tuesday-Saturday 5 to 10. Reservations accepted; major credit cards. Cozy cellar style restaurant in a bunkered bungalow. Italian specialties such as homemade *gnocci, chioppino and canneloni,* plus fresh seafood, steaks and lamb specials. Good-sized Italian and American wine list.

WHERE TO SLEEP

Carson Station Hotel Casino • ⌒⌒ $$
900 S. Carson St. (P.O. Box 1966), Carson City, NV 89701; (800) 528-1234 or (702) 883-0900. Doubles and singles $45 to $85, suites $100. Major credit cards. A Best Western motel with Carson Station casino and **restaurants** adjacent. Ninety good-sized modern rooms, each with its own balcony; TV, room phones.

City Center Motel • ⌒⌒ $$
800 N. Carson St., Carson City, NV 89701; (800) 338-7760 or (702) 882-5535. Doubles $36 to $45, plus low-cost room-dining-gaming packages. Major credit cards. Basic, modern rooms with TV, room phones and sun deck. Part of the Carson Nugget across the street; **restaurants** and casino listed above.

Days Inn • ⌒⌒ $$$ ∅
3103 N. Carson St., Carson City, NV 89701; (800) 325-2525 or (702) 883-3343. Doubles $55 to $60, singles $35 to $45. Major credit cards. Attractive motel with 62 good sized, well-appointed rooms with TV, video rentals, room phones.

Desert Hills Motel • ⌒⌒ $$ ∅
1010 S. Carson St. (at Tenth), Carson City, NV 89701; (800) NEVADA-1 OR (702) 882-1932. Doubles $39 to $89, singles $35 to $79, suites $49 to $149; weekly winter rates. Major credit cards. Country-style 33-unit motel with TV movies, phones, some waterbeds. Honeymoon suites with in-room spas. Pool, outside hot tub; pets OK. Carson Station Casino adjacent.

Hardman House • ⌒⌒ $$ ∅
917 N. Carson St., Carson City, NV 89701; (800) 626-0793. Doubles $45 to $60, singles $36 to $50, suites $65 to $90. Major credit cards. A 62-unit motel with TV, room phones; refrigerators, microwaves and wet bars in some suites; VCRs available.

Motel Orleans • ⌒⌒ $$ ∅
2731 S. Carson St., Carson City, NV 89701; (800) 626-1900 or (702) 882-2007. Doubles $39 to $46, singles $30 to $38. Major credit cards. A 58-unit motel with TV, room phones, pool and spa.

Ormsby House • ⌒⌒⌒ $$
600 S. Carson St., Carson City, NV 89701; (800) 648-0920 or (702) 882-1890. Doubles $46 to $59, singles $40 to $45. Major credit cards. Good-sized,

comfortable rooms, contemporary furnishings with Victorian touches; TV, room phones. In hotel tower behind casino with full gaming facilities and **restaurants** (listed above.)

Silver Queen Inn ● △ $$ ∅

201 W. Caroline St. (at Curry, behind state museum), Carson City, NV 89701; (800) NEVADA-1 or (702) 882-5534. Doubles $34 to $46, singles $29 to $44. Major credit cards. Basic 35-room motel with TV and room phones.

WHERE TO CAMP

Camp-N-Town ● *2438 N. Carson St., Carson City, NV 89701; (702) 883-1123. RV sites; water and electric $14, full hookups $16.50. Reservations accepted; MC/VISA.* On northern edge of town, some pull-throughs. Showers, coin laundry, pool and spa, bar with slots, pay phones, convenience store, game room.

Comstock Country RV Resort ● *5400 S. Carson St. (just south of Highway 395/50 junction), Carson City, NV 89701; (800) NEVADA-1 or (702) 882-2445. RV and tent sites; full hookups $18, no hookups $14. Reservations accepted; MC/VISA.* Large RV park in rural setting, with many pull-throughs. Full hookups, showers, coin laundry, groceries, Propane, picnic tables, pool and spa, pay phones, tennis and basketball courts, rec room, playground, shuffleboard and horseshoes.

Carson Nugget ● *507 N. Carson St., Carson City, NV 89701; (702) 882-1626.* Free RV parking is offered in one of the Nugget lots, two blocks off Carson Street at Fall and Telegraph; no hookups or facilities.

ANNUAL EVENTS

Pow Wow & Native American Arts & Crafts Fair, first weekend of February, third weekend of April and first weekend of October, (702) 885-9759; in Stewart Indian Colony gymnasium.

Carson City Founder's Festival, last weekend of February, (702) 885-8461; banjo and fiddle jamboree, arts and crafts, foods.

Stewart Indian Museum Arts & Crafts Fair and Pow Wow, third weekend of June; (702) 882-1808; dancing, hand games, Native American foods and crafts.

Pony Express Ride re-creation & Kit Carson Rendezvous, mid-June, (702) 687-4507 or 687-7410; Pony Express re-enactment; wagon train from Reno to Carson City; costume pageant with food booths, live country music, fast-draw contests, amateur boxing other events.

Capitol City Fair, third weekend of July at Carson City Fairgrounds; (702) 882-4460 or 887-3942; carnival, entertainment, livestock show and other county fair fare.

NORTH OF CARSON CITY

If you head north on Highway 395, you'll enter the **Washoe Valley** and skim the edge of **Washoe Lake,** or the former Washoe Lake, if the multi-year drought hasn't eased by the time you read this.

A right onto State Route 428 (East Lake Boulevard) takes you along the lake's eastern edge to **Washoe Lake State Park.** It offers no-hookup campsites for $6, day use for a dollar and a boat launch and pier that currently begins and ends on dry land. The lake is that distant gleam you see across the sagebrush. You can loop around the lake or backtrack to Highway 395 and follow State Route 429 to a Comstock millionaires' mansion.

Bowers Mansion County Park ● *Open mid-May through October; (702) 849-0644. Twenty-minute tours every half hour, 11 to 4:30; adults $2, kids under 13, $1.* Uneducated mule skinner Lemuel Sanford Bowers and boardinghouse operator Eilley Orrum Hunter Cowan had side-by-side claims in the Comstock. They married, pooled their wealth and began building their $200,000 granite mansion in 1864. Sadly, Sandy died of silicosis three years later. Eilley converted the mansion into a hotel and tried to run it profitably. But mostly, she ran it into the ground, and she died penniless in 1903.

Shorn of its hotel fixtures and furnished to the 1860s (with some of the Bowers' original stuff), the mansion offers visitors a good look at the good life of the Comstock. A visitor center museum provides glimpses of local history, with exhibits on Tahoe logging flumes and Comstock mining.

Continuing north of Highway 395, you'll pass the hamlet of **Washoe City** and—a bit beyond—**Steamboat Hot Springs,** where you can take a sizzling dip in soothing mineral water. You're now in **Steamboat Valley,** cradled between the Lake Tahoe's Sierra Nevada (reached by the dramatically levitating **Mount Rose Highway**) and Virginia City's Sun Mountain (reached by equally spiraling **Geiger Grade**).

Steamboat Valley blends into the **Truckee Meadows,** that flat place between the mountains that cradles the Biggest Little City in the World. But that's in the next chapter.

Bed & breakfast inns

Two country style inns, not historic but comfortable and nicely situated, may tempt you to linger in the Washoe Valley.

Deer Run Bed & Breakfast ● ⌒⌒ $$$$ ØØ
5440 East Lake Blvd. (eight miles north; East Lake Boulevard east off U.S. 395), Washoe Valley, NV 89704; (702) 882-3643. Doubles $75 to $85. Two rooms with private baths; full breakfast. MC/VISA. Modern "passive solar" home on a working ranch near Washoe Lake. Lots of room for strolling, hiking and in winter, ice skating on a nearby pond and cross country skiing. Sitting room with TV and library; pool, gardens and pond.

Winters Creek Ranch Bed & Breakfast ● ⌒⌒ $$$$ ØØ
1201 N. U.S. Highway 395 (Bowers Mansion exit, 10 miles north), Washoe Valley, NV 89704; (702) 849-1020. Doubles $75 to $105. Three rooms with private baths; full breakfast. Cape Cod mansion on an historic 1850s horse ranch, in a secluded pine-shaded setting on the edge of Toiyabe National Forest. Rooms furnished with Victorian and American antiques; one has an Art Deco 1930s look. Private, stocked fishing pond, riding horses, hiking."

EAST OF CARSON CITY

If you've forgotten that tree-shaded Carson City and its surrounding ranchlands are in a desert, a drive east on Highway 50 will return you to arid reality. Sage and creosote bush share a dry and hilly landscape with scattered businesses, light industry and homes that comprise Carson's ugly eastern edge.

This is the quickest route from Carson to Virginia City. Seven miles out, a left turn onto State Highway 341 takes you up **Gold Canyon** through the weathered mining towns of **Silver City** and **Gold Hill.** Before doing this, however, you may want to continue east through **Dayton** to the ruins of **Fort Churchill**, Nevada's first Army of the West facility.

Dayton offers visitors little except historical curiosity and a few old stone buildings. The Emigrant Trail branched off here, with the north fork heading over Donner Pass and the southern fork passing through Carson City to Walker Pass. Young men of the Pony Express hurried through here, as did a stage line.

With all this traffic, it's logical that Dayton became one of Nevada's first settlements. It was first labeled Gold Creek after gold was discovered in a nearby ravine in 1849. It became Hall's Station when Spafford Hall set up a trading post in 1853, then Dayton in honor of surveyor John Day, who laid out the townsite. The town began jumping when silver poured down from the Comstock to be processed at mills along the Carson River. It became the Lyon County seat in 1862, then lost that honor in 1909 to Yearington. During the interim, with the Comstock mines closed, the town withered to practically nothing, and most of that burned in an 1870 fire.

Dayton is now a rather scruffy bedroom suburb of Carson City. A drive down Main Street will reveal a few old stone buildings and **The Old Corner Bar,** noted for history of a more recent vintage. The town and the ranch lands hereabouts were used in the filming of Clark Gable and Marilyn Monroe's *The Misfits,* and the bar brims with movie memorabilia. The adjacent **Misfit Touchdown Club** serves passable fare at reasonable prices, open daily from 7 a.m. to 9 p.m.

A couple of miles east of Dayton, look for an historical landmark sign on your left, telling of the town of **Sutro** and the **Sutro Tunnel.** As the Comstock Mines above probed more deeply into the earth, they began filling with water. Adolph Sutro, a San Francisco cigar magnate with little engineering experience but grandiose ideas, proposed a tunnel from the mines to the foothills of Sun Mountain near Dayton. This would relieve them of their water and provide easy egress for the silver. Sutro built a substantial town at the base, hoping to reap great profits by milling the silver delivered through his conduit. But William Sharon, who controlled the ore-hauling Virginia & Truckee Railroad and owned an interest in other smelters, kept delaying the project.

The tunnel—16 feet wide, 12 feet high and four miles long—wasn't completed until 1878, when the Comstock was about played out. Sutro sold out and returned to San Francisco, and his namesake city withered in the desert sun. Fragments remain, along with the impressive concrete-faced entrance to the tunnel. Unfortunately, it's now in private hands, behind a locked gate.

Beyond Dayton, you have two options for the Fort Churchill run. Highway 50 takes you quickly and smoothly 27 miles to **Silver Springs** at Highway 95-A. From here, an eight-mile trip south delivers you to the fort. (As you approach Silver Springs, watch for the **Ramsey-Weeks Cutoff** just beyond the school; it takes you directly to 95-A, saving a few miles.)

The second route is both shorter and bumpier. A few miles beyond Dayton, fork to the right onto Fort Churchill Road. You may add some bunions to your buns, since this is the washboardiest road we encountered in all of Nevada. *Ickybod,* our faithful Volkswagen camper, was near hysterics by the time we touched pavement again, at the edge of the state park.

However, it's an interesting trek, taking you along the Carson River, over the original Pony Express route. If you like things remote, you'll be content in this outland of desert and faraway ranches. We paused to let Ick rest while we enjoyed a riparian picnic lunch among the willows of the river.

Fort Churchill State Park • *Visitor center open daily 8 to 4:30 (sometimes closed in the off-season); free.* **Campsites** *with water, pit potties, picnic tables and dump station.* When the Pyramid Lake Paiutes began demanding their rights in the '1850s, the U.S. government sent the Army of the West to put things in order. Then in 1860, Nevada's first military post was constructed and named for Army inspector-general Sylvester Churchill. A site on the old Bucklands ranch was selected, since it straddled the Emigrant Trail. From here, the pony soldiers could sally forth to protect way stations and pioneers from the disgruntled Indians. It also served as a Pony Express stop.

It is today a fascinating ruin—a collection of rounded adobe walls melting back into the adobe soil. Roof beams and most of the other wood was pilfered decades ago by neighboring ranchers. What remains is a sort of Stonehenge with windows. Paths lead among the ruins and signs indicate what you'd see if there was anything to see. A visitor center, constructed as Civilian Conservation Corps project during the Depression, offers displays and graphics concerning the Pony Express, transcontinental telegraph, the Pyramid Lake wars and life at a remote Army outpost. Although the visitor center may be closed during the off-season, there's still plenty to see as you ruminate among the ruins of the fort.

Virginia City

Population: about 700 **Elevation: 6,220 feet**

We'll begin by saying that we really don't like Virginia City—or at least, what it has become. It's tacky, it's filled with tourists and the junk they buy, it's riddled with phony museums and poor taste and it's about as authentic as a Hong Kong Rolex.

However, we aren't suggesting that you bypass this historic town. By all means, pay the place a visit! Even if you're offended by touristic excess, you'll be fascinated by its weather-worn buildings, cantilevered onto a hillside like a terraced vineyard of history. You can tour Victorian mansions and former silver mines, and take a train ride through history. And you'll be intrigued by the stories the town has to tell. Of course, many of them are just that—stories, exaggerations, wild guesses and campfire talk.

Mark Twain set the pattern when he began reeling off his picturesque prose as a writer for the *Territorial Enterprise*. But he was only kidding. (As an editor used to tell me during my newspaper days, jokingly: "Never mind the facts, just get the story!")

Twain spent two years writing for the *Enterprise*, starting in September of 1862. He'd been prospecting in the mining camp of Aurora, to the east, sending humorous items to the newspaper under the pen name of "Josh." He adopted his much more famous name while at the *Enterprise*. As he recalled in a letter to the *Daily Alta Californian* in 1877:

"'Mark Twain' was the nom de plume of one Captain Isaiah Sellers, who used to write river news for the New Orleans Picayune. He died in 1863 and as he could no longer need that signature, I laid violent hands upon it without asking permission of the proprietor's remains."

About 40 years ago, two other writers, Lucius Beebe and Charles Clegg, bought the old *Enterprise* and began promoting Virginia City as a tourist destination. Entrepreneurs rushed in to convert tattered buildings into phony saloons that never existed, with names borrowed from somewhere else. They raided antique stores and junk shops and set up "museums" in the back. Tour guides began herding camera-clutchers around town, rattling off figures, some with no basis in fact.

Although Virginia City is now just an overworked tourist trap, it *was* Nevada for a few wild decades. It set a pattern of high-spirited free thinking, independence and entrepreneurial fervor that continues to this day. Fortunately, the rest of the state pursues its prosperity with much better taste.

THE WAY IT WAS • Serious prospecting in the region began in the early 1850s in Gold Canyon and Six-Mile Canyon above Dayton. The argonauts were looking for gold, and kept shoveling that famous blue mud aside. Two brothers were the first to assay the mud and learn that it contained rich silver deposits. Hosea and Ethan Allen Grosch, sons of a New York minister, had come west with mineralogy books, assayers tools and chemicals. Instead of casting the blue stuff aside, they analyzed it.

"Our first assay was one-half ounce of rock," they wrote home in 1857. "The result was $3,000 of silver to the ton."

However, silver mining required lots of cash and the pair had none. So, they kept their little secret and pecked away at their gold claim, hoping to

---

A TALE OF TWO NEVADAS

There's a bit of historical irony in the word "nevada," which is a Spanish adjective meaning snow-covered. Early explorers applied it to the bold snowcapped mountain range on the rim of the Great Basin. One of California's first gold rush towns, dating from 1848, also was called by that name, along with the county in which it sat.

When two gentlemen from the Comstock came over the mountains in 1859 to have the area's mysterious "blue mud" checked, they took it to J.J. Ott, an assayer in Nevada, California. Ott's findings—that it was a rich blend of silver sulfide—caused a tidal wave of action in both California's Nevada and Nevada's Nevada (which was then called Carson County, Utah Territory). Nevada, California, was practically deserted in the rush to the Comstock.

After Utah Territory was sliced in half to create two new dominions, the western chunk was named "Nevada," which irritated the folks of Nevada, California, and confused map makers. (Actually, most locals on the Nevada side wanted to name their new state Washoe.) To help sort things out, the name of the California gold camp was changed to Nevada City.

Thus, if you travel to the northern reaches of the Golden State's gold country, you'll encounter the attractive little community of Nevada City, California, seat of Nevada County, nestled in the Sierra Nevada foothills, just across the mountains from Nevada.

Did you follow that?

raise capital for a mining company. It was not to be; they died within months of each other in that same year. Hosea succumbed to blood poisoning from a pick wound in his foot and Ethan expired in a Sierra Nevada blizzard, trying to reach San Francisco to find some investors.

Two years would pass before the main lode was discovered farther up the hill. A pair of Irish lads, Peter O'Reilly and Patrick McLaughlin, hiked to the head of Gold Canyon and began working the mouth of a small spring. Gold glittered in their rusty pans! A ne're-do-well and braggart, Henry T. Paige Comstock, noted their good fortune and insisted that he'd already filed claim on that particular ravine. The fast-talking Comstock was able to strike a deal with the naive Irishmen. They would continue working the claim and Comstock, the "rightful" owner, would share in the proceeds.

So the pair kept working and Comstock kept talking. He called it his claim so often that others began referring to "Comstock's mine."

For the record, it was still a gold mine. Others filed claims nearby, including Sandy Bowers and his wife-to-be, Eilley Cowan. They all cast aside the blue-black mud until two gents named Stone and Harrison, who were headed for the California gold fields, took some samples with them. In Nevada City, they showed it to assayer J.J. Ott. The rest, of course, is quick history. Sandy and Eilley became the Comstock's first millionaires (see Bowers Mansion above), and others rushed in for a share of the wealth.

A proper christening

The story of the naming of the town that grew up around "Comstock's mine" sounds pretty far-fetched, but it's cute. A rummy named James "Old Virginny" Finney gets the credit, according to Beebe and Clegg:

"One night, this prophetic ancient was taken in wine and, on the way home to his shack, tripped and fell, smashing a bottle of whisky he was carrying as a precaution against the night air and altitude. Reluctant to let the liquor disappear into the earth without having some good of it, he turned the catastrophe into a christening party and then and there named the tent town Virginia City.

Another source says he uttered: *"I christen this spot Virginny Town!"* The name later was formalized to Virginia, in homage to Finney's home state.

It seems, then, that the lode and the town were named for miscreants who had contributed nothing to their fortunes. No wonder latter-day Virginia City was so ripe and ready for the fathers of bogus saloons and other tourist traps!

None of these early figures profited much from Sun Mountain's treasure. Comstock sold his share for $11,000 and piddled it away in Montana, dying there penniless. McLaughlin was talked out of his stake for a mere $3,500, although O'Reilly held out for $40,000. Both men died broke. Old Virginny perished in a fall from a horse, demonstrating that a drunk should never get that high off the ground.

Most of the Comstock fortunes were made by corporate barons who had the money, power and manipulative zeal to create huge mining companies. Among them were **George Hearst,** whose son William Randolph founded the Hearst newspaper empire, and **William Sharon,** sent by the Bank of California's **William Ralston** in 1864 to "straighten out the mess" when mining yields slowed and several companies defaulted on their loans. Sharon loaned them more money, then foreclosed. The bank took over the mines, tunneling ever deeper and finding more silver. For seven years, the

Bank of California's "Ralston Ring" virtually owned Virginia City. Other principals were **John Mackay** (pronounced "Mackie"), who broke the Bank of California monopoly by developing or gaining control of rival mining operations, and his partners **James Flood** and **William Fair** (whose heirs started San Francisco's Fairmont Hotel chain). Mackay contributed substantially to the founding of the University of Nevada in Reno, whose Mackay School of Mines is named in his honor.

Many of these men retired to San Francisco's Nob Hill and contributed substantially to that city's growth. Meanwhile, those who did the all the work labored under miserable conditions. They were paid the princely sum of $4 a day to keep on digging, equivalent to $250 today. As the mines penetrated deeper, they reached geothermal areas where temperatures topped out at 140 degrees. Working in rotating shifts, they'd sweat and dig for a few minutes then be lifted to the top to cool down with ice water. They drank as much as three gallons of water a day, which may have contributed to the eventual flooding of the mines.

Inevitably, the mines began to play out. The great silver lode, about four miles long and a few feet to a few hundred yards wide, pitched downward at a steep angle. As the shafts were burrowed deeper, it became increasingly more difficult to keep air pumped in and water pumped out.

Ninety percent of the town burned to the dirt in 1875, but there was still enough silver around to rebuild it. Within two years, however, the mines became too deep and thus too difficult to work. The Cornish pumps were shut off, water flooded the shafts, the millionaires went off to their mansions in California and the miners went off to mostly die of silicosis.

Virginia City didn't have the decency to die, however. Small companies re-worked the tailings, providing a few jobs for those who stayed on. Then in 1937, the tourist gimmickry was started by Paul Smith, a New York hotel man. He opened the first of the so-called museums, salvaging "authentic" artifacts from the rubble and shacks. The town went into a coma during World War II after the government banned all non-essential mining operations. Gasoline rationing discouraged tourists from visiting Smith's Museum of Memories. Then along came the erudite New York writing team of Beebe and Clegg. They were followed by Ben Cartwright, Hoss, Little Joe and Adam. For 239 television episodes, the burning map of *Bonanza's* Ponderosa Ranch and a make-believe Virginia City were projected into several million living rooms weekly.

Viewers didn't question the fact that Little Joe rode his pinto into Virginia City most afternoons, then returned to the ranch in time for supper— even though the ranch was near Lake Tahoe and the town was 24 miles away, down one steep hill and up another one.

But then, most folks aren't too concerned with reality in Virginia City, even when it's pretend reality.

THE WAY IT IS ● What's left of Virginia City sits just where the miners abandoned it, terraced into the steep flanks of Mount Davidson, the highest promontory of Sun Mountain. The most interesting approach is on State Route 341, which twists steeply upward through Gold Canyon. You'll be following the tracks of those 1850s miners who first came looking for quick riches.

— photo courtesy **Nevada Historical Society**

The Comstock mines and a sketch of Phillip Deidesheimer's square-set timbering illustrate this old lithograph. Called in from the California mines to solve the problem of cave-ins, the young engineer developed this technique, which became universal. It also led to the annihilation of most of nearby Lake Tahoe's forests.

The tourist gimmicks begin very quickly. Less than a mile from Highway 50, the **Chocolate Nugget Candy Factory** invites you to try some of its sweet specialties. You can watch the stuff being made through a picture window from the retail shop. Even better than its candies are huge, hand-dipped ice cream bars, multi-coated with thick chocolate and weighing about a pound (it seems). The trick on a hot day is to get through one before you wind up wearing part of it.

Beyond the candy factory, you climb past the tailing dumps, derelict headframes and sagging shacks of **Silver City,** now a virtual ghost town. Just above is **Gold Hill,** somewhat more intact, with a handful of people occupying what's left of its houses. An historic marker discusses the bad luck of the Grosch brothers, who made their silver find here. Stop in for a drink and perhaps plan dinner at the **Gold Hill Hotel**. Built in 1859, it's oldest hostelry in the state. It's been spruced up and filled with period furnishings and its Crown Point Restaurant gets good reviews from locals.

Beyond Gold Hill, the highway rears back and pitches upward at a 15 percent grade, not recommended for RVs and trucks. (There's an alternate route branching off near Gold Hill.) Then suddenly, you emerge onto a terrace and Virginia City spreads before you, sticking stubbornly to the steep slope. Tailing dumps from yesterday's frantic mining activity rise from the valley below and the hills above. Your route levels out now, following the brow of the hill along C Street, Ole Virginny's main drag.

Coming up quickly on your right, the **Sharon House** and castle-like **Fourth Ward School** speak of Virginia's days of glory. A bit farther along, also on the right, are the chamber of commerce **Visitors Bureau** and the ticket office for **Virginia & Truckee** railroad excursions. They're both housed in an 1874 V&T bullion car that hauled processed silver and prosperous mine officials down the hill. The visitor's bureau is open daily in summer, 10 to 4, with shorter hours in the off-season, if any. (It was closed on a Friday in March.)

Farther along C Street is the Virginia City that millions of tourists know and maybe even love. About the only thing authentic here are the post office and a few Victorian mansions. Although the town is a national historic site, everything is privately owned. Little has been done to preserve the town's historic integrity.

Step right up, folks! Welcome to the Fudge Factory, the shooting gallery, the T-shirt specialty shops, the gem shops, the jewel shops, the junk shops. In a holiday mood? Step into the Forever Christmas Authentic Virginia City Souvenir Shop (huh?) and the Yuletide Christmas Shop, home of Dickens Village.

Ya say ya like museums? Listen, have we got museums! We've got your Gambling Museum, your Mark Twain Museum of Memories, your Mark Twain Museum (without memories?), your Assay Office Museum, your Comstock Firemen's Museum, your Red Light Museum, your Grant's General Store Museum, your Territorial Prison Museum and your Wild West Museum.

Ya say ya wanna see Mark Twain's desk? The very place where he sat and composed those amazing words? Have we got a deal for you! Yessir, we've got *two* Mark Twain's desks. Not just one genuine, bona fide authentic Mark Twain's desk, but two! Now, where else—I ask you, sir—where else can you find a deal like that?

If you visit on a summer weekend, you'll find that museums outnumber available parking places. Virginia city draws a million visitors a year, and they come as tourists, not as gamblers. Although the dozen or so saloons and wanna-be saloons along C Street have slots and video pokers, there are no serious table games in this town.

More interesting and certainly more authentic than C Street's museums is "Millionaires Row." It's a block above, along B Street south of Union Street, where several fancy Victorians survive. Noteworthy among them is **"The Castle,"** carefully restored, opulently furnished and open to tours.

While you're up there, drive north on B Street, noting on your left the elaborate Italianate stone façade of the 1877 **Storey County Courthouse,** still in use, and open weekdays from 8 to 5. Note also the statue of Justice, *without* a blindfold. Continue on B, then turn left (uphill) onto Taylor Street and follow it toward the water tanks and a large white "V" whitewashed onto the hillside. (You'll swerve right onto Stewart, then swing left again.)

From here, dirt roads lead to the heights, offering impressive views of the town's tin rooftops, the spires of **St. Mary's** and **St. Paul's** churches and the gopher-riddled mining valley beyond. Squint carefully to the southeast and you'll see the headframe of the **Combination Mine,** the most prominent in the area. Most of the dirt roads up here are suitable only for four-wheel drives, although they make perfectly good hiking trails. For a

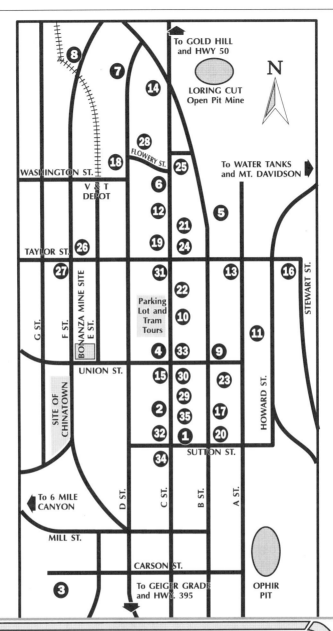

VIRGINIA CITY

DIRECTORY

1. Assay Office Museum
2. Bonanza Saloon
3. Cemeteries
4. Bucket of Blood Saloon
5. The Castle
6. Chamber of Commerce
7. Chollar Mansion (B&B)
8. Chollar Mine
9. Courthouse
10. Delta Saloon
11. Kennedy/Spaulding House
12. Firemen's Museum
13. Fire Monument (1875)
14. Fourth Ward School
15. Julia C. Bulette Saloon (Red Light Museum)
16. King Mansion
17. Knights of Pythias Hall
18. Mackay Mansion
19. Mark Twain's Memories
20. Miners' Union
21. Old Washoe Club
22. Palace Saloon (Gambling Museum)
23. Piper's Opera House
24. Ponderosa Saloon (Underground Mine)
25. Presbyterian Church
26. St. Mary's Catholic Church
27. St. Paul's Episcopal Church
28. Savage Mansion
29. Silver Queen Saloon
30. Silver Stope
31. Territorial Enterprise
32. Union Brewery
33. Visitors Bureau
34. The Way It Was Museum
35. Wild West Museum

particularly awesome vista, press on to the top of Mount Davidson, which will require bush-whacking through the sage. Plan on a huffing-puffing one or two-hour hike, depending on the state of your lungs.

You can see a fair chunk of northwestern Nevada from here—Reno with Bally's Casino highrise to the northwest; the Pah Rah Mountains of the Great Basin and maybe a hint of Pyramid lake filtered through Reno's haze in the northeast; the Washoe Valley and a piece of the lake to the west, with Slide Mountain and Mount Rose—the front range of the Sierra Nevada—beyond. Up there somewhere is the Ponderosa Ranch, and isn't that Little Joe's pinto trekking across the valley floor?

Now, turn east and stare down at the town. Aloof from the phony signs and historical lies, try to imagine it as it was. During its boom days, Ole Virginny was terraced according to class, in descending order, of course. Naturally, the wealthy of Millionaires Row had the best view, along A and B streets. Down on C Street, the six-story International Hotel would have risen toward you, housing the first elevator west of Chicago; locals called it the "rising room." The miners shacks and whores' cribs were just below the business district, along D and E, while a good-sized Chinatown was relegated to F Street, down among the mines.

And the mines! Imagine them not as empty, ugly tailing dumps, but as pulsating industries filling their owners pockets with silver and the air with pollution. A massive mill with a forest of smokestacks rose over the Combination Shaft. Headframes reached skyward from the Ophir, the Mint, the Hale & Norcross and the Gould & Curry. Although most of the mines are down in the vale, the original **Ophir Pit,** where those Irish lads first found gold and then silver, is just off A Street, now just an oversized coyote hole. Driving along A, you'll see the shallow pit above you.

Down to the left were—and still are—the town's collective **cemeteries**. They were segregated like the town: Catholic, Masonic, Protestant, Jewish, Irish, Mexican, Chinese. After you've descended the heights, drive down Carson Street and walk among the headstones. They say that the first 88 men resting here died violently before a resident lived long enough to expire from natural causes. A exaggeration? Who knows? Dead men tell no tales.

THE BEST ATTRACTIONS & TOURS

NOTE: The Castle, Fourth Ward School, Virginia & Truckee train rides, Chollar mine tour and Piper's Opera House are closed in the off-season.

The Castle • *70 South B St.; (702) 847-0275. Guided tours 10 to 5 July 1 through Labor Day and 11 to 5 in May and September, closed the rest of the year. Adults $2.75, kids 6 to 12, 25 cents.* This board and batten cream and brown structure is one of the most beautifully furnished mansions around, and it's nearly all original. Take the 30-minute tour and admire the Italian marble fireplaces, alabaster and hand-painted Dutch vases, rosewood bed, Czechoslovakian crystal chandeliers and silver door knobs. Everything is immaculate; everything museum quality. The mansion and its furnishings are nearly flawless because it has passed through only three owners since it was built in 1868 by the superintendent of the Empire Mine.

Fourth Ward School • *C Street, south end; (702) 847-0975. Daily 10 to 5, mid-May to mid-October. Admission $2.* Even the schools were fancy during Virginia City's heyday. Gray with burgundy trim and a Mansard roof, this place looks more like an opulent Victorian home. When it was built for

$100,000 in 1876, it had the first indoor plumbing of any school in Nevada, plus drinking fountains and a piped-in heating system. First through 12th grade classes were conducted here until 1936. It's now one of the city's finer archives, with exhibits in the form of school lessons, crafted by the Nevada State Museum. They include full-dimensional models of mining equipment, graphics and photos concerning the Comstock, the people who lived here and how they were entertained.

Marshall Mint's Assay Office Museum • *98 North C St. (at Sutton); (702) 847-0777. Daily 10 to 5; donation $1.* It's one of the two best small museums in town (along with the gambling museum below), featuring a nice, cleanly displayed collection of minerals. It includes rarely seen raw silver specimens, some beautiful free gold and a blacklight exhibit of glow-icky minerals, plus some elegant jade, ivory and turquoise carvings.

Nevada Gambling Museum • *Palace Emporium Mall, 22 South C (near Taylor); (702) 847-9022. Daily 10 to 5; $1.50.* Housed in a former saloon, it offers a large collection of old gaming machines, early poker machines, a chuck-a-luck cage, a faro table with an explanation of how the game is played and exhibits on card cheaters and their techniques. Cut-away slot machines offer a peek at how these contraptions work. This is a *museum*, not a collection of dusty junk.

Ponderosa Saloon Underground Mine Tour • *106 South C St.; (702) 847-0757. Daily 10 to 5; adults $3, kids $1.50, families $7.50.* You'll learn all about drifts, stopes, raises, cuts, shafts and even winzes during this interesting 30-minute tour of the old Best and Belcher Mine. Equally interesting is the fact that the entry is through a storefront (the unauthentic Ponderosa Saloon), proving that the miles of tunnels went over, under, around and certainly through Virginia City. Your affable guide will demonstrate the dim grimness of early-day mining by dousing the lights and lighting a candle—the only source of glimmer for the miners. And they were swinging heavy hammers at hand-held drill bits! You'll also learn that not all the Comstock mines made their owners rich. The Best and Belcher yielded exactly $438!

Piper's Opera House • *B and Union streets; (702) 847-0433. Mid-May through October, Daily 11 to 3. Admission $2.* Still owned by the original family, the opera house was built in 1885 by John Piper. One of the west's finer opera houses in its time, it played to the likes of Maude Adams, Lillian Russell, Edwin Booth, Lola Montez and her protegè Lotta Crabtree. Patrons paid $20 for box seats at a time when a full meal cost 15 cents. Undergoing restoration, it still has its original acoustical canvas walls, cantilevered boxes and suspended balcony. The stage floor was canted upward to give the audience a better view of the proceedings. The terms "upstage" and "downstage" supposedly originated from this Piper tilt.

St. Mary's of Nevada Catholic Church • *E and Taylor streets; (702) 847-0797. Open to visitors daily from 9 to 5. Mass daily at 8 a.m., Saturday at 4 and Sunday at 10:30.* This splendid structure is the town's most visible—and probably most beloved—landmark, with its squared Gothic bell tower jutting skyward. It's still an active church and its solid-cast silver bell is rung for mass, echoing through this yesterday boom town like a voice from the past. Step inside to admire the lofty vaulted ceiling, stunning stained glass windows and elaborate Gothic altar.

Virginia City tour • *Phone (702) 786-0866. Departs Delta Saloon parking lot every 30 minutes on the hour and half hour, daily 9 to 6 (from 10 to 4:30* in the off-season). Adults $3, kids 6 to 12, $1.50. The best thing about this tour aboard an open-air "replica San Francisco trolley" is the narration, which is the most accurate spiel you'll hear in this tourist town. Each of the three guides, Lee Mayfield, Carl Kuttle and Chick DiFrancia, conducted extensive research to get their facts straight. They share them during this 20-minute drive around the town as they point out the assorted historic sites.

Virginia & Truckee train ride • *Ticket office on South C, opposite the post office; depot at Washington and F streets; (702) 847-0380. Late May through September, departures from 10:30 a.m. to 5:45 p.m. Adults $4, kids $2, all-day pass $8.* This may be the best four dollars you'll spend in town, for it puts you aboard one of America's most historic short line railways. Powered by the "technology of the times," the old steamer chugs down to Gold Hill and back, following the route of the famous bullion cars. The conductor points out historic sites and regales folks with stories of the Comstock as the train winds carefully along the steep track.

The Way It Was Museum • *113 North C (at Sutton); (702) 847-0766. Daily 10 to 6; adults $2, kids free; MC/VISA.* This is the largest and busiest of the town's museums, housed in an "old" weathered shed built in 1958. The collection is neither professionally done nor orderly, but it's so extensive that it's worth the price. Further, you can sit through three short videos on the town, taken from TV's *American Frontier* series. The museum's eclectic clutter includes collections of minerals, old medicines and notions, antique dolls, mining equipment and firearms. Note the 3-D model of the incredible webwork of 700 miles of mine shafts burrowed into the surrounding hills.

THE REST

Chollar Mine Tour • *South F street; (702) 847-0155. Adults $4, kids 14 and under $1.* Inside the Chollar (pronounced "collar"), you'll see examples of square-set timbering developed in the Comstock by California mining engineer Phillip Deidensheimer to prevent cave-ins. The tour doesn't penetrate very deeply into the mine, although you'll see some good examples of mining equipment and learn about underground techniques in the Comstock.

Firehouse Museum • *51 South C St. (at Washington); (702) 847-0717. May through September, 10 to 5; donations.* Focal point in this small museum is the hand-drawn 1856 Knickerbocker pumper and hose carts, used by Liberty Engine Company Number 1. Old fire hats and other smoke-eaters' regalia complete the collection.

Mackay Mansion Tour • *129 S. D St. (south of Washington); (702) 847-0173. Daily 10 to 4. Adults $3, kids under 12, $1.* The oldest surviving home in Virginia City, this two-story square-shouldered structure was built in 1860 as the mining office for the Gould and Curry Company. It later was occupied by George Hearst and then by John W. Mackay, the richest miner in the Comstock. You'll be greeted on entry by a mineral exhibit, then you'll pass through rooms furnished to the period.

Mark Twain Museum of Memories • *C and Taylor streets; (702) 847-0454. Daily 10 to 5, longer hours in summer; suggested donation $2.* Run by the Virginia Historical Society, this place rivals The Way It Was Museum for the extent and dustiness of its clutter. Some of the exhibits even attempt to be thematic. They include a telegraph office, V&T baggage office and bottled and canned items on a general store's shelves. Perhaps the highlight is a stuffed Mark Twain at his desk, issuing some of his wit via Hal Holbrook.

— photo courtesy Nevada Historical Society

The silver mines of Virginia City were huge, polluting industries, as illustrated in this lithograph of the "Combination Mine."

Mark Twain Museum • *Territorial Enterprise building, 109 South C (between Union and Taylor); (702) 847-0525. Daily 10 to 5; admission $1.50* Ne'er the Twains shall meet? This ramshackle display in the dark and dingy basement of the *Territorial Enterprise* offers the second authentic Mark Twain desk. Who are we to dispute it? This is, after all, the real *Territorial Enterprise*. Other exhibits include the newspaper's water-powered press, an 1894 Linotype machine, type cases and non-related items such as bottles, a phone switchboard and the skeleton of a midget horse. Don't fail to miss the indoor commode labeled: "Mark Twain sat here."

Red Light Museum • *Julia C. Bulette Saloon, 5 North C St. (near Union); (702) 847-9394. Adults $1.* This sad excuse for a museum is in the creaky but not creepy basement of a saloon named for a beloved whore who was strangled in her bed in 1867. Although prostitution is a worthy subject for—uh—sociological study, there is little here that's revealing, or interesting. You can see some oldstyle naughty nudie photos, a crib scene with a mannequin male about to drop his drawers for the lady in repose, some vintage condoms, old medical equipment and a tray full of glass eyes.

Vintage condoms? Try not to think about it.

INTERESTING SALOONS

Despite their venerated look, most of Virginia's saloons are relatively new, at least compared with the age of the town. Since they're tourist oriented, most close around 6 in the evening, so the old boom town is inappropriately peaceful after dark. The Union Brewery is one of the few places with the decency to act like a real Western watering hole and whoop it up after nightfall.

Bucket of Blood Saloon • *One South C St.; (702) 847-0322.* The name isn't pretty, but the scores of vintage lamps hanging from the ceiling are. The saloon is named for an earlier establishment in town, and has a nice collection if antique slot machines. A picture window offers an impressive view down toward the mining dumps.

Delta Saloon • *18 South C. St.; (702) 847-0789.* The Delta is one of the largest and spiffiest places in town, with knotty pine walls, a handsome backbar decorated by game trophies, lamps and artifacts dangling from the ceiling. Check out the old photos and prints on the walls, including portraits of the Irishmen who started it all. Have a look at the famous Suicide Table. It's famous mostly because there's a sign heralding it about every 200 feet as you drive up the hill. The Delta also has the cleanest potties in town, and it's one of the few saloons that keeps properly late hours.

Silver Queen • *28 North C St.; (702) 847-0468.* The main attraction in this place is a poorly-done 16-foot portrait of a lady wearing a gown covered with 3,261 real silver dollars. The Queen also has one of the town's more elaborate bars and backbars. Should you want to be wed in a vintage costume, the folks here will provide the clothes and get you hitched in a little Victorian chapel in back.

Union Brewery • *North C near Sutton.* This place brews its own beer in the basement and the stuff must be great because patrons really whoop it up at night. Although the blaring jukebox is inappropriate to the period, the Union is one of the few saloons dating back to the Comstock days. It even has sawdust on the floors. Considering the intensity of the harmless nighttime revelry, it might be yesterday's furniture.

Old Washoe Club • *112 South C St.; (702) 847-9300.* The most authentic and historic of the town's bars, the Washoe dates back to 1875. The Comstock leisure class hung out here, and in the private Millionaires' Club upstairs. It was reached by the world's tallest unsupported spiral staircase (says the *Guinness Book of World Records*). You can't climb the old spiral but you can quaff a beer downstairs and admire the copper-colored pressed tin ceiling, crystal chandeliers and attractive carved bar.

WHERE TO DINE

Crown Point Restaurant • ☺☺☺ $$$

In Gold Hill Hotel; (702) 847-0111. Continental; dinners $11.50 to $23; full bar service. Dinner Tuesday-Sunday from 5:30, Sunday champagne brunch 10:30 to 2:30; combined dinner and historic lectures on Tuesdays. Reservations accepted; MC/VISA. Nicely restored Victorian dining room in Nevada's oldest hotel, with wainscoting, print wallpaper and pink nappery. Menu items range from basil scampi and veal paprika to *coque a vin*. Check out the great old bar downstairs with its rough brick floor and interior stone walls.

Julia C. Bulette Saloon and Cafe • ☺ $

5 North C St. (near Union); (702) 847-9394. American; meals $5 to $11; full bar service. Lunch and dinner daily; no credit cards. Simple fare served in a made-to-look-old saloon named for everybody's favorite fallen angel; Booths with a canyon view. Menu ranges from corn dogs to sirloin tips.

Sharon House Restaurant • ☺☺ $$

25 Taylor St. (just up from C); (702) 847-9495. American-Continental; dinners $10 to $18; full bar service. Nightly 5 to 10. Old-timey dinner house above the Ponderosa Saloon; not fancy but nicely refurbished with red wallpaper, beaded globe lamps and the like.

Silver Stope Restaurant • ☺☺☺ $$$

25 North C St.; (702) 847-9011. American-Continental; dinners $13 to $20, early bird special for $7.95; full bar service. Wednesday-Monday 11 a.m.

to 9 p.m. MC/VISA. One of the town's older restaurants, dating from 1946. It's cleverly fashioned like a mining stope with log and rock-filled walls and ceilings. Eclectic menu ranges from teriyaki to Cornish game hens, plus and a whopping miner's platter of crab, lobster and steak for $38.

Solid Muldoon's Saloon Restaurant • ☺ $$

65 North C St.; (702) 847-0135. Basic American; dinners $5 to $15; full bar service. Daily 6 a.m. to 2 a.m. No credit cards. Good ole' boy cafe, locally popular, with checkered tablecloths and a funky Western look. Simple menu lists prime rib, chicken fried steak, pork chops and a few pasta dishes.

WHERE TO SLEEP

Chollar Mansion Bed & Breakfast • ⌂⌂⌂ $$$ Ø

565 South D St. (P.O. Box 889), Virginia City, NV 89440; (702) 847-9777. Doubles and singles $65 to $100. Three rooms, one with private bath; full breakfast. No credit cards; checks accepted. Home and office of the Chollar Mine superintendent, built in 1861 and restored to Victorian finery. Rooms are furnished with American and Victorian antiques. Some of the original facilities are still intact, such as the paymaster's booth and a 164-square-foot arched vault where the bullion was stored.

Edith Palmer's Country Inn • ⌂⌂⌂ $$$ ØØ

P.O. Box 576, Virginia City, NV 89440; (702) 847-0707. Doubles $65 to $80, singles $60 to $70. Five rooms, three with private baths; full breakfast. MC/VISA, AMEX. Nicely restored Victorian with country-style furnishings. Elaborate gardens and impressive views of the town and valley. The structure was built in 1862 as a residence and wine wholesaler's facility.

Gold Hill Hotel • ⌂⌂⌂ $$

In Gold Hill; mailing address P.O. Box 304, Virginia City, NV 89440; (702) 847-0111. Doubles $40 to $80, kitchenette suites $80 to $135. MC/VISA. Some private, some share baths. Nevada's oldest hotel, built in 1859 and nicely refurbished. Period furnishings in the rooms; some with fireplaces, wet bars and balconies. Three guest house suites have kitchen units and amenities such as a fireplace and grand piano. **Crown Point Restaurant** and oldstyle saloon (listed above). Bookstore featuring Western Americana.

WHERE TO CAMP

The RV Park • *Carson Street, below C; P.O. Box 846, Virginia City, NV 89440; (702) 847-0999. RV and tent sites; full hookups $18 in summer, $14 in the off-season; no hookups $12; tent camping $4 per person.* Just below the historic district; showers, coin laundry, convenience store and pay phones.

ANNUAL EVENTS

Call the Chamber of Commerce at (702) 847-0311 for details.

Comstock Preservation Weekend in May; historic celebration.

Tour of the Comstock and **Fireman's Muster** in June; costumed guided tours and demonstrations of antique fire equipment.

Fourth of July Celebration; old time festivities with parade, food booths, games, arts and crafts.

International Camel Races in September; Virginia City's biggest celebration with camel races, old time music, crafts, food booths and such.

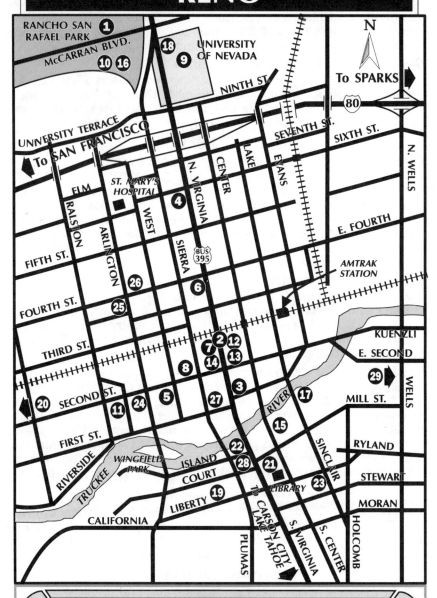

"Last night, the era of legal gambling came to an end. The once opulent and brightly-lit saloons along Commercial Row were locked up forever this morning. Gambling was duely laid to rest with the carnival atmosphere of an Irish wake." — **A September 30, 1910, Reno newspaper story**

Chapter Seven

RENO
Still the biggest little city

One is tempted to compare Reno and Las Vegas, since they're Nevada's two largest cities and most popular tourist destinations. In fact, 95 percent of the state's residents and visitors gather about these two communities.

If you think in numbers, there's no comparison. Greater Las Vegas will soon top a million residents while Reno's Truckee Meadow is hovering somewhere around 250,000. About 3,000 people move to the Reno area each year; the southern city gets that many *every month*. Las Vegas draws about 22 million visitors a year, Reno-Tahoe about seven million.

Pictorially, Reno wins hands down. It's an attractive little city with tree-shaded streets and a compact downtown cluster of highrises along the banks of the Truckee River, all sitting at the base of the Sierra Nevada. With its mini-metropolitan core and surrounding suburbs, it continues to be the "Biggest Little City in the World." Tahoe's skiing, hiking and water sports are a short drive away. Rand McNally recently rated the Reno-Tahoe area number one for outdoor recreation. The American Economic Review ranks Reno-Sparks among the country's top five cities for urban quality.

Desert-rimmed Las Vegas is gaudy, lively, the center of the action, but pretty it ain't. However, it offers a much greater variety of entertainment, including the big, flamboyant and sexy revues. The two towns are similar price-wise, although Las Vegas probably has a slight edge in overall room prices.

You can sense the slower pace in Reno. The casinos generally are less crowded—and less monstrous, except for the 2,000-room Bally's. There's not the promotional intensity here; hawkers aren't shoving discount coupons in your face and you don't find fake "visitor centers" staffed by tourism hustlers. Reno is a more conservative town, without the rows of "adult literature" racks that dominate Las Vegas sidewalks.

The visitor, then, has two obvious choices, and both are excellent ones. You go to Reno-Tahoe for relaxation and scenery, and to Las Vegas for serious partying.

THINGS TO KNOW BEFORE YOU GO

BEST TIME TO GO • Reno's 4,490-foot elevation gives it a cool spring and autumn, wrapped around warm summers. Book well ahead for summer visits; this place gets *busy* then! Winters are crisp, clear and quite palatable. Expect occasional gusty snowfalls, but the stuff usually doesn't last. It's beautiful here then, with the frosted backdrop of the Sierra Nevada.

WHAT TO SEE • The National Automobile Museum, University of Nevada campus and its Mackay Mining Museum, Harold's Club Gun Collection, Liberty Belle Saloon slot machine collection, Nevada Historical Society Museum and the Wilbur D. May Museum.

WHAT CASINOS TO SEE • In Reno, Bally's for its vast opulence, Harrah's and the Flamingo Hilton for their glitzy style, Fitzgerald's for its Irish excess, Circus Circus for its big top gimmickry, the cute little southern accented Riverboat, the stylish Eldorado, the sleek, lush new Peppermill, the Nevada Club for its great 1950s look and tiny Western style Old Reno Casino. In Sparks, the stylish tucked-under-the-freeway John Ascuaga's Nugget.

WHAT TO DO • Learn to gamble at one of the casino's gaming lessons; stroll the wetland trails of the Oxbow Nature Study Area and the desert-to-riparian woodland path at Rancho San Rafael Park, catch a sky show or wide-screen film at the Fleischmann Planetarium and stop by Friday night to peek through its telescope; hike the Truckee River Trail from Reno to Sparks.

Useful contacts

General information and lodging: Dial (800) FOR-RENO

Reno-Sparks Convention & Visitors Authority, P.O. Box 837, Reno, NV 89504-0837; (702) 827-7366. It operates the Nevada Welcome Center in **Town Center Mall** at First and Sierra streets; Sunday-Thursday 10 to 6 and Friday-Saturday 10 to 9; (702) 333-2828.

Reno Chamber of Commerce, 275 N. Virginia St., Reno, NV 89501; (702) 329-3558. Visitor center open weekdays from 9 to 4:30 the year around, plus 9 to 2 on Saturday from April through November; closed Sundays.

Sparks Chamber of Commerce, B Street at Pyramid Way, Sparks, NV 89432; (702) 358-1976. Open weekdays 8 to 5.

Reno area radio stations

KBUL-FM, 98—country
KHIT-FM, 104.5—country
KINX-FM, 91.3—Christian
KNEV-FM, 95.5—easy listening, news and sports
KRNO-FM, 107—soft hits
KRQZ-FM, 96—rock
KUNR-FM, 88.7—Nat'l Public Radio

KCBM-AM, 1230—CNN news and sports
KHIT-AM, 1590—country
KOH-AM, 650—music, news and sports
KCBM-AM, 1230—CNN news and sports
KRNO-AM, 1230—soft hits

Incidentally, you often hear a reference to Reno-Sparks as if it were one place. It is, geographically; Sparks is a suburb of Reno, separated by the name and not much else. Four miles east, it has a small casino complex in its attractive Victorian style downtown. John Ascuaga's Nugget is the dominant gaming complex here. We'll meet Sparks at the end of this chapter.

THE WAY IT WAS • As dissimilar as they are today, Reno and Las Vegas had similar beginnings. Both were way stations boosted to cityhood by railroads; both began with railroad- sponsored building lot sales.

Reno is much older, since it's on the routes of the early emigrant trail and the historic Central Pacific Railroad. Until recently, it was much larger as well. During a good part of this century, Reno was Nevada's biggest city while Las Vegas was a dusty railroad crossing.

When the first emigrants trekked over the Great Basin, the Truckee River was both a godsend and a barrier. It provided water and graze as the settlers prepared for their assault of the Sierra Nevada. However, it had to be crossed—often repeatedly. One early journal records that wagon trains had to ford the river *forty times* in the laborious haul up Truckee Canyon toward Donner Summit. These repeated crossings contributed to the fatal delay of the Donner party, trapped on the wrong side of the Sierra by an early snowstorm in 1846. They were following a route that had been blazed two years earlier by Captain Elisha Stevens. The river was named either for the group's Indian guide or for a northern Paiute chief, depending on which history book you read. The term means "all right" or "very well."

Considering the river barrier, it's not surprising that Reno began as a toll crossing. Fords, ferries and log bridges spanned the stream. The most notable of these was Charles Fuller's toll bridge, erected in 1859. With competition from other crossings, he didn't do terribly well. After two years, he sold out to 33-year-old New York entrepreneur Myron Lake. With more business acumen and foresight, Lake beefed up Fuller's trading post operation, improved the bridge and gained franchise for a toll road that crossed his bridge and the valley. Once all this was in place, he pocketed $60,000 in tolls within 18 months.

Money talks, and he talked Central Pacific surveyors into re- directing their course through the Washoe Valley to "Lake's Crossing." His bait was 80 acres for a townsite, which the railroad auctioned off on May 9, 1868. The town was named for Civil War General Jesse L. Reno, killed at the Battle of South Mountain in 1863. It was the custom of the day to name new town sites after Civil War heroes. Reno was particularly revered because he remained loyal to the Union even though he was a native Virginian, like Robert E. Lee.

Had he lived to see his namesake city, he'd have been displeased with the way locals pronounced it. The name was Anglicized from the French *Renault,* like the car, and the accent should be on the last syllable. However, the town became RE-no, right up there with Ge-NO-ah and VER-dai. ("Them furriners shore talk funny, don't they, Ned?")

Rail traffic and the nearby Comstock silver boom insured the new town's success. Reno took the county seat from Washoe City in 1871 and the state university from Elko in 1886. After Virginia City's silver shriveled, Reno became the dominant community in Nevada, a role it enjoyed until Benny Siegel invented the Las Vegas Strip after World War II.

— photo courtesy **Nevada Historical Society**

Renoites gathered for a final night of gambling on September 30, 1910, after the pastime had been outlawed. It returned with a flourish in 1931.

America's first cross-country highways, the Victory and Lincoln, were both completed in the 1926. One passed through Reno; the other just to the south. They're now known as Interstate 80 and U.S. 50. To mark their completion, a steel arch was erected over Virginia Street (Marvin Lake's old toll road) and dedicated on October 23, 1926. No, it didn't say "The Biggest Little City in the World." Electric lights spelled out: "Reno Transcontinental Highways Exposition, June 25 to August 1." They promoted a festival planned for the following year. The famous slogan came later (see box).

For the first half of this century, Reno's history was pretty much Nevada's history, since it was the principal city. Although it was no wild mining town, it was hardly an unaware angel, either. Prostitutes' cribs flourished along Lake Street and gambling, technically illegal, was practiced openly. The "fight of the century" between Jim Jeffries and Jack Johnson in 1910 gave the biggest little city national recognition.

But some folks fussed about the town's unsavory reputation and began pushing for reform. Gambling was driven underground, the whores were driven out and the entire state outlawed drinking in 1918, two years before the Volstead Act. However, an anti-reformer, E.E. Roberts, was elected mayor in 1923, backed by wealthy political bosses. Reno became sin city again, a virtual mini-Chicago during the Roaring Twenties. Baby Face Nelson hung out here, and there was talk of Mafia money funding the local power brokers.

When the stock market crash created a national hangover, it caught Nevada in the middle of a prolonged drought, so the state was doubly wounded. Then quickie divorces and gambling were legalized to boost the economy in 1931, and Reno's fortunes took off.

Two Nevada gaming pioneers, honest men with no mob connections, brought gambling out of dingy Douglas Alley and built attractive casinos on

Virginia Street. Raymond "Pappy" Smith and his two sons Raymond Jr., and Harold opened their casino in 1935. They scattered "Harold's Club or Bust" signs across the highways of the nation.

William Harrah opened a bingo parlor in 1937 and began acquiring small casino saloons. He launched his fancy Harrah's in 1946, the same year that Benny Siegel's Fabulous Flamingo opened its doors down south. Having no mob to fear, Bill Harrah lived until 1978, expanding his casino empire and accumulating the world's largest automobile collection.

Perhaps more than anyone else, Harrah and the Smith families brought respectability to Nevada gaming parlors and truly made Reno the Biggest Little City in the World. Neither family is involved with the properties now. Harold's was sold to Howard Hughes' Summa corporation in 1970, then to Reno's Fitzgerald family of Fitzgerald's Casino. Harrah's empire was sold to Holiday Inn, whose executives dealt off two-thirds of the 1,200-vehicle auto collection. However, although they donated the best to Reno's new National Automobile Museum.

Split city

Reno became the divorce capitol of the world after the much-publicized marital severings by Mary Pickford, Cornelius Vanderbilt and Jack Dempsey. Tabloids called it "Reno- vation." Newly-single ladies would ritualistically toss their wedding rings into the Truckee River from the Virginia Street bridge, a short walk from the courthouse.

"Two thousand matrimonial invalids now crowd this sagebrush metropolis," read a tabloid of the day. *"They're waiting for the new quickie divorces, spending over $5 million a year and bringing the state of Nevada the biggest boom it has known since gold rush days."*

While wide-open Las Vegas took off in the desert following World War II, Reno fathers again became image-conscious. They passed legislation in 1947 limiting casinos to the heart of downtown. (It has since been repealed.) The town diversified, attracting small industries and warehousing, lured by the state's lack of inventory tax. The convention and visitors bureau linked Reno to Lake Tahoe, touting the region as an all-season vacation area, where folks could ski in winter and hike and boat in summer. It was, they said, a place where one can play something besides craps and roulette.

It still is.

THE WAY IT IS • Today's Reno is either rolling merrily along or just holding its own, depending on the prejudices of those you talk with. One does not sense the dynamics of Las Vegas here; no mega-casinos are rising from the dirt. In fact, several older ones—the Mapes, Riverside, Onslow and Pioneer—have closed.

There is some expansion. The Clarion Hotel-Casino opened a 160-room tower recently and the Peppermill is enlarging its casino. Harrah's is in the midst of a major remodeling project to blend four separate casinos into a single 69,000 square foot gaming area. The closed Riverside is supposed to be the object of a $10 million restructuring, although there was little activity in early 1992. Beyond the casinos, the Wingfield Park Amphitheater opened in 1992 near the new Truckee River Walk downtown and a state-of-the-bowling-art eighty-lane "National Bowling Stadium" is planned for the mid-1990s.

Getting there and getting around

Centrally fixed on Freeway 395 and Interstate 80, Reno is easily reached from the four points of the motorist's compass. It's about 225 miles from **San Francisco**, 470 from **Los Angeles**, 450 from **Las Vegas**, 525 from **Salt Lake City**, 580 from **Portland** and 730 from **Phoenix**.

Once there, you'll be greeted by a simple layout. I-80 and U.S. 395 freeway form a ragged "X" just east of downtown. North-south running Virginia Street is the main drag, paralleled by one-way Center Street (northbound) and Sierra Street (southbound). Most of the casinos are within this grid, between Fifth Street and the Truckee River. If you've been to Las Vegas, you'll see a resemblance between downtown Reno and Glitter Gulch. After you've parked, you can stroll to most Reno casinos except Bally's which is to the east, off Freeway 395, and a couple that are farther south on Virginia Street.

To reach downtown from Interstate-80, simply take a Sierra or Virginia street exit and head south. From Freeway 395, shift onto I-80 west, go about a mile and a half and do the same thing. I-80 is sunken as it goes through Reno and is thus surprisingly unobtrusive. It passes almost unnoticed between downtown and the **University of Nevada Reno** campus.

More attractive from afar, downtown is something of a jumble of oversized blocks of hotel towers and parking structures, some linked by catwalks. As successful outfits such as **Harrah's, Circus Circus** and the **Flamingo Hilton** expanded, they devoured smaller casinos and other businesses. The "front" of Harrah's on Virginia Street, for instance, occupies an old stone bank building. **Visitor parking** is not really a problem, despite downtown's compactness. In addition to the casino parking structures, several private lots offer all-day parking for $2 to $6. Summer weekends can be a challenge, however.

For a good overview of Reno's innards and edges, get on **McCarran Boulevard** and just keep driving. It forms a squared oval around the entire city. You can pick it up from North Virginia Street, just beyond UNR.

Reno-Cannon International Airport is about four miles southeast of downtown, reached by Freeway 395 (East Plumb Lane exit). It's served by **America West**, (800) 247-5692; **American**, (800) 443-7300; **Continental,** (800) 525-0280; **Delta,** (800) 221-1212; **Northwest,** (800) 225-2525; **United,** (800) 241-6522 and **USAir**, (800) 428-43322, plus some feeder and charter carriers. Book your flight through a travel agent, who will know of the best fares and special fly-sleep-gamble packages that casinos may be offering.

Airport Transportation is provided by **Airport Minibus** (786-3700). **Showboat Lines** (324-5333) and the **Las Vegas-Tonopah-Reno Stage** (323-3088) run between the airport and Lake Tahoe's casinos.

Amtrak and **Greyhound** both serve the city. Amtrak's California Zephyr follows the historic Central Pacific route, with a downtown depot two blocks east of Virginia Street. When the train comes to town, it's literally a traffic-stopper. For reservations, call (800) USA-RAIL. The Greyhound depot is at 155 Stevenson at west Second; (702) 322-7056.

Incidentally, several firms offer "Gambler's Special" buses to Reno, with rebates and coupons that make the trip virtually free. They're particularly popular from San Francisco, Oakland and Sacramento; give your travel agent a ring.

Transit, public and otherwise

Citifare is the local bus system (348-RIDE), operating hub-like out of the Downtown Transportation Center at Fourth and Cedar streets. Service is 24 hours and the fare is 60 cents; a dollar for zones; exact change, of course. **Whittlesea Checker** (323-3111), **Yellow Deluxe** (331-7171) and **Reno-Sparks Cab** (333-3333) are the largest taxi companies.

Virtually all major **rental car** companies operate in Reno, most with offices at the airport. A couple of local outfits that might give you better rates are **Apple Rent-A-Car,** (800) 537-9034 and (702) 329-2137 and **Western Rent A Car,** (702) 828-3456.

Getting hitched

Reno has lost its title as America's marrying capital to Las Vegas, but it's still easy to tie the knot here. The marriage bureau in the old Grecian style **Washoe County Courthouse** at Virginia and Court Streets (opposite the Pioneer Center for the Performing Arts) is open daily, 8 a.m. to midnight. The license fee is $35. A rackful of brochures here will direct you to nearby wedding chapels and, in case there's an early crisis, to family counseling services. For a quick and cheap marriage, go right out the back door to the **Commissioner of Civil Marriages** at 195 S. Sierra Street. The knot-tying fee there is only $25 weekdays and $30 weekends and holidays.

Where to shop

Reno isn't as rampant with souvenir shops as Las Vegas, although there are several downtown. **Woolworth's** on Virginia Street near First is as good as any and cheaper than most. The **Pioneer** souvenir store at Second and Virginia is worth a look mostly for the building it occupies—an old masonry structure with a clock tower outside and pressed tin ceilings within. Upstairs is the **Gambler's Book Store,** (786-6209) with titles on everything you ever wanted to know about the games people play and the history of gambling. The **Casino Dealers' School** occupies the same floor, in case you want to learn more about this business.

For general shopping, **Park Lane Mall** (825-7878) is at south Virginia Street and Plumb Lane, a couple of miles beyond downtown. It has 94 shops and restaurants, anchored by Sears and Weinstock's. A bit farther south, past the Reno-Sparks Convention Center, is **Meadowood Mall** (827-8450) at South Virginia and McCarran Boulevard. Its anchors are Macy's and JCPenney and it offers more than 70 other stores and restaurants.

If you're a bargain-hunter (who isn't?), follow I-80 two miles past **Sparks** and take the Sparks Boulevard exit to **Nevada Factory Outlets.** It's home to several discount shops and **Sierra Trading Post,** our favorite stop for outdoor clothing, backpacks and such. The complex is open Monday-Saturday 10 to 7 and Sunday 10 to 6.

AFFORDABLE RENO

Our "Affordable Las Vegas" section in Chapter 3 covers the basics for a thrifty Nevada vacation. We'll review them briefly, edited for Reno. Of course, the bargain seasons are reversed. Reno's best room buys are in the Summer while the Las Vegas high season is winter.

• Book your trip through a travel agent, who will know of the best room rates and assorted gamblers' specials.

- Room prices in casino hotels often rival those in non-gaming hotels and motels, and you might as well be where the action is.
- Practice "Couponamania" by picking up coupons good for freebies and discounts. Visitors bureaus usually have them, and non-gaming lodgings generally pass them out as well.
- Pick up free tourist guides, whose ads often feature bargains; they may contain coupons as well. The most popular is *Showtime,* available in racks or stacks just about everywhere you turn. It also lists shows, restaurants, upcoming events and other items of interest to visitors.

Bargains with no coupons attached.

Here are a few examples of discount goodies you can enjoy in Reno; you'll find dozens more:

Nugget — A 99-cent pancake and egg breakfast.
Eldorado — Steak and lobster dinner for $9.99.
Circus Circus — Hickory Pit has a $6.95 one-pound prime rib dinner. Circus Circus also has the buffet in town: $2.29, $2.99 and $3.99.
Sundowner — A $1.95 spaghetti dinner.
Sands Regency — Steak and lobster $8 at Palm Court Restaurant.
Flamingo — Eggs, biscuits and gravy breakfast $2 at Sierra Crossing; also shrimp scampi and chicken breast $4.99.
Comstock — Steak and lobster $7.99 at the Miners Cafe.
Old Reno casino — Five free nickels just for walking in.
Fitzgerald's — Discount coupons are given with a "Lucky Forest" visit.
Riverboat Casino — Lunch $2.99, prime rib $5.99, breakfast $1.99.

THE RENO ABCs

All phone numbers (702) unless otherwise indicated

Auto clubs—Reno office of the Nevada Division of the California State Automobile Association (AAA) is at 199 E. Moana Lane; 826-8800. The National Automobile Club has an emergency road service number in Carson City; 882-3800.

Babysitting—Two agencies that provide sitting service in your hotel/motel room or at their facilities are Dial-A-Sitter (359-8051) and Professional Sitter Service (356-7823).

Big rooms—Reno has only four major showrooms, compared with more than a dozen in Las Vegas. Bally's has Broadway musicals, the Flamingo Hilton has an adult dance revue while Harrah's and John Ascuaga's Nugget in Sparks feature headliners.

Bus service—See **Transit,** above.

Cash machines—Virtually every casino has credit card cash advance machines and autotellers that will respond to your bank card. The autotellers are a much better deal, operated by local banks and charging only a dollar per transaction. Credit card machines charge as much as 10 percent of the amount advanced. For a better cash advance deal, take your MasterCard or VISA to any issuing bank during regular hours.

Checks and credit—Most casinos will cash out of state checks if you apply at the cashier's cage and give them 24 hours to verify your account. If you're in the high roller category, you also may be able to establish credit, then you merely sign an IOU for chips. (See **A day in the life of a high roller** in Chapter 2.)

Dental services—Misery with a molar? Call the 24-hour Dental Referral Service at 322-6886.

Gambling lessons—Among the casinos offering gaming lessons are Bally's, Circus Circus, Fitzgerald's, the Flamingo Hilton and Peppermill. Also contact the **Reno/Tahoe Gaming Academy** 348-7403 and **Gamblers' Book Store,** (800) 323-2295 or (702) 786-6209, both at 195 Virginia St. (second floor, at Second Street) or **Bobby Kees gambling seminars,** 856-2600.

Hotel reservations—The Reno-Sparks Convention & Visitors Authority will find you a room, toll-free. Call (800) FOR-RENO.

Medical services—Washoe County uses the 911 number for medical and other emergencies. Hospitals with 24-hour emergency rooms are Washoe Medical Center at 77 Pringle Way, 328-4140; and St. Mary's Regional Medical Center, 235 W. Sixth St., 789-3188. For non-emergency medical referrals, call the Washoe County Medical Society at 825-0278.

Newspaper—The *Reno Gazette-Journal* covers the local and national scene for Northern Nevada. It publishes an excellent guide to entertainment, dining and casino action in the Sunday *Best Bets* magazine. You'll often find it as a give-away in casinos, in case you don't want to buy the three-pound Sunday paper.

Pets—Few casino hotels allow them; some smaller motels do. Boardings services are offered by the Nevada Humane Society, 331-5770; Fantasia Pet Hotel, 322-1199 and Sentry Kennels, 786-8161.

Police services—Dial 911 in an emergency. Otherwise, the Reno Police Department number is 334-2121; Nevada Highway Patrol is 688-2500.

Poison emergency—Call the Poison Control Center, St. Mary's Regional Medical Center, 789-3013.

Road conditions—Call the Nevada Highway Patrol at 793-1313.

Show reservations—These can be made through individual hotels, or through BASS (829-8497), Sierra Select a Seat (784-4444) or Ticketron (348-7043).

Visitor information—Call (800) FOR-RENO or (702) 827-7662 to find out what's happening and to make room reservations. That's the number for the Reno-Sparks Convention & Visitors Authority, which operates a **Nevada Welcome Center** in **Town Center Mall** at First and Sierra streets. Enter through the Sierra Street doorway and take a quick left. Hours are Sunday-Thursday 10 to 6 and Friday-Saturday 10 to 9; call (702) 333-2828. The Reno Chamber of Commerce has a visitor' bureau in the **Downtown Events Center** at 275 Virginia St. (at Commercial Row), open weekdays 9 to 4:30 the year around, plus 9 to 2 Saturdays from April through November. It's closed Sunday; (702) 329-3558. Two local information guides, available free at most casino hotels are ***Showtime*** and the *Reno Gazette-Journal's **Best Bets*** magazine.

ON TOUR: INNER & OUTER RENO

Reno's casinos are so closely grouped that most folks simply park and walk. To see the few outer-area gaming parlors and the town's other attractions (described later in greater detail), follow the verbal dotted line we've outlined below.

From downtown, head north over the sunken I-80 freeway on Virginia Street. You'll immediately encounter the handsome old and new brick build-

— photo courtesy Reno News Bureau

Reno's gaming towers glitter at the base of the Sierra Nevada foothills.

ings of the **University of Nevada**. Note the round cast concrete **Lawlor Events Center** on your right. Just beyond, also on your right, is a common parking lot shared by the **Nevada Historical Society Museum** and **Fleischmann Planetarium.**

Continue north less than half a mile, cross McCarran Boulevard and take the next left into the eastern section of **Rancho San Rafael Park.** A hiking trail leads to a **Basque memorial** and a riparian woodland (see **Reno's Parks** below). Now, reverse your route, pass McCarran again and fork right onto Sierra Street, then turn right into the lower section of the park (near a white arch.) Here, you'll find the **Wilbur D. May Museum, arboretum** and kids' **Great Basin Adventure** theme park.

Return to Sierra, cross back over the freeway and drive about half a mile to Second Street. Follow Second just over a mile, and fork left onto Dickerson Road. This takes you past a junky assemblage of auto upholstery shops and small warehouses to **Oxbow Park Nature Study Area,** a delightful Truckee River retreat. Reverse yourself on Dickerson and stay on Second, headed back toward Virginia Street. Three blocks short of Virginia, note the delightfully ornate **St. Thomas Aquinas Cathedral,** on your right at the southwest Corner of Arlington.

Go right on Virginia and you'll cross the Truckee River and see the **Raymond I. Smith Truckee River Walk** on your right, then the copper-colored geodesic **Pioneer Center for the Performing Arts** and **Washoe County Courthouse** opposite one another. Two blocks to your left, tucked against the river at Mill and Lake streets, is the **National Automobile Museum.**

Pressing south on Virginia Street for about a mile, you'll pass the new **Peppermill Casino** on your right, then the **Clarion Hotel Casino** on your left and the **Reno-Sparks Convention Center** just beyond. There's nothing of interest there unless you're attending a convention, although you might like to see the **Lake Mansion,** where town founder Myron lived. It's on the southern edge of the center's parking lot E.

RENO — 243

Come back up Virginia, turn right onto Moana Lane (the next major intersection), go east about half a mile and start north onto Freeway 395. You'll see **Reno-Cannon International Airport** on your right. About a mile and a half beyond is the monolithic **Bally's** casino tower, surrounded by nothing except its parking lots and reached by the Mill Street Avenue off ramp.

Return to the freeway and follow it to the I-80 interchange, go east briefly and take the Nugget Avenue exit. You're in downtown **Sparks**, occupied mostly by **John Ascuaga's Nugget**. The cute little **Victorian Square** and **Sparks Museum** are opposite the Nugget on B street, along with the rest of the town's casinos. Good old I-80 will deliver you swiftly back to downtown Reno.

THE CASINOS

Our ratings, explained in more detail under this heading in the Las Vegas chapter, are for casino explorers and gamblers, not necessarily for lodgers. We list prices for a double room here; you'll find more specifics under **Where to sleep**. The **K** symbol marks casino resorts of particular appeal to kids, and Ø indicates places with non-smoking gaming areas.

Most of the city's restaurants are in casino hotels, and we list them here. Dining salons located outside casinos are covered farther down in this chapter, under **Where else to dine**.

Bally's ● ☺☺☺☺ K Ø

2500 E. Second St.; (800) 648-5080 or (702) 789-2000. Renoites are probably growing weary of our comparisons, but Bally's is the only local casino resort with the look, feel and immensity of a major Las Vegas Strip hotel. It's Reno's only true destination resort, with 2,000 rooms, a monster casino, 40-shop mall, bowling alley, health clubs, tennis courts, Olympian swimming pool, twin movie theaters, a wedding chapel, a "big room" and two other showplaces, the area's only comedy club, five restaurants and a full-service RV park. (Bally's Camperland was our headquarters for much of the Reno research.)

The place exudes glistening class, particularly when you walk down the sweeping red-carpeted "hall of mirrors" staircase, beneath a giant chandelier, en route to the downstairs shopping arcade. If all this sounds like a surreal movie set, the comparison is apropos. The place originally was the MGM Grand. It is, incidentally, one of the best-planned gaming resorts in the state. Most of the restaurants are conveniently located along a landing above. It's a good family place, too, with its movie theaters, bowling alley and large video arcade.

Casino: It's roomy, with high ceilings to absorb the noise. Obviously, all the games, slots and videos are here—thousands of them, plus a large sports book and keno lounge. Massive chandeliers above the gaming tables add a touch of European casino elegance to this 100,000-square-foot facility.

Entertainment: At this writing, Broadway shows were being presented in the Ziegfeld Room; headliners sometimes appear as well. Catch a Rising Star is the comedy club and live entertainment issues from the Confetti Cabaret and Leo's Lair lounge.

Dining: Take your pick from five restaurants: **Marco Polo** for Chinese and Italian, $7 to $15, weekdays 11:30 to 2:30 for lunch and nightly from 5 for dinner; **Caruso's** for upscale Italian, $13 to $20, dinner Friday-Tuesday

6 to 11; **Café Gigi** for French and American, $10 to $25, nightly from 6; **The Bounty,** a shellfish and seafood cafe, $5 to $12, daily 11 a.m. to 11 p.m. and the upscale, clubby **Steakhouse,** $16 to $21, serving dinner nightly. There's a 24-hour **coffee shop** and **Grand Buffet** as well.

Rooms: Doubles range from $69 to $95.

Cal Neva ● ☺☺

38 East Second at North Virginia Street; (702) 323-1046. A Reno oldtimer, the Cal Neva has been around since 1947. During most of those years it was owned by Leon Nightingale, one of Reno's most generous philanthropists; he expired in 1990. The medium-sized gaming parlor, stacked onto three floors, has a pleasing railroad theme. From the mezzanine balcony, the place appears to be a railroad yard turned casino.

It's popular with low rollers, with lots of nickel slots and $1 table minimums and two-bit craps. One lucky cuss was a *high* roller several years ago; he set a world's record by winning $6.8 million on a slot machine.

Dining: Cal Neva has some of the best food prices in town. The 24-hour **Hauf Brau** dishes up ribs and sandwiches from $2.50 to $5; a prime rib dinner is only $4.95. The **Top Deck** restaurant under a greenhouse roof is a bargain as well, with dinners from $5 to $7.

Circus Circus ● ☺☺ K ∅

500 N. Sierra St. (at Fourth); (800) 648-5010 or (702) 329-0711. Although this place spreads over several blocks like some pink mechanical monster, the Reno Circus Circus is much smaller than the original in Las Vegas. It's less glittery inside was well. Otherwise, it's the same bit: a family-oriented low rollers' casino with circus acts, a huge carnival midway and cheap hotel rooms. The giant clown and lollipop sign and the pink-accented towers are a noticeable—although certainly not noteworthy—downtown landmark.

Casino: Large and rather confusing in layout, it has $2 table minimums, a sports book, poker room, lots of nickel slots and videos and some non-smoking tables. Free craps, blackjack and roulette lessons are offered in the casino and on a TV channel in the rooms. The toga-clad drink girls look like they drifted down from Caesars Tahoe.

Entertainment: Just look up and you'll see it. Aerial acts and other circus feats are performed daily from 11 a.m. to midnight in a quasi-bigtop above the casino. (There's a roof and net in case someone's grip slips.) Also, the Hickory Pit Lounge features live music, usually a vocalist.

Dining: Predictably, food prices are a bargain here. The **Hickory Pit** serves American fare, $7 to $16, from 5 to 11 p.m., including a $6.95 one-pound prime rib dinner. The **Three-Ring Circus** is the 24-hour coffee shop and the **Buffet** is the cheapest in town: $2.29 breakfast, $2.99 lunch and $3.99 dinner, with a Friday seafood buffet for $5.99.

Rooms: Doubles range from $28 to $46.

Clarion Hotel Casino ● ☺☺

3800 S. Virginia St. (just north of the Reno-Sparks Convention Center); (800) 762-5190 or (702) 825-4700. It's a jungle in here, but a lavender one? Originally a Quality Inn and expanded to the tune of $25 million in 1991, the Clarion is a curious blend of Polynesian and purple. Check out the 30-foot indoor waterfall cascading into the tropical flora (no fauna). Facilities include a mid-sized casino with a hotel, pool, par course and health club.

Casino: The gaming venue offers the usual table games with $2 and $3 starts, plus slots and videos starting at a nickel. With its thatched roofs over the casino, chandeliers, purple neon tubing and glossy black mirrored glass, the effect is *deco moderne* goes to Hawaii."

Entertainment: Live music issues from two lounges called the Center Stage and Clarion Lounge, and couples can trip lightly in the Dance Lounge.

Dining: It's informal here; the **Pizza Cafe**, with a mod-California look, serves what it says, plus pasta; dinners $7 to $16; daily 11:30 to 2 a.m. The tropical **Purple Parrot** is the 24-hour place, with American plus a couple of Italian and Oriental dishes for $8 to $17. Both have non-smoking areas.

Rooms: Doubles are $49 to $64.

Comstock Hotel Casino • ☺☺

200 W. Second St. (at West Street); (800) 648-4866 or (702) 329-1880. The Douglass family wants you to feel right at home in its mid-sized casino—if your home happens to be an 1870s silver camp. Descended from an old Virginia City family, the Douglass clan has created a Western-theme casino with pioneer town façades and elevators resembling mine shaft lifts.

Casino: With its high ceilings, it's reasonably ventilated, even on busy weekends. Table games start at $2 and some of the slots kick out a thousand bucks with a single feed. Between TV races in the sports book, watch for the audio-animated character that perform 24 hours a day. There's also a poker parlor and for the kids, a video arcade.

Dining: The 24-hour joint is the **Miners Cafe,** with special dinners from $3.50 and regular entrées $6 to $8. **Amigo's Mexican Restaurant** serves south of the border dishes from nightly from 5 to 11; $4.25 to $8.50, plus two-for-one combos. **Hatch Brother's Deli** serves light fare from 7 a.m. to midnight.

Rooms: Doubles $34 to $64; half price on Thursdays.

Eldorado Hotel Casino • ☺☺☺

Fourth and Virginia streets; (800) 648-4597 or (702) 786-5700. Like the Comstock, the large and successful Eldorado was founded by folks with deep Nevada roots. Don Carano's great-grandfather Bernardo Ferrari was a Comstock cook in Virginia City. His father Ben Carano was a railroad clerk in Reno, who bought a tiny plot of land on Virginia Street in 1929. That plot has blossomed into one of the town's largest, glossiest and most successful casino hotels. The family also owns a state-of-the-art winery, Ferrari-Carano, in California's Sonoma County. (But that's another story in another book, ***The Best of the Wine Country,*** at your favorite bookstore, $12.95.)

Casino: The gambling venue is bright, cheerful and lively, with running lights and mirrored, coffered ceilings. Although it's often crowded, it's quite spacious, a pleasant place to invest your dollars. Tables start at $2; slots and videos at a nickel. There's a sports and race book and mini-baccarat, plus a kids' video parlor and—for trivia fans—the world's largest roulette table, capable of seating 40 people.

Entertainment: The Cabaret Lounge, open to the casino, features a variety of entertainers—the up-and-coming and the nearly forgotten, from Kristine & the Sting to the Sons of the Pioneers. (Shouldn't that be the Grandsons of the Pioneers by now?)

Dining: Eldorado rivals Bally's for its restaurant assortment, and most are centrally located on the second floor. There's **Eldorado Grill & Rotis-**

serie, primarily American, $8 to $22.50, daily 7 a.m. to 11 p.m.; **La Strada,** Northern Italian, $9.25 to $19.50, nightly from 5; the plush American-continental **Vintage,** $17.50 to $22, Thursday-Monday from 5; **Tivoli Gardens** 24-hour coffee shop; the 24-hour fast-food **Choices** and the **Market Place** buffet.

Rooms: Doubles range from $40 to $90.

Fitzgerald's Casino/Hotel • ☺☺ Ø

255 N. Virginia St. (at Commercial Row); (800) 648-5022 or (702) 785-3300. If ya gotta have a gimmick, Fitzgerald's certainly has one: The place is as Irish as Paddy's pig, with Lucky Lane, the Lucky Bar and the Lucky Forest, where patrons turn in coupons for a free pull on a prize machine. (Coupons are passed out in front.) The forest is filled with good luck charms, such as a horseshoe, magic lamp, wishing well, a Buddha who's tummy must be rubbed for good fortune, plus lots of lucky rocks from Erin. Named for Lincoln Fitzgerald, who opened the Nevada Club back in 1947, this luck-ridden place dates from 1978.

Casino: Amidst a sea of shamrocks and other things green, you'll find all the essential gaming devices, starting at $1 for red dog and $2 for blackjack, plus lots of nickel slots and videos. It has no-smoking gaming tables. Note the antique slot machine exhibit on the second floor, and the Irish armor just outside the buffet line; hopefully, it brought its wearer good luck.

Entertainment: Combos issue sounds from Fitzgerald's casino lounge, called the Lucky Bar, of course.

Dining: The Fitz has one of the town's cheaper **buffets,** $2.99 breakfast, $3.99 lunch and $5.99 dinner. **Molly's Garden Restaurant,** with an Irish country look, serves essential American fare 24 hours a day; $8 to $13.

Rooms: Doubles are $20 to $48 weekdays and $50 to $80 weekends.

Flamingo Hilton • ☺☺☺

255 N. Sierra St. (at West Second); (800) 432-3600 or (702) 322-1111. While not as fabulous as its pink parent in Las Vegas, the local bird is nonetheless one of Reno's glitzier fun parlors. Actually, it's not a direct descendant. It began as Del Webb's Sahara in the 1970s, became a Hilton property in 1981 and went Flamingo pink in 1989. Its neon spectacular along Sierra Street is the gaudiest exterior in town; note the rather striking flamingo frieze. The place is large as well as flashy. Counting a recent reach onto Virginia Street, it's tentacled over three blocks.

Casino: This place is nearly as bright inside as out—a large, cheerful casino with high coffered and mirrored ceilings and lots of pinkness. It serves both high and low rollers, with low end slots and table games, plus some $5 to $100 slots.

Entertainment: "Heavenly Bodies" is an adult T&A show in the Flamingo Showroom, available in early dinner and late cocktail versions ($19.95 or $17.50). The Showspot Lounge features live groups and singers, and the Top of the Hilton lounge usually has a singer on tap.

Dining: The **Top of the Hilton** is one of Reno's *in* places, with sky-high vistas and lofty prices—$15 to $28. This elegant affair is Reno's only rooftop restaurant, well worth the treat; dinner 6 to 11, plus a 9:30 to 2 Sunday brunch. **Emperor's Garden** is a new Chinese place at 240 N. Sierra, across the street but linked to the Hilton; $7 to $13; open 11 a.m. to 3 a.m. **Sierra Crossing** serves American fare, $5 to $11 with some budget specials; open 24 hours. **Food Fantasy** is the 7 a.m. to 10 p.m. buffet.

Rooms: Doubles wander from $59 to $219.

Harold's Club • ☺☺

250 N. Virginia St. (at Commercial Row); (702) 329-0881. And now we come to the legendary place in a legendary location, right at the base of Reno's "Biggest Little City" sign. By reputation, Harold's is the biggest little casino in town, dating from 1935 when it was opened by "Pappy" Smith and his boys. We've already discussed their cross-country "Harold's Club or Bust" signs. (Most are now in signboard heaven, up there with Burma Shave.)

The Smiths pioneered many features which are routine today in the gaming business: the "eye in the sky" and other anti-cheating devices to keep both sides honest, free drinks for handle-pullers and junkets for high rollers. Feminists of the world, rejoice: Harold's was also the first place to employ woman dealers, during World War II. And Californians take note: the idealized western mural out front was painted in 1949 to commemorate the California Gold Rush centennial. And of course, everyone knows about the famous Harold's Club Gun Collection, which is now in its own personal museum space (see **The best attractions** below). Originally, it was displayed in cases on the casino walls. What everyone may not know is that most of the stuff was accumulated not by the Smiths but by R.M. Stagg, owner of the Roaring Camp Saloon.

Casino: As in many legendary places, there's more history and substance than glimmer to Harold's. Oak paneling, period photos and Western artifacts give it the properly venerated look. Tables and machines run the full range and you can play some still-working mechanical slots dating from the 1950s. In addition to the gun collection, you'll find a fine gathering of old slots and music-making machines on the mezzanine.

Dining: The fancy place is the seventh-floor **President's Car,** $12 to $20, serving American-continental fare from 5 to 11 Friday-Tuesday; it's a warm and clubby simulated railroad lounge car with a great view. **Nevada Annie's** is as Western American as its name, serving 4 to 10 p.m. Wednesday-Sunday, $7 to $14.

Harrah's Reno • ☺☺☺ Ø

219 Center St. (at Second Street); (800) 648-3773 or (702) 786-3232. The second of Reno's historic "H" clubs, this large (and growing) establishment started small, opened by William Harrah 1946. As we mentioned above, Harrah's is now owned by the Holiday Inn Corporation, which apparently likes the Harrah name. Specifically, those bean-counters like the clean, honest and upscale image that Bill Harrah brought to the industry. "America's innkeeper" has opened new casinos in Atlantic City and Laughlin under the Harrah brand, and it recently changed the name of its Holiday Casino in Las Vegas to Harrah's Las Vegas.

Casino: One of Reno's largest gaming refuges, the Harrah's complex spreads over a couple of blocks, making it a bit hard to find your way around. However, it's worth a couple of wrong turns to explore this attractive place with its high coffered ceilings and spacious gaming areas. It has a high roller look and indeed attracts some of the town's more earnest gamblers. Yet Mom and Pop Nebraska can still find nickel machines and videos and even a few dollar blackjack tables. It has a non-smoking gaming area.

Entertainment: Harrah's has one of Reno's few big rooms, which alternates between headliners and small Vegas-style revues. "Stage Struck" and a sexy-sounding something called "High Voltage" were playing when we were in town. The Vintage Court Lounge and Rendezvous Bar offer combos, singers and keyboard tinklers.

Dining: The restaurants, like the rest of Harrah's, are widely scattered. Seek out the *Italian moderne* **Andreotti**, $9 to $13, Thursday-Monday from 5. Or try the very upscale Western American **Steak House,** $19 to $30, lunch weekdays 11 to 12:30 and dinner nightly 5 to midnight; or the never-closing **Garden Room** for upscale coffee shop fare, $7 to $12. **Oriental Garden** is obviously Chinese, $9 to $15; and the Skyway is the **buffet.**

Rooms: Doubles drop to $69 during slow periods, and rise to $120.

Holiday Hotel Casino • ☺☺

Between Mill and Center streets, south bank of the Truckee: (800) 648-5431 or (702) 329-0411. If you like your gaming action at river's edge, you might swing by this attractive mid-sized casino, which sits right on the banks of the Truckee, near the National Automobile Museum. With the closing of the Riverside, it's the only river-view casino in town.

Casino: Bright and modern with mirrored ceilings and red and black carpeting, the casino offers the usual range of slots and video poker, keno and the only bingo parlor in downtown Reno. The casino lounge offers views of the river.

Dining: The **Shoreroom Restaurant,** is just that, offering tables with a river view. The menu focuses on American steaks, chicken, chops and such, and the place is open 24 hours.

Rooms: Doubles range from $30 off-season to $95 during holidays.

Horseshoe Club • ☺

229 N. Virginia St. (near Second Street); (702) 323-7900. Bob Cashell's small sawdust joint is an oldstyle casino with an air curtain out front and lots of nickel slots inside, plus one craps and a few blackjack tables. It's popular with locals and food prices at the back room **Silver Spur Cafe** are a bargain, starting with a hot dog and long neck Bud for $1.99.

John Ascuaga's Nugget • See Sparks at the end of this chapter.

Nevada Club • ☺☺☺

224 N. Virginia St. (fused to Harold's Club); (702) 329-1721. This is one of my favorite places in town, a little jewel of a 1950s joint with old nickel-plated mechanical slots, vintage movie posters and photos. It's "the way Reno used to be," says a sign on its purple façade. Further, it's low-roller's heaven, with $1 blackjack, lots of nickel machines and even penny slots.

Dining: The **Coffee Shop** (that's what it's called, folks) carries the 50s theme, with prices to match. You'll see local business types perched on counter stools beside the glass brick wall, chatting with a waitress wearing a little white apron, sipping their coffee and downing cheap hamburger steak. It's open from 11 a.m. to 9 p.m.; dinners $4 to $8.

Nugget Casino • ☺

233 N. Virginia St. (near Second Street); (702) 323-0716. Next door to the Horseshoe, the Nugget is a near twin in temperament and facilities. Locally popular, it's a low-roller joint with a single blackjack table and ranks of nickel slots and videos. Check out the red Naugahyde **diner** where cooks in tall white hats dish up "hangover omelettes" for $5.25, pancake and egg breakfast for 99 cents, and an "Awful Awful" hamburger (awful big, awful good) for $3.50.

Old Reno Casino • ☺☺
44 W. Commercial Row (just off Virginia Street); (702) 322-6971. This place earns two grins because it's so darned cute—a tiny casino jammed between empty buildings at the backside of Fitzgerald's. Walls are packed with hunting trophies, old bottles and pioneer artifacts. It's a handle-puller's haven, stuffed with nickel slots and videos, and rare penny slots. There's no food, but the drinks are cheap: $1.25 for a hit, 75 cents for a beer and 50 cents for soda pop.

Peppermill • ☺☺☺
2707 S. Virginia St. (near Plumb Lane, a mile south of downtown); (800) 648-6992 or (702) 826-2121. The Peppermill represents the next generation of Nevada casinos—a flashy new place on the outskirts of downtown. The hotel tower is sleekly modern and the bright, busy casino is—well, the phrase nouveau-muted-garish comes to mind. The look is high tech disco with lots of soft red and blue lights, smoked mirror glass and reflective ceilings. Facilities include a health club, swimming pool and spa.

Casino: Payouts are generous and promotions and slot tournament are frequent, so the place has a large local following—with the sound level to prove it. You'll find lots of nickel slots and videos, plus all the usual tables, manned and womanned by dealers wearing sparkly vests to match their surroundings. Further, this glitzy joint has the sexiest cocktail waitresses north of Las Vegas, maybe even north of Tierra del Fuego.

Entertainment: You mean, other than watching a cocktail waitress approach? Check out two of the most sensuous bars in town. The Lounge has deep, plush seats around huge hexagonal fish tanks and the Fireside offers seating around burbling cauldrons spouting gas flame. Both are dimly lit and done in muted red, blue and turquoise, looking like sets for *Superman XVI*. The Casino Cabaret offers live entertainment.

Dining: Island Buffet, which features seafood and prime rib nights; it's pricey at $9.99 to $14.99 but locals say it's worth it. For more elegance, try **Le Moulin,** serving American and continental dishes nightly 5 to 11, $10 to $20. The 24-hour **coffee shop** is predictably attractive, with more of those blues and reds; dinners $8.50 to $16. An **International Food Court** is due for the summer of 1992.

Rooms: Prices range from $49 for motor queens (sounds like a haven for racing molls) to $135 for tower kings.

Riverboat Hotel & Casino • ☺☺☺
34 W. Second St. (at Sierra); (800) 888-5525, (800) 321-4711 or (702) 323-8877. This charming little place chugged into Reno in 1988, propelled by its Mississippi riverboat paddlewheel and a reputation for friendly service. It is thus popular with locals, and visitors are drawn by the pleasingly garish riverboat façade and canopied entry.

Casino: It's bright and cheerful, the way a casino might look if it sprouted from a sunny bayou. Simulated trees are nestled against slot machines and plastic willows dangle from the ceiling. Despite its stylish Southern plantation look, it's a low roller retreat with $1 blackjack, ten-cent roulette and 20-cent craps and, of course, ranks of nickel slots and videos.

Dining: Food prices are a bargain, particularly when the menu drops to half price at the **Riverboat Restaurant** from 11 p.m. to 4 a.m. Daytime prices are reasonable as well, starting at $1.99 for a full breakfast and $4.99 for a chicken and rib dinner; it's open 24 hours. The **Oyster Bar** might be the town's best seafood place, with tasty *cioppino* for $6.

Rooms: From $25 weekdays off-season up to $75 in summer.

Sands Regency ● ☺☺

345 N. Arlington Avenue (Third Street); (800) 648-3553 or (702) 348-2200. Although they aren't as well known as other gaming pioneers, the Cladianos family has been in business here since 1932. Greek immigrants Antonia and Pete arrived broke and optimistic, bought five slot machines and kept going from there. Their gaming parlor has grown to a good-sized casino and 1,000-room hotel, now operated by the third generation. It's Las Vegas in style and scatter, although not as glitzy as its southern counterparts. Amenities include a health club and swimming pool.

Casino: Although it lacks dash and flash, it's a comfortable, spacious place to play, with $2 blackjack minimums, roulette, craps, a sports book and nickel-to-dollar slots and videos.

Dining: The Cladianos family has provided for your dining pleasure the easy way, by inviting in the franchises: **Tony Roma's** ($5.45 to $13, nightly from 4), **Baskin-Robbins** and **Winchell's Doughnuts.** For something other than ribs, pecan swirl and dunkers, there's the 24-hour **Palm Court** with very good prices—$6 to $13 for complete dinners; and **Antonia's**, American-Greek-Italian, $6 to $13, dinner Thursday-Monday.

Rooms: They start at $26 off-season, rising to $54 and beyond.

Sundowner ● ☺☺

450 N. Arlington Ave. (at Fourth); (800) 648-5490 or (702) 786-7050. Without a lot of glitter but with a solid down-home Western look and attitude, the Sundowner seems to do quite well, despite its location several blocks from Virginia Street. **Casino:** Nothing really catches the eye here. In fact, the term "faded" comes to mind. (Maybe it's the tired beige carpeting.) Yet, low table limits, generous slots and cheap rooms draw them in. Table games start at $2 and the joint offers the usual array of games and devices.

Dining: The **G.K. Steakhouse** is quite elegant, compared with the look of the rest of the place; dinner prices are $14 to $24. The 24-hour **Coffee Shop** has loss-leaders like $1.98 spaghetti and other dinner prices from $4.25 to $11. The Garden Gazebo is the pig-out **buffet.**

Rooms: As we said, they're a bargain, starting at $29 and rising to $48.

The Virginian ● ☺☺

140 N. Virginia St. (between First and Second); (800) 874-5558 or (702) 329-4664. Although it appears to be one of the Virginia Street oldtimers, this place is relatively new and apparently doing well in its key downtown slot. It's small, friendly and modern with Western touches. With the demise of the Riverside, Mapes and Onslow, it's the first casino you encounter coming from the south on the main drag.

Casino: Stacked onto three small floors, it's a prim little gaming parlor, with lots of nickel slots and videos and low stakes table games.

Dining: M.K.'s Ranch Restaurant issues inexpensive lunches from 11 to mid-afternoon and dinner from 5 to 11; fare is essential American with entrées from $5 to $9. A 24-hour **Snack Bar** serves ordinary food at below ordinary prices. **Rooms:** From $32 to $44 for doubles.

THE BEST ATTRACTIONS

Fleischmann Planetarium • *1600 Virginia Street (north side of the UNR campus); (702) 784-4812 or 784-1 SKY. Weekdays 8 to 5, weekends 10:30 to 5 (open in evenings for shows). Small science museum free; wide-screen movies and sky shows $5 for adults and $3.50 for kids and seniors; call for schedule. Public telescope viewing Fridays from 8:30 p.m. to 9:30.*

Housed in a structure resembling a space age saddle, this busy center offers lots of things skyward, plus those ultra-wide screen films enjoyed in tilt-back seats. In the science museum, you can admire a one-ton meteorite, quiz yourself astronomically on a computer (I got a D-) and study a solar system model (not to scale, or Pluto and Uranus would be in the parking lot). You can look for the Copernicus crater on a large moon globe, check out weather instruments and feed a gravity well that eats your change in a slow spiral. Before you leave, stop at the gift shop and check out its intriguing scientific gadgets.

Harold's Club Gun Collection • *250 N. Virginia St. (at Commercial Row); (702) 329-0881. Free; open 24 hours.* What a wonderful bunch of killing devices! A National Rifle Association redneck will think he's died and gone to heaven, fully armed. Among the devices of death are a 1675 German wheelock musket, a 1590 Austrian sporting rifle (killing is a sport?), beautifully ornate pearl-inlaid dueling pistols from 1580 Italy, Buffalo Bill Cody's Remington "long range" rifle (great for slaughtering buffalo), and a gold-encrusted shotgun made in 1865 for King Willhem III of The Netherlands. For you Western six-shooter fans, check out the Navy Colt Dragoon percussion-cap revolver (I have one for parade use only). You'll see assorted other Colts and Winchesters and Remingtons, displayed with biographies of their makers. Across the way from this second floor museum, you'll find a nice collection of antique slots and old music-making machines.

National Automobile Museum • *10 Lake St. (at Mill Street); (702) 333-9300. Daily 9:30 to 5:30. Adults $7.50, seniors 62 and over $6.50, kids 6 to 18, $2.50.* **Wheels Cafe** *with outdoor tables, lunches $5 to $7. One-hour guided tours start at 11:55 a.m. and 1:55 p.m. Mixed-media film on the history of the motorcar; gift shop filled with things automotive.*

This is as close to perfection as a themed museum gets, and it's certainly the world's finest auto museum. Not the biggest, just the finest. Cars are grouped logically by era, and walkie-talkie earphones give you an overview of each period. Some of these fine road machines are parked along mock streets appropriate to their time, complete with Burma Shave signs and a Union 76 service station. Exhibits begin in a blacksmith shop, which is logical since this is where the first cars were made.

And the cars! Check out the 1890 Philion steam carriage, the 1902 curved dash Oldsmobile runabout, Henry Ford's first 1903 Model-A and a dashingly handsome red and black 1913 Stutz Bearcat. Moving right along, admire Buckminster Fuller's Dymaxion that looks like a low-budget missile, a rare Tucker and a wonderfully ugly Chrysler Airflow. Finish with a 1981 24-karat gold-plated DeLorean, then walk back to your nondescript Belchfire V-6 and drive away, feeling automotively fulfilled.

252 — CHAPTER SEVEN

Nevada Historical Society Museum • *1650 N. Virginia St. (north side of the UNR campus); (702) 789-0190. Monday-Saturday 8 to 5. Free; donations appreciated.* Nevada the place is presented here, in neat and logical order, from the rocks that shaped it to the climate that makes it what it is. People exhibits travel from the 1200 B.C. nomadic hunters to the Desert Archaic tribes through the Anasazi, Paiutes, Shoshone and Washo, right up to the whites who ruined one culture to establish another. You meet the first Nevadans, like Joe Walker, John C. Frèmont, Jedediah Strong Smith and Peter Skene Ogden. Carriages, cast iron stoves and high-wheel bicycles take

---

RENO'S ARCHES OF TRIUMPH
(At least, none of them have fallen)

One of America's most enduring landmarks is simply known as the "Reno Arch," which spans Virginia Street at Commercial Row. It would be more accurate to say "Reno's arches," since the present one is the sixth design to occupy this spot.

Reno arches go back to 1899, according to Nevada Historical Society curator Phillip I. Earl. A temporary structure was erected near the Truckee River bridge to honor troops of the First Nevada Volunteer Cavalry, returning from Spanish-American War combat in the Philippines. In 1910, journalists covering the Johnson-Jeffries heavyweight fight suggested that Reno was worthy of recognition as the "biggest little city in the world." The phrase appeared on banners carried by the Reno Moose Lodge contingent in parades in Chicago and Minneapolis in 1914. However, it still wasn't in general use.

The arch that made Reno famous—or visa versa—was dedicated on October 23, 1926, to herald completion of the Lincoln and Victory transcontinental highways. It bore bulb-lit slogan promoting an exposition planned the following summer. After the celebration, the sign came down but the arch remained.

Later, the Reno City Council sponsored a contest for a slogan to promote the city and enhance the arch. The winning entry came from one G.A. Burns of Sacramento, and you can guess what it said.

"The winning slogan is by no means original," a council member admitted, "but it better describes the city in a few words." Light bulbs painted the slogan across the arch and Governor Fred Balzar lit the sign on the evening of June 25, 1929.

Six versions of the Reno Arch have appeared on three different frameworks since then. The first neon sign went up in 1934, spelling out a green "Reno" with no slogan. Nobody liked it much, so the endearing phrase was added a year later.

The current version is based on a sketch submitted by Ad Art designer Charles Barnard of Stockton, Calif. Constructed in 1987 by the famous Young Electric Sign Company of rival Las Vegas, it's 48 feet high, with nine-foot neon letters and 2,000 light bulbs. What happened to the first arch? It was dismantled. However, the 1935 version is being refurbished and will grace the entrance to Paradise Park .

you through the last century and into this one. There's lots of stuff on mining, of course, focusing on the "Rush to Washoe" that created today's Nevada, and on the development of gambling, which brings all you tourists.

Housed in a modern finned building, this rates among the best museums in the state. It offers an extensive library of books, old periodicals and photos, available to serious scholars and guidebook writers on a budget. (And thank you, very much.)

Wilbur D. May Museum • *1502 Washington Street (in Rancho San Rafael Park); (702) 785-5961. Open 10 to 5 Tuesday-Sunday in summer and Wednesday-Sunday in winter. Adults $2, kids and seniors $1. Adjacent arboretum and Great Basin Adventure theme park open May through October.* This fine exhibit center is a showplace for a remarkable man's achievements and generosity. It's one of the West's nicer better privately endowed museums, fashioned as a opulent ranch house, similar to May's Double Diamond ranch

— above: Betty Woo Martin; below Nevada Historical Society

What a difference a few decades make! Downtown Reno and the legendary arch, now and in the summer of 1947.

outside Reno. There's no attempt at interpretation here; no test will be given later. Just stroll through and enjoy the professionally done exhibits.

The scion of the May Company, Wilbur spent much of his life traveling and this exhibit center is filled with his trophies. Check out a room filled with enough hunting trophies to give a Sierra Club member heart seizure, the rifle and pistol collection, African weapons and shields and Oriental carvings; and say hello to a grinning shrunken head. This place is a Ripley's Believe It or Not! museum with class. Pick up a brochure and read about the legend of the water hole that changed this remarkable man's life. May, a longtime Reno resident and philanthropist, was planning this museum complex when he died in 1982.

After you're museumed out, adjourn to the nearby **arboretum** and send the kids off to the **Great Basin Adventure,** a playground and theme park.

THE REST

Liberty Belle Museum, Saloon and Restaurant ● *4250 S. Virginia St. (in front of the Reno-Sparks Convention Center) (702) 826-2607. Monday-Friday 11 a.m. to midnight, Sunday 4 to midnight. Free.* Who's better qualified to accumulate a fine collection of old slot machines than the grandsons of the inventor? (See box.) The Liberty Belle Saloon, operated by Marshall and Frank Fey, has become a virtual museum of slots and other gaming devices. The star of the show is Grandfather Charles Fey's first Liberty Bell slot, invented in 1899. Since this place charges no admission, it's probably the best museum deal in the state. Buy a drink and browse to your heart's content, or schedule dinner or lunch; the food's excellent (see dining listing below). You could easily spend a couple of hours here, admiring these wonderfully ornate old machines. And note that the roof is filled with old carriages and wagons. These two boys just can't seem to stop collecting.

Nevada Museum of Art (E.L. Wiegand Museum) ● *160 W. Liberty Street (at Sierra); (702) 329-333. Tuesday-Saturday 10 to 4, Sunday noon to 4. Adults $3, students and seniors 50 and older $1.50, free for all on Fridays.* Starkly modern inside and out, the state-operated Wiegand Museum features rotating exhibits of Nevada artists and those beyond. The permanent collection focuses primarily on paintings, drawings and bronzes of the American West. The museum's striking interior—refrigerator white walls, track lights and black painted ceiling ducts and girders—provides the ideal environment for display.

University of Nevada campus and Mackay Museum of Mines Museum ● *Museum open weekdays 8 to 5; free; (702) 784-6988. Campus directory available at a kiosk at the Center Street entrance.* The 200-acre University of Nevada campus is an island of scholastic calm next to the gaming glitter of downtown. Take Center Street north (the only direction it goes) across the freeway and onto the campus. Stroll beneath century-old oaks, admiring the thorny beauty of a rose garden and the dignity of UNR's fine old brick buildings. The university has the look of a venerable Ivy League school, completely unlike its larger, flashier UNLV cousin down south (no basketball scandals, no mod buildings).

Since mining made Nevada, it's not surprising that the **Mackay Museum of Mines** has one of the finest rock collections in the state, along with exhibits on mines and mining techniques. It was closed when we visited, being completely redone for a July 1992 reopening, so it should be spanking new when you stop by. Also worthy of investigation are the 1886 **Morrill Hall,** which housed all 56 students and two teachers when the university came here from Elko, the **Jot Travis Student Union** and the **Getchell Library.** The food's ample and cheap at the **Dining Commons.**

NUGGETS

Lake Mansion • *Virginia Street and Kietzke Lane, southern edge of parking lot E at the Reno-Sparks Convention Center.* Town founder Myron Lake occupied this square-shouldered colonial style white mansion, built in 1877. It's a grand if stern-looking structure, with a wrap-around porch and widow's walk atop the roof. Adjacent is the little white Glendale school house, the oldest in the state (1864). It was moved here from next-door (and now defunct) Glendale. The mansion and school were closed when we visited, but these things change.

Pioneer Center for the Performing Arts • *100 S. Virginia St. (at Mill Street); For show schedules and ticket information, (702) 329-2552.* This structure, housed in a copper-colored geodesic dome, is worth a pause as you prowl about the lower end of downtown.

Raymond I. Smith Truckee River Walk • *South Virginia Street at the river.* With the Truckee trickling through town, Reno cries out for a river walk in the style of San Antonio's great *Paseo del Rio.* But this short section is rather overdone, with its lavender and pink steel pipe structures and designer garbage cans. It looks more like the entrance to a low-budget world's fair. However, it *is* a nice place to relax along the river, if you don't mind Post Neo-Classic American Tune Town Garish.

St. Thomas Aquinas Cathedral • *310 W. Second (at Arlington); (702) 329-2571. Sanctuary open from 7 a.m. to 5 p.m. daily; Sunday masses at 7:30, 9:30. 11:30, 5:15 and 7 (Spanish), weekday masses at 7 a.m., 12:10 and 5:15.* Admire the elaborate Italianate twin towers of this 1907 jewel, then step inside for instant escape from downtown hubbub. Elaborate stained glass windows tell the story of Catholicism in Nevada, starting from Farther Garces' trek. An elaborate mural of the Adoration of the Lamb fills the curved altar ceiling.

Washoe County Courthouse • *Virginia and Court streets; marriage information (702) 328-3275. Marriage bureau open daily 8 a.m. to midnight.* More marriage licenses have been issued at this Grecian style courthouse than at any other facility of its size in America. Unlike some of Nevada's handsomely restored county office buildings, this staid 1911 sandstone structure with a green copper dome doesn't offer much in the way of visitor appeal. However, you can step inside to admire its old marble halls and terrazzo tile floors, and watch the giggling couples waiting to have their bonding license issued.

RENO'S PARKS

It would not be an exaggeration to call Reno the city of parks. For a community of its size, it has a remarkable number of public greeneries—51 separate park sites and a huge chunk of elemental desert. Further, it the only city in Nevada to earn the National Arbor Day Foundation's Tree City USA designation for its "commitment to urban forestry."

To learn which parks offer what recreational facilities, call the Park and Recreation Department at (702) 334-2260. Here's a brief view of some of the more interesting ones.

256 — CHAPTER SEVEN

Riverside parks • Three public parks line the Truckee downtown, offering quick release from urban pressures. **Wingfield Park,** with benches and picnic tables, occupies an island reached by bridges off Arlington Avenue. It's flanked by **Riverside Park,** with a playground, tennis and basketball courts. **Raymond I. Smith Truckee River Walk,** really more of a square than a walk, has places to sit, relax and read.

Truckee River Trail • *Go east on Second Street to the Kuenzli Street fork.* A streamside hiking, jogging and biking path follows the river five miles from **Broadhead Memorial Park** downtown, past the MGM Grand to a point beyond Sparks.

Idlewild Park • *Take First Street west to Riverside Drive and follow the signs.* This large park occupies a bend in the river about a mile east of Virginia Street. Built for the 1927 Transcontinental Highway Exposition (of Reno Arch fame), it offers a playground, picnic areas, baseball and volleyball facilities and Nevada's only **Municipal Rose Garden.** Peak blooming period for the 2,400 plants (representing 560 varieties) is mid-June through late August. The **Idlewild Park Kiddieland** is open daily from 11 to 6 May through Labor Day, then weekends and holidays the rest of the year; (702) 329-6008.

Oxbow Nature Study Park • *Drive west on Second Street, fork left onto Dickerson and follow it to the end. Daily 8 a.m. to sunset; nature trails, picnic tables and potties.* This riparian jewel shelters a slice of riverbank and marshland two miles west of downtown. More than a mile of paths wind beneath cottonwoods and alders, through tule marshes and alongside the river. Some lead to river and marsh overlooks, where signs explain the their ecological significance. For a park sandwiched between a light industrial area and across-the-river condos, Oxbow shelters a remarkable variety of wildlife—mostly waterbirds, treebirds, squirrels and a few volunteer rabbits that look suspiciously domesticated. This is a great place to sit, relax and watch the cattails grow.

Rancho San Rafael Park • *Just north of the UNR campus and west of Virginia Street.* Reno's own personal patch of desert, Rancho San Rafael covers 408 acres. It's mostly undeveloped, since pro and anti-growth factions have been deadlocked since the land was purchased by a voter-approved bond issue in 1979. The southern chunk, below McCarran Boulevard, shelters the **Wilbur D. May Museum** and **Arboretum,** and the **Great Basin Adventure** theme park. Other facilities include a picnic area, par course and riding stables (329-RIDE). The larger northern chunk, reached by crossing McCarran on Virginia Street then turning left, is primarily open space, with great views back at the city. A hiking trail from the far end of the parking lot leads past a **Basque memorial** and down to a **riparian woodland** along Evans Creek. It's dry most of the year but damp enough to support groves of cottonwoods, willows and tules, which in turn shelter assorted birds and burrowing critters. A web work of trails—some planned, some unauthorized—takes you along both sides of the stream bed and up to a 1917 flume that watered early Reno farms.

Virginia Lake Park • *Go south two miles on Virginia Street, right onto Plumb Lane then left onto Lakeside Drive.* Thirty-two acres rimmed by suburban Reno offer a good sized lake, walking/jogging/biking trails, a par course and picnic areas. The place is busy with birds, and duck-feeding is a major activity. Watch where you step.

ACTIVITIES
All numbers (702) unless otherwise indicated

BALLOONING • To soar aloft, contact Aerovision Balloons, 747-4144; Balloon Adventure Company, 826-5858; Instead Sky Sports, 972-6493; Reno Balloon Race, 786-1181 or Zephyr Balloons, 329-1700.

BICYCLE RENTALS • Bobo Sheehan's, 786-5111; Just Cruisin' Bicycle Rental, 348-4646 and Reno Bicycling Center, 329-BIKE.

GOLF • These Reno-Sparks courses are open to the public:

Northgate Golf Club, 1111 Clubhouse Dr., Reno; 747-7577. Green fees $37 for 18 holes, $30 for nine, less in the off-season.

Wildcreek Golf Course, 3500 Sullivan Lane, Sparks; 673-3100. Fees $37 for 18 holes, $20 for nine, less in the off-season.

Brookside Municipal Golf Course, 700 S. Rock Blvd., Sparks; 322-6009. Nine holes, single round $3.50, double round $6.

Lakeridge Golf Course, 1200 Razorback Dr., Reno; 825-2200. Fees $46 including cart, off-season $28 including cart.

Rosewood Lakes, 6800 Pembroke Dr., Reno; 685-2892. Fees $22 for 18 holes, golf carts $16 (optional).

Sierra Sage Golf Course, 6355 Silver Lake Rd., Reno; 972-1564. Fees $18 weekdays (nine holes $12) and $21 weekends (nine holes $15); carts $18 for 18 holes, $9 for nine.

Washoe County Golf Course, 2601 S. Arlington Ave., Reno; 785-4286. Fees $13 in summer, $12 in the off-season; carts $18.

HORSEBACK RIDING • Rent your trusty steeds at Bull Creek Ranch, 345-7500; Corky Prunty's Horseback Riding, 345-RIDE; More Horses, 331-0606; Rancho San Rafael, 329-RIDE or Western Riding Stables, 343-0104.

SIGHTSEEING TOURS • Among local tour operators are Hardy & Associates Scenic Tours, (800) 627-8222 or (702) 329-3114; Reno Tahoe Company, 348-7788; Gray Line, (800) 822-6009 or (702) 329-1147; and Sierra West Limousine Service, 329-4310. Also, the Reno/Tahoe Gaming Academy has behind-the-scenes casino tours for $5; call 348-7403.

SOARING • Catch a glider ride from Soar Reno, 972-7627.

TENNIS • You'll find courts at Bally's Reno, 789-2145; Lakeridge Tennis Club, 827-4500; Lakeside Tennis Club, 831-5258; Reno Park and Recreation Department, 334-2260; Reno YMCA, 329-1311; Sparks Recreation Department, 359-7930 and Washoe County Parks Department, 785-6133.

ANNUAL EVENTS

Reno Rodeo, late June at the Livestock Events Center; 329-3877.

Hot August Nights, in early August; (800) FOR-RENO; downtown street fair.

Nevada State Fair, early August, Livestock Events Center; 322-4424.

Ben Hogan Golf Tour, September, Northgate Golf Club; 747-7577.

Great Reno Balloon Race, early September, Rancho San Rafael Park; 826-1181.

National Championship Air Races, mid-September at Reno/Stead Airport; 972-6662; one of America's major air shows.

National Senior Pro Rodeo Finals, mid-November, Livestock Events Center; 323-3073.

Festival of Trees, mid-December, downtown Reno; (800) FOR-RENO.

CHARLES FEY & THE LIBERTY BELL

Every time you pull a handle on a slot machine or feed a quarter to a hungry video poker game, you can thank Bavarian immigrant Charles August Fey. He invented the first three-reel automatic payout slot machine, the Liberty Bell, in San Francisco in 1899.

You can see that device and more than 200 other antique gaming machines by visiting the Liberty Belle Saloon and Restaurant at 4250 S. Virginia Street in Reno. The San Francisco-Reno link is no coincidence; the Liberty Belle is owned by Fey's two grandsons, Marshall and Frank.

"Grandfather was one of several San Francisco tinkerers working on gaming machines in the late 1900s," said Marshall, author of **Slot Machines: The First 100 Years.** "Those were the wild days of the Barbary Coast and just about anything was legal. Coin operated gaming devices enjoyed immense popularity then."

The first reeled "nickel-in-the-slot" machines were poker games. A deck of 50 cards was attached to five wheels, similar to a Rolodex file, and a poker hand appeared in a viewing window. Fey wanted to build an automatic payout poker machine "but that wasn't feasible with the technology of the day, so he developed a three-reeler," said Marshall.

Since it couldn't display a five-card poker hand, he used other symbols, including the Liberty Bell, a patriotic icon that the Bavarian immigrant greatly admired. Today's cherry, lemon and orange symbols evolved from machines that dispensed gum, after gambling devices became illegal. "The fruit represented the flavors of the gum, and the jackpot bar was the gum wrapper," Marshall explained.

Grandfather Fey was the last of 16 children born to a Bavarian schoolmaster and his wife. At age 14, he worked as a lathe operator in Munich, which began a lifelong love for mechanics. A year later, he fled Germany to avoid the draft. "The threat of conscription into Otto von Bismark's Army of the German Empire made the lure of freedom...irresistible," Marshall writes in his book. By 1885, he had worked his way to San Francisco. Intrigued with the city's many mechanical gaming machines, he began tinkering in his basement. This eventually led to the grandfather of today's slot machines.

In 1955, Marshall and Frank opened a bar in San Mateo, south of San Francisco. To compliment its Gay Nineties theme, they began collecting old gaming machines. As the collection grew, they decided to move to the only state where these devices were still legal. They opened the Liberty Belle Saloon in Reno in 1958.

You'll often find them around the place most evenings, and they'll happily answer your questions about the intriguing world of gambling devices. If you decide to buy Marshall's $29.95 encyclopedic history of slot machines, hardbound and lavishly illustrated, he'll likely offer to autograph it for you.

WHERE ELSE TO DINE

Most of the town's restaurants are in casinos, included with the listings above. Reno also offers a goodly selection of other dining venues, from family Basque and essential Italian to upscale French and gourmet American.

American

Famous Murphy's • ☺☺☺ $$ Ø

3127 S. Virginia St. (a mile south of downtown); (702) 827-4111. American, mostly seafood; dinners $12 to $18; full bar service. Lunch daily 11 to 2, dinner 5 to 10, Sunday brunch 10 to 2. Reservations accepted; major credit cards. Lively Irish-theme twin restaurant with a burger-chowder-steamers bar open for lunch, and a dining room for dinner. Menu romps from fresh fish and shellfish to ribs and pasta; topped off with homemade desserts.

Liberty Belle Saloon & Restaurant • ☺☺☺ $$

4250 S. Virginia St. (near Reno-Sparks Convention Center) (702) 826-2607. American; dinners $8 to $25; full bar service. Lunch weekdays 11 to 2:30, dinner nightly 5 to 10. MC/VISA. Hearty American fare such as southern fried chicken, seafood, steaks and chops served in an appealing San Francisco-Victorian setting, with carved woods and leaded glass. Diners are surrounded by a collection of 200 antique gaming machines (see **Attractions** above).

Little Waldorf Grill • ☺☺☺ $

1661 N. Virginia St. (opposite UNR's Lawlor Events Center); (702) 323-1926. American and Basque; dinners $8 to $11; full bar service. MC/VISA, AMEX. Great oldstyle saloon and family restaurant with "semi-Basque" dinners with soup, salad and Basque beans; plus other menu items. It's a locally popular place, particularly for the UNR Wolf Pack, who's memorabilia and class photos tattoo the walls. The adjacent saloon functions as a sports bar.

PJ's Saloon • ☺☺ $ Ø

1590 S. Wells Ave. (near Park Lane Mall); (702) 323-6366. Tex-Mex and American; dinners $6 to $12; full bar service. Breakfast weekdays 7 to 11 and weekends 8 to noon, lunch and dinner Monday-Saturday 11 to 9, closed Sunday night. MC/VISA. Lively Western bistro with a busy menu ranging from "breakfast burritos" and "monster muffins" to barbecued ribs, *fajitas* and Tex-Mex specials for lunch and dinner. A local hangout.

Rapscallion Seafood House • ☺☺☺ $$ Ø

1555 S. Wells Ave.; (702) 323-1211. Seafood; dinners $11 to $19; full bar service. Lunch weekdays from 11:30, dinner nightly 5 to 10:30, Sunday brunch 10 to 2. Reservations accepted; MC/VISA, AMEX. Appealing old San Francisco style place with warm woods, stained glass and cozy booths. Extensive seafood menu with daily fresh fish specials; a locally popular *fishhause*.

Asian, Mideastern

Ichiban Restaurant • ☺☺ $$

635 N. Sierra Ave.; (702) 323-5550. Japanese; dinners $10 to $15; full bar service. Nightly from 5. Reservations accepted; major credit cards. "Americanized Japanese" restaurant in Oriental garden setting. Conventional Japanese fare, plus teriyaki steaks and table-side knife-swinging "cooking shows" *a la* Benihana. Also a sushi bar.

Kyoto Restaurant • ☺☺ $$ ∅
915 W. Moana Lane (Moana West Shopping Center); (702) 825-9686. Japanese; dinners $12 to $14; full bar service. Open daily, lunch 11:30 to 3 and dinner 5 to 10. Reservations accepted; MC/VISA, AMEX. Tokyo-modern restaurant trimmed with Japanese art and artifacts. It features savory *yakitori,* a skewered barbecued delicacy. Also *sushi* and several *tempura-sushi* combination dinners.

Sanpa Indian Restaurant • ☺ $ ∅
3374 Kietzke Lane; (702) 829-1537. East Indian; dinners $6 to $12; wine and beer. Monday-Saturday 11 to 9:30, closed Sunday. Reservations accepted; major credit cards. Small, inexpensive place specializing in vegetarian and meat Marsala curries; other India fare ranging from hot and spicy to mild. Dose up on *dosas, pakoras, kebobs* and *tandoori* specialties.

Szechuan Garden • ☺☺ $
903 W. Moana Lane (in Moana West Shopping Center); (702) 827-6333. Chinese; dinners $7 to $13; full bar service. Daily 11:30 a.m. to 10 p.m. MC/VISA, AMEX. Shopping center-modern Chinese restaurant specializing in spicy Szechuan and Mandarin cuisine, with a particular accent on broiled fish and other seafood. Try the *kung pao shrimp,* or the *mushu pork* wrapped in "Chinese tortillas."

Palais de Jade • ☺☺☺ $$
960 W. Moana Lane (Moana West Shopping Center); (702) 827-5233. Chinese; dinners $9 to $20; full bar service. Daily 11 a.m. to 10 p.m. Reservations accepted; MC/VISA, AMEX. Northern Nevada's fanciest Chinese restaurant, done in black and white, with red accents (for good luck) and Chinese artifacts. Extensive menu runs the gamut of *cuisine de China,* focusing on spicy Szechuan and Hunan fare, plus milder Cantonese offerings.

Basque

Louis' Basque Corner • ☺☺☺ $$ ∅
301 E. Fourth St. (at Evans, two blocks off Virginia); (702) 323-7203. Family-style Basque; dinners $14 to $15; full bar service. Lunch Monday-Saturday 11 to 2, dinner Monday-Saturday 5:30 to 10 and Sunday 4:30 to 9:30. Major credit cards. One of Nevada's legendary Basque restaurants, serving seven-course dinners at family style tables; all you can eat with gratis wine. Dishes reflect both French and Spanish Basque cooking.

Pyrenees Bar & Grill • ☺☺☺ $$
California and Flint streets; (702) 329-3800. Basque- American; Basque dinners $13.50, other entrées $10 to $16; full bar service. Lunch weekdays 11 to 2, dinner nightly 5:30 to 10. Reservations accepted; MC/VISA, AMEX. Upscale Basque restaurant occupying a two-story turn of the century columned mansion; the look is old world Spanish. Family-style Spanish-French Basque dinners, or order from an American menu of steaks, chops, chicken and fish.

European

Bavarian World • ☺ $$
595 Valley Rd. (at Sixth Street); (702) 323-7646. German- Bavarian; dinners $8 to $16; wine and beer. Lunch and dinner Monday-Saturday; closed Sunday. MC/VISA. Folksy Bavarian-style cafe serving inexpensive and hearty

portions of *sauerbraten, schnitzel* and *bratwurst*, plus American chicken and fish dishes. This versatile little place also features a bakery and deli.

Le Table Française • ☺☺☺☺ $$$ ∅
3065 W. Fourth St. (two miles west); (702) 323-3200. French-American; dinners $20 to $28.50; full bar service. Dinner nightly 6 to 10. Reservations accepted; MC/VISA, AMEX. Nevada's oldest and possibly finest French restaurant, owned since 1974 by award- winning Chef Yves Pimparel, former executive chef of San Francisco's Le Trianon. Elegant place with French Provincial dècor and museum-quality antiques. Changing menu featured classic French dishes, plus flown-in fresh fish and black Angus beef.

Italian

Casanova's Restaurant • ☺☺☺ $$ ∅∅
1695 S. Virginia St. (south end, a block north of Plumb Lane); (702) 786-6633. Italian-American; dinners $12 to $20; full bar service. Lunch weekdays 11:30 to 2:30, dinner nightly 5 to 11. Reservations accepted, essential on weekends. Major credit cards. Stylish and cozy restaurant *a la* early San Francisco with dressy waitstaff, antiques, stained glass and curtained booths. Wide range of pasta and other Italian dishes, plus steaks and wild game such as venison, quail and pheasant. Smoke-free dining room. Music for dancing Friday and Saturday.

Columbo's Riverfront • ☺☺ $$
145 W. Truckee River Lane (downtown, between Sierra and Arlington); (702) 323-7004. Italian; dinners $12 to $23; full bar service. Dinner nightly from 6; bar and light snacks until 7 a.m. No reservations; MC/VISA, AMEX. Intimate bistro with an Art Deco style, overlooking the river. Varied Italian menu plus several steak dishes. Live piano bar Friday-Saturday.

La Trattoria • ☺☺ $$
719 S. Virginia St.; (702) 323-1131. Italian; dinners $9 to $14; wine and beer. Monday-Saturday 5 p.m. to 10 p.m. Reservations accepted; MC/VISA. Cozy family-owned cafè featuring fresh "home grown" stuffed pastas, plus old country style *cacciatores, Parmagianas* and such. Try the steak ravioli in wine sauce or the stuffed eggplant in marinara sauce. Good wine list.

Mexican

El Borracho • ☺☺ $ ∅
1601 S. Virginia St. (south end at Plumb Lane); (702) 322-0313. Mexican; dinners $8 to $12; full bar service. Daily except Tuesday, 11 a.m. to 11 p.m. Reservations accepted; major credit cards. Longtime local favorite, awarded silver medal in a restaurant industry rating. Extensive menu featuring pork *carnitas*, chicken *fajitas* and 11 different shrimp dishes.

La Pinata • ☺ $ ∅
1575 Vassar St. (at Kietzke Line in Town and Country Plaza); (702) 323-3210. Mexican; dinners $6 to $10; full bar service. Daily 11 a.m. to 10 p.m. Reservations accepted; MC/VISA, AMEX. Colorfully decorated family place serving a wide range of typical *Latino* dishes. Mexican buffet weekdays from 11:30 to 1:30, and on Friday and Saturday nights.

Miguel's Fine Mexican Food • ☺☺ $ ∅
1415 S. Virginia St. (south end, at Mount Rose Street); (702) 322-2722. Mexican; dinners $6.50 to $7.75; full bar service. Sunday-Thursday 11 to 9,

262 — CHAPTER SEVEN

Friday-Saturday 11 to 10. Reservations accepted Sunday-Thursday; major credit cards. Long-established family owned restaurant with lively "early Tijuana-UFO" dècor. *Carne Asada* is a specialty; tasty *sopatillas* come with every meal. Extensive Mexican menu plus steaks and hamburgers.

WHERE TO SLEEP

Listings are mostly casino hotels, which we feel are the preferred places to stay in Nevada's gaming centers. You're here to party, so why not sleep near the action? Casino hotels generally are very good buys, often cheaper than non-gaming aligned places, although we list some of those as well.

Scores of relatively inexpensive motels line south Virginia Street and others are clustered near the downtown area along Virginia, Center, Lake, Sierra and Arlington.

Most hotels and motels without gaming parlors offer discount coupon books to various casinos. Virtually every hotel and motel in town has a dual rate structure; rooms are cheaper Sunday through Thursday and higher Friday and Saturday; rates often are higher in summer, lower in winter.

NOTE: Because of Reno's smaller room count and summer popularity, rooms often are more scarce here than in Las Vegas from June through Labor Day. Book well in advance. Lower prices in listings generally indicate weekday, off-season rates. The Ø symbol denotes properties with non-smoking rooms or floors.

Rooms for $70 and up

Bally's Reno ● ⌂⌂⌂⌂ Ø

2500 E. Second St., Reno, NV 89595; (800) 648-5080 or (702) 789-2000. Doubles $69 to $95, suites $100 and beyond. Major credit cards. The 2,000 rooms in this mega-casino are large and cheerfully decorated with picture-window views of the mountains and countryside. Full amenities in the rooms and in the surrounding casino complex—the only true destination resort in town. Pool, spa, health club, tennis courts, movie theaters and bowling alley.

Harrah's Reno ● ⌂⌂⌂ Ø

219 Center St., Reno, NV 89501; (800) 648-3773 or (702) 786-3232. Doubles from $69, luxury doubles $115 to $130, suites $210 to $375. Major credit cards. Conservative color schemes mix with luxurious appointments in Harrah's 565 rooms. Large and comfortable rooms are among downtown's finest. Attached casino offers a headliner room, cabaret entertainment and several restaurants.

Rooms from $50 to $69

Best Western Airport Plaza ● ⌂⌂⌂ Ø

1981 Terminal Way (adjacent to Reno-Cannon Airport), Reno, NV 89502; (800) 648-3525 or (702) 348-6370. Doubles $58 to $68, suites $190 to $220. Major credit cards. Attractive 270-unit hotel; stylish rooms with TV movies, phones; several suites; swimming pool, sauna, spa, exercise room, restaurant and small casino (slots only).

Clarion Hotel Casino ● ⌂⌂⌂ Ø

3800 S. Virginia St., Reno, NV 89502; (800) 762-5190 or (702) 825-4700. Doubles $54 to $125, singles $49 to $125, suites $125 to $295. Major *credit cards.* Color-coordinated rooms with modern décor to match the flashy new casino downstairs, with all the usual amenities; pool, spa, health club.

Eldorado Hotel Casino • ⌂⌂⌂ ∅
Fourth and Virginia (P.O. Box 3399), Reno, NV 89505; (800) 648-5966 or (702) 786-5700. Doubles $35 to $99, suites $110 to $175. Major credit cards. Sleek new hotel tower offering view rooms from the heart of downtown, with TV movies and other amenities; pool and spa. Full casino facilities and several restaurants below.

Flamingo Hilton-Reno • ⌂⌂⌂
255 N. Sierra St. (P.O. Box 1291), Reno, NV 89504; (800) 648-4882 or (702) 322-1111. Doubles $59 to $219, suites to $245. Major credit cards. Nicely subdued white and green rooms are quieter than the gaudy pink gaming palace below. Six hundred units with TV movies, phones and the usual upscale amenities. Full casino facility with restaurants and the like.

Peppermill Hotel Casino • ⌂⌂⌂ ∅
2707 S. Virginia St., Reno, NV 89502; (800) 282-2444 or (702) 826-2121. Doubles $49 to $84, to $135 for tower kings, suites $79 to $500. Major credit cards. Very attractive color-coordinated rooms in glossy new casino resort with fitness center, swimming pool, restaurants and full gaming facility.

Rooms from $25 to $49

Best Western Daniel's Motor Lodge • ⌂ ∅
375 N. Sierra St. (downtown area), Reno, NV 89501; (702) 329-1351. Doubles $40 to $64. Well-located 82-unit motel with large rooms; TV, room phones.

Circus Circus Hotel/Casino • ⌂⌂ ∅
500 N. Sierra St. (P.O. Box 5880), Reno, NV 89513; (800) 648-5010 or (702) 329-0711. Doubles $28 to $46. Major credit cards. More than 1,600 modest but nicely-done rooms in a pair of think-pink towers rising above the striped circus tent casino.

Comstock Hotel Casino • ⌂⌂ ∅
200 W. Second St., Reno, NV 89501; (800) 824-8167 or (702) 329-1880. Doubles $39 to $64, suites $225 to $295. Recently added hotel tower brings room count to 130; large and comfortably furnished with Western décor to match the casino. Amenities include a spa, sauna and exercise room.

Days Inn • ⌂ ∅
701 E. Seventh St., Reno, NV 89512; (800) 942-3838. Doubles $25 to $75. Major credit cards. A 137-unit motel with good low-end off-season rates for its near-downtown location. Basic but clean and well-equipped rooms with TV, phones; swimming pool.

Executive Inn • ⌂ ∅
205 S. Sierra St. (downtown), Reno, NV 89501; (800) 648-4545 or (702) 786-4050. Doubles $25 to $69. Major credit cards. A good mid-downtown base of operations; all rooms have microwaves and refrigerators, plus TV, room phones; covered parking; pool.

Fitzgerald's Casino/Hotel • ⌂⌂ ∅
255 N. Virginia St. (P.O. Box 40130), Reno, NV 89504; (800) 648-5022 or (702) 785-3300. Doubles $28 to $92. Major credit cards. A 350-unit down-

town hotel, towering over a casino with full gaming and restaurant facilities. Simple, nicely done rooms with TV movies and phones.

Holiday Hotel Casino • ⌒⌒

P.O. Box 2700 (on the river, between Mill and Center), Reno, NV 89501; (800) 648-5431 or (702) 329-0411. Doubles $30 to $66. Major credit cards. Modern 193-room casino hotel on the banks of the Truckee, with TV, room phones; three two-room suites. Many rooms have river views.

Riverboat Hotel & Casino • ⌒⌒ ∅

34 W. Second St., Reno, NV 89501; (800) 888-5525 or (702) 323-8877. Doubles from $25 and to $75. Major credit cards. Pleasing color coordinated rooms with Tiffany-style lamps and other touches to match the Old South casino motif; gaming and dining facilities below.

Sands Regency Hotel Casino • ⌒⌒ ∅

Arlington Avenue at Third Street, Reno, NV 89501; (800) 648-3553 or (702) 348-2200. Doubles from $26 off-season, from $54 high season, suites and kitchenettes $110 to $225. Major credit cards. Old family-owned casino hotel with some motel and newer hotel units. Rooms range from standard to somewhat luxurious, including bridal suites and three efficiencies. Facilities include swimming pool, health spa and several restaurants.

Sundowner Hotel/Casino • ⌒⌒ ∅

450 N. Arlington Ave., Reno, NV 89503; (800) 648-5490 or (702) 786-7050. Doubles $29 to $48. Major credit cards. Modest but clean and neat rooms with TV, room phones and other essentials, with casino and dining facilities below; swimming pool.

Virginian Hotel Casino • ⌒⌒

140 N. Virginia St., Reno, NV 89501; (800) 874-5558 or (702) 329-4664. Doubles $32 to $44. Major credit cards. A good buy, right on Virginia Street; the 120 bright and new rooms are color coordinated and comfortable with the usual amenities. Full gaming and dining facilities downstairs.

Wonder Lodge • ⌒

430 Lake St. (near downtown); (702) 786-6840. Doubles $30 to $52. Major credit cards. Well-located 63-unit motel two blocks from casinos; good-sized rooms with TV, phones; swimming pool.

WHERE TO CAMP

Bally's Camperland • *2500 E. Second St., Reno, NV 89595; (800) 648-5080 or (702) 789-2129. RV sites only, full hookups $17. Reservations accepted; major credit cards.* Showers, convenience store, dump station, Propane and gasoline, coin laundry. Part of Bally's Reno complex with access to full resort facilities, including tennis, pool and health club.

Chisum Trailer Park • *1300 Second St. (about a mile west of downtown), Reno, NV 89503; (702) 322-2281. RV sites; full hookups $14.50. Reservations accepted; MC/VISA.* Old but clean RV park on the Truckee River with tree-shaded sites; showers, dump station, pay phone, laundry. Some pull-throughs.

John Ascuaga's Nugget • *B Street and Pyramid Way, Sparks.* Free RV parking on the far end of the Nugget's eastern lot; no facilities available, except refuse cans.

Sparks

Population: 53,400 **Elevation: 4,407 feet**

Although it's fused to Reno's east suburbs, Sparks is a separate city, founded in 1904 as a site for Southern Pacific Railroad's maintenance facility. It was named for Governor "Honest John" Sparks, a flamboyant Texas Ranger, Indian fighter, rancher and cotton farmer turned politician. Apparently not as honest as his name, he left his family penniless. His house of cards financial world collapsed when he died in office in 1908.

Sparks would offer no reason to visit if it hadn't been for two Idahoans, Dick Graves and John Ascuaga. Graves opened the Nugget Casino here in 1955 and installed Ascuaga, son of a Basque sheepherder, to manage it. Young John was so successful—and presumably so thrifty—that he bought the place just three years later. Ascuaga's Nugget today is one of the most successful casinos in Nevada, dominating what little there is of downtown Sparks. Basically, the casino and its parking lots occupy one side of B Street and Sparks occupies the other.

The once-drab little town decided it needed sprucing up, so its redevelopment agency spent $1.7 million in 1988 to convert a four-block area along B Street into **Victorian Square.** It's not the sort of place you'd drive dozens of miles to see, but it is attractive, with a few refurbished turn-of-the-century brick and masonry buildings, wrought iron, sculptures and old-style park benches.

Most of the town's casinos surround Victorian Square. Also here for your enjoyment are the oldstyle 1931 federalist revival **Courthouse, Lillard Railroad Park** with some greenery and a monument to Nevada's early Chinese. The **Sparks Museum,** with an ordinary but neat collection of pioneer artifacts and early Sparks photos, is open Wednesday-Sunday 1 to 4; free. The **Sparks Chamber of Commerce,** open weekdays 8 to 5, occupies a turn-of-the-century railroad style depot at B Street and Pyramid Way.

THE CASINOS

John Ascuaga's Nugget • ☺☺☺☺ Ø

1100 Nugget Ave., Sparks, NV 89431-9905; (800) 648-1177 or (702) 356-3300. It is appropriate to say that one of Reno's two finest casino resorts is in Sparks. The Nugget doesn't have Bally's extensive facilities and massive size. However, it rivals its near neighbor in all-around spiffiness, service and that catch-all phrase, general amenities. The restaurants, casino and rooms are immaculate and the service is prompt and cheerful. It's obviously staffed by a bunch of happy campers. John himself likes to stroll through his mini-city, chatting with the help, asking how things are going, and making sure things are going well.

Casino: We aren't sure if Mr. Guinness has been notified, but the Nugget has the world's only casino built under a freeway. I-80 rumbles overhead, splitting the casino complex in two, but there's really no rumble. Strolling about the large and open gaming area, you'd never know that 18-wheelers were breaking the speed limit right over your head. The casino is quite appealing, with strip lighting, floral carpeting and mirror paneled ceilings. All the games and machines are here, along with a race and sports book, bingo parlor and stylish poker room.

Entertainment: The Nugget's Celebrity Room books the big names of showbiz. Lesser-knowns make live music in the Casino Cabaret. Also, check out Trader Dick's Bar. With a thatched roof and sarong-clad cocktail waitresses, it would have brought a grin to the face of the long-departed Trader Vic Bergeron of San Francisco.

Dining: Overall, this may be the best collection of casino restaurants in the state. Take your pick: The **Rotisserie** features American entrées from $14 to $18, serving lunch Monday-Saturday and dinner nightly; the **Farmhouse** is a steak, prime rib and seafood place, $8 to $14, lunch weekdays and dinner nightly; **Trader Dick's** has Polynesian and Szechuan dishes, $10 to $17, lunch and dinner; the **Steak House Grill** is elegant and clubby, open nightly for dinner; the rural-trimmed **General Store** is the 24-hour place, $6.50 to $14.50 and the **Oyster Bar** serves everything from raw oysters to fish filets, amidst lanyard and halyards, $9 to $14, daily from 11 a.m. The Nugget **buffet** is rated among the best in the area.

Rooms: The 1,000 lodging units run the gamut from inexpensive motel rooms to plush highrises with a view well beyond that freeway. Prices begin as low as $30 and range up to $89 for luxury tower doubles. Resort amenities include an Olympian pool, health club, spa, barber and beauty shop and shopping facilities in the casino.

Silver Club Hotel Casino • ☺☺

1040 B Street (P.O. Box 3567), Sparks, NV 89432; (800) 648-1137 or (702) 358-4771. Across Victorian Square from the Nugget, the newly remodeled Silver Club is an appealing mid-sized casino with a rural turn-of-the-century America look. With its high ceilings, the casino a spacious place, with a selection of low-limit tables and nickel slots and videos. There are pool tables and dart boards on the balconied second floor.

Dining: The attractive **Victoria Steakhouse** has a $7.95 steak special and other American fare from $9 to $14. The 24-hour **Town Square** offers good prices like prime rib for $4.99, and other complete dinners up to $10. The **Whistle Stop Buffet** is a bargain, too: $3.95 for breakfast and lunch, $4.95 for din-din. **Rooms:** An basic motel wing out back offers doubles from $35 to $43.

Three smaller casinos extend west from the Silver Club:

The Mint • It's an ordinary looking little joint with a few slots and a basic coffee shop with good prices: $4.95 prime rib, $3.25 ham hocks and such.

Treasury Club Casino • This small place has a cute turn-of-the-century front in keeping with Victorian Square. You'll find assorted low-roller slots and videos inside. Its **Rio Grande Cantina** is an attractively rustic place serving mostly American fare, despite it's name. You can get *fajitas* and chili Colorado, however. Hours are 7 a.m. to 10 p.m. and in has some good buys, such as a $1.49 breakfast and $3.95 prime rib.

B Street Gambling Hall • This attractive place also carries the Victorian Square theme, with a Gay Nineties look and a small assortment of table games and slots. The 24-hour restaurant is **Giudici's,** offering American and Italian fare from $4 to $10. The 99-cent shrimp cocktail and $3.95 veal Marsala are good buys.

"To a wearied frame and tired mind, what refreshment there is in the neighborhood of this lake! The air is singularly searching and strengthening. The noble pines, not obstructed by underbrush, enrich the slightest breeze with aroma and music." — **Theologian Thomas Starr King, 1863**

CHAPTER EIGHT
LAKE TAHOE
Pine tree playground

Come with us now to one of the most popular and heavily-used alpine recreational areas in America—in both winter and summer. The Lake Tahoe Basin, shared by California and Nevada, draws upwards of six million visitors a year. Come looking for pretty scenery and reams of activities, but don't come looking for solitude. (Although you can find that if you hike far enough into the surrounding woods.)

The irony here is that Nevada, noted for its garish flamboyance, appears to be much kinder and gentler to its share of the lake than California. It is perhaps a pity that the state controls only 29 miles of its 71-mile shoreline.

Much of the eastern shore is occupied by Lake Tahoe Nevada State Park, national forest lands and the planned community of Incline Village. This has deterred the unbridled development which has spoiled much of the California shoreline. "Cal-Tahoe" consists mostly of a disjoined string of motels, service stations and other small businesses, simmering in their own sea of asphalt. As the beautiful Tahoe Basin gained popularity during the 1950s and 1960s, folks rushed in by the thousands to get their own piece of paradise while there was still some left.

It was a classic example of humanity fouling a very pretty nest.

Of course, what we really have here is irony upon irony. Although most tourist facilities are on the California side, a good share of the *tourists* are lured by casino clusters at Crystal Bay and Stateline, on the north and south shores.

In belated attempts at damage control, the Nevada-California Tahoe Regional Planning Authority was formed a couple of decades ago. It has placed strict limits on future growth and design. Fortunately, 85 percent of the greater Tahoe Basin is public land, so visitors can still retreat to their own personal patch of pristine—if second-growth—ponderosas. The basin offers hundreds of national forest campsites and hundreds of miles of hiking trails. (However, 85 percent of the lakeshore is privately owned.)

THINGS TO KNOW BEFORE YOU GO

BEST TIME TO GO ● Obviously, it depends on whether you want to ski or you want to hike and play in the woods. If gambling is your game, we'd recommend going in winter because the area is more beautiful and less crowded, with lower room rates. Both I-80 and U.S. 50 are cleared after winter storms, so you should be able to get into the basin. (Expect awesome skier traffic jams on weekends, however.) Folks who get snowed in for a couple of days generally don't complain. Their bosses might, but they don't.

WHAT TO SEE ● Mostly what you see is the view, the same one that inspired Mark Twain. As you drive the lake, plan stops at Sand Harbor and Ponderosa Ranch on the north shore, the viewpoint at Logan Shoals and the Spooner Lake on the east side, then drive on around the California side to Emerald Bay, Tahoe's finest single vista.

WHAT CASINOS TO SEE ● The woodsy elegant Cal Neva and upscale Hyatt Regency at north shore, and the "Big Four" at Stateline—Harvey's, Harrah's, the Horizon and Caesars Tahoe.

WHAT TO DO ● Take the Ponderosa Ranch hayride that ends with a big cowboy breakfast, scramble down to the Tahoe shore at Logan Shoals, hike a piece of the Tahoe Rim Trail from the Spooner Summit trailhead, and of course camp, boat, swim (brrr) and hike to your heart's content in summer, and fall down in the snow in winter.

Useful contacts

General information and lodgings: Dial (800) GO-TAHOE

Reno-Sparks Convention & Visitors Authority, P.O. Box 837, Reno, NV 89504-0837; (702) 827-7366

Lake Tahoe Basin Management Unit, U.S. Forest Service, 1052 Tata Lane (Box 8465), South Lake Tahoe, CA 95731; (916) 544-6420.

Tahoe-Douglas Chamber of Commerce, P.O. Box 7139, Stateline, NV 89449. Visitor center in Roundhill Shopping Mall open weekdays 9 to 5 and Saturdays 10 to 4.

Sierra Ski Marketing Council, P.O. Box 9137, Incline Village, NV 89450.

South Lake Tahoe Chamber of Commerce, 3066 Lake Tahoe Blvd., South Lake Tahoe, CA 95702; (916) 541-5355.

Tahoe North Visitors and Convention Bureau, P.O. Box 5578, Tahoe City, CA 96145; (800) 824-6348.

Reno/Tahoe, P.O. Box 9038, Incline Village, NV 89450

Lake Tahoe area radio stations

Most Reno radio waves reach easily into the high pines. Also, you can tune in these local stations:

KRLT-FM, 93.9—light rock
KZFF-FM, 102.9—top 40
KOWL-AM, 1490—music & news
KTHO-AM, 590—music & news

THE WAY IT WAS • Nevada was not always so kind to its share of the lake. During the 1860's "Rush to Washoe," 98 percent of the eastern side's timber was cut to shore up the silver mines and to build the towns of Virginia City, Carson City and Reno. The logs were fired down flumes to the valley below, and later hauled on a narrow gauge extension of the Virginia & Truckee Railroad. Until that time, this amazingly clear mountain-rimmed lake slept peacefully among the pines. The few outsiders who visited here came to admire, not to plunder.

"As it lay there with the shadows of the mountains brilliantly photographed upon its still surface, I thought it must surely be the fairest picture the whole earth affords," wrote Mark Twain, who visited here in 1861.

Tectonic shifting set the stage for the lake when the Sierra Nevada and Carson Range were uplifted about 25 million years ago. Faulting caused the land between to sink, creating the Tahoe Basin. About 20 million years later, volcanic flows sealed the northern end. Ice Age glaciers crept in, then retreated and left the beginnings of a huge lake in their wake, about 10,000 years ago. As rain and snow raised the water level, it seeped through the porous lava at the northern shore, creating an outlet for the Truckee River. That "leak" has now been formalized with a dam that controls the flow of drinking and irrigation water to the Washoe Valley.

John C. Frèmont apparently was the first outsider to see the lake, following the course of the Truckee in 1844. He gave it the unbecoming name of Lake Bonpland to salute a French explorer. It then became Lake Bigler in honor of California's third governor. But John Bigler turned out to be a rather unsavory character and a bit of a tippler.

"Nothing could have been in worse taste than in applying to a liquid so beautifully clear and cool the name of one who so detested water," penned California historian Hubert Bancroft.

Finally, cartographers chose a Washo term whose meaning is vague. Tahoe may mean limpid water, big water, high water, falling leaf or edge of the lake—*Da Ow A Ga*. (Mark Twain insisted that Tahoe was Paiute for "grasshopper soup.") The California legislature—presumably after consulting the Nevada legislature—made Lake Tahoe the official name in 1928. Northern Californians, who comprise 75 percent of Tahoe's visitors, simply call it The Lake, as San Francisco is The City.

After Washoe mining interests stripped the Nevada side of most of its timber, the area lay relatively undisturbed. A few reclusive millionaires built mansions among the trees, but the lack of a road network discouraged regular visitation. A rough road reached the north shore from Truckee shortly after the turn of the century. The Lincoln Highway nipped the south shore in the 1920s and resort building began in earnest. It became fashionable to "go up to the lake" for the weekend, or for the summer if one could afford it.

Sacramento meat wholesaler Harvey Gross opened a tiny bar with three slot machines just inside the Nevada line in 1944. Others followed, setting the stage for the area's future as a major gaming destination.

THE WAY IT IS • The vision of Tahoe beguiles the eye and its statistics boggle the mind. It's the largest alpine lake in North America and the second largest in the world, measuring 21.6 by 12 miles, with 71 miles of shoreline (76 road miles). (Peru's Lake Titicaca is larger and higher, but murkier.) Further, it's the second deepest lake in the U.S., after Oregon's

Crater Lake, averaging 1,000 feet. At its deepest point, 1,645 feet, the bottom is lower than the elevation of Carson City.

If an aquatic supergopher got down there and started burrowing, the resulting leak would flood an area the size of Nevada with more than two feet of water. The lake holds roughly 40 trillion gallons, enough to supply America's domestic needs for five years. (Don't get any wild ideas, Arizona!)

Further, the lake is incredibly clear, as you will certainly note when you explore its shoreline. Plants, which need sunlight to make fuel, have been found growing 400 feet below the surface. Unfortunately, runoff from the construction frenzy of the 1950s and 1960s introduced nutrients that encouraged algae growth. The water has lost an average 25 feet of its clarity.

The lake's volume is so massive that it acts as its own insulator. Surface water temperature rarely rise above 60 degrees, even in August. Most attempts at swimming are rather brief. Six hundred feet below the surface, the water remains a constant 30 degrees. The lake's mass also prevents it from freezing in winter, except at sheltered inlets like Emerald Bay.

GETTING THERE

You have a choice of four approaches from Nevada: Interstate 80, then south from Truckee; Mount Rose Highway from a point south of Reno off U.S. 395; good old Highway 50 from Carson City over Spooner Summit; and Kingsbury Grade from the Minden-Gardnerville Area.

Those who make this trip often say **Mount Rose Highway** is the most spectacular, since it enters the basin at the highest paved point on the rim, at 8,900-foot **Mount Rose Summit.** The views of the Washoe Valley below and the lake ahead are predictably awesome. Pause to drink them in (sorry about that) before spiraling down to **Incline Village. Kingsbury Grade** is a twisting, scenic spiral that tops out at **Daggett Summit,** 7,374 feet, then drops steeply into **Stateline**. Since it's a major highway, many of the curves have been engineered out of **U.S. 50** as it rises swiftly from the Washoe Valley and glides over **Spooner Summit** at 7,146 feet. It hits the eastern shoreline midway between Incline and Stateline.

We've chosen **I-80** for our approach because of it's great historic significance. Much of the Westward Movement was funneled through here, up twisting Truckee Canyon, over Donner Summit and on to California. This was John Frèmont's choice, following directions from the Paiute Indians of Pyramid Lake. The first wagon trains used this route, although the drop down the other side was so precipitous that the wagons had to be taken apart and lowered in pieces.

Even though the Donner Party suffered its winter of horror here in 1846, it remained the route of choice for emigrants who followed. Historians estimate that 30,000 gold-seekers passed through here in 1849. When young engineer Theodore Judah sought a route for the western end of the transcontinental railroad, he chose this route as well. Built primarily by Chinese labor, it was so well engineered that it is still used today.

The nation's first coast-to-coast road, the Victory Highway, followed the same route, generally on canyons opposite the gently twisting rails. Today it is I-80, the only freeway through the Sierra Nevada. It climbs quickly as it heads east out of Reno toward the border hamlet of **Verdi.** The tiny town offers two final chances to gamble, at a pair of casinos set a couple of miles inside the border.

Boomtown Hotel/Casino • ☺☺
P.O. Box 399, Verdi, NV 89439; (800) 648-3790 or (702) 345-6000. Major credit cards. The midsize Boomtown, with an old Western façade, offers all the table games, lots of nickel slots and videos, a poker room, gift and souvenir shop. The 24-hour **restaurant** has a basic American menu with meals ranging from $7 to $11. Simply attired, comfortable **hotel rooms** are $37 to $46. There's also an **RV park** with full hookups from $13 to $16.

Gold Ranch • ☺
Verdi; (702) 345-0556. Just beyond Boomtown, this is a dinky but cute little Western themed place with an Arco service station, a row of slots, two blackjack tables, small gift shop and a mini-mart. Its restaurant (dinners $6 to $8) has a local reputation for cheap and tasty food.

If you're Tahoe-bound, you'll turn south from I-80 onto State Highway 267 at **Truckee**, California. You'll thus fall short of **Donner Memorial State Park** near Donner Lake, and **Donner Pass** above it. The memorial is certainly worth a stop, with a museum that outlines the tragedy of the Donner Party. You may recall that some survivors resorted to cannibalism to get through a horrible winter. The museum also has exhibits on the transcontinental railroad, emigrant trail and area logging. It's open daily 10 to 4 (closed for lunch during the off-season); admission $2; (916) 587-3841. There's also a **campground** adjacent, and picnic areas.

Truckee is an appealing forest hamlet, with an oldstyle business district well preserved from its days as a major provisioning center for the Central Pacific Railroad. The route south from here climbs steeply to 7,179-foot Brockway Summit and—*there it is!*

Your first view of this giant *lapis lazuli* gem, shimmering from a mountain-rimmed basin, is filtered through the pines. Anyone seeing Lake Tahoe for the first time has to feel some sort of emotional rush. Of course, if you approach from the California side on Highway 50, and your first view is filtered through McDonald's golden arches, the visual impact is diminished somewhat.

Curving down toward the lake, you hit the shoreline between **Tahoe Vista** and **Kings Beach,** on State Highway 28. Both are typical California lakefront collections of motels, summer cabins and real estate offices. **Kings Beach State Recreation Area** consists of a sandy beach, boat launch, picnic area and restrooms. Next-door **Brockway,** population 125, consists mostly of lakefront condos.

THE NORTH SHORE & INCLINE

You're first clue that you've entered Nevada is a sign identifying the midsized **Cal-Neva Lodge and Casino**. You're in the town of **Crystal Bay,** consisting mostly of the Cal-Neva and a few smaller gaming parlors.

From Crystal Bay, the highway climbs a bit, affording views of the lake over condo rooftops. A mile or so beyond Crystal Bay, fork to the right onto Lakeshore Drive and you'll be delivered into **Incline Village.** You immediately note the community planning here that is lacking on the California side. Although this is no pristine wilderness, homes and businesses are carefully tucked among the trees and lakeside condos march in a rather orderly fashion down to the shoreline. Most structures are dressed in properly muted browns and greens, going through the motions of forest camouflage.

— photo courtesy Heavenly Ski Resort

The shimmering sapphire of Lake Tahoe is particularly stunning in winter.

Your shoreline drive takes you through this appealing community to **Incline Beach,** offering a play area and picnic tables shaded by lakeside pines. A snack bar is open in summer. Just beyond, on your left, is **Hyatt Lake Tahoe,** the most elegant and pricey casino resort on this end of the lake. Opposite is **Country Club Mall,** with a couple of restaurants, assorted boutiques and real estate offices.

If price were no object, this would be our place of choice on the lake. Our second selection would be the rustic **Cal-Neva.** We prefer the wooded, quieter north shore to the crowded, highrise glitter of the southern end.

This area was named for the Great Incline Tramway, completed in 1874 to hoist logs to the summit of Incline Mountain, where they were fired down a flume to Washoe Valley mills. After the forest was stripped from this land, it was mostly ignored until the Crystal Bay Development Company arrived in 1960 to begin building a planned community. Incline is easily the most attractive and prosperous town on the lakeshore, now numbering about 6,500 presumably contented residents.

Its most famous "resident" is a fictitious ranch inspired by history's most popular TV western series. Since we followed Shoreline Drive, we missed **Ponderosa ranch,** which sits up on Highway 28. If you're a *Bonanza* fan or/and you've got kids in tow, you won't want to miss it. We describe the place in detail below.

NORTH SHORE CASINOS, DINING & LODGING

Cal Neva Lodge • ☺☺☺

Two Stateline Rd. (P.O. Box 368), Crystal Bay, NV 89402; (800) CAL NEVA or (702) 832-4000. *Major credit cards.* This handsome chalet style casino is the smallest one in the state to earn our "Three Grin" award. You'll smile, too, as you step into this refined yet woodsy place, which was renovated in the early 1990s. One of Nevada's oldest lodges, the Cal Neva dates from 1927. Frank Sinatra owned a piece of it in the 1960s but the Nevada Gaming Commission jerked his license for allowing Sam Giancana to hang out there. That seemed a bit over-reactive, considering that gang bosses practically *owned* Las Vegas.

The term "dramatically rustic" may come to mind as you explore this place, particularly when you step into the Indian Room. It's a stately space, with a high-pitched log beam ceiling and a massive fieldstone fireplace, often crackling. With a fine Washo Indian exhibit, hunting trophies and overstuffed couches, it has the feel of one of those elegant old national park lodges. And there are no distracting gaming machines in this quietly elegant space. The Cal Neva *really* hugs the state line; straddles it, in fact. A border stripe runs through the Indian Room fireplace, with gold on the California side and Silver for Nevada—a nice touch.

Casino: With an oldstyle bar offering a view of the lake, we were more tempted to sit and sip than gamble. There are machines a- plenty, of course, along with roulette and craps, several blackjack tables and a poker room.

Entertainment: The Frank Sinatra Celebrity Showroom hosts midrange luminaries such as hypnotist Pat Collins and—who else?—Frank Sinatra, Jr., and his band.

Dining: Cal Neva's early American style gourmet room, **Sir Charles,** serves continental fare from $15 to $25, nightly from 5 (weekends only in the off-season). The **Lakeview Restaurant** is certainly that, offering seating indoors and on a deck above the lake when weather permits; dinners $7 to $15; daily 7 a.m. to 11 p.m. (with seasonal variations).

Lodging: The rooms, all with a lake view, are stylishly done in a blend of early American and modern. Doubles range from $99 to $149, suites (including cabins and chalets) are $199 to $259.

Crystal Bay Club • ☺

Highway 28 (at the state line), Crystal Bay, NV 89402; (702) 821-0512. MC/VISA. This small casino and restaurant next to Cal Neva has been around since 1936. It's a blend of early rustic and 1960s modern, offering one craps and roulette and several blackjack tables, plus slots and videos. The **Steak and Lobster House** serves dinner nightly from 6 (with early bird specials the first half hour), steaks, chops and chickens, $10 to $28 with most entrées in the teens. There's a 24-hour **coffee shop** as well, with dinners ranging from $8 and slightly up.

Tahoe Biltmore • ☺☺

Highway 28 (P.O. Box 115), Crystal Bay, NV 89402: (800) 245- 8667 or (702) 831-0660. Major credit cards. Across the highway from the Cal Neva, this inviting mid-sized place has a sort of Mystic Seaport/Balboa Island look with a rounded glass front and blue-white color scheme. The **casino** has the requisite one craps, one roulette and several blackjack tables with a $2 start, plus the machines. There's a kids' video parlor here and live entertainment in the Aspen Lounge. The Biltmore offers free overnight **RV parking** on a lot above. The attractive **dining** room, sort of Art Deco seaport with soft colors, serves nightly dinners from $4 to $10, plus a 99-cent breakfast and cheap lunches.

Lodging: Room rates range from $27 to $33 in a motel unit and $33 to $44 in the casino hotel.

Hyatt Regency Lake Tahoe ● ☺☺☺
Lakeshore Boulevard at Country Club Drive (P.O. Box 3239), Incline Village, NV 89450; (800) 233-1234 or (702) 831-1111. Major credit cards. With its sleek chalet style façade rising above the pines, the Hyatt looks right at home in Lake Tahoe's most attractive community. The large casino resort went through a couple of earlier incarnations before settling in as one of the Hyatt chain's upscale Regency properties.

Casino: It's an interesting mix of woodsy class and flash—a kind of dark elegance with red and blue neon, accented by pine cones with twinkle-light needles. One decorator touch is particularly striking: crystal chandeliers with circles of neon on their backsides, reflecting into coffered mirrored ceilings. The essential table games are here; betting minimums start at $2 and you'll find a few nickel machines, plus a poker parlor.

Entertainment: Singers, combos and the like perform in the Stage Bar, and Hugo's Rotisserie features live music.

Dining: Down by the lake with a view thereof, **Hugo's** is among the more elegantly rustic gourmet rooms on the lake. It offers American-continental fare, $17 to $28; Sunday-Thursday 6 to 10 and Friday-Saturday 6 to 10:30. **Ciao Mein** is Italian-Chinese, as dictated by that catchy name, with $14 to $26 dinners served Wednesday-Sunday 6 to 10. The 24-hour **Sierra Cafe** has a busy menu, mostly American; $5 to $14. The **Hyatt Buffet** is worth the $7.95, $8.50 and $15 breakfast, lunch and dinner prices.

Lodging: The Hyatt offers an assortment of handsomely-appointed accommodations, starting with tower room doubles from $229 to $279, lower in the off-season. Suites and lakeside cottages range from $450 to $900. Amenities at this full-service resort include a pool, sauna and spa, tennis courts, golf at two nearby courses, and a private beach with boat rentals.

THE ATTRACTION

Ponderosa Ranch ● *State Highway 28 (P.O. Box AP), Incline Village, NV 89450; (702) 831-0691. May through October 9:30 to 5. Adults $9.50; kids 5 to 11, $7.50 and toddlers $2.* It's difficult to discern where one fable ends and the other begins at the legendary home of TV's Cartwright family. They galloped into 400 million living rooms, speaking 12 different languages during 239 episodes of *Bonanza* from 1959 until 1973. Sadly, only one member of the fictitious family of a father and three sons, Pernell Roberts (Adam), is still alive. However the legend of *Bonanza* seems destined to last forever. Nearly half a million people visit the so-called Ponderosa Ranch each year.

Wanna-be cowboys and *Bonanza* trekkies can explore a simulated Western town and the Cartwright ranch house; view a collection of antique cars, farm equipment and carriages; have an old timey photo taken; meet friendly critters at the Pettin' Farm and watch a shoot-out. You can ride a hay wagon into the timber for a chuck wagon breakfast. Or chomp into a Hossburger, washed down with suds from a tin cup (which you can take home).

"Ponderosa Ranch: The Tourist Attraction" came after the TV series started, the brainstorm of Bill and Joyce Anderson. They owned a chunk of timber above the lake and decided to create the tourist ranch after studio officials used the area for location shooting. In a classic art imitates art move, they duplicated the Hollywood sets, with the cooperation of studio officials. Later, some filming was done at the ranch, giving tourists occasional opportunities to meet Ben, Hoss, Little Joe and Adam.

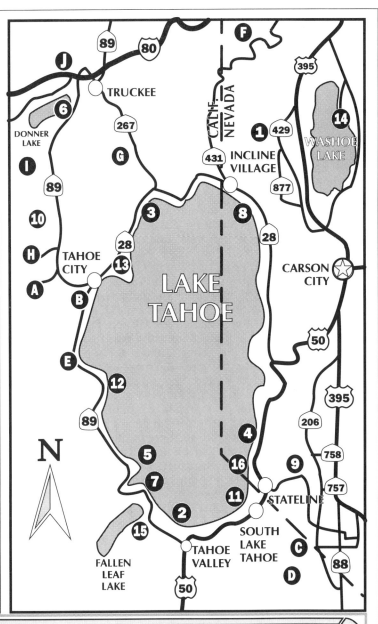

THE UNSPOILED EAST SHORE

Beyond Incline, Lakeshore Drive rejoins Highway 28. You'll enter **Lake Tahoe Nevada State Park** in the basin's most pristine section. Let your eyes travel down through the pines to the boulder-strewn shoreline. Then peer across the great sapphire oval to the opposite shore, embraced by the snow-dusted granite peaks of the Sierra Nevada. You'll understand why Mark Twain called this "the fairest picture the whole earth affords."

The highway alternately hugs the shoreline, then climbs higher for an aerial view. Roadside parking areas invite you to pull over for a more studied view (letting those less view-struck motorists pass). At several points, you can scramble down to the shore to peer into the clear ice blue depths.

Sand Harbor is an inviting public beach with picnic tables, potties, ranger station (open summers only) and a boat launch. Day use fee is $4 per vehicle and $1 for walkers and bikers. Just beyond, you enter "rural Carson City" (Carson is a combined city/county). And beyond that, a turnoff to the left leads a short distance to **Spooner Lake.** This little tree-rimmed pond has a picnic area and potties, plus 55 kilometers of groomed cross-country ski trails in winter; entry is $3 per car and $1 for walkers and cyclists. A sign advises you that it was named for Michele E. Spooner, a French entrepreneur who started the lumber industry here in the 1850s. His operation later was taken over by the Tahoe Lumber & Fluming Company, which became part of the legendary Virginia & Truckee Railroad.

Highway 50 joins the eastern shore just beyond Spooner Lake, bringing with it a quick increase in traffic. However, the area is still relatively free of development, except for the private community of **Glenbrook,** tucked down by Tahoe's edge. An historical landmark at the Glenbrook turnoff discusses a lumbering operation based here in the 1860s.

If you'd like to hike the **Tahoe Rim Trail,** follow Highway 50 east a short distance to **Spooner Summit,** where you can pick up the Nevada-side trailhead. This wonderful pathway, being built by volunteers, will encircle the lake when it's completed in mid-decade. It will meander 150 miles through thick ponderosa groves, old Washo hunting grounds and former Basque sheep camps, entering six counties, three national forests and—of course—two states. If you'd like to learn of its progress, or pitch in and help *make* it progress, contact: The Tahoe Rim Trail, P.O. Box 10156, South Lake Tahoe, CA 95731; (916) 577-0676.

Logan Shoals Vista Point is a fine place to pause and admire the view. It offers your last chance to commune with the lake before you return to civilization. By scrambling carefully down through the trees, you can reach the water's edge, here cobbled by giant boulders that are favored retreats of summer sun-lovers. In this undeveloped area, the water is amazingly clear, a soft turquoise at the edge, turning to a deep blue offshore. A trail leads both directions from here along most of the length of the state park's three-mile lake front.

Beyond Logan Shoals, **Cave Rock** offers a boat launch and beach area, adjacent to the tiny community of the same name. **Zephyr Cove,** one of the area's oldest resorts and appropriately funky, is a good base of operations for lake play. Surrounded by national forest land, it was built in the early 1900s. The complex offers a restaurant, lodges and campgrounds (listed below), marina and boat landing, forested beach and picnic area. The

M.S. Dixie is berthed here, offering excursions across the lake to Emerald Bay (see **Lake cruises** below).

Zephyr Cove Resort • ☺
760 Highway 50 (P.O. Box 830), Zephyr Cove, NV 89448; (702) 588-6644. MC/VISA, AMEX. Rustic lodge rooms range from $45 to $50 for doubles up to $75 for a mini-suite sleeping six. Bungalows and cottages go from $39 to $85 for two, up to $185 for a two-story chalet that sleeps eight, with a kitchen, fireplace, living room and four bedrooms. All accommodations have private baths; many have decks or porches. The **restaurant** serves American fare such as chicken fried steak and liver and onions, full dinners $7 to $15, daily 7:30 a.m. to 9:30 p.m. (from 7:30 to 3 p.m. November through May); non-smoking tables available. The **marina** offers boat docking, a mile of beach, fishing charters and rentals of boats, parasails and jet skis. A stable and beachside bar and grill are open in summer. Other facilities include a general store, video arcade, gift shop and winter snowmobile center with rentals.

The forest service's **Nevada Beach** is just beyond Zephyr Cove, down Elks Point Road, with lakeside picnic areas and campsites (closed in winter). Opposite the turnoff is **Round Hill Shopping Center,** a weathered old mall with some nice little shops and a restaurant or two. It also shelters the **Tahoe-Douglas Chamber of Commerce,** open weekdays 9 to 5 and Saturdays 10 to 4.

Beyond Round Hill, you round a corner and there they are—four glass towers rising from what's left of the trees like giant, windowed cereal boxes. Welcome to Glitter Gulch of the Pines!

THE SOUTH SHORE & STATELINE

If you're a gambler, you'll probably like the setting, certainly prettier than downtown Reno or the Las Vegas strip. We'll add that the tower restaurants offer some of the finest views in the state. So do the rooms, which are particularly opulent (and pricey) at the larger casino resorts.

Of course, if you're a conservationist, you may be appalled at what's happened to the lake's south shore. Little survives of the natural terrain here. Stateline is a crowded collection of the Big Four highrise casinos—Caesars Tahoe, Harrah's, Harvey's and the Horizon—plus a few smaller ones. What space is left is taken up mostly by parking lots and parking structures.

Across the border, stretching into a cluttered California infinity, are the service stations, motels, cafes and other small businesses of South Lake Tahoe. You'll even see a few trees here and there—without which this business strip might as well be in Hayward or Hackensack.

The history of Stateline is the history of Harvey and Llewellyn Gross. They opened their Wagon Wheel Saloon and Gambling Hall in 1944, with the only gas pump between Placerville and Carson City. Harvey kept the pump open for 24 hours by posting a "ring bell for service" sign. When the bell buzzed, a dealer would come out to gas up the car and, of course, invite the occupants to come in and relax for a spell. Llewellyn provided food service by cooking meals at home and walking them down to the six-stool bar.

Stateline had no phones, utilities, sewer service or fire department. The Grosses were instrumental in getting these started, along with the Tahoe Airport on the California side. Harvey also campaigned for an all-winter road over Echo Summit. When California drug its bureaucratic feet, he and several neighbors would hike up to the pass with show shovels and clear the road by hand. Legend has it that Harvey would trudge up ahead, plant a bottle in the snow and urge his friends to shovel for refreshments.

The Stateline pioneer died in 1983.

SOUTH SHORE CASINOS, DINING & LODGING

Harvey's Resort Hotel/Casino • ☺☺☺ ∅

P.O. Box 128, Stateline, NV 89449; (800) 553-1022 or (702) 588-2411. Major credit cards. The oldest casino resort on Lake Tahoe is now the largest and most opulent. A $100 million tower addition in 1986 increased the room count to 740. Although the complex is handsome, it looks like an architectural mistake, since the blue-tinted glass addition is fused to the original brown structure.

Casino: It's the largest on the lake, roomy and glitzy, with red neon wagon wheels in alcove ceilings to mark the days when it was Harvey's Wagon Wheel. "The party's at Harvey's" theme carries throughout, with confetti banners and lots of flash. This is a complete gaming venue, with a baccarat parlor, Premiere Slot Pavilion with $5, $25 and $100 machines, race and sports book and poker room, plus the full range of slots and videos.

Entertainment: Scaled down versions of Broadway shows ("Ain't Misbehavin'" in 1992) alternate with headliners in the Emerald Theater. Live music emanates from the Emerald Party Lounge and Llewellyn's.

Dining: The headliner is the 19th floor **Llewellyn's,** an eye-catching space with chandeliers, marble, brocaded chairs and a striking lake view. The fare is international, $10 to $25, with lunch and dinner daily and a Sunday brunch. Others are the **Sage Room,** preserving a bit of the original Wagon Wheel, steaks and chops, $16.25 to $28.50, dinner nightly; **Seafood Grotto,** $7 to $26, lunch and dinner daily; **El Vaquero,** Mexican fare with fresh fish and a do-it-yourself taco cart, $3.25 to $14; lunch and dinner daily; **Pizzeria,** $4 to $7, lunch and dinner; **Classic Burgers** with a great 1950s look, from midday through late night; and the **Garden Buffet,** serving breakfast, lunch and dinner.

Lodging: Elegantly done rooms, many with lake views, range from $90 to $170 for doubles and $175 to $475 for suites. All include a free buffet breakfast. Non-smoking rooms available. Resort amenities include swimming pools, spa and health club, tennis courts, a lake-view wedding chapel, video arcade for kids, specialty shops, barbershop and beauty salon.

Caesars Tahoe • ☺☺☺ ∅

P.O. Box 5800, Stateline, NV 89449; (800) 648-3353 or (702) 588-3515. Major credit cards. Although it's properly stylish and posh, the high-in-the-sky Caesars is modest when compared with the Las Vegas original. Caesar Augustus is out front to greet you, with a rolled up winning casino ticket in his hand, but that's about the extent of the marble statuary. The layout is rather curious here. Although the motor entrance is logically located, the street entrance sends people into the race and sports book, then on a broken-field stroll through the casino to the hotel desk and restaurants.

Casino: The pleasing, low-ceiling, high-roller gaming space runs the gamut from $3 blackjack tables to mini $2 baccarat, plus the usual dice and roulette and ranks of slots and videos. Although it lacks the opulence of its Vegas cousin, it doesn't lack those sexy toga-clad drink girls.

Entertainment: Circus Maximus features top headliners, while lesser groups perform in the Emperor's Lounge, and magicians do their magic in Caesars Cabaret. Nero's 2000 is a dance club with live music.

Dining: Like Harvey's, this place offers a wide choice. The clubby **Broiler Room** serves steak, seafood and Cajun, $14.50 to $30, dinner nightly; **Pisces** is the seafood place of course, $11 and up, Thursday-Monday 6 to 11; **Empress Court** features a mixed Asian menu, $12 and up, Friday-Tuesday 6 to 11; **Primavera** is a pool side Italian place, $11 to $18, Tuesday-Saturday 6 to 11 and **Cafe Roma** is the 24-hour space with an American-continental menu.

Lodging: The 440 rooms and suites are predictably opulent with the prices to prove it. They range from $115 to $175 for doubles and $300 to $650 for suites. All have refrigerators, and the hotel has a non-smoking floor. Resort amenities include a Romanesque indoor spa with a lagoon style swimming pool, weight and exercise room, racquetball and tennis courts, a large shopping arcade and a kids' video parlor.

Harrah's Lake Tahoe ● ☺☺☺ Ø

P.O. Box 128, Stateline, NV 89449; (800) 553-1022 or (702) 588-2144. Major credit cards. With a brown textured façade that tries to blend with the woodsy setting, Harrah's is the most handsome of the resort towers here. Guests love its amenity-rich, oversized rooms, each with two bathrooms. However, it has been out-glittered by the new look at Harvey's. Last year, it was dropped from five to four diamonds by heartless AAA critics. (We assume this doesn't cause the same suicidal reaction suffered by French chefs when they lose a Michelin star.)

Harrah's is the second oldest major hotel at the lake after Harvey's. William Harrah bought the Gateway Club at Stateline in 1955, then followed with the purchase of the Stateline Country Club and Nevada Club. From these latter two sites sprouted today's imposing Harrah's Lake Tahoe complex.

Casino: Facilities in this large, busy gaming center include $3 blackjack, craps, roulette, wheel of fortune and a poker room with pai gow. There's also a race and sports book and something really radical for a casino—a clock above the main entrance! The place has no smoking tables.

Entertainment: The South Shore Room alternates between Broadway shows and headliners, and the Summit Lounge features live music. The Stateline Cabaret offers adult revues, currently "Bare Essence" (a little play on words there).

Dining: The 18th floor **Summit** is a dressy American-continental place with awesome views, $15 to $30, nightly 6 to 10 (until 11 Friday-Saturday). Grouped together on the ground floor are **Andreotti**, regional Italian, $10 to $20, Wednesday-Sunday 5:30 to 10; **Asia**, serving Pacific Rim fare, $8 to $20, nightly 4 to 10; and **Sierra**, the 24-hour place with a basic American menu, $7.50 to $11.50. The clubby, lake-view **Friday's Station** serves steak and seafood, $19 to $37, nightly 5:30 to 10; and the **Forest Restaurant** serves a **buffet** with lake vistas.

Lodging: If you simply must have twin bathrooms equipped with TV and phones, then your party's at Harrah's. Prices for these and other amenities are not modest, starting at $105 for doubles and ranging up to $175, suites $145 to $225. No-smoking rooms available. Resort amenities include a health club, shops, beauty salon and kids' video arcade.

Horizon Casino Resort ● ☺☺☺

P.O. Box C, Stateline, NV 89449; (800) 648-3322 or (702) 588-6211. Major credit cards. Despite its sleek new look, the Horizon has gone through several manifestations. It dates from 1965, when it was Del Webb's Sahara. It became the High Sierra, then was purchased by William Yung of Kentucky in 1990. He spent about $12 million create its present slick appearance.

Casino: It's one of the prettiest around, with off-white coffered ceilings, fancy chandeliers and vivid red and white gaming tables and chairs. One finds all the essential table games, and slots and videos from a nickel up.

Entertainment: Two shows alternate at the Golden Cabaret. The "Bottoms Up" comedy revue is a good buy, $12 including buffet dinner. It cycles nightly with the *very* adult "Zoom!", described as "an erotic centerfold fantasy." Live band music issues from the Convention Center lounge.

Dining: The dressy place is **Beaumont's,** serving steaks and seafood for $20 to $30, nightly 6 to 10:30. **Le Grande Buffet** comes in brunch and dinner versions, and **Four Seasons** is a 24-hour $7 to $13.50 coffee shop.

Lodging: Like the casino, the hotel lobby is striking, with marble floors and mirrored walls. Newly renovated rooms offer the usual amenities, from $72 to $107 for doubles; more for suites. No-smoking rooms are available. Resort goodies include a swimming pool, hot tubs and kiddies' wading pool.

Bill's Lake Tahoe Casino ● ☺

Highway 50, Stateline, NV 89449; (702) 588-2455. Every gaming center needs a low rollers' joint, and Bill's fills the bill. Sandwiched between Harrah's and Caesars, Bill's is billed as the "quarter capital of Nevada," meaning that it's a pretend sawdust joint filled with slots and videos. It's owned by Harrah's (dba Holiday Inn). Step through the old fashioned air curtain, pick up a bag of free popcorn and take a pull on nine-by-nine-foot "Big Bertha," touted as the world's largest free-pull slot machine. Dining chores are handled by McDonald's, offering 99-cent all you can eat waffles, and Benigan's coffee shop, not much more expensive.

Lakeside Inn and Casino ● ☺☺ ∅

Highway 50 at Kingsbury Grade (P.O. Box 5640), Stateline, NV 89449; (800) 624-7980 or (702) 588-7777. Major credit cards. This friendly, rustic little place is a bit farther east, providing a retreat from the overbuilt commotion at stateline. It's a nice woodsy package with a small casino, 24-hour restaurant and 123 rooms. The pleasant casino with wood paneled walls and laminated ceiling beams offers lots of nickel slots and videos, plus blackjack and craps. The 24-hour **Timber House Restaurant** serves a $5.99 prime rib dinner, Mexican and American fare from $6 to $16, plus $3 breakfast and $4 lunch specials.

Lodging: Nicely done rooms, some with stone wall accents, range from $59 to $89. A $99 package ($75 in winter) gets you weeknight accommodations, prime rib dinner, breakfast, champagne and a $10 gaming rebate.

WHERE ELSE TO DINE
(North, east and south shores)

The Chart House ● ☺☺ $$$ ∅

392 Kingsbury Rd., Stateline; (702) 832-7223. American; dinners $13 to $23; full bar service. Sunday-Friday 5:30 p.m. to 10, Saturday 5 to 10:30. Reservations accepted; major credit cards. Aquatic-woodsy dining room with a panoramic lake view. Versatile steak, seafood and prime rib menu, with a large all-you-can-eat salad bar.

Chinese Flower Drum • ☺☺ $$
120 Country Club Mall (opposite Hyatt), Incline Village; (702) 831-7734. Chinese, primarily Mandarin; dinners $9 to $13; full bar service at adjacent Paddlewheel Saloon. Daily 7:30 a.m. to 8 p.m. MC/VISA, AMEX. A good-size restaurant partitioned to provide more intimate seating. Busy menu features seafood dishes and several spicy Szechuan entrèes; combination dinners are good buys.

Hacienda de la Sierra • ☺☺ $ ∅
931 Tahoe Blvd., Incline Village; (702) 831-8300. Mexican; dinners $5 to $10; full bar service. Summer 11 to 10 daily, winter 4 to 10. MC/VISA, AMEX. Locally popular place with a woodsy-tropical look; outdoor deck and patio entertainment in summer. Wide range of Mexican dishes; specialties include *fajitas* and *carnitas de la Sierra* (mildly spiced chunks of pork or turkey served with Mexican condiments and tortillas).

BED & BREAKFAST INN

Haus Bavaria • ⌂⌂⌂ $$$$ ∅∅
593 N. Dyer Circle (P.O. Box 3308), Incline Village, NV 89450; (702) 831-6122. Doubles $72 to $90, singles $72 to $80. Five rooms, all with private baths; full breakfast. MC/VISA, AMEX. Attractive European style guest house with rustic wood paneling, modern teak furnishings and German bric-a-brac. All rooms have balconies with mountain views. Lake Tahoe is within walking distance, with a private beach and swimming pool for guests.

WHERE TO CAMP

The Lake Tahoe basin has hundreds of national forest campsites, mostly away from the lake on the California side. That doesn't imply plentiful camping and RV parking, however. They fill up quickly in summer and many are closed in winter. For details on camping and other outoor activities, contact: **Lake Tahoe Basin Management Unit,** P.O. Box 8465, South Lake Tahoe, CA 95731.

Nevada Beach is the only lakeside national forest campground on the east shore. It's a *very* tough ticket in summer, since it doesn't accept reservations. Fees are $10 for camping and $2 per vehicle for day use. It's open Memorial Day through Labor Day.

Free RV parking is offered by the Tahoe Biltmore at Crystal Cove. However, signs at Stateline casinos forbid overnight RVing, threatening to have them towed. (This conjures a vision of a couple sleeping peacefully in their Winnebago while it's being whisked away in the middle of the night.) Banned from resort parking, south shore RVers must resort to regular campgrounds. There's one near the lake on the Nevada side:

Zephyr Cove Resort • *P.O. Box 830, Zephyr Cove, NV 89448; (702) 588-6644. RV and tent sites; full hookups $22 a day or $140 a week, tent sites $15 a day or $95 a week. Reservations accepted; MC/VISA, AMEX.* It's pricey and a bit scruffy, but it's in a woodsy setting and you *can* reserve a spot. Facilities include showers, picnic tables and barbecues, pay phones, coin laundry, dump station, groceries, provisions and the many facilities of the adjacent resort (listed above, under **East shore**).

Several commercial campgrounds are on the California side, not too many miles from the Stateline casinos. For a list, contact the **South Lake Tahoe Chamber of Commerce,** 3066 Lake Tahoe Blvd., South Lake Tahoe, CA 95702; (916) 541-5355.

LAKE CRUISES

M.S. Dixie • *P.O. Box 1667, Zephyr Cove, NV 89448; (702) 588-3508. Emerald Bay cruise $12 for adults and $4 for kids, champagne brunch cruise $16 for adults and $7.50 for kids, sunset dinner dance cruise (kids not recommended), $31 with dinner. Mid-April through October. MC/VISA, AMEX.* Cruises are aboard a refurbished 1927 paddlewheeler that saw service on the Mississippi. Glass bottom for underwater viewing.

Tahoe Queen • *P.O. Box 14327, South Lake Tahoe, CA 95702; (800) 23-TAHOE or (916) 541-3364. Emerald Bay cruise $14 for adults and $5 for kids, dinner dance $18 for adults and $9.50 for kids (plus dinner from $14.95); all year. Also winter ski shuttle to North Shore, adults $18, kids $9. MC/VISA, AMEX.* The "Queen" is a triple-deck oldstyle, newly constructed paddlewheeler, with glass bottom for viewing.

North Tahoe Cruises • *700 N. Lake Blvd. (P.O. Box 7913) Tahoe City, CA 96145; (916) 583-0141. Shoreline cruise, champagne continental breakfast cruise and Emerald Bay cruise, all $13 for adults and $5 for kids; also $12 adults-only "Casino Fun Package" cruise to Crystal Bay. Late April through November.* Sleek motor launches sail along the western shore, near several historic sites.

OTHER LAKE TAHOE ACTIVITIES
All numbers (702) unless otherwise indicated

BOATING • Lake Tahoe boat rentals are available from North Shore Sailing Inc., (916) 546-4333; North Tahoe Marina, (916) 546-8248; Sand Harbor, (702) 831-0494 and Zephyr Cove Marina, (702) 588-3833.

FISHING • Numerous outfits offer charter fishing on the lake. For a list, contact: Lake Tahoe Visitors Authority, (916) 544-5050.

GOLF • Sky high links on the Nevada side are Edgewood at Tahoe, Stateline, 588-3042, $100 for unlimited play per day, including cart; Glenbrook Golf Course, Glenbrook, 749-5201, nine-holes, twice-around $35 in summer, $30 the rest of the year; Incline Village Championship Course, 832-1144, $85 in summer and $75 the rest of the year, including cart; Incline Village Executive Course, open May through September, $45 including cart.

SIGHTSEEING • For tours between Tahoe and Reno and around the lake, contact Reno Tahoe Company, 348-7788; Showboat Lines, 588-6633; Gray Line of Reno & Lake Tahoe, (800) 822-6009 or (702) 329-2877 and Travel Systems, 588-4277.

WINTER SPORTS

The most complete information source for Tahoe Basin winter sports is the ***Skier's Planning Guide****,* P.O. Box 9137, Incline Village, NV 89450, with descriptions of major ski areas, casino resorts and ski packages. For a packet of travel and ski information, write: **Reno/Tahoe,** P.O. Box 9038, Incline Village, NV 89450. A newsprint guide, *Ski Tahoe* is available free at most casinos, ski shops and many other stores at the lake, with area maps, listings of ski resorts and discount coupons. Another good winter sports information source is the **Lake Tahoe Basin Management Unit,** P.O. Box 8465, South Lake Tahoe, CA 95731.

Most Tahoe Basin ski areas are in California; we list those in both states for your reference.

DOWNHILL SKIING • Alpine Meadows, (916) 583-4232, all day lift ticket $38; Granlibakken, (916) 583-4242, $12; Heavenly (sections on California and Nevada sides, above Stateline), (916) 541-1330, $38; Homewood, (916) 525-7256, $29; Mount Rose Resort (includes Incline), (702) 849-0706, $28; Northstar, (916) 562-1330, $38; Squaw Valley, (916) 583-6985, $38; Sugar Bowl, (916) 426-3651, $33 and Tahoe Donner, (916) 587-9400, $20.

CROSS COUNTRY • Squaw Creek, (916) 583-8951, trail pass $10; Diamond Peak, (702) 832-3249, trail pass $10; Eagle Mountain Nordic, (916) 389-2254, $11; Northstar, (916) 562-1330, $13; Royal Gorge, (916) 426-3871, $16; Tahoe Donner, (916) 587-9484, $13; Tahoe Nordic Ski Center, (916) 583-0484, $12; Hope Valley, (916) 694-2266, free; Lake Tahoe Winter Sports Center, (916) 577-2940, $5; and Spooner Lake, (702) 749-5349, $9.50.

SNOWMOBILE RENTALS • The basin has more than 500 miles of groomed and ungroomed snowmobile trails. Call these outfits for rental prices: Eagle Ridge Outfitters, (916) 587-9322; Zephyr Cove Snowmobile Center, (702) 588-3833; Mountain Lake Adventures, (702) 831-4202; Lake Tahoe Winter Sports Center, (916) 577-2940 and Snowmobiling Unlimited, (916) 583-5858.

SLEDDING AND SNOW PLAY • Hansen's Resort, 1360 Ski Run Blvd., South Lake Tahoe, (916) 544-3361, use fee, equipment rentals; Granlibakken, (916) 583-4242, free, equipment rentals; North Tahoe Regional Park end of National Avenue in Tahoe Vista, free; Incline Village, near the golf course driving range, free; Mount Rose Summit on Mount Rose Highway, free; Spooner Summit on Highway 50, free.

ANNUAL EVENTS

Snowfest, late February to early March at north shore, (800) 824-6348; Western America's largest winter carnival.

Music at Sand Harbor, July at Sand Harbor State Park, Incline Village, (916) 583-9048; live rock music, reggae and new wave jazz are performed at lakeside.

Shakespeare at Sand Harbor, August, (916) 583-9048; the Bard's works performed on an outdoor stage.

Valhalla Arts & Music Festival and **Starlight Jazz & Blues Festival,** June to early September at Lake of the Sky Amphitheater at the Tallac Historic Site above Camp Richardson, California side, (916) 542-4166 or 541-4975.

Cool September Days, early September at Stateline and South Lake Tahoe; (702) 588-8575; community celebration with car show, poker run and other activities (contrasting Reno's Hot August Nights).

Ski season opening: Thanksgiving is traditional opening for Tahoe Basin's ski resorts.

Winter Festival of Lights, Thanksgiving through March at Stateline and South Lake Tahoe (916) 541-5255; merchants and homes decorated with outdoor lights.

TAKING A RIDE ON THE CALIFORNIA SIDE

To complete your Tahoe experience, take the 76-mile loop around the lake. Although much of it is heavily impacted by those scattered little towns, you'll find swatches of forest and scenic shoreline sections, and you'll discover the finest viewpoint on the entire lake. If you're here in winter, check to make sure the west side road is open, since it's sometimes closed by winter storms; call (916) 577-3550.

After wading through the long commercial strip of **South Lake Tahoe**, you'll come to a "Y" where U.S. 50 branches off to climb Echo Summit to take all those Californians back home. Steer to the right onto State Highway 89, called Emerald Bay Road at this point. For heaps of information on the Tahoe Basin, stop at the **Forestry Supervisor's Office** at 89870 Emerald Bay Road; it's open the year around, weekdays from 8 to 4:30.

Just beyond, you'll pass through **Camp Richardson,** one of the senior resorts on the lake. This comfortably rustic old place still has rooms to let, along with a large 230-unit campground; call (916) 541-1800. **Tallac Historic Site** is a venerable shingle-sided retreat that hosts summer concerts (see **Annual events** above). Just beyond, on your right, is the octagonal **Lake Tahoe Visitors Center** (closed in winter) in the **Pope-Baldwin Recreation Area,** with picnic areas, hiking trails and a stream profile chamber.

Enclosed in national forest lands, the lakefront is wooded and unspoiled in this area. After passing a succession of campgrounds and picnic areas, you'll round a bend and see stunningly beautiful **Emerald Bay.** This narrow inlet cradling a wooded island at the base of tree-thatched cliffs is one America's the most photographed spots. It has, in fact, been declared a National Natural Landmark.

Beyond, at **Vikingshome Viewpoint,** you can hike a steep trail down to a castle-like lakeside home built in 1929. Now forest service property, it's open for tours from mid-June through Labor Day, 10 to 4; adults $2, kids $1. Just beyond is the large **D.L. Bliss State Park** with a sandy beach, hiking trails and summer naturalist programs; day use fee is $5. From here, you pass through the hamlet of **Meeks Bay** and hit **Sugar Pine Point State Park,** one of the few lakeside camping areas kept open in winter.

Civilization, such as it is, has claimed the shoreline from this point on. Highway 89 peels off at **Tahoe City,** passing **Squaw Valley** and joining I-80. Your lakeside route becomes Highway 28, carrying you uneventfully past wooded little communities of **Carnelian Bay** and **Tahoe Vista** to **King's Beach.**

And isn't this where we came in?

Surrounded by lofty mountains, contents almost unknown, but believed to be filled with rivers and lakes which have no communication with the sea; deserts and oases which have never been explored."
— John C. Frêmont's notes on the Great Basin, about 1844

CHAPTER NINE
THE I-80 CORRIDOR
Cowboys and Paiutes

ONE OF AMERICA'S most famous pathways cuts across northern Nevada, rising and falling with the gentle swells of the desert, dancing around clustered mountains that stand like geological afterthoughts in the Great Basin.

Most travelers hurry along Interstate 80, anxious to reach the partying promise of Reno-Tahoe, or anxious to get away, having been partied out. However, a pause here and there, an overnight stop in a remote town, a detour onto a side road will reveal some of Nevada's more interesting nuggets.

The route itself begs closer examination. I-80 is not just another expenditure of federal gasoline tax funds. It was blazed more than a century and a half ago as mountain men and then emigrants followed Indian and game trails, seeking an avenue to the Pacific. Early guidebooks called it the Emigrant or Humboldt Trail. As tens of thousands of 49ers headed for the gold fields of the Golden State, it earned a third name—the California Trail.

The Central Pacific Railroad came this way in the 1860s, reaching eastward to link up with the Union Pacific at Promontory, across the great salt flats in Utah. The busy emigrant trail became Nevada's State Highway 1, then the Victory Highway in 1926 and U.S. 40 in 1958. After President Eisenhower launched the interstate highway system in 1956, the route gained its present title—Interstate 80. Appropriately, it's also called the Dwight D. Eisenhower Highway. The last link of I-80 wasn't completed until 1983.

The Victory Highway and Lincoln Highway (U.S. 50 through central Nevada) had engaged in a spirited competition for interstate status. Associations made up of boosters from communities along the two routes erected signs and bought billboards to promote theirs as the best route across Nevada. U.S. 40, although 30 miles longer than U.S. 50, carried more traffic, so that route got the nod when the interstate system was laid out. It probably didn't help when a *Life Magazine* article in 1986 called U.S. 50 the "loneliest road in America." We shall travel that lonely byway in the next chapter.

286 — CHAPTER NINE

Meanwhile, back to the busy I-80 corridor—busy, at least, when compared with Highway 50. It will carry you through one of the world's largest desert sinks, which we discussed in some detail in our opening chapter. The Great Basin is a high plateau with a hump in the middle, covering most of Nevada, slices of California, Oregon and Idaho the salt flats of Utah. A mon-

---

THINGS TO KNOW BEFORE YOU GO

BEST TIME TO GO • Late spring through late fall. Don't be misled by northern Nevada's "desert" status. It's high desert with most towns over 4,000 feet, so summers are quite bearable. Winter, on the other hand, is *winter*. Although main highways are kept open, many smaller roads are closed by snow, and most of the Humboldt National Forest's high country is out of reach. Nasty blizzards can blow through here in winter, so check weather reports before striking out.

WHAT TO SEE • Marzen House Museum and circular Pershing County Courthouse in Lovelock; historic Unionville south of Winnemucca and Paradise Valley to the north; Humboldt Historical Museum and Buckaroo Hall of fame in Winnemucca; Northeastern Nevada Museum in Elko; historic Lamoille south of Elko; the border town of Jackpot; old gaming machines and pedestrian bridge in State Line-Silver Smith casinos and Bonneville Speedway Museum in Wendover.

WHAT TO DO • Explore the lonely shores and visit the pyramid of Pyramid Lake; picnic beside the Humboldt River at Rye Patch State Recreation Area west of Winnemucca; eat a Basque dinner in Winnemucca or Elko; drive and hike through Lamoille Canyon in the Ruby Mountains; drive the Bonneville Salt Flats east of Wendover.

Useful contacts

Elko Chamber of Commerce, Box 470, Elko, NV 89801; (702) 738-7135.

Fernley Chamber of Commerce, 85 E. Main St. (P.O. Box 1606), Fernley, NV 89408; 575-4459.

Humboldt National Forest, Supervisor's Office, 976 Mountain City Highway, Elko, NV 89801; (702) 738-5171.

Pershing County Chamber of Commerce, P.O. Box 821, Lovelock, NV 89419; (702) 273-7213.

Pyramid Lake Indian Reservation, Visitor Services, Sutcliffe Star Route, Reno, NV 89510; (702) 476-0132.

Wendover Visitor & Convention Bureau, P.O. Box 2468, Wendover, NV 89883; (800) 426-6862 or (702) 664-3414.

Winnemucca Convention & Visitors Bureau, 50 Winnemucca Blvd. West, Winnemucca, NV 89445; (702) 623-5071.

Area radio stations

KELK-FM, 93.5, Elko—classic rock
KLKO-FM, 93.5, Elko—classic rock
KWNA-FM, 92.7, Winnemucca—rock

KELK-AM, 1240, Elko—light rock
KWNA-AM, 1400, Winnemucca—country and Western

ster topographical trap, it captures every river flowing into it, wrings it dry and leaves it to die in alkaline sand. It is hardly a barren place, however. Its pine-thatched mountains harbor alpine lakes and high glacial valleys. Basin lakes nurture huge trout and those ill-fated rivers feed rich agricultural valleys before disappearing into the sand.

Civilization, as we label it, is shed quickly when you follow I-80 away from the Reno-Sparks mini-megalopolis. Venturing northeast, you dip into the remote heart of the lonely Great Basin. In this space, it takes 40 acres to feed a cow, several square miles to support a human and a ton of rock to get an ounce of gold. Towns are small and widely spaced. Many are seats of government for upper Nevada's huge, thinly- populated counties.

This rough land of sagebrush, bunchgrass and creosote bush is marked by occasional stacks of baled hay and ranch houses huddled beneath clusters of cottonwoods. Blue-gray mountain ranges stand on far horizons, seeming to float the surface swells of the beige desert. They're often powdered with winter snow, standing in dazzling relief against a crisp, cold sky—a vision from a Marlboro billboard.

Many I-80 corridor towns—notably Lovelock, Winnemucca, Battle Mountain and Elko—are experiencing a corporate mining boom of late. Advanced refining techniques permit companies to turn a profit from open pits yielding only traces of gold. Silver, lead, dolomite and even limestone also are mined hereabouts.

Before the modern miners came, this was cowboy country. Just about any town of any account still conducts an annual rodeo. Between ridin' and ropin', buckaroos gather in Elko for the annual cowboy poets convention.

Before the cowboys came, the Paiutes looked on apprehensively as dusty strings of wagons creaked across the basin. Ignoring the surrounding hills where later arrivals would find gold, the pioneers pushed resolutely toward the great barrier of the Sierra Nevada, headed for California.

The Truckee River traces the first part of our route and we will follow it to its terminus in the Great Basin. It's one of the few streams in America that trickles from one lake (Tahoe) and terminates in another (Pyramid).

NORTHEAST TO PYRAMID LAKE

East of Sparks, Interstate 80 follows the river through shallow but rough Truckee Canyon, which gave both emigrant trains and railroad builders fits more than a century ago. The canyon is pretty if not awesome. Brushy desert hills rise from the curling stream. Groves of cottonwoods, poplars and an occasional farmer's field line the river's banks.

Two roadside "attractions" are worth noting. That innocuous **Mustang** freeway sign at Exit 23 near a large auto wrecking yard directs frisky travelers to the legendary whorehouse of Joe Conforte. It made headlines a few years ago when banks threatened to close it down, proving that even sin isn't recession-proof. Should you be driven by curiosity or other urges, you might detour up the twisting, somewhat scenic road to see if Joe paid off his debtors. As you follow I-80 deeper into Truckee Canyon, watch on your left for a **scenic view** turnout where a sign explains what we just told you above, about the history of the river and the route.

The canyon narrows toward its eastern end, then ejects you onto Dodge Flat as you approach the hamlets of **Fernley** and **Wadsworth**, flanking both sides of I-80. This is a broad agricultural valley, watered by the turn-of-the-century Newlands Reclamation Project. Extending southeast from here to Fallon, this area is popularly regarded as the "Oasis of Nevada."

Wadsworth is little more than a slight widening of the freeway frontage road, with a couple of false front stores and a saloon or two. It's a gateway to **Pyramid Lake** on the Indian reservation of the same name.

Fernley is a bit larger, a neon blip in this irrigated desert. It serves as a provisioning center for local farmers and ranchers, and it offers bedrooms to employees of the nearby Nevada Cement Company and Eagle Picher diatomaceous earth processing plant, west on I-80. (Should you wonder, diatomaceous earth isn't really earth. It's composed of superfine fragments of single-celled diatom shells, useful in filtering and insulation.)

The Truckee River swings north at Fernley, headed for its final resting place in Pyramid Lake. State Highway 447 follows its course, entering **Pyramid Lake Indian Reservation** at Wadsworth. The lake lies wholly within Indian land. You're back in bunchgrass desert here, having left the rim of the Oasis of Nevada.

The highway swings away from the river, then nudges it again near **Numana Fish Hatchery and Visitor's Center.** Open daily from 10 to 2, the hatchery is operated by the Pyramid Lake Paiute Tribe. One can learn a bit about the tribe, the lake's troubled history and trout-rearing at the visitor's center. If the center is closed when you arrive, the grounds may be open and you can stroll about the rearing tanks, staring down at millions of wriggling fingerlings who face a grim future of frying pan avoidance.

Continuing northward, you soon catch your first glimpse of the lake—a silver-blue satin sheen, glowing in the desert. Anaho Island, its Mexican hat shape floating on the silvery mist, stands boldly in the foreground. Pyramid has been called "the most beautiful desert lake in North America." However, be prepared to employ a different set of adjectives when you explore its shoreline.

No green oasis, Pyramid Lake is a shimmering anomaly in a sea of dusty, beige desert. Its sandy alkaline shoreline does not encourage growth; no clumps of palms or stands of grass grace its banks. They are instead marked with outerworldly clumps and spires of off-white tufa, formed as calcium carbonate precipitates from the water as the lake level drops. Unfortunately and ominously, the level has been dropping for years, first by the hand of nature as the climate became drier and now by the hand of man as a growing, thirsty Nevada diverts water from the Truckee.

THE WAY IT WAS • Although it's one of the largest fresh-water lakes in America, 27 miles long and covering 170 square miles, Pyramid is but a puddle of its former self. It's the largest remnant of Lake Lahontan, a primeval sea that covered 8,600 square miles 50,000 years ago. With finger-like bays reaching between the Great Basin's mountains, Lahontan covered much of western Nevada and smothered Susanville's Honey Lake in northeastern California.

Early Americans dwelt along Pyramid Lake's shoreline as much as 11,000 years ago, living in tufa caves and fishing for huge Lahontan trout. They were rather advanced for their time, expert tule reed weavers who even fashioned duck decoys. Called the Lovelock People, they probably were absorbed into the Paiute tribes that began moving into the area about four centuries ago.

John C. Frèmont was the first outsider to view this shimmering desert sea. Marching his entourage south from eastern Oregon in early 1844, he topped a desert mountain rise and saw the great "green sheet of water." He scouted the shoreline, noted a great stony upthrust as imposing as the Pyramid of Cheops and gave this inland sea its present name. Native Americans, employing their more lyrical language, called it *Ku-yui Pah,* the spawning place of the huge cutthroat trout. Frèmont's party was served an Indian banquet of these 30-pound fish, which he called "salmon trout," a name he gave to the present-day Truckee River.

The California gold discovery in 1848 brought thousands through Paiute territory. Some settled in the area, indiscriminately killing game and occupying Indian lands. Winnemucca, a major chief of the Northern Paiutes, negotiated a treaty with the intruding whites in 1855. However, discovery of silver in the nearby Comstock Lode brought more intruders, and the Treaty of Friendship soon was pushed to the breaking point.

It was shattered in 1860 when white traders violated several Indian women, and avenging Paiutes killed them and burned their trading post. Chief Winnemucca's son Numaga tried to negotiate another accord, but a group of armed squatters fired upon his peace party. The Paiutes retreated into a canyon, took position and annihilated the wildly charging irregulars.

The Pyramid Lake War raged for two years, until Winnemucca and Nevada territorial governor James Nye arranged an informal peace. Sporadic outbreaks continued, with the Indians inevitably on the losing end. Finally, in 1874, President Ulysses S. Grant "gave" the Paiutes what they already owned—a half million acre reservation surrounding Pyramid Lake.

THE WAY IT IS • The Paiutes still own the lake and they serve as genial hosts to visitors. However, they remain on the losing end of "progress." Starting with the Derby Dam project in 1905 that created the Fernley-Fallon oasis, Truckee River water is continually being diverted. More than half the river's flow has been redirected to serve thirsty and growing Reno and its surrounding agricultural belt. The lake has dropped nearly a hundred vertical feet in this century.

The lake's caretakers, like their ancestors before, don't care much for development. They've kept the shoreline remarkably free of marinas and other clutter. Two small, prim communities, **Nixon** on the lake's southeastern tip and **Sutcliffe** on the western shore, serve the needs of the Paiutes and Pyramid Lake visitors.

The barren shoreline and perforated tufa formations lure wilderness strollers and dry campers. Many folks, however, come here to *fish.* Thanks to the Paiutes' successful hatchery program, one can land 15-pound descendants of Frèmont's salmon trout, which essentially are landlocked salmon.

Most Pyramid Lake visitors head for **Sutcliffe**, where they can purchase tribal permits for fishing, boating and camping. Costs are modest: $5 for informal camping along the shoreline and $6 for boating and fishing. Long-term permits are available as well. Day use is a mere dollar, which can be paid at a self-service station as you enter the lake's perimeter.

Permits are sold at the **Pyramid Lake Ranger Station** on the edge of Sutcliffe, open Tuesday through Sunday from 7 a.m. to 5:30 and Monday 7 to 3:30 (476-0123) or at **Pyramid Lake Store,** open daily from 6 to 7.

The best provisioning center is **Crosby Lodge,** a busy little complex offering groceries, a gift and book shop, fishing tackle, a bar, a campground with hookups and showers, and motel rooms. Motel units, cabins and a couple of parked trailers are $36 to $48 for doubles, $24 for singles and up to $60 for family groups. Campsites are $14 with hookups and $8 without. All reservations are made in the store, which is open Monday-Thursday 7 to 8, Friday-Saturday 7 to 9 and Sunday 7 to 7. It accepts MasterCard and VISA.

Pavement delivers you to Sutcliffe, then it ends eight miles north at **Warrior Point Park**, with picnic shelters and primitive campsites. Reasonably smooth dirt and gravel roads take you on north, although they don't circle the lake. Follow signs to **The Needles**, tufa-coated pinnacles, and **Hot Steam Well,** a steam geyser that leaks hot mineral water into the lake. If you have an entrenching tool handy, you can dig your own personal hot tub and alternate between soaking and scampering into the cool, slightly briny lake water.

To reach the eastern shore follow Highway 447 through Nixon, then turn left onto an unpaved road. If you're willing to take a few bumps, you'll reach Frèmont's 450-foot **Pyramid,** a formation resembling a Russian folk doll called **The Great Stone Mother** and a fascinating moonscape of tufa shapes. Immediately opposite is **Anaho Island,** a national wildlife refuge. Here, hundreds of cormorants and pelicans seem determined to paint the island as white as the shoreline tufa.

If you, like we, follow roads just because they're there, you can continue north on Highway 447 to the California border. It takes you through one of Nevada's most remote corners, along the shoreline of **Lake Winnemucca,** another piece of Lahontan that dried up within this century, and across the edge of the **Black Rock Desert** that terrorized early emigrants. The route passes through the pleasantly funky hamlet of **Gerlach** and into the pine-crested **Warner Mountains** at the California-Nevada border.

PYRAMID LAKE TO LOVELOCK

As you drive northeast from Fernley on I-80, you enter—in presumed air-conditioned comfort—the dreaded **Forty-mile Desert**. During the great rush for gold, this was one of the wickedest stretches along the California Trail. Travelers had followed the brackish but drinkable Humboldt River until it withered and died, disappearing into the fractured alkaline mud of the Humboldt Sink. From there, they faced 40 miles of desert with no water and no graze for their oxen. Shifting sand buried wagons to their hubs and hot desert gales scoured the faces of the plodding pioneers.

The fearful route took exhausted travelers along the barren foothills of the Humboldt Range above the Carson Sink, then branched off to deliver them either to the Truckee or the Carson rivers.

"As we advance we find dead oxen, remains of wagons, carts, harness and baggage strewn along the trail in profusion," Bernard J. Reid wrote of his 1849 crossing. *"Panic had evidently overtaken the emigrants ahead of us. In their distress, loss of cattle, hunger, thirst and fatigue, they seem to have cast everything away to save life. We begin to fear our guide book has deceived us, and that we have made a fatal mistake in (choosing) the road."*

This guidebook does not deceive, and promises a swift crossing on I-80 as it skirts the edge of Forty-mile Desert. In fact, *speed* is the problem here. Because of the monotonous terrain and arrow-straight freeway, this stretch through the infamous barrens has one of the highest single-car accident rates in the country.

If you'd like to sample the equally bleak terrain of the **Carson Sink**, turn south onto U.S. Highway 95 toward Fallon, 34 miles northeast of Fernley. This marks the dying gasp of the Carson River, trickling northeastward from the Sierra Nevada. It's ironic that these two desert streams, seeping toward one another, ran out of fuel just a few miles apart. Four dozen centuries ago, both dusty sinks were very liquid arms of Lake Lahontan.

Lovelock

Population: 2,310   **Elevation: 3,903 feet**

The Lovelock agricultural valley offers refreshing green relief from the Forty-mile Desert. Fifty-seven miles northeast of Fernley, it draws its agricultural water from the withering Humboldt River.

One is tempted to guess that it draws its name from Nevada's early days as a marriage mill. In fact, it is named for one of the most ambitious and versatile itinerants ever to set foot in the sandy deserts of the West.

THE WAY IT WAS • In 1847, Welsh-born George Lovelock wed an English lass with a wonderful name, Mill Marry Forest, and promptly hauled her off to Australia. He worked the copper mines, spent a stint in Hawaii then in 1850, they surfaced in San Francisco, where George learned carpentry. They later adjourned to Sacramento and thence to the Sierra Nevada foothills. In 1866, they struck out for Nevada, bought 320 acres and water rights on the Humboldt River, built a stage station and started farming. When the Central Pacific Railroad came through in 1868, Lovelock donated 85 acres for a townsite, with the agreement that it be named for him.

This short, stocky, full-bearded Episcopalian ran a hotel, dug some of Nevada's first irrigation canals, dabbled in mining, operated stores and always voted Republican. "Uncle George" started each morning with a nip of quinine powder and a cup of tea. He was never sick a day in his life, until pneumonia put him away in 1907 at the age of 83.

After George's reluctant departure, ranching and farming continued in the valley, despite uncertainties of the drought-prone Humboldt River. The completion of Rye Patch Dam in 1936 assured Lovelock's future.

THE WAY IT IS • Lovelock is a quiet island of contented civilization midway between the gaudy lights of Reno and Winnemucca. The oldstyle downtown area is weathered but not quite shabby. Several business have closed but this does not suggest that Lovelock is withering; they've merely moved to the suburbs. Interior Nevada's resurgence in open pit mining and Lovelock Valley's feed grain crops keep the economy perking along at a reasonable pace.

Two attractions, the Pershing County Museum in the Marzen House and the county courthouse, are reasons enough to leave I-80. To visit them, take the west side freeway exit (105), cross under the freeway onto Cornell Avenue. You'll see the museum in a square-shouldered, two-story mini-mansion on your left; it's just west of the Lovelock Inn. The mansion also houses the **Pershing County Chamber of Commerce** with its usual offering of brochures and maps, including a walking tour of old downtown buildings. Its open Tuesday through Sunday from 9 to 4 (273-7213).

From the museum, continue a mile down Cornell to the town's only stoplight, turn left and you'll see the beehive domed, yellow-brick courthouse.

Pershing County Courthouse • *Main at Central, Lovelock; (702) 273-2753. Open weekdays 8 to 5.* When area residents persuaded the Nevada legislature to carve Pershing County out of Humboldt County in 1919, they decided to build a suitable monument to their accomplishment. What emerged was a roundhouse court—one of only two such structures still in use in the country. Step inside and follow the circular hallway around the courtroom. County offices occupy the outer rim, so if you miss one, just keep walking and it'll come around again. (It's an ideal environment for bureaucrats who don't know if they're coming or going.) If court's not in session, peek into the main courtroom beneath the beehive dome. It's a handsome study in polished wood, with an unusual curved jury box.

Pershing County Museum • *Cornell Avenue at I-5 exit 105; (702) 273-7144. Tuesday-Sunday 9 to 4; free; donations appreciated.* The structure is the most interesting element of the museum. Built by Joseph Marzen in the late 1870s as headquarters for his Big Meadows Ranch, it has been carefully restored by the Pershing County Museum Board. The interior is a study in 19th century finery, with print wallpaper, decorative borders, ornately carved wood and lace curtains. Museum exhibits, not very disciplined but clean and neat, range from old advertising signs to turn of the century kitchen utensils to a penny slot machine.

Lovelock isn't exactly glitter gulch; only two small casinos function here. Smoky **Jax Casino** at 485 Cornell Avenue (273-2288) has a handful of slot machines, a single blackjack table and a restaurant (see below). A bit larger and fancier, **Sturgeon's Casino** at 1420 Cornell (273-2971), has a pair of blackjack tables, slots, video poker, a game room for kids, plus a coffee shop, restaurant and Best Western motel (see below).

WHERE TO DINE

Andy's Coffee Shop • ☺ $

Fourth and Cornell. American; meals $5 to $9; wine and beer. Breakfast, lunch & dinner. Oldstyle restaurant that's been dishing up stable American fare since the 1940s. Try Peggy Rose's liver and onions or juicy roast beef; also noted for its whopping breakfasts.

Fiesta Room • ☺☺ $$

In Sturgeon's Casino, 1420 Cornell Ave.; (702) 273-2971. Mexican-American; meals $7 to $24; full bar service. Dinner 6 to 10 in summer, 5 to 9 in winter; coffee shop open 24 hours. Reservations accepted; MC/VISA. Attractive dining room featuring enchiladas and such, good Mexican seafood dishes, plus American steaks, chicken, chops and ribs.

Jax Restaurant • ☺ $$

In Jax Casino, 485 Cornell Ave.; 273-2288. American; dinners $7 to $15; full bar service. Daily 6 a.m. to 10 p.m. Reservations not needed; MC/VISA. Family style diner featuring teriyaki steak, prime rib, scampi and such.

WHERE TO SLEEP

Best Western Sturgeon's Motel • ⌂⌂⌂ $$

1420 Cornell Ave. (P.O. Box 56), Lovelock, NV 89419; (800) 528-1234 or (702) 273-2971. Doubles $40 to $58, singles $35 to $55, spa rooms $63. Major credit cards. An attractive 74-unit motel, part of the Sturgeon's Casino complex. Nice-sized rooms, some with spa tubs. Indoor pool.

Lovelock Inn ● ⌂⌂ $$ ∅
P.O. Box 757 (I-80 west exit), Lovelock, NV 89419; (702) 273-2937. Doubles $34 to $42, singles $32 to $38, kitchenettes $38 to $48, suites $65 to $85. Major credit cards. Attractive older 37-unit inn on extensive grounds; free continental breakfast, in- room coffee, TV, room phones.

Super 10 Motel ● ⌂ $$ ∅
1390 Cornell Ave. (P.O. Box 819), Lovelock, NV 89419; (702) 273-2228. Doubles $27 to $32, singles $21 to $27. MC/VISA, AMEX, DISC. A 10-unit motel with simple but neat rooms; TV, room phones; refrigerators and microwaves in some units.

WHERE TO CAMP

KOA Lovelock Kampground ● *1500 Cornell Ave. (Highway 40 East & I-80; P.O. Box 541), Lovelock, NV 89419; (702) 273-2276. Full hookups $16.15, water and electric $15.25, tent sites $14.35, cabins $20.65. Reservations accepted; major credit cards.* Full-service RV park with 70 spaces, mostly pull-throughs. Showers, picnic tables and barbecues, TV hookups, pay phones, laundry, provisions, Propane and gasoline, dump station and swimming pool.

Rye Patch Recreation Area ● *Exit 129 off I-80, 25 miles northeast, Star Route 1, Lovelock, NV 89419; (702) 538-7321. RV and tent sites $5, boat launching $5, day use $2. No reservations or credit cards.* Attractive riverside campsites near Rye Patch dam with flush potties, picnic tables and barbecues. Pit toilets only in winter, for a $2 camping fee. Fishing, boating and swimming.

LURES BEYOND LOVELOCK

Giant Tufa Park ● *Off Pitt road, northwest of Lovelock.* Several tufa survivors of Lake Lahontan stand in the desert a few miles from town, like hunched troops in a petrified army. To reach them, drive north on Central Avenue (North Meridian), turn left (west) onto Pitt Road for less than a mile, then go right on a gravel road.

Lovelock Cave and Leonard Rock Shelter ● *South of town; directions available from the Chamber of Commerce.* One of the first Great Basin prehistory sites to be excavated, Lovelock Cave is a 40-foot tufa hollow occupied by early man about 4,000 years ago. It was discovered in 1887, then excavated after the turn of the century, yielding tons of bat guano and a trove of Indian relics. Leonard Rock Shelter, an even older site, is marked with standing tufa shapes and petroglyphs. It was explored by the University of California at Berkeley in the 1950s and determined to be 6,000 years old.

LOVELOCK TO WINNEMUCCA

The desert becomes more rumpled as you continue northeast from Lovelock on I-80. The West Humboldt Mountains present a beige barrier to your right. The main Humboldt range, often dusted with winter snow, fills the far horizon.

About 25 miles from Lovelock, **Rye Patch Dam and Recreation Area** offers camping, picnicking (see listing above), fishing and—if the weather's proper—swimming. Take Exit 129 to the left, cross the dam and you'll see the first camping and picnicking area, just down river. A second camping area, with pit toilets, is upstream alongside the reservoir. The 63-foot homogeneous earth-fill dam was completed in 1936. Its 179,000 acre-foot reservoir keeps Lovelock and its surrounding agricultural lands blooming.

On the right as you continue along I-80, you'll see a mountain being devoured by the **Florida Canyon Gold Mine** operation. This is one of the many new open pit mines that has boosted interior Nevada's economy in the past decade. At the Mill City exit (149), take a hard right and follow arrow-straight State Highway 400 south. Tucked in behind the Humboldt Mountains, this slim paved road takes you to a pair of hidden hamlets.

After a few miles, note the historical marker for **Star City.** Once a lively mining camp, it's located seven miles up a dirt road, at the base of the handsome, near-symmetrical Star Peak. Little survives of the town. It's worth a visit only if you enjoy driving along bumpy roads for the privileges of poking among crumbling foundations and rusty mining gear.

Seventeen miles from your I-80 turnoff, Highway 400's pavement ends. Hang a right and bump three miles into the folded flanks of the Humboldts to **Unionville.** Unlike Star City, it is still very much a town, albeit a shabby one. It's an interesting study in weathered wood, junk cars and satellite TV dishes, bringing the world to people who have chosen to withdraw from it. If it were located on the outskirts of a big city, Unionville would be called junky; here in the mountains, it's quaint. There is, incidentally, no business district. The few dozen residents must trek to Winnemucca for supplies.

The town began rather auspiciously, at the site of an 1861 silver strike. Three clusters of cabins developed: Upper Town, Dixie and Lower Town or Union. Later merged as Unionville, it became the seat of Humboldt County. Then the silver expired, a planned railway bypassed it and the town went to sleep. A growing Winnemucca snatched the county seat in 1873.

Among the hopefuls lured to early Unionville was one Samuel S. Clemens. He arrived with three partners in early 1862, filed a claim and began hacking futilely at a chunk of mountain. Gaining nothing but blisters and sweat, they sold their interest in the mine. Clemens moved on, eventually winding up at the Virginia City *Territorial Enterprise.*

"We built a small, rude cabin in the side of the crevice and roofed it with canvas," he wrote, *"leaving a corner open to serve as a chimney, through which the cattle used to tumble occasionally, at night, and mash our furniture and interrupt our sleep."*

Stone fragments of the cabin remain, near the Pershing County Youth Center, in a small park at the upper end of town.

If the town today is homely, its setting is striking. Unionville is scattered for nearly two miles along the grassy, poplar-shaded banks of Buena Vista Creek in a shallow V-canyon, twisting down from the Humboldts. If you've brought a four-wheel-drive or sturdy hiking boots, you can pursue the deteriorating road into the high country. Not all of Unionville is shabby. A few of the homes are tidily-tended, particularly a cheery yellow and white Victorian, part of a bed and breakfast complex.

Old Pioneer Garden • ⌒⌒ $$ ØØ

Unionville (Imlay), NV 89418; (702) 538-7585. Doubles $65 to $85, singles $44 to $65. Six rooms; some share, some private baths. Full breakfast. No *credit cards. Also dinner served for $7.50.* In "downtown" Unionville, it offers a pleasing mix of antiques and relics in its simple but comfortable rooms. The complex, consisting of a pair of restored 130-year-old guest houses and a two-unit cottage with a fireplace, sits in a tree-shaded hollow just above the stream. A creekside gazebo invites fair-weather lingering.

Winnemucca

Population: 6,250   **Elevation: 4,280 feet**

Continuing northeast on I-80, you'll know when you're nearing Winnemucca. "Not just another pretty face," proclaims a large billboard, exhibiting a Groucho Marx mask. "Winnemucca. Proud of it!" insists another.

In the mid-1980s, local casino owner Bob Cashell sponsored 15 of these billboards to lure visitors to Winnemucca and help the town survive its silly name complex. Cashell has since moved on and most of the signs went to other uses, although the county now maintains five of them.

THE WAY IT WAS ● One of Nevada's oldest settlements, Winnemucca began life in 1850 as Frenchman's Ford, a toll crossing of the Humboldt River for California-bound gold seekers. A decade later, nearby hills began yielding their own treasures. The settlement became a provisioning center for surrounding mines and cattle ranches.

The arrival of the railroad in 1868 assured the town's position on the map. In that same year, the name was changed to honor the great Paiute chief who had worked so valiantly to make peace with the intruding whites. There is no record of Chief Winnemucca spending much time in his namesake town, since he ranged mostly in northwestern Nevada and northeastern California. He died in California's Lassen County in 1882. Presumably, he was aware that those who had destroyed his way of life had named a village in his honor.

The town's leading citizen was George Nixon, a former Central Pacific Railroad telegraph operator who opened a bank here in 1886. He eventually built an empire that included the First National Bank of Nevada (now part of First Interstate), Winnemucca's *Silver State* newspaper and major mining operations in Tonopah and Goldfield. He was elected to the U.S. Senate in 1903 and served until his death in 1912 at the age of 52, after an unsuccessful spinal meningitis operation. The old Nixon opera house and Winnemucca Grammar School are among the young entrepreneur's legacies.

Another group of "citizens" left their mark on Winnemucca, although it was rather fleeting. One of America's last oldstyle Western bank robberies occurred here on September 19, 1900. A gang of outlaws rode into town, stuck a gun in George Nixon's face and rode off with $32,640 from his bank. Popular legend insists that it was Butch Cassidy, the Sundance Kid and their Wild Bunch. Why, they even sent Nixon a portrait of themselves, dressed in finery bought with their stolen gold, the legend insists.

More sober historians say that Cassidy never came near the place and that the photo was sent by Pinkerton detectives to see if Nixon could identify the robbers. But never mind cold reality. Winnemucca still celebrates Butch Cassidy Days to honor the great bank robbery. Now, if they could only get Robert Redford to show up.

THE WAY IT IS • Mining, ranching and the first solid set of casinos this side of the Oregon border have pumped a lot of vitality into old Winnemucca. The town's four casinos might be regarded as a tribute to former Humboldt County State Assemblyman Phil Tobin. In 1931, the 29-year-old cowboy turned politician sowed the seeds for the Nevada we know and love today. To help create jobs during the Depression, he introduced the bill permitting wide-open gambling.

West Winnemucca Boulevard is a literal glitter gulch, although most of the sparkle comes from motel signs. Sitting at the juncture of I-80 and U.S. 95, the town is a popular stopover on the long trek across the Great Basin.

Winnemucca is a curious mix of old brick and new neon, cradled between mountains in a ranching and agricultural valley. Despite the glitter, it's still a down-home kind of town drawing heavily on its Western roots. It's the kind of place where the appliance shop sells hunting licenses, where J.C. Penney is still a brick-front clothing store.

Locals like to call it the "Buckaroo Capital of America." To prove their point, they started a Buckaroo Hall of Fame in the Winnemucca Convention Center in 1991. Unusually large for a small-town convention center, it covers nearly a full city block, between Winnemucca Boulevard, Bridge, Second and Melarkey streets. Should you wonder about the rather ornate façade, part of the center occupies the now-defunct Star Casino building.

The center is a good starting point, for it houses the **Chamber of Commerce,** open weekdays 8 to 12 and 1 to 5 (623-2235). Here, you can pick up brochures and maps, and buy reproductions of those billboards on T-shirts and bumper stickers—"Winnemucca: If you don't stop, who will?" "Winnemucca: free admission" and "Four billion people have never been here."

One local lure not listed in the brochures is the **red light district**. If you're curious, continue a block beyond the convention center to Baud Street, turn left and follow it a block to Second Street. Tucked discreetly around the corner to your right are Simone de Paris, My Place, Pussycat Saloon and Penny's. The latter takes MasterCard and VISA, according to a window sign. Another sign, in a large parking lot beyond this shabby little courtyard of legal sin, tells truckers to park elsewhere if they're hauling cattle. It also asks them not to leave their motors running, which may or may not be a double entendre.

Winnemucca's tree-shaded streets lined with sturdy old homes are worth a browse. Among other interesting structures are the Spanish-baroque **St. Paul's Catholic Church** at Fourth and Melarkey, the old Basque **Martin's Hotel** near the tracks at Commercial and Lay streets and the red brick and white masonry **Winnemucca Grammar School** at Fifth and Lay. Just beyond on Lay, note the imposing private home with pressed tin exterior walls.

THE ATTRACTIONS

Humboldt Historical Museum • *Jungo Road and Maple Avenue (off Highway 95, just north of town); (702) 623-2912. Weekdays 10 to 4, Saturday 1 to 4, closed Sunday. Free; donations appreciated. Gift shop open Monday, Wednesday and Friday 11 to 2.* Perched on a hill in Pioneer Park above town, the county museum occupies the 1907 New England-style St. Mary's Episcopal Church and a modern brick structure behind. An adjacent gift

WINNEMUCCA

DIRECTORY
1. Buckaroo Hall of Fame, Visitor Center, Casinos
2. Humboldt County Courthouse
3. Humboldt Historical Museum
4. Nixon Opera House, Redwood Tree Slice
5. Red Light District
6. Winnemucca Hotel

shop is housed in a false front feed store. Most of the county's museum funds obviously went into the smart new brick and smoked glass structure. Exhibits here include an imposing mural of turn-of-the-century Winnemucca, an organ from nearby Paradise Valley and a shining 1907 Schacht, one of the county's first motorcars. The museum in the church is a rather disorganized clutter. You'll find the usual collection of old photo albums, period costumes, early telephones and Paiute and Shoshone woven baskets and projectile points.

Buckaroo Hall of Fame ● *30 W. Winnemucca Blvd. (at Bridge street) in the convention center; (702) 623-2225. Weekdays 8 to 4; free.* Started by cowboy artist Carl Hammond, the museum offers a collection of Western-style paintings and bronzes, plus biographies and memorabilia of the area's noteworthy cowboys. Exhibits are in several display cases set into the walls of the convention center's east hall, adjacent to the Chamber of Commerce visitor center. To be inducted into the hall, one must have been born before 1900, lived within a 200-mile radius of Winnemucca and have been a real cowboy, making his living in the saddle.

There are no cowgirl inductees yet.

Nixon Opera House and City Art Gallery • *Winnemucca Boulevard at Melarkey Street; (702) 623-6330. Gallery open Tuesday, Thursday, Friday and Saturday 1 to 4. Free.* This sturdy 1907 brick and masonry building was one of Senator Nixon's gifts to the town. After a stint as a movie theater, it was threatened with demolition until townsfolk came to its rescue in the early 1980s. A fund-raising drive is underway to restore it to its former glory. Meanwhile, the city's art gallery occupies the basement.

NUGGETS

Butch Cassidy marker • *First Federal Savings & Loan, corner of Fourth and Bridge streets.* Citizens need to believe that Cassidy and Sundance rode into town to relieve Nixon's First National Bank of its gold, so they erected a monument to the event. The present structure replaces Nixon's original one-story red brick bank, which later served as the office of the *Humboldt Star*.

"Highway to the Sea" redwood monument • *Winnemucca Boulevard at Melarkey Street, in front of the Nixon Opera House.* Sitting high and certainly dry in the desert, Winnemucca's citizens longed for a direct route to the ocean. After decades of lobbying, the Winnemucca-to-the-Sea highway was completed in 1962, running through southern Oregon to Crescent City, California. When a storm washed a giant chunk of redwood ashore in Crescent City two years later, citizens there sent a slice to Winnemucca to honor their asphalt link.

Humboldt County Courthouse • *Fifth and Bridge streets.* Completed in 1919, this imposing structure is a typical bit of Thomas Jefferson neo-classical style with its Greek pediments and columns.

THE CASINOS

Parker's Model T Casino • ☺☺

1130 W. Winnemucca Blvd.; (702) 623-2588. Used brick, wood paneling and old photos give Parker's an attractive Old West look. Slots, blackjack, a motel and pool comprise its facilities. **Dining:** The **Model T Restaurant** is open 24 hours, dinners $7 to $12; MC/VISA.

Red Lion Casino and Hotel • ☺☺

721 W. Winnemucca Blvd.; (800) 633-6435 or (702) 623-2565. This medium-sized low-rise gaming parlor is spruced up with chandeliers, stained glass and floral carpeting. Plenty of slots, blackjack tables and a roulette wheel keep the hopeful coming. Facilities include a motel, restaurant and swimming pool. **Dining:** The 24-hour **Red Lion Restaurant** offers interesting variations on American fare, such as finger steaks dipped in tempura batter; dinners $7 to $16; major credit cards.

Sundance Casino • ☺

33 W. Winnemucca Blvd.; (702) 623-3336. Sundance has the usual ranks of slots and a few gaming tables, and it claims to offer the loosest poker bar in town. With a smoky, dingy interior, there's little else to recommend it.

I-80 CORRIDOR — 299

Winners Hotel and Casino • ☺
West Winnemucca Boulevard and Lay Street; (702) 623-2511. This busy place offers the full range of gaming devices, including roulette, craps and blackjack, plus hotel rooms. **Dining:** The casino a 24-hour **coffee shop**, plus **Grandma's Kitchen**, nightly 5 to 10; dinners $7 to $14; MC/VISA.

WHERE ELSE TO DINE

Two Basque hotels, the Winnemucca and Martin's, serve traditional family-style food in historic settings; they're popular with locals and visitors. Most of the other significant eating establishments are in the casinos.

Flyin' Pig Barbecue • ☺☺ $$
1100 W. Winnemucca Blvd. (Raley's Shopping Center); (702) 623-4104. American barbecue; meals $3.75 to $11; full bar service. Daily from 11 a.m. MC/VISA. Tasty hickory smoked chicken and pork barbecued dinners and sandwiches. They're served in a cheery Art Deco atmosphere of black and white tile floor, black lacquered chairs and ceiling fans.

Hotel Winnemucca Restaurant ☺ $$
95 Bridge St.; (702) 623-2908. Basque; regular dinners $5 to $11.50, Basque dinners $12; full bar service. Daily noon to 1 and 6:15 to 9. Major credit cards. Start with a sip of Picon punch and admire the beautifully ornate back bar. Then adjourn to a family-style table in the large, unadorned dining room to tackle a hefty Basque dinner. Less expensive but not as extensive as the Martin Hotel prix fixe meals.

Martin Hotel • ☺ $$
Melarkey and Railroad streets; (702) 623-3197. Basque; dinners $10 to $16; full bar service. Lunch weekdays 11 to 2, dinner nightly 5 to 10. MC/VISA. Go for the food, not for the austere pressed-tin decor of this 100-year-old Basque hotel restaurant. The prix fixe dinner includes entrèe, soup, salad, , veggies, two Basque side dishes, wine, coffee and (gasp) dessert.

Mike's Ristorante and Cantina • ☺ $$
47 E. Winnemucca Blvd.; (702) 623-3021. Mexican-Italian; dinners $6 to $12; full bar service. Weekdays 10 to 10, Saturday 7 to 10, closed Sunday. MC/VISA, AMEX. As the name suggests, this simple little place offers a mix of smashed beans and rice and pasta dishes, launched with a bowl of minestrone or *albondigas*. Menu specials include homemade raviolis and lasagna, chimichangas, deep fried ice cream and "awesome" morning omelets.

Ormachea's Basque Dinner House • ☺☺ $$ ØØ
180 Melarkey St.; (702) 623-3455. Basque-American; dinners $9.50 to $15; full bar service. Tuesday-Saturday 6 to 10. MC/VISA. Cozy restaurant in an attractive cottage-style building, serving family-style Basque dinners plus American entrèes such as steaks, seafood and chicken. Basque dinners include soup, salad, potatoes, French bread, wine and dessert.

WHERE TO SLEEP

Motel 6 • ⌒⌒ $$ Ø
1600 W. Winnemucca Blvd., Winnemucca, NV 89445; (505) 891-6161 or (702) 623-1180. Doubles $34 to $36, singles $28 to $30. Major credit cards. Large 103-room motel with TV movies, room phones and a pool. Some non-smoking rooms.

Nevada Motel • ◠ $$
635 W. Winnemucca Blvd., Winnemucca, NV 89445; (702) 623-5281. Doubles $30 to $60, singles $20 to $40. Major credit cards. A 28 unit motel near downtown; TV movies, room phones and pool.

Pyrenees Motel • ◠ ø
714 W. Winnemucca Blvd., Winnemucca, NV 89445; (702) 623-1116. Doubles $40 to $60, singles $35 to $50. Major credit cards. Well-maintained 46-unit motel with TV, room phones, refrigerators. Near downtown and casinos.

Scott Shady Court • ◠ $$
400 First St. (P.O. Box 670), Winnemucca, NV 89445; (702) 623-3646. Doubles $45 to $52, singles $35 to $40. MC/VISA, AMEX, DIN. Attractive 78-unit motel with TV movies, room phones, indoor pool, sauna and children's playground.

Val-U-Inn ◠ $$$ ø
125 E. Winnemucca Blvd., Winnemucca, NV 89445; (800) 443-7777 or (702) 623-5248. Doubles $55, singles $49.50. Major credit cards. Well-maintained 81-unit motel in downtown area; TV, room phones, pool, sauna and steam room, continental breakfast.

WHERE TO CAMP

Hi-Desert RV Park • *5575 E. Winnemucca Blvd. (half miles south of exit 180), Winnemucca, NV 89445; (702) 623-4513. Full hookups $18, tent sites, $13. Reservations accepted; MC/VISA.* Some pull-throughs, barbecues and tables, flush potties and showers, dump station, phone, laundry, groceries and snacks, RV supplies, Propane, pool, rec hall and playground.

Parker's Model T RV Park • *1130 W. Winnemucca Blvd., Winnemucca, NV 89445; (702) 623-2588. RV sites, call for rates.* New RV park under construction; ready in summer of 1992; will have showers and flush potties; access to adjacent Parker's Model T Casino facilities.

Westerner Trailer Lodge • *800 E. Fourth St. (a block off Winnemucca Boulevard), Winnemucca, NV 89445; (702) 623-2907. RV sites, full hookups $12.* Some pull-throughs; showers, flush potties, playground, phone, dump station.

KOA Winnemucca Kampground • *5255 E. Winnemucca Blvd. (exit 178), Winnemucca, NV 89445; (702) 623-5797. RV and tent sites, full hookups $18. Reservations accepted; MC/VISA.* Some pull-throughs, barbecues and tables, showers, dump station, pay phone, coin laundry, TV hookups, groceries, playground, horseshoes, game room, pool, Propane and RV parts.

ANNUAL EVENTS

For details, call the chamber of commerce at 623-5071.

Winnemucca Mule Show and Races, last weekend of May.

Winnemucca Basque Festival, mid-June; Basque dances and foods.

Red Mountain Indian Pow Wow, late June in McDermitt; a gathering of Indian tribes from several Western states.

Western Art Roundup and Winnemucca Rodeo, Labor Day weekend; Nevada's oldest rodeo.

Pari-mutuel horse and mule racing, last two weekends of September.

NORTH TO PARADISE VALLEY & McDERMITT

U.S. 95 north from Winnemucca leads to the Oregon border hamlet of **McDermitt** and the **Fort McDermitt Indian Reservation**. These offer little of visitor interest, although two attractions en route are worth a pause. **Paradise Valley,** reached by forking right onto State Highway 290, 22 miles north of Winnemucca, is one of the more attractive rural hamlets in the state. Bypassed by "progress," it has preserved a pair of old steepled churches and a deserted yet still-intact false front business district.

Beyond Paradise Valley, the highway takes you into the **Santa Rosa-Paradise Peak Wilderness** of Humboldt National Forest. You can get particulars on camping and hiking in the area at the **Paradise Valley Ranger Station.**

WINNEMUCCA TO ELKO

Meanwhile back on I-80, the one-hour drive from Winnemucca to Battle Mountain will be uneventful, as will be your arrival. While it's probably a perfectly pleasant place for Great Basin residents, Battle Mountain offers little excuse for the visitor to linger.

Two minor points of interest may catch your attention en route. **Golconda,** 16 miles east of Winnemucca, is comprised of a handful of tired buildings at the site of a 1860s hot springs. Several mines were worked in the surrounding hills and a large open pit gold mine, to the south and out of sight, is still active. **Valmy** a few miles beyond, isn't noted for anything except a Bruce Springsteen album cover. An LP released in 1981 shows The Boss with a 1965 Ford Fairlane ragtop at the Valmy Auto Court. The idea was to depict Middle America, although the middle of nowhere would be more appropriate. A copy of the album cover, autographed to longtime Valmy resident Gene DiGrazia, sits on a cluttered shelf above the cash register in Valmy's Shell Station mini-mart.

Statistics and other guidebooks say that **Battle Mountain** is booming, profiting from the resurgence in mining activity hereabouts. From a visitor standpoint, however, it offers little. What one sees in this town of 7,000-and-growing is a random scatter of houses on a downslope from I-80.

Downtown, reached by taking one of two freeway exits to Front Street, has more of an organized look. Little changed from its formative years as a railroading center, the compact oldstyle business section stretches about four blocks, and some of the new prosperity is evident in its neat and tidy look. The cheek-to-cheek storefronts, including two casinos, appear to be thriving. Two small casinos here, the **Owl Club** and **Nevada Club,** offer a few slots and a small restaurant each.

Returning to I-80 and continuing eastward, you'll climb a couple of mountain passes and pass some imposing peaks, reminding you that the Great Basin is not giant saucer but a plateau with a hump in the middle. **Summit** and **Emigrant** passes carry you more than a mile high, then you drop down to **Carlin,** only slightly lower. Once an Asian farming settlement called Chinese Gardens and later a stop on the Central Pacific, Carlin today is but a slight widening of the road. Its small, shabby business district has little of visitor interest.

It does offer a grim page in Nevada's history book. In 1890, Elizabeth and Joseph Potts murdered one Miles Faucett (who may have been her ex-lover) and buried him in the basement of their Carlin home. They sold the house and moved to Rock Springs, Wyoming. The new owner felt a ghostly presence, so he dug around—literally—and found Faucett's remains. The Potts were extradited from Wyoming, tried for murder and hanged in Elko. Elizabeth thus gained the dubious distinction of being the first woman legally executed in the Pacific states.

"Faucett's ghost rattled and clattered
And made an awful din.
For in that house in Carlin,
The Potts had done him in."

This cheerful campfire song gives us cause to end our pause in Carlin and continue over this high desert to Nevada's fourth largest city.

Elko

Population: 12,586 **Elevation: 5,060 feet**

Spread across the floor of a shallow valley, Elko is the thriving hub of northeastern Nevada and the largest community between Reno and Salt Lake City. It's a handsome old town with a sturdy brick business district and residential streets shaded by mature trees.

This booming cowtown, sheeptown and rail division center began life as a place to pause and party, and it continues this role today. In fact, the practice of booking big-name acts in casinos, which has made Nevada the world's entertainment center, started right here. While we're not suggesting that *this* fits your definition of entertainment, Elko also has more lawful brothels than any other city in the U.S.

THE WAY IT WAS ● Curiously, no one is sure how Nevada's fourth largest city earned its name. It may have been a Shoshone expletive or a Romanized version of "elk," from the herds which once grazed hereabouts.

Central Pacific's rails reached this area around Christmastime, 1868. Officials decided it would be a good townsite, so they began selling lots right after New Year's. With a bit of mining activity in the hills and hundreds of thousands of acres of cattle graze in the surrounding valley, Elko grew quickly. By March it was the county seat with more than 2,000 residents. It boasted a sturdy red brick courthouse before the end of the year. Within five years, it was picked as the site for the University of Nevada.

Beneath all this propriety, Elko was a wild, wicked Western frontier town where cattlemen and sheepmen brawled over saloon girls on Saturday night, sobered up on Sunday and fought over grazing rights on Monday. Bloody range wars flared between cowmen and Basque sheepmen, like plots from low-budget Western movies.

The tent camp cowtown burned back to the dirt in 1870 and a sturdier brick Elko emerged. The area evolved into Nevada's largest cattle and sheep center. Ranches became multi-million dollar empires the likes of TV's *Dallas*. Elko cattleman Lewis Rice Bradley was elected governor in 1870, starting a pro- ranching political policy that ruled the state for decades. Sheep ranchers, too, became wealthy. Local sheepman Pedro Altube was regarded as the "father of Basques in America." More colorful was multi-millionaire sheepman Pete Itcaina. He stopped in the Silver Dollar Club for a drink one day, got mad because the service was too slow, bought the place and fired the bartender.

When Nevada gambling was legalized in 1931, the Newton Crumley family installed a casino in Elko's historic Commercial Hotel. A decade later, Newton, Junior, made history when he hired noted nightclub entertainer Ted Lewis to perform, followed by legendary bandleader Paul Whiteman. Lewis' opening act on April 26, 1941, changed the face of Nevada-style entertainment forever.

THE WAY IT IS • Although big-name entertainers soon bypassed little Elko in favor of Las Vegas and Reno, gaming remains popular, since this is the only sizable town between Salt Lake City, Boise and Phoenix. Dice tables and modern mining operations started a boom that carries into this decade. It doubled its population in the 1980s and likely will match it again by the new century.

Elko is an easy town to navigate, laid out in a typical grid. It's a wide open town, and we don't mean sinful. The railroad tracks recently were shifted south to the banks of the Humboldt River. The old division yard between Commercial and Railroad streets have been converted into a huge public parking lot, with nary a meter in sight.

Most of the casinos and motels are in this downtown core. Idaho Street is the main drag. Red Lion, the largest casino, is near the eastern freeway interchange. There are few empty storefronts in old Elko. Although shopping centers occupy the suburbs, ample parking and the casino center has encouraged many businesses to stay downtown. Some of the town's fine old homes stand along **Court Street,** one block away and parallel to Idaho.

The **Chamber of Commerce,** in a rustic brick building at 1601 Idaho Street next to the museum, is open weekdays from 9 to 5 (738-7135).

THE BEST ATTRACTION

Northeastern Nevada Museum • *1515 Idaho St.; (702) 738-3418. Monday-Saturday 9 to 5, Sunday 1 to 5. Free; donations accepted. Large gift shop with a good book selection.* The best museum outside of Las Vegas-Reno, this is a roomy, bright and professional repository of northeastern Nevada memories. It's located in a severely modern trapezoidal masonry building on the eastern side of town. Out front is one of its more interesting attraction—a log, fieldstone and sod-roofed 1860 Pony Express station, moved intact from Ruby Valley to the south.

Within the museum, you'll find a large room used for rotating exhibits, backdropped by an imposing wooden bar from Hallack Station, east of here. Other wings offer a Nevada time line, mockups of a school room and a 19th century kitchen, old printing presses, artifacts from an early Chinatown, gems and minerals and the usual Native American baskets and projectile points. An excellent modern-day mining exhibit features a slide show of the open pit process, from blasting and terracing to extracting ounces of gold from tons of ore.

The rest

J.M. Capriola Saddle Shop • *Fifth and Commercial streets; (702) 738-5816. Daily 9 to 5.* Master saddlemaker Guadalupe S. Garcia created fancy riding gear for Presidents and other notables here until his retirement in 1932. Although the firm was sold to others, son Les still turns out leather finery. This two-story place is the total cowboy shop, where you can get a Stetson, silver belt buckle, boots, shirts, Levi's, harness and of course the lat-

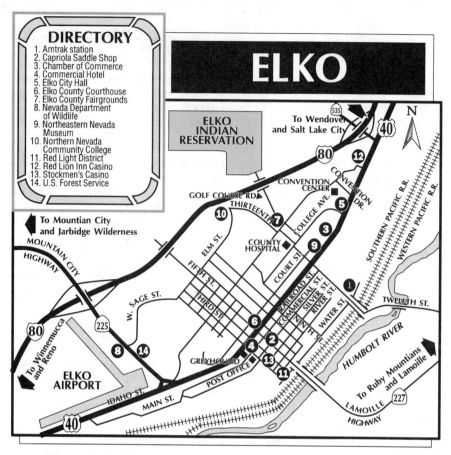

est trendy double-weave saddle blanket. Western paintings and photos line the walls and a book department offers more volumes about cow-punching than we ever thought had been written.

Commercial Hotel ● *345 Fourth St.; (702) 738-3181*. This is where the Nevada glitter began, when Ted Lewis' jazz band and Rhythm Rhapsody Revue played to packed houses in 1941. Red hot mama Sophie Tucker, the Dorsey Brothers, Ozzie Nelson's orchestra and Lawrence Welk followed. Dating from 1869, the Commercial is the state's third oldest operating hotel. Unfortunately, the glitz is gone and it's now a bit scruffy. However, this old-style saloon is certainly worth a visit. Check out the portraits and biographies of Western gunfighters and the stuffed giant polar bear (presumably not a Nevada hunting trophy).

Nuggets

Elko City Park ● *College Avenue behind the museum*. If you're visiting Elko on a toasty summer day, you might want to retreat to this large, shady park and its public swimming pool. Much of civic Elko surrounds it: a community college, city hall, fairgrounds and convention center.

Elko County Courthouse ● *Idaho and Sixth streets*. This is one of rural Nevada's more intriguing civic structures, with a Greek columned front topped by a beehive dome. It was built on this site in 1910 to replace the original, erected here in 1869 when Elko County was carved from Lander County. The courthouse has to cover a lot of territory; Elko is the sixth largest county in America.

THE CASINOS

Red Lion • ☺☺
2065 Idaho St.; (702) 738-2111. Elko's largest casino provides plenty of glitz and glitter. The Red Lion actually is two casinos, on opposite sides of Idaho Street, along with a large hotel complex. It offers "mini-Las Vegas style revues," all the basic table games, scores of slots and three lounges. **Dining:** American-continental fare is served at **Misty's,** dinners $8 to $15; lunch weekdays 11:30 to 1:30 and dinner nightly from 5. The Lion also has a 24-hour **coffee shop.** Major credit cards.

Stockmen's • ☺☺
340 Commercial St.; (702) 738-5141. Not quite but nearly as attractive as the Red Lion, Stockmen's also has herds of slots, all the essential gambling games, live entertainment and a hotel. **Dining:** The plush **Stockmen's Dining Room** serves American fare nightly 5 to 9:30; $8 to $13. There's also the usual all- night **coffee shop.** Major credit cards.

Commercial Hotel • ☺
345 Fourth St.; (702) 738-3181. This venerable place rates high historically, although it's rather smoky and dingy, with more glitter outside than in. It has lots of slots, blackjack, poker and roulette, plus inexpensive hotel rooms. **Dining:** There's a 24-hour **coffee shop,** of course, and the **Brand Room** serves American fare nightly, $8 to $13.

WHERE TO DINE

El Simpatico • ☺ $
2515 Mountain City Highway; (702) 753-6222. Mexican; dinners $6 to $11; wine, beer and margaritas. Daily 11 to 9. MC/VISA. Small family style place on highway north of town; noted for its well-prepared *Latino* dishes and tasty margaritas.

Gratton's Fine Dining • ☺☺☺ $$$ ØØ
217 Idaho St.; (702) 738-2170. Continental; dinners $15 to $35; full bar service. Lunch weekdays 11 to 2, dinner Monday- Saturday 5 to 10, closed Sunday. Reservations advised; Major credit cards. This is as close as Elko gets to dining elegance, and it's pretty nice. Cozy and stylish restaurant in a Spanish-style turn of the century home. Intimate dining rooms; several smoke free; crackling fireplace in the lounge. Frequently-changing menu features assorted European entrées such as chateaubriand and cioppino, plus some nicely prepared American steaks and chops.

Showboat Catfish Restaurant • ☺☺ $
1396 Idaho St., in Rancho Plaza; (702) 753-8686. Southern-style seafood; dinners $5 to $10; wine and beer. Monday-Saturday 11 to 9, closed Sunday. No credit cards A great little place if you like Cajun-Creole style seafood. Pond-raised catfish are featured, served with corn on the cob and maybe even grits. Also featured are Cajun grill, shrimp dinners and hamburgers.

Basque dining
The home of the National Basque Festival is, of course, home to several Basque restaurants. Toki Ona offers a Basque-American mix. Three more traditional family-style Basque places are close together along Silver Street, three blocks south and parallel to Idaho Street.

Toki Ona • ☺☺ $$ ØØ
1550 Idaho St.; (702) 738-3214. Basque-American; dinners $8.25 to $15; full bar service. Daily 6 a.m. to 10:30 p.m. MC/VISA. Family style service in a newer restaurant; more attractive than the typically austere Basque cafes. Traditional Basque dinners include soup, salad and spaghetti for $14. Smoke- free dining room.

Biltoki Basque-American Dinner House • ☺ $$
405 Silver St.; (702) 738-9691. Dinners $10 to $22; full bar service. Daily 4 to 10. Like Toki Ona, it offers American fare, along with Basque dinners.

Nevada Dinner House • ☺ $$
351 Silver St.; (702) 738-8485. Dinners $10 to $15; full bar service. Daily except Monday from 3 p.m. Family-style Basque dinners.

Star Hotel • ☺ $$
246 Silver St.; (702) 738-9925 or 753-8696. Dinners $10.50 to $17; full bar service. Lunch weekdays 11:30 to 2, dinner Monday- Saturday 5 to 9:30, closed Sunday. Basque-American fare; at the same location for 80 years.

WHERE TO SLEEP

Key Seven Motel • △ $$
605 W. Idaho St. (Mountain City Highway), Elko, NV 89801; (702) 738-8081. Doubles $30 to $44, singles $26 to $40. Major credit cards. A 33-unit motel with TV, room phones, room refrigerators and microwaves.

National 9 Toppers Motel • △△ $$ Ø
1500 Idaho St. (near city park); Elko, NV 89801; (800) 524-9999 or (702) 738-7245. Doubles $36 to $48, singles $28 to $38. Major credit cards. A 33-room motel with TV movies, room phones, refrigerators and microwaves. **Toki Ona** restaurant adjacent; see listing above.

Star Lite Motel • △ $$ Ø
411 Tenth St. (Idaho Street), Elko, NV 89801; (702) 738-8018. Doubles $32 to $42, singles $28 to $36. Major credit cards. A well-maintained 20-unit motel with TV, room phones and refrigerators; free airport pickup.

Super 8 Motel • △△ $$ Ø
1755 Idaho St. (near city park), Elko, NV 89801; (800) 800-8000 or (702) 738-8488. Doubles $44.88 to $71, singles $35.88 to $41.88, suites $65 to $71. Major credit cards. Attractive 75- unit motel with TV, room phones and courtesy shuttle to casinos.

WHERE TO CAMP

East Elko Double Dice RV Park • *3730 E. Idaho St. (Exit 303, then left at light), Elko, NV 89801; (702) 738-5642.* Full hookups $17, tent sites $10. Reservations accepted via phone credit card; MC/VISA, DISC. A 140-unit RV park with many pull-throughs, showers, picnic tables and barbecues, TV and phone hookups, pay phones, laundry, Propane and dump station. Free shuttle to casinos and shopping.

Hidden Valley Guest & RV Resort • *Coal Mine Road (Freeway exit 314), Elk NV 89801; (702) 738-2347.* Full hookups $10, water and electric $10, no hookups $5. Reservations accepted; no credit cards. A three-acre park with 37 pull-throughs, flush potties (no showers), barbecues, TV hookups, dump station, horseshoes, trout pond and rec hall.

Valley View RV Park • *Highway 40 E. (about 1.5 miles east), Elko, NV 89801; (702) 753-9200. Water and electric $15, no hookups (tents) $10. Reservations accepted; MC/VISA.* Well-kept park with paved streets, pull-throughs, swimming pool and playground, showers and laundry and TV.

ANNUAL EVENTS

For details, call the chamber at 738-7135.
Cowboy Poetry Gathering the last weekend of January.
Western Heritage Festival and **Elko Mining Expo,** June.
National Basque Festival, Fourth of July weekend; nation's largest.
Silver State Stampede, July; Elko's annual rodeo.
Elko County Fair, Labor Day weekend.

THE JARBIDGE WILDS AND THE RUBIES

A pair of side trips from Elko will take you to the **Jarbidge Wilderness Area** in the north and the **Ruby Mountains** to the south. To pick up maps and detailed information on these areas, stop by the **Humboldt National Forest** office at 976 Mountain City Highway (Fifth Street from downtown Ely). It's open weekdays 8 to 5; phone (702) 738-5171.

Tucked up against the Idaho border, the Jarbidge area has changed little with the passing decades. Check out the old mining town of **Tuscarora,** the pretty **Independence Valley** beyond and the tree-rimmed town of **Mountain City.** To the east, reached only by dirt road, is the isolated village of **Jarbidge,** surrounded by one of America's most remote wilderness areas.

The **Ruby Mountains** are more easily reached. These imposing crests, which form a dramatic backdrop to the town, are less than an hour's drive. Head south on Fifth or Twelfth streets which blend into Lamoille Highway. After a dozen miles, take a right onto Lamoille Canyon Road and follow it into the spectacular alpine reaches of **Lamoille Canyon.** Also check out the pretty town of **Lamoille** at the base of these 11,000-foot peaks. With a national forest map, you can follow dirt roads to the far side of the "Rubies" to explore the **Ruby Marshes** waterfowl area.

ELKO TO WELLS AND UP TO A JACKPOT

East from Elko, Interstate 80 follows the curving course of the Humboldt River, snug against the foothills of the Rubies. The river and highway then brush the skirts of the adjoining Humboldt Mountains, swing past their northern tip and enter wide Independence Valley. Here, a branch of the river issues from the ground in a series of springs, which provided a popular pausing place for the California-bound.

A town that seems ready to run dry, **Wells** sits like a weary old man in the sun at the junction of I-80 and U.S. 93. It's a pity that the town appears moribund, for it must have been a handsome place at one time. An entire block of 19th century brick and masonry stands intact, yet abandoned. The only movement here is an occasional passing tumbleweed. A few businesses do function downtown and quite a few more are active at Four Corners, where highways 93 and 80 cross. The town's location at this junction and a bit of mining and ranching in the area keep it on the map.

Wells got its unimaginative name from the nearby Humboldt Wells, the previously noted emigrant watering hole. The Central Pacific chose the wells as a division point and town slowly, almost reluctantly, took shape.

Should you care to gamble, the choices are four: **Chinatown Casino** at 455 S. Humboldt Ave. (752-2101), is one of the few we've encountered with an Asian theme, despite the Chinese love of gambling. It has a Chinese-American restaurant, motel and RV park. **Old West Inn Casino** is downtown at 465 Sixth St. (752- 3888); it's Western rustic, with slots, a restaurant and motel. **Four Way Cafe and Casino,** out near the freeway at the Highway 40- 93 junction (752-3344), is the largest of the four, with a full range of table games, rows of slots, a gift shop and restaurant. Nearby is **The Ranch,** (752-3384), housed in a drab stucco structure that's considerably brighter inside. It has the usual slots, a dice table, three blackjack tables and the Feedlot restaurant.

If you're curious to see one of Nevada's senior border gambling towns—established only for that purpose—head northward on Highway 93 toward the Jackpot. Not *a* jackpot. *The* Jackpot. The route climbs 6,274 feet over **Hunters Draw Summit**, across a high and lonely desert, past an occasional juniper and into the town named for every handle-puller's wish.

Jackpot

When Idaho banned the last of its slot machines in 1956, Don French of Garden City, a sin center just outside of Boise, went south. He built the Horseshu Casino at an empty highway crossing on the Idaho-Nevada border. It did so well that Pete Piersanti moved his Cactus Pete's to the border from Mineral Springs, 12 miles south.

Although the two clubs prospered from passing Highway 93 traffic, no real town developed around them. The name Jackpot—inspired by Carl Hayden, who handles PR for both casinos—didn't appear on maps until a couple of decades ago. For a time, the area was listed on Elko County maps as Unincorporated Town Number One.

After 40 years, the place seems to be booming. Cactus Pete just spent $10 million on a 200-room hotel tower and a place called Barton's Club 93 has undergone a complete face-lift. The likes of Rich Little, Charlie Pride and the Captain and Tennille are regulars in Jackpot.

However, as far as a town is concerned, there is still no here here. We found no subdivisions other than a few double-wides and clusters that suggested portable classrooms. The single supermarket is the General Store, part of the Horseshu.

Do the girlies of the girlie shows fade like shapely dust devils into the desert at dawn? Perhaps they grab a few winks in the hundreds of hotel rooms, between tourist shifts. Or does everyone commute to Twin Falls, Idaho, 50 miles north?

Jackpot rivals Wendover in offering the most modern and liveliest casinos in northern Nevada. Few of the inland city gaming parlors match the size, glitter and amenities of these state line fun houses.

Cactus Pete's • ☺☺☺

(800) 442-3833 or (702) 755-2321. With its plush carpeting, Southwestern decor and gleaming give-away cars parked above slot carousels, Pete's could hold its own with most Reno- Tahoe-Las Vegas casinos. It's all here: "big room" shows featuring headliners, hundreds of slots and the full array of table games, topped off by a 300-room tower hotel. There's even an 18-hole **golf course** adjacent. **Plateau** is Pete's gourmet room, with dinners

$10 to $18, Wednesday-Sunday 5 to 11. There's also a 24-hour **coffee shop** and a buffet. **Rooms** are $40 to $100; Major credit cards.

Barton's Club 93 • ☺☺

(702) 755-2341. Smaller than Pete's, Club 93 is tackily resplendent in its new dress of strip lighting, neon piping, carpeting and general all-around glitter. Most of the table action—blackjack, roulette and craps—happens in a sunken pit amidships. **Bartons** restaurant is open 24 hours, serving thrifty dinners from $5 to $10 and a buffet. Major credit cards.

Four Jacks • ☺

(702) 755-2491. Smoky, small and friendly, Jacks is more akin to the folksy casinos inland. Its western-style interior includes the usual platoons of slots, table games and a **Mexican-American restaurant** with a pianist (nice touch) at the entrance. Dinners are $5 to $9, served 24 hours. Major credit cards.

Horseshu • ☺☺

(702) 755-7777. Across Highway 93 from Pete's and now under the same ownership, Jackpot's senior casino offers a pleasing Western look. It's all a-trim with fake bat-wing doors, cowboy hats, lariats and horseshoes. Ranks of slots, craps, blackjack, roulette and keno will satisfy all betting urges. It offers a frontier style **dining room** with dinners $5 to $9, open 24 hours and a 120-room **hotel,** doubles $35 to $100. Major credit cards.

WHERE TO CAMP

Spanish Gardens RV Park • *P.O. Box 259, Jackpot, NV 89825; (800) 422-8233, (702) 755-2333 or CB channel 13. Full hookups $10.95 ($8.95 in the off-season). Reservations accepted; MC/VISA.* Well-tended small park with showers, laundry, free cable TV; shuttles to casinos and golf course.

WELLS TO WENDOVER

Meanwhile, back on busy I-80, the drive east from Wells takes you over the highway's highest rise, 6,967-foot **Pequop Summit**. You brush a few junipers at this elevation and pass down through a rock-ribbed canyon into the **Goshute Valley.**

The mountains ahead belong to the Toano Range. That conical promontory is **Pilot Peak,** a 10,716-foot landmark named by John C. Frèmont in 1845. This was the Fujiyama, the Matterhorn, the Pike's Peak to California-bound emigrants. Perched rather nobly and perhaps haughtily on the edge of the great Utah salt flat, it signaled the end of a grueling three-day desert crossing. It promised the beginning of graze for the oxen, shade and respite for the travelers and water for everybody.

The Wendovers

And suddenly, you're out of the brushy, rolling, mountain-rimmed desert. Below and beyond stretches an impossibly level off-white flatness—the great empty bottom of primeval Lake Bonneville. Here, thirst-crazed bullocks wilted and died in the world's greatest salt lick, emigrants stumbled and squinted blindly in an alkaline hell. Here, where travel once took an agonizing eternity, land speed records are now set.

On a hot day, the heat shimmers from the great white flatness, casting mountain ranges adrift, creating lakes where there are none, distorting light and thus all vision. At the edge of this sits the twin towns of Wendover, NV/UT. With their neon glitter, they must appear as an illusion to today's migrants, streaking across the flats, anxious to end the endless expanse.

The Utah border encloses the Bonneville Salt Flat as if it were proper Mormon property. No Mormon principles disturb the Nevada border town, however. It offers a Utah backslider's first shot at legal sin.

THE WAY IT WAS • Despite its glossy casinos, Wendover was not born of gambling. The town, split between Utah and Nevada, emerged at the turn of the century as a supply and watering center for the Western Pacific Railroad—the water being piped from the base of Pilot Peak.

As early as 1914, automotive engineers began using the nearby salt flats to fulfill their need for speed. Wendover became a hangout for racing freaks. Gary Gabolich's *Blue Flame Special* streaked over the proper pair of flying miles (one in each direction) at 622.407 mph in 1971.

Highway 40, predecessor to I-80, pushed across the salt flats in the 1920s, shortly followed by an energetic young man named Jim Smith. He opened a service station and repair shop, then received one of Nevada's first gaming licenses in 1931. The **Silver Smith Casino**, largest and glitziest on the border, is still operated by his descendants.

The Army Air Corps arrived in 1940 to develop Wendover Field, one of the largest and most remote military bases in the world, straddling the Utah-Nevada border. GIs had the choice of pulling the slot handles at Jim Smith's Stateline Casino or taking a long bus ride to Ely, Elko or Salt Lake City for liberty. Bob Hope, visiting the base, called it "Alcatraz with tents."

However, it was ideal for its assigned purpose, to train heavy bomber crews for World War II. Three and a half million acres offered plenty of room for bombing practice. Late in that war, the base hosted the most famous crew of all, the 509th Composite Group. (See box.)

THE WAY IT IS • The two Wendovers line either side of old Highway 40, now a frontage road to I-80. Since the casinos must stay on the western side, most of the other businesses have gone east. Utah's Wendover is thus the commercial tail that wags Nevada's gambling dog.

Housing, such as it is and much of it prefab and double-wide, occupies the surrounding treeless desert. Despite its 90-year heritage, Wendover, like Jackpot, looks like it just got off the train. The only things green are a golf course and all that money the travelers leave behind.

Little remains of the old Wendover Field, which is used now only for emergency landings and occasional maneuvers. A portion of it was sold in 1977 to Wendover for general aviation use.

THE ATTRACTIONS

Bonneville Speedway • *Off I-80 exit 4 on the Utah side.* You can see where the fastest men alive drive by heading into Utah, then going five miles north. Watch carefully for signs and traffic. You wouldn't want to be broadsided by something approaching the speed of sound. In theory, you'd never hear what hit you. The famous speedway, 80 feet wide and ten miles long, is marked by black lines. You may see a speed trial, or you may see nothing but a lot of salt. (The last time we visited, freight rigs were running speed tests. Without their trailers, they could really fly.)

WENDOVER'S SINISTER SECRET

When the Army Air Corps arrived at Wendover in 1940, it was a dusty hamlet of about 125 souls. Jim Smith's gas station, motel and State Line Casino comprised most of the business district.

Of course, the Army wasn't here to party. The huge base, straddling the Nevada-Utah border, was used to train hundreds and pilots and crewmen for B-17 and B-29 heavy bombardment. Then in the spring of 1944, the program was suspended and the facility was used briefly for fighter training.

That fall, a squadron of fifteen B-29s arrived, under the command of Lieutenant Colonel Paul Tibbets. A cloud of secrecy settled over the base. All phone calls, written material and even conversations were monitored.

"I was baffled by the presence of naval officers at Wendover, hundreds of miles from sea," recalls William B. Wolfan. Now a Chicago journalist, he served as assistant public relations officer for the base. "Then there were two individuals who sat across from me at the officer's club dining table. One was a thin, frail-looking man who said little except to ask me to pass the mashed potatoes."

Later, he learned that the skinny one was Dr. J. Robert Oppenheimer, head of the Los Alamos Atomic Bomb Laboratory in New Mexico. The other was the lab's Norman Ramsey, who would later win the Nobel Prize for physics. They were here to prepare two B-29s, the Enola Gay and Bock's Car, to deliver a cargo that would forever change the world.

The Superfortresses were stripped of all armament except a tail gun, to increase their speed and mobility. They had to be nimble to out-climb enemy fighters and evade the shock waves after delivering their lethal loads. The world's first two atomic bombs, *Little Boy* and *Fat Man*, were never at Wendover. They were still being perfected in the Los Alamos "Manhattan Project." Pilots used dummy bombs in practice drops over the Utah Salt Flats and California's Salton Sea.

The ground crew of the 509th left Wendover in April of 1945. The B-29s departed a month later, headed for Tinian in the South Pacific. No one at the base, indeed almost no one in the 509th, knew why they had been at Wendover.

On July 16, 1945, an atomic bomb was successfully exploded at Alamagordo, New Mexico. Three weeks later, on the morning of August 6, Lieutenant Colonel Tibbets pushed forward the throttles on the Enola Gay. It began rolling down the runway at Tinian, headed for Hiroshima, Japan.

You'll likely see some action if you visit during **Speed Week** the third week of August, then **The World of Speed** the following month. Take binoculars, a wide-brimmed hat and lots of Mountain Dew.

Bonneville Speedway Museum • *Utah side; (801) 665-7721. Open from 10 to 6, daily June to mid-September, weekends only the rest of the year; $2.* Photos, clippings and artifacts herald the accomplishments of the *Blue*

Flame Special, Mormon Meteor, Green Monster and similar swifties. The museum also offers a small collection of carriages, fast and fancy cars, including a 1960 Rolls Royce Silver Cloud.

Welcome Center and Peace Memorial • *Nevada side; Wendover Boulevard and Highway 93; (702) 664-3414. Wednesday-Sunday 8:30 to 5.* This is where you load up on brochures and casino discount coupons. More interesting is a wall exhibit concerning the 509th Composite Air Group, a crew of 2,000 that secretly prepared to blast the world into the Atomic Age. Outside is a Peace Memorial erected in 1990—an ironic gesture, since 200,000 souls died in Hiroshima.

Wendover Field Tour • *Call (702) 664-3414 for details.* Free tours of the abandoned hangars, barracks and runways of Wendover Field are given by personnel of the Wendover Welcome Center.

THE CASINOS

Peppermill Casino • ☺☺

680 Wendover Blvd.; (702) 664-2255. This is an interesting place with a red and black glossy decor, sort of a modernistic Gay Nineties look. It has the usual array of slots and tables and it's noted for a huge budget-priced **buffet**. The garden style **Peppermill Restaurant**, open 24 hours, serves steak and lobster specials, prime rib and other fare from $6 to $10.

Red Garter Casino • ☺

Wendover Blvd.; (702) 664-2111. It seems that every gaming center has to have its down-home, smoky, sawdust joint. Folksy little Red Garter fills that role here. A frontier town façade and Western style interior, slightly worn, give it the proper look. The slots must be loose, because the place is always jammed.

Silver Smith/State Line • ☺☺☺

101 Wendover Blvd.; (702) 664-2221. These two posh playpens, owned by the Smith family, nudge the border on opposite sides of Highway 40, linked by a pedestrian skyway. For a quickie tour, start on the State Line side, admire the old gambling machine exhibit and check out a great sports bar with a score of TV screens set into paneled walls. Then cross over the bridge, enjoying views of the salt flats. From a landing on the other side, you'll get a nice high-angle look at a glittering casino in action. The twin complex has it all: hundreds of slots, big shows, naughty little shows, restaurants and hotel rooms.

Dining: Restaurants include the fancy **Salt Cellar,** with American and continental fare, $15 to $25, nightly 5 to 10; the **White Swan,** American with prime rib specials, $15 to $25, Sunday-Thursday 5 to 10, Friday-Saturday 5 to 11 and Sunday brunch 10 to 2; the 24-hour **Pantry** featuring American and Mexican food, $5 to $10; and the 24-hour **Bonneville Room Coffee Shop.**

Travel Center Casino at Nevada Crossing Hotel • ☺☺

1045 Wendover Blvd.; (702) 664-4000 The look is low budget high tech, with lots of ribbed stainless steel and glass. It targets the heavy trucker traffic on I-80 with a large service facility and even a "trucker's spa" downstairs. (A steam bath with a CB?) It also offers a slot machine that plays "Yankee Doodle," and a general store. The 24-hour **coffee shop** features prime rib and other American fare, $5 to $14.50.

WHERE TO SLEEP

Nevada Crossing Hotel • ⌒⌒ $$ ∅
1035 Wendover Blvd. (P.O. Box 2457), Wendover, NV 89883; (702) 664-2900. Doubles and singles $31 to $39, kitchenettes $41 to $58. Major credit cards. A 137-unit hotel linked to the Travel Center casino and truck stop. TV, room phones; indoor pool and spa. Non-smoking rooms.

Peppermill Inn • ⌒⌒ $$
850 Wendover Blvd., Wendover, NV 89883; (800) 648-9660 or (702) 664-2255. Doubles and singles $39 to $55, suites $90 to $120. Major credit cards. A 90-unit hotel with distinctive red and black decor; TV, room phones. Restaurant and casino adjacent.

Silver Smith Hotel & Resort • ⌒⌒ $$ ∅
P.O. Box 729 (101 Wendover Blvd.), Wendover, NV 89883; (800) 648-9668 or (702) 664-2231. Doubles and singles $39 to $49. Major credit cards. New 120-unit resort with TV movies, room phones, pool, tennis courts and complete spa with exercise equipment, sauna and tanning beds. Full casino facilities with several restaurants; catwalk to State Line Casino facilities.

State Line Hotel & Casino • ⌒⌒ $$ ∅
P.O. Box 789 (101 Wendover Blvd.), Wendover, NV 89835; (800) 648-9668 or (702) 664-2221. Doubles and singles $39 to $49, kitchenettes $52 to $62, suites $81 to $91. Major credit cards. Attractive 248-room casino hotel with TV movies, room phones, pool and spa. Full casino facilities with several restaurants; catwalk to Silver Smith Hotel Casino facilities.

WHERE TO CAMP

Wendover KOA • *1220 Camper Drive (off Wendover Blvd., P.O. Box 2397), Wendover, NV 89883; (702) 664-3221. Full hookups $22, water and electric $20, no hookups and tent sites $13. Reservations accepted; MC/VISA, DISC.* Campground near Red Garter Casino, offering showers, picnic tables and barbecues, TV, pay phones, laundry, provisions, Propane, dump station, swimming pool, horseshoes. playground and casino shuttle.

State Line RV Park • *P.O. Box 789 (Wendover Boulevard at First Street), Wendover, NV 89883; (702) 664-2221, extension 695. Full RV hookups $13 weekdays and $16 weekends. Reservations accepted; MC/VISA, AMEX.* A 56-space RV park adjacent to State Line Casino with showers, picnic tables, TV, pay phones, laundry and dump station. Guests can use spa and tennis facilities at State Line and Silver Smith casinos.

— **Don W. Martin**
Rumors that Nevada is mostly a treeless wasteland have been greatly exaggerated. The view is from U.S. Highway 6 between Ely and Tonopah.

"They were swift phantoms of the desert who swept across the landscape like the belated fragment of a storm."

— Mark Twain's description of Pony Express riders

Chapter Ten
U.S. 50 CORRIDOR
A lonely highway and a lonesome county

The whims of history and topography gave Highway 50 second billing to I-80 as the chosen corridor across Nevada's Great Basin. The northern route got the Emigrant Trail, the railroad, the freeway and most of the publicity. The trail through central Nevada got the Pony Express and an unfortunate nickname: "The loneliest road in America."

Both were explored in the earliest days of the quest West. And both were determined to be passable—barely.

In the 1820s, Peter Skene Ogden scouted the northern approach and legendary mountain man Jedediah Strong Smith struggled eastward from present-day California across the central route. Since it lacked the northern route's rivers, Smith nearly died of thirst—hardly a recommendation for further trail development. Later, Joseph Walker made a more detailed exploration of the upper route. It became the avenue of choice for California and Oregon-bound wagon trains of the 1840s and 1850s.

After this Emigrant Trail had become something of a covered wagon freeway, one Howard Egan surveyed a route that roughly followed Smith's erratic trek. It was mapped by Captain James Simpson in 1859 and became known as the Overland Route. Weaving between a series of north-south mountain ranges, it was more suited to horses and never became popular as a wagon trail.

Although attention continued to focus on the Emigrant Trail, the Overland Route had its moments of glory, particularly when it was chosen as the route of the Pony Express. But when the pony mail was discontinued after a year and a half, the future seemed grim for this route across central Nevada. Only the long, thin wires of the transcontinental telegraph, which had followed the route of the ponies and thus put them out of business, kept the Overland Trail on the map.

However, prospectors found silver near present-day Austin in 1862 and lead-silver ore around Eureka two years later. Fortune hunters literally beat a path to their doors. Major copper mining operations developed near Ely after the turn of the century, assuring a future for the old pony trail.

315

THINGS TO KNOW BEFORE YOU GO

BEST TIME TO GO • Like I-80, U.S. 50 passes through high desert, so spring to late fall is the preferred visitor season. Winters are generally clear but often bitterly cold, sometimes with blizzard conditions. The route is kept open, but you could be caught in a winter storm, so check weather reports before venturing forth.

WHAT TO SEE • Churchill County Museum in Fallon; Berlin Ichthyosaur State Park in the ghost town of Berlin; old downtown Austin; county courthouse in Eureka; Copper Pit mine overlook in Ruth; Nevada Northern Railway Museum in Ely and nearby Ward Charcoal Kilns and Cave Lake State Park; Lehman Caves and other attractions at Great Basin National Park; the eroded shapes of Cathedral Gorge State Park and the mission revival Caliente railroad station.

WHAT TO DO • Sign up for a trip to Hidden Caves at Fallon's Churchill County Museum; climb Sand Mountain just east of Fallon; follow the petroglyph trail at Hickison Petroglyph Recreation Site; hike to the Cold Springs Pony Express Station west of Austin and the trails through the formations of Cathedral Gorge; catch a ride on the "Ghost Train of Old Ely"; hike to the bristlecone forest in Great Basin National Park; drive through Rainbow Canyon east of Caliente.

Useful contacts

Austin Chamber of Commerce, P.O. Box 212, Austin, NV 89310; 964-2200.

Bureau of Land Management, Ely District Office, HC 33, Box 150, Ely, NV 89301; (702) 289-4865; for information on Baker archaeological site tours.

Caliente Chamber of Commerce, P.O. Box 255, Caliente, NV 89008; (702) 726-3129.

Churchill County Chamber of Commerce, 100 Campus Way, Fallon, NV 89406; (702) 423-2544.

Eureka Chamber of Commerce, P.O. Box 14, Eureka, CA 89316; (702) 237-5484.

Great Basin National Park, Baker, NV 89311; (702) 234-7331.

Lincoln County Tourism Chair, P.O. Box 255, Caliente, NV 89008; (702) 726-3209.

Pioche Chamber of Commerce, P.O. Box 553, Pioche, NV 89043; (702) 962-5544.

White Pine Chamber of Commerce, 636 Aultman St., Ely, NV 89301; (702) 289-8877.

Area radio stations

KELY-AM, 1230, Ely—country
KVLV-AM, 980, Fallon—country-Western
KBXS-FM, 92.7, Ely—adult contemporary
KELY-FM, 101.7, Ely—mostly rock, some Top 40
KLNR-FM, 91.7, Panaca—National Public Radio; news, talk and classical music
KSVC-FM, 95.7, Richfield, Utah—mostly country
KVLV-FM, 99.3, Fallon—adult contemporary

Then came the motor car and the need for something better than rutted wagon trails. The Overland Trail got one of two transcontinental routes, the Lincoln Highway (U.S. 50). However, the larger railroad-supported communities along the Victory Highway lured more auto traffic—four times as much, according to a traffic count conducted in Wendover in 1939. As World War II loomed, Congress saw the need for a national defense highway system and picked the Victory as the best route to California. Like a benched quarterback, Highway 50 was cast into a permanent role as a back-up.

Old towns along the Overland Trail, already shrinking from dwindling mining activity, would shrivel even more in the decades that followed. A 1986 *Life Magazine* article, branding the Lincoln Highway as America's loneliest, should have been the final affront.

However, business people along this neglected route turned the insult into an asset. Assisted by state tourist officials, they assembled a *Highway 50 Survival Kit*. It's available from chambers of commerce and merchants, listing attractions and services along the route. Folks who have a "Survival Map" postcard validated at businesses and visitor centers along the route can send it in and receive a bumper sticker attesting to their daring trek.

Out on the highway, "Loneliest Road in America" signs invite motorists to shun I-80 freeway and drive where the solitary pony riders once galloped.

Actually, the route isn't really *that* lonely. Provisioning centers of Fallon, Austin, Eureka and Ely are one to two hours' drive apart, like modern Pony Express way stations. Ghost towns, semi-ghost towns, mountain ranges and a brand new national park give today's road warriors plenty to explore.

You will, of course, encounter long stretches where your only companion will be your car radio, if it's strong enough to pull in distant stations. Our most reliable kilowatt *compadre* was KSVC-FM from Richfield, Utah, 95.7 on your dial. *Ickybod*, our little green VW camper, hummed along to the "Overdrive Top Ten Country Countdown." Actually, we prefer the "lonely road" and its funky towns to life in the fast lane on that northern route.

Driving along Highway 50, you'll encounter several Pony Express markers and an occasional way station ruin. The only intact station, ironically, is in Elko on I-80. It was moved there as a museum exhibit from Ruby Valley, just north of Highway 50. Interestingly, there is little reference to the transcontinental telegraph, which *really* tied together the loose ends of 19th century America.

After completing our trek across Nevada, we'll head south on Highway 93 to visit Lincoln County. If Highway 50 is Nevada's loneliest road, then rarely visited Lincoln County is probably its loneliest corner. However, with the stunning badlands formations of Cathedral Gorge and the tough and weathered old mining town of Pioche, it's certainly worth the trip.

CARSON CITY TO FALLON

Heading west from Carson City, Highway 50 skims the edge of Sun Mountain and passes through Dayton, which we explored in Chapter 6, then moves into the now-familiar Great Basin Desert.

At the junction of highways 50 and 95 Alternate, the crossroads hamlet of **Silver Springs** offers a small casino called Piper's, with a combination motel and restaurant. Just beyond is **Lahontan State Recreation Area**, rimming the 10,000-acre Lahontan Reservoir on the Carson River. This large pond offers several beaches, boat launches, picnicking and camping areas

318 — CHAPTER TEN

along its 70-mile shoreline. Day use fee is $2; camping and boat launching are. Some sites offer showers and others have pit potties only.

If you like things green, savor the farmlands you're about to enter as you approach Fallon. Fed by the reservoir, this is the "Oasis of Nevada," the only serious agricultural swatch along Highway 50 between Carson City and the Utah border. In a good runoff year, Lahontan Reservoir can store nearly 300,000 acre feet of water.

The reservoir is a key element of the Newlands Reclamation Project, named for Nevada Congressman Francis Griffith Newlands. He devoted much of his political career to water conservation for the thirsty, growing West. For a decade, he worked for passage of the Federal Reclamation Act, which in 1902 laid the foundation for the U.S. Reclamation Service.

Naturally, the Newlands project was the agency's first, begun in 1903, with the construction of Derby Dam and a diversion channel from the Truckee to the Carson River. Lahontan Dam was completed in 1914, bringing 70,000 acres under irrigation.

Fallon

Population: 4,500 **Elevation: 4,000 feet**

Hardly lonely at this point, Highway 50 carries you into Fallon, about 15 miles east of Lahontan Reservoir. While most of Nevada's towns gained fame for their gaming or their gold and silver mines, Fallon for years was noted for its cantaloupes. Specifically, Hearts o' Gold cantaloupes.

Even though the Newlands Project brought water to this area, called the Carson Sink Valley, the soil was too alkaline for most agricultural uses. After several false starts, farmers found that cantaloupes, properly fertilized, did quite well. In recent years, however, alfalfa has become the crop of choice.

THE WAY IT WAS • Although most emigrant trains followed the Truckee River to the north, a few chose the Carson River Route. Asa and Catherine Kenyon opened a trading post here in 1855 to serve settlers who'd survived the Forty-Mile Desert. It became known as Ragtown, either because the dusty pioneers finally could wash their clothes and spread them to dry, or because the settlement consisted mostly of ragged tents. Another version suggests that emigrants cast aside unwanted belongings here, preparatory to the difficult pull over the looming Sierra Nevada.

This first settlement didn't survive, although a few other hamlets sprouted in the area. Churchill County was carved from this desert sink in 1861 with the seat at Buckland Station. Later, it was shifted to the mining camp of La Playa, and then to Stillwater, an early farming center near Stillwater Marsh.

Late in the 19th century, settlers diverted water from the Carson River and established a few ranches in the area. One of these ranchers was Mike Fallon, who settled here in 1896. After passage of the reclamation act in 1902, Fallon sold his land to State Senator Warren Williams, who laid out a town named in honor of the pioneer rancher.

Growing with the Newlands Reclamation Project, the new town won the county seat from Stillwater in 1903. Local legend says that Stillwater officials were sore losers and refused to surrender the records, so Fallon folks spirited them away in the dark of night. With its fourth and final move into a courthouse that it still occupies, the Churchill County seat holds the record as the most mobile seat of government in Nevada. The local government has a second distinction. It operates the Churchill County Telephone System, the only county-owned phone company in America.

THE WAY IT IS • Except for the backdrop of the Sierra Nevada, Fallon might be a quiet midwestern farm town. Maine Street, named for Senator Williams' home state, is lined with two-story brick and false front stores. Neither booming nor busting, it holds is own as a provisioning center for the Oasis of Nevada and a stopover for Highway 50 and 95 traffic. The two highways cross paths in the middle of town.

Although not a tourist town, Fallon offers a noteworthy museum, certainly worth a pause. Also check out the white clapboard, Greek-columned courthouse at Maine and Williams Avenue, final resting place for the Fallon County records. Fallon Naval Air Station is three miles south of town, off Highway 95. It's closed to visitors, but you can drive the perimeter fences and watch the black darts of jets take off and land (sometimes in tight formations), if that sort of thing amuses you.

Highway 50 becomes West Williams Avenue as you approach from Carson City. To reach the museum, turn right onto Maine Street and go south through the heart of town for just over half a mile. And why does the museum façade have a familiar look? It's housed in an old Safeway store.

To learn more about Fallon and surrounds, stop at the **Chamber of Commerce** in the convention center adjacent to the campus of Western Nevada Community College. Take a hard left from West Williams onto Auction Way at an Exxon service station opposite the **Depot Casino,** then hang a right onto Campus Way. The chamber is open weekdays from 9 to 5.

THE ATTRACTIONS

Churchill County Museum • *1050 S. Maine St.; (702) 423-3677. Summer: Monday-Saturday 10 to 5, Sunday noon to 5; October through May: Monday-Saturday 10 to 4 and Sunday noon to 4, closed Thursday. Free; donations accepted.* Although not professionally arranged, this is an appealing archive, with a large number of interesting, uncluttered exhibits in the roomy interior of the former Safeway. Much of the stuff focuses on the turn of the century, when Fallon came to be. We liked some of the specialty exhibits, such a manganese purpled glass, a full-scale Paiute reed dwelling with assorted artifacts within and about, 19th century safes and vaults and several furnished pioneer rooms. The museum's best exhibit details the exploration of—and displays artifacts from—nearby Hidden Cave.

Churchill County Courthouse • *Williams Avenue and Maine Street; open weekdays 8 to 5.* Built in 1903, this white clapboard structure, with a Greek column and pediment façade, is still in use. It is thus one of the oldest continually-active government buildings in Nevada.

THE CASINOS

The town has four midsize casinos. supported mostly from the folks at the Naval Air Station. All are on Williams Avenue, west of Maine Street.

Bonanza Inn Casino • ☺

855 W. Williams Ave.; (702) 423-6031. It's a drab and smoky little gaming parlor, although a sign proclaims the loosest slots in town. A motel, **restaurant** and RV park are part of the complex.

The Depot Casino • ☺☺
875 W. Williams Ave.; (702) 423-2311. The look is old western railroad depot, with mustard yellow trim and a clock tower. It's dimly lit inside, with railway station signs dangling from the ceiling. Offerings include several ranks of slots and blackjack. **La Cocina** is a locally popular Mexican-American restaurant, serving daily from 7 a.m.; dinners $6 to $11; MC/VISA.

Nugget Casino • ☺☺
Maine and Williams Avenue; (702) 423-3111. Looking more like an old-style casino with a glittering light bulb marquee, the Nugget catches the downtown shopping crowd. Only slightly scruffy, it offers the usual table games and slots. **Nugget Steakhouse** serves dinner 5 to 11 nightly; $8 to $14 and the **Prospector coffee shop** is open 24-hours. MC/VISA.

Stockman's Casino • ☺☺
1560 W. Williams Ave.; (702) 423-2117. This is a low-key casino for low rollers, featuring lots of nickel slots and ten-cent keno. It offers dice and blackjack, plus a large dance floor that gets lively come Saturday night. **Steakhouse Lounge** is the town's most attractive restaurant, open nightly 5 to 10; $6 to $17; there's also a 24-hour **coffee shop.** MC/VISA.

WHERE ELSE TO DINE

El Simpatico • ☺☺ $
118 E. Williams Ave.; (702) 423-6522. Mexican; dinners $7 to $13; full bar service. Daily 11 to 2 and 4 to 10. MC/VISA. Neat looking little casino with barnboard interior and brilliant serape designs on booths. Usual Mexican fare, plus Gringo steak dinner and rather tasty *carne asada* and *fajitas.*

Los Rosalas • ☺☺ $
125 S. Maine St.; (702) 423-7268. Mexican; dinners $5.25 to $10; wine, beer and margaritas. Open daily; summer 11 to 10, winter 11 to 9. No credit cards. Simple little family cafe with very good food for the price. Beef *con papas* (steak and Mexican fried potatoes) and *fajitas* are among its specialties.

The Waterhole • ☺☺ $$
111 Allen Rd. (near Raley's shopping center); (702) 423-3051. American-Italian-Mexican; dinners $6 to $12; full bar service. Lunch Sunday-Friday 11 to 2, dinner Sunday-Thursday 5 to 10 and Friday-Saturday 5 to 11, closed Tuesday. MC/VISA. Western style restaurant with a busy menu, wandering from steaks, chops and chicken to lasagna and minestrone.

Woolgrowers • ☺☺ $$ ø
60 W. Center St.; (702) 423-8585. French Basque; dinners $7.50 to $14; full bar service. Lunch Tuesday-Wednesday from 11:30, dinner Monday-Saturday 5 to 9, closed Monday. Reservations accepted; MC/VISA, AMEX. Traditional hearty Basque dinners, built around leg of lamb, roast beef, sweetbreads, salmon and steak, served family-style. Attractive new restaurant; cocktail lounge with live entertainment.

WHERE TO SLEEP

Lariat Motel • △ $$ ø
850 W. Williams Ave. (P.O. Box 649), Fallon, NV 89406; (702) 423-3181. Doubles and singles $30 to $48. MC/VISA. An 18-unit motel with good-sized rooms; TV, room phones; pool.

Uptown Motel • △ $$ ∅
180 W. Williams Ave. (near Maine), Fallon, NV 89406; (702) 423-5151. Doubles $32 to $41, singles $26 to $32, kitchenettes $35 to $41. Major credit cards. Small 22-unit motel with TV, room phones, some room refrigerators and microwaves; pool.

Western Motel • △ $$
125 S. Carson St. (P.O. Box 290), Fallon, NV 89406; (702) 423-5118. Doubles $34 to $40, singles $30. Major credit cards. A 22-unit motel, one block from U.S. 50-95 intersection; TV movies, room phones; small pool.

ANNUAL EVENTS

Wild Bunch Stampede and Rodeo, Memorial Day; (702) 423-6006.
Nevada International Invitational Rodeo, second weekend of July; (702) 423-3986.
All Indian Stampede and Pioneer Days, late July; (702) 423-3968.
Churchill County Fair and Pioneer Days, second weekend of August; (702) 423-5121.
Cantaloupe Festival, Labor Day weekend; (702) 423-2544.

BEYOND FALLON

Grimes Point and Hidden Cave • *Eleven miles southeast of Fallon, off U.S. 50. Hidden Cave tours conducted by Churchill County Museum on the second and fourth Saturday of each month, starting at 10; free. Call 423-3677 for details.* Grimes Point, across U.S. 50 from the Fallon Naval Air Station, offers one of Nevada's finest petroglyph formations. A path, maintained and signed by the Bureau of Land Management, leads past dozens of pre-Columbian scratchings on basaltic boulders. Man spent a long time leaving sundry scratchings here; these pre-history writings date from 5000 B.C. to 1500 A.D. **Hidden Cave** is nearby but the desert road markings are confusing, so it's best to sign up for the twice-monthly two-hour museum tour. Discovered in the mid-1920s by a group of school children, it has proven to be one of Nevada's richest archaeological finds. Excavations have yielded hundreds of pre-history artifacts and rock writings.

Stillwater Wildlife Management Area • *Fifteen miles northeast of Fallon on State Highway 116; P.O. Box 1236, Fallon, NV 89406; (702) 423-5128.* This wetland is a major stop on the Pacific Flyway, hosting as many as 200,000 waterfowl. There are no elaborate visitor facilities, but with patience and a good pair of binoculars, one can see a host of white-faced ibises, pelicans, swans, teals, redheads, gadwalls and gad knows what else.

To reach it, head east on U.S. 50, then turn north onto the Stillwater Road (Route 116). Stair-stepping through the desert farmlands, the route takes you to the edge of **Fallon Indian Reservation.** Its Round House Gallery displays and sells Native American arts and crafts. A few miles beyond is tiny **Stillwater,** once the county seat.

FALLON TO AUSTIN

Before leaving busy Fallon for lonely Highway 50, pick up a useful single sheet of paper produced by the Churchill County Museum and Bureau of Land Management. With the self-explanatory title of *Archaeological, Historical and Recreational Sites Along U.S. Highway 50*, this handy sheet will guide you to just what it says. Copies are available at the museum and the chamber of commerce.

Heading east on U.S. 50, you quickly shed the green fields of Fallon and the highway begins to live up to its name. **Grimes Point** petroglyph site appears about the time you clear the farmland and the runways of Fallon Naval Air Station. A few miles beyond, the ragged, hilly horizon flattens into a great off-white expanse—the alkaline remains of **Carson Lake.** The highway skirts along **Eight Mile Flat** on the lake's northeastern edge. As you clear the salt flat's eastern shore, the silky curves of **Sand Mountain** appear ahead and to your left. Nearby are the ruins of **Sand Springs Pony Express Station.**

The station site has been enclosed as a desert study area, where interpretive signs describe the geology, climate, beetles and other bugs of this hostile terrain. Only the rock walls of the pony stop survive. More signs tell you about life during the days of the desert phantoms.

Sand Mountain, a procession of sand dunes right out of *Lawrence of Arabia*, is a favorite weekend playground as dune buggies swarm over it like happy mechanized scarabs. If you choose a quieter time, you can trudge to the top of one of Sand Mountain's razor ridges, listen to the singing sands and admire this fragile wilderness of sensual shapes. Watch in wonder as the desert wind whips up spumes, like waves at play on a granular ocean.

Beyond Sand Mountain, you pass between the **U.S. Naval Electronic Warfare Training Area** and **Area Baker 17** of the U.S. Naval Target Area. You'll see no Top Gun action however; the hotshot Navy pilots practice for their future Desert Storms far from the highway.

If you'd like to go from a lonely highway to a lonelier one, turn south onto State Route 361 and follow it 29 miles to **Gabbs.** It's a company town built in the 1940s at the site of a huge magnesium mine. Although mining is sporadic, the little town survives, with its prim company houses and a few businesses.

East from Gabbs, State Highway 844 takes you up and over 6,947-foot Green Springs Summit in the **Paradise Range,** down into pretty little Ione Valley, then into the ruggedly handsome **Shoshone Mountains.** This a floating alpine island of Toiyabe National Forest and one of four side-by-side ranges dangling southward from U.S. 50. Climbing into the Toiyabe foothills, you encounter a state park with a dual purpose.

Berlin Ichthyosaur State Park

This remote park, in a 7,000-foot pinyon-juniper zone at the end of a four-mile unpaved road, preserves the remnants of Berlin, a turn-of-the-century mining town. It also shelters something a bit older—fossil remains of 225 million-year-old Ichthyosaurs. They were sea-going reptiles (literally "fish lizards") of the early Mesozoic Era. This arid region was at that time an extension of the primeval Pacific Ocean.

Berlin is one of the best-preserved of Nevada's ghost towns, with a goodly collection of wood-frame houses and stores and a large stamp mill. Although gold and silver mining activity in the area dates from the 1860s, the Berlin Mine and its attendant company town wasn't established until 1895. It bustled briefly, supporting about 250 miners and merchants. The Berlin Mine produced more than 40,000 ounces of gold before the vein fizzled out in 1911.

The local ichthyosaurs were undisturbed by all this mining activity. It was erosion, not a miner's pick, that led to their discovery in 1928. It proved to be the largest collection of the largest ichthyosaurs ever found in America. A campground and fossil shelter is a short distance beyond the ghost town. Signs along the way tell you what you're seeing, and more signs in the shelter point out details of the dig, which began in 1954.

Icky was an imposing critter—a 50-foot air-breathing sea-going carnivore with long beak-like jaws lined with needle-sharp teeth. Well suited to his salty element, he survived for 150 million years on a diet of careless fish. Classified as a reptile, he was replaced in the evolutionary scheme of things by toothed whales and dolphins. A life-sized bas relief gives you an idea of the scope of these 50-ton beasts of the briny.

From Berlin, you can follow a long gravel road northeast and eventually hit Highway 50 just west of Austin, or you can retrace your route on Highway 844 and 361. If you choose the gravel, you'll pass through the attractive **Reese River Valley**, flanked by the Shoshone Mountains and the Toiyabe Range. This route takes you through the old gold mining town of **Ione,** interesting because many of its ancient buildings were spruced up during a mining resurgence in the early 1980s.

Assuming you're returned to U.S. 50, you'll pass an assortment of Pony Express and other historic markers as your route weaves among the northern toes of the **Shoshone Mountains**. This wild area of bunchgrass desert, rocky crags, windy passes and distant alpine peaks is so desolate it's beautiful. That *Life Magazine* writer who said there was nothing out here had never driven Highway 50 on a crisp winter day; had never seen the snowcapped peaks and the high, blue windless sky.

Cold Springs, about 40 miles shy of Austin in Edwards Creek Valley, was a busy little hamlet a century ago. It served as a Pony Express, stagecoach and transcontinental telegraph station. You'll see several markers indicating their sites.

Ruins of the Cold Springs Freight and Telegraph Relay Station are on the left side of the highway, protected by a chain-link fence. Just beyond on the right, an interpretive ramada discusses the Cold Springs pony stop; a 1.5 mile trail will take you there. It's worth the hike, since it's one of the largest Pony Express ruins between St. Jo and Sacramento.

From Cold Springs, Highway 50 climbs 6,348 feet over **New Pass Summit** then drops down into the **Reese River Valley**. You begin climbing again, into the steep flanks of the Toiyabe Range. Sitting halfway up the mountain, tucked into Pony Canyon, is one of the most dramatically situated towns in Nevada.

Austin

Population: 450   **Elevation: 6,575 feet**

One wonders why Austin built itself into a steep hillside instead of down in the inviting valley. But then gold and silver love to hide in narrow granite canyons, so men must seek it there.

Cantilevered against the slope, the town presents rather dramatic photo opportunities, particularly with two church spires reaching skyward from surrounding houses and trees. With its weathered brick, stone and wood frame buildings, this is the penultimate rustic Western mining town.

324 — CHAPTER TEN

THE WAY IT WAS • The story goes that William Talcott, a former Pony Express rider working at the Jacobs Springs stage stop, found a silver vein while seeking some stray horses in Pony Canyon in 1862.

Austin soon become one of the busiest and rowdiest mining communities in Nevada. Money flowed so fast and freely that a 50-pound sack of flour was auctioned off for $275,000 in 1864. The funds went to the Sanitary Relief Fund, forerunner of the American Red Cross. Store owner Rueul Gridley had carried the sack, festooned with ribbons, from one end of town to the other as a payoff of an election bet. He decided to auction it off for charity. The free-spending miners kept re-selling it among themselves until they set an all-time record for 50 pounds of flour.

When they weren't selling flour, the miners were lying to one another. They formed the Sazarac Liars Club that met weekly to swap the biggest fibs west of Chicago. The club and its tall tales became fodder for Oscar Lewis's *The Town that Died Laughing*.

More than $50 million in gold and silver was pulled from local mines and Austin's population peaked at 10,000 before the ore ran out in the early 1870s. Shortly after the silver discovery, Austin became the seat of new Lander County, a position it held for more than a century. Then in 1979, county residents voted to move it north to Battle Mountain. Stubborn Austin residents appealed all the way to the Nevada Supreme Court before finally losing in 1980.

THE WAY IT IS • The **Lander County Courthouse** still stands, as one of the town's more substantial buildings. And it's still active, functioning as a governmental annex that serves this part of the huge 5,721 square mile county. It also serves as the local tourist bureau. Visitors can pick up brochures and a historical newsletter from a rack just inside the door.

Like many other central Nevada towns, Austin is enjoying a modest economic boost from renewed mining activities. However, it's not evident from its comfortably worn look. Mostly people are drawn here because it's about as far from anywhere as one can get, located near the state's geographic center. It's 110 miles from Fallon and 70 miles from Eureka.

Approaching Austin from the west, you'll first pass an old-fashioned boot hill, then the highway snakes through the terraced downtown area and switchbacks to the top of 7,484-foot Austin Summit.

Greater Austin offers the predictable collection of stone, brick and wooden false front, with a couple of refueling stops for your vehicle and yourself. The **Gridley Store,** scene of the flour sack episode, survives. Another noted landmark is a skinny, square stack of stone called **Stoke's Castle.** Sitting on a hillside just south of Main Street, it more resembles a low-budget blockhouse than a palace, however. It was built in 1897 by wealthy miner Anson P. Stokes and occupied for only a few months. To reach it, turn south onto Castle Road at the west end of town and drive about half a mile upward.

Continuing up the Highway 50 switchbacks, pause frequently to look back over your shoulder. A couple of turnouts here offer Austin's best views. As you depart, look to your right for the only modern structure in town, the blue metal **Shoshone Turquoise Shop** (964-2641). Shopkeepers mine their own turquoise nearby and fashion it into a nice assortment of baubles. The place also has a mineral exhibit and assorted Indian jewelry.

WHERE TO DINE & SLEEP

Carol's Country Kitchen ● ☺☺ $$ ∅
Main Street; (702) 964-2493. American; dinners $6 to $13; full bar service. Daily 6 a.m. to 9 p.m. in summer; 11 to 8 in winter. Major credit cards. Remarkably cute little cafe all a- clutter with 19th century collectables. Housed in an 1890 storefront, it's a combined cafe and Americana museum. All foods are freshly prepared and the busy menu ranges from inexpensive stews to steaks, chops and fish, plus Mexican and Chinese dishes.

Lincoln Motel ● △ $$
28 Main St., Austin, NV 89310; (702) 964-2698. Doubles $32 to $38, singles $26. Major credit cards. A 17-unit motel in downtown Austin with TV and room phones. Adjacent **International Cafe and Bar** serves from 6 a.m. to 9 p.m.; American fare; dinners $6 to $13; full bar service; housed in one of the oldest hotels in Nevada.

Pony Canyon Motel ● △ $ ∅
P.O. Box 86 (Highway 50, west end), Austin, NV 89310; (702) 964-2605. Major credit cards. A 10-unit motel with TV movies, room phones and a conference room with a refrigerator. Mini- market adjacent.

ANNUAL EVENTS

Gridley Days Fiddlers Contest, mid-June; 964-2200.
Nevada Day and Halloween Celebration, October 31; 964-2200.

AUSTIN TO EUREKA

East of Austin, you cross over a pair of mountain passes, Austin Summit and Scott Summit. The U.S. Forest Service's **Bob Scott Campground** is near the latter, sitting among the pines and junipers, offering RV and tent spaces and flush potties.

This area is in a disconnected swatch of **Toiyabe National Forest**. It's disconnected because the rest of the forest reserve is in the eastern foothills of the Sierra Nevada, more than a hundred miles to the southwest. Most of the other island mountain ranges of north, central and eastern Nevada belong to Humboldt National Forest.

The **Toiyabe** and **Toquima mountain ranges** extend south from here; Toiyabe is an impressive 100-mile-long ridge, much of it more than 10,000 feet high. A Shoshone word, it means either black mountain or big mountain; perhaps big, black mountain. With their thick juniper-pinyon cover, many of these peaks appear to be both in the right light. Paved State Highway 376 will take you south between the Toiyabe and Toquima ranges to Tonopah. Views from this highway are predictably awesome and it's an easy drive, since it runs with the north-south grain of the mountains. The region around 11,775-foot **Arc Dome** was set aside recently as Nevada's largest federal wilderness area, covering 115,000 acres.

Highway 50 east of Austin carries you through 70 miles of this high desert wilderness before it encounters any civilization of any kind—that being Eureka. Not even a ghost town breaks the pattern of loneliness. There is one interesting stop en route, however.

Hickison Petroglyph Recreation Site is just beyond Hickison Summit, preserving a group of 3,000-year-old rock scratchings. Watch for the Bureau of Land Management's sign on the left, about 15 miles beyond Scott

Summit. Less than a mile off the highway, it's an appealing place, with a picnic area and campground tucked among pinyons and rocky ridges. One of these ridges, just north of the parking area, has a few prehistoric etchings. Unfortunately, many have been defaced and over-written with contemporary scrawls. Sadly, to invite public viewing is to invite vandalism. A rock-lined path leads from the base of this 30-foot cliff to another outcropping, where a careful search will reveal a few more geometric writings of the past. The path then ends at a rancher's fence.

As you continue east, the tumbled desert terrain settles a bit, finally smoothing out into **Diamond Valley** as you approach an interesting bit of weathered civilization with a nasty past.

Eureka

Population: 800   **Elevation: 6,481 feet**

A slightly larger version of Austin and equally scruffy, old Eureka occupies a shallow basin, cradled between the Fish Creek and Diamond mountains. It is an unlovely town with an unlovely history, once called the "Pittsburgh of the West" because of its polluting blast furnaces.

Eureka is certainly worth a prowl, since its main drag and twisted side streets are lined with 19th century buildings. The architectural jewel in its thorny crown is the 1879 **Eureka County Courthouse,** perhaps the best-preserved public building in Nevada. The first major lead and silver producing district in America, the area has been declared a national historic landmark. Tailing dumps and blackened slag heaps mark the site of one of Nevada's busiest mining centers.

THE WAY IT WAS • Fanning out from Austin, prospectors found silver veins in this shallow draw in 1864. However, it contained too much lead to be processed profitably. Later, high-temperature blast furnaces were developed to get the lead out. The Eureka boom began in earnest in the early 1870s. It its peak, the town topped 10,000 population, making it briefly the second largest city in Nevada. In 15 years, Eureka mines yielded more than $40 million worth of silver, $20 million in gold and lots of lead.

Unfortunately, this wealth was won at a terrible cost to the environment and to human lives. Eureka apparently was a *very* nasty place. Arsenic and lead fumes from the blast furnaces poisoned the atmosphere, killing wildlife, plants and occasionally people. The furnaces were charcoal-fired and the landscape was stripped of trees for 50 miles around to feed hungry kilns.

The charcoal-makers were mostly impoverished Italian-Swiss immigrants called *carbonari*. Mine owners paid them only 13 cents a bushel for their charcoal, so they formed the Eureka Coalburners Protective Association and demanded an increase. In August, 1879, a sheriff's posse confronted a hundred *carbonari* and opened fire. When the gun smoke cleared, five strikers lay dead and six others were wounded. Murder charges were filed against the posse then later dropped, suggesting who controlled the courts in early-day Eureka. With the strike broken, the price of charcoal fell further and production dwindled to nothing. A fire ravaged downtown, some of the mines were flooded and the last of the smelters shut down in 1891.

THE WAY IT IS • Eureka never quite went to sleep, since it was on the main highway, and it was served by a railroad until 1937. No other town challenged it for the county seat because there *are* no other towns of significance in remote Eureka County. A few mines are working again, bringing tax bonuses to the weathered old town. Some of it was spent on a meticulous renovation of the Eureka County Courthouse, and more is earmarked for restoration of the Opera House in the early 1990s.

The **Eureka Chamber of Commerce** is in the Eureka Sentinel Museum, behind the courthouse at Bateman and Monroe streets. It's open weekdays 11 to 5, Saturdays 10 to 4 and Sundays noon to 4. You can pick up a historic walking tour map that will tell you more than you ever wanted to know about the old town. If the chamber- museum is closed, you can get a map from a rack just inside the courthouse.

THE ATTRACTIONS

Eureka County Courthouse ● *Main and Bateman streets; (702) 237-5262. Weekdays 8 to 5.* Time your Eureka stop for a weekday so you can admire the beautifully refurbished interior of this two-story red brick structure. It's a study in polished woods, wainscoting and ornately carved paneling. The second-floor courtroom is one of the most attractive you'll see anywhere, with globe chandeliers, copper-colored pressed tin ceiling and thick burgundy drapes. Along the spotless hallways, oldstyle hand-lettered signs mark offices where county employees hunch over computer terminals and copy machines amidst yesterday furnishings. Although this isn't a museum, employees will happily answer your questions.

Eureka Sentinel Museum ● *Bateman and Monroe streets; (702) 237-5484. Weekdays 11 to 5, Saturdays 10 to 4 and Sundays noon to 4. Free; contributions appreciated.* This two-story beige brick building housed the *Eureka Centennial*. It was published from 1879 until 1960 by three generations of the Skillman family. A museum with typical pioneer relics and historic exhibits occupies the front portion, along with the Chamber of Commerce. Exhibits are done in an interesting "read all about it" newspaper style. The still-intact if somewhat dusty newspaper office is the back of the building. Visitors can prowl among Linotype machines, type cases and old presses.

A NUGGET

Eureka Opera House ● *Main and Bateman streets.* This red brick false-front structure may be refurbished as a new convention center by the time you read this. Or it may be as we left it, as the unused Eureka Theatre. It was built in 1880, intended to be a union hall. However, the union went on strike and ran out of money. The town took over its construction, converting it to an opera house and community center. In 1913, it became the Eureka Theatre, showing silent films and then talkies until 1958.

WHERE TO DINE

Owl Club & Steak House ● ☺ **$$**

10231 Main St., Eureka; (702) 237-5280. American; dinners $6.50 to $13; full bar service. Daily 5 a.m. to 9 p.m. No credit cards. Steaks, chops and chicken served in an 18th century structure. Adjacent saloon features a 150-year-old bar, a few slots and a blackjack table or two.

WHERE TO SLEEP

Jackson House ● △ **$$**

10209 Main St., Eureka, NV 89316; (702) 237-5518. Doubles $34.54, singles $30.24. Basic accommodations at the head of a creaking stairway in an

1877 hotel. The downstairs area is scruffily interesting, with a brass-railed bar, rough barnboard walls, candelabra chandeliers and a **restaurant** which may or may not be open.

Parsonage House • ⌒⌒ $$$
Spring and Bateman streets (P.O. Box 99), Eureka, NV 89316; (702) 237-5756. Doubles or singles $50, including continental breakfast; no credit cards. Complete kitchen unit with separate bedroom, two queen beds, TV and room phones, built into old Victorian cottage.

Ruby Hill Motel • ⌒ $$
10326 Main St., Eureka, NV 89316; (702) 327-5339. Doubles $38 in summer and $27.70 in winter, singles $27.70 in summer and $23.95 in winter. No credit cards. A basic 11-unit motel with in-room TV and not much else.

ANNUAL EVENT
Eureka County Fair, second weekend of August; (702) 237-5326.

EUREKA TO ELY

East of Eureka, Highway 50 lives up to its high lonesome billing. You see not a shred of civilization as it hurries across desert basins and climbs four mountain passes—**Pinto, Pancake, Little Antelope** and **Robinson**. Your elongated roller-coaster ride carries you from sage to pinyon-juniper woodlands and back to sage. The trees on Pinto Summit are second growth since the original stand fell victim to the *carbonari* axes.

About five miles east of Pinto Summit, graveled State Route 20 leads south to **Fish Creek,** scene of the bloody posse attack on the carbon-makers. Only a few scattered pieces of charcoal and some charcoal pits remain to mark the area, so it's really not worth the dusty drive.

Robinson is the highest pass along the route, topping out at 7,588 feet. From there, perhaps feeling like astronauts of the 1960s, you drop down onto a moonscape.

Ruth mining district

Decades of mining activity have torn the earth asunder around the small town of **Ruth** and it continues today. This is copper country, the richest operation of its type in Nevada. Decades of open pit mining have left a badlands of green, yellow and rust slag heaps, mining terraces, tailing dumps and open pits that rival craters on the moon. Some of the tailings are being re- worked to sift out gold and silver overlooked by earlier copper smelting operations.

Two of the world's largest open mines, the **Liberty** and **Copper Pit,** are in this area, and visitors are allowed on the rim of the latter. To explore this huge mining district, turn south off Highway 50 just short of Ely, following signs to Ruth. Built early in this century as a company town, this nondescript scatter of frame houses sits among mining terraces and tailing dumps like a low budget moon colony. A general store and pair of saloons comprise the business district.

Continue through town on Main Street, following it into this netherworld of mine tailings. Above the town, the road becomes hardpack dirt and fragments of old asphalt, easily navigable by the family sedan. Within a mile or two, it blends to the right onto a newer asphalt road which takes you through the **Magma Nevada Mining Company** operation.

Watching carefully for monster trucks, follow "mine overlook" signs to the brink of Copper Pit, one of the larger of America's manmade holes. The gaping pip spirals hundreds of feet into the earth, exposing wounds of green and yellow. One corner of the cavity was being worked when we visited. From our vantage point, the giant trucks looked like Tonka toys.

Slag heaps of contorted earth extend in every direction from the rim of Copper Pit. The area is practically treeless, like the no man's land of a battlefield. The distant ridge of the White Pine Mountains mark the eastern horizon, looking pristine and aloof from all this. It's particularly striking with a dusting of winter snow.

NOTE: Heed all signs carefully as you drive through this area! You wouldn't want to confront an ore truck whose tires probably outweigh your Belchfire Six.

The paved road that took you through the Magma mining complex will return you to Highway 50. From there, it's a short drive through Robinson Canyon to the hillside town that was born of all this earthly destruction.

Ely

Elevation: 6,431 feet **Population: 6,000**

A sturdy blue collar town of sturdy red brick and masonry, Ely isn't thriving as it was a century ago, but it certainly is surviving. Although mining activity has slumped, the town has become a destination of sorts: home to an important railway museum and gateway to the new Great Basin National Park.

Three major highways converge here, creating confusion for newcomers and a modest boon for hotel and restaurant owners. If you're traveling anywhere in east central Nevada, it's hard *not* to pass through Ely. There is, of course, Highway 50, stretching for 3,000 miles from Sacramento to Washington. Highway 6 angles in from the southwest and U.S. 93 intersects Highway 50 on its long journey from the Mexican to the Canadian border. The three highways are stacked atop one another on Seventh Street as they travel through Ely.

THE WAY IT WAS ● Ely was slow a-birthing. For decades, prospectors knew the copper was here. However, neither the technology nor the money was available to profitably pull in from the ground.

The Pony Express and transcontinental telegraph passed far to the north, dodging the Schell Creek Mountains that form a barrier to Ely's eastern flank. Silver was found in the area and a settlement was established in 1868 to accommodate thousands of hopefuls. The strike didn't amount to much and early Ely plugged along, supported by small gold and silver mines and a ranch or two.

White Pine County was chipped from huge Lander County in 1869, with the mining community of Hamilton as its seat. Then Hamilton went bust and, adding injury to insult, the courthouse burned in 1885. Ely still wasn't much, but it was the only town in the game, so it got the county seat in 1887.

Two young drifters with only 75 cents between them seemed unlikely candidates to start Ely's wheel of fortunes. However, in September of 1900, Edwin Gray and David Bartley convinced locals that they were wealthy entrepreneurs and started picking up mining options around present-day Ruth.

ELY

DIRECTORY
1. Bristlecone Convention Center (Bristlecone Pine Exhibit)
2. Copper Queen Casino
3. Ely City Park
4. Hotel Nevada and Jailhouse Casinos
5. Nevada Northern Railway Museum
6. Red Light District
7. White Pine Chamber of Commerce
8. White Pine County Courthouse
9. White Pine Public Museum

Working the claim for two years, they found a good pocket of copper, but they lacked the funds and skills to mine it profitably.

Finally, a *real* entrepreneur came along. Mark Requa, son of a Comstock millionaire, started the White Pine Copper Company, buying up the Gray and Bartley claims. Then, in a case of big fish being swallowed by bigger fish, the Nevada Consolidated Copper Company arrived in 1906. The powerful firm bought out Requa and started investing the millions of dollars necessary for a serious mining operation. Finally, giant Kennecott Copper Company took over in 1933.

U.S. 50 CORRIDOR — 331

Environmental regulations and declining copper deposits finally closed the venture in 1979. But if the investors cried, they did it on the way to the bank. Nevada's longest-lived and richest mining operation yielded one *billion* dollars.

While the investors left town to seek solace in their penthouses, Ely hit the predictable skids. Population, which had peaked at 12,000, dwindled to nearly half. White Pine County struggled along with one-fourth of its work force out of work.

THE WAY IT IS • Determined to survive the loss of their mining industry, Ely officials looked to tourism for salvation.

They became eager participants in the Highway 50 promotion, and they convinced Kennecott to donate facilities of its Nevada Northern Railway to the community as a tourist lure. Opened to the public in 1987, the main railyard of this ore-hauling short line has become eastern Nevada's most-visited living museum. The recent expansion of Lehman Caves National Monument into Great Basin National Park draws additional visitors to the area.

Despite its nest of highways, Ely is reasonably easy to navigate if you remain semi-alert. Highway 50 becomes Aultman Street as it approaches the community. The brick-front **Chamber of Commerce** is on the left at 636 Aultman, near Sixth in the heart of downtown; hours are 9 to 5 weekdays.

After clearing the business district, Aultman curves slightly, and you'll see the **White Pine Public Museum** in a white cinderblock building on the left (at Ogden Avenue). Beyond Seventh Street, Aultman becomes Avenue F. Turning left from F onto Eleventh Street delivers you to the **Nevada Northern Railway Museum.**

You will note on the accompanying map that Ely has two sets of numbered streets that seem to repeat themselves. As we said, you have to remain at least semi-alert.

Back at the intersection of Aultman and Seventh, a turn southeast puts you onto eastbound U.S. 50, along with highways 93 and 6. They all come together here before going their separate ways. East of Ely, this bundle becomes the Pioche Highway.

Should you be curious (and you probably shouldn't, even though it's been a long, lonely drive), the town's **red light district** is on the western edge, a block from Aultman at Second and High streets. The Stardust Ranch, Green Lantern and Big Four are clustered here. A young lady wearing a warm smile and little else beckoned from the Stardust's doorway as I drove past on a chilly evening. I declined to stop, needing to check out attractions of another sort.

THE ATTRACTIONS

Nevada Northern Railway Museum • *Avenue A at 11th Street East; (702) 289-2085. Railyard tour $2, steam train and diesel train rides $8 to $12, less for kids and seniors. Open daily 9 to 4. Tours and train rides from May through October and on some holiday weekends. MC/VISA.* The neatest thing about this museum is that it isn't one. It's a fully-intact early 20th century railroad complex that happens to be open to visitors.

Forty-five minute tours, conducted hourly, take tourists through giant maintenance sheds big enough to hold the Graf Zeppelin, past water towers, freight and passenger depots and into the roundhouse. During the off-season, you can wander about on your own. The huge railyard, covering dozens of acres, offers a treasure trove for train buffs. Become acquainted with a black Baldwin steam locomotive so big that it's almost intimidating. Then check out a snowplow train, flat cars, freight cars, tanker cars, passenger cars, a yellow diesel locomotive and a couple of cabeese. The complex also includes the handsome East Ely Passenger Station, a freight station and the Rail Place gift shop specializing in railroading memorabilia and folk crafts.

An assortment of train rides is offered summer. You can take the 1910 Baldwin steamer, the "Ghost Train of Old Ely," on a 14-mile round trip into the Keystone mining district. Or, catch the Highliner, an Alco RS-3 diesel ore hauler that takes you on its original route to an old smelter. Nevada Northern Railway was established in 1906 by Nevada Consolidated Copper to haul ore to Ely from mines at Cobre and Copper Flat. Taken over in the Kennecott buy-out, it also ran passenger service and even carried workers' kids to Ely High School until 1941.

White Pine Public Museum • *2000 Aultman St.; (702) 289-4710. Weekdays 9 to 4:30 and weekends 10 to 4. Free; donations appreciated.* More of Nevada Northern's rolling stock is parked outside the county museum, notably a big black Baldwin steam locomotive. Inside, several rooms are a-clutter with old saddles, Shoshone projectile points, china, silver, farm equipment, stuffed critters, early-day photos and a large doll collection. The closest thing to a disciplined display is an interesting exhibit about the use of lamps in history, from miner's headlamps to police lanterns.

Bristlecone pine exhibit • *Bristlecone Convention Center, 150 Sixth St. (near the Chamber of Commerce); (702) 289-3720.* A cross-section of a 4,900-year-old bristlecone pine cut down in 1964 is on display in Ely's convention center. It apparently was the world's oldest living thing when it fell to the ax. Rings are marked with historic events paralleling the tree's life, from Egyptian pyramid construction to the 20th century.

THE CASINOS

Copper Queen • ☺☺
Seventh at Avenue I; (702) 289-4884. This is a stylish little place, with wood paneling, brick columns and an indoor pool and spa at one end. Hotel rooms are off second-floor balconies, giving guests an aerial view of the action. The casino offers ranks of slots but no gaming tables. **Evah's Copper Kitchen**, across the street from the Queen, is done in cheery rural Americana with white bentwood chairs and Casablanca fans, serving from 6 a.m. to 9 p.m.; dinners $8 to $17; major credit cards.

Hotel Nevada • ☺
501 Aultman St.; (702) 289-6665. It's the town's requisite old-timey casino, housed in a 1908 hotel. Towering six stories, it's the tallest building between Ely and Carson City. The gaming room is predictably rustic, offering slots, blackjack and hotel rooms. The **restaurant** serves inexpensive American fare, $6.50 to $12; open 24 hours; MC/VISA, DISC.

Jailhouse Casino • ☺
540 Aultman St.; (702) 289-3033. This is an attractive oldstyle place with brick interior walls and globe chandeliers. It has motel rooms, lots of slots and a bit of blackjack. The **Jailhouse Restaurant** is open 6 a.m. to 10 p.m., specializing in prime rib and other American grub; $6.50 to $14.

WHERE ELSE TO DINE

Senoritas Restaurant • ☺ $ ∅

489 Aultman (at Fifth); (702) 289-8262. Mexican; dinners $6 to $13; full bar service. Daily 5 to 9:30 p.m. MC/VISA, AMEX. Family-style restaurant focusing on fajitas and tamales.

Silver State Restaurant • ☺☺ $$

1204 Aultman (Twelfth); (702) 289-2712. American-Mexican; dinners $6 to $13; no alcohol but it can be brought in. Daily 6 a.m. to 9 p.m. No credit cards. Cute country-style restaurant with vinyl booths, print wallpaper, hunting trophies and a wall filled with glossy, wonderfully tacky decorative clocks. Locally popular, featuring chicken, chops and steaks plus several Mexican *combinaciòns*.

WHERE TO SLEEP

Best Western Main Motel • ⌂⌂ $$ ∅

1101 Aultman St., Ely, NV 89301; (800) 528-1234 or (702) 289-4529. Doubles $38 to $52, singles $33 to $46, suites $48 to $65. Major credit cards. Well-maintained 19-unit motel with TV movies, room phones and some room refrigerators. Non-smoking units.

Bristlecone Motel • ⌂ ∅

700 Avenue I Ely, NV 89301; (702) 289-8838. Doubles $36 to $40, singles $30 to $34. Major credit cards. A 31-unit motel near downtown with TV, room phones and refrigerators.

Copper Queen • ⌂⌂⌂ $$$ ∅

701 Avenue I, Ely, NV 89301; (702) 289-4884. Doubles $43 to $62, singles $39 to $50. Major credit cards. A particularly appealing 64-unit casino hotel with TV, room phones. Some rooms off second-floor balconies overlooking the casino. Swimming pool, spa, cocktail lounges and restaurant (listed above). Non-smoking rooms.

Fireside Inn • ⌂⌂ $$

McGill Highway (three miles north on U.S. 93), SR 1, Box 2, Ely, NV 89301; (702) 289-3765. Doubles $38, singles $31. MC/VISA, AMEX. Attractive, inexpensive 15-unit motel with TV, room phones. Small casino and **restaurant** serving American and Italian fare; dinners $7 to $12; daily 5 p.m. to 10 p.m. (11 on Saturdays); full bar service.

Grand Central Motel • ⌂ ∅

1498 Lyons Ave., Ely, NV 89301; (702) 289-6868. Doubles $28 to $30, singles $26 to $28. MC/VISA, DISC. Basic lodging in a 13-unit motel with TV, room phones and some room refrigerators.

Jailhouse Motel & Casino • ⌂⌂ $$

540 Aultman St., Ely, NV 89301; (702) 289-3033. Doubles $45 to $51, singles $39 to $43. Major credit cards. A 47-unit motel adjacent to casino with TV and room phones.

Bed & breakfast inn

Steptoe Valley Inn • ⌂⌂⌂ $$$ ∅∅

P.O. Box 151110 (220 E. 11th St), East Ely, NV 89315; (702) 289-8687. Five rooms, all with private baths. Full breakfast. Doubles $69 to $75, singles

334 — CHAPTER TEN

$58. MC/VISA, AMEX. Appealing B&B housed in a 1907 grocery store; rebuilt in 1990, with the old market's façade still intact. Rooms named for local pioneers; furnishings range from early American to "modern country cottage." Rather elegant Victorian library and dining room.

WHERE TO CAMP

KOA of Ely • *Pioche Highway (SR 5, Box 3), Ely, NV 89301; (702) 289-3413. RV and tent sites; rates $14.50 to $18.50. MC/VISA.* Well-maintained RV park with mostly pull-throughs; store, laundry, showers, gasoline and diesel, Propane, volleyball and horseshoe pits and playground.

ANNUAL EVENTS

Railfair, Memorial Day weekend; (702) 289-2085.
White Pine Rodeo, first weekend of June; (702) 289-8513.
White Pine Basque Festival, late July; (702) 289-8586.
Ely's Pony Express Days, late August; (702) 289-8877.
White Pine County Fair, fourth weekend of August; (702) 289-8877.

ELY TO GREAT BASIN NATIONAL PARK

As you begin your final leg of Nevada's segment of Highway 50, take time to check out a couple of interesting features before continuing to Great Basin National Park. Five miles east of Ely, watch for a sign indicating "Cave Valley Road and Ward Mining District." Gravel but easily navigable, it takes you 11 miles across a desert basin to one of the more curious leftovers from the early mining days.

Ward Charcoal Ovens State Historic Monument • *Off Cave Valley road; free.* If the terrain around Ruth seems outerworldly, then the six Ward charcoal ovens might have been dwellings for space aliens. They're huge cones of fitted rough stone, 30 feet high and 27 feet in diameter. You almost expect Yoda to come waddling out of one of them, mumbling to himself. In late light, you can imagine that they're six giant gnomes, huddled together. We talked earlier of the *carbonari* who produced charcoal for the Eureka smelters. They used crude pits, but developers of the early mining town of Ward went a step further, constructing these striking conical towers to convert wood into charcoal.

The town of Eureka, up in the foothills, has long since vanished. However, the sturdy cones are virtually intact, and could be fired up tomorrow should the need for charcoal arise. You'll also discover, as you explore inside and stare up at the smoke hole in the roof, that they make ideal echo chambers. Overnight camping is permitted here, although there are no facilities.

You have choices as you leave the coneheads. You can retrace your route to Highway 50, continue east briefly, then turn north into **Cave Lake State Park.** Or you can retreat about a mile from the kilns, turn right onto another gravel road and pick up Highway 50 farther down the line.

Cave Lake is a striking little jewel, tucked high into the flanks of the Schell Creek Range. Even if you aren't camping or fishing, take time to enjoy this 7,300-foot alpine setting and perhaps follow an interpretive trail through the pinyon-juniper forest. Campsites, complete with flush potties and hot showers, are $5 per night.

Back on Highway 50, you begin a long, straight and subtle climb toward Conners Pass in the Schell Creek Range. The terrain begins shedding sage-

The 30-foot-high Ward Charcoal Ovens near Ely resemble giant beehives.

brush and bunchgrass in favor of pinyons and juniper. As you top the pass, one of Nevada's best known peaks looms into view, like a lost continent of Atlantis emerging from the desert basin of Spring Valley.

Snowcapped **Wheeler Peak,** looking a bit like a blunted Matterhorn, reaches 13,061 feet skyward from the Snake Range. It's the centerpiece of Great Basin National Park which, you will soon discover, is more mountain than basin. At a Y-junction called **Major's Place,** Highway 93 spins off to the south, leaving you with 50 and 6.

Passing through Spring Valley, the route swings sharply north to avoid the barrier of the Snake Range. An historical marker invites you to explore the remnants of **Oceola,** a few miles up a bumpy gravel road; it's a gold camp that was established in 1872. Today's visitor will see only rusting machinery and a couple of headframes. From the Oceola marker, Highway 50 carries you over 7,154-foot **Sacramento Pass** and into **Snake Valley.** Shortly, a sign at a fork in the highway invites you to turn right onto State Route 487 to Baker and Great Basin National Park.

A small scatter on the eastern foothills of the Snake Range, **Baker** functions as the gateway to the park. Only recently elevated from its status as Lehman Caves National Monument, Great Basin receives few overnight visitors. Thus Baker has developed none of the peripheral services found outside most park gates. A motel and a couple of restaurants and saloons—not always open—constitute the scruffy, tree-shaded hamlet's commercial offerings. The **Silverjack Motel** (324-7323) has doubles from $32 to $35 and it accepts MC/VISA. For grub, there's the **Outlaw Restaurant**, serving basic American grub from $6 to $13. The Western-style joint is open daily from 10 a.m. to midnight and it takes MC/VISA.

Great Basin National Park

State Highway 488 draws you arrow-straight from Baker toward the inviting, overlapping pyramids of the **Snake Range**. One of the newest of America's national parks, Great Basin offers a stunning ecological slice of this part of the world. Mostly vertical, the 77,000-acre park reaches 8,000 feet from a high desert basin to the second highest peak in Nevada. It covers all of the Great Basin's five climate zones.

One of America's most complex limestone caverns, a rare bristlecone pine forest, Nevada's only active glacial basins and the awesome beauty of subarctic granite await the visitor. Most of the park's features—even the top of Wheeler Peak—can be reached by non-technical day hikes. The highest paved road in Nevada takes visitors up to 10,000 feet and hiking trails cover the rest. The visitor center is just inside the boundary, in a pinyon-juniper zone where the alluvial foothills begin rumpling into the mountains.

Park essentials • *Visitor center open daily from 9 to 5 (longer hours in summer when candlelight tours are scheduled). Ninety-minute Lehman Cave tours conducted hourly during the summer and on the half hour summer weekends. The rest of the year, they begin at 9, 11, 2 and 4. Group size is limited to 30 and you may have to wait a bit in summer, so make your reservation as soon as you reach the park. Tour prices $3 for adults, $2 for kids 6 to 15 and $1.50 for Golden Age and Golden Access passport holders. Spelunking trips $6.*

Lehman Caves Gifts and Cafe, 8 to 5 in summer, comprises the park's total commercial facilities. The park has three **campgrounds**: Lower Lehman Creek, Upper Lehman and Wheeler Peak. Lehamn sites have running water, no hookups at $5 per night. Wheeler Peak Campground, with pit potties and no running water, is free, and it offers spectacular views of the countryside. Lower Lehman, easily reached by RVs, is open the year around; the others are closed by winter snow. For general information, contact : **Great Basin National Park**, Baker, NV 89311; (702) 234-*7331*.

In addition to the regular cave tours, 45-minute historical candlelight tours are scheduled daily at 6 p.m. in the summer. Three-hour spelunking trips begin Saturday and Sunday at 1:30; they require advance reservations. The candlelight tours are particularly inviting. Rangers sometimes assume the character and garb of late 19th century guides, who took people through the cave when it was still in private hands. Candle lights in tin cans add an atmosphere of ghostly authenticity to the outing.

Caves of wondrous beauty

Among other summer ranger activities are bristlecone pine walks that depart Wheeler Peak Campground trailhead daily at 9 a.m., patio talks at the visitor center, and evening campfire programs.

We've visited virtually all of the western America's major caverns and have found few as beautifully complex as Lehman Caves. The subterranean wonderland tour begins in the Gothic Room, bristling with thousands of stalactites, stalagmites and other things limestone. Images of a cobweb-cloaked attic in a Transylvanian mansion occur, or perhaps a scene from a subterranean *Phantom of the Opera*.

After the cave's discovery in 1885 by rancher Absalom Lehman, he and other guides *did* bong out melodies on the stalactites. They obviously weren't terribly concerned about protecting this underground wonderland. A newspaper article reported: *"Abe Lehman of Snake Valley reports he and others have struck a cave of wondrous beauty. The cave was explored for about 200 feet when the points of the stalactites and stalagmites came so close together as to offer a bar to their further progress. They will again explore the cave armed with sledgehammers to break their way into what appears to be onother (sic) chamber."*

Fortunately, today's park service guides enforce a look but don't touch policy. Ideal conditions, the perfect balance of carbon dioxide, oxygen and seeping water, have created an amazing variety of structures here. You'll see columns, draperies, bacon, argonites and helictites, soda straws and the rare shield formation, resembling a large discus with tentacles. Lustrous, marbled flowstone forms a wall along a narrow corridor, like the shelf of a subterranean reef. In other rooms, "cave popcorn" clings to stalactites, stalagmites and columns, creating a *Fantasia* forest.

"I like to think," said our guide, "that after we've locked the entry doors at night, the formations come alive and begin singing and dancing."

Since the park was established, visitors are discovering that there is much more to this area than the limestone caves. The 10,000-foot-high park road gives visitors a head-start into the high country. Assorted hiking trails branch into the wilds, taking the foot-loose set into a rare bristlecone pine forest and to the top of the peak itself.

Bristlecones, probably the world's oldest living things, are surprisingly accessible here. A hike of less than two miles from Wheeler Peak Campground delivers you to one of three groves in the park.

Looking like gnarled *bonsai*, bristlecones grow near the treeline, clinging tenaciously to life in a rocky, cold, wind-whipped environment. It is this mean circumstance that allows them to live so long, according to experts. Since they're one of the few plants able to survive here, they have this subarctic climate zone to themselves. Thus, they're not crowded by botanical competitors. Their thick, dense bark resists insects and their thin, scattered ranks discourage forest fires.

How old is old if you're a bristlecone? A specimen from the White Mountains of California is thought to be the world's most ancient living thing, with an estimated age of 4,600 years. That takes it back beyond the pyramids, *twice* as far back as the oldest California redwood.

We mentioned earlier that there is more mountain than basin to Great Basin National Park. This is a concession to local ranchers and mining interests, who opposed a large desert preserve, fearing the loss of their lands. To keep everyone happy, the proposed park borders were shrunk from a planned 174,000 acres to 77,000. The shrink-back excluded most of the basin; it included only national forest land and the Wheeler Peak Wilderness Area. After decades of efforts by conservationists, Great Basin was established in 1986 as the 49th of America's natonal parks.

Baker Village Archeological Site

Brigham Young University and the Ely office of the Bureau of Land Management began excavating an archeological site just north of the town of Baker in 1990. At this writing, they may be offering tours of the site, which consists of several pit houses. Clues thus far suggest that this Baker Village site was occupied around 1050 A.D. by a group called the Frèmont people, hunter-gatherers who roamed much of the Great Basin. To learn if tours are being conducted, contact: **Bureau of Land Management,** Ely District Office, HC 33, Box 150, Ely, NV 89301; (702) 289-4865.

If you continue east on Highway 50 from Great Basin National Park, you'll soon arrive in Utah. Perhaps in keeping with its "Loneliest road in America" role, Highway 50's departure from Nevada is marked only by a small complex called the **Border Inn.** Westbound travelers can legally pull their first slot machine handles here; the small saloon has no other gaming devices. The inn offers modest motel rooms for $27 and a family-style cafe serves grub from 6 a.m. to 10 p.m.

If the state boundary signs are accurately placed here, one eats, drinks and gambles in Nevada, then gets gas and sleep in Utah. That does seem appropriate.

SOUTH TO LINCOLN COUNTY

One of the Nevada's most remarkable geological formations, Cathedral Gorge, is about 100 miles below our present locale. It's between the tough old mining town of Pioche and the hot springs area of Caliente, in remote Lincoln County. To explore this intriguing area—and perhaps turn your Highway 50 escapade into a loop trip—head south from Major's Place on U.S. 93, appropriately called the Great Basin Highway.

This another lonesome highway, with nary a service station between Majors and Pioche, 81 miles south, so prepare your car accordingly. You'll skim over the toes of the Eagan Range to the west and the Snake and Wilson Creek mountains to the east. It's a pleasantly scenic route, rising and falling between between bunchgrass desert and pinyon pines.

Pioche

Population: approximately 400   Elevation: 6,060 feet

An appealing scatter of an old mining town, Pioche is tucked among tailing dumps and abandoned headframes in a steep slope of the Highland Mountains. Its business district, a mix of false fronts and brick fronts just off Highway 93, tilts sharply uphill. Informational signs tacked to every building of historic significance will help your exploration.

Pioche's history is typical for a rowdy Nevada mining camp. Silver ore was discovered in 1869 and a town soon bloomed atop the tailing dumps. Named for a San Francisco banker who financed the first mines, Pioche soon gained dubious fame as one of the wildest of Nevada's early towns. Historians say nearly 50 men died from violence before anyone got around to expiring from natural causes. Several perished in 1871 when a powder dump exploded, destroying most of the town.

After the blast, Pioche was rebuilt and boasted a population of more than 10,000 at its peak. The predictable decline followed, and it was little more than a ramshackle ghost town for decades. It enjoyed a brief resurgence during World War II when some of the mines were re-opened for their manganese and tungsten. Tourism, a dab of mining and area ranching keep the town barely alive these days.

To see Pioche's lures, take the first turnoff, Highway 320, about three miles north. The route carries you past the red brick **Million Dollar Courthouse** and **Masonic Hall,** then blends into the tilt-up Main Street, passing assorted other 19th century structures. The **Lincoln County Museum** occupies one of Main Street's store fronts. A few doors higher up is **Commerce Cottage,** a little green clapboard information center operated by the Chamber of Commerce. It's open Monday-Saturday 11 to 3 in summer. Hours are shorter and sometimes non-existent the rest of the year.

Continue up Main Street, then swing left above the business district, following a Highway 93 sign. Just below the crest of a hill, you'll see the weathered wooden **Pioche Tram** station on your left. Its rusting steel cables, with tram buckets still dangling, lead over a ridge and down to the valley below.

Now, retrace your route down Main Street and follow it to the right past the tough old **Overton Saloon,** the weathered **Gem Theatre** (still showing movies), the **Opera House** and **Pioche School**. You'll shortly encounter the glistening white Art Deco **Lincoln County Courthouse,** completed in 1938 to replace the brick financial debacle. Parked nearby is "Old Faithful," narrow gauge steam locomotive #279. Built before the turn of the century, it hauled ore and other essentials until 1927. From here, you can pick up Highway 93 and continue your southward jaunt.

THE ATTRACTIONS

Lincoln County Museum • *Main Street; (702) 962-5207. Monday-Saturday 10 to 4, Sunday 1 to 5, shorter hours in the off-season. Free; donations appreciated.* This busy place is a typical small-town museum and then some. You can consume an hour or so studying its eclectic clutter of bottles, mantle clocks, an old printing press and Victrola talking machine, historic photos, mining equipment and minerals, pioneer relics and gawd knows what else. It's neither professional nor organized, although it certainly offers a remarkable assortment of yesterday memories. The hundreds of items fill cases, walls and corridors of two large rooms.

The Million Dollar Courthouse • *Lacour Street. Open April through October, Sunday-Thursday 10 to 5 and Saturday 9 to 5.* The name of Lincoln County's original courthouse does not reflect its luxury. It is rather a commentary on the financial debacle of its construction. Completed in 1871, it was supposed to have cost $16,000, but overruns and skimming by county officials ballooned the price to $26,000. With no funds to cover the overage, the county issued junk bonds. However, it had no funds to pay either the interest or principle. The debt increased to $400,000 by 1890, more than two-thirds of the county's assessed valuation. Officials wanted to default but the state wouldn't let them. When the bonds were finally paid off in 1938, the debt had exceeded a million dollars. By that time, the aging structure had been condemned, replaced by the new Art Deco courthouse. Visitors, escorted by volunteer docents, will see historical exhibits and assorted county offices, the sheriff's department and courtroom, furnished to the period. A grim, dungeon-like jail is out back.

Pioche Tramway • *Upper Main Street.* This rusting, weather-blackened structure is one of Nevada's more interesting mining relics. It's actually a latter-day creation, built by Pioche Mine Company in 1923 to carry ore from Treasure Hill Mine to Godbe's Mill in the valley below. Since gravity did most of the work, pulling full buckets downhill while pushing the empties up, only a five horsepower motor was needed to set the contraption in motion. At the base of the sagging tram house, you'll see the complex set of gears that made the thing work. When the operation closed in the late 1930s, the crew simply shut off the little motor, walked away and left everything exactly as you see it today—with the added corrosion of 50 years.

Incidentally, as you depart Pioche on U.S. 93, you'll drive right under the bucket line. Smokestacks and ruin walls of the old smelter are just east of the highway.

WHERE TO DINE

Silver Cafe • ☺ $

Main Street (opposite Overton Hotel & Bar); (702) 962-5124. American and Mexican; dinners $5 to $12. Daily 7 a.m. to 8 p.m. No credit cards. Basic family-style cafe with counter and a few booths, offering a choice of chicken, chops and steaks or Mexican smashed beans and rice. It's not fancy, but portions are ample and the folks are friendly.

Uptown Deli • ☺ $

Main Street (opposite the museum); (702) 962-5811. Deli fare; meals $3 to 5; no alcohol. Monday-Thursday 10 to 6, Friday- Saturday 10 to 7, closed Sunday. No credit cards. Simple soup and sandwich joint with a couple of tables. It's a good place to build a picnic lunch for your upcoming visit to Cathedral Gorge State Park or Rainbow Canyon.

WHERE TO CAMP

Lincoln County RV Park, Pioche • *Several RV slots available free, just behind the Lincoln County Courthouse.* Water and garbage receptacles; no hookups. Seven-day limit.

If you're in a fishing mood or you happen to have a boat in tow, you might check out a couple of state parks in the area, both off State Highway 322 east of Pioche. **Echo Canyon** encloses a mile- high wilderness hiking area, a campground and a reservoir stocked with trout and crappies. Another stocked reservoir is at **Spring Valley State Park,** sitting at the base of Government Peak at the end of the highway.

Continuing south from Pioche on the Great Basin Highway, you lose altitude quickly, dropping from a pinyon-juniper zone and back into the sagebrush desert. After ten miles, you'll encounter a remarkable geological formation, visible to your right from the highway. This gorgeous gorge might occupy you for the better part of a day if you're in a hiking mood. The first turnoff takes you to a viewpoint; the second into the main park.

Cathedral Gorge State Park

Park Essentials • *Picnicking and hiking $1, No fee for "just looking." Camping $2; shaded sites with water, barbecues and picnic tables, flush potties in summer, pit toilets in winter; no hookups.*

Although the name suggests a watercourse weaving through a narrow chasm, Cathedral Gorge is not that at all. It's rather shallow and wide, with walls only a few hundred feet high. They have eroded into a stunning display of fluted cliffs and serpentine gullies, like a scene from *Dune*. This may be the most amazing example of erosion you'll see anywhere— with tens of thousands of overlapping spires, pinnacles, columns and fins.

If you take the first park turnoff from Highway 93, you'll arrive at **Miller's Point;** the sign is very small, so watch for it. Here, you'll find picnic tables, pit potties and an awesome view. You're looking down into Meadow Valley Wash, which leads into the main chasm. From the gazebo viewpoint, it resembles a cross between South Dakota's Badlands and a mini-Grand Canyon.

The main park entrance is just under two miles south. The road here skims the base of wonderfully eroded and stratified cliffs and ends at a picnic area among the pinnacles. From here, a trail leads toward the canyon then branches in two direction. Hike half a mile to the right and you'll climb a narrow ravine and some wooden steps up to Miller's Point. The left fork takes you on a four-mile round trip into the main chasm, ending at a campground. It's an easy trek across the level floor of the valley. You'll want to branch off frequently to explore the base of the cliffs.

Before leaving the picnic area, take time to squirm through **Moon Caves** and **Canyon Caves**, serpentine slots that penetrate a hundred or more feet into the cliff faces. These amazing erosion channels are just a cou-

— Don W. Martin

Erosion and wind have created an outer-space landscape at Cathedral Gorge State Park on Nevada's eastern edge.

ple of feet wide in places, rising straight-away to the cliff tops, more than a hundred feet above your head. They're so narrow in spots you'll have to shed your fanny pack to get through. If you had an extra pork chop for dinner last night, don't even try.

As you explore Cathedral Gorge, similes start flitting through your mind's eye: an upside down and inside out limestone cavern, the undersea castle in *The Little Mermaid,* weathered Greek statues still on their pedestals, *Fantasia* temples, armies of petrified gnomes, a thousand praying hands, a coral reef—drained and left to dry in the sun.

Some of the formations are free-standing, only a few feet high. You can have someone take your picture beside your own personal pinnacle. The area is best seen and photographed in early morning and middle to late afternoon, since the slanting sun accents the ribbed shapes. When we visited, we hung around until sunset, watching the shadows intensify as they crept up the canyon walls.

How it came to be: A million years ago, this area was a valley rimmed by the same mountains you see today. Then the climate turned wet and a huge lake filled the valley floor. During a millennia of rainstorms, fine silt and sand washed down from the mountains, depositing a layer of mud 1,400 feet deep. When the present arid climate evolved a few hundred centuries ago, the lake dried up and seasonal rains began creating the complex maze of rills, gullies and other watercourses. The superfine silt, easily dissolved, is gradually being flushed into Lake Mead, a hundred miles south.

342 — CHAPTER TEN

Half a mile below Cathedral Gorge, you'll encounter the turnoff to **Panaca,** a quiet farm community about a mile off Highway 93. There's no compelling reason to visit this hamlet, other than for historical curiosity, and to view an oddly green limestone butte that rises from its middle. One of the oldest settlements in Nevada and the first in the southern part of the state, Panaca was founded by Mormons in 1864. It has changed little through the decades, persevering as an island of peaceful civilization, surrounded by green fields which in turn are surrounded by endless desert.

A 14-mile drive south from Panaca delivers you to an exemplary early-day railroad town, the most handsome depot this side of Los Angeles and a multi-colored canyon.

Caliente

Population: about 400   **Elevation: 4,398 feet**

In our Las Vegas chapter, we discussed the role played by Montana copper king William Clark in southern Nevada's development. After years of struggle, this strong-willed entrepreneur opened rail service between Los Angeles and Salt Lake City in 1905. Since engines were steamers in those days, water sources were vital. Like Las Vegas, Caliente was born a railroading town because of its springs. Also, the adjacent Rainbow Canyon offered a passable route through the mountains into Utah.

Caliente and Las Vegas both were established in 1905 as division points for Clark's San Pedro, Los Angeles and Salt Lake Railroad. With plentiful food from the nearby Panaca farmers, plus mineral springs to attract visitors and a more benign climate, Caliente fared much better than dusty Las Vegas during its earliest days. Its population approached 2,000 by 1907, double that of the desert city to the south.

Then floods through Rainbow Canyon wrecked a million dollars worth of track that year; more floods destroyed a 100 miles of the line in 1910. It was feared that Clark's railroad might have to be abandoned, and Caliente along with it. However, money was found to elevate the tracks to avoid future flood damage and the railroad survived. Eventually, it became a part of the huge Union Pacific operation, and it remains so today.

The replacement of steamers with diesel locomotives eliminated Caliente's reason to exist. Fortunately, farming, nearby mining and the lure of the hot springs have kept the little community chugging along.

It wears its railroad heritage handsomely. As you enter Caliente from the north on Spring Street (Highway 93), note the long row of modest little matched cottages on your left. They were built for railroad employees decades ago and are still occupied by town residents. As the highway kinks onto Front Street, you'll see a much grander sight—the penultimate mission revival **Caliente Railroad Station**. It's all dressed up with a tile roof, a scalloped facade and Spanish arch windows and doorways.

Caliente is eastern Nevada's most attractive community, with this stately depot and a neatly tucked-together business district. The old station now houses city offices, the municipal court and library. The **Chamber of Commerce** operates its "RSVP" visitor center here, sharing space with an art gallery; both are open weekdays from 9 to 5. The old station still offers passenger service, hailing the Los Angeles-Salt Lake City train once each day, once each way. Incidentally, when the chamber office is closed, you can pick up local brochures in the **AMTRAK** lobby, which is open daily.

If you'd like to take to the local waters, cross the tracks on the north side of town and follow signs to **Hot Springs Motel.** You can sit and simmer in deep Japanese-style hot tubs for $5, or you can rent a room (see below) and have the soaker thrown in as part of the deal. Baths are open to the public daily 8 a.m. to 10 p.m. The tubs are a bit weathered and some tiles are missing but never mind that. After a wearying drive or a long day playing tourist, soaking in that silky 115-degree water is absolute luxury. Also, it doesn't have that nose-twitching sulfur smell of many mineral baths.

When you've finished exploring the station and the rest of this prim little railroading town (and perhaps soaked your cares away), take time to check out nearby **Rainbow Canyon.** This impressive geological gallery of multi-colored strata was carved by Clover Creek. It provides thoroughfare for both the historic railroad and a 21-mile paved highway. To reach it, drive through town and turn left by an attractive brick Mormon church onto State Highway 317. You can pick up a milepost brochure from the chamber's RSVP room or from local merchants.

Caliente is a handy base for exploring the surrounding deserts and modest mountain ramparts. To learn more about the countryside, stop in at the **Bureau of Land Management Office** off Highway 93 on the southern edge of town. It's open weekdays from 9 to 5; phone 726-3105.

THE ATTRACTIONS

Union Pacific Depot • *Downtown; Chamber of Commerce RSVP Room, (702) 726-3129. Weekdays 9 to 5; AMTRAK depot open daily.* The classic Spanish- California depot was designed by noted Los Angeles architects John and Donald Parkinson. It was completed in 1923 at a cost of $86,300 and originally offered a restaurant and a 50-room hotel. The handsome oak-trimmed lobby, now the waiting room for AMTRAK's *Desert Wind,* is something of a museum. You'll find photo displays and graphics concerning the construction of the Los Angeles-Salt Lake Railroad, a mural of Rainbow Canyon and a southern Nevada history mural.

Rainbow Canyon • *South of Caliente, along Highway 317.* Twenty-one miles of paved highway take you past a rich geological panorama, with pastels ranging from chalky whites through the entire brown scale to yellow, pea soup green, russet and almost-orange. While not awesome (a term we reserve for Cathedral Gorge), Rainbow Canyon is certainly a striking display of sculpted, colored rock. The most impressive feature comes near the end, as the chasm narrows into the vertical, chocolate brown walls of **Grapevine Canyon**. Clover Creek has some inviting little willow glens in its bends, so you might want to bring a picnic lunch and linger a while.

While the canyon's railroad tracks and several trestles are high and dry, the road dips down into the creek bed on concrete crossings. They often overflow when the seasonal creek is in season, so use caution during rainstorms. The pavement and the ravine both quit half a mile beyond Bradshaw's **End of the Rainbow Ranch**. Dirt roads continue on from here.

WHERE TO DINE & SLEEP

Knotty Pine Cafe • ☺☺ **$**

690 Front Street (at First); (702) 726-3194. American; dinners $6.50 to $15; full bar service. Daily 7 a.m. to 8 p.m.; no credit cards. Cute little diner with a knotty pine interior (naturally), oldstyle counter with stools, plus

Naugahyde booths. Good old American menu with liver and onions, pork chops and such; lots of full meals under $10. Adjacent "casino" is a busy bar with a short row of video poker and slot machines.

Hot Springs Motel • △ $$

Off Spring Street (across the tracks, north end), Caliente, NV 89008; (800) 266-4468 or (702) 726-3777. Doubles, singles and kitchenettes $27.50 to $31. MC/VISA. Recently refurbished old spa; simple but neat rooms with TV. Room price includes hot mineral baths in deep Japanese-style tiled tubs.

Shady Motel • △ $$

430 Front St. (P.O. Box 186), Caliente, NV 89008; (702) 726-3106. Doubles and singles $25 to $27, up to six people $38, kitchenettes $10 extra. Major credit cards. Clean and neat little place with cable TV and room phones.

WHERE TO CAMP

Young's RV Park • *Highway 93 (south end of town, beside Bureau of Land Management office); 726-3418. Full hookups, $10.* Picnic tables and barbecues, flush potties and showers, dump station; some pull-throughs.

If you decide to make this journey to eastern Nevada a round trip, head west from Caliente on U.S. 93. Then take State Highway 375 across the state's lonely middle to U.S. 6 and thence to Tonopah. Top off your tank first, since the next gas stop is 80 miles away at tiny Rachel (and the pumps don't stay open late). Beyond Rachel, it's 110 dry miles to Tonopah.

Folks may boast that Highway 50 is the loneliest road in America, but it's downright crowded when compared with State 375. In a pair of crossings, we met one car as we drove east and none when we returned west. Rachel is the only town on the entire 190-mile Caliente-Tonopah stretch, and it's nothing but a handful of mobile homes and a shack or two.

As you depart Caliente, you'll climb through a pretty rock-ribbed canyon to the pinyon-juniper highlands of **Oak Springs Summit.** At 6,231 feet, it's the highest pass you'll encounter on this jaunt, and the only place where you'll see a tree. The rest of the trip is a long trek across flat desert basins, up shallow mountain passes and down into more basins. Often, you can see the thin thread of highway before you, reaching 20 or more miles across a valley to the next range of hills.

The scenery along this route consists of distant mountains on the horizon and a zillion acres of bunchgrass, salt brush, creosote bush, Utah sage and an occasional steer. You'll be glad to see scruffy old Tonopah. In case you're skipping ahead, **Chapter 5** takes you to and through this historic mining town.

LINCOLN COUNTY ANNUAL EVENTS

Lincoln County Rodeo in Alamo, May; (702) 726-3333.
Pioneer Days Celebration in Panaca, July; (702) 728-4666.
Heritage Days Celebration in Pioche, late July; (702) 962-5544.
Lincoln County Fair in Panaca, mid-August; (702) 726-3333.
Meadow Valley Days in Caliente, late September; (702) 726-3129.

Chapter Eleven
GLOSSARY

A NEVADA GAMING DICTIONARY

Action—The level of gambling activity in a casino. Thus the term: "Going where the action is."

Bankroll—A stake; the amount of money one has committed to gambling.

Betting right—A wager that the shooter will win in craps.

Betting wrong—A wager that the shooter will lose.

Bill—A gambler's term for a hundred-dollar bill. "I lost three bills last night."

Boxman—The person who supervises a craps table.

Break the deck—Reshuffle the cards in blackjack; sometimes done to foil a card counter.

Burn a card—Removing one or more cards from the top of a deck and placing them face up on the bottom; commonly done in blackjack and poker after the cards are shuffled.

Bust card—The term given to the two, three, four, five or six as the dealer's upcard in blackjack. So called because it's a lousy point to hit.

Bust hand—A blackjack hand totaling 12 to 16; also called a "hard hand."

Buy-in—The amount of money a player exchanges for chips, usually referring to buying into a poker game.

Cage—Casino cashier; also the wire bowl that holds the numbered ping-pong balls in keno.

Call bet—A wager made verbally. In poker, a "call" is a bet that matches the previous player's wager.

Caller—The person who runs a keno game by operating the blower and calling out the selected numbers.

Callman—The person who runs a baccarat game.

Carousel—An island of slot machines with an attendant in the middle.

Carpet joint—Fancy casino; one that caters to high rollers.

Casino checks—Slang for gaming chips used by a particular casino.

Catches—The numbers picked by a player that come up on the casino board.

Change colors—To exchange casino chips for those of a different denomination, thus a different color.

Checks—slang for casino chips.

Chemin de Fer—A variation of baccarat, played now only in Europe; the term is French for "railroad."

Cold dice—A pair of dice that isn't making the shooter's point.

Combination bet—In roulette, a bet on more than one number, using a single chip.

Come bet—A wager that a craps shooter will make his point after his come out roll.

Come out—A craps shooter's first roll. "Shooter coming out" is a common call at a craps table.

Comp—Slang for "complimentary" or freebies given to high rollers, visiting journalists and even occasionally to authors of guidebooks.

Crap out—In Craps, to hit a two, three or 12 on your come out roll.

Craps shoot—Any venture in which the outcome is a gamble, such as writing guidebooks.

Croupier—French term for the operator of a roulette game.

345

Double down—An additional bet, equal to the original, that a blackjack player can make after seeing his first two cards. He is permitted to take only one additional card.

Drop—The amount of cash collected from bettors at a particular casino table, which is placed in a "drop box" below.

Easy way—A point made in craps without paired numbers, such as getting a six with a four and two or five and one instead of a three and three, which is the "hard way."

Edge—The mathematical advantage that a casino has in any given game; generally called the house edge or house advantage.

En prison—A rule permitting a roulette player to let his bet ride or surrender only half of it if a zero or double-zero comes up.

First baseman—The player sitting at the dealer's left in blackjack.

Floorman—Supervisor of a pit or cluster of gaming tables, usually applied to blackjack.

Fold—To throw in a poker hand.

Free odds—A bet made with a pass or come bet in craps; it's so called because the house gives even odds.

Front line—The pass line in craps.

Front money—Funds put up by a player to establish credit in a casino.

Full house—In poker, three of a kind plus a pair.

Goose—The tube where keno balls collect, forced there by the blower.

Grind—Casino slang for a low-roller; one who bets small amounts. A **grind joint** is a casino catering to them.

Hard total—The total of a blackjack hand without an ace, or a hand in which the ace is counted as one point.

Hard way—Making your point in craps with paired numbers, such as a three and three for a six; any other combination is the "easy way."

High rollers—High-stakes gamblers, generally given preferential treatment in casinos.

Hit—To request another card from the dealer in blackjack.

Hold—The casino's take; the amount of money it "withholds" from gamblers.

Hole card—The blackjack dealer's card turned face down. Also, face down cards in various poker games, such as seven card stud.

Hot roller or **hot shooter**—A craps player who keeps winning by rolling sevens or making his point. He has a "hot hand."

House—The universal term for a casino, its employees and its funds. One "bets against the house" and "plays against the house." If you win, you're then playing with the house's money.

House advantage or **edge**—The mathematical edge that a casino has in a particular game.

Insurance—A blackjack wager in which you bet that a dealer with an ace showing has a blackjack.

Juice—Connections; the power that comes from knowing the right people. During the gangland era, it referred to people who'd attained power through bribery and payoffs.

Marker—An IOU marked with the amount of debt a player has incurred.

Money wheel—Another term for the Big Six or wheel of fortune.

Natural—A blackjack hand scoring 21 on the initial deal; also called a blackjack.

Nickel chips—Slang for $5 gaming tokens.

Nut—The overhead; the amount a casino must make to break even. A casino doing poorly has a "tough nut to crack."

On the stick—To become the stickman in craps, since dealers take turns. Thus the term: "Getting on the stick."

Paint—Slang term for face cards.

Pass—A bet that a craps shooter will throw a seven on his come out roll.

Pass line—The area on a craps layout where pass bets are made.

Pass posting—The practice, obviously illegal, of attempting to place a bet after the results are known.

Pat hand—An excellent hand, one in which the player requests no additional cards.

P.C.—Percentage, as it relates to the house advantage.

Pit—The employee-only area within a cluster of gaming tables. The **pit boss** is the supervisor of these tables.

Press a bet—To increase a bet after a win.

Push—A player's hand that ties the dealer's hand; usually called a draw with the bet carrying over into the next round.

RFB—The ultimate comp—free room, meals and drinks.

Right bettor—A player in craps who bets the shooter will make his point.

Royal flush—In poker, a ten, jack, queen, king and ace of the same suit; the highest possible hand.

Sawdust joint—Low budget casino, as opposed to a carpet join.

Score—A verb; to win big.

Seven-out—Rolling a seven after the initial throw, which then becomes the shooter's losing point.

Shift boss—The executive in charge of a particular shift, who answers to the casino manager.

Shill—A casino employee who poses as a player to keep the action going. Also called a ringer, particularly if he's part of a scam to encourage others to gamble.

Shoe—An open-ended box holding several decks of cards, used in baccarat and multiple-deck blackjack.

Shoot—A completed round of craps, in which the shooter makes or fails to make the point.

Silver—Slang for dollar chips or tokens, or silver dollars used for gambling.

Slots—Slang term for slot machines.

Snapper—Slang for a natural or blackjack.

Soft hand or ***soft total***—A blackjack hand in which the ace may be counted as one or eleven.

Splitting pairs—A blackjack option in which a player can turn two of a kind into two separate hands.

Spots—Slang for the numbers a keno player marks on a ticket.

Stickman—The dealer who runs the craps game, using a hooked stick to retrieve the dice and push them toward the shooter.

Stiff—A blackjack hand from 12 to 16, which is difficult to hit without busting. Also a cheapskate who doesn't tip for services rendered.

Stiffed—To be stiffed is to receive no tip for providing food, drink or other service.

Straight—In poker, five cards in numerical sequence, such as four through eight, or a ten, jack, queen, kind, ace.

Straight flush—A straight with all cards of the same suit.

Straight ticket—A simple keno ticket with no combination bets.

Straight up bet—A roulette bet on a single number.

Strip—Universal term for the Las Vegas Strip, the casino row along Las Vegas Boulevard.

Strip poker—A poker game in which participants' clothing is used for bets; not practiced in casinos but possibly in hotel rooms.

Stud poker—A poker game in which some of the cards are dealt face up and others face down.

Surrender—To give up on a bad blackjack hand and lose half your bet, permitted in some casinos.

Systems—Various methods used to try and improve gambling odds. Card-counting and doubling losing bets are "systems."

Table hopping—Switching gaming tables in an attempt to change one's luck.

Tapped out—Slang for going broke, gambling away your entire stake or bankroll.

Third baseman—The person sitting at the dealer's far right in blackjack.

Toke—slang for a tip.

Tom—Las Vegas slang for a stiff or a poor tipper.

Twenty-one—Alternate name for blackjack.

Unit—A measure used by gamblers to set the size of their wagers, usually based on the minimum bet at a particular game.

Upcard—The blackjack dealer's card that is dealt face up.

Vigorish or ***vig***—A fee collected by the house from a winning hand in a betting round, usually in baccarat and poker; also the term to describe the house edge.

Wrong bettor—One who bets against the shooter in craps, betting that the house will win.

OTHER USEFUL NEVADA BOOKS

FOR BOOKS ON GAMBLING, SEE THE END OF CHAPTER 2.

History

The Green Felt Jungle by Ed Reid and Ovid Demaris, © 1964, Pocket Books, New York, N.Y. A scathing look at Las Vegas of the 1950s and the mobsters who ran it.

Howard Hughes in Las Vegas by Omar Garrison, © 1970, Lyle Stuart. An intimate study of the reclusive billionaire's stay in Glitter City.

Inside Las Vegas by Mario Puzo, © 1987, Charter Books, New York, N.Y. A breezy yet heavy-handed look at Glitter City, by the author of *The Godfather*.

Las Vegas Behind the Tables! by Barney Vinson, © 1988, Gollehon Press, Grand Rapids, Mich. A behind-the-scenes look at Nevada gambling, written by a former casino executive.

Las Vegas: Compass Discover America series by Deke Castleman with photography by Michael Yamashita, © 1991. Compass American Guides, 6051 Margarido Dr., Oakland, CA 94618. Attractive color guide to Las Vegas with well-written history of the town, its casinos and casino characters.

Las Vegas: As It Began—As It Grew by Stanley W. Paher, Nevada Publications, Las Vegas, Nev. A detailed and affectionate look at the city, by a long-time resident and historian.

Mark Twain: His Life in Virginia City by George Williams III, © 1990, Tree by the River Publishing, P.O. Box 935, Dayton, NV 89403. Detailed account of the famed author's days in the Comstock, filled with quotes by Twain and his contemporaries.

Rosa May: The Search for a Mining Camp Legend by George Williams III, © 1980, Tree by the River Publishing, P.O. Box 935 VC, Dayton, NV 89403. A biography of a Virginia City and Bodie, California, prostitute, with details on the lives of mining camp "fallen angels."

The Tough Little Town on the Truckee: Reno by John M. Townley, © 1983, Great Basin Study series. Very readable account of Reno, its environment and its formative years."

The Town That Died Laughing by Oscar Lewis, © University of Nevada Press, Reno, Nev. The classic tale of Austin, its liars' club and its notorious newspaper, the *Reese River Reveille*.

Virginia City: Its History and Its Ghosts by Phyllis Zauner, © 1989, Zanel Publications, P.O. Box 1387, Sonoma, CA 95476. A pictorial look at historic Virginia City, with lots of photos and lithographs.

Touring

The Best Cat Houses in Nevada by J.R. Schwartz, © 1991, Straight Arrow Publishing, P.O. Box 1092, Boise, ID 83701. A detailed locator guide to the state's legal sanctuaries of sex, with rather graphic details on services performed. Informative but rather crudely written.

The Best of the Sierra Nevada by Gerald W. Olmstead, © 1991, Crown Publishers, New York, N.Y. Focusing on the mountain region between Nevada and California, it offers brief coverage of the east shore of Lake Tahoe, Carson City, Virginia City, Gardnerville-Minden and Reno.

The Complete Lake Tahoe Guidebook, © 1990, Indian Chief Publishing House, Tahoe City, Calif. A guide to both the Nevada and California shores of the lake.

Dining Out in Las Vegas by Elliot S. Krane, © 1991, Krane and Associates, 2822 Bridgepointe Drive, Las Vegas, NV 89121-4147. Detailed reviews of more than 200 Las Vegas area restaurants.

Hiking the Great Basin by John Hart, © 1980, Sierra Club Books, San Francisco, Calif. Typically detailed and well-written Sierra Club guide to the state's mountain and desert wilderness.

The Nevada Desert by Sessions S. Wheeler, © 1971, Caxton Printers, Ltd., Caldwell, Idaho. History and explorations of Nevada's Great Basin deserts.

Touring Nevada: A Historic and Scenic Guide by Mary Ellen and Al Glass, © 1983, University of Nevada Press, Reno, Nev. Driving trips over the state's back roads, with details on history and attractions.

INDEX

Main listings bold face

Airports, major, 22, 73, 74, 85, 238, 243, 277
Aladdin Hotel & Casino, 91, 152
Amtrak, 22, 74, 85, 118, 238
Anasazi Indians, 15, 67, 128, 159, 161, 252
Arizona, 14, 15, 21, 67, 68, 164, 168
Arizona Charlie's Hotel & Casino, 118, 153
Atomic testing, 21, 72, 131, 185, 311
Austin, 24, **323**

Bally's Las Vegas, 92, 150
Bally's Reno, 243, 262
Barbary Coast Hotel & Casino, 93, 152
Basque restaurants, 199, 200, 259, 299, 305
Basques, 17, 185, 197, 198, 242, 256, 265, 276, 296, 300, 302, 306, 307, 334
Beatty, 185
Berlin Ichthyosaur State Park, 322
Binion, Benny, 90, 112
Binion's Horseshoe Hotel & Casino, 112, 153
Block 16 red light district, 69, 70, 71, 90
Boardwalk Hotel & Casino, 93, 153
Bonneville Speedway Museum, 311
Boomtown Hotel/Casino, 271
Boulder City/Hoover Dam Museum, 166
Bourbon Street Casino, 93
Bowers Mansion County Park, 217
Boyd, Sam, 112, 118
Bus service, Greyhound, 22, 74, 85, 118, 238

Caesars Palace, Las Vegas, 93, 151
Caesars Tahoe, 278
Cal Neva, Reno, 244
Cal Neva, Tahoe, 272
Caliente, 342
California, 14, 15, 16, 21, 22, 25, 33, 67, 83, 180, 220, 267, 277, 284
California gold rush, 12, 16, 62, 68, 183, 221, 247, 289
California Hotel & Casino, 112, 154
California Trail, 16, 290
Carson, Kit, 16, 206, 211, 216
Carson City, 17, 21, 22, 30, 198, 202, 205, **206**, 269, 276
Carson Nugget, 212
Carson Station casino, 212
Cathedral Gorge State Park, 340
Central Nevada Museum, 192
Central Pacific Railroad, 235, 238, 271, 285, 291
Churchill County Museum, 319
Circus Circus
 Las Vegas, 95, 154
 Reno, 244, 263
Clarion Hotel Casino, 244, 262
Clark, William, 69, 74, 88, 118, 183, 186, 342
Clark County Heritage Museum, 128
Colorado Belle, 171
Comstock, Henry T. Paige, 221
Comstock Hotel Casino, 245, 263
Comstock Lode, 12, 13, 17, 20, 24, 33, 205, 207, 218, **219**
Crystal Bay, 267 282
Curry, Abraham Z., 206, 209, 211

Death Valley, 137, 185, 186, 189
Desert Inn, 96, 151
Desert Valley Museum, 182
Divorce laws, 13, 19, 23, 71, 236, 237
Don Laughlin's Riverside Hotel & Casino, 169
Dunes Hotel & Country Club, 96, 152

349

Edgewater Hotel & Casino, 170
El Cortez Hotel, 113, 154
El Rancho Hotel & Casino, 97, 154
El Rancho Vegas, 70
Eldorado Hotel Casino, 245, 263
Elko, 24, **302**
Ely, 24, **329**
Emigrant Trail, 19, 202, 206, 218, 219, 235, 271, 285, 315
Emigrants, 16, 22, 205, 235, 270, 285, 290, 309, 318
Ethel M Chocolate Factory tour, 136
Eureka, 24
Eureka Sentinel Museum, 327
Eureka , 326
Excalibur, 67, **98**, 154

Fabulous Flamingo, 20, 70, 71, 72, 87
Fallon, 18, 19, 288, **318**
Fire Department Museum, Carson City, 211
Fitzgerald's, Las Vegas , 113, 156
Fitzgerald's, Reno, 246, 263
Flamingo Hilton
 Las Vegas, 99, 152
 Laughlin, 170
 Reno, 246
Fleischmann Planetarium, 251
Fort Churchill Park, 219
Four Queens Hotel Casino, 114, 156
Fremont Hotel & Casino, 114, 156
Frèmont, John C., 14, 16, 68, 252, 269, 270, 289,
Frontier Hotel & Gambling Hall, 100, 156

Gambling
 early days of, 19, 70, 130, 131, 135, 236, 253
 history of, 32
 legalizing, 19, 20, 22, 69, 303
 organized crime, 20, 71
Gass, Octavius, 68
Genoa, 17, 198, **202**, 206

Genoa Courthouse Museum, 203
Gold Coast Hotel & Casino, 119, 156
Gold River Gambling Hall & Resort, 172
Gold Spike Hotel Casino, 115, 158
Golden Nugget Hotel & Casino, 115, 152
Golden Nugget-Laughlin, 172
Goldfield, 18, 24, **189**
Golf, 138, 257, 282
Governor's Mansion, Carson City, 212
Great Basin, 13, **14**, 16, 17, 185, 235, **285**, 293, 296, 301, 315
Great Basin National Park, 14, 30, 329, **334**
Guinness World of Records Museum, 129

Hacienda Hotel, 100, 156
Harold's Club, 247
Harold's Club Gun Collection, 251
Harrah, William, 71, 237, 247
Harrah's Del Rio, 172
Harrah's Lake Tahoe, 279
Harrah's Las Vegas, 101, 152
Harrah's Reno, 247, 262
Harvey's Resort Hotel/Casino, 278
Hawthorne, 194
Hearst, George, 221, 228
Hidden Cave, 321
Holiday Hotel Casino, 248, 264
Hoover Dam, 19, 67, 70, 131, 159, **162**
Horizon Casino Resort, 280
Hughes, Howard, 20, 96, 100, 107, 151, 175, 237
Humboldt Historical Museum, 296
Hyatt Regency Lake Tahoe, 274

Imperial Palace, 102, 156
Imperial Palace Auto Collection, 129
Incline Village, 267, 270, 271

Jackie Gaughan's Plaza, 117, 157
Jackpot, 308
Jarbidge Wilderness, 307
Jean and Stateline, 180
John Ascuaga's Nugget, 265
Jubilee show, 124

Kidd Marshmallow Factory tour, 136
King Arthur's Tournament, 124

Lady Luck Casino Hotel, 116, 157
Lake, Myron, 235
Lake Lahontan, 13, 15, 195, 288, 291, 293
Lake Mead, 70, 137, 161
Lake Mead National Recreation Area, 30, 159, 161, **163**
Lake Mohave, 163, 164, 167, 173
Lake Tahoe, 14, 15, 22, 23, 30, 168, 210, 237, **267**
Las Vegas, 12, 15, 18, 19, 20, 21, 22, 24, 26, 29, 30, 64, **65**, 159, 233, 237, 342
Las Vegas Club Hotel & Casino, 116, 157
Las Vegas Hilton, 102, 151
Las Vegas Mormon Temple, 129
Las Vegas Museum of Art, 132
Las Vegas Natural History Museum, 132
Las Vegas Springs, 68, 69
Last Frontier Hotel, 70
Laughlin, 74, 159
Laughlin, Don, 168
Laughlin, town of, 168
Lehman Caves, 335
Liberace Museum, 129
Liberty Belle Museum, 254
Lied Children's Museum, 130
Lincoln County Museum, 339
Lincoln Highway, 19, 269, 285, 317
Lost City Museum, 161

Lovelock, 291
Lyon County Museum, 196

Mackay, John W., 222, 228
Mackay Museum of Mines, 254
Main Street Station casino, 117
Marjorie Barrick Museum of Natural History, 130
Marriage laws, 13, 19, 21, 23, 71, 75, 77, 239
Maxim Casino, 103
McDermitt, 301
Mesquite, 181
Mexico, 15, 16, 67
MGM Grand Hotel, 67
Minden-Gardnerville, 197
Mineral County Museum, 195
Mirage, the, 11, 53, 67, **103**, 155
Mojave Desert, 14, 67, 85, 185, 189
Mormon settlement, 13, 17, 68, 90, 128, 132, 164, 181, 202, 205, 310
Mormon Station, 17, 202, 206
Mount Charleston recreation area, 155, 174, **177**, 179, 185

National Automobile Museum, 251
Nevada Banking Museum, 131
Nevada City, California, 220
Nevada Gambling Museum, 227
Nevada Historical Society Museum, 252
Nevada Northern Railway Museum, 331
Nevada State Capitol, 209
Nevada State Museum, Las Vegas, 131
Nevada State Museum (Carson Mint), 209
Nevada State Railroad Museum, 210
New Mexico, 68, 311
Northeastern Nevada Museum, 303

Old Mormon Fort, 132

Old Nevada and Bonnie Springs, 175
Omnimax Theater, Caesars Palace, 131
Ormsby House casino hotel, 213
Overland Trail, 19, 315, 317
O'Sheas Casino, 105

Pahrump Valley Winery, 176
Paiute Indians, 14, 15, 68, 128, 129, 161, 176, 195, 196, 213, 235, 252, 270, 287, 288, 289, 297, 319
Palace Station Hotel Casino, 119, 156
Paradise Valley, 301
Peppermill, 249, 263
Pershing County Courthouse, 292
Pershing County Museum, 292
Pioche, 338
Pioche Tramway, 339
Pioneer Club, 117
Pioneer Hotel & Gambling Hall Laughlin, 171
Piper's Opera House, 227
Ponderosa Ranch, 274
Ponderosa Saloon Underground Mine Tour, 227
Pony Express, 12, 16, 198, 202, 203, 205, 216, 218, 219, 303, 315, 317, 322, 323, 324, 329, 334
Prostitution, 13, 24, 25, 71, 177, 229
Pyramid Lake, 16, **288**

Rainbow Canyon, 343
Ramada Express, 170
Red light districts, 13, 25, 189, 296, 331
Red Rock Canyon, 174
Reno, 12, 15, 17, 19, 21, 30, 71, 113, 135, 168, 210, 222, 233
Reno, Jesse L., 235
Rhyolite, 18, 183, **187**
Rio Casino & Suite Hotel, 120, 151
Ripley's Believe It or Not! museum, 131

Riverboat Casino, 249, 264
Riviera Hotel, 105, 153
Ruby Mountains, 14, 307
Ruth mining district, 328

Sahara Hotel & Casino, 106, 153
Salt Lake City, 14, 17, 18, 68, 205, 206, 238, 302,
Sam's Town Hotel & Gambling Hall, 120, 157
Sands Hotel, 107, 151
Sands Regency, 250, 264
Santa Fe Hotel & Casino, 121, 157
Sharon, William, 218, 221
Showboat Hotel Casino, 121, 157
Siegel, Bugsy, 20, **71**, 99, 113, 152, 235
Sierra Nevada, 13, 14, 16, 29, 194, 197, 233
Silver City Casino, 108
Skiing, 179, 283
Slots A Fun, 108
Smith, Jedediah Strong, 16, 161, 195, 252, 315
Smith, Raymond and sons, 20, 71, 237, 247
Southern Nevada Zoological Park, 134
Sparks, 233, 243, **265**
Spring Mountain Ranch State Park, 174
Stardust Hotel, 108, 153
Stateline, Lake Tahoe, 267, 270, **277**
Stewart, Archibald and Helen, 68, 69
Stewart Indian Museum, 210
St. Mary's of Nevada Catholic Church, 227
Sundowner Hotel/Casino, 250, 264

Tennis, 139, 257
Territorial Enterprise, 205, 219, 229, 294
Tobin, Assemblyman Phil, 19, 20, 296
Tonopah, 13, 18, 24, 69, 183, **190**
Transcontinental Highways, 236, 256, 317
Transcontinental railroad, 12, 17, 270, 271

351

Transcontinental telegraph, 12, 219, 315, 317, 323, 329
Treasure Island resort, 67
Tropicana Hotel & Casino, 109, 153
Truckee River, 14, 17, 25, 233, 235, 237, 242, 264, 269, 287, 288
Twain, Mark (Samuel Clemens), 162, 213, 219, 224, 269, 276, 294

University of Nevada, 254
Utah, 13, 17, 181, 202, 220, 285, 309, 337

Vacation Village Casino Hotel, 110, 158
Valley of Fire State Park, 161
Vegas Vic neon sign, 135
Vegas World Hotel & Casino, 111, 157
Victory Highway, 19, 270, 285, 317
Virginia City, 17, 18, 24, 205, 208, **219**, 235
Virginia & Truckee Railroad, 183, 198, 207, 209, 210, 218, 224, 226, 228, 269, 276
Virginian Hotel Casino, 250, 264

Walker, Joseph, 16, 195, 252, 315
Walker Lake, 14, 183, 195
Ward Charcoal Ovens Historic Monument, 334
Washo Indians, 269, 273, 276
Washoe County Courthouse, 255
Way It Was Museum, 228
Wendover, 310
White Pine Museum, 332
Wilbur May Museum, 253
Winnemucca, 24, 183, 287, 294, **295**
Winnemucca, Chief, 289, 295
Wynn, Steve, 67, 104, 115, 130, 172

Yerington, 196
Young, Brigham, 17, 68, 202, 206

REMARKABLY USEFUL GUIDEBOOKS
by Don and Betty Martin

Critics praise the "jaunty prose" and "beautiful editing" of Don and Betty Martin's travel guides. You can order their other popular books or additional copies of **The Best of Nevada** by sending a personal check or money order to Pine Cone Press. If you wish, the authors will autograph your book. Indicate the dedication you'd like them to write.

INSIDE SAN FRANCISCO — $8.95

This is the ideal pocket guide to everybody's favorite city. Compact and complete, it covers San Francisco's attractions, activities, shopping, nightlife, restaurants and lodging. Maps, photos and walking tours help folks find their way. **248 pages**

SAN FRANCISCO'S ULTIMATE DINING GUIDE — $9.95

The Martins surveyed the *real* dining experts to compile this upbeat guide: chefs and other restaurant personnel, hotel concierges, cafe critics and community leaders. It lists more than 300 restaurants in the city and nearby communities. **224 pages**

THE BEST OF ARIZONA — $12.95

This comprehensive guide covers attractions, dining, lodgings and campgrounds in the Grand Canyon State. Maps and scenic driving routes direct visitors to Arizona's wonders. A special "Snowbird Directory" helps retirees plan their winters under the Southwestern sun. **336 pages**

COMING TO ARIZONA — $12.95

This is an all-purpose relocation guide for job-seekers, retirees and winter "Snowbirds" planning a move to Arizona. It provides useful information on laws, real estate, taxes, job markets, education and leisure time activities. Dozens of cities are featured, with data on climate, population, housing prices and other essentials. **232 pages**

THE BEST OF THE WINE COUNTRY — $12.95

This comprehensive tasters' guide covers more than 250 California wineries, from Napa, Sonoma and Mendocino to Monterey, Santa Ynez and Temecula. It features tasting notes and locator maps, plus specifics on winery facilities, tours and gift shops. It also covers restaurants, lodgings and other Wine Country attractions. **304 pages**

THE BEST OF THE GOLD COUNTRY — $11.95

It's a "complete, witty and remarkably useful guide to California's Sierra gold rush area and old Sacramento." This informative book takes visitors along historic Highway 49, covering its old mining towns, attractions, cafes, campgrounds, gold rush hotels and other lodgings. **240 pages**

Include $1 postage and handling for each book; California residents add proper sales tax. Please give us a complete mailing address and a phone number, in case there's a question about your order.

**Send your order to: *Pine Cone Press*
P.O. Box 1494, Columbia, CA 95310**

**THE MARTIN GUIDES ALSO ARE
AVAILABLE AT MOST BOOK STORES**